THE
unofficial GUIDE®
ᵀᴼCalifornia
with Kids

6TH EDITION

THE *unofficial* GUIDE®

TO California with Kids

6TH EDITION

COLLEEN DUNN BATES *and*
SUSAN LaTEMPA

WILEY

Please note that prices fluctuate in the course of time and that travel information changes under the impact of many factors that influence the travel industry. We therefore suggest that you write or call ahead for confirmation when making your travel plans. Every effort has been made to ensure the accuracy of information throughout this book, and the contents of this publication are believed to be correct at the time of printing. Nevertheless, the publishers cannot accept responsibility for errors or omissions, for changes in details given in this guide, or for the consequences of any reliance on the information provided by the same. Assessments of attractions and so forth are based upon the authors' own experiences; therefore, descriptions given in this guide necessarily contain an element of subjective opinion, which may not reflect the publisher's opinion or dictate a reader's own experience on another occasion. Readers are invited to write the publisher with ideas, comments, and suggestions for future editions.

Published by:
John Wiley & Sons, Inc.
111 River Street
Hoboken, NJ 07030-5774

Produced by Menasha Ridge Press

Cover design by Michael J. Freeland

Interior design by Vertigo Design

For information on our other products and services or to obtain technical support, please contact our Customer Care Department within the United States at 800-762-2974, outside the United States at 317-572-3993, or by fax at 317-572-4002.

John Wiley & Sons, Inc., also publishes its books in a variety of electronic formats. Some content that appears in print may not be available in electronic formats.

ISBN 978-0-470-38002-4

Manufactured in the United States of America

5 4 3 2 1

CONTENTS

LIST *of* MAPS

ACKNOWLEDGMENTS

THANKS TO LITERARY AGENT Betsy Amster for bringing us a project that has been so rewarding for our entire families. Thanks to Pam Brandon, author of *The Unofficial Guide to Florida with Kids,* who provided long-distance counsel, perspective, and laughs. Thanks to the publications that have sent us traveling with our families, especially *Westways, Journey,* the *Los Angeles Times, Travel & Leisure, Food & Wine, Working Mother, Parenting, FamilyFun,* and the *San Jose Mercury News.* Thanks to the folks at Menasha Ridge Press, especially Bob Sehlinger and Molly Merkle; they are surely the kindest souls in publishing. And, most importantly, thanks to our traveling companions: Daniel, Patricia, and Irene Milder; Pat Taylor; Darryl, Erin, and Emily Bates; Ellie Dunn; and the camping families at Sequoyah School.

ABOUT
the AUTHORS

LOS ANGELES NATIVE **Colleen Dunn Bates** is the author of many books, including *Hometown Pasadena: The Insider's Guide* and *Storybook Travels: From Eloise's New York to Harry Potter's London, Visits to 30 of the Best-Loved Landmarks in Children's Literature,* which she cowrote with Susan LaTempa. She lives in Pasadena with her husband, Darryl Bates, and their two daughters.

Culver City resident **Susan LaTempa** wrote *Storybook Travels* with Colleen, has written for many national magazines, and is now an editor for the *Los Angeles Times*. Susan and her husband, Dan Milder, have two daughters.

INTRODUCTION

OUR FAMILIES *and* TRAVELS

FROM COLLEEN

MY MOTHER IS NEVER HAPPIER than when she's planning a trip, and I inherited that longing and joy. God knows it wasn't easy to take our brood anywhere—my parents had six kids in seven years, and I'm not sure how they ever got us dressed, let alone out of the house. But they did. From our Los Angeles home, we crammed into the station wagon and went to Yosemite, Palm Springs, Big Bear, and Disneyland. We rented an RV and camped the entire length of the state. We skied Mammoth and Tahoe. We flew to San Francisco, two at a time. And we went to the beach, from Malibu to San Onofre, chasing the waves that my father, and later we kids, loved so much.

Now my husband, Darryl, and I are doing it with our own two teenagers, Erin and Emily. We've rented a beach house, stayed in a fancy San Francisco hotel, taken Amtrak to San Diego, skied in Mammoth and Tahoe, snorkeled at Catalina, and camped in the Anza-Borrego Desert. We've gone beyond California's borders to Hawaiian beaches, a French country house, and Rocky Mountain ski towns. We've had mishaps, and stress, and a lifetime supply of whining, but we've never had a bad trip, and we've had lots of great ones. We've learned how to plan drives around Emily's essential rest times and set the stage to minimize Erin's fear of the unknown. And we've learned how to weave our grown-up desires and interests into those of our children, further fusing us as a family. (We've also learned how to take the occasional adult trip away from the kids . . . but that's another book.)

I will never tire of exploring California. My children are perpetually panting for a new outing in our home state. From the trail atop Half Dome to the splash at the end of Splash Mountain, California is a great gift to the traveling family.

FROM SUSAN

AS I WRITE THIS, I get up from the desk from time to time to check on the laundry—an extra load this week because my daughter Irene and I have just returned from a trip to San Francisco and need some of our things for school and work tomorrow. Teenager Irene hasn't learned the joys of packing light yet, so I shake my head over the size of the pile of laundry. But even at her young age, Irene has learned that travel is a special joy, that it's a great good fortune to substitute pictures in your head for place-names in a book. This trip brought forth her memories of previous family travels, and Irene shared with me her perspective on such adventures as our family's two-week car trip through Mendocino and the redwoods, and a more recent biking weekend in the Santa Ynez Valley. Her reminiscences this week reminded me again how children hold dear the most unexpected moments (often forgotten by adults) of a vacation, and how, more than anything, travel is a kind of practice that allows a child to learn to face other new experiences and be free to explore in all parts of her or his life.

My own earliest memories of California are a child's images of giant pinecones and picnic tables at highway rest stops. But I have to admit that for the most part I ignored my first chances to appreciate the state's spectacular scenery as I sat next to my brother in the backseat of the station wagon, bologna sandwiches floating in the ice chest at my feet. Today my family travels frequently throughout the state—Irene and I joined by my husband, Dan, and older daughter, Patricia. We've summer-vacationed in Mammoth and Sequoia, in Oxnard and Mendocino. (Admittedly, we sometimes take two summer vacations!) We've had Christmas week or winter weekends away from home, and spring break has been a traditional time to travel with Grandma— once to La Jolla, once to Coronado. We've headed out to see natural wonders in Death Valley and to play on the waterslides at Hurricane Harbor. We've seen and done enough for me (with a little help from the kids' sharper memories) to contribute half the material in this book. But we haven't seen it all yet.

The **DYNAMICS** of **FAMILY TRAVEL**

DON'T EVEN THINK ABOUT planning a family trip until you answer this question: what does each member of the family want to get out of the vacation?

It seems like a simple question, but it'll take more time and thought to answer than you might realize. It means assessing your current relationship with your kids and your spouse. It means taking stock of your children's passions and fears, as well as your own.

It means attaching a budget to everyone's wishes. And it invariably means compromise.

Start by asking yourself some questions. Is this vacation an opportunity for togetherness, for time alone for you while the children are entertained, or for a little of each? Are you a single dad who doesn't get to see the kids much? Are you an at-home mom who never gets a break? Are you looking for exhilarating adventures or a laid-back getaway? Do you want intellectual stimulation for you and the kids? How well do your kids handle spontaneity?

Because your family's dynamics change with every birthday, the answers may surprise you. One child may be more ready for adventure than you've realized; another might be more ready for peace and quiet than you think.

THE PLEASURES OF PLANNING

IT'S BEST TO DECIDE what you want to do and come up with some options to start the ball rolling. Then call a family meeting and include your kids in the planning process. Let everyone ask questions. Show some brochures or books about the places you have in mind so they'll feel as though they have enough information to be taken seriously. Pull out maps and a globe. Jump on the Internet. Teenagers in particular are quite vocal about expressing their choices, and they appreciate it when they can influence the planning process. The getaway is much more enjoyable when everyone wants to be there.

This shared planning time can be a great routine to continue as the trip itself gets under way. Remember, your kids may not be able to easily visualize your destination or the plane ride or cab ride you'll take on the way. And if you're traveling from place to place during your vacation, each new day dawns on the unknown. So keep the brochures and guidebooks handy, and break the itinerary down into manageable chunks. Offer an advance agenda every now and then, referring again to your original planning sessions ("Remember how we thought that the Bubbling Brook Motel sounded like a good one?") and letting the kids develop anticipation rather than anxiety.

It's essential to be realistic when you plan a family vacation. Parents of young children may have to concede that the days of romantic sunsets are over for a while if there's a toddler tugging at their shorts. With infants and toddlers, the best vacations are the simple ones. They don't much need to see the sights; the idea is to be somewhere comfortable and intriguing for the adults, with a pleasant environment in which to relax and enjoy your children. In California, such destinations as Mission Bay or Monterey are ideal for parents of the youngest group of kids. School-age kids revel in attractions created for their enjoyment—theme parks, amusement parks, arcades, rides. The metropolitan regions can also be a blast with elementary-age kids. Teens may seem reluctant, but if a pilgrimage to a special point of interest for them (a certain skateboard shop, a movie-star hangout) is included, the whole trip becomes "worthwhile." And they thrive in safe, explore-it-on-your-own situations such as a tour of Alcatraz or a Gold Country town.

LESS IS MORE THAN ENOUGH

AS YOU PLAN, we urge you to leave plenty of downtime in the schedule. Some of our families' most memorable moments are simple breakfasts on the beach or early evening walks to nowhere, when the conversation naturally flows. Kids treasure moments, not places or days. Give your children plenty of room to run and play; a morning collecting seashells or an afternoon at the hotel pool can be more satisfying than standing in line at a crowded theme-park attraction.

unofficial **TIP**
A good rule of thumb may sound stringent: no more than two activities in a day.

If you spend the morning at a museum and plan to go to dinner at Universal CityWalk, go back to the hotel in the afternoon to rest and swim. If you're driving from San Francisco to Monterey, make your reservations for the aquarium the next day. Then you can stop on the way at the lighthouse and the artichoke fields and the funny little town that time forgot. Remember that travel itself is an activity.

Also, plan some activities that allow you to take a break from each other. Quarters get a little close after a week together in a hotel room, particularly if your children are of significantly different ages. Schedule an afternoon in which Mom and Dad split duties, giving each other a break; take advantage of child and teen programs offered in many resorts to allow an evening alone with your spouse. Everyone benefits from a little elbowroom.

RECONNECTIONS

FAMILY VACATIONS ARE A NECESSARY INDULGENCE in today's hurried-up world, a time for togetherness without the day-to-day distractions. Whether it's a car trip on a budget or a transcontinental flight, it's a time to reconnect with your family, especially teenagers. And the best times are the serendipitous moments—a heart-to-heart conversation on an evening hike or silly "knock-knock" jokes while standing in line for the roller coaster. Roles are relaxed when schedules are flexible, and kids can have the opportunity to see their parents as interesting companions, not just bossy grown-ups. We all can learn from one another when there's time to listen and when we take the time to see the world through a loved one's eyes.

A seasoned traveler friend once scoffed at the notion of traveling with young children, "since they don't remember anything." We couldn't disagree more.

Susan's children have often mentioned the hours spent sitting at the mouth of the Klamath River watching the incredible sight of sea lions, pelicans, Native American fishermen, and one ambitious, wet dog, all competing for the salmon swimming into the river from the ocean.

When Colleen's daughter Erin was 7, she struck up an intense friendship with a boy on a Hawaiian beach, and when they returned to their respective homes in California and Michigan, they kept in touch by e-mail. Given the open hearts and all the innocence of childhood, new impressions may sink in even more deeply with kids than with adults.

Our children have a greater understanding of the rest of the world as a result of traveling to new places and experiencing new ideas. And siblings have formed a special bond from traveling together, a bond less likely to be formed at home, where they have separate classrooms, separate friends, and separate bedrooms.

As parents, it's up to us to be sure there's some fun in a trip for each member of the family. And as a family, we all need to remember to indulge our traveling companions from time to time. Remember, your responses to challenges on the road—delayed flights, long lines, unsatisfactory accommodations—will influence the way your children will deal with frustrations. Be patient, be calm, and teach your children these important lifelong skills.

Vacations are times for adventure, relaxation, shared experiences, time alone—whatever your family decides. Our goal with this book is to evaluate each destination with that in mind—recognizing that your family has needs, based on ages, backgrounds, and interests, that are quite different from any other family's—and to provide you with some structure to analyze your family's needs and create a vacation that works.

unofficial **TIP**
It's stressful enough to get a kindergartner out the door to school each morning, so don't keep up the stress on vacation.

We have traveled the world with our children, from France and Holland to the Hawaiian Islands and the Rocky Mountains. Yet some of our most wondrous trips have been in our own backyard: hopping a San Francisco cable car, bodyboarding on a Santa Barbara beach, playing hide-and-seek in a redwood forest. We can't imagine ever tiring of exploring our home state, whether we're stalking the newest amped-up amusement park or finding the next best beach.

This book is not meant to be a compendium of every family-priced hotel or every advertised attraction, though we have striven to cover a variety of interests for a variety of ages. Instead of compiling a family-travel Yellow Pages, we've edited out the less worthy places to better draw attention to the destinations that will make your trip a hit.

Dozens of families have contributed their opinions to this book; it is evaluative and opinionated, and it offers advice about the best ways for families to have fun together and to further relationships.

Survival Guide for Little Kids

THINK SMALL Little ones love little pleasures: splashing in the hotel pool, cavorting in the lobby, stacking up rocks on the beach. Don't overload them.

SEEK CREATIVE TRANSPORTATION   For young children, getting there is often more fun than being there. When Emily was 3 years old, her greatest joy and memory from our gala two-week Hawaiian vacation was the open-air Wiki Wiki shuttle at Honolulu International Airport—she positively shook with excitement during the ride. Seek out the ferries, trolleys, shuttles, trains, surreys, and double-decker buses, and you'll be rewarded with a cheap thrill that's as much fun for little ones as a Disneyland ride.

LIMIT THE SHOPPING   Our rule at attractions is a firm one: no shopping, not even looking, until we are leaving the place. Young children can get consumed by and panicky about choosing a souvenir, and they'll enjoy the museum or theme park more if they can focus on the activities, not the trinkets.

GIVE THEM A VOICE   Even a 4-year-old will benefit from feeling as if he has some control over his vacation. Let him make simple choices for the family—such as "Should we walk to the beach or ride the trolley?"

ALLOW FOR LOTS OF DOWNTIME   Bring books or quiet hobbies to amuse yourself during nap times or playtimes. Remember, a child's ability to tackle the big world is much more limited than yours.

ACCEPT SOME SLOWNESS   As any parent who's gotten a child ready for school in the morning can attest, kids are used to being rushed. And kids, like adults, need a break from it. If they're happy playing in their pajamas for an extra half hour, the museum can wait. Conversely, accept that the times you like to be more leisurely—such as dinnertime—lead to impatience in children.

Survival Guide for School-age Kids

GIVE THEM THEIR OWN SPACE   Whether it's a backpack, a carry-on train case, or one of those shoe-bag-like hanging pockets that fits over the car seat in front of them, each kid needs a portable room of his or her own in which to stow gum, cards, books, cameras, and souvenirs.

MAKE A NEW ROUTINE   At least until middle-school years, most kids do best with a certain amount of predictability, so it's a kindness to create little travel routines and rituals within your changed life. Knowing that his parents will always stop sightseeing by 3 p.m. to swim (or will never check out without one last hour in the pool) is a comforting thought to many a fourth-grader. Knowing that you will have $5 spending money each day can do away with shopping anxiety. Having set turns as map reader can add some fun to a hundred-mile drive.

AVOID EATING BREAKFAST OUT   Many savvy traveling parents never eat breakfast in a restaurant. School-age kids are at their brightest and best in the morning, and waiting for table service at a ho-hum restaurant can start the day on the wrong foot. We carry fruit, cereal, milk, and juices in coolers or to kitchenettes, or pop for room service—it's the least expensive and most wonderfully indulgent time to do so.

BEWARE BEFUDDLED EXPECTATIONS School-age kids are old enough to have some reference points but young enough to have great gaping holes in their mental pictures of the world. Our kids have imagined that they'd find matzo ball soup instead of chocolate at Ghirardelli Square (thinking it was Jerry's Deli); they've worried that the car would tumble down the cliff on a winding mountain road; they've expected to see gold nuggets in the bottom of the creek in Gold Country. Ask what's going on in their minds. Listen. Don't overpromise.

WATCH THE DIET It's fun to let vacation be a time of special treats, but overindulgence in junk food, sweets, and caffeinated drinks may contribute to behavioral changes in kids who aren't sleeping in their own beds and are full of adrenaline as it is.

REMEMBER THAT KIDS HATE SCENERY Drive them through it if you must, but don't make them actually look at too much of it.

GIVE THEM A SHIP'S LOG A roll of tape and a blank book are all that's needed to turn ticket stubs, menus, brochures, and postcards from a clutter of trash into a wonderful scrapbook that's always ready to be shared and enjoyed.

HOTELS AND MOTELS ARE NOT JUST FOR SLEEPING Allow time for getting ice, playing in the pool, reviewing all items and prices in the minibar, packing and unpacking, using the hair dryer, putting laundry into the laundry bags, trying out the vending machines, etc.

HIT THE PLAYGROUNDS Check your maps and ask ahead about public playgrounds with climbing and sliding equipment, and on days when you'll be sightseeing, driving, or absorbing culture, allow for an hour's lunch or rest stop at the playground. Even on city vacations, try to set aside at least one day for pure physical fun at a beach or water park or ski slope.

JUST SAY YES TO RANGER TOURS These tours are often designed with schoolkids in mind. We'd never have tasted sand flies at Mono Lake or seen a tarantula up close at Anza-Borrego Desert State Park if we hadn't checked the schedule at the state or national park information center and made a point to join the ranger walk.

Survival Guide for Teenagers

DON'T TRY TO FOOL THEM Don't try to tell them they'll have more fun with you than with their friends. They won't. But if you offer them the possibility of doing things they might want to tell their friends about later, they'll be interested.

RESPECT THEIR CULTURE Let your teenager play an active role in planning the vacation. Ask her opinion of your arrangements. Often our daughter will offer a great suggestion or an alternative that we may not have considered. And look for pop-culture landmarks—movie locations or palaces of fashion or music or sport. Add a ball game to the itinerary.

NIGHT MOVES   A vacation is a great time to go with your teenager to a music club or a midnight movie, or on a moonlight hike. Go to the theater or the ballet; check out a jazz club. If you have other kids needing earlier bedtimes, let the parents switch-hit on going out at night with the older kids.

GIVE THEM OPTIONS   You don't need to go everywhere with everyone. If your younger child wants to go see the dinosaurs at the museum, this is the time for a split plan: Dad and son see the dinosaurs; Mom and daughter shop or take in a movie or a play. If you have a teenager who appreciates her sleep time, let her snooze late at least one morning. Slip out with younger siblings and take a walk or read a book. Also, set wake-up time before everyone says good night so that there are no grouchy morning risers (at least not because they've been awakened too early).

GIVE THEM FREEDOM   Before age 12, kids are bound to parents, preferring to stay in your orbit; when adolescence hits, they're programmed to push away from you. Choose a vacation spot that is safe and controlled enough to allow them to wander or spend time with other teenagers. If you can't do that, look for an afternoon or evening at a controlled hangout such as Universal CityWalk or Pier 39. Give them the night to themselves at Disneyland or Knott's. Send them off to the ranger campfire by themselves at Yosemite; sign them up for an afternoon's photography workshop in Big Sur.

COMPROMISE ON THE HEADPHONE THING   Headphones can allow teens to create their own space even when they're with others, and that can be a safety valve, but try to agree before the trip on some non-headphone parameters so you don't begin to feel as if they're being used to keep other family members and the trip itself at a distance. If you're traveling by car, take turns choosing the radio station or CD for part of the trip.

DON'T MAKE YOUR TEENAGER THE BUILT-IN BABYSITTER   It should be a family vacation—a time for reconnecting, not for avoiding the kids. A special night out for parents also should be special for the children; let them order videos and room service, for example, or participate in a few age-appropriate hotel programs.

MAKE PEACE WITH SHOPPING   Look for street markets and vintage stores; spend some time in surf shops and record stores. If you go with your teenager, you may find that the conversation in such an environment flows easily. Or hit the outlets—many a summer vacation has included a day of back-to-school shopping.

JUST SAY YES TO AT LEAST ONE BIG-TICKET EXCURSION   Teenagers will get a lot out of a half-day adventure. What on the surface appeared to be expensive tours (often available through the hotel sports desk or concierge) turned into memorable and important experiences for our kids that we as parents were simply not able to offer by ourselves. A raft ride, a desert Jeep tour, a kayak and snorkel trip, a horseback trail ride—each took us far into the country we were exploring, and each was worth every cent. Or let the teenager sign up for a lesson: surfing, sailing, rock climbing. One of our daughters took a remarkable rope-climbing course that had her swinging through the trees in Mammoth.

A Word on Homework

Both our elementary-school and high-school kids have faced a load of homework or a special project that had to be worked on during vacation time. If a surprise major assignment comes up and plans can't be changed, there will be an unavoidable strain on the trip. Parents should consider strategies such as bringing along a laptop computer, scheduling vacation fun in half-day chunks so that the homeworked kid gets some work and some play, and/or including a marathon session at a library at the vacation spot. You can also shamelessly beg the teacher for a reprieve, but make that a last resort.

The Secret to Visiting Art Museums

Wandering through room after room of paintings and sculptures is numbing to children. They need a focal point and a sense of adventure. Before your visit, find out what some of the major works on display are, and locate pictures of them. Perhaps the museum will mail you a brochure with pictures, or you can look online or get an art book from the library. Let each child pick one or two works to sleuth out. They can learn a little about the artist and the work in question, and then when you visit the museum, they can go on a hunt for "their" artwork.

A Few Words for Single Parents

Because single parents generally are working parents, planning a special getaway with your children can be the best way to spend some quality time together. But remember, the vacation is not just for your child—it's for you, too. You might invite along a grandparent or a favorite aunt or uncle; the other adult provides nice company for you, and your child will benefit from the time with family members.

Don't try to spend every moment with your children on vacation. Instead, plan some activities for your children with other children. Look for hotels with supervised activities, or research the community you'll be visiting for school-vacation offerings at libraries, recreation centers, or temple or church day camps. Then take advantage of your free time to do what you want to do: read a book, have a massage, take a walk or a catnap.

Tips for Grandparents

A vacation that involves generations can be the most enriching experience for everyone, but it is important to consider the needs of each

unofficial **TIP**
If planning a child-friendly trip seems overwhelming, try **Grandtravel** (☎ 800-247-7651; **www.grandtrvl.com**), a tour operator–travel agent catering to kids and their grandparents.

family member, from the youngest to the oldest. Here are some suggestions.

• If you're planning to travel alone with your grandchildren, spend a little time getting to know them before the vacation. Be sure they're comfortable with the idea of traveling with you if their parents are not coming along.

• It's best to take one grandchild at a time, two at the most. Cousins can be better than siblings because they don't fight as much.

• Let your grandchildren help plan the vacation. Be flexible, and don't overplan.

• Discuss mealtimes and bedtime. Fortunately, many grandparents are on an early dinner schedule, which works nicely with younger children. Also, if you want to plan a special evening out, be sure to make the reservation ahead of time. Stash some crayons and paper in your bag to keep kids occupied.

• Gear plans to your grandchildren's age levels, because if they're not happy, you're not happy.

• Choose a vacation that offers some supervised activities for children in case you need a rest.

• If you're traveling by car, this is the one time we highly recommend headphones. Teenagers' musical tastes are vastly different from most grandparents', and it's simply more enjoyable when everyone can listen to her or his own style of music.

• Bring a night-light.

• Carry a notarized statement from parents for permission for medical care in case of an emergency. Also, be sure you have insurance information.

• Tell your grandchildren about any medical problems you may have so they can be prepared if there's an emergency.

• Many attractions and hotels offer discounts for seniors, so be sure to check ahead of time for bargains.

• A cruise may be the perfect compromise—plenty of daily activities for everyone but shared mealtimes.

For Travelers with Disabilities

Facilities for the physically challenged are plentiful in California. All public buildings have some form of access for people who use wheelchairs. In addition, many public buses are equipped with wheelchair lifts. Also, most of the state's attractions offer facilities and services for those with physical challenges, and many hotels have specially equipped rooms. The state's three most popular cities have guides for the physically challenged: in San Diego, call ☎ 858-279-0704; in Los Angeles, call ☎ 323-957-4280; and in San Francisco, call ☎ 415-391-2000.

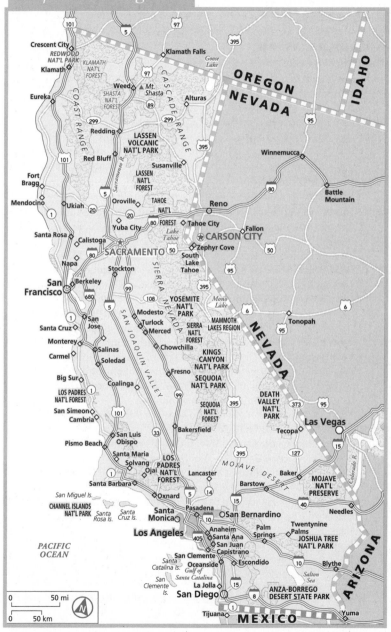

california at a glance

HOW *the* UNOFFICIAL GUIDE WORKS

ORGANIZATION

OUR INFORMAL POLLS show that most families tend to choose a vacation spot based on geography—a place that's new and different, or familiar and comfortable. So we've divided California into eight regions, with family-friendly information for each region. The chapters are organized geographically, from south to north. For great places to stay within those regions—resorts, hotels, campgrounds—see the "Family Lodging" sections within each chapter; kid- and parent-pleasing dining is recommended in the "Family-friendly Restaurants" sections in each chapter.

The regions break down as follows:

- **San Diego County** From Tijuana to Carlsbad, and inland to Anza-Borrego, this region centers on the San Diego metropolitan area and beaches.
- **Orange County** From San Clemente in the south to Costa Mesa in the north, this region includes such beloved beach destinations as Newport, Laguna, and Dana Point, as well as Disneyland and Knott's Berry Farm.
- **Los Angeles and Vicinity** This huge urban area centers on the nation's second-largest city and includes such satellite towns as Palm Springs, Pasadena, Redondo Beach, Big Bear, and Santa Monica, as well as such suburban amusements as Magic Mountain.
- **The Central Coast** North of LA lies this rich collection of beaches and small-town escapes, starting in Ventura, continuing through Santa Barbara and San Simeon (Hearst Castle), and going north through the wilds of Big Sur to the aquarium in Monterey.
- **The Sierra Nevada** Mountain fun awaits in this large region, from Yosemite's Half Dome to Sequoia's trees to sparkling Lake Tahoe. This region also includes Death Valley on the Sierra's eastern boundary.
- **The San Francisco Bay Area** Along with the great City by the Bay, this region includes adventures in the East Bay (Berkeley), San Jose, and Marin County as far north as Point Reyes.
- **Gold Country** Inland from San Francisco, this region encompasses the capital city, Sacramento, and wanders through the gold-rush towns flanking the western Sierra Nevada.
- **Northern California** A vast, rural area rich in national and state parks, this region stretches from Bodega Bay up through the redwoods to the Oregon border and over to Mount Shasta.

WHAT'S THERE TO DO BESIDES DISNEYLAND?

EACH REGIONAL CHAPTER recommends the best beaches, parks, family outdoor adventures, and attractions, ranging from theme parks to science museums. We've also included serendipitous sidebars on offbeat places that you'll want to know about, from children's theaters in LA to the old schoolhouses of the Gold Country.

If you're looking for some healthy family bonding, stretch beyond the man-made attractions. Have a sense of adventure and plan some activities that are new and exciting—not necessarily strenuous, but memorable. Each region has specific spots for the following activities.

CAMPING   We've selected a few choice family-friendly campgrounds throughout the state. If it's your family's first experience, you might opt for a cabin; we list them in many state parks.

BIKING   For beginners, we have recommended miles of paved bicycle trails; older kids will like the mountain biking spots we've found. You don't even have to bring your own bike; you can rent one at many resorts and bike shops, and many shops have trailers for rent for small children (ages 5 and under) to travel safely behind you—these are much safer than bicycle seats. Know that helmets are the law for children, and it is strongly advised that all cyclists wear helmets.

unofficial **TIP**
Cycling is one of the best ways to experience an area firsthand and can be enjoyed year-round in much of California.

SURFING   The wave is king (or queen) in many parts of California, so we've recommended the best surfing classes and camps for kids, as well as good beaches for wave riders of all kinds, including bodyboarders.

WHALE WATCHING   Wintertime visitors won't want to miss a whale-watching trip, offered up and down the California coast. Even if you don't spot one of the great gray whales, you'll surely enjoy dolphins, seals, seabirds, and an exhilarating ride on the Pacific Ocean.

HIKING   California is a hiker's paradise; we've concentrated on the easiest spots suitable for kids, from urban nature hikes to Sierra trails.

KAYAKING AND WHITEWATER RAFTING   From kayaking the coves of the north coast to rafting the wilds of the American River, these are wonderful bonding adventures for families with kids older than age 5 or 6.

WHAT'S "UNOFFICIAL" ABOUT THIS BOOK?

THE MATERIAL IN THIS GUIDE originated with the authors and researchers and has not been reviewed, edited, or in any way approved by attractions, restaurants, and hotels we describe. Our goal is to help families plan a vacation that's right for them by providing important details and honest opinions. If we found a family-oriented destination to be dreary or a rip-off, we simply didn't include it.

Readers care about the author's opinion. The author, after all, is supposed to know what he or she is talking about. This, coupled with the fact that the traveler wants quick answers (as opposed to endless alternatives), dictates that authors should be explicit, prescriptive, and, above all, direct. The *Unofficial Guide* tries to be just that—it spells out alternatives and recommends specific courses of action. It simplifies complicated destinations and attractions and allows the traveler to feel in control in the most unfamiliar environments. The objective of the *Unofficial Guide* is not to have the most information or all the information, but to have the most accessible, useful information, unbiased by affiliation with any organization or industry.

This guide is directed at value-conscious, consumer-oriented families who seek a cost-effective, though not spartan, travel style.

The *Unofficial Guide* Rating System for Attractions

Our system includes an "appeal to different age groups" category, indicating a range of appeal from one star (★ star), "don't bother," up to five stars (★★★★★), "not to be missed."

Letters and Comments from Readers

We expect to learn from our mistakes, as well as from the input of our readers, and to improve with each book and edition. Many *Unofficial Guide* users write to us asking questions, making comments, or sharing their own discoveries and lessons learned. We appreciate all the input, both positive and critical, and encourage our readers to continue writing. Readers' comments and observations are frequently incorporated into revised editions of the *Unofficial Guide* and contribute immeasurably to its improvement.

How to Write the Authors

Colleen Dunn Bates and Susan LaTempa
The Unofficial Guide to California with Kids
P.O. Box 43673
Birmingham, AL 35243
unofficialguides@menasharidge.com

When you write, be sure to put your return address on your letter as well as on the envelope—sometimes envelopes and letters get separated. And remember that our work takes us out of the office for long periods of time, so forgive us if our response is delayed.

Reader Survey

At the back of this guide, you will find a short questionnaire that you can use to express opinions concerning your California visit. Clip the questionnaire out along the dotted line, and mail it to the above address.

The *Unofficial Guide* Web Site

The Web site of the *Unofficial Guide* Travel and Lifestyle Series, providing in-depth information on all *Unofficial Guides* in print, is at **www.theunofficialguides.com.**

GETTING READY *to* GO

WEATHER AND WHEN TO GO

CALIFORNIA'S CLIMATE VARIES TREMENDOUSLY from region to region, but in general it is a temperate state, suitable for year-round visiting. The deserts (Palm Springs, Anza-Borrego) are brutally hot in late summer, and the far north is rain soaked in winter, so avoid those areas then. Otherwise, travelers have a lot of flexibility. You can always count on warmth and sun in Southern California from mid-June through October, though the coastal areas can get fogged in during early summer (the "June gloom"); the San Francisco Bay Area is more unpredictable, with its chilly fog that's sent many a summer visitor scurrying to the Gap to buy a sweatshirt. (The average daily August temperature in LA, for instance, is 82°F, while in San Francisco the average is just 69°F.)

We're most fond of visiting Los Angeles in May or October, when there's plenty of warm sun but not too much smog or blazing heat. If you're staying at the beach, know that May and June are often gray and overcast; the beach cities of San Diego, Newport, Laguna, Santa Barbara, and Santa Cruz shine in the peak of summer—July, August, and September are best—when days are long and the Pacific warms up. We like San Francisco best in winter, especially around the holidays, when it is festive and mildly brisk, or in September, when the fog is minimal. The mountains, from the southern Sierras to the Cascades, are wonderful year-round, from the ski days of February to the hikes of August.

In general, popular tourist sights are busier on weekends than weekdays, and Saturdays are busier than Sundays. Locals say the least crowded time to visit theme parks is on a rainy weekday in the winter.

Of course, family travel schedules often revolve around school holidays, which tend to be the busiest times to travel. But consider taking your children out of school for special family trips—a well-planned week of family travel is just as enriching as five days in a classroom. Make it clear that traveling is a privilege, and agree that all missed work must be made up upon return. Talk with teachers ahead of time.

PACK LIGHT

WE LIMIT OURSELVES to one carry-on bag and one backpack each, no matter what the duration of the trip or how we are traveling. (The exception is a ski or snow trip, which demands bulky clothes.) If you have small children, stashing an extra T-shirt and pair of shorts in your backpack comes in handy in emergencies. A California trip generally is casual, though you may want to pack one nice outfit for a special evening out.

Make a list of necessities, and let the kids pack their own bags (subject to your inspection). T-shirts, shorts, and bathing suits are perfect in the warmer regions, but never travel without a jacket or

Web Sites for California-bound Kids

Kids from about age 8 and up will connect more with a trip if they're part of the planning. One of the ways for them to plan is to explore the Internet. Here are our favorite Web sites to prepare for a trip within California:

Alcatraz Island–Golden Gate NRA	www.nps.gov/Alcatraz
Birch Aquarium at Scripps	aquarium.ucsd.edu
California Division of Tourism	www.visitcalifornia.com
California images	oac.cdlib.org/search.image.html
California history	www.californiahistory.net
California State Parks	parks.ca.gov
Caltrans driving information	dot.ca.gov
Channel Islands National Park	www.nps.gov/chis
Donner Party	www.donnerpartydiary.com
Exploratorium	www.exploratorium.edu
Gold Country guide	www.malakoff.com/goldcountry
Gold Rush	www.isu.edu/~trinmich
Golden Gate Bridge	www.goldengate.org
Hearst Castle	www.hearstcastle.org
International Surfing Museum	www.surfingmuseum.org
Marine Mammal Center	www.tmmc.org
Monterey Bay Aquarium	www.mbayaq.org
National Park Service	www.nps.gov
Northern California information	www.shastacascade.org
Redwoods: California's redwood canyons	www.savetheredwoods.org
San Diego Zoo and Wild Animal Park	www.sandiegozoo.org
Santa Cruz Beach Boardwalk	www.beachboardwalk.com
Zeum	www.zeum.org

unofficial **TIP**
Bring a "surprise bag" for young travelers. Sticker books, a card game, or a new book is a perfect lightweight diversion to bring out when everyone's patience is wearing thin.

sturdy sweatshirt. California weather is fickle, and you may be surprised with cold. Bring a small bottle of detergent for hand washing. The vacation will be much more enjoyable if you don't have a bunch of bags to haul around busy airports or hotel lobbies.

Let your children pack their own backpacks, then ask them to wear them around the house to test how comfortable they will be on a long trip. Our children have become savvy packers, aware that each piece counts. Of course, you should check their bags before departing, just to be sure the essentials are all there.

REMEMBERING YOUR TRIP

WHEN YOU CHOOSE A DESTINATION, write or call for information (info sources are listed in each chapter). The travel brochures can later be used as part of a scrapbook commemorating your trip.

Purchase a notebook for each child and spend time each evening recording the events of the day. If your children have trouble getting motivated or don't know what to write about, start a discussion; otherwise, let them write or draw, whatever they want to do to remember the day's events.

Collect mementos along the way and create a treasure box in a small tin or cigar box. Months or years later, it's fun to look at postcards, seashells, or ticket stubs to jump-start a memory.

Add some inexpensive postcards to your photographs to create an album, and then write a few words on each page to accompany the images.

Give each child a simple digital or disposable camera to record his or her version of the trip. Our 5-year-old snapped an entire series of photos that never showed anyone above the waist—his view of the world (the photos are priceless).

These days, many families travel with a camcorder, though we don't recommend using one—parents end up viewing the trip through the lens rather than enjoying the sights. Take it along if you must, but record only a few moments of major sights (too much is boring anyway). Let the kids shoot and narrate.

Even better, because it's more compact, carry a palm-sized digital recorder and let everyone describe his or her experiences. Hearing a small child's voice years later is so endearing, and those recorded descriptions will trigger an album's worth of memories, far more focused than what most novices capture with a camcorder.

GETTING THERE

BY CAR

DRIVING IS CERTAINLY THE MOST ECONOMICAL way to travel, but if you're covering a lot of miles, it's time-consuming and can try the patience of every passenger. For starters, don't pull any punches with your kids about just how long you'll be in the car.

If it's a long trip, leave before daylight. Bring small pillows and blankets (we use our children's baby blankets), and let the kids snooze. When they're fully awake a few hours down the road, stop for breakfast and teeth brushing.

Bring along books, crayons, paper, and a couple of laptop games (though not the electronic kind with annoying beeps). Parents can

unofficial **TIP**
Be sure you have maps,
and chart your trip
before you leave home.
Share the maps with the
children so that they'll
understand the distance
to be covered.

stash a few surprises to dole out along the way: sticker books, action figures, magazines. We take along a deflated beach ball to blow up, a Frisbee, or a Koosh ball for impromptu playtimes at rest stops.

The most significant California highway is **Interstate 5,** which runs from Mexico to Oregon, connecting San Diego, Los Angeles, Sacramento, and Mount Shasta. It's fast and convenient, but frequently dreary; the stretch from LA to San Francisco is particularly numbing. **Highway 1 (CA 1)** is the oceanfront road that starts and stops throughout the state; it's worth the detour and time to drive it through the Big Sur area. **US 101** heads in roughly the same direction as I-5, connecting LA to the Oregon border, but is far more charming (and slower), passing through farm and beach towns.

Traffic is a force to be reckoned with in California's urban areas, and you should plan around it. Don't even think about driving across LA or over San Francisco's Bay Bridge at 5:30 p.m.

Seat belts for drivers and front-seat passengers are required by law in California. Child car safety seats are mandatory for children under 4 years of age or weighing less than 40 pounds.

Snacks are great, but leave the drinks (preferably water, since it doesn't stain or get sticky when spilled) until the last moment, or else frequent restroom stops will prolong the journey. Rest areas can be found all along California's major highways, and most of them are open around the clock. Pack a picnic for mealtimes, and everyone can take a walk or stretch.

Small pillows and your own CDs or iPods make the journey peaceful. Take turns and let everyone choose a favorite. If kids fight over music, make them take turns choosing. Ditto for movies on a portable DVD player. To settle seat fights, we rotate turns, either weekly or daily, for who gets to choose a seat first.

Don't forget to always lock your car, and never leave wallets or luggage in sight. Keep valuables locked in the trunk.

BY TRAIN

AMTRAK BRINGS EASTERNERS to California via Chicago and Denver aboard the *Zephyr,* via New Orleans and San Antonio aboard the *Sunset Limited,* and via Chicago and Kansas City aboard the *Southwest Chief.* Northwesterners can train down on the *Coast Starlight,* which runs from Seattle to Los Angeles. Amtrak also runs popular commuter and vacationer trains from LA north to San Luis Obispo and south to San Diego, and from the San Francisco Bay Area north to Auburn and south to Bakersfield.

We've taken long train trips, and for youngsters, it's interesting for about the first hour of a many-hour trip. But with books, games, and activities to occupy the time, it's a leisurely and relatively inexpensive way to travel, with time to unwind and spend quality moments with your family. You can stand up and stretch, or go for a walk, and there's more legroom than in an airplane or car (and no traffic jams). Plus,

unofficial **TIP**
If you opt for a longer train trip, book first class and a sleeping car.

many trains offer sleeping and dining cars, but remember: some trips can be mighty long, and the fare is not much less than cut-rate airfares.

Amtrak offers a children's discount—kids ages 2 through 15 ride for half price when accompanied by a full-fare-paying adult. Each adult can bring two children for the discount; one child under the age of 2 rides free with every adult ticket purchased.

If you're arriving in LA by train, you'll need a car to get around, so reserve one in advance. It's entirely possible, however, to arrive in San Francisco, Santa Barbara, and San Diego and enjoy your stay without a car.

For reservations and information, call ☎ 800-USA-RAIL or log on to the Internet at **www.amtrak.com.**

BY PLANE

MAJOR AIRLINES SERVE EVERY PART OF CALIFORNIA, so choosing a flight is a matter of time and economics. Booking as far in advance as possible can save hundreds of dollars for a family of four. When you book your tickets, be sure to get your seat assignments. Request bulkhead seats for small kids who won't be entertained by a movie but might be able to move around a bit. Although far-front seats are

preferred for the most part, be sure to ask how the movie is shown; if you're more than a few rows back from a small screen, it can be hard to enjoy the film.

Takeoff and landing bother some children's ears, particularly if they have a cold. Look for plastic earplugs designed to ease the pain of ear pressure. They come in children's sizes and are available at travel stores, drugstores, and airport sundry stores. We've found them to be highly effective. One pair lasts for at least two flights; they cost $2 or $3 per pair. You can also bring gum for older children or a bottle or sipper cup for babies and toddlers. A washcloth heated with hot water from the restroom and held to ears will also help the younger ones who can't tolerate earplugs. Most of your fellow passen-

unofficial **TIP**
Pack a few nutritious snacks and a small bottle of water. If you or your child wants or needs a special meal, be sure to call the airline at least 48 hours in advance to request it. Remember that you can no longer bring gels and liquids—including juice boxes—on board; visit **www.tsa.gov** for the latest security restrictions.

gers would agree that the best babies on airplanes are sleeping babies, so, if possible, book your flights around nap times, which assures a peaceful flight for you and a happy child as you land.

Bring your own child-safety seat; though airlines allow children under 2 years of age to fly free on a parent's lap, it's much safer if they're strapped in a safety seat (and they're much more likely to nap, giving you a break). A car seat must have a visible label stating it is approved for air travel.

IF YOU RENT A CAR

THE CAR IS KING IN CALIFORNIA, so rental rates are competitive, and every major company is represented at the larger airports. Recreational vehicles, four-wheel-drives, and convertibles can also be rented, though they are considerably more expensive. To rent a car, you will need a valid driver's license, proof of insurance, and a major credit card. Some companies have minimum age requirements.

Ask about extras. Many companies offer GPS, cell phones, satellite radio, ski racks, area maps, and child-safety seats (California law says that any child who is less than 40 pounds or under 4 years old must sit in a safety seat).

If there are more than four in your family, you might want to consider renting a minivan. They cost a little more, but the comfort is worth it.

FAMILY LODGING

HOTELS, MOTELS, AND RESORTS

IN EACH REGIONAL CHAPTER, you'll find our favorite family hotels, motels, and resorts. Note that we said favorite *family* hotels, not favorite hotels, period—many wonderful retreats were excluded because they're aimed at romantics or businesspeople, and they would make any parent of an energetic 4-year-old feel like a leper. We've reviewed only places that particularly catch our fancy or seem suitable for families, and we've striven to find places with character. If you don't see an accommodation in the region you wish to visit, call the toll-free number of your favorite chain to find out what it offers.

Tips on Hotels, Motels, and Resorts with Kids

First, there has to be a pool. After that, you get some choices.

One room or two? Large or small? Upscale hotel or basic motel? Old or new? There are pros and cons with each of these overnight options, and we've found that on different days on the same vacation, we might make different choices.

Overall, one of the hardest things for some of us parents to adjust to is being awake when the kids are asleep but not wanting to leave them alone in the room. Although adjoining rooms are a good option in some hotels, they're not offered everywhere, and the choice between one or more rooms for a family always seems to come up.

CHILDPROOF YOUR ROOM

When you arrive at the hotel, some childproofing may be in order. Be sure that both the front door and any patio or balcony doors and windows can be securely locked and bolted. Some hotels offer electrical-outlet coverings if you have toddlers, and protective covers for sharp furniture corners. They also will remove glass objects or other knickknacks that might be easy for a toddler to break. And if the minibar is stocked with junk food and alcoholic beverages, it should be locked.

So we try, on an extended family vacation during which we're moving from place to place, to book ourselves into several different kinds of facilities and have different solutions. In a hub city where we're not expecting to be in a picturesque setting, we look for a business-suite chain, especially on the weekends, when discounts are often offered (but check to see that all amenities, such as breakfasts, continue). The price for a spacious suite may be the same as for a cramped room at the motel down the street, and it's great to be able to watch the late show while the little ones snooze.

Big landmark hotels or luxury hotels with character are worth the splurge for us if the location is workable, and they might come at the end of a road trip, when the only choices in small-town stops on the way have been inexpensive roadside motels. Our kids tell us they like the excitement of big hotels (it's almost like a theme park, they say) and even enjoy "the neat old stuff" in some establishments. And room service is God's gift to traveling parents. But we also always ask about the executive, concierge, or butler floor of this kind of establishment, because the lounge areas often offer breakfast, coffee, snacks, and wine at various hours. For one thing, it's convenient for grabbing a muffin for a kid in the room; for another, it's a place for parents to escape to, like a living room, without being far away.

The all-American motel is, of course, a favorite with families. No need to find a bellman—you park in front of your room and unload only what you need. Kids love roaming the corridors for ice, getting soda from the machines, and spotting other children. Lack of towel service poolside may be compensated for by the existence of a coin laundry. At this kind of hostelry, we might opt for one room, but we'd request a room near the pool with a patio or veranda. Proximity to the pool allows kids of a certain age to come and go; the patio extends the living space nicely.

CHILDREN'S PROGRAMS

MANY LARGE HOTELS OFFER supervised programs for children, some complimentary, some with fees. We've included several hotels throughout California that offer exemplary activities.

Chain-hotel Toll-free Numbers

This guidebook gives details on some of the hotels in California with outstanding children's programs. However, for your convenience we've listed toll-free numbers for the following hotel and motel chains' reservation lines:

Best Western	☎ 800-780-7234 United States and Canada
Comfort Inn	☎ 877-424-6423 United States and Canada
Courtyard by Marriott	☎ 888-236-2427 United States and Canada
Days Inn	☎ 800-329-7466 United States
Doubletree	☎ 800-222-TREE (8733) United States
Econo Lodge	☎ 800-424-6423 United States
Embassy Suites	☎ 800-EMBASSY (362-2779) United States and Canada
Fairfield Inn by Marriott	☎ 800-228-2800 United States
Four Seasons	☎ 800-819-5053 United States and Canada
Hampton Inn	☎ 800-HAMPTON (426-7866) United States and Canada
Hilton	☎ 800-HILTONS (445-8667) United States
Holiday Inn	☎ 888-HOLIDAY (465-4329) United States and Canada
Howard Johnson	☎ 800-I-GO-HOJO (446-4656) United States
Hyatt	☎ 800-233-1234 United States and Canada
Loews	☎ 800-23-LOEWS (235-6397) United States and Canada
Marriott	☎ 888-236-2427 United States and Canada
Quality Inn	☎ 877-424-6423 United States and Canada
Radisson	☎ 888-201-1718 United States and Canada
Ramada Inn	☎ 800-272-6232 United States
Renaissance Hotels	☎ 888-236-2427 United States and Canada
Residence Inn by Marriott	☎ 888-236-2427 United States
Ritz-Carlton	☎ 800-542-8680 United States and Canada
Sheraton	☎ 800-325-3535 United States and Canada
Wyndham	☎ 877-999-3223 United States

If you decide to take advantage of the kids' programs, call ahead for specific children's events that are scheduled during your vacation. Ask about cost and the ages that can participate; the best programs divide children into age groups. Make reservations for activities your child might enjoy (you can always cancel after arrival).

After check-in, stop by and visit with the kids'-program staff. Ask about counselor-child ratio and whether the counselors are trained in first aid and CPR. Briefly introduce your children to the staff and setting, which typically will leave them wanting more, thereby easing the separation anxiety when they return to stay.

Some hotels offer in-room babysitting, but if your hotel does not, there is a national, non-profit referral program called **Child Care Aware** that will help you locate a good, high-quality sitter. Call ☎ 800-424-2246, Monday through Friday, 6 a.m. to 4 p.m. Pacific Time, or see **www.childcareaware.org.**

CAMPING

WE'VE INCLUDED A SMALL but choice collection of California campgrounds—ones that are easily accessible, fun for children, and not too demanding of parents (we consider bathrooms and running water, for instance, to be essential). Camping can be a wonderful family experience, slowing down the pace so you can all take pleasure in the small things, from fishing in a stream to chasing butterflies. And, of course, camping takes you to California's most beautiful places for very little money.

Most of these campgrounds are state properties, and all are popular; for those that take reservations, make them early. Reservations are accepted seven months in advance, and the good campgrounds often book up fully seven months ahead; call **ReserveAmerica** at ☎ 800-444-7275 or visit **www.reserveamerica.com.**

Tips on Camping with Children

We've had wonderful family camping trips—and horrible ones. Basically, if you are regular campers and your children are used to it from birth, you'll be happy at any of the campgrounds we suggest. If you're not regular campers, we'd recommend the motel option while your children are between infancy and the age of at least 3, maybe 4. As young as 6, Colleen's daughters rolled up their own sleeping bags, rinsed their own cups, and hiked a couple of miles, but at age 2 they mostly ate rocks, cried, and slept about four hours a night (tent living can greatly upset the routines of sensitive toddlers).

One of Colleen's daughters attends a school that organizes many camping trips, and we've adopted the school's camp rules in our families, because they maximize safety and comfort. They are as follows:

unofficial **TIP** Be sure to ask if the babysitter is licensed, bonded, and insured. To ease your children's anxiety, tell them how long you plan to be away, and be sure they feel good about the person who will be caring for them. Finally, trust your own instincts.

unofficial **TIP** Camping is a superb opportunity to teach kids independence and self-reliance. If they're all expected to help out and the adventure aspect is played up, they'll help prepare food, pitch tents, and do camp chores.

- No one is allowed to leave the campsite (even to go to the bathroom) without a whistle. Children wear the whistle around their necks; adults can carry it as they like. The whistle is blown only in an emergency, which can range from a twisted ankle to getting lost.

- Hats and sunscreen must be worn on all outings.
- Water must be carried on all outings.
- No playing, exploring, or hiking until the morning campsites are tidied and breakfast dishes are done.

Finally, recognize that camping is tiring, and after a few days of sleeping on the ground, tempers of both children and adults can get frayed. After two or three nights of roughing it, nothing cheers up a family like clean hotel sheets, a swimming pool, and a restaurant hamburger.

FAMILY-FRIENDLY RESTAURANTS

WE LOVE FOOD AND LOVE TO EAT OUT, and our kids love to eat out, too, but rarely do we agree on what constitutes a good restaurant. We like comfort, good service, creative cooking, and a nice glass of wine. They like noise, cups with lids, and as much fried food as possible. Hence the challenge: to put together a roster of restaurants throughout the state that make both parents and children happy. We had more success in some areas than others; some parts of the state don't have much more than coffee shops and chains, so you'll have to make do. Other areas, however (especially the San Francisco Bay Area, the Central Coast, and the LA area), are rich in kid- and parent-friendly dining.

You'll note that few major chain restaurants and no chain fast-food restaurants are found in the listings that follow. We encourage you to skip McDonald's whenever possible and make the effort to patronize local places—not only is it better for your health, but you're also more likely to get a feel for an area when you sit with the locals and eat a burrito or dim sum or pancakes. As for the big chain restaurants, we find most of them to be soulless and dull. There are exceptions, especially such smaller chains as Islands, Rubio's, and Ruby's, all of which are good family restaurants with California flair.

The major tourist areas all seem to have Hard Rock Cafes and Planet Hollywoods, but we cover those rarely—after all, if you've been to one Hard Rock, you've been to them all. Your hotel in San Francisco, LA, San Diego, or Orange County can steer you to one of them.

Tips on Dining Out with Children

BE REALISTIC ABOUT AGE LIMITS   We ate at elegant restaurants when our children were sleeping infants in car seats. By the time toddlerhood hit, we restricted ourselves to good-quality fast food (such as taquerias), child-friendly ethnic restaurants (Chinese, Cuban, Mexican, etc.), and take-out food enjoyed in park picnic areas. We began restaurant training in earnest at about age 4, the dawn of a years-long process of gentle reminding about napkins on laps, feet off chairs, and proper butter-knife etiquette. We expect to have achieved success around the junior year of college.

DON'T BATTLE A PICKY EATER   You'll never win this one. If everything looks yucky, get them some plain rice and plain bread. Enjoy your food with gusto, and if the kids get hungry enough, they'll break down and ask to try some.

LOOK BEYOND THE KIDS' MENU   The vast majority are monotonous and unhealthy, consisting mostly of burgers, deep-fried chicken, and French fries. Encourage experimentation in the grown-up menu, and ask if it's possible to order smaller portions of the "adult" food.

REMEMBER THE TAILGATE   We had more fun eating on a tailgating vacation than perhaps any other. Grocery stores, delis, upscale gourmet shops, and mini-marts are all stocked with foods that seem almost too decadent to buy at home—but if you're tailgating, you have to go for the convenience foods. So we'd get take-out salads and chicken, made-to-order sandwiches, sushi, poached salmon, fresh baguettes, imported cheeses, and exotic fruits. The price was still less than that of a bad meal at a roadside coffee shop.

WATCH THE IN-BETWEENERS   When they feel too old for (or don't like) the children's menu but can't really eat a big meal, some parental diplomacy is in order, or the in-betweener will be taking one bite from a huge order of whatever and then stopping, overwhelmed. Some kids will agree to splitting or sharing a meal, but let them choose most of it. Sometimes it's just a matter of ordering three meals for four people, so you avoid huge quantities of leftovers (which you can't take home when you're traveling) and yet allow for some tasting of different things.

SOUP, SOUP, SOUP   Not only is it comforting and homey, but soup also is often a tasty, nutritious, affordable basis for a kid's meal that needs only an appetizer to complete it.

LET THEM BE WEIRD   One man we know is still grateful to his parents for letting him order hamburgers at breakfast, and conversely, how many people are cheered up by a nice breakfast at 7 p.m.? As much as possible, let your kids enjoy the get-what-you-want pleasure of restaurant eating as part of their vacation. Remember, they're also missing home, routine, and the certainty of their daily meal rituals.

FREE CALIFORNIA PUBLICATIONS FOR VISITORS

FOR DESTINATION AND STATEWIDE VISITORS' information, contact the **California Division of Tourism,** P.O. Box 1499, Sacramento 95812; ☎ 916-444-4429 or 800-862-2543; **www.visitcalifornia.com.** For publications detailing the exceptional state park system, contact the

California State Park System, Department of Parks and Recreation, P.O. Box 942896, Sacramento 94296; ☎ 916-653-6995 or 800-777-0369; **parks.ca.gov.** To reserve a state campground, call ☎ 800-444-7275; for a federal campground, call ☎ 877-444-6777; or, for both, see **www .reserveamerica.com.**

PART ONE

SAN DIEGO COUNTY

WHAT AN INTERESTING TOEHOLD SAN DIEGO COUNTY has on the continent—right at the edge, where travelers must choose between the ocean and a foreign country if they keep going. The eastern part of the county is home to the enormous **Anza-Borrego Desert State Park.** The coastal area is the population center, with the city of **San Diego** (the second-largest municipality in the state) dominating. The northern part of the county (before the huge military base at **Camp Pendleton** takes over the map) is dotted with golf courses. To the south, of course, is Mexico.

unofficial **TIP**
Families will find San Diego County easy to like. It has everything California is supposed to have—palm trees, beaches, a multicultural population, unlimited outdoor recreation, sophisticated cultural offerings, and good Mexican food.

We've taken our kids to San Diego County in all seasons and for lots of different kinds of vacations. We've ridden the train from **LA** and stayed in downtown San Diego, riding the trolley to the **San Diego Zoo** and shopping in **Horton Plaza.** We based ourselves in **Carlsbad** to visit the **Wild Animal Park** and **Legoland** and enjoyed a bonus of gorgeous beach time. We've lolled in a fancy **Coronado Island** resort's outdoor spa after biking all over the island and taking the ferry back and forth just for fun. And we've sat in the gentle tidal waters of **Mission Bay** while a happy toddler splashed next to us. You see where this is headed, of course. It'll take more than a single vacation to even begin to sample San Diego's charms.

If it's your first visit to the San Diego area and you're arriving in summer, a four-day itinerary with a base at one of the Mission Bay resorts is ideal. **SeaWorld** is right in Mission Bay, so that's one day's outing. Pick among the zoo, the Wild Animal Park, a **Balboa Park** museum or two, **Old Town,** and **Legoland California** for another two days of fun. Finish with a day dedicated to water sports and beach fun. If the attractions that most interest you are Legoland and the

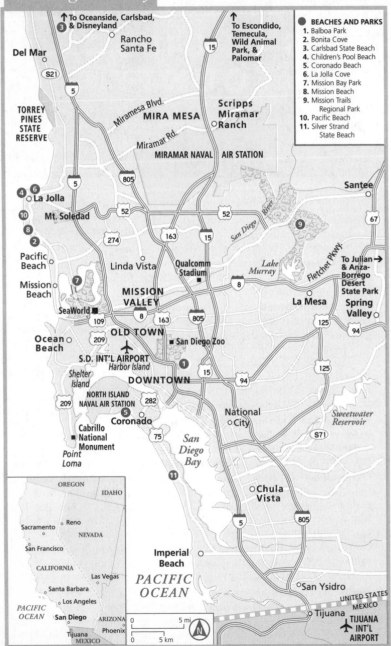

san diego county

↑ To Oceanside, Carlsbad, & Disneyland
3

Rancho Santa Fe

Del Mar

S21

5

↑ To Escondido, Temecula, Wild Animal Park, & Palomar

15

BEACHES AND PARKS
1. Balboa Park
2. Bonita Cove
3. Carlsbad State Beach
4. Children's Pool Beach
5. Coronado Beach
6. La Jolla Cove
7. Mission Bay Park
8. Mission Beach
9. Mission Trails Regional Park
10. Pacific Beach
11. Silver Strand State Beach

TORREY PINES STATE RESERVE

Miramesa Blvd.

MIRA MESA

Scripps Miramar Ranch

Miramar Rd.

MIRAMAR NAVAL   AIR STATION

5

805

4 **6** La Jolla
10
Mt. Soledad
8
2

52

52

163

15

San Diego River

9

Fletcher Pkwy.

Santee

67

Pacific Beach

Mission Beach

274

Linda Vista

Qualcomm Stadium

Lake Murray

To Julian & Anza-Borrego Desert State Park →

7

SeaWorld

109

MISSION VALLEY

8

163

805

8

La Mesa

Spring Valley

125

94

Ocean Beach

209

OLD TOWN

San Diego Zoo

S.D. INT'L AIRPORT
Harbor Island

1

15

94

125

Shelter Island

DOWNTOWN

NORTH ISLAND NAVAL AIR STATION

209

282

5 Coronado

National City

Sweetwater Reservoir

S71

Cabrillo National Monument

Point Loma

75

San Diego Bay

11

Chula Vista

5

805

OREGON

IDAHO

Sacramento

Reno

NEVADA

San Francisco

CALIFORNIA

Las Vegas

Santa Barbara

Los Angeles

PACIFIC OCEAN

San Diego

ARIZONA

Tijuana

MEXICO

Phoenix

Imperial Beach

PACIFIC OCEAN

San Ysidro

UNITED STATES
MEXICO

Tijuana

TIJUANA INT'L AIRPORT

0   5 mi

0   5 km

N

Wild Animal Park and you like a small-town setting, consider staying up the coast in **Carlsbad.** Families traveling with convention-goers won't be disappointed with the ever-improving downtown area and can try out the car-free itineraries described below. Visitors with another day should add a **Borrego Springs** visit, a **Tijuana** excursion (*note:* passports are required to enter Mexico), or (in early spring) a whale-watching boat trip.

GETTING THERE

BY PLANE   San Diego International Airport, also known as **Lindbergh Field,** is served by most major airlines; ☎ 619-231-2100; **www.san .org**) and is just northwest of downtown.

BY TRAIN   Amtrak makes its final southbound stop in San Diego, delivering travelers from as far north as Seattle. From LA, the trip is less than three hours on the popular, well-patronized **Pacific Surfliner** commuter line (frequent departures morning and afternoon). Excellent public transportation from the train station makes a trip without a car possible. Call ☎ 800-USA-RAIL, or visit **www.amtrak.com** or **www.amtrakcalifornia.com.**

BY CAR   Interstate 5, which runs from Canada to Mexico, is the main freeway heading into San Diego. It's also reached from the north by **Interstate 15,** which passes through the Riverside area and connects to **Interstate 10,** and by **Interstate 8,** which heads east to Arizona. A car is not necessary to enjoy central San Diego, but it's great to have if you want to explore the farther reaches.

Car-free Sightseeing

Although San Diego and its suburbs are spread generously over many acres, and motorists will find their way along good roads and modern freeways, the city has also created a network of public transportation that permits easy access to major attractions, many of which are in a comparatively concentrated geographic area. The weather's almost always sunny and mild, so the journey from place to place is a pleasant jaunt; and because the city does a brisk convention business, the various trams, trolleys, and ferries have enough patronage to justify frequent, convenient runs.

If you think you'd like to do San Diego without a car (arriving by train, for example), you'll need to stay downtown, in Coronado, or near Old Town in order to easily combine the attractions mentioned here into a network. You can also simply take a taxi or municipal bus to the first boarding point of the day.

Here's a sample no-car itinerary: Board the **Old Town Trolley Tours** bus at your hotel in Coronado and ride it (enjoying the guide's descriptions of passing sights) to **Balboa Park.** Spend a morning at the zoo, then take the free Balboa shuttle to the **Space Museum,** then reboard the Old Town Trolley and continue to Old Town. Save the historic buildings for another day, but enjoy a Mexican meal and some shopping, then take the **San Diego Trolley** to downtown, changing to another trolley to **Seaport Village.** At Seaport Village, let the kids play some games and get an ice-cream cone, then get on the ferry to cross the water to Coronado and your hotel.

You might think the Old Town Trolley Tours bus (with narration and music) is corny, but it sure is convenient. It goes to most of the major attractions, and you can get on and off at ten stops, including Old Town, the **Embarcadero, Seaport Village,** Horton Plaza, Coronado, and Balboa Park. For locations of stops and a timetable, call ☎ 800-868-7482 or 619-298-8687, or visit **www.historictours.com.** Fare is $32 adults, $16 ages 4 to 12; age 3 and under free. **Metropolitan Transit Service's Transit Store** (102 Broadway, downtown San Diego; ☎ 619-234-1060 or 511; **transit.511sd.com**) is a center of information about buses, Coaster (coastal light rail), and the San Diego Trolley. The center is open from 9 a.m. to 5 p.m. weekdays; closed weekends. The new 511 system, sponsored by a coalition of transit entities, operates a free phone (just dial 511) and Web service (see above) with one-stop information about transportation options throughout the county. The Day Tripper Transit Pass, available as a one- ($5), two- ($9), three- ($12), or four-day ($15) pass, is sold here. There is no charge for children age 6 and under. One-day passes can also be purchased at trolley stations and the ferry landing.

The **San Diego Trolley** (☎ 619-233-3004; automated info line, ☎ 619-685-4900) operates daily from 5 a.m. to midnight, with service every 15 minutes most of the time. Tickets are dispensed from automated machines at each station. The **Blue Line** extends from Old Town through downtown to the Mexican border. The **Orange Line** covers the Harbor Drive area and goes to Seaport Village, to the convention center, and through downtown and the **Gaslamp Quarter,** including **Petco Park,** home of the San Diego Padres baseball team. The **Green Line** links to the Blue Line and heads for **Qualcomm Stadium,** home of the San Diego Chargers football team, via Mission Valley. Fares are $1.25 to $6. There is free daily tram-shuttle service around Balboa Park.

The **San Diego–Coronado Ferry** (☎800-442-7847 or 619-234-4111; **www.sdhe.com/san-diego-bay-ferry.html**) runs between downtown San Diego's Broadway Pier (1050 North Harbor Drive, at Broadway) and the Ferry Landing Marketplace on Coronado at First Street and B Avenue. The crossing is 15 minutes, and the ferry leaves San Diego every hour on the hour from 9 a.m. to 9 p.m., returning from Coronado every hour on the half hour. One-way fares are $3.50 per person, and reservations are not needed.

The **San Diego Water Taxi** (Fish Harbor Pier, Seaport Village, 891 West Harbor Drive; ☎ 619-235-8294; **www.sdhe.com/san-diego-water-taxi.html**) offers on-call service daily from 3 p.m. to 10 p.m., and transports people to various spots around the bay, including Shelter Island,

Harbor Island, Coronado, and Chula Vista; fares start at $7 but can vary by destination.

HOW TO GET INFORMATION BEFORE YOU GO

- **Anza-Borrego Desert State Park Visitors Center**   200 Palm Canyon Drive, Borrego Springs 92004; ☎ 760-767-5311; **parks.ca.gov**
- **Balboa Park Visitors Center**   1549 El Prado, San Diego 92101; ☎ 619-239-0512; **www.balboapark.org**
- **Border Station Parking and Tourist Information**   A commercial park-and-shuttle service at the Mexican border; 4570 Camino De La Plaza, San Ysidro 92173; ☎ 619-428-1422; **www.borderparking.com**
- **Carlsbad Convention & Visitors Bureau**   400 Carlsbad Village Drive, Carlsbad 92008; ☎ 800-CARLSBAD or 760-434-6093; **www.carlsbadca.org**
- **Coronado Visitor Center**   1100 Orange Avenue, Coronado 92118; ☎ 619-437-8788; **www.coronadovisitorcenter.com**
- **San Diego Convention & Visitors Bureau**   2215 India Street, San Diego 92101; ☎ 619-232-3101; **www.sandiego.org**
- **Tijuana Tourism Board**   ☎ 800-025-0888; **www.seetijuana.com**

CHILD CARE AND BABYSITTING

Marion's Childcare (10491 Pine Grove Street, Spring Valley; ☎ 619-303-4379 or 888-891-5029; **www.hotelchildcare.com**), a long-established agency providing in-room child care, works with concierges all over town.

The BEST BEACHES and PARKS

ANZA-BORREGO DESERT STATE PARK   This 600,000-acre park is home to bighorn sheep, roadrunners, and, in the spring, amazing wildflower displays; it's rich with riding and hiking trails for families with desert and wilderness experience. For a stop on a driving tour of San Diego County, the visitors center offers a fine slide presentation and lots of great children's books on desert flora and fauna. Open daily October through May, on weekends and holidays only June through September. Visitors center: 200 Palm Canyon Drive, Borrego Springs; ☎ 760-767-5311; **parks.ca.gov**.

BALBOA PARK   San Diego has taken the urban park to new heights, going beyond outdoor recreation to create a compact cultural hub that no other American city can rival (except, of course, Washington, DC). In the heart of the city, not far from downtown, Balboa is home to 14 museums (many are reviewed later), the world-famous San Diego Zoo, and five theaters (including the Old Globe). You'll also find outdoor pleasures,

unofficial **TIP**
Before you visit any of Balboa Park's destinations, hop on the free tram that cruises the park, both to get oriented and to give your kids a cheap thrill.

including picnic areas, three playgrounds, and botanical gardens, along with amusements such as a miniature-train ride, a carousel, and a butterfly-theme ride for kids age 5 and under. Open daily 9:30 a.m. to 4:30 p.m., 5 p.m in summer; free parking. The Web site offers packages such as the Passport to Balboa Park for $65 adults, $36 children ages 3 through 12, which gets you into 13 attractions plus the zoo ($39 and $21 without the zoo). Visitors Center: House of Hospitality building, 1549 El Prado; ☎ 619-239-0512; **www.balboapark.org.**

BONITA COVE   Within Mission Bay Park, near **Belmont Park** and **Mission Beach,** you'll find this outdoor paradise for young children. The calm, shallow water is friendly even to toddlers, and there's a playground, a grassy picnic area, and sand to dig. For information, call ☎ 858-694-3049 or visit **www.sandiego.gov/park-and-recreation.**

CARLSBAD STATE BEACH   A broad sand beach with a wide, concrete bike and skating path, this is a great summertime beach for families—there's typically enough surf to have fun in, but it's rarely rough. Just south of the beach is Agua Hedionda Lagoon, a calm, wave-free spot for swimming, fishing, and boating. Lifeguards, restrooms, showers. For information, call ☎ 760-438-3143; **carlsbad.ca.us/beaches.**

CHILDREN'S POOL BEACH   Still known by the name given it by locals who brought kids to play in the quiet surf, this beach is now home to herds of sea lions. Families stop by to look down on the hundreds of huge, protected creatures from a high vantage point. End of Jenner Street, 850 Coast Boulevard, La Jolla; ☎ 619-221-8901; **www.sandiego .gov/lifeguards/beaches.**

CORONADO BEACH   San Diego's widest beach, Coronado is so big that it absorbs even the largest crowds comfortably. Good for swimming, bodyboarding, people-watching, and basic beach fun, it is guarded by the looming Hotel del Coronado. There are volleyball courts, fire pits on the north end, changing rooms, lifeguards in summer, showers, and pay parking at the hotel or free parking on the streets. For beach information, call ☎ 619-437-8788 or 866-599-7242; **www.coronadovisitorcenter.com.**

LA JOLLA COVE   A drop-dead gorgeous jewel of a beach, in a cove protected by cliffs, La Jolla Cove seems smaller than ever in peak season, when crowds get intense. But don't let that keep you from enjoying the tide pools, the calm, clean water, the excellent snorkeling, and the grassy picnic areas. Next door is Boomer Beach, an expert-bodysurfing spot that's dangerous for most but great for pros, or for watching the locals put on a show. Changing rooms, lifeguard. Coast Boulevard to Scripps Park, La Jolla. For information, call ☎ 619-221-8901; **www .sandiego.gov/lifeguards/beaches.**

MISSION BAY PARK   Although major resorts and hotels line Mission Bay, a calm-water tidal area that curls and curves for many acres, the bay's park is a huge public playground, with grassy meadows and picnic areas sloping down to sandy beaches (many areas with no waves!), as well as several marinas servicing the 4,235-acre aquatic sports area. There are designated areas for each sport (swimming, sailing, windsurfing, kayaking, waterskiing, and fishing). And paved bike paths dot the grassy areas and run along the shore. Free parking lots adjacent; no overnight parking or camping. Fires allowed in designated fire containers on beaches. The playground at Tecolote Shores was especially designed for disabled children. For more information, call ☎ 619-276-8200 or 858-694-3049, or log on to **www.sandiego .gov/park-and-recreation/parks/missionbay.**

MISSION BEACH   If you have older kids who want to be where the action is, head to this two-mile-long shoreline on the ocean side of Mission Bay. Teenagers are plentiful here, playing volleyball, skating on the boardwalk, bodyboarding in the sometimes-rough surf (riptides are common), and flaunting the latest surf wear. On the boardwalk right in the center of the beach is Belmont Park amusement park (see profile, page 43). Changing rooms, showers, lifeguards. Mission Boulevard, Mission Bay; for information, call ☎ 619-221-8900; **www .sandiego.gov/lifeguards/beaches.**

MISSION TRAILS REGIONAL PARK   See "Hiking" under "Family Outdoor Adventures."

PACIFIC BEACH   Locals call it the Strand, and locals are plentiful on hot summer days, of which San Diego has many. (Consequently, parking is a challenge.) It has everything a big public beach should have, from a fishing pier to a biking and skating path to bodyboard rentals to lifeguards; surfers are limited to one area, so swimmers don't have to battle them for wave space. The many restaurants and shops of the neighborhood of Pacific Beach are a short walk away. Changing rooms, showers, restrooms (but no public restrooms between Pacific Beach Drive and Mission Beach). Mission Boulevard, San Diego; for information, call ☎ 619-221-8900; **www.pacificbeach.org.**

SILVER STRAND STATE BEACH   Three things make this state park a good beach for families: the surf and riptides are fairly calm; parking is plentiful here, unlike at the city beaches; and the shoreline sparkles with millions of tiny silver shells, which enchant many children. This two-mile-long beach connects the isthmus of Coronado (no, it's not really an island) to the mainland's Imperial Beach, and it's quieter than the beach in front of the Hotel Del Coronado. The broad, shallow shoreline allows for lots of safe scampering in gentle waves (or in no waves on the bay side), as well as good clamming and surf fishing. If you visit in winter, know that the location invites wind and chill, so dress warmly. Dogs are not allowed on the beach, in the tunnels, or on the bay side. Parking is free, and RV camping (reservations required) is available for $25 to $30; no tent camping. Restrooms, showers, lifeguards. Follow signs off CA 75; for information, call ☎ 619-435-5184; **parks.ca.gov.**

FAMILY OUTDOOR ADVENTURES

BICYCLING AND SKATING   On some bright summer days, it seems that every San Diegan is on skates, bikes, or skateboards, making good use of the endless paved paths that wend around Mission Bay and along the beaches. Mission and Pacific Beaches are particularly fun to cruise, but in season they can get intimidatingly crowded and speedy for the training-wheel set. For a quieter, beautiful, long ride, follow the path along the Coronado shoreline through Silver Strand State Park. The Mission Bay paths are also good for younger children. On Coronado Island, you can rent bikes and skates from **Bikes and Beyond,** Ferry Landing Marketplace; ☎ 619-435-7180; **www.hollands bicycles.com.** In the Mission Bay area, get gear from **Mission Bay Sportcenter,** Hyatt Regency Mission Bay Spa & Marina, 1441 Quivira Road; ☎ 619-221-9264; **www.missionbaysportcenter.com.**

BOATING   Even novices can learn to sail in the calm waters of Mission Bay, and every weekend, they're out there doing it. Boats and lessons are offered at **Mission Bay Sportcenter,** 1010 Santa Clara Place; ☎ 858-488-1004; **www.missionbaysportcenter.com.** At the Dana Hotel on Mission Bay (1710 West Mission Bay Drive), there's **Adventure Water Sports;** ☎ 619-226-8611; **www.adventurewatersports.com**), offering motorboats, kayaks, and aqua cycles.

FISHING   Oceangoing fishing charters are plentiful in San Diego, but with kids we prefer a cheaper, lower-key outing—we head for one of the several fetching piers, where licenses are unnecessary and fish are often caught. The piers at Pacific Beach and the Coronado Ferry Landing are good ones, and both have bait-and-tackle shops.

HIKING   Serious hiking opportunities abound in the region, but with kids in tow, our favorite destination is **Mission Trails Regional Park** (1 Father Junipero Serra Trail, San Diego; ☎ 619-668-3275; **www .mtrp.org**). This inland, 5,800-acre urban park has 35 miles of trails for hiking, mountain biking, and horseback riding, and some of the trails are paved to accommodate strollers and wheelchairs. Pick up a map at the visitors center. If your kids are sturdy, tackle the trail to San Diego's highest peak, a 1,600-foot climb that pays off with a 360-degree view of the city.

SNORKELING   California's clearest waters are found in **La Jolla Cove,** a protected part of the San Diego–La Jolla Underwater Park. For swimming children old enough to manage a mask and snorkel (typically age 7 and up), a snorkeling adventure is mind-blowing, as interactive a nature experience as they'll ever have. See La Jolla Cove listing in "The Best Beaches and Parks" for location details; if you don't have snorkel gear, you can rent it from **La Jolla Kayak** 2199 Avenida de la Playa, La Jolla; ☎ 858-459-1114; **www.lajollakayak.com**).

SURFING   Surfing's popularity has exploded in the last few years, and so the choices for surf lessons and camps are numerous. One of our favorites is the **San Diego Surfing Academy** (☎ 800-447-SURF or 760-230-1474; **www.surfsdsa.com**), which makes fine use of the gentle waves at South Carlsbad State Beach in its private lessons for kids (age 8 and up) and adults; also note that its summertime surf camps can be attended for just a day or two. On Mission Beach, Pacific Surf School (☎ 858-488-2685; **www.pacificsurf.org**) offers frequent group lessons for a reasonable $55 to $65. Also highly recommended is **La Jolla's Surf Diva** (☎ 858-454-8273; **www.surfdiva .com**), known for its classes for girls and their moms, but boys are welcome, too. If you want to try it on your own, rent a soft-foam longboard from the rental concessions at Pacific Beach and go for it.

WATERSKIING AND WINDSURFING   On the ocean side of Mission Bay is some of the best windsurfing in California; on the bay side is superb waterskiing. For instruction and equipment for both sports, you can contact the **Mission Bay Sportcenter** (1010 Santa Clara Place; ☎ 858-488-1004; **www.missionbaysportcenter.com**); open daily, 9 a.m. to 7 p.m. The staff can also get you started on a surfboard, personal watercraft, or kayak. Another good spot for waterskiing lessons and rentals (as well as whale-watching excursions) is **Seaforth Mission Bay Boat Rentals** (1641 Quivira Road; ☎ 619-223-1681; **www.seaforthboat rental.com**).

 WHALE WATCHING   The Pacific gray whale swims past San Diego from December through mid-March, and blowhole and breech sightings are common. In fact, so confident is one outfitter, **H&M Landing** (2803 Emerson Street, San Diego; ☎ 619-222-1144; **www.hmlanding.com**), that it guarantees a whale sighting or you get a voucher for another outing. Family trips are typically three hours long. If you'd rather scout whales from dry land, head to the Cabrillo National Monument on Point Loma (see profile, page 44).

A **CALENDAR** of **FESTIVALS** and **EVENTS**

January

WHALEFEST   *Birch Aquarium at Scripps, La Jolla.* January and February. Special exhibits and hands-on activities teach kids about whales; ☎ 858-534-FISH; **aquarium.ucsd.edu**.

February

HERITAGE DAY PARADE   *San Diego.* Late February. Celebrates the city's rich ethnic diversity; ☎ 619-262-0334; **www.heritageday parade.org**.

WILDFLOWER BLOOMS   *Anza-Borrego Desert State Park.* The blooms hit sometime between early February and late April, and they last only for a few weeks; ☎ 760-767-5311; **parks.ca.gov.**

March

OCEAN BEACH KITE FESTIVAL   *Ocean Beach.* Sponsored by the Kiwanis for more than 50 years. Kite decorating (9 a.m. to noon) and flying, as well as a parade (plus free hot dogs). Bring your own kite; ☎ 619-531-1527.

April

GASLAMP QUARTER EASTER BONNET PARADE & HAT CONTEST   *Fifth and L streets, San Diego.* A charity event held the weekend before Easter. Hat-making workshop, Easter egg hunt, parade, and treats; ☎ 619-233-5008; **www.gaslamp.org.**

OPENING DAY, SAN DIEGO PADRES BASEBALL   *Petco Park.* ☎ 619-795-5000; **padres.mlb.com.**

SAN DIEGO EARTHFAIR   *Balboa Park.* Earth Day festival with lots of activities for children; ☎ 858-272-7370; **www.earthdayweb.org.**

May

FIESTA CINCO DE MAYO   *Old Town State Park, San Diego.* A two-day party with music, entertainment, food, booths, and kids' activities; ☎ 619-296-3236; **www.fiestacincodemayo.com.**

CARLSBAD VILLAGE STREET FAIRE   *Carlsbad.* Some 90,000 people fill this small town for its twice-a-year (May and November), one-day blowout, which includes children's rides, a pancake breakfast, farmers' market–style vendors, live music, and international foods; ☎ 760-931-8400; **www.carlsbad.org.**

INDIAN FAIR   *San Diego Museum of Man, Balboa Park.* Native Americans from across the country gather to share tribal ceremonies, stories, music, foods, and crafts, with hands-on projects for children; ☎ 619-239-2001; **www.museumofman.org.**

June

SAN DIEGO COUNTY FAIR   *Del Mar.* Carnival rides, flower shows, animals, arcades, and nationally known musical performers; ☎ 858-755-1161; **www.sdfair.com.**

July

ANNUAL FESTIVAL OF THE BELLS   *Mission Basilica.* Weekend-long festival celebrating the anniversary of the founding of Mission Basilica San Diego de Alcala. Includes food, music and dance performances, llama rides, and games; ☎ 619-283-7319; **www.missionsandiego.com.**

FOURTH OF JULY EVENTS   *La Jolla:* a free concert at Scripps Park followed by a fireworks show; ☎ 858-454-1600; **www.lajollabythesea.com.**

Coronado: a parade, free concert in Spreckels Park, and fireworks; ☎ 619-437-8788; **www.coronadovisitorcenter.com.**

U.S. OPEN SANDCASTLE COMPETITION *Imperial Beach Pier.* Sandcastles like you've never seen 'em, along with a parade and evening fireworks. Children have their own competition; ☎ 619-424-6663; **www.usopensandcastle.com.**

MOVIES BEFORE THE MAST *Star of India.* Nautically themed, family-friendly movies are screened on board this historic sailing ship in July and August; ☎ 619-234-9153; **www.sdmaritime.org.**

August

CHULA VISTA ANNUAL DOWNTOWN LEMON FESTIVAL *Chula Vista.* Food and crafts; ☎ 619-422-1982; **www.cvdba.com.**

WORLD BODYSURFING CHAMPIONSHIPS *Oceanside Pier and Beach.* Bodysurfers from around the world put on a show; ☎ 760-722-1534; **www.worldbodysurfing.org.**

September

FLEET WEEK *San Diego.* An extended tribute to the military with many events that extend well into October, including ship and submarine tours, a ship parade, and an air show; ☎ 619-858-1546; **www .fleetweeksandiego.org.**

October

OKTOBERFEST *Holiday Park, Carlsbad.* Since Carlsbad was originally a German settlement named Karlsbad, this is the Oktoberfest event to attend; ☎ 760-434-6093; **www.rotaryoktoberfest.org.**

November

DEL MAR FAIRGROUNDS HOLIDAY OF LIGHTS *Del Mar.* Drive your car around the racetrack and view more than 400 holiday displays; ☎ 858-755-1161; **www.sdfair.com/holidayoflights.**

CARLSBAD VILLAGE STREET FAIRE *Carlsbad.* The fall version of this semiannual event (see May listing); ☎ 760-931-8400; **www .carlsbad.org.**

MOTHER GOOSE PARADE *Main Street, El Cajon.* Hundreds of thousands of spectators jam into El Cajon for this decades-old parade honoring fairy tales, children, and Mother Goose rhymes; ☎ 619-444-8712; **www.mothergooseparade.org.**

December

LA JOLLA CHRISTMAS PARADE AND HOLIDAY FESTIVAL *Downtown La Jolla.* Floats, marching bands, and Santa, followed by a carnival and street fair; ☎ 858-454-5718; **www.lajollabythesea.com.**

SAN DIEGO

San Diego IS THE ONE DESTINATION IN CALIFORNIA that combines an ocean-resort feel with big-city culture and activities. You can lie on the beach at **Coronado** and 20 minutes later be downtown at a major rock concert. You can spend the morning in a museum as you might in other cities, but after lunch you'll be skating along Mission Bay. While you watch your little one ride the carousel at **Shoreline Village,** you'll admire the bay on one side and the skyscrapers of the financial district on the other.

More cosmopolitan than Santa Barbara and easier to navigate than LA, San Diego is an ideal introduction to Southern California. The big-deal attractions (**San Diego Zoo, Wild Animal Park, SeaWorld**) are indeed world-class; the historic areas (**Old Town,** the **Maritime Museum** ships) are colorful and inviting; there are wonderfully located concentrations of hotels and motels (**Mission Bay, Coronado**); north of town are some beautiful, laid-back beach towns for day trips or overnight escapes (**La Jolla, Carlsbad**); and the residents are relaxed and casual.

unofficial **TIP**
If you'll be in San Diego for at least a week, renting a beach house is the way to go.

FAMILY LODGING

Best Western Blue Sea Lodge
707 Pacific Beach Drive, San Diego; ☎ 800-BLUE-SEA or 858-488-4700; www.bestwestern-bluesea.com; $159–$279 off-season, $229–$319 in summer

THE EXTERNAL ARCHITECTURE may be hideous, but the location can't be beat: the boardwalk and the soft sand of Pacific Beach are right in front, Mission Bay is just around the corner, and the neighborhood is full of cafes, restaurants, and beach shops. Furthermore, a recent remodeling spruced up the interior, adding a colorful surfer theme and 26 new rooms, bringing the room count up to 128. The ocean-view suites are big enough for families, and many rooms have kitchens. Extras include free wireless Internet, a small pool, a spa, a cheerful cafe, and rental bikes. Reserve at least two months in advance for summertime visits.

Catamaran Resort Hotel & Spa

3999 Mission Boulevard, Mission Bay; ☎ 800-422-8386 or 858-488-1081; www.catamaranresort.com; $159–$799; packages with SeaWorld or various sporting adventures offered

THIS LARGE MISSION BAY RESORT has live parrots in the tropical-decor lobby, spacious rooms (many with sliding glass doors to patios and bayside), outside pizza-delivery service, and a location convenient to SeaWorld. It's not as glitzy as some other San Diego–area resorts, but it is a beach and water-sports paradise—wear your bathing suits and board shorts and head for the hotel pier for rentals and lessons in kayaking, windsurfing, diving, and more, or go to the bayfront beach for swimming and volleyball; wave lovers can just walk across Mission Boulevard to get to Mission Beach. Among the offerings for adventurous teens is sea-cave kayaking.

Embassy Suites San Diego Bay

601 Pacific Coast Highway, San Diego; ☎ 800-EMBASSY or 619-239-2400; www.essandiegobay.com; $189–$717

IF YOU WANT TO BE DOWNTOWN (not a first choice for beach-loving families, but it has its appeal), this is a good place to stay. It has all the family comforts that the chain is known for (two-room suite, two TVs, sleeper sofa, refrigerator, microwave, free breakfast); it's close to the trolley line, the Embarcadero, and Seaport Village; and it's not far from Balboa Park. There is a pool, but, curiously, it is indoors.

Hotel del Coronado

1500 Orange Avenue, Coronado; ☎ 800-HOTEL-DEL or 619-435-6611; www.hoteldel.com; $335–$535; suites $700 and up

INCREDIBLY POPULAR WITH MANY TRAVELERS, this huge (692 rooms, six restaurants) resort complex on Coronado Island offers lodgings from vintage-historic rooms to modern beachfront suites. Some kids find the main Victorian building kind of creepy, its dark hallways often crowded with busloads of day-trippers. But there's plenty of sunshine out by the (crowded) pool and on the beach, where supervised kids' programs and activities (some free, most costing $15 to $65, depending on activity) are held in spring and summer and during the Christmas holidays. Teens have a new lounge, with computers, video games, a pool table, and music, and they get such active options as surf lessons, kayaking, and biking. The full line of sports and water equipment is available to rent, and there are child-care services and children's menus. This is no place for the budget conscious—you'll pay dearly for everything from parking to food—but for some it's worth it to be in the middle of the history and the beach action.

Loews Coronado Bay Resort

4000 Coronado Bay Road, Coronado; ☎ 800-815-6397 or 619-424-4000; www.loewscoronadobay.com; $339–$369; suites $575 and up

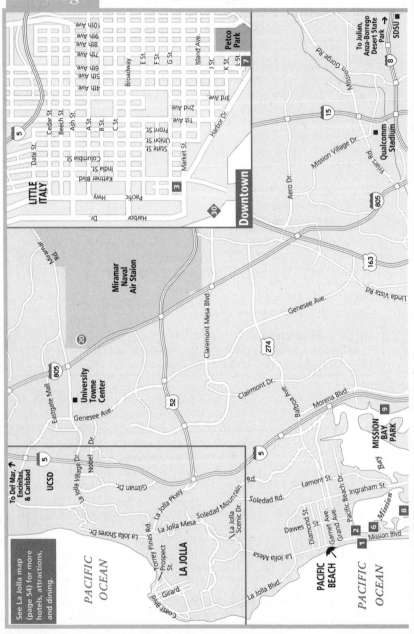

san diego

PACIFIC
OCEAN

See La Jolla map
(page 54) for more
hotels, attractions,
and dining.

To Del Mar,
Encinitas,
& Carlsbad

UCSD

5

LA JOLLA

Coast Blvd.

Girard

Prospect
St.

Torrey Pines Rd.

La Jolla Shores Dr.

La Jolla Mesa

La Jolla Blvd.

La Jolla Pkwy.

La Jolla Village Dr.

Nobel Dr.

Gilman Dr.

805

Eastgate Mall

University
Towne
Center

Genesee Ave.

52

Soledad Mountain Rd.

Soledad Rd.

La Jolla
Scenic Dr.

Rd.

20

Miramar
Naval
Air Staion

Miramar Rd.

Claremont Mesa Blvd.

Genesee Ave.

Clairemont Dr.

274

Balboa Ave.

Morena Blvd.

Clairemont Dr.

Aero Dr.

Mission Village Dr.

Friars Rd.

15

805

163

Linda Vista Rd.

Mission Gorge Rd.

8

To Julian,
Anza-Borrego
Desert State
Park

SDSU

Qualcomm
Stadium

Qualcomm
Stadium

9

MISSION
BAY
PARK

Mission Bay

Morena Blvd.

Lamont St.

Ingraham St.

Pacific Beach Dr.

Grand Ave.

Garnet Ave.

Diamond St.

Dawes St.

2

1

6

Mission Blvd.

8

PACIFIC
BEACH

PACIFIC
OCEAN

5

5

LITTLE
ITALY

Date St.

Cedar St.

Beech St.

Ash St.

A St.

B St.

C St.

Columbia St.

India St.

Kettner Blvd.

State St.

Union St.

Front St.

Market St.

Harbor Dr.

Pacific Hwy.

Harbor
Dr.

10th Ave.

9th Ave.

8th Ave.

7th Ave.

6th Ave.

5th Ave.

4th Ave.

3rd Ave.

2nd Ave.

1st Ave.

Broadway

E St.

F St.

G St.

Island Ave.

J St.

K St.

L St.

Petco
Park

7

3

30

Downtown

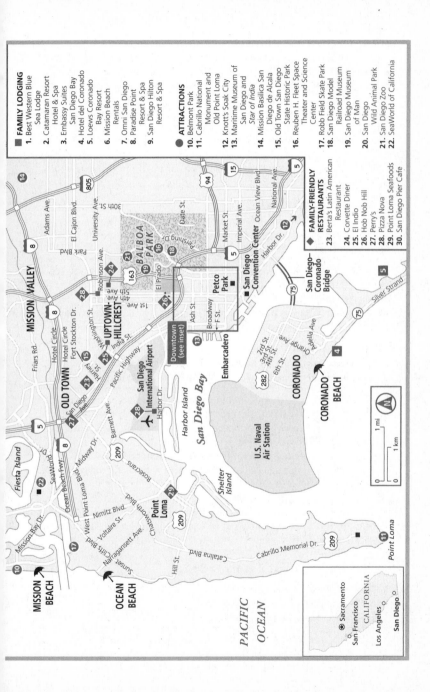

■ FAMILY LODGING
1. Best Western Blue Sea Lodge
2. Catamaran Resort Hotel & Spa
3. Embassy Suites San Diego Bay
4. Hotel del Coronado
5. Loews Coronado Bay Resort
6. Mission Beach Rentals
7. Omni San Diego
8. Paradise Point Resort & Spa
9. San Diego Hilton Resort & Spa

● ATTRACTIONS
10. Belmont Park
11. Cabrillo National Monument and Old Point Loma
12. Knott's Soak City
13. Maritime Museum of San Diego and Star of India
14. Mission Basilica San Diego de Alcala
15. Old Town San Diego State Historic Park
16. Reuben H. Fleet Space Theater and Science Center
17. Robb Field Skate Park
18. San Diego Model Railroad Museum
19. San Diego Museum of Man
20. San Diego Wild Animal Park
21. San Diego Zoo
22. SeaWorld of California

◆ FAMILY-FRIENDLY RESTAURANTS
23. Berta's Latin American Restaurant
24. Corvette Diner
25. El Indio
26. Hob Nob Hill
27. Perry's
28. Pizza Nova
29. Point Loma Seafoods
30. San Diego Pier Cafe

THIS UPSCALE, MODERN, 440-room resort looks at first like a business hotel, but it is actually totally family-friendly. Located on its own little peninsula on Coronado Island, it's far from the taco bars and shops of Coronado Village, but there's plenty to keep families happy right at the resort. There's a nice pool area (three pools, one of which is adults-only) with a great snack bar; on Friday nights, a 9- by 12-foot screen shows family movies while kids float on inner tubes. You'll also find a spa (for grown-ups), a playground, a game room, PBteen lounge-spa, and sailboat and bike rentals; beautiful Silver Strand State Beach is a short walk. The Loews Loves Kids activities program for ages 4 to 12 (summers and holidays) is $80 for a full day and $55 for a half day, with sibling discounts, and there is an in-room babysitting service as well as baby-proofing kits. The casual restaurant and room service have kids' menus, but save the fine-dining room for adults.

Mission Beach Rentals
747½ San Fernando Place, Mission Beach; ☎ 858-488-3100;
www.missionbeachmanagement.com;
weekly rentals in summer $550–$6,000 per week

A LONG-ESTABLISHED RENTAL AGENCY with a good supply of beach houses, apartments, and condos. All but the smallest studios are ideal for families, with kitchens, living rooms, and homelike comfort; some condos have such amenities as pools and spas. Locations include Mission Bay and Pacific Beach.

Omni San Diego
675 L Street, San Diego; ☎ 888-444-6664 or 619-231-6664;
www.omnisandiegohotel.com; $259–$369; suites $500 and up

LINKED BY A SKYBRIDGE to Petco Park (home of Padres baseball), this gleaming new tower has a great location for those who need to be near the Convention Center or want to be in the Gaslamp Quarter or at a baseball game (some rooms even look right into the stadium!). Its 511 rooms include 27 family-fitting junior and one-bedroom suites, all decorated with a cool white-on-beige palette and all complete with such modern frills as video games, pay-per-view movies, and wireless Internet. The pool deck is decidedly urban, with modern buildings all around, but it's kid-friendly and has a good cafe with a children's menu. The San Diego Trolley stops right in front, so you can easily get to Old Town, Seaport Village, and the Mexican-border transit center.

Paradise Point Resort & Spa
1404 West Vacation Road, San Diego; ☎ 800-344-2626 or
858-274-4630; www.paradisepoint.com;
$259–$509 off-season, $356–$631 summer

THIS IS NO PLACE FOR FANS OF INTIMATE LITTLE HOTELS—462 low-slung, recently rehabbed, 1970s-vintage rooms, five pools, tennis courts, a volleyball court, an 18-hole putting course, and much more are spread over a tropically landscaped, 44-acre island in Mission Bay. But it's a good place on a lovely bayside beach for an active family resort vacation. Summertime brings the daily Kids Camp, where kids ages 3 to 12 experience everything from Hula Hoop lessons to making ice cream; the cost is $100 for a full day, including lunch (the littlest ones have a morning program only). Teens get nighttime activities and lots to do on their own, from sunbathing at the beach to cruising the video arcade. Many rooms have kitchens; all have patios or terraces. Bike and pedal-boat rentals, children's menus, sauna, fitness center, packages with local attractions.

San Diego Hilton Resort & Spa
1775 East Mission Bay Drive, San Diego; ☎ 800-221-2424 or 619-276-4010; sandiegoresort.hilton.com; $239 (and up) off-season, $279 (and up) in season; children stay free in parents' room

PART HIGH-RISE, PART BUNGALOW COMPLEX, this 357-room resort hotel on Mission Bay caters to families, with all sorts of kid-friendly amenities. The Kids Klub program is $12 per hour. (It's less like day care and more like organized fun, so many kids just join in for an hour or two to take part in the activities that most attract them.) The over-11 set gets its own Teen Time program, which includes mixers. Fun facilities include the huge swimming pool, the little-kid wading pool, pathways for biking and skating (rentals available), the beach, the tennis, and the water-sport rentals. Many of the large rooms have terraces or patios, as well as wet bars and refrigerators. Children's menus are available.

■ ATTRACTIONS

Belmont Park

APPEAL BY AGE	PRESCHOOL ★★	GRADE SCHOOL ★★★★	TEENS ★★
YOUNG ADULTS ★★★		OVER 30 ★★	SENIORS ★★

West Mission Bay Drive and West Mission Boulevard, Mission Bay; ☎ 858-488-1549; www.giantdipper.com

Hours *Summer:* Sunday–Thursday, 11 a.m.–11 p.m.; Friday and Saturday, 11 a.m.–midnight. *Off-season:* Monday–Thursday, 11 a.m.–8 p.m., Friday–Sunday, 11 a.m.–10 p.m. **Admission** Free to the park; ride prices vary. **Touring time** Average 3 hours with swimming; minimum 1 hour. **Rainy-day touring** Yes, for indoor facilities. **Restaurants** Concessions. **Alcoholic beverages** No. **Disabled access** Limited on rides. **Wheelchair rental** No. **Baby-stroller rental** No. **Lockers** No. **Pet kennels** No. **Rain check** No. **Private tours** No.

DESCRIPTION AND COMMENTS   Part old-fashioned seaside amusement park, part modern playground, this fun zone is particularly appealing to school-age kids and teens; many of the games and rides are too difficult or scary for young children, though there is a small kiddie area. The showpieces are the 1925 wooden roller coaster and the wooden replica of a Looff carousel; our kids particularly liked steering the little boats around the miniature harbor. The Plunge, a gigantic indoor saltwater pool, is worth a dip, if only to experience Wyland's impressive underwater whale mural. Arcades, video games, a movie theater, and shops ring the rides.

Cabrillo National Monument and Old Point Loma

APPEAL BY AGE	PRESCHOOL ★★	GRADE SCHOOL ★★★★	TEENS ★★★
YOUNG ADULTS ★★★★		OVER 30 ★★★★	SENIORS ★★★★

Point Loma, south on Catalina Boulevard, San Diego; ☎ 619-557-5450; www.nps.gov/cabr

Hours Daily, 9 a.m.–5 p.m.; open later in summer. **Admission** $5 per car or $3 per person walk-in. **Touring time** Average 2 hours; minimum 1 hour. **Rainy-day touring** Not good. **Restaurants** Vending machines. **Alcoholic beverages** No. **Disabled access** Yes. **Wheelchair rental** Yes, free. **Baby-stroller rental** No. **Lockers** No. **Pet kennels** No. **Rain check** No. **Private tours** No.

DESCRIPTION AND COMMENTS   This falls under the scenery category, which typically bores kids, but ours enjoyed this outing as much as we did. Reached after driving past the airport through Shelter Island, a huge Navy base (some of which is operational and some abandoned), and Point Loma, this point of land several hundred feet above the ocean seems like the end of the world. As you stand on the point's bluff, the Pacific stretches eternally to your right, while the whole of San Diego Bay spreads out straight ahead and to the left. The kids loved looking through the coin telescope for close-ups of the many incoming and outgoing military ships and planes, commercial planes, and pleasure boats (in winter and spring, this is also a great vantage to spot gray whales). Then we walked higher up the point to the tiny old 1855 lighthouse; what enthralled our 8-year-old was not the light itself, but the preserved (behind glass) living quarters of the lighthouse captain, his wife, and two sons. A steep trail down to tide pools is a worthy outing with older kids, and the visitors center has displays on the history of Juan Cabrillo's discovery of San Diego.

Knott's Soak City

APPEAL BY AGE	PRESCHOOL ★★	GRADE SCHOOL ★★★★	TEENS ★★★
YOUNG ADULTS ★★		OVER 30 ★★	SENIORS ½

2052 Entertainment Circle, Chula Vista; ☎ 619-661-7373; www.soakcityusa.com

Hours May and June: daily, 10 a.m.–6 p.m.; July and August: daily, 10 a.m.–7 p.m.; September: daily, 10 a.m.–5 p.m. **Admission** $30 adults, $20 children ages 3–11; after 3 p.m., $20 for adults and kids; parking $8–$12. **Touring time** 4–6 hours; minimum 1 hour. **Rainy-day touring** Yes. **Restaurants** Snack bar. **Alcoholic beverages** No. **Disabled access** Yes. **Wheelchair rental** No. **Baby-stroller rental** No. **Lockers** Yes. **Pet kennels** No. **Rain check** No. **Private tours** No.

DESCRIPTION AND COMMENTS   This 1950s-themed water park celebrates the surf-loving California fantasy. A highlight is the Coronado Express, a family raft ride that rushes down almost 700 feet of twists and turns into a splashdown pool. Among the 22 other rides are tube slides, body slides, speed slides, a wave pool, and a lazy river for folks who just want to kick back and float.

Mission Basilica San Diego de Alcala

APPEAL BY AGE	PRESCHOOL ★	GRADE SCHOOL ★★	TEENS ★★
YOUNG ADULTS ★★	OVER 30 ★★★		SENIORS ★★★

10818 San Diego Mission Road, San Diego; ☎ 619-283-7319; www.missionsandiego.com

Hours Daily, 9 a.m.–4:45 p.m., except Thanksgiving and Christmas. Tours are Monday–Friday, 9 a.m.–2 p.m.; call ☎ 858-565-9077 between 12:30 p.m. and 2:30 p.m on Monday and Thursday only for reservations. **Admission** $3 adults, $2 seniors, $1 children ages 6–12. **Touring time** Average 1 hour; minimum 30 minutes. **Rainy-day touring** Yes. **Restaurants** No. **Alcoholic beverages** No. **Disabled access** Yes. **Wheelchair rental**. No. **Baby-stroller rental** No. **Lockers** No. **Pet kennels** No. **Rain check** No. **Private tours** Self-guided audio tour.

DESCRIPTION AND COMMENTS   This was the first of the California missions, and it still serves as an active parish church. It's a short stop for most families because the museum area is small, but the grounds are lovely, and the church sanctuary is a fine example of the folkloric quality of mission architecture.

Old Town San Diego State Historic Park

APPEAL BY AGE	PRESCHOOL ★★★	GRADE SCHOOL ★★★★★	TEENS ★★★★
YOUNG ADULTS ★★★★½	OVER 30 ★★★★½		SENIORS ★★★★½

Bounded by Wallace, Congress, Twiggs, and Juan streets, San Diego; ☎ 619-220-5422; parks.ca.gov

Hours Daily, beginning at 10 a.m. for historic houses; most shops open until 9 p.m. **Admission** Free; donations appreciated. **Touring time** Average a half day; minimum 3 hours, with a meal and minimal shop browsing. **Rainy-day touring** Not great; outdoor paths, unpaved areas. **Restaurants** Surrounding. **Alcoholic beverages** In some restaurants. **Disabled access** Yes. **Wheelchair rental** No. **Baby-stroller rental** No. **Lockers** No. **Pet kennels** No; leashed pets allowed. **Rain check** No. **Private tours** Yes.

DESCRIPTION AND COMMENTS   Shops and restaurants occupy many of the landmark buildings that surround the official state-historic-park section of Old Town, so the kids may never know they're being educated when you come here. The park showcases aspects of San Diego's past from 1821 to 1872, when the area was first under the Mexican and then later the American government. The original town plaza is the focal point of the pedestrian-only zone; it is surrounded by restored homes with furnishings of the period, a smithy and stable, a courthouse, a schoolhouse, a dental museum, a drugstore museum, and a newspaper museum. Free tours are conducted daily at 11 a.m. and 2 p.m. by costumed docents at the visitors center in the Robinson-Rose House (4002 Wallace Street). The Bazaar del Mundo—shops and cafes surrounding a courtyard—often has mariachis and costumed dancers performing.

Reuben H. Fleet Science Center

APPEAL BY AGE	PRESCHOOL ★★★	GRADE SCHOOL ★★★★	TEENS ★★★★
YOUNG ADULTS ★★★★		OVER 30 ★★★★	SENIORS ★★★★

1875 El Prado, Balboa Park, San Diego, near San Diego Zoo;
☎ **619-238-1233; www.rhfleet.org**

Hours Monday–Thursday, 9:30 a.m.–8 p.m.; Friday, 9:30 a.m.–9 p.m.; Saturday and Sunday, 9:30 a.m.–8 p.m. Summer hours vary. **Admission** Price varies depending on IMAX movies attended: $8–$16.50 adults, $7–$14 seniors age 65 and over and children ages 3–12, free for children under age 3; first Monday of each month (holidays excluded) is Senior Monday, with $5 admission for seniors to exhibits and 1 IMAX film. **Touring time** Average 2 hours; minimum 1 hour. **Rainy-day touring** Yes. **Restaurants** Yes. **Alcoholic beverages** No. **Disabled access** Yes. **Wheelchair rental** No. **Baby-stroller rental** No. **Lockers** No. **Pet kennels** No. **Rain check** No. **Private tours** No.

DESCRIPTION AND COMMENTS   Of the many, many fine museums in Balboa Park, this is the hardest to find—despite its tremendous appeal to families, it is not mentioned on any of the directional signs posted in the park. (*Hint:* It's across the fountain plaza from the Natural History Museum, en route to the zoo.) This is an excellent hands-on science museum, where kids can touch, feel, experiment, and explore. The special exhibits are always first-rate, and they sometimes stay for a long time; recent examples included interactive exhibits on high-definition television and the science of seeing, and a "flight" through the human heart. Big-screen IMAX Dome films, usually about nature and/or space, are shown daily in the adjacent theater, and they are invariably worth seeing—but note that the noise and special effects may scare small children. This place can get mobbed, so try to visit on a school day after lunch, when the field trips have all returned to school.

Robb Field Skate Park

APPEAL BY AGE	PRESCHOOL ★	GRADE SCHOOL ★★★	TEENS ★★★★
YOUNG ADULTS ★★★		OVER 30 ½	SENIORS –

2525 Bacon Street, San Diego (Ocean Beach); ☎ 619-525-8486;
www.sandiego.gov/park-and-recreation/centers/robbskate.shtml

Hours Monday–Friday, 1 p.m.–dark.; Saturday and Sunday, noon–dark. **Hours** subject to change; call to verify hours. **Admission** $5 for a day pass; three-month multiuse pass $30. **Rainy-day touring** No. **Restaurants** No. **Alcoholic beverages** No. **Disabled access** Limited. **Wheelchair rental** No. **Baby-stroller rental** No. **Lockers** No. **Pet kennels** No. **Rain check** No. **Private tours** No.

DESCRIPTION AND COMMENTS Top local skateboarders helped the city of San Diego come up with a winning street-course design for this popular, 40,000-square-foot concrete paradise. It has something for all skill levels, including a combo bowl, a volcano shaped like an octagon, and rails, ledges, and blocks galore. Pay for a day pass at the entrance office and ollie away. Helmets and pads are required; the park office has a limited supply of gear you can check out with an ID. Parents need to fill out an entrance application and sign a liability release that stays on file for return visits. To get there, take the Sunset Cliffs exit from Interstate 8, then turn right on West Point Loma Boulevard and right on Bacon Street, which leads to the park. We often let our teens skate here (it's totally safe and gated, with staff supervising at all times) while one of us takes the preschoolers across the street to the playground, or the doggie to the off-leash beach next to the field.

 ## Maritime Museum of San Diego and *Star of India*

APPEAL BY AGE	PRESCHOOL ★★★	GRADE SCHOOL ★★★★½	TEENS ★★★★½
YOUNG ADULTS ★★★★		OVER 30 ★★★★½	SENIORS ★★★★½

1492 North Harbor Drive, San Diego; ☎ 619-234-9153; www.sdmaritime.com

Hours Daily, 9 a.m.–8 p.m.; Memorial Day through Labor Day, open until 9 p.m. **Admission** $14 adults, $11 seniors 62 and older, $11 active military with valid ID, $8 ages 6–17, free for children age 5 and under. **Touring time** Average 3 hours; minimum 1 hour. **Rainy-day touring** Not good. **Restaurants** No. **Alcoholic beverages** No. **Disabled access** Limited. **Wheelchair rental** No. **Baby-stroller rental** No. **Lockers** No. **Pet kennels** No. **Rain check** No. **Private tours** No.

DESCRIPTION AND COMMENTS The picture in our minds of the cozy passenger cabin of the square-rigged *Star of India,* an 1863 merchant sailing ship, is as fresh as it was the day we stepped into the officers' and passengers' area. As we talked to the children about what it might have been like to sail across an ocean on a ship like this, the wooden floor beneath us gently rose and fell with the waves. *Star of India* is one of five historic ships at the Maritime Museum; the others are an 1898 ferryboat, a 1914 harbor pilot boat, an early-1970s Soviet submarine, and a 1904 steam-powered luxury yacht. Visitors walk or scramble up and down the ships, in and out of decks and holds, seeing ropes and engines and sailors' bunks. In summer, such nautical film classics as *Captain Blood* are projected onto a ship's sail for an evening of unusual entertainment.

San Diego Model Railroad Museum

APPEAL BY AGE	PRESCHOOL ★★★★	GRADE SCHOOL ★★★★	TEENS ★★★
YOUNG ADULTS ★★★★		OVER 30 ★★★★	SENIORS ★★★★

1649 El Prado, Balboa Park, San Diego; ☎ 619-696-0199; www.sdmrm.org

Hours Tuesday–Friday, 11 a.m.–4 p.m.; Saturday and Sunday, 11 a.m.–5 p.m. **Admission** $6 adults, $5 seniors over 65, $3 students 15 and over, $2.50 military on active duty, free for children under age 15; free first Tuesday of the month for San Diego County residents. **Touring time** Average 2 hours; minimum 1 hour. **Rainy-day touring** Yes. **Restaurants** Sandwich shop. **Alcoholic beverages** No. **Disabled access** Yes. **Wheelchair rental** No. **Baby-stroller rental** No. **Lockers** No. **Pet kennels** No. **Rain check** No. **Private tours** No.

DESCRIPTION AND COMMENTS   We've seen many a grown man get far more excited about model trains than any kid does, and this museum caters to both groups. The country's largest collection of model trains winds through elaborate miniature countrysides and towns, some of which represent historical periods in Southern California. This fascinates some kids but makes others insane because they're not allowed to touch—so take them to the Toy Train Gallery, where they can work the controls of Lionel O-Gauge toy trains and push Brio wooden trains on their tracks.

San Diego Museum of Man

APPEAL BY AGE	PRESCHOOL ★★	GRADE SCHOOL ★★★★	TEENS ★★★★
YOUNG ADULTS ★★★		OVER 30 ★★★	SENIORS ★★★

1350 El Prado, Balboa Park, San Diego; ☎ 619-239-2001; www.museumofman.org

Hours Daily, 10 a.m.–4:30 p.m.; closed Christmas, Thanksgiving, and New Year's Day. **Admission** $10 adults, $7.50 children ages 13–17 and seniors, $5 children ages 3–12, free for children under age 3. **Touring time** Average 3 hours; minimum 1 hour. **Rainy-day touring** Yes. **Restaurants** No. **Alcoholic beverages** No. **Disabled access** Yes. **Wheelchair rental** No. **Baby-stroller rental** No. **Lockers** No. **Pet kennels** No. **Rain check** No. **Private tours** No.

DESCRIPTION AND COMMENTS   If your kids aren't fascinated with the history of man and woman, they will be after a visit to this cool museum, home to mummies, skeletons, and life-size, very realistic (often naked) re-creations of our predecessors going back to early Africa. Weekends bring live demonstrations of crafts and cooking from cultures around the world, and the Children's Discovery Center offers changing hands-on displays keyed to the museum's collection, allowing kids to, for instance, dress up like ancient Egyptians.

San Diego Wild Animal Park

APPEAL BY AGE	PRESCHOOL ★★★★	GRADE SCHOOL ★★★★½	TEENS ★★★★
YOUNG ADULTS ★★★★½		OVER 30 ★★★★½	SENIORS ★★★★½

15500 San Pasqual Valley Road, Escondido; ☎ 760-747-8702 or 760-738-5067 (TDD); www.sandiegozoo.org

Hours *Summer:* daily, 9 a.m.–8 p.m. (grounds open until 9 p.m.). *Winter:* daily, 9 a.m.–4 p.m. (grounds open until 5 p.m.). **Admission** $28.50 adults, $17.50 children ages 3–11, free for children age 2 and younger; combination tickets for the San Diego Zoo and Wild Animal Park: $60 adults, $43 children ages 3–11; parking $9 and $14 for RVs. **Touring time** Average two-thirds of a day; minimum a half day. **Rainy-day touring** Some shows and exhibits close. **Restaurants** Yes.

Alcoholic beverages Yes. **Disabled access** Yes. **Wheelchair rental** Yes. **Baby-stroller rental** Yes. **Lockers** Yes. **Pet kennels** Service animals only. **Rain check** No. **Private tours** Photo Caravan, age 8 and older, $90–$230 plus admission.

DESCRIPTION AND COMMENTS   Although it's actually in Escondido, about 45 minutes northeast of downtown, we're putting this in the San Diego section because San Diego heads up the name and it'd be confusing otherwise. This is a unique animal-viewing experience, designed to replicate what you'd see if you were visiting animal parks in Africa. The animals roam freely in herds over many acres of land similar to an African savannah, and the visitors observe from an open-sided, soft-wheeled tour vehicle that travels 2.5 miles through the park's 21,000 acres. The 30-minute Journey into Africa ride (sometimes too long for toddlers) departs from Simba Station, between the Lion Camp and Heart of Africa exhibits. Unless you are a member or purchase a Best Value ticket, the ride is not included in admission; tickets cost $10 per adult, $6 for children ages 3 to 11. A theme park–like Nairobi Village and Mombasa Lagoon area feature more traditional exhibits as well as animal shows presented in an African-village setting, and visitors can relax at cafes—and, of course, shop. A walk-through exhibit, Condor Ridge, showcases endangered North American bird species; more heart-pounding is the new Cheetah Run Safari, where you get to watch cheetahs run at full speed up close (limited hours; call for reservations). There's also a pleasant play area for younger kids, with slides and climbing equipment, also themed. For a more in-depth adventure, consider the Beastly Bedtime and other themed sleepover programs (☎ 619-718-3000 or 800-407-9534), over-night family camping experiences for parents and children age 4 and over; the cost runs $109–$179 adults and $89–$109 for children.

We like to hike the two-mile Kilimanjaro Safari Walk through some of the park's most scenic areas. We always take a picnic and binoculars, and rest near Kilima Point, with restrooms, a drinking fountain and fantastic views of African herds roaming the fields below. We also advise that you watch little children carefully on some of the viewing platforms; one is a three-story-high, circular platform with wood rail-ings that attract climbing kids like magnets.

If you're planning to visit both the San Diego Zoo and the Wild Animal Park more than once a year, consider a membership for yourself and your children—it's probably cheaper, and you get other benefits as well. For details, call or go to the Web site.

 # San Diego Zoo

2920 Zoo Drive, Balboa Park, San Diego;
☎ **619-234-3153 or 619-231-1515; www.sandiegozoo.org**

Hours Daily, 9 a.m.–4 p.m. (grounds open until 6 p.m.). *Summer:* open until 8 p.m. with grounds closing at 9, but animals generally go to sleep at dusk; call

☎ 888-MY-PANDA for current panda-viewing schedule. **Admission** *Regular admission:* $24.50 adults, $16.50 children ages 3–11, free for children age 2 and under. *Deluxe admission* (includes bus tour and sky tram): $34 adults, $24 children ages 3–11, free for children age 2 and under. **Touring time** Average 6 hours; minimum 2 hours. **Rainy-day touring** Some shows and exhibits close. **Restaurants** Yes. **Alcoholic beverages** Yes. **Disabled access** Yes. **Wheelchair rental** Yes. **Baby-stroller rental** Yes. **Lockers** Yes. **Pet kennels** Service animals only. **Rain check** No. **Private tours** V.I.P. Tours go behind the scenes: call ☎ 619-718-3000 or 800-407-9534.

DESCRIPTION AND COMMENTS   This legendary zoo has been exhibiting rare species since 1915 and now has more than 4,000 animals of 900 species. Unbarred enclosures and sensitive landscaping (Dr. Seuss used to sketch in the cactus gardens here) have been the norm at this 100-acre facility for many years, but trying to see everything means a lot of walking. The narrated bus tour gives a good overview in just 35 minutes; best viewing is from the left side. The giant pandas Bai Yun and the now-deceased Shi Shi became parents in 1999 to Hua Mei (currently in China), the first panda cub born in captivity in the West since 1990, and their home is well worth a look. Bai Yun has since given birth to three other cubs at the San Diego Zoo. Also don't miss the new Monkey Trails and Forest Tales, a naturalistic home for more than 30 rare African and Asian monkeys, reptiles, pygmy hippos, and birds. Between June and September, the zoo opens at 9 a.m. (great if you have your own early birds) and stays open until 9 p.m. for nocturnal animal viewing and special entertainment programs.

unofficial **TIP**
Trying to see everything at the San Diego Zoo means a lot of walking—we head right for the Children's Zoo, built to a 4-year-old's scale; here, kids can pet creatures and see the newborns.

☀ SeaWorld of California

APPEAL BY AGE	PRESCHOOL ★★★★	GRADE SCHOOL ★★★★½	TEENS ★★★★
YOUNG ADULTS ★★★★½		OVER 30 ★★★★½	SENIORS ★★★★½

500 SeaWorld Drive, Mission Bay; ☎ 800-25-SHAMU or 619-226-3901; www.seaworld.com

Hours *Fall–spring:* daily, 10 a.m.–dusk. *Summer:* daily, 9 a.m.–11 p.m. **Admission** $61 adults, $51 children ages 3–9; parking $12. **Touring time** Average 6 hours; minimum 3 hours. **Rainy-day touring** So-so; most attractions are outdoors. **Restaurants** Yes. **Alcoholic beverages** Beer garden. **Disabled access** Yes. **Wheelchair rental** Yes. **Baby-stroller rental** Yes. **Lockers** Yes. **Pet kennels** Yes. **Rain check** No. **Private tours** Yes.

DESCRIPTION AND COMMENTS   Part theme park, part zoo, part serious animal rescue and research program, SeaWorld has an appeal that cuts across age groups and interests—just try to find someone jaded and cynical enough to not be thoroughly wowed and charmed by the dolphin show, in which smiling dolphins perform amazing acrobatic feats and deliberately splash the audience. Over in Shamu's stadium, a huge crowd roars its approval when the killer whales leap far into the sky, ask for the extra-large bucket of fish, and serve as living surfboards for trainers. Popular attractions are *Clyde and Seamore's Risky Rescue,* a sea-lion, walrus, and otter show, and *Sesame Street Presents Lights, Camera, Imagination!,* a 3-D film and live special-effects experience.

Our 5-year-old loved adventuring through the aquarium tunnel under the shark tank, and the sight of our shivering but deliriously happy 8-year-old after a Shamu soaking will stay with us for years. (Her little sister, however, was shocked into shrieking tears by the coldness of the water, so don't forget a change of clothes for less-tough little ones.) Bring a disposable, waterproof camera—even if you don't sit in the Soak Zone at a show, you're bound to get wet riding the Shipwreck Rapids rafts or plunging into the waterway on the thrilling Journey to Atlantis ride. Buy (or bring) a thin vinyl poncho if you don't want to walk around dripping from head to toe. For a break, head to the new two-acre *Sesame Street* Bay of Play, where Elmo, Cookie Monster, and friends preside over a vast complex of pirate ships, three kid-friendly rides, and other play areas.

SeaWorld also gets points for going a little beyond the deep-fried, junk-food theme-park basics—at some of the snack carts, you can get a tasty fresh-fruit smoothie for a cooling, healthy snack that kids love.

In summer, the park stays open later and jazzes things up with live music, a circus show, and special night performances. But we prefer getting dolphin-splashed under a hot San Diego sun.

FAMILY-FRIENDLY RESTAURANTS

Berta's Latin American Restaurant
3928 Twiggs Street, Old Town, San Diego; ☎ 619-295-2343; www.bertasinoldtown.com

Meals served Lunch and dinner. **Cuisine** Mexican. **Entree range** $8–$17. **Kids' menu** No. **Reservations** Recommended for 6 or more. **Payment** All major credit cards.

BERTA GOES WAY BEYOND the tourist-Mexican standards to offer the best from Chile (lamb stew), Guatemala (shrimp in spicy salsa), Spain (paella), and practically every other Spanish-speaking country. Kids will like the cheese empanadas, quesadillas, and flan, and parents will like the Argentinean rib-eye steak and Brazilian seafood with tomatoes, peanuts, ginger, coconut, and chiles. Beer and wine only.

Corvette Diner
3946 Fifth Avenue, San Diego; ☎ 619-542-1476; www.cohnrestaurants.com

Meals served Lunch and dinner. **Cuisine** American. **Entree range** $8–$13. **Kids' menu** Yes. **Reservations** Not accepted. **Payment** All major credit cards.

HUGELY POPULAR WITH LOCAL FAMILIES, this 1950s diner camps it up with a live DJ, a magician, wisecracking waitresses, and blaring oldies rock. The decor is equally over the top: neon, chrome, a soda fountain, and an actual Corvette. The food is retro diner: meat loaf, chicken-fried steak, burgers, corn dogs, PB&Js, and root beer floats. Our kids beg to go back.

El Indio

3695 India Street, Old Town, San Diego; ☎ 619-299-0333; www.el-indio.com

Meals served Breakfast, lunch, and dinner. **Cuisine** Mexican. **Entree range** $6–$11. **Kids' menu** Yes. **Reservations** Not accepted. **Payment** MC, V.

TORTILLA CHIPS ARE THE CLAIM TO FAME of this beloved institution—they're so good that people buy them as souvenirs and ship them home. Originally a tortilla factory in 1940, the Old Town location is notable for its bare-bones outdoor seating, as well as its claim to have invented the word *taquito*. Other than the fabulous chips, the food is workaday (but tasty) Cal-Mex; try the carne asada, the vegetarian tamale, the nachos deluxe, and, of course, the handmade tortillas. Beer and wine only.

Hob Nob Hill
2271 First Avenue, downtown San Diego; ☎ 619-239-8176; www.hobnobhill.com

Meals served Breakfast, lunch, and dinner. **Cuisine** American. **Entree range** $8–$20. **Kids' menu** Yes. **Reservations** Recommended. **Payment** All major credit cards.

SINCE 1944, HOB NOB HILL has been dishing out home cooking, and it still looks as though it's 1944 inside: red Naugahyde booths, chintz curtains, glass pie cases, and waitresses who know their way around a coffeepot. The location is convenient to nowhere, but that doesn't stop this place from being San Diego's favorite breakfast restaurant, home to very good Western omelets, pancake sandwiches, roast-beef hash, and cinnamon rolls. Dinner is of the turkey-croquette variety, and it's popular with the early-bird-special crowd.

Perry's
4610 Pacific Highway, Old Town, San Diego; ☎ 619-291-7121

Meals served Breakfast and lunch. **Cuisine** American/Mexican. **Entree range** $7–$9. **Kids' menu** Yes. **Reservations** Not accepted. **Payment** D, MC, V.

THE BEST PLACE IN OLD TOWN for breakfast, Perry's serves an odd but appealing mix of Mexican (huevos rancheros), Italian (frittatas), and American (French toast) cooking; the children's menu is the usual pancake–hot dog roster. The food is cheap, tasty, and generously served, and there's a crowd on weekends.

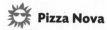 **Pizza Nova**

3955 Fifth Avenue, downtown San Diego; ☎ 619-296-6682; 5050 North Harbor Drive, Point Loma, San Diego; ☎ 619-226-0268; 954 Lomas Santa Fe Drive, Solana Beach; ☎ 858-259-0666; www.pizzanova.net

Meals served Lunch and dinner. **Cuisine** Italian/Californian. **Entree range** $9–$18. **Kids' menu** Yes. **Reservations** Recommended. **Payment** All major credit cards.

WINNER OF *San Diego* MAGAZINE'S BEST PIZZA award, this small chain makes very good wood-fired pizzas, ranging from classic pepperoni to pizza pies with lox or Thai shrimp. Pastas, salads, and special-occasion desserts are also offered, along with kid-sized pizzas. The original branch at Point Loma has water views and an appealing funkiness.

Point Loma Seafoods

2805 Emerson Street, San Diego (Point Loma); ☎ 619-223-1109; www.pointlomaseafoods.com

Meals served Lunch and dinner. **Cuisine** Seafood. **Entree range** $8–$14. **Kids' menu** Yes. **Reservations** Not accepted. **Payment** All major credit cards.

FOR DECADES, PEOPLE HAVE LINED UP in droves at the Point Loma Seafoods counter to pick up what most locals consider the freshest seafood around. The casual, family-owned market and eatery sits right on the water in Shelter Island Harbor and specializes in locally caught fish straight from the boats. Our kids devour the fish-and-chips, and teens hanker for the fish tacos, crab cakes, and shrimp platters with coleslaw and fries. If you're staying at a place with a barbecue or cooking facilities, this is the place to fetch tonight's dinner ingredients. We love to sit at a table on the patio. This place closes by 6:30 p.m., so dine early if you're coming for dinner.

San Diego Pier Cafe

885 West Harbor Drive, downtown San Diego; ☎ 619-239-3968; www.piercafe.com

Meals served Lunch, dinner, and weekend brunch. **Cuisine** Seafood/American. **Entree range** Lunch, $9–$18; dinner, $13–$28. **Kids' menu** Yes. **Reservations** Only for 6 or more. **Payment** All major credit cards.

IT MAY LOOK LIKE A TOURIST TRAP, given the Seaport Village location, but the food is better than it needs to be at this family favorite. Perched on the end of a small pier next to an old boathouse, it's a wonderful place for watching seagulls fly past, with the Coronado Bridge in the background; try to snag an outdoor table, especially if you have restless kids. The clam chowder, fresh fish, and fish tacos are all tasty, and the all-American breakfasts are particularly good; the children's menu includes fish-and-chips.

la jolla

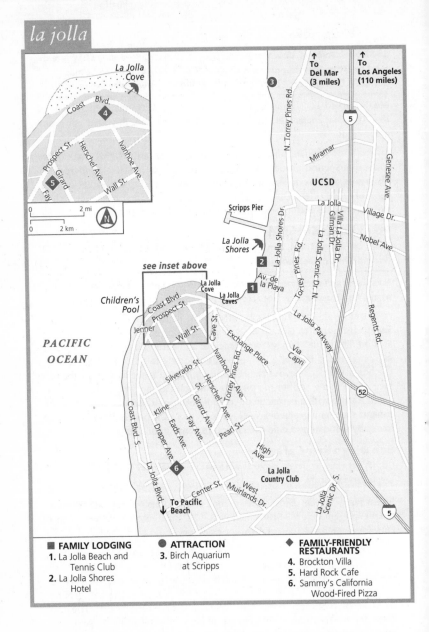

To
Del Mar
(3 miles)

To
Los Angeles
(110 miles)

La Jolla Cove

Coast Blvd.

4

Prospect St.

Herschel Ave.

Ivanhoe Ave.

5

Girard

Fay

Wall St.

0 — 2 mi
0 — 2 km

N

N. Torrey Pines Rd.

Miramar

UCSD

La Jolla

Villa La Jolla Dr.

Gilman Dr.

La Jolla Scenic Dr.

Village Dr.

Nobel Ave.

Genesee Ave.

5

Scripps Pier

La Jolla Shores

La Jolla Shores Dr.

Torrey Pines Rd.

La Jolla Scenic Dr. N.

2

see inset above

La Jolla Cove

La Jolla Caves

Av. de la Playa

1

La Jolla Parkway

Via Capri

Regents Rd.

Children's Pool

Coast Blvd.
Prospect St.

Jenner

Wall St.

Cave St.

Exchange Place

PACIFIC OCEAN

Silverado St.

Ivanhoe Ave.

Herschel Ave.

Torrey Pines Rd.

52

Kline

St.

Girard Ave.

Coast Blvd. S.

Draper Ave.

Eads Ave.

Fay Ave.

Pearl St.

High Ave.

La Jolla Country Club

6

La Jolla Blvd.

Center St.

West Muirlands Dr.

La Jolla Scenic Dr. S.

To Pacific Beach

5

■ **FAMILY LODGING**
1. La Jolla Beach and Tennis Club
2. La Jolla Shores Hotel

● **ATTRACTION**
3. Birch Aquarium at Scripps

◆ **FAMILY-FRIENDLY RESTAURANTS**
4. Brockton Villa
5. Hard Rock Cafe
6. Sammy's California Wood-Fired Pizza

LA JOLLA

A SOPHISTICATED VILLAGE perched above a dramatic public beach, **La Jolla** isn't the kind of place you might think to take your kids—unless they are precocious, design-conscious shoppers. But look beyond the expensive shops and restaurants to discover La Jolla's spectacular cove (see "The Best Beaches and Parks") and the low-key, family-friendly resorts right on the gorgeous main beach. And the aquarium at **Scripps Institute** is worth a stop if you haven't seen one of the larger aquariums in Monterey or Long Beach. La Jolla is a few miles north of central San Diego, about a ten-minute drive.

FAMILY LODGING

La Jolla Beach and Tennis Club

2000 Spindrift Drive, La Jolla; ☎ 800-640-7702 or 858-454-7126; www.ljbtc.com; $379–$809 off-season, $379–$1,500 summer

THIS IS THE SORT OF OLD-MONEY BEACH retreat where Pasadena families have been summering for decades. It's decidedly unglamorous, even motel-frumpy, but once you get to know the place, its charms are seductive. The best draw is its own gorgeous beach, close to but just far enough away from the mob scene at La Jolla Shores public beach, and notable for one of the shallowest, most family-friendly shorelines in California. There's also a large pool tucked into a wind-protected courtyard. Supervised activities in summer for kids ages 3 and up include swim meets, treasure hunts, and craft making. The club can set you up so you can have your own beach barbecue. Other on-site fun includes a large collection of quality tennis courts (tennis is taken very seriously here) and a par-three golf course.

La Jolla Shores Hotel

8110 Camino del Oro, La Jolla; ☎ 866-392-8762 or 858-459-8271; www.ljshoreshotel.com; $219–$399 off-season, $389–$699 in season; children under 12 stay free

LA JOLLA SHORES HOTEL doesn't have supervised children's activities, which is just fine with its many loyal patrons—with a beach this lovely and kid-friendly, who needs a kids' program? The tile-roofed Spanish-style hotel, a sibling of the La Jolla Beach and Tennis Club, is right on the same wonderful beach (with a boardwalk, good bodyboarding, and a gentle shoreline for little kids) and next door to a public park and playground; families also make good use of the pool, whirlpool, two tennis courts, Ping-Pong, and upscale restaurant, which has a children's menu. Wet, hungry kids can get a grilled cheese sandwich delivered poolside. The 128 rooms have a no-frills, beachy-rattan decor, with refrigerators, coffeemakers, and wooden balconies; 19 of the larger rooms have kitchenettes.

ATTRACTIONS

Birch Aquarium at Scripps

APPEAL BY AGE	PRESCHOOL ★★★★	GRADE SCHOOL ★★★★	TEENS ★★★
YOUNG ADULTS ★★★	OVER 30 ★★★★		SENIORS ★★★★

2300 Expedition Way, La Jolla; ☎ 858-534-3474; aquarium.ucsd.edu

Hours Daily, 9 a.m.–5 p.m.; closed Thanksgiving, Christmas, and New Year's Day. **Admission** $11 adults; $9 seniors; $8 college students; $7.50 University of California, San Diego, staff and children ages 3–17; under age 3 free; 3-hour free parking. **Touring time** Average 1 hour; minimum 30 minutes. **Rainy-day touring** Yes. **Restaurants** Concessions. **Alcoholic beverages** No. **Disabled access** Yes. **Wheelchair rental** Yes. **Baby-stroller rental** No. **Lockers** No. **Pet kennels** No. **Rain check** No. **Private tours** Yes.

DESCRIPTION AND COMMENTS   The museum is perched on a bluff high above the blue Pacific, and the outdoor touch tank is on a balcony boasting one of the most extraordinary views ever. Parents will find themselves admiring their offspring as the strong sunlight glints on their heads while gulls circle overhead and the kids concentrate on sea stars. Meanwhile, inside, dramatically dark hallways are lined with glowing aquariums, lit from behind to best showcase the jellyfish, lobsters, and other marine species. There's also a theme-park moment—a simulated submersible ride—but be warned that the ride might be too scary for kids under age 6. If your kids want to prepare for a visit, have them go to the Web site.

FAMILY-FRIENDLY RESTAURANTS

  Brockton Villa

1235 Coast Boulevard, La Jolla; ☎ 858-454-7393; www.brocktonvilla.com

Meals served Breakfast, brunch, lunch, and dinner. **Cuisine** American. **Entree range** Lunch, $11–$21; dinner, $16–$35. **Kids' menu** Yes. **Reservations** Recommended; a day in advance. **Payment** All major credit cards.

THE PERFECT FUNKY BEACH RESTAURANT, the Brockton Villa is pure San Diego. Breakfast or lunch at this 1894-vintage white clapboard beach house perched over La Jolla Cove will evoke beach summers of your childhood, or at least of your fantasy childhood. While you take in the ocean view, you can feast on the city's best French toast, scented with orange; warming oatmeal; a great turkey sandwich; or the popular cioppino.

Hard Rock Cafe
909 Prospect Street, La Jolla; ☎ 858-456-7625; www.hardrock.com

Meals served Lunch and dinner. **Cuisine** American. **Entree range** $9–$25. **Kids' menu** Yes. **Reservations** For groups of 8 or more only; expect to wait. **Payment** All major credit cards.

IF YOU'VE BEEN TO ONE HARD ROCK, you've been to them all. But for a 12-year-old, there's no such thing as too many trips to the Hard Rock. Like the others, it's a loud place, perhaps too loud for the very young; the small patio is a bit quieter. The ribs, burgers, and chicken are tasty, but it's the T-shirts that most kids remember.

Sammy's California Wood-Fired Pizza
702 Pearl Street, La Jolla; ☎ 858-456-5222; www.sammyspizza.com

Meals served Lunch and dinner. **Cuisine** Californian. **Entree range** $10–$17. **Kids' menu** Yes. **Reservations** For 6 or more only. **Payment** All major credit cards.

THIS IS THE PARENT OF A BRIGHT, yuppified San Diego chain dedicated to the California pizza: small pies flavored with such things as goat cheese, grilled zucchini, and barbecued chicken. They are utterly delicious and can be paired with tasty Caesar salads. Kids have their own menu of minipizzas, and they can decorate a paper pizza with crayons. Come early to beat the considerable crowds.

DEL MAR *and* CARLSBAD

THE RACETRACK AT **Del Mar** is the famed adult draw here, but plenty of families frequent Del Mar and never place a bet. Instead, they head for the broad, white-sand beach between 15th and 29th streets, and the quaint little downtown area. We've used it as a base for visiting the **Wild Animal Park**—still a half-hour drive, but along scenic country roads from here. Downtown San Diego is a 15- to 20-minute drive south outside of rush hour, but be warned that increasing traffic on I-5 can greatly lengthen that trip.

A half hour north of San Diego, **Carlsbad** is a quiet community that has typically attracted the upscale-golfing set (think the senior George Bush), but it became more family-friendly when **Legoland** came to town. What with this major theme park; the clean, beautiful state beach; and two swell kid-friendly resorts (the upscale Four Seasons and the charming Carlsbad Inn), Carlsbad is turning into a lovely family destination away from the San Diego crowds. If you're in town in spring (March through May), don't pass up a quick trip to the 50 acres of colorful blooms at **The Flower Fields** (Carlsbad Ranch); ☎ 760-930-9123; **www.theflowerfields.com**.

unofficial **TIP**
Families seeking beautiful beaches with fewer crowds than in urban San Diego are increasingly heading for Carlsbad.

FAMILY LODGING

Carlsbad Inn
3075 Carlsbad Boulevard, Carlsbad; ☎ 800-235-3939 or 760-434-7020; www.carlsbadinn.com; $169–$189 off-season, $240–$350 summer

A CHARMING IF QUIRKY (what's with the Tudor thing in sunny California?) beach resort, the Carlsbad Inn offers a lot of bang for the buck. Accommodations include family-size junior suites and spacious condos; the pool and spa area is fronted by a broad, green lawn; and terrific Carlsbad Beach is just across the road. On site are a playground, a frozen-yogurt shop, a Mexican restaurant, Ping-Pong, a fitness center, bikes, and beach toys, and Carlsbad's shops and restaurants are an easy walk. The hotel organizes activities for kids (sand-dollar painting, root-beer-float making) and seniors (financial planning, bus trips to Mexico).

Clarion Del Mar Inn

720 Camino del Mar, Del Mar; ☎ 800-451-4515 or 858-755-9765; www.delmarinn.com; $119–$159 off-season, $199–$299 summer

THERE'S A SNAPSHOT OF OUR KIDS in the pool area of this motel, and the brightness of their smiles is matched by the bright flowers everywhere around them—real home gardens, not institutional landscaping. A landmark along the Pacific Coast Highway and popular lodging for the horse professionals frequenting the racetrack (just count the trailers in the parking lot), this 80-room faux-Tudor place has some unusual homey touches. Afternoon tea is served in real china cups by a woman with a genuine English accent, and the decor is heavy on horse pictures and red plaid. The beach isn't too far of a walk.

Four Seasons Resort at Aviara

7100 Four Seasons Point, Carlsbad; ☎ 800-819-5053 or 760-603-6800; www.fourseasons.com/aviara; $405–$595 low season, $395–$615 high season, suites $775 and up; special packages sometimes available; children stay free in parents' room

IT MAY NOT HAVE A BEACH—South Carlsbad beach is a couple of miles away—but this expensive resort has just about everything else: a gorgeous golf course, tennis, a swimming pool, a health club, a spa, high-end restaurants, ocean views, walking/jogging trails around the neighboring Batiquitos lagoon and bird sanctuary, and luxuriously outfitted rooms. Like almost all Four Seasons resorts, this one is out to corner the upscale family market. Children are won over from the moment of check-in: waiting for them in the room are cookies and milk, and their names are spelled out with sponges in the bathroom. The free Kids for All Seasons program goes far beyond the video-room basics—warm, well-qualified counselors take kids on nature walks and for swims in the pool; kids also enjoy storytelling in a tepee, make their own postcards, and pet and feed the program's mascot, Avie the frog. Available for kids ages 4 to 12, the program is offered daily in summer, weekends and school vacations in spring, and weekends the rest of the year.

San Elijo State Beach Campground

On US 101, Cardiff-by-the-Sea; ☎ 800-444-7275 or 760-753-5091; parks.ca.gov; campsites $25–$44

IN SPIFFY CARDIFF-BY-THE-SEA, just south of Carlsbad and about 20 minutes north of San Diego's Mission Bay, this campground is beautifully set on a small bluff above the beach, with most of the tent campsites overlooking the ocean. You won't get any privacy out here in the open (the beachfront road runs right by), but you'll get a lot of beach beauty and

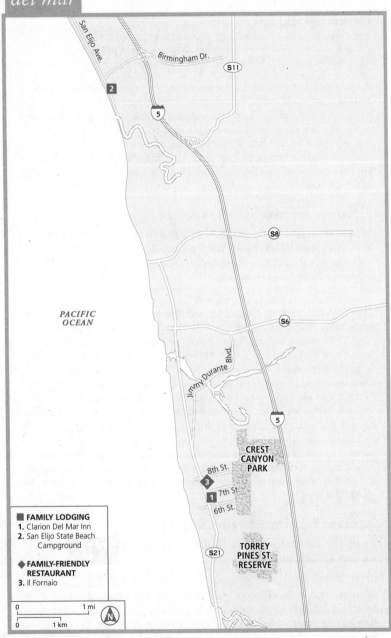

del mar

PACIFIC
OCEAN

San Elijo Ave.

Birmingham Dr.

S11

2

5

S8

S6

Jimmy Durante Blvd.

5

CREST
CANYON
PARK

8th St.

3

7th St.

1

6th St.

S21

TORREY
PINES ST.
RESERVE

■ FAMILY LODGING
1. Clarion Del Mar Inn
2. San Elijo State Beach
   Campground

◆ FAMILY-FRIENDLY
RESTAURANT
3. Il Fornaio

0 _____ 1 mi
0 _____ 1 km

N

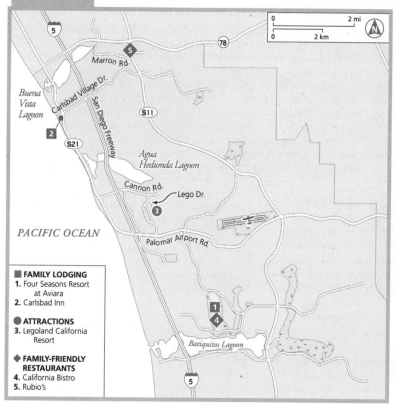

■ FAMILY LODGING
1. Four Seasons Resort
  at Aviara
2. Carlsbad Inn

● ATTRACTIONS
3. Legoland California
  Resort

**◆ FAMILY-FRIENDLY
RESTAURANTS**
4. California Bistro
5. Rubio's

fun for very little money. Summertime always books up seven months in advance, so reserve early. Hot showers, flush toilets, lifeguards, barbecues, lots of nearby restaurants.

▐ ATTRACTIONS

Legoland California Resort

APPEAL BY AGE	PRESCHOOL ★★★★½	GRADE SCHOOL ★★★★½	TEENS ½
YOUNG ADULTS ★★		OVER 30 ★★	SENIORS ★★

1 Legoland Drive, Carlsbad; ☎ 760-918-5346; www.legoland.com

Hours Vary daily; call ahead or check Web site for correct hours. **Admission** $60 adults, $50 children ages 3–12 and seniors; discounts for parents or Southern California residents are sometimes offered. Parking is $10 cars, $11 campers/ RVs, $5 motorcycles, preferred $20. **Touring time** Average 5 hours; minimum

3 hours. **Rainy-day touring** Limited. **Restaurants** Yes. **Alcoholic beverages** No. **Disabled access** Yes. **Wheelchair rental** Yes. **Baby-stroller rental** Yes. **Lockers** Yes. **Pet kennels** Yes. **Rain check** No. **Private tours** No.

DESCRIPTION AND COMMENTS   When it opened in 1999, this theme park held little appeal for older kids, especially older kids who aren't into Legos. There were no thrill rides, and to a 14-year-old, thrill rides are the only reason to go to a theme park. Over the past few years, however, the Lego-land folks have added attractions and developed the property to broaden the park's appeal. It's now a full-on resort, with two new hotels and the adjacent Sea Life (separate admission), a two-story, 36,000-square-foot aquarium with interactive exhibits and play areas designed to educate visitors about underwater life in California's rivers, lakes, streams, and oceans. Still, for the most part, this friendly place remains best suited for kids under 12—and, of course, Legomaniacs of all ages.

unofficial **TIP**
Arrive right at opening time, do the Sky Cruiser, driving school, and rides first, indulge in some quiet-time building activities, have lunch, explore Mini-land, burn off lunch in the Hideaways and Pirate Shores, then leave at the hottest part of the day, in the early afternoon, to hit the beach in Carlsbad for a refreshing family swim.

The theme here, of course, is Legos, the little, primary-colored plastic bricks out of which chil-dren (and adults) make everything from houses to Star Wars vehicles. The showpiece is Miniland, which is perhaps the most appealing part of the park for adults and older Lego-loving kids, if a bit frustrating for little ones, who aren't allowed to touch. Many regions of the United States have been meticulously re-created with more than 20 million Lego bricks. Lego boats chug in the New England harbor, subway trains run under Rockefeller Center in Manhattan, rockets get ready to launch from Cape Canaveral, and cars drive down the streets of Beverly Hills. It's pretty astounding. In the Florida Miniland, kids can race remote-control minicars around a replica of Day-tona International Speedway.

Our kids' hands-down favorite attraction is the driving school, which takes Disneyland's Autopia to the next level. Kids from ages 6 to 13 attend a brief class on driving safety and rules of the road and are then rewarded with a driver's license (these are treasured by 6-year-olds). In a Volvo-sponsored Lego car, they drive scaled-down city streets, stopping at signals and staying in their lanes like real drivers. Kids ages 3 to 6 get their own, smaller-scale driving school as well.

Otherwise, your child's favorite area will depend on age and inter-ests. The littlest ones like the Duplo building area, while the oldest ones like Mindstorms in the Imagination Zone, where they can build robotics vehicles. In this same area, kids are often allowed to help the master builders with whatever they're currently creating. After a session of quiet building, head over to the Hideaways in Castle Hill, a terrific climbing and play structure, or to the new Pirate Shores—and make sure to change into bathing suits! This new water-play area is a huge hit for 8-year-olds and up, offering waterslides, mock pirate battles, water jets, and a water-play place stocked with soaker devices galore. Younger kids might be happier at Explore Village, which includes the Dino Island, where they can dig for "remains" of prehistoric dinosaurs and ride the moderately thrilling Coastersaurus.

Other rides include the fairly tame Castle Hill Dragon roller coaster (an ideal thrill for 5- to 8-year-olds), the very tame Lake (great for pre-schoolers), and the fun Aquazone Wave Racer personal watercraft ride, a good one for older kids. The Technic Coaster will amuse the big kids, though it's still no match for Magic Mountain's megacoasters. The Sky Cruiser, which putters around high over Fun Town, isn't worth it if the line is long, which it often is. If your kids really want to ride Sky Cruiser, head over there as soon as you arrive.

Legoland gets huge kudos for making the food far more palatable and healthful than at any other theme park. Pastas, sandwiches, and salads (including a great fruit salad for kids) are made fresh to order, and the various restaurant spaces are inviting, with plenty of shade from the often-hot Carlsbad sun.

FAMILY-FRIENDLY RESTAURANTS

California Bistro

Four Seasons Resort at Aviara, 7100 Four Seasons Point, Carlsbad; ☎ 760-603-3773; www.fourseasons.com/aviara

Meals served Breakfast, lunch, dinner, and Sunday brunch. **Cuisine** Californian/American. **Entree range** Lunch, $10–$20; dinner, $25–$45. **Kids' menu** Yes. **Reservations** Recommended. **Payment** All major credit cards.

A RARE "NICE" RESTAURANT that's as comfortable for children as adults, this casual eatery is a find for families seeking a relaxed dinner out. In a beamed, high-ceilinged, California-chic dining room with an ocean-view terrace, the staff dotes on kids, bringing them coloring supplies and children's menus; babies and toddlers get a high chair and spill mat. Our kids flipped for the tortilla chip–crusted crab cakes from the grown-up menu, then returned to the safety of the children's menu for burgers and fries; we loved the roasted asparagus salad and the organic king salmon with a lentil vinaigrette. Good vegan and vegetarian choices, too, even for kids.

Il Fornaio

Del Mar Plaza, 1555 Camino del Mar, Del Mar; ☎ 858-755-8876; www.ilfornaio.com

Meals served Lunch, dinner, and Sunday brunch. **Cuisine** Italian. **Entree range** Lunch and dinner, $11–$32. **Kids' menu** Yes. **Reservations** Advised. **Payment** All major credit cards.

FOR AN UPSCALE FAMILY MEAL with a sunset ocean view you won't soon forget, head to this accomplished chain. A different region of Italy is featured monthly, and those specials are always the best, but the regular menu of risottos, pasta, bruschetta, grilled fish, and salads is delicious, too. Children are welcomed and given their own menu, with such things as Italian-style macaroni and cheese.

Rubio's

2604-A El Camino Real, Carlsbad; ☎ 760-434-6298; www.rubios.com

Meals served Lunch and dinner. **Cuisine** Mexican. **Entree range** $5–$12. **Kids' menu** Yes. **Reservations** Not accepted. **Payment** MC, V.

BORN IN SAN DIEGO, this order-at-the-counter chain is now found all over the West, and for good reason: the food is fresh, healthy, cheap, and tasty, appealing to kids and grown-ups alike. Known for its soft fish tacos, it also has a good chopped salad, generous wraps, peppery beans, and burritos and tacos filled with grilled mahimahi, savory carnitas, and grilled shrimp.

☀ SIDE TRIP:
Anza-Borrego Desert State Park

MANY SOUTHERN CALIFORNIANS manage to achieve middle age without even realizing that this 600,000-acre desert park is hiding right in their midst. Inland about two hours from San Diego, Anza-Borrego is a wilderness preserve, desert playground, and wildflower paradise in spring; the only town, Borrego Springs, still doesn't have a traffic signal, though it has a few hotels and amenities. Our favorite excursions are the extremes: either sleeping in relative luxury at La Casa del Zorro or sleeping under the stars at the state campground. Either way, pack a picnic (including lots of drinking water), have the kids wear swimsuits under their clothes, and spend a day hiking up the Palm Canyon Trail. This child-friendly destination was overwhelmed by a flash flood in 2004 that took out many of the palms and swimming holes, but the intrepid scrambler will still find a few palm oases and water. Before your hike, stop by the visitors center in Borrego Springs so your kids will know which sorts of cacti, birds, and wildflowers to hunt for. Avoid the area from June through October, when the heat can be brutal. Visitors center is at 200 Palm Canyon Drive, Borrego Springs, ☎ 760-767-5311; **parks.ca.gov.** Open daily October through May; on weekends and holidays June through September.

FAMILY LODGING

Borrego Palm Canyon State Campground

2 miles north of Borrego Springs (check Borrego Springs visitors center for directions); reservations: Reserve America, ☎ 800-444-7275, www.reserveamerica.com; campsites $15 without hookups, $24 with hookups. *Note:* This campground is inside Anza-Borrego Desert State Park.

QUIET CAMPSITES ARE SCATTERED among the ocotillo, mesquite, and barrel cactus, close to the trailhead to Palm Canyon, an easy hike that kids love. When not on the trail, they can scramble up the hillside, hunt for lizards, and, at night, count the shooting stars. Hot showers, flush toilets, barbecues, fire pits, and drinking water are available.

La Casa del Zorro Desert Resort and Spa

3845 Yaqui Pass Road, Borrego Springs; ☎ 760-767-5323 or 800-824-1884; www.lacasadelzorro.com; $240–$1,220 off-season, $360–$1,500 high season

MORE LUXURIOUS THAN THE NO-FRILLS town and empty expanse of state park would suggest, this is a fine place to recover from a long, hot hike up Palm Canyon. Swim in the pool, play tennis, rent a bike, or stay cool in one of the large, handsome, family-size villas or casitas, many of which have one or two bedrooms, refrigerators, and microwaves. Children's activities are sometimes scheduled on weekends. Rates plummet in the depths of summer. Good restaurant.

PART TWO

ORANGE COUNTY

NATIONALLY, ORANGE COUNTY IS BEST KNOWN as the home of **Disneyland Resort,** expanded with the addition of **Disney's California Adventure** and a dining and entertainment complex called **Downtown Disney.** But while the Magic Kingdom is certainly one of the county's great draws, it's in singularly unattractive Anaheim, which hardly epitomizes the California dream. The dream is here, however—you just have to head south to the beach towns. Traditionally a side trip for California visitors, the county is now a destination in and of itself, or a generous series of stops on the north–south coastal route.

Home to more than 3 million people, Orange County is dense with suburban tract developments and strip malls. The lure is the county's 42 miles of coastline, peppered with lots of lively public beaches. On the north end of the county's coast is **Huntington Beach,** aka Surf City, a sun-bleached suburb known for its pier, its surf contests, and its relaxed friendliness. On the south end is **San Clemente,** a bit too far from the business hubs of Irvine and San Diego to have become an affluent suburb—despite its prime oceanfront location, it remains a welcoming, regular-folks beach town, although prosperity is creeping in. In between these are such visitor meccas as mission-centric **San Juan Capistrano,** artsy **Laguna Beach,** and posh **Newport Beach,** along with beautiful, lesser-known beaches, endless family sporting adventures, and some way-cool attractions.

If you've never visited Orange County, we advise spending a few days in the North County theme-park area, then driving 20 to 45 minutes southwest to stay in one of the coastal towns described in this chapter (Newport, Laguna, Huntington, or the South County towns) for a few days. From any of these locations, you'll be no more than a 45-minute drive to **Wild Rivers** or the big shopping malls . . . or, even better, you can simply enjoy beach life closer to your home base. From campgrounds to luxury resorts to house rentals, there are a lot of ways to hit the beach in the Big Orange.

orange county

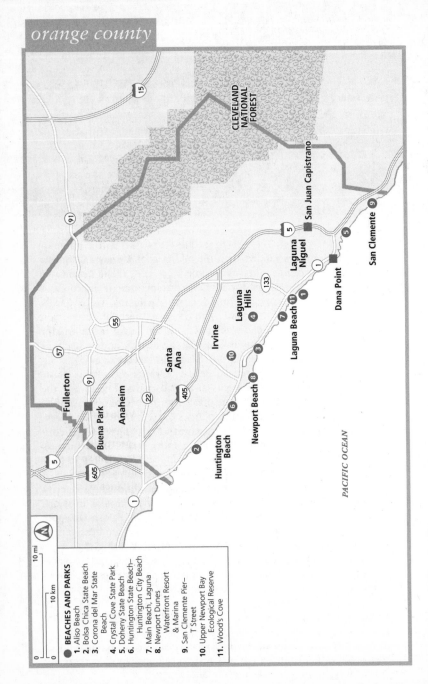

CLEVELAND
NATIONAL
FOREST

San Juan Capistrano

San Clemente ⑨

Laguna
Niguel ⑤

Dana Point

Laguna
Hills ④

133

Laguna Beach ⑪ ①
⑦

Irvine

⑩

Santa
Ana ③

405

Newport Beach ⑧

22

⑥

Anaheim

Huntington
Beach ②

Fullerton

Buena Park

57

91

55

PACIFIC OCEAN

15

91

57

5

605

①

BEACHES AND PARKS
1. Aliso Beach
2. Bolsa Chica State Beach
3. Corona del Mar State
   Beach
4. Crystal Cove State Park
5. Doheny State Beach
6. Huntington State Beach–
   Huntington City Beach
7. Main Beach, Laguna
8. Newport Dunes
   Waterfront Resort
   & Marina
9. San Clemente Pier–
   T Street
10. Upper Newport Bay
    Ecological Reserve
11. Wood's Cove

10 mi

10 km

GETTING THERE

BY PLANE Orange County is served by **John Wayne Airport** (☎ 949-252-5200; **www.ocair.com**), just off Interstate 405 in Irvine, inland from Newport Beach. Many major airlines fly into John Wayne; those that don't serve **Los Angeles International Airport** (☎ 310-646-5252; **www.lawa.org/lax**), about 20 miles north on the 405 from Irvine.

BY TRAIN Amtrak delivers passengers throughout Orange County, with stops in Fullerton, Anaheim, Santa Ana, Irvine, San Juan Capistrano, and San Clemente, connecting between Union Station in Los Angeles and downtown San Diego. If you're not doing Disneyland, one of the best possible day trips from LA is to take the train to the San Juan Capistrano or San Clemente stations (there's also a stop at **Angel Stadium of Anaheim** for an afternoon of baseball in the most family-friendly stadium in Southern California). The San Juan station is in the heart of the mission area of town, and between the station and the mission are shops and cafes. We had a mother–daughter day with friends this way and couldn't have had more fun. The San Clemente stop (only on selected trains) is at the beach and pier, so you really can wear your suits, bring a beach chair, enjoy a day at the beach and lunch at the pier, and then return to the big city. Call ☎ 800-USA-RAIL or go to **www.amtrak.com** for details.

The same route is served during commuter hours by **Metrolink** (☎ 800-371-5465; **www.metrolinktrains.com**), which is considerably cheaper than Amtrak but lacks food service and weekend travel.

BY CAR Two major freeways cut through Orange County. **Interstate 5,** which heads north to Canada and south to Mexico, runs right past Disneyland, San Juan Capistrano, and Dana Point; the **405,** which splits off from the 5 and follows a coastal route north, will get you to Newport and Huntington Beach. The **San Joaquin Hills Toll Road** (CA 73) gives riders a fast, traffic-free route from Irvine to San Juan Capistrano, via Laguna (for $5.25, $4.50 off peak, $4.25 weekends).

unofficial **TIP**
While the Pacific Coast Highway can make for a pretty drive, it slows to a creep in some areas and is not a good long-distance artery.

HOW TO GET INFORMATION BEFORE YOU GO

- **Anaheim–Orange County Visitor and Convention Bureau**
  800 West Katella Avenue, Anaheim 92802; ☎ 714-765-8888; **www.anaheimoc.org**
- **Huntington Beach Conference and Visitors Bureau**
  301 Main Street, Suite 208, Huntington Beach 92648; ☎ 800-729-6232 or 714-969-3492; **www.hbvisit.com**
- **Laguna Beach Visitors Bureau** 252 Broadway, Laguna Beach 92651; ☎ 800-877-1115 or 949-497-9229; **www.lagunabeachinfo.org**

- **Newport Beach Conference and Visitors Bureau**   1200 Newport Center Drive, Suite 120, Newport Beach 92660; ☎ 800-94-COAST; **www.newportbeach-cvb.com**
- **Orange County Tourism Council**   P.O. Box 6850, Fullerton 92834; ☎ 714-278-7491; **www.visitorangecounty.net**

SITTERS UNLIMITED

A HOME-BASED CHAIN BUSINESS, this organization will find you a licensed, bonded, experienced babysitter. For the south Orange County area, call ☎ 949-635-0906; for north, central, and inland Orange County, call ☎ 714-444-1400; in the Newport–Costa Mesa area, call ☎ 949-650-1166; **www.sittersunlimited.com.**

A **CALENDAR** of **FESTIVALS** and **EVENTS**

March

FESTIVAL OF WHALES   *Dana Point*. Early March. First-rate (and free!) open-air rock, blues, and jazz concerts, a pancake breakfast, and a street fair on the weekends. Loads of great kid activities, which change each year but might include kayaking and sailing lessons, ocean crafts, and a rubber-ducky race. A parade features such amusements as lobster jugglers, and at the ranger-led campfire, kids learn about whales and marine life. Whale-watching trips leave from the Dana Point Harbor. Call for details; ☎ 888-440-4309 or 949-472-7888; **www.dpfestivalofwhales.com.**

GLORY OF EASTER   *Crystal Cathedral, Garden Grove*. Late March to mid-April. A gala Passion play with live animals, special effects, and a cast of more than 100 in a spectacular church; ☎ 714-544-5679; **www.crystalcathedral.org.**

RETURN OF THE SWALLOWS   *Mission San Juan Capistrano*. Mid-March. They ain't what they used to be, but that doesn't stop a good time from happening. Street fair, Mexican food, shows, live music; ☎ 949-234-1300; **www.missionsjc.com.**

April

KOREAN FESTIVAL   *Garden Grove*. A three-day cultural fair with kiddie rides, a parade, and great food; ☎ 714-638-1440.

May

IMAGINATION CELEBRATION   *Countywide*. An arts festival for young children, teens, and their parents, with lots of hands-on workshops, performances, and exhibits; ☎ 714-556-5160; **www.ocimaginationcelebration.org.**

July

HUNTINGTON BEACH FOURTH OF JULY PARADE AND PIER FESTIVAL *Main Street, Huntington Beach.* Several hundred thousand people attend this all-American parade in the morning; most stick around for the beachfront fireworks show after dark; **www.hb4thofjuly.org.**

OLD GLORY BOAT PARADE *Newport Beach.* July 4; ☎ 949-673-5070 or **www.alyc291.com.**

ORANGE COUNTY FAIR *88 Fair Drive, Fairgrounds, Costa Mesa.* A classic county fair; ☎ 714-708-3247; **www.ocfair.com.**

SAN CLEMENTE OCEAN FESTIVAL *San Clemente Pier area.* A weekend of family fun, including a kids' surf contest, rubber ducky race, fishing derby, sand sculpting and tandem surfing contest, supports a number of local charities. Mid-July; ☎ 949-440-6141 or **www.oceanfestival.org.**

SAWDUST ART FESTIVAL *Laguna Beach.* The funkier cousin to the upscale Festival of Arts, this craft-oriented festival particularly appeals to teenagers; ☎ 949-494-3030; **www.sawdustartfestival.org.**

U.S. OPEN OF SURFING AND BEACH GAMES *Huntington Pier, Huntington Beach.* Late July. If your kids are surfers (or wannabes), they'll want to check out this acclaimed surf contest; also features skateboarding and BMX competitions; ☎ 424-653-1900; **www.go211.com/usopenofsurfing.**

September

TALL SHIPS FESTIVAL *Ocean Institute, Dana Point.* Weekend after Labor Day. Grand old tall ships sail into the harbor; families can get aboard one of the ships and sail in the great parade (reservations are essential; call the number below). You can also tour old ships, learn how to sail a square-rigger, listen to live sea chanteys, and see the work of nautical artisans; ☎ 949-496-2274; **www.tallshipsfestival.com.**

October

SANDCASTLE CONTEST *Corona del Mar Beach.* Kids and adults (including professionals) create amazing works in sand; ☎ 949-729-4400; **www.newportbeach.com.**

December

CHRISTMAS AT THE MISSION *Mission San Juan Capistrano.* Early December. The season kicks off with Christmas music, entertainment, and refreshments; ☎ 949-234-1300, ext. 322; **www.missionsjc.com.**

CHRISTMAS BOAT PARADE *Newport Harbor.* Seemingly all of Newport turns out to watch some 200 decorated, Christmas-lighted boats parade by; ☎ 949-729-4400; **www.christmasboatparade.com.**

The BEST BEACHES and PARKS

 ALISO BEACH   Like its sister beach (Main Beach) to the north, Aliso Creek is so picturesque that it's beloved of film crews. The sand sweeps in a gentle, golden arc, and kids frolic on the playground and in the waves. Barbecues, picnic tables, restrooms, easy metered parking, and lifeguards in summer. 31131 South Pacific Coast Highway, Laguna Beach; ☎ 949-923-2280; **www.ocparks.com/alisobeach.**

BOLSA CHICA STATE BEACH   A long, substantial, sometimes-windy strip of sand between the ocean and the Pacific Coast Highway, Bolsa Chica is between towns rather than in towns, and backing it on the other side of the highway is Bolsa Chica Ecological Reserve, a bird sanctuary that's somewhat renowned. So families day-tripping or camping here can have some pretty pure all-nature days (bring binoculars). They are, however, within an easy bike ride of Huntington Beach's surf shops, movies, and taco joints, and both the overnight and day-use areas access a snack bar. The thrill of bonfires at night is available here, too. Barbecue pits, lifeguards in summer, camping, showers, concessions. Pacific Coast Highway between Warner and Seaport avenues; ☎ 714-846-3460; **parks.ca.gov.**

CORONA DEL MAR STATE BEACH   Also known as Big Corona, this is one of Southern California's prettier beaches, with cliffs behind, the sparkling Pacific ahead, and a rock pier into the sea. Lifeguards, bathrooms, a snack bar, volleyball courts, barbecues. Ocean Boulevard and Iris, Corona del Mar; 949-644-3151; **parks.ca.gov.** The neighboring beach is known as Little Corona, but its formal name is Corona del Mar Marine Life Refuge. When the tide is low, you can explore fascinating marine life pools; call for a schedule of kid-friendly ranger tours; ☎ 949-644-3038.

CRYSTAL COVE STATE PARK   Developers are encroaching on the heretofore unspoiled land surrounding these 2,791 acres of bluffs, chaparral canyon, and open land—not to mention 3.5 miles of coastline—between Laguna Beach and Corona del Mar; a new luxury hotel and golf course have arrived, and a housing development on the inland side is under construction. But this is still one of the most amazing open stretches south of Santa Barbara, and much of it is protected. Inland are miles of trails beloved by mountain bikers and hikers; on the beach is superb tide pooling in the rocky stretches. Docents hold nature walks on Saturday and Sunday mornings. 8471 Pacific Coast Highway; ☎ 949-494-3539; **parks.ca.gov.** Parking is $10. Primitive camping is available (bring your own water, and take everything out), or you can rent one of the wonderful renovated cottages; ☎ 800-444-7275 or **www.crystalcovebeachcottages.org** (see Family Lodging).

DOHENY STATE BEACH   After San Onofre, this is the second-best Southern California beach for kids (or adults) to learn how to surf, thanks to the long, gentle waves that break just south of the Dana Point Harbor breakwater. This is also a great beach for a day trip, especially if you reserve one of the extremely popular barbecue-equipped picnic sites in advance, (call Reserve America, ☎ 800-444-7275; **www .reserveamerica.com**). There's only one problem—the ocean has been off limits more and more days in recent years for high bacteria counts, so there's a chance of disappointment, especially after a rainstorm. Rolling green lawns dotted with picnic areas are interwoven with pedestrian and bike paths; all this fronts a broad sand beach equipped with pro-quality volleyball courts, a snack bar, showers, and, in summer, both lifeguards and a concession that rents bodyboards, surrey bikes, inline skates, and other amusements. Near the entrance to the beach is a small but worthy interpretive center with an indoor tide pool and 3,000-gallon marine aquarium system. 25300 Dana Point Harbor Drive, Dana Point; ☎ 949-496-6171; **parks.ca.gov.**

HUNTINGTON STATE BEACH–HUNTINGTON CITY BEACH When the surf is really booming, your kids will need to stay out of the water, but they'll have a blast watching the surfers put on a show, especially on the north side of the magnificent, 1,800-foot-long pier. Typically, however, the waves aren't too forbidding. The city and state beaches adjoin each other, with the Bolsa Chica wetlands (see left) connecting via a fun bike path from the state beach. This is a classic white-sand California beach, great for everything from castle making to bodysurfing to fishing on the pier. Summer lifeguards, a snack bar, bathrooms, a bike path, barbecue pits, concessions. State beach is on Pacific Coast Highway at Magnolia Avenue; ☎ 714-536-1454; **parks.ca.gov.**

MAIN BEACH, LAGUNA BEACH This is the beach you've seen in a million commercials for everything from cars to sunscreen—it's the idealized California beach. A compact, gently sweeping arc in the heart of Laguna Beach, it's famed for its old-fashioned lifeguard tower (painted ad nauseam by local artists), its near-NBA-level pickup basketball games, its volleyball courts, its swimming, and, most of all, its people-watching. At the north end, you'll find the Glenn East Vedder Ecological Reserve, which continues north to Crescent Bay Drive. Pick up a tide chart at the visitors center, visit at low tide, and discover wonderful tide pooling; make sure children understand before you start that this is a marine preserve, so nothing may be removed, not even a shell. Older kids may want to join you in a snorkeling tour of the reserve at higher tide. Take younger ones to the south end of the beach, where there's a nifty playground. Summer lifeguard service, showers, and restrooms. Restaurants, ice-cream parlors, and shops are plentiful, but parking is not. Pacific Coast Highway at Broadway, Laguna Beach; ☎ 800-877-1115; **www.lagunabeachinfo.org.**

NEWPORT DUNES WATERFRONT RESORT & MARINA The Disneyland of beaches, this chic, private, RV-oriented campground is also a very fun day trip with young children. There's loads of clean, white

unofficial **TIP**
We like to stake out a spot south of the San Clemente Pier, closer to the restrooms, showers, and snack bar.

sand, a wave-free lagoon in which sits a big fiberglass whale (the kids can swim to the whale), a good playground, and even decent shell hunting. A concession rents pedal boats, kayaks, and other watercraft, and you can even get a hot indoor shower. Snack bar, food shop, lifeguards, tent camping (but no stakes), RV camping. Admission is $16 per car. 1131 Back Bay Drive, Newport Beach; ☎ 949-729-3863 or 800-765-7661; **www .newportdunes.com.**

SAN CLEMENTE PIER–T STREET A superb day-at-the-beach destination, T Street beach lies south of the San Clemente Pier; Amtrak trains stop right here a couple of times a day, making this a fun car-free trip from LA or Anaheim. It's a great beach for all ages— the shore break area is broad and shallow, with gentle waves that amuse toddlers to no end; farther out are some of the best bodysurfing–bodyboarding waves for miles (surfboards are banned in some areas after 10 a.m., to protect the kids). Avenida Del Mar and Avenida Victoria, San Clemente; ☎ 949-361-8264; **www.beachcalifornia.com/ sanclem.html.** The Marine Safety Headquarters on the pier can be reached at ☎ 949-361-8261.

UPPER NEWPORT BAY ECOLOGICAL RESERVE Bring bikes or your sneakers to explore the 700 acres of pristine peace in the midst of developed Newport Beach. The bird population is astounding; look for great blue herons and snowy egrets, and see how many different kinds of ducks you can spot. The Newport Bay Naturalists & Friends provide guided tours and interpretive programs for families. Back Bay Drive off Jamboree Road, Newport Beach; ☎ 949-640-6746; **www .newportbay.org.**

WOOD'S COVE If Laguna's Main Beach is too crowded, head over to this lesser-known gem, hidden by dramatic bluffs. Kids love climbing the many rocks and hunting for crabs and other sea critters. Bathrooms, summer lifeguards. Pacific Coast Highway at Diamond Street, Laguna Beach; ☎ 800-877-1115 or 949-497-9229; **www.lagunabeachinfo.org.**

FAMILY OUTDOOR ADVENTURES

BICYCLING AND INLINE SKATING Cycling, skating, and scootering are passions with countless Orange County families, and for good reason—the county is zigzagged with miles of easy, dedicated paths, especially near the beaches. One of our favorite family rides is the path from **Huntington State Beach** north to **Bolsa Chica,** where you can watch birds in the wetlands. Or you can ride south from

Huntington all the way to **Newport Beach,** a beautiful ride for 10-and-ups who can pedal a few miles. Another great one is the **Back Bay Drive** bike path, which wanders through the Upper Newport Bay Ecological Reserve (see "The Best Beaches and Parks," page 72). Finally, you can ride along the **Balboa Peninsula** in Newport, stopping to watch the gnarly bodysurfing waves at the Wedge on the south end of the peninsula. Then take your bikes over to **Balboa Island** on the ferry, explore the tiny island, have a snack, ferry back, and ride north along the peninsula to Newport Pier. You can get outfitted in rental skates, bikes, and protective gear at **Balboa Bikes & Beach Stuff** (601 East Balboa Boulevard on Balboa Peninsula; ☎ 949-723-1516; **www .balboabikes.com**); in Huntington Beach, check out **Team Bicycle Shop** (8464 Indianapolis Avenue; ☎ 714-969-5480).

Mountain bikers will want to check out the trails in and around Laguna's **Crystal Cove State Park** (see "The Best Beaches and Parks") If you need mountain bikes, you can rent them at **Laguna Beach Cyclery** (240 Thalia Street; ☎ 949-494-1522; **www.lagunabeachcyclery.com**).

BOATING   Puttering around **Newport Harbor** in a rented boat can be big fun for young sailors. Pick up a small sailboat ($45 per hour), electric boat, motorboat, or kayak at **Balboa Boat Rentals** in Newport Harbor (☎ 949-673-7200; **www.boats4rent.com**) and set out for a tour of the harbor's many nooks and crannies. Most of the smaller boats are not allowed out of the harbor.

FISHING   Fun, affordable seagoing fishing trips are run out of Dana Point Harbor by **Dana Wharf Sportfishing and Whale Watching** (34675 Golden Lantern; ☎ 949-496-5794; **www.danawharfsportfishing.com**). A half-day trip is $39 for adults and $25 for kids under age 12, with rods and reels renting for another $12; fishing licenses are available for $13. The crew will help neophytes, and any fish you catch (there are calico bass, sand bass, rock cod, mackerel, even the occasional shark out there) will be filleted and packaged for you. Whale-watching trips are also offered in season. If you're based in Newport, try **Newport Landing Sportfishing** (309 Palm Street, Suite A, Balboa; ☎ 949-675 -0550; **www.newportlanding.com**).

HIKING   There's more than beaches to Orange County's outdoors—there's also a surprising amount of high-quality hiking. The best trails for families are in the **Laguna** area; good ones are also found near **San Juan Capistrano,** but fear of mountain-lion attacks sometimes forces rangers to prohibit children from the trails. Our favorite family hike, other than the tide-pooling–rock-climbing adventures at **Dana Point** and **Crystal Cove** (see "The Best Beaches and Parks"), is the three-mile round-trip trek in Moro Canyon at Crystal Cove State Park; for details, call ☎ 949-494-3539 or go to **www.crystalcovestatepark.com**.

PARASAILING   Adventurous teens (maybe you, too) will get a huge thrill out of a parasail trip—they'll be lofted like a human kite, tethered to the deck of a boat, to soar over the ocean for a 12-minute ride that seems much longer. The best place to try it is **Balboa Boat Rentals** (510 East Edgewater, Balboa; ☎ 949-673-7200; **www.boats4rent.com**).

SURFING AND OCEAN SPORTS   The explosion of lessons, classes, and camps in recent years makes surfing easy to try. A good program is sponsored by the city of San Clemente: half-day surf classes (and private lessons) for kids and adults in the easygoing waves of North Beach. **JP's Surf Camp** runs the program for the city; ☎ 949-361-8264 or 949-547-2088; **www.jpssurfcamp.com.** For more options, see "Surf Camp," below.

unofficial **TIP**
No kid should visit Orange County without trying surfing.

TIDE POOLING   An afternoon spent scrambling over rocks hunting for crabs, anemones, shells, sea stars, and maybe even an octopus is often a highlight of a trip. Orange County has several great locations, so look under a specific beach heading for recommendations. See our profiles of Corona del Mar Beach, Crystal Cove State Park, and Main Beach in "The Best Beaches and Parks," and also see the **Ocean Institute** attraction profile in the South County section. You can pick up a tide chart at any of the dozens of surf, fishing, or boat stores in any of the beach towns. Make sure your kids understand that if the tide pools are part of a preserve, nothing may be removed, not even an empty shell—a hermit crab may need it for a home later.

WHALE WATCHING   Much anticipated by local schoolchildren each year, and celebrated with a terrific festival in **Dana Point,** whale-watching season arrives each January and lasts through March. These boat trips are fun half-day outings for kids of all ages; even if you aren't lucky enough to spot a herd of migrating gray whales, you're sure to see dolphins and sea birds and get great views and a feel for the vast Pacific. Trips depart from the harbors in Dana Point (☎ 949-496-2274) and Newport (☎ 949-673-1434). The Dana Point trips are run by the Ocean Institute (**www.ocean-institute.org**), and the Newport trips are run by **Davey's Locker–Sport Fishing and Whale Watching** (**www.daveyslocker.com**) with curious kids in mind.

SURF CAMP

NOTHING SYMBOLIZES CALIFORNIA MORE THAN SURFING, yet few sports are more challenging to master. Enter the surf camp, which offers several days or more of intense instruction, along with a lot of camaraderie and fun. After a week at any of these Orange County camps, your kid will be a real surfer. And don't be afraid to try it yourself—it's one of the simplest, purest thrills in the sporting world. Some camps offer one-day sessions.

SUPER SURF CAMP   Part of the excellent California Junior Lifeguards Program, these one-week day camps (ages 8 through adult) are offered during spring break and throughout summer. Based at Huntington State Beach, Newland Street and Pacific Coast Highway, this is a great way to get to know the ocean. Your kids (or your whole family) will learn not only surfing or bodyboarding, but also the essentials of first aid, CPR, lifeguarding, and ocean safety. The price is moderate, and it includes free loaner boards and wet suits for those who don't have their own. If you have a daughter, take note that even though surfing may seem boy dominated, 35% to 40% of the camp participants are girls. Huntington Beach; ☎ 714-901-9030; **www.jrlifeguards.com.**

SUMMER SOUL SURF CAMP   This Billabong-sponsored camp isn't fancy—home base is the scruffy campgrounds of San Clemente State Park—but it's a lot of fun, very well run, and, best of all, the surfing is done at San Onofre, home of the most learner-friendly waves in the state. Former longboard champ Josh Baxter and Chris Bamum (and their staff) teach kids to surf and offer such extras as outrigger canoe surfing, skateboard outings, and art sessions. Little ones (ages 4 to 6) can attend a one-day camp that will get them up on a surfboard; older ones (up to age 17) enjoy five-day sessions that can be done as either day camps or sleepovers. Private lessons also offered. San Clemente; ☎ 800-522-1352; **www.summersoulsurfcamp.com.**

SURF ACADEMY   Founded and run by former surfing champ (and mother of five) Mary Setterholm, this LA-area operation has grown to include a rich roster of surfing-related events and activities. You can take private surf lessons or even lessons on how to swim in the ocean. Saturdays are devoted to surf classes for women and girls age 7 and older, Sundays to classes for families of all ages, and summer weekdays to terrific, reasonably priced surfing and bodyboarding day camps for kids. Camps and lessons are held at Huntington Beach, Santa Monica, and El Segundo; ☎ 877-599-7873; **www.surfacademy.org.**

FINDING *a* HOME *in* ORANGE COUNTY

RENTING A BEACH HOUSE

FROM ANY OF THE LOCATIONS BELOW, you can make easy day trips to Disneyland, Knott's, Wild Rivers, or the other Orange County amusements—but your kids will have just as much fun on the beach and in the ocean, and you may be happiest staying put. If you have younger children, try sleepy Capistrano; if you have teenagers, you're better off in Newport or Laguna, where they'll find more close-by shops, amusements, and other teens.

BURR WHITE REALTY   With more than 30 years of experience renting beach houses, this Newport firm is the best source for a beach house on the Balboa Peninsula; it has choices on the oceanfront, for

unofficial **TIP**
If you've got a week or more to spend, a beach house is the way to go. True, you have to do your own dishes and daily housekeeping, but you can get plenty of room for a family right on the sand, for less than a comparably located hotel, and you can save more money by eating a meal or two a day at home.

wave fans, and on the bay front, for those who prefer gentler waters, and less expensive ones in between, for those on a budget who don't mind walking a block to the beach. August prices for a three-bedroom waterfront house range from $2,200 to $10,000 a week, depending on the property. The beach is less secluded and private than Capistrano, but there's more action for teens. 2901 Newport Boulevard, Newport Beach; ☎ 800-944-0952; **www.burrwhite.com.**

CAPISTRANO REALTY   Between San Clemente and Dana Point lies one of Orange County's few private beachfront communities, perhaps the only one in which every house sits on the sand. This agency is the primary source for renting a house along guard-gated, one-and-a-half-mile Beach Road, which parallels the Pacific Coast Highway just across the (frequently traveled) railroad tracks. Although hardly cheap, the houses rent for much less than in the Malibu colony or Del Mar: A high-quality three-bedroom, two-bath place might go for $2,500 a week in June and $5,000 in August. Cycling families, note that you can ride from Beach Road all the way to Dana Point Harbor (about three miles) on a flat, protected, oceanfront route; a vendor at the public beach at the beginning of the road rents bikes, surreys, and skates. Houses on the north end of the road have the largest sand beach; those on the south end have the best swimming for children, but note that erosion is making the beach rockier. 34700 Pacific Coast Highway, Capistrano Beach; ☎ 800-397-6931 or 949-496-5353; **www .socalvacation.com.**

LAGUNA PROPERTIES   This Laguna Beach agency offers weekly and monthly vacation rentals in Laguna and surrounding towns, including Dana Point. 1096 South Coast Highway, Laguna Beach; ☎ 888-393-6533 or 949-494-8057; **www.lagunaproperties.biz.**

SOUTH COUNTY:
San Clemente, Dana Point, and San Juan Capistrano

LOW ON A-LIST AMUSEMENTS BUT HIGH ON BEACH FUN, the towns in southernmost Orange County aren't well known to the tourist trade. That's just fine by the locals, who get to enjoy clean, sunny beaches and small-town appeal. We have a number of friends who live within walking distance of LA's beaches but who drive an hour or more south to San Clemente's **T Street** every Saturday in summer because its water is cleaner, its beach more picturesque, and its surf better for both little kids and bodysurfers.

San Clemente is the southernmost town in this area, and it's a great place to spend a beach day. Amtrak trains stop right in front of the pier and beach, making it a fine car-free day trip from LA or Anaheim. Although it has begun to gentrify, it's still a real beach town, populated by retirees and middle-class families, with a classic pier, a public beach with all the amenities, and a sunny downtown with great surf shops, a few interesting boutiques, and Mexican restaurants.

Dana Point, a few miles north, is centered on a large pleasure-craft harbor (see attraction profile, page 82). The heart of town itself is a rather dispiriting collection of late-model storefronts along the Pacific Coast Highway (PCH), but if you look carefully you'll find a few shops that surf-fascinated kids will adore, including **Hobie, Girl in the Curl** (for female surfers), and **Killer Dana.** Along with the usual streets, a bike path follows **San Juan Creek** from its end point—the bird sanctuary–estuary between **Doheny State Beach's** campground and public park—about three flat miles into **San Juan Capistrano,** the handsome mission town in which even the fast-food restaurants have red-tile roofs.

The mission is San Juan's main draw, and it's one of the state's loveliest and most interesting to children. From the mission, you can walk to the train depot and let kids run through the old train cars that make up the station and station restaurant; across the train tracks are a few of the town's oldest houses, including some adobes, as well as a sweet little petting farm and pony ride that local kids love.

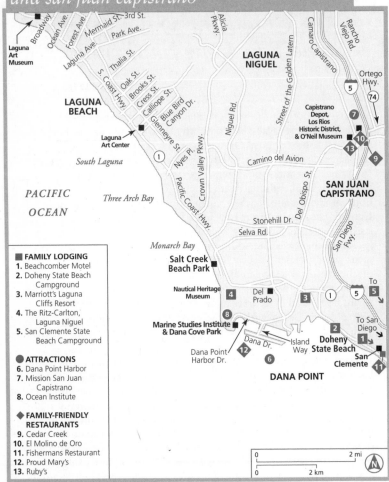

south county: san clemente, dana point, and san juan capistrano

FAMILY LODGING
1. Beachcomber Motel
2. Doheny State Beach Campground
3. Marriott's Laguna Cliffs Resort
4. The Ritz-Carlton, Laguna Niguel
5. San Clemente State Beach Campground

ATTRACTIONS
6. Dana Point Harbor
7. Mission San Juan Capistrano
8. Ocean Institute

FAMILY-FRIENDLY RESTAURANTS
9. Cedar Creek
10. El Molino de Oro
11. Fishermans Restaurant
12. Proud Mary's
13. Ruby's

FAMILY LODGING

Beachcomber Motel

533 Avenida Victoria, San Clemente; ☎ 888-492-5457 or 949-492-5457; www.beachcombermotel.com; $125–$375, weekly rates available

A VINTAGE 1940S BEACH MOTEL, the red-tile-roof Beachcomber has just 12 rooms and a killer location on a grassy bluff overlooking San Clemente beach and the pier. The amenities are few: a vending machine instead of a coffee shop, and the blue Pacific instead of a pool. The prices are high for a basic motel (maid service, for example, is provided only "as needed"). But even the studios have kitchenettes and can house a family of four, and the one-bedrooms can handle as many as seven people. Each unit also has its own little front porch with a fabulous ocean view. The beach below is one of the best for family fun in Southern California. This motel books up months in advance for summer, so plan ahead.

Doheny State Beach Campground

25300 Dana Point Harbor Drive, Dana Point; ☎ 949-496-6171; www.dohenystatebeach.org; reservations: Reserve America, ☎ 800-444-7275; www.reserveamerica.com; campsites, $9–$25; parking rates are established by park

IT'S SMALL, IT HAS NO RVS (no hookups), and it's right on one of the most family-friendly beaches in Southern California, so this tent campground is booked months in advance for weekends and summer. Because it's so compact, don't expect much peace and quiet, but do expect to find lots of other families skating and cycling the bike paths, playing volleyball, learning to surf the famed, gentle waves, barbecuing, visiting the small indoor aquarium, and exploring the neighboring Dana Point Harbor. Be warned that this part of the ocean has had a number of health-related closures in the past couple of years.

Laguna Cliffs Marriott Resort & Spa

25135 Park Lantern, Dana Point; ☎ 800-228-9290 or 949-661-5000; www.marriott.com; $229–$750, suites $600 and up

A CAPE COD–STYLE HOTEL that sprawls over a bluff with views from Dana Point to San Clemente, this resort has had several changes in management, but it has remained a very good family resort no matter who's in charge. From the extensive lawns, paths lead down to a pine-dotted city park above the harbor, with a children's playground, an excellent basketball court, and lawns popular with kite flyers. On site are two pools, lots of room to run around, a fitness center, and a spa. The children's menu is available for both the restaurant and room service. Doheny State Beach is a third-of-a-mile walk, but the walk back is up a steep hill, so if you have little ones, you might consider driving (which means paying for parking).

The Ritz-Carlton, Laguna Niguel

1 Ritz-Carlton Drive, Dana Point; ☎ 800-241-3333 or 949-240-2000; www.ritzcarlton.com; $500–$700; 4 people allowed in a room ($50 per extra guest); children under 18 stay free

THIS IS PARADISE FOR KIDS and their parents, as long as they've got plenty of money and don't mind a setting that's more formal than California beach. A few hundred guest rooms, elegant restaurants, lounges, lobbies, and meeting rooms are spread along a bluff overlooking a soft-sand beach; everywhere are lawns and flowers and walkways, along with the expected pools, spas, a fitness center, spa facilities, and tennis courts (golf is adjacent).

Your 6- to 12-year-old children can join in the Ritz Kids program ($80 a day), which includes swimming, beach games, arts and crafts, tide pooling, and trips to the Ocean Institute; if you crave a grown-up meal, the hotel offers Kids' Night Out on Friday and Saturday, when youngsters are served dinner and entertained with movies or live performances (such as puppet shows). The Dana Pool Cafe offers a good children's menu, which is also available through room service.

San Clemente State Beach Campground

3030 Avenida del Presidente, San Clemente; ☎ 949-492-3156; parks.ca.gov; reservations: Reserve America; ☎ 800-444-7275; www.reserveamerica.com; campsites $25–$34

POPULAR WITH SURFERS and beach-loving families, this is a well-equipped (hookups, fire rings, hot showers, flush toilets) campground on a bluff overlooking the beach; the trail down is easily manageable for kids, though the littlest may whine heading back up (consider bringing a wagon). A fine beach for bodyboarding, surfing, splashing, and general beach fun.

❚ ATTRACTIONS

Dana Point Harbor

APPEAL BY AGE	PRESCHOOL ★★★	GRADE SCHOOL ★★★	TEENS ★★★
YOUNG ADULTS ★★★		OVER 30 ★★★	SENIORS ★★★

Golden Lantern off Pacific Coast Highway, Dana Point; ☎ 949-923-2255; www.danapointharbor.com

Hours Shops and restaurants open daily; hours vary. **Admission** Free. **Touring time** Average 4 hours including lunch or dinner; minimum 1 hour. **Rainy-day touring** Not great. **Restaurants** Many. **Alcoholic beverages** Yes. **Disabled access** Yes. **Wheelchair rental** No. **Baby-stroller rental** No. **Lockers** No. **Pet kennels** No. **Rain check** No. **Private tours** No.

DESCRIPTION AND COMMENTS   More an afternoon's destination than an attraction, the harbor is home to a fine museum (the Ocean Institute; see profile) and a kid-beloved outdoor cafe, Proud Mary's (see page 85). The harbor is also the place to head out for a whale-watching, fishing, or personal-watercraft expedition (rentals available). You can also skate, cycle, or walk the pedestrian paths linking the shopping, eating, and boating areas, and explore the little caves, tide pools, and rocky shoreline on the far west end of the harbor. On a sunny day, the hippest place to be is the terrace front of the Scoop Deck, an ice-cream parlor next door to a coffeehouse. Locals and their many dogs join visitors to sit and watch the passing parade of inline skaters, sailors, and walkers.

 ### Mission San Juan Capistrano

APPEAL BY AGE	PRESCHOOL ★★	GRADE SCHOOL ★★★	TEENS ★★★
YOUNG ADULTS ★★★		OVER 30 ★★★	SENIORS ★★★★

Visitors Center, 31882 Camino Capistrano, San Juan Capistrano;
☎ **949-234-1300; www.missionsjc.com**

Hours Daily, 8:30 a.m.–5 p.m.; closed Thanksgiving, Christmas, and Good Friday afternoon. **Admission** Self-guided tours: $9 adults, $8 seniors, and $5 children ages 3–11; docent tours $8. **Touring time** Average 2 hours; minimum 1 hour. **Rainy-day touring** Some; outdoors may be difficult. **Restaurants** Nearby. **Alcoholic beverages** No. **Disabled access** Yes. **Wheelchair rental** 2 chairs to borrow. **Baby-stroller rental** No. **Lockers** No. **Pet kennels** No. **Rain check** No. **Private tours** Guided tours $8 all ages.

DESCRIPTION AND COMMENTS Perhaps the most fully restored of the mission chain, with the most to see in the way of demonstrations and living, working, sacred, and exhibition areas, San Juan Capistrano is also an enclosed, parklike setting that makes it an easy place to keep track of kids while they scramble and skip around a bit. The mission buildings are laid out around two enclosed courtyards, and the rooms you see are on the ground level with a simple step in and out of the adobe doorways. Parents of very young children don't even have to bother with the lectures; instead they can wander past the tables full of ancient tools and bits of leather and such that are set out especially for little ones to touch and examine. On the second Saturday of each month, the mission holds Living History Day, which is worth a visit—docents dress and act in character as Native Americans and missionary priests. Check the Web site for hands-on activity days for kids.

 Ocean Institute

	PRESCHOOL ★★★	GRADE SCHOOL ★★★★	TEENS ★★★
APPEAL BY AGE			
YOUNG ADULTS ★★★	OVER 30 ★★★		SENIORS ★★★

24200 Dana Point Harbor Drive (far western end of harbor), Dana Point;
☎ **949-496-2274; www.ocean-institute.org**

Hours Store open daily, 9 a.m.–5 p.m.; facility open for field trips Monday–Friday, 8 a.m.–5 p.m. **Admission** $6.50 adults, $4.50 children ages 3–12, free for age 2 and under. **Touring time** Average 30 minutes; minimum 30 minutes. **Rainy-day touring** No problem inside; difficult near tide pools. **Restaurants** Nearby. **Alcoholic beverages** No. **Disabled access** Yes. **Wheelchair rental** No. **Baby-stroller rental** No. **Lockers** No. **Pet kennels** No. **Rain check** Excursions only. **Private tours** Yes.

DESCRIPTION AND COMMENTS The name suggests an aquarium center, but while plans are afoot to add tank space, that's not what this place is about. It's a quirky, intriguing collection of marine-centered activities and sites, from the tide pools out on the shoreline to tours of a historic tall ship. Inside is a simple, docent-staffed touch tank, allowing kids to hold a sea star or tiny crab, along with a gift shop and such whale memorabilia as a fully reconstructed skeleton hanging overhead. Across the lawn outside is the home dock of *The Pilgrim*, site of overnight field trips for seemingly every fifth-grade class in Southern California; on

Sundays you can tour the ship, which will bring your child's Captain Hook fantasies to life. Parent–child overnighters are offered sporadically in summer; call for information.

Even cooler, at least for the 8-to-teen set, is a trip aboard the R/V Sea Explorer, a state-of-the-art research ship complete with underwater remote cameras. Outings include the Marine Mammal trip (best during whale-watching season) and our favorite, the Bioluminescence Night Cruise, a two-hour trip in search of glowing fish, plankton, and glowworms.

Finally, the institute supervises (and sometimes leads tours of) the wonderful tide-pooling preserve on its northern edge, at the base of the actual point. Our kids have spent many happy hours exploring the life here and hiking the rocky but easy trail that hugs the bluff, leading to several kid-sized caves and even more tide pooling.

FAMILY-FRIENDLY RESTAURANTS

Cedar Creek
26860 Ortega Highway, San Juan Capistrano; ☎ 949-240-2229; www.cedarcreekinn.com

Meals served Lunch, dinner, and Sunday brunch. **Cuisine** American. **Entree range** Lunch, $11–$18; dinner, $11–$31. **Kids' menu** Yes. **Reservations** Not accepted on Friday and Saturday nights. **Payment** AE, MC, V.

IDEALLY LOCATED ACROSS THE STREET from Mission San Juan Capistrano, this place has the prettiest patio in town, all brick and greenery and Mission influenced, with a fireplace for chilly evenings. Unlike the Cedar Creek in Laguna, this one welcomes children with such things as special menus and booster seats. The well-prepared food is solid American with a bit of modernity (there's a rare grilled-ahi sandwich as well as a terrific burger). Later, evenings often bring live music and what passes for a singles scene in San Juan, so families are best coming for lunch and early dinner.

El Molino de Oro
31886 Plaza Drive, San Juan Capistrano; ☎ 949-489-9230

Meals served Breakfast, lunch, and dinner. **Cuisine** Mexican. **Entree range** $5–$12. **Kids' menu** Yes. **Reservations** Not accepted. **Payment** D, MC, V.

ALMOST HIDDEN IN A STRIP MALL south of the mission (look for the Starbucks to find it), this tortilleria and cafe makes the best Mexican food in town. There's always a line at the counter, and the plastic tables on the sidewalk fill up fast, thanks to the fresh, homemade tortillas and hearty, cheap, delicious burritos, soft tacos, enchiladas, and more. Our picky kids love the cheese quesadillas and fresh chips.

Fishermans Restaurant

San Clemente Pier, 611 Avenida Victoria, San Clemente;
☎ **949-498-6390; www.fishermansrestaurant.com**

Meals served Breakfast, lunch, and dinner. **Cuisine** American/seafood. **Entree range** Breakfast, $5.25–$11.25, lunch $8.95–$20, dinner $13.25–$35.95. **Kids' menu** Yes. **Reservations** Not accepted. **Payment** All major credit cards.

IDEALLY LOCATED ON THE SAN CLEMENTE PIER, steps from the Amtrak station and in the middle of great public beaches, this seafood-focused bar and grill is jam-packed on summer weekends, and the wait for an out-door table can run 90 minutes. In summertime, the best deal is the Sunset Dinner—on weeknights from 4 to 6 p.m., you can get a full dinner (calamari steak, salmon, pasta) for $14.95. There's a respectable breakfast and an inexpensive children's menu.

 ## Proud Mary's

34689 Golden Lantern, Dana Point Harbor; ☎ **949-493-5853; www.proudmarysrestaurant.com**

Meals served Breakfast, lunch, and dinner. **Cuisine** American. **Entree range** Breakfast, $5–$8; lunch, $6–$12; dinner, $9–$20. **Kids' menu** Yes. **Reservations** Not accepted. **Payment** All major credit cards.

OUR KIDS WERE HEARTBROKEN when they heard that Proud Mary's was destroyed by a fire—and now they're relieved to hear that it was about to reopen after a total renovation. This has been their favorite restaurant for years. For one thing, all lunches come with a small bag of potato chips. For another, the children's menus are great to color, and they can hang them on the inside wall when finished. Best of all, the patio tables overlook the fishing boats, coastline, and harbor walkway, which is always packed with kids, dogs, and adults on weekends. While waiting for their chicken fingers, they can wave to departing fishing boats and watch crabs scurry on the rocks below. We love it, too, because of the enlarged, fire-pit-warmed patio, the view, and the superb hamburger, Ortega chile–turkey sandwich, and breakfasts.

Ruby's

31781 Camino Capistrano, San Juan Capistrano; ☎ **949-496-7829; www.rubys.com**

Meals served Breakfast, lunch, and dinner. **Cuisine** American. **Entree range** Breakfast, $7–$12; lunch and dinner, $8–$12. **Kids' menu** Yes. **Reservations** Not accepted. **Payment** All major credit cards.

A MULTISTATE CHAIN that grew out of the Newport Beach original, Ruby's is another rider on the 1940s-nostalgia bandwagon, and kids can't get enough of it. Booths are big, red, and shiny, children's cheeseburgers come in car-shaped cardboard boxes (complete with toy), and a model train chugs around the ceiling. The food is generic, inexpensive, and more fun for children than parents (though it makes kids happy).

LAGUNA BEACH *and* NEWPORT BEACH

THE ANTIDOTE TO THE TRACT-HOUSE STERILITY of Orange County is **Laguna Beach.** This hilly, meandering town is funky, artistic, and utterly charming. It's known more as a beach-town retreat for artists, art lovers (including devotees of the bizarre **Pageant of the Masters,** where people dress in costume and re-create famous paintings), and couples (straight and gay) seeking a romantic weekend. Don't look for such amusements as theme parks or kid-oriented museums, but do spend time exploring some of its 30 jewellike beaches, many hidden at the base of steep bluffs. If you choose Laguna as a beachy base for exploring Orange County, know that **Newport** is only about a 15-minute drive north, **Dana Point** about a 15-minute drive south, and **Disneyland** and **Knott's Berry Farm** are some 30 minutes inland. Add more time to the drives in July and August, when central Laguna sees wicked traffic.

Newport Beach is the nouveau-riche capital of California. It oozes prosperity, with seemingly more Mercedes-Benzes than in all of Germany. Although this can be irritating for less materialistic families, prosperity does have its advantages. Newport has miles of wide, clean, well-maintained beaches, a yacht harbor stocked with pretty boats, bike paths galore, some of the country's best shopping, good restaurants, and fetching little Balboa Island, almost a toy beach-village.

In some social circles, families have rented Newport beachside cottages for generations, which can be a fine idea (see "Renting a Beach House," page 77). **Balboa Peninsula** is a particularly nice place to be, with its bay and ocean beaches, bike path, pier, pedal boats on the bay, ferry, and **Fun Zone.** Teens especially love Balboa and Newport, because there's always life (and other teens) on the boardwalk and the beach. Don't miss a morning visit to the **Newport Pier** to watch the dory fishermen row in and unload their morning catch—kids find it enthralling. (They'll also like watching the fishing families on the pier, catching their dinners.) If you don't have a week

unofficial **TIP**
Laguna is an excellent base for beach vacations with teens and preteens, who will love the shopping (beads, tie-dyes, surf wear, locally made jewelry); the snack, coffee, and yogurt vendors; the hip cafes; and the fellow-teen watching.

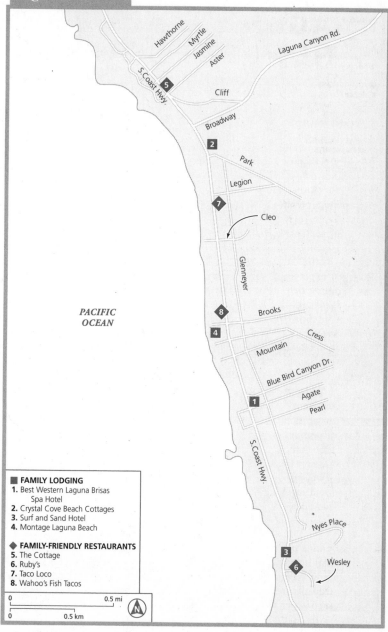

laguna beach

Hawthorne
Myrtle
Jasmine
Aster
Laguna Canyon Rd.
S. Coast Hwy.
Cliff
Broadway
Park
Legion
Cleo
Glenneyer
Brooks
Cress
Mountain
Blue Bird Canyon Dr.
Agate
Pearl
S. Coast Hwy.
Nyes Place
Wesley

PACIFIC
OCEAN

■ FAMILY LODGING
1. Best Western Laguna Brisas
   Spa Hotel
2. Crystal Cove Beach Cottages
3. Surf and Sand Hotel
4. Montage Laguna Beach

◆ FAMILY-FRIENDLY RESTAURANTS
5. The Cottage
6. Ruby's
7. Taco Loco
8. Wahoo's Fish Tacos

0   0.5 mi
0   0.5 km

N

newport beach

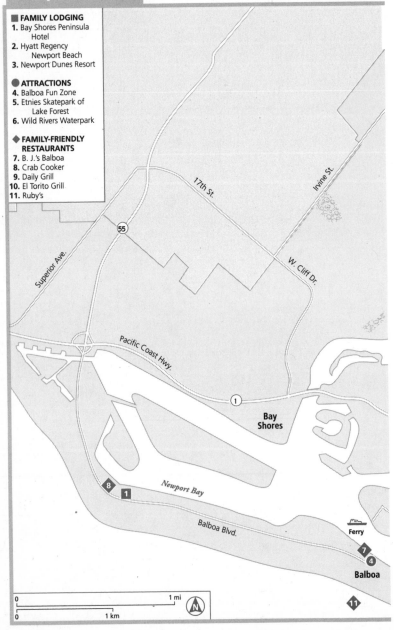

■ **FAMILY LODGING**
1. Bay Shores Peninsula Hotel
2. Hyatt Regency Newport Beach
3. Newport Dunes Resort

● **ATTRACTIONS**
4. Balboa Fun Zone
5. Etnies Skatepark of Lake Forest
6. Wild Rivers Waterpark

◆ **FAMILY-FRIENDLY RESTAURANTS**
7. B. J.'s Balboa
8. Crab Cooker
9. Daily Grill
10. El Torito Grill
11. Ruby's

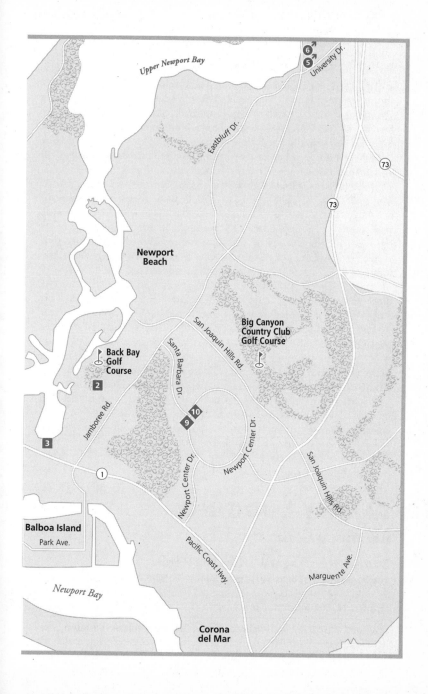

or the inclination to rent a house, one of the hotels or the campground at **Newport Dunes** will also make a fun family base. The theme parks of the North County are only about 20 minutes away.

MALL MANIA

A QUARTET OF DISTINCTIVE MALLS makes Orange County a shopper's destination. We prefer **Fashion Island** in Newport Beach (Newport Center Drive between Jamboree and MacArthur, Newport Beach; ☎ 949-721-2000; **www.shopfashionisland.com**), because it's open-air and visually appealing, with good restaurants (the **Hard Rock Cafe** is, of course, where kids want to go). See profiles for **Daily Grill** and **El Torito Grill** under "Family-friendly Restaurants."

In Costa Mesa, **South Coast Plaza** (3333 South Bristol Street, Costa Mesa; ☎ 800-782-8888 or 714-435-2000; **www.southcoastplaza.com**) is a huge, glitzy mall that sells everything imaginable. Younger kids will want to play in the **Disney Store** and the other toy stores; older ones can hit the dozens of fashion-oriented shops and department stores. A good on-site restaurant choice is the **Wolfgang Puck Cafe,** home to great salads, chic pizzas, and a children's menu.

Middle schoolers infatuated with skateboard culture will love **The Block at Orange** (City Drive off I-5 or the CA 22 freeway; ☎ 714-769-4000; **www.theblockatorange.com**), home not only of all the best surf and swimwear shops in Southern California, but also of **Vans Skate Park,** an indoor facility where skateboarders and inline skaters can pay by the hour to skate the two "swimming pools" and the many ramps and other structures. There's also a movie megaplex, and adults can cool their heels at some surprisingly good cafes.

Older teens will want to head down the street to the **Lab Anti-Mall** in Costa Mesa (2930 Bristol Street, Costa Mesa; ☎ 714-966-6660; **www.thelab.com**), a small, outdoor collection of teen and Gen-X/Y shops—**Urban Outfitters, CrewSalon, Great Laundry** (a Japan-based T-shirt store), **Eye Society**—that sort of thing. Nose rings and skateboards are the norm here.

FAMILY LODGING

LAGUNA BEACH

Best Western Laguna Brisas Spa Hotel
1600 South Coast Highway, Laguna Beach; ☎ 888-296-6834 or
949-497-8306; www.lagunabrisas.com; $140–$240;
kids age 12 and under stay free

YOU GET GOOD BANG for not too many bucks at this well-located hotel right across the street from a pretty beach (parents of toddlers note that it's a fairly steep walk down to the sand). It's impeccably maintained and has a nice pool on the ocean-view rooftop terrace, as well as a decent Continental breakfast, flat-screen LCD TVs, free wireless Internet, free parking and refrigerators and coffeemakers in the rooms. The downside is the noise from Coast Highway, so ask for a room on one of the upper floors. No restaurant, but you'll find plenty of good places to eat within walking distance.

 ## Crystal Cove Beach Cottages

Los Trancos at Pacific Coast Highway, Newport Coast; ☎ 800-444-7275; www.crystalcovebeachcottages.org; $121–$185 for 4 people; $22–$32 for each additional person

MODEST BOARD-AND-BATTEN COTTAGE RESORTS like this once dotted this coastline, but they eventually gave way to condominiums, resort hotels, and mansions—all but Crystal Cove, that is. This new state park just north of Laguna Beach recently refurbished 13 of its 46 1920s- and 1930s-era cottages and put them up for rental, and the demand has been overwhelming—you won't find a better oceanfront deal in California. The charming, whitewashed cottages sleep four to nine, with rudimentary kitchens, generous porches, and access to a fabulous state beach and the funky Beachcomber Cafe. They are reserved just like state campgrounds, through ReserveAmerica, which means you need to start speed-dialing at 7:55 a.m. on the first of the month seven months before the month you hope to visit; even then, your chances aren't great, especially for summer. But it's worth the effort. Over time the state hopes to renovate the remaining cottages and add them to the rental pool.

Montage Laguna Beach

30801 South Coast Highway, Laguna Beach, ☎ 866-271-6953 or 949-715-6000; www.montagelagunabeach.com; $695–$2,200; children under age 18 stay free

THIS LOW-SLUNG, CRAFTSMAN-STYLE RESORT HOTEL has usurped the Ritz-Carlton as the luxury Orange County beach hotel. It's a stunning property, both architecturally and geographically, with pathways along the landscaped bluffs above the green-blue coves below, which are easily accessed by paved trails. The 30-acre property has three pools, including one for kids and a lap pool for adults; restaurants; a posh spa; and all sizes of rooms and suites, all equipped with DVD players and wireless Internet access. The kids' program, called Paintbox, has full-day ($75) and half-day ($50) options, both of which include lunch and such hip activities as miniyoga and plein-air painting. Weekend evenings bring kids'-night-out events, and the hotel will organize great (if pricey) family adventures, ranging from surfing to belly dancing.

 ## Surf and Sand Hotel

1555 South Coast Highway, Laguna Beach; ☎ 888-869-7569 or 949-497-4477; www.surfandsandresort.com; $400–$650, suites $600–$1,400; kids under age 18 stay free

THIS SMALL-SCALE RESORT IS MOST NOTABLE for its exceptional location perched on the rim of the Pacific; from some rooms, you might feel as if you're shipboard. Although it is a quiet, subtly elegant place, it also manages to welcome families. Many rooms, from the least expensive ones with two queens to the oceanfront kings with pullout sofas, can handle a family of three or four; the large Catalina minisuites can easily handle four. Along with 500 feet of beautiful beach, there's a fancy spa, a pool, summertime children's activities, and Splashes, a good Mediterranean restaurant (with children's menu) facing the beach. Main Beach is a mile north, but there are plenty of cafes and shops nearby.

NEWPORT BEACH

Bay Shores Peninsula Hotel
1800 West Balboa Boulevard, Newport Beach; ☎ 800-222-6675 or 949-675-3463; www.thebestinn.com; $400 and up in summer, suites $480 and up; kids under age 12 stay free in parents' room

LOCATION IS KING, say real-estate agents, and this recently renovated motel has location in spades—it's one block to Newport Bay and, in the other direction, one block to the ocean-side beach. To make up for the lack of a pool, the motel supplies everything you need for the beach, including towels, bodyboards, chairs, toys, DVD players. The 25 surf-themed rooms are relatively small; four of you can fit in a room with two doubles, but just barely. But you don't come here to hang out in your room.

Hyatt Regency Newport Beach
1107 Jamboree Road, Newport Beach; ☎ 800-233-1234 or 949-729-1234; newportbeach.hyatt.com; $200 and up; half-price adjoining rooms sometimes available

THE NEARBY FOUR SEASONS may be a bit swanker, but for families, this is the best resort hotel in Newport. It's attractive and upscale but not too fussy; the 403 rooms and suites are spread over 26 acres, surrounded by lawns, flowers, trees, and all sorts of amusements—such as the three pools (one just for kids), or the tennis courts, Ping-Pong table, shuffleboard court, or nine-hole golf course. Or the bike-rental shop, which will steer you to the path connecting to the superb Upper Newport Bay Ecological Reserve (see "The Best Beaches and Parks," page 72). The amusements at Newport Dunes (detailed in the next entry) are just across the street, and shuttles will deliver your family to Balboa's Fun Zone and Fashion Island.

Newport Dunes Resort
1131 Back Bay Drive, Newport Beach; ☎ 949-729-3863; www.newportdunes.com; reservations, ☎ 800-765-7661; tent sites and RV sites $68–$130 in summer, higher on holidays

THIS PRIVATE CAMPGROUND is so much fun for families that it rates its own listing under "The Best Beaches and Parks." Along with all the amenities described there, it has RV and tent sites (freestanding tents only—no stakes allowed), windsurfing lessons, picnic facilities, barbecues, changing rooms, a restaurant, a market, and a boat launch. Reservations for the summer are taken from January 1 on, so call early for a prime time.

ATTRACTIONS

 Balboa Fun Zone

APPEAL BY AGE	PRESCHOOL ★★★	GRADE SCHOOL ★★★★	TEENS ★★★
YOUNG ADULTS ★★		OVER 30 ★★	SENIORS ★★

600 East Bay Avenue, Balboa; ☎ 949-673-0408; www.thebalboafunzone.com

Hours 11 a.m.–10 p.m. **Admission** Free; rides are $1.50–$3. **Touring time** Average 3 hours, with ferry ride; minimum 1 hour. **Rainy-day touring** No. **Restaurants** Yes. **Alcoholic beverages** Yes. **Disabled access** Yes. **Wheelchair rental** No. **Baby-stroller rental** No. **Lockers** In laser tag. **Pet kennels** No; leashed pets only. **Rain check** Yes. **Private tours** On the boats.

DESCRIPTION AND COMMENTS   On the waterfront near the Balboa Pier and Balboa Pavilion is a little amusement park full of old-fashioned small-town charm. There's a Ferris wheel, a merry-go-round, bumper cars, a moon bounce, arcade games, laser tag, and such art projects as spin paintings. One of our fondest childhood memories is getting a "Balboa bar," a precursor to the Häagen-Dazs bar, which is as popular as ever.

Almost as fun as the Fun Zone is a ride over to Balboa Island on the Balboa Island Ferry (☎ 949-673-1070; **www.balboaislandferry.com**), which leaves right near the Fun Zone. It's a short, picturesque, little-kid-size ride to the island; kids ages 5 to 11 ride for just 50¢, and adults ride for $1; cars with driver are $2, and passengers are extra. The island itself doesn't have much for kids, but if you bring bikes over on the ferry, it's great fun to pedal around the Lilliputian streets.

Etnies Skatepark of Lake Forest

APPEAL BY AGE	PRESCHOOL	GRADE SCHOOL ★★★★	TEENS ★★★★½
YOUNG ADULTS ★★		OVER 30 ★	SENIORS –

20028 Lake Forest Drive, Lake Forest; ☎ 949-916-5870; www.etniesskatepark.com

Hours Daily, 10 a.m.–10 p.m. **Admission** Free with signed waiver from parent; children age 8 and under must have a parent present. **Touring time** Average 3 hours; minimum 1 hour. **Rainy-day touring** No. **Restaurants** No. **Alcoholic beverages** No. **Disabled access** Yes. **Wheelchair rental** No. **Baby-stroller rental** No. **Lockers** No. **Pet kennels** No. **Rain check** No. **Private tours** Private parties allowed.

DESCRIPTION AND COMMENTS   In the kid-friendly south-OC suburbs is a public skate park that's worth a detour for skateboarding or BMX-bike-riding kids. It's an extensive and well-designed public park with everything a skater or rider could want: deep bowls, shallow bowls, stairs, ramps, rails, ledges . . . and it's all free. Lake Forest is easily reached off I-5 between Anaheim and San Clemente. Good summer-camp programs, too.

Wild Rivers Waterpark

APPEAL BY AGE	PRESCHOOL ★★★★½	GRADE SCHOOL ★★★★½	TEENS ★★★★½
YOUNG ADULTS ★★★★		OVER 30 ★★★★	SENIORS ★★★

8770 Irvine Center Drive, Irvine; ☎ 949-788-0808; www.wildrivers.com

Hours *Mid-June to early September:* open daily 10 a.m.–8 p.m.; limited hours from mid-May to the prime season and in the postseason through September. **Admission** $32, $20 for children 48" tall or shorter and $20 for adults, $15 for children after 4 p.m. in summer; parking, $10 **Touring time** Average 4 hours, 6 for school age and up; minimum 2 hours, 4 for school age and up. **Rainy-day touring** No. **Restaurants** Yes. **Alcoholic beverages** No. **Disabled access** Limited. **Wheelchair rental** No. **Baby-stroller rental** No. **Lockers** $6 plus $1 deposit small, $10 plus $1 deposit large. **Pet kennels** No. **Rain check** No. **Private tours** No.

DESCRIPTION AND COMMENTS   When Anaheim starts to swelter and the sand burns your feet at Balboa, consider a trip to this first-rate water park, which has something for every age group. At about a foot deep, Pygmy Pond keeps the little ones happy, with its small, not-scary waterslides, inner-tube rides, gorilla swing, and climbing structure that shoots out water. Older, braver kids will go for Surf Hills, which they can belly-slide down; the swimming pool with a water-basketball hoop; and the wave pools, which generate real waves. The bravest of all can tackle the vertical drops, rapids, and enclosed tunnel slides. All in all, there are more than 40 rides, along with two swimming pools. If you don't want to eat at the restaurants, you can use the picnic area outside the entrance.

FAMILY-FRIENDLY RESTAURANTS

LAGUNA BEACH

The Cottage
308 North Coast Highway, Laguna Beach; ☎ 949-494-3023; www.thecottagerestaurant.com

Meals served Breakfast, lunch, dinner, and Sunday brunch. **Cuisine** American. **Entree range** Breakfast and lunch, $6–$17; dinner, $12–$35. **Kids' menu** Yes. **Reservations** Accepted. **Payment** All major credit cards.

THERE'S ALWAYS A CROWD at this handsome old Arts and Crafts bungalow in north Laguna, thanks to the family-style conviviality and generous, simple food. Breakfast is the real draw (and the most crowded), not because the waffles and eggs are that memorable (they're fine), but because it's hard to find a solid breakfast in this upscale town.

Ruby's
30622 South Pacific Coast Highway, Laguna Beach; ☎ 949-497-7829; www.rubys.com

Meals served Breakfast, lunch, and dinner. **Cuisine** American. **Entree range** Breakfast, $7–$12; lunch and dinner, $8–$12. **Kids' menu** Yes. **Reservations** Not accepted. **Payment** All major credit cards.

SOUTH OF THE TOWN CENTER—which means parking is free and plentiful—this is the hottest kid restaurant in Laguna. The gleaming 1940s and 1950s cars in the parking lot set the stage for the neo-sock-hop theme: oldies music, big vinyl booths, uniformed waitresses, old Coke ads, model trains, and shameless catering to children, who find the food to be way more delicious than their parents do.

Taco Loco
640 South Coast Highway, Laguna Beach; ☎ 949-497-1635

Meals served Lunch and dinner. **Cuisine** Mexican. **Entree range** $5–$20. **Kids' menu** No. **Reservations** Not accepted. **Payment** All major credit cards.

IF YOUR TEEN WANTS to hang with the coolest surfers, come to this sidewalk cafe, where you'll find the best Mexican street food in town, along with hip Southwestern and Californian dishes; you can have a calamari quesadilla while your kids try a carne asada burrito. The food is so good that regular customer Jimmy Buffett hired the owner to cater his road tours.

Wahoo's Fish Tacos
1133 South Coast Highway, Laguna Beach; ☎ 949-497-0033; www.wahoos.com

Meals served Lunch and dinner. **Cuisine** Mexican. **Entree range** $4–$10. **Kids' menu** Yes. **Reservations** Not accepted. **Payment** MC, V.

EVERYBODY LOVES WAHOO'S: little kids, who get their own menu; big kids, who love both the food and the grunge surfer decor; parents, who can have fresh-fish (not fried) tacos or burritos and a cold Corona while the kids have quesadillas and fries; and Laguna's surfers, who would surely starve if not for Wahoo's tasty, cheap Mexican food with a Hawaiian accent (the "da plate" lunch specials are good). This is an order-at-the-counter, throw-a-T-shirt-over-your-bathing-suit kind of place, in a prime spot between Main Beach and the Surf and Sand Hotel.

NEWPORT BEACH

B.J.'s Balboa
106 Main Street, Balboa Peninsula; ☎ 949-675-7560

Meals served Lunch and dinner. **Cuisine** Italian. **Entree range** Lunch and dinner, $10–$25. **Kids' menu** Yes. **Reservations** Not accepted. **Payment** All major credit cards.

TASTY, THICK-CRUST PIZZA is the draw here, as is the great location a half block from Balboa Pier. Other pluses are a pretty good salad bar, kid-sized pizzas and pastas, and boisterous camaraderie. Expect a wait, especially on summer weekends.

The Crab Cooker

2200 Newport Boulevard, Newport Beach; ☎ 949-673-0100; www.crabcooker.com

Meals served Lunch and dinner. **Cuisine** Seafood. **Entree range** $8–$30. **Kids' menu** No, but there is a "Light Eaters" plate. **Reservations** Not accepted. **Payment** AE, D, V.

A CLASSIC BEACH DIVE, The Crab Cooker is beloved of locals and tourists alike. The plates are paper, the prices are mostly rock bottom, and the food (mesquite-grilled fresh fish, clam chowder, crab legs, sourdough bread) is mighty fine. Expect to wait in line.

Daily Grill
Fashion Island, 957 Newport Center Drive, Newport Beach; ☎ 949-644-2223; www.dailygrill.com

Meals served Lunch, dinner, and Sunday brunch. **Cuisine** American. **Entree range** Lunch, $10–$22; dinner, $13–$30; Sunday brunch, $19 adults, $9 kids. **Kids' menu** Yes. **Reservations** Yes. **Payment** All major credit cards.

SUCCESS CAME QUICKLY to this small California chain of updated bar and grill restaurants, thanks in part to its recognition that baby boomers like to take their kids out to eat. Little kids get their own menu, big kids can get a chicken potpie or turkey meat loaf, and parents can get an adult beverage and wonderful crab cakes. Avoid the pastas.

El Torito Grill
Fashion Island, 951 Newport Center Drive, Newport Beach; ☎ 949-640-2875; www.etgrill.com

Meals served Daily, lunch and dinner; Sunday, buffet brunch. **Cuisine** Southwestern. **Entree range** Lunch, $8–$14; dinner, $10–$17; Sunday brunch, $17 adults, $8 kids. **Kids' menu** Yes. **Reservations** Not necessary. **Payment** All major credit cards.

MORE SOUTHWESTERN than Mexican, this offshoot of the El Torito chain of Mexican restaurants is a bit more upscale than its parent, but it's still family oriented. Colorful, noisy, and friendly, it's a good spot for nachos, fajitas, red-corn taquitos, great carnitas, and spicy chicken dishes. Parents get hand-shaken margaritas, and the kids get coloring supplies and their own burritos and tacos, as well as such standards as chicken fingers; children's meals even come with fresh fruit.

Ruby's

☎1 Balboa Pier, Newport Beach; ☎ 949-675-7829; www.rubys.com

Meals served Breakfast, lunch, and dinner. **Cuisine** American. **Entree range** Breakfast, $7–$12; lunch and dinner, $8–$12. **Kids' menu** Yes. **Reservations** Not accepted. **Payment** All major credit cards.

THE ORIGINAL OF THE 1940S-DINER CHAIN (also see profiles under Laguna and San Juan), this Ruby's is also the best located, smack on the end of the Balboa Pier. Get a table outside, soak in the view, drink a chocolate shake, and have a good time.

HUNTINGTON BEACH

MILES FROM THE FREEWAYS, Huntington Beach, the original Surf City and the archetypal beach town, is as lively as it gets because the pier and the commercial section of town are contiguous. This means beachgoers can roll up their towels and head across the street to get a frozen yogurt or shop for surf wear. It also means an ongoing sense of festivity, enhanced by the city's near-constant schedule of concerts and art fairs during the summer. Do you have kids who never want to come out of the water? You don't have to hassle them here. Huntington Beach is one of the few places where you can still build a fire on the beach (it's open until 10 p.m.), so grab a fire ring early in the day and bring hot dogs, marshmallows, guitars, and blankets for an unforgettable summer evening. To learn more about the beach, see **Bolsa Chica** and **Huntington State Beaches** under "The Best Beaches and Parks."

FAMILY LODGING

Hilton Waterfront Beach Resort
21100 Pacific Coast Highway, Huntington Beach; ☎ 800-822-SURF or
714-960-7873; www.hilton.com; $300–$400 summer,
$200–$269 winter; kids under 18 stay free

ITS HIGH-RISE DESIGN doesn't suit low-key Huntington Beach, but otherwise this 248-room hotel is a convenient resort, across the highway from the beach, with pedestrian and bike access to the bike trails and sand. The rooms are attractive and comfortable, the views can be great, and between the beach and the pool, kids have plenty to do. Family amenities include children's activities, babysitting services, bike rentals, a pool, and tennis courts.

ATTRACTIONS

 International Surfing Museum

APPEAL BY AGE	PRESCHOOL ★	GRADE SCHOOL ★★	TEENS ★★★
YOUNG ADULTS ★★★	OVER 30 ★★★		SENIORS ★★★

**411 Olive Street, Huntington Beach; ☎ 714-960-3483;
www.surfingmuseum.org**

Hours Monday–Friday, noon–5 p.m.; Saturday and Sunday, noon–6 p.m.
Admission $2 adults, $1 students and seniors, children age 6 and under free.
Touring time Average 1 hour; minimum 30 minutes. **Rainy-day touring** Yes.
Restaurants Nearby. **Alcoholic beverages** No. **Disabled access** Yes. **Wheelchair
rental** No. **Baby-stroller rental** No. **Lockers** No. **Pet kennels** No. **Rain check**
No. **Private tours** No.

DESCRIPTION AND COMMENTS   At this friendly little museum, the history of
surfing is told via old photographs, text, surf music, trophies, old surfboards, even Dick Dale's guitar. After your visit, walk down the block to
see the Surfer's Walk of Fame. Note that the star ratings apply only if
you're interested in surfing; otherwise the museum's a snooze.

FAMILY-FRIENDLY
RESTAURANTS

Alice's Breakfast in the Park
**6622 Lakeview Drive, Huntington Beach; ☎ 714-848-0690;
www.breakfastinthepark.com**

Meals served Breakfast and lunch. **Cuisine** American. **Entree range** $6–$9. **Kids'
menu** Yes. **Reservations** Recommended on weekends. **Payment** No credit cards.

BREAKFAST IS OFTEN a kid's favorite meal to eat out, especially a breakfast
like this: huge cinnamon rolls, scrambled eggs, pancakes, and other such
treats, served on a patio next to the lake in Huntington Central Park, so
kids can run around and feed the ducks between bites. After breakfast (or
lunch), spend a couple of hours exploring the lovely park and the excellent
library.

Savannah at the Beach
**315 Pacific Coast Highway, Huntington Beach; ☎ 714-374-7273;
www.culinaryadventures.com**

Meals served Lunch, dinner, and Sunday brunch. **Cuisine** Cal-Mex seafood.
Entree range $16–$45. **Kids' menu** No. **Reservations** Good idea for brunch.
Payment All major credit cards.

THIS HANDSOME EATERY is beautifully situated at the foot of the pier on
the sand. Because it's often hard to enjoy a family meal at one of the more
casual (and less expensive) restaurants across the street (which are typically
crowded and difficult to manage with little kids), Savannah can be a peaceful alternative. The casual tropical decor welcomes families in shorts and
T-shirts; lunch is served until 4 p.m. Try a chicken taquito appetizer for a
child; other options range from wild mushroom pizzas to fresh fish entrees.

huntington beach

■ **FAMILY LODGING**
1. Hilton Waterfront
   Beach Resort

● **ATTRACTION**
2. International Surfing
   Museum

◆ **FAMILY-FRIENDLY
RESTAURANTS**
3. Alice's Breakfast
   in the Park
4. Savannah at the Beach

39

Main St.

**HUNTINGTON
CENTRAL PARK**

Slater Ave.

Golden West

Central Park Dr.

3

*Huntington
Lake*

Garfield Ave.

**Sea Cliff
Country Club**

Edwards St.

Talbert Ave.

Springdale

**BOLSA CHICA
WETLANDS**

1

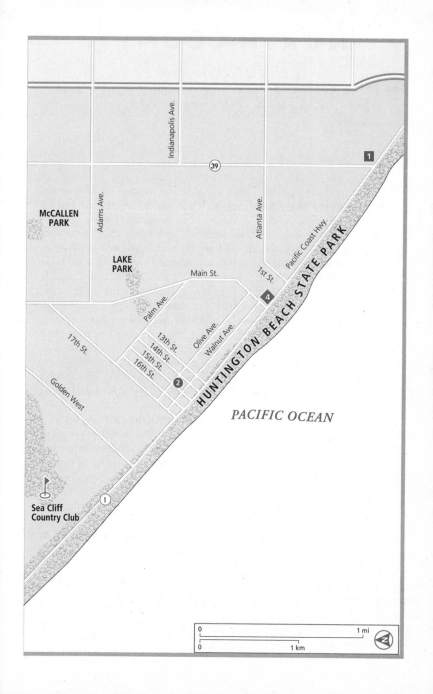

NORTH COUNTY:
Anaheim, Buena Park, and Santa Ana

THE INLAND AREA OF NORTHERN ORANGE COUNTY would not be on any tourist's list if not for the ever-expanding **Disneyland Resort–Knott's Berry Farm** nexus. It's a sprawl of several former agricultural town centers, now linked by residential areas that are generally more working class than the expensive neighborhoods by the sea. It's an ethnically diverse region: **Santa Ana** is home to many Latino immigrants, and **Westminster** is known for its large Vietnamese community. But northern Orange County is not exactly famed for its natural beauty—Anaheim is notable for its 150-plus hotels, most of which are cardboard-box motels (although some now qualify as vintage examples of 1950s and 1960s kitsch architecture), and **Buena Park** is flat and featureless, an easy place to get lost in under the glaringly reflected summer sun. But if you have kids, you'll be forced to visit the North County, because that's where you'll find Disneyland Resort and Knott's Berry Farm, along with such lesser amusements as **Adventure City** and the **Medieval Times** theme restaurant.

By all means, plan an overnight stay in Anaheim; Disneyland is best enjoyed over a two-day period, with a cool, quiet hotel room to which the family can retreat. Note that in season, Angels baseball games at **Angel Stadium of Anaheim Stadium** and Ducks hockey games at **Honda Center** are nearby, and that the water park at Knott's, **Soak City,** offers the contrast of a day of water play.

If you have very young children, under age 5, they will enjoy the woodsy atmosphere and gentle rides of **Camp Snoopy** at Knott's or the birthday-party-park feel of **Adventure City** more than a bewildering day in the crowds swirling through the hugeness of Disneyland.

Just know that the beach is a half-hour drive or more, and the fun here is man-made. After a couple of days doing the theme-park thing in the North County, head to the beach communities to experience another side of the OC.

unofficial **TIP**
Don't try to fit Universal Studios, Disneyland, and Knott's into a sequential three-day period. Theme parks need the space of some nature days in between, or it will all be a blur to your kids.

FAMILY LODGING

Candy Cane Inn
**1747 South Harbor Boulevard, Anaheim; ☎ 800-345-7057 or
714-774-5284; www.candycaneinn.net;
$99–$139 standard, $109–$189 deluxe**

A GOOD BARGAIN well placed near Disneyland's parking lot, this motel is
freshly spruced up and now has such luxurious touches as down comforters
and plantation shutters. It's worth the modest splurge for a deluxe room,
which comes with a fridge and coffeemaker. One of the deluxe rooms can
sleep five if you pay an extra $10 for a rollaway. Rates include a Continen-
tal breakfast and shuttles to Disneyland. Outside are a heated pool, a spa,
and a wading pool for little ones. Ask about packages including Disneyland
tickets. Free parking.

Disneyland Hotel
**1150 Magic Way, Anaheim; ☎ 714-778-6600 or 714-956-6425;
disneyland.disney.go.com; $260–$320 (changes every season)**

A GIGANTIC ANNEX to the park, located just past the Downtown Disney
monorail station, offering clean, comfortable, reasonably updated rooms
in which to sleep off too many long lines. Younger children will enjoy a
stay here as much as a trip across the street, thanks to the several pools,
the little faux-sand beach complete with pedal boats, the fish ponds, the
gift shops, and Goofy's Kitchen (see page 116). Children under age 17 stay
free in parents' rooms; ask about hotel-park packages. And remember that
most days, guests here are allowed into Disneyland an hour before the
ordinary folk, which alone is worth a stay in busy times.

Disney's Paradise Pier Hotel
**1717 South Disneyland Drive, Anaheim; ☎ 714-999-0990 or
714-956-6425; disneyland.disney.go.com; $245–$360
(changes every season)**

LIKE THE DISNEYLAND HOTEL, this is officially part of the park. We prefer
it to its sibling, because it's less than half the size and is therefore quieter
and less overwhelming, with more attractive rooms. The food is better,
too. There aren't as many amusements, but you can make do with the pool,
workout room, video games, several restaurants and lounges, and shops, as
well as direct access to Disneyland.

Disney's Grand Californian Hotel
**1600 South Disneyland Drive, Anaheim; ☎ 714-635-2300 or
714-956-6425; disneyland.disney.go.com; $230–$685**

THIS LUXURY RESORT has supplanted the Disneyland Hotel as Disneyland's
prestigious lodging property. Even Disney haters have had to concede that
it's a mighty handsome place. Designed in the Craftsman style of a rustic

north county: anaheim, buena park, and santa ana

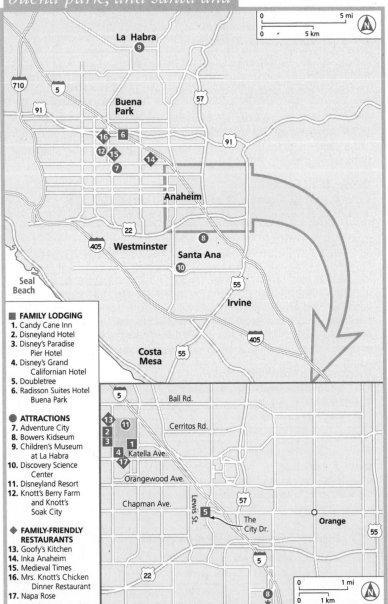

■ FAMILY LODGING
1. Candy Cane Inn
2. Disneyland Hotel
3. Disney's Paradise
   Pier Hotel
4. Disney's Grand
   Californian Hotel
5. Doubletree
6. Radisson Suites Hotel
   Buena Park

● ATTRACTIONS
7. Adventure City
8. Bowers Kidseum
9. Children's Museum
   at La Habra
10. Discovery Science
    Center
11. Disneyland Resort
12. Knott's Berry Farm
    and Knott's
    Soak City

**◆ FAMILY-FRIENDLY
   RESTAURANTS**
13. Goofy's Kitchen
14. Inka Anaheim
15. Medieval Times
16. Mrs. Knott's Chicken
    Dinner Restaurant
17. Napa Rose

national-park lodge (think of Yosemite's Ahwahnee), it has 750 spacious rooms—some with an extra daybed for kids—and offers three swimming pools (one with a tree slide and one shaped like Mickey Mouse), a high-end health club, and upscale (but family-friendly) restaurants. If you long for dinner without the kids, they'll be happy at Pinocchio's Workshop, an evening child-care center in the hotel. Hotel guests have their own entrance to California Adventure, and Disneyland is right across the way.

Doubletree
100 The City Drive, Orange; ☎ 800-222-8733 or 714-634-4500; www.doubletreehotels.com; $200–$500 (breakfast extra); kids under age 18 stay free in parents' room

THIS UPPER-MIDLEVEL HOTEL gives Disney-bound families a lot of bang for the buck. Aside from the nice but basic pool, there's a cool outdoor lagoon that's the size of several pools; other extras include two tennis courts, a fitness center, Nintendo in every room, free shuttles to Disneyland and local malls, in-room coffeemakers, and packages that include Disneyland tickets. The 454 rooms (and 11 suites) are well equipped and reasonably large. The Block mall is a short walk away.

Radisson Suites Hotel Buena Park
7762 Beach Boulevard, Buena Park; ☎ 888-201-1718 or 714-739-5600; www.radisson.com; $149 and up; check for specials

ONE OF THE BEST THEME-PARK experiences we ever had was a day at Knott's with two nights at this place, when it was an Embassy Suites. This 202-suite facility is a four-story building surrounding a landscaped courtyard with pool and spa, and it's within walking distance of Knott's. (The Disney parks are a shuttle ride away.) We checked in the night before, enjoyed the generous buffet breakfast in the dining room (included in room rate), left the car in the (free) lot, and headed to Knott's. When we'd had our fill of the park, we got a take-out chicken dinner from Mrs. Knott's (far better than dining in, really), called the hotel shuttle, and returned to the hotel. We ate dinner in our dining area in the suite, then headed down (with bunches of other families) for a night swim and whirlpool soak. All rooms have free wireless Internet, two flat-screen TVs, microwaves, fridges, and sleeper sofas.

▌ ATTRACTIONS

Adventure City

APPEAL BY AGE	PRESCHOOL ★★★★	GRADE SCHOOL ★★★	TEENS ½
YOUNG ADULTS ★		OVER 30 ★	SENIORS ½

1238 South Beach Boulevard, Anaheim; ☎ 714-236-9300; www.adventurecity.com

Hours *Off-season:* Friday, 10 a.m.–5 p.m.; Saturday, 11 a.m.–8 p.m.; Sunday 11 a.m.–7 p.m.; *Summer:* Monday–Thursday, 10 a.m.–5 p.m.; Friday, 10 a.m.–7 p.m.;

Saturday, 11 a.m.–9 p.m.; Sunday, 11 a.m.–8 p.m. **Admission** $14, $10 for seniors, free for children age 1 and under; includes face painting, puppet shows, and theater. **Touring time** Average 3 hours; minimum 2 hours. **Rainy-day touring** Not great. **Restaurants** Basic. **Alcoholic beverages** No. **Disabled access** Yes. **Wheelchair rental** No. **Baby-stroller rental** No. **Lockers** Yes. **Pet kennels** No. **Rain check** No. **Private tours** Yes.

DESCRIPTION AND COMMENTS   All it takes is that first visit to Disneyland with a 3-year-old to understand that the Magic Kingdom is really for older kids—it can be overwhelming and very scary, overrun with huge, mute cartoon characters and dark, fast rides. Enter this compact kiddie land in Stanton (next door to Anaheim), adjacent to Hobby City, a retail center for collectors and hobbyists. It's designed with the 3-year-old in mind, and while it's a dreadful bore for teens, it's heaven for little ones.

The roller coaster is small and not too intense, and the mini–Ferris wheel is so tame it's called the Giggle Wheel. In the Rescue Ride, youngsters get to dress up in firefighter and police gear, climb in a kid-scale fire truck, and listen to dispatcher calls. Trains are a big deal here, from the 1938 open-air choo-choo ride that circles the park to the Thomas the Tank Engine play island. When it's time to sit down, head for a puppet show or one of the entertaining (to young ones) stage shows. Needless to say, this place is extremely popular for birthday parties. Be warned that there's an arcade, in the Chuck E. Cheese vein, so steer game-ticket-obsessed kids clear.

Bowers Kidseum

APPEAL BY AGE	PRESCHOOL ★★★	GRADE SCHOOL ★★★★	TEENS ★★
YOUNG ADULTS ★★	OVER 30 ★★		SENIORS ★★

1802 North Main Street, Santa Ana; ☎ 714-480-1520; www.bowers.org/visit/kidseum.jsp

Hours Tuesday–Friday, 10 a.m.–3 p.m.; Saturday and Sunday, 11 a.m.–4 p.m.; hours may be expanded in summer. **Admission** $6 for everyone age 3 and older, free for age 2 and under. **Touring time** Average 2½ hours; minimum 1 hour. **Rainy-day touring** Yes. **Restaurants** Yes. **Alcoholic beverages** No; only at Tangata cafe. **Disabled access** Yes. **Wheelchair rental** Yes, free. **Baby-stroller rental** No. **Lockers** Items can be checked. **Pet kennels** No. **Rain check** No. **Private tours** By appointment.

DESCRIPTION AND COMMENTS   A companion to the Bowers Museum of Cultural Art down the street, this modest interactive museum brings to life the culture and art of Asia, Africa, and the Native Americans for elementary-age kids. They can try on masks, go into the Time Vault (an old bank vault), put on puppet shows in the theater, play strange musical instruments, and pretend to grind corn with an old stone mortar and pestle. Some of its best offerings are special events—storytelling, art classes, craft workshops—so call for a schedule before you plan a visit. Locals note the regular classes for preschoolers and lower-elementary kids.

The admission fee also includes the nearby museum, so if your older kids are ready for more, browse through and look at its beadwork, carvings, sculptures, and costumes from around the world.

Children's Museum at La Habra

APPEAL BY AGE	PRESCHOOL ★★★★	GRADE SCHOOL ★★★★	TEENS ★★
YOUNG ADULTS ★		OVER 30 ★	SENIORS ½

301 South Euclid Street, La Habra; ☎ 562-905-9793; www.lhcm.org

Hours Tuesday–Friday, 10 a.m.–4 p.m.; Saturday, 10 a.m.–5 p.m.; Sunday, 1–5 p.m. **Admission** $6 for age 2 and older. **Touring time** Average 2½ hours; minimum 1 hour. **Rainy-day touring** Yes. **Restaurants** Picnic area and restaurants nearby. **Alcoholic beverages** No. **Disabled access** Yes (except for but 1 room). **Wheelchair rental** No. **Baby-stroller rental** No. **Lockers** Cubbyholes. **Pet kennels** No **Rain check** No. **Private tours** No.

DESCRIPTION AND COMMENTS   On more than one occasion, we've loaded the kids in the car and headed to La Habra, bypassing the other children's museums closer to home. It occupies an old Union Pacific depot in a quiet neighborhood, and it's full of wonderful hands-on activities. Our kids' favorite is the theater area, complete with costumes, a stage, and a lighting booth for impromptu performances. They also love the front half of a city bus, to drive, ride, and scramble in; the full-size train caboose; the kid-scale supermarket; the Dentzel carousel; and the science experiments. There's always a new interactive temporary exhibit, and there's a separate play area for those under age 5.

Discovery Science Center

APPEAL BY AGE	PRESCHOOL ★★	GRADE SCHOOL ★★★★	TEENS ★★★★
YOUNG ADULTS ★★★		OVER 30 ★★★	SENIORS ★★★

2500 North Main Street, Santa Ana; ☎ 714-542-2823; www.discoverycube.org

Hours Daily, 10 a.m.–5 p.m.; store, daily, 11 a.m.–5 p.m.; **Admission** $13 adults, $10 seniors age 55 and over and children ages 3–17; additional $3 for admission to 4-D Movie Theater (3-D films plus fog, wind, and other physical effects); parking $3; adult supervision required for children under age 13. **Touring time** Average 3 hours; minimum 1 hour. **Rainy-day touring** Yes. **Restaurants** Yes. **Alcoholic beverages** No. **Disabled access** Yes. **Wheelchair rental** No. **Baby-stroller rental** No. **Lockers** Yes. **Pet kennels** No. **Rain check** No. **Private tours** No.

DESCRIPTION AND COMMENTS   This newish, interactive science museum is packed with 100 of the latest and greatest in cool, hands-on, science-based exhibits and experiences. What better way than to lie on a bed of nails to learn that the larger the area over which a force is distributed, the less pressure is exerted on any one point? Kids can hoist themselves with pulleys, redirect an eight-foot-tall tornado by walking through it, experience an earthquake in the Shake Shack, learn about waves by touching the spinning Lariat Chain, work as "research assistants" in the very cool new Dino Quest area, and make their hair stand on end by putting one hand on the Van de Graaff generator. Special exhibits have included such things as Par for the Planet, an 18-hole miniature golf game in which kids learn about the natural world, from butterfly metamorphosis to water pollution. And unlike at many science museums, the preschool set gets its own area, complete with age-appropriate science, art, and dress-up activities.

Food service is limited, alas, to a Pizza Hut Express and a Taco Bell Express, and there isn't an outdoor picnic area. But that's a small quibble, given that this place is such a wonderful addition to Orange County.

 ## Disneyland Resort

| APPEAL BY AGE | PRESCHOOL ★★★ | GRADE SCHOOL ★★★★½ | TEENS ★★★★½ |
| YOUNG ADULTS ★★★★½ | | OVER 30 ★★★★ | SENIORS ★★★ |

Disneyland Park, Disney's California Adventure Park, Downtown Disney, 1313 South Harbor Boulevard, Anaheim; ☎ 714-781-4565; disneyland.disney.go.com

Hours *Year-round:* daily, 10 a.m.–6 p.m.; hours extended as early as 8 a.m. and as late as 1 a.m. during busy seasons; hours vary seasonally. **Admission** *One-day pass:* $69 age 10 and over, $67 seniors (age 60 and over), $59 children ages 3–9, free children age 3 and younger. **Touring time** *Disneyland Park:* average 16 hours–2 days; minimum 7 hours. *Disney's California Adventure:* average 8 hours–1 day; minimum 5 hours. **Rainy-day touring** Yes—a mildly rainy day can be great at the parks, because the crowds disappear and many rides are indoors. **Restaurants** Yes. **Alcoholic beverages** At Disney's California Adventure and in Downtown Disney restaurants only. **Disabled access** Yes. **Wheelchair rental** $10; electric carts $35; $20 deposit (not offered at Downtown Disney). **Baby-stroller rental** $10 (not offered at Downtown Disney). **Lockers** $7–$15. **Pet kennels** $20; no overnight. **Rain check** No. **Private tours** Yes.

DESCRIPTION AND COMMENTS   In February 2002, the Walt Disney Company unveiled its second theme park, Disney's California Adventure, on the Disneyland property. The opening capped an ambitious expansion of Disneyland that also included new hotels and Downtown Disney, a dining, shopping, and entertainment complex. The entrances of Disneyland Park and Disney's California Adventure face each other across a palm-studded pedestrian plaza called the Esplanade. The Esplanade begins at Harbor Boulevard and runs west, passing into Downtown Disney, which you can visit without paying admission. From Downtown Disney the pedestrian thoroughfare continues to the new monorail station and to the Disneyland and Paradise Pier hotels.

Disney's California Adventure, known as DCA among Disneyphiles, is built on 55 acres (including a sizable carve-out for the Grand Californian Hotel), quite small by modern theme-park standards. The theme, celebrating all things (OK, OK, most things) Californian, is infinitely flexible, allowing Disney to offer diverse attractions that would not go well together under any other umbrella. Unfortunately, there's precious little new technology at work in Disney's newest theme park. Of the headliner attractions, only one, Soarin' Over California (a simulator ride), breaks new ground. All the rest are recycled, albeit popular, attractions from Disney's Animal Kingdom and Disney's Hollywood Studios in Florida. When you move to the smaller-statured second half of the attraction batting order, it gets worse. Most of these attractions are little more than off-the-shelf midway rides spruced up with a Disney story line and facade.

Seen from overhead, Disney's California Adventure is arrayed in roughly a fan shape around the park's visual icon, Grizzly Peak (yet another of Disney's "mountains"). At ground level, however, the park's layout is not so obvious. From the Esplanade you pass through huge block letters spelling "California" and under a whimsical representation of the Golden Gate Bridge, over which the monorail passes. To your left and right you'll find Guest Services as well as some shops and eateries.

Comparable to Main Street at Disneyland Park, but not as long, the entranceway leads to a central hub where pedestrian thoroughfares branch like spokes to the various theme areas. "Lands" at DCA are called "districts," and there are three of them. A left turn at the hub leads you to the Hollywood Pictures Backlot district of the park, celebrating California's history as the film capital of the world. All other paths lead to the Golden State district of the park. Golden State is a somewhat-amorphous combination of separate theme areas that showcase California's architecture, agriculture, industry, history, and natural resources. Within the Golden State district you'll find Condor Flats by taking the first right before the hub. Grizzly Peak will likewise be to your right, though you must walk two-thirds of the way around the mountain to reach its attractions. The entrances to A Bug's Land and Bountiful Valley Farm branch off the central hub at about two o'clock, as does Golden Vine Winery. The remaining two Golden State theme areas, The Bay Area and Pacific Wharf, are situated along a kidney-shaped lake and can be accessed by following the walkway emanating from the hub at seven o'clock and winding around Grizzly Peak. The third district, Paradise Pier, recalls seaside amusement parks of the first half of the 20th century. It is in the southwest corner of the park, across the lake from The Bay Area.

From a competitive perspective, Disney's California Adventure is an underwhelming shot at Disney's three Southern California competitors. The Hollywood section of DCA takes a hopeful poke at Universal Studios Hollywood, while Paradise Pier offers midway rides à la Six Flags Magic Mountain. Finally, the whole California theme has for years been the eminent domain of Knott's Berry Farm. In short, there's not much originality in DCA, only Disney's now-redundant mantra that "whatever they can do, we can do better."

We can't possibly do Disneyland and its two theme parks justice in this space; for the complete and inside scoop, pick up our sister book,

disneyland park

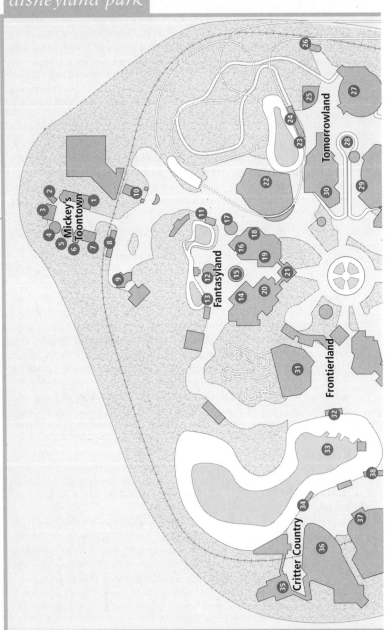

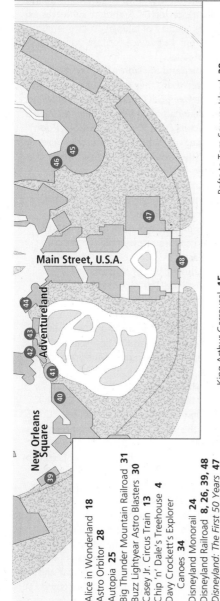

Main Street, U.S.A.

Adventureland

New Orleans Square

Rafts to Tom Sawyer Island **38**
Riverboat and Sailing Ship **32**
Roger Rabbit's Car Toon Spin **1**
Sleeping Beauty Castle **21**
Snow White's Scary Adventures **20**
Space Mountain **45**
Splash Mountain **36**
Star Tours **29**
Storybook Land Canal Boats **11**
Tarzan's Treehouse **41**
Tom Sawyer Island **33**

King Arthur Carrousel **15**
Mad Tea Party **17**
The Many Adventures of
   Winnie the Pooh **35**
Matterhorn Bobsleds **22**
Mickey's House **3**
Minnie's House **2**
Miss Daisy, Donald's Boat **6**
Mr. Toad's Wild Ride **16**
Peter Pan's Flight **19**
Pinocchio's Daring
   Journey **14**
Pirates of the
   Caribbean **40**

Alice in Wonderland **18**
Astro Orbitor **28**
Autopia **25**
Big Thunder Mountain Railroad **31**
Buzz Lightyear Astro Blasters **30**
Casey Jr. Circus Train **13**
Chip 'n' Dale's Treehouse **4**
Davy Crockett's Explorer
   Canoes **34**
Disneyland Monorail **24**
Disneyland Railroad **8, 26, 39, 48**
Disneyland: The First 50 Years **47**
Dumbo the Flying Elephant **12**
Enchanted Tiki Room **44**
Fantasyland Theatre **9**
Finding Nemo Submarine
   Voyage **23**
Gadget's Go Coaster **5**
Goofy's Playhouse **7**
Haunted Mansion **37**
Honey, I Shrunk the Audience **46**
Indiana Jones Adventure **42**
Innoventions **27**
It's a Small World **10**
Jungle Cruise **43**

The Unofficial Guide to Disneyland. If you have children and you're breathing, you know the basics of what Disneyland Park has to offer—from the atmospheric charms of Pirates of the Caribbean to the thrills of Splash Mountain, and the foregoing discussion of DCA should suffice as an overview of the new park. Therefore, instead of taking you through both parks in detail, we'll give you some tips and advice for how to best plan for the parks with each age group of kids.

1. **Four-year-olds want to go to Disneyland Park** only because their parents or their preschool friends tell them they want to go. In its research, *The Unofficial Guide to Disneyland* found that more than half of all kids that age are afraid of the characters (that is, Mickey, Goofy, Pooh) that roam the park, which often catches parents by surprise. (But wouldn't you be alarmed if a mute, stuffed [but clearly alive] creature four times your size loomed near?) If your dream dictates that you take your little one to Disneyland Park, that's fine, but realize that the park is really designed for kids age 7 and older.

   > *unofficial* **TIP**
   > Much of Disneyland Park is overwhelming, exhausting, and scary for kids under age 6.

   Disney's California Adventure is aimed at an even more mature audience. Although it offers several children's play areas, it has comparatively little to offer 4-and-unders.

2. **Consider a stay at a Disney hotel during busier seasons**—or at a non-Disney hotel within walking distance. The monorail access back and forth (to Disneyland Park only) is also a fun and convenient way to break up the day. Kids object less strenuously to leaving for a few hours in the heat of the afternoon if it's to ride the monorail to take a swim (and of course a nap). The restaurants in the hotels and at Downtown Disney are less crowded than the food service areas in the parks during peak times, too.

3. **Nearly 15 million people a year visit Disneyland,** and on some days it seems as if every one of them is waiting in your line. We locals know that the best time to visit is in the first three weeks of December. (Conversely, the parks' busiest season is the week between Christmas and New Year's.) The next-best times to visit are from September to mid-November, January 4 through early March, and the week after Easter to Memorial Day (although we remember a particularly nasty crowd one early May weekday). Thursdays are the quietest day, and days that start with a drizzle (not pouring rain) are ideal. Visiting the Disneyland parks on a July weekend is a nightmare. Trust us. Don't do it.

4. **Not all lines are created equal.** Disneyland Park's oldest rides were built in the 1950s, before it was known how huge the crowds of visitors would be, so they aren't set up to move large numbers of people quickly. Although these Fantasyland rides are no longer popular with the teen set, families (especially local parents who remember going on these rides as kids) often line up for Snow White or Peter Pan—and it can take forever to get in. Keep an eye out for when these lines are shortest. The rides built in the late 1960s—Small World, Pirates of the

Caribbean, the Haunted Mansion—have outdoor plaza areas built to accommodate lines that move more quickly. The newest rides—Indiana Jones, Splash Mountain, Tomorrowland rides—were built knowing that much of the ride time is spent in line, so the waiting areas are part of the ride structure itself (you won't see them from the entrance area), decorated and sometimes offering a bit of entertainment.

At Disney's California Adventure, ride capacity and efficiency were sacrificed for eye appeal. Taking a step backward, Disney loaded the park with midway rides, infamous for slow loading and long waits. Of 11 rides, only 2 move crowds efficiently. Fortunately, most of the shows and theater attractions can accommodate large numbers.

5. Here are our recommended sample days, by age group:

Under 6 To do Disneyland right with young children, think small and plan carefully. To avoid meltdowns, visit the park of your choice for a half day and then return to your hotel for a swim and a nap, returning in the afternoon refreshed. Don't wander around the parks aimlessly, but head straight to the attractions best suited to young kids. At Disneyland Park with 6-and-unders, we go right to Fantasyland and do Dumbo, Peter Pan, Pinocchio, Alice in Wonderland (usually twice, because there's no line), and, depending on their scary-tolerance, Mr. Toad's Wild Ride. Then it's lunch and a peaceful trip on It's a Small World, which is so cool and calm it makes for a good rest stop. Refreshed, we head to Mickey's Toontown to see Minnie's House, ride the dinky roller coaster, jump in Goofy's Playhouse, ride the trolley, and, if they aren't especially timid, do Roger Rabbit. (But if the crowds are bad, we skip Toontown altogether, as it's impossible to understand its village setup when it's mobbed with people.) Then it's time for a cool drink and a souvenir stop near the exit gates, and the day is done. Any more with young kids is asking for trouble. Also with little ones, we establish a firm shopping policy. To prevent hours of panicked browsing through gift shops, we let our kids buy one toy or souvenir, but only at the very last stop before leaving. Before that, no shopping allowed.

At Disney's California Adventure, there is comparatively little of particular interest to the 6-and-under crowd, except for Flik's Fun Fair, a collection of diminutive rides for little ones.

Early Elementary For this age at Disneyland Park, we recommend a day alternating rides with shows and theme areas. Assuming that there's a too-scary limit for these kids but that they like a little thrill, we try to get them on Pirates of the Caribbean, Haunted Mansion, Indiana Jones, and Thunder Mountain as their "big" rides worth waiting in line for. Between the rides, we give them at least an hour for Pirate's Lair on Tom Sawyer Island (ride the raft over the water, run around the parklike trails, see the fort) and take them to Winnie the Pooh, the *Enchanted Tiki Room,* a live show, Tarzan's Treehouse, and short-wait experiences such as the excellent *Honey, I Shrunk the Audience.* We also schedule the nighttime parade and (if they're late stayer-uppers) the unbelievably wonderful fireworks spectacle over the waters in Frontierland. Getting good parade-type seats on the curbs, refreshments, and a chance to browse a souvenir shop while waiting (and while another family member saves places) make for a pretty good interlude. The park's live entertainment is excellent, and it imparts more of the Disney spirit this age group looks for than long hours in line for high-speed thrills.

At Disney's California Adventure, head first for Soarin' over California, then for the Paradise Pier district of the park to the new *Toy Story* Midway Mania attraction. After that, sample the rides on the pier that appeal to your kids, then backtrack and catch Grizzly River Run, using FASTPASS. Save shows and theater attractions for last.

Older Elementary–Preteen   This age group, as is befitting, benefits from a half-and-half day. Kids age 10 and older with watches or cell phones can be allowed to go off on their own in the parks for a few hours at a time, meeting parents (with younger kids to look after?) at designated times and places. When you arrive at the park of your choice, discuss the park layout and the locations of some key sites. Set early mealtime meeting places at a sit-down restaurant, and when you rendezvous, allow enough time for the kids to calm down and for you to assess their energy level. Let them have a half-hour leeway on the meeting time, so if they're in line for something, they don't have to get out to meet you; if you've picked a sit-down restaurant, you can relax comfortably while you wait for them. This age group can skip the parade and hustle off to the big-deal rides during that time, when the lines will be shorter. Another thing we've done with this group (because they like to go over and over again on a favorite ride) is bring a book and park ourselves on a bench while they do the rides and come check with us from time to time.

Teen   One of the few occasions when an ideal teen schedule fits into the world, a teen's trip to Disneyland should be almost the opposite of everyone else's. Don't make them get up early, but rather let them arrive at the park of their choice in late morning or early afternoon and stay until it closes (midnight or later in summer). Teens own the parks after dusk, and parents will love knowing that there's a safe place for kids this age to roam. (This is even more true of Knott's Berry Farm; see profile.) If you have preteens and teens and you're staying at a Disneyland hotel, you can even retire with the preteens and let the teens walk or ride the last monorail back to the hotel.

The *Unofficial Guide to Disneyland,* also published by John Wiley & Sons, offers in-depth information on both Disneyland Park and Disney's California Adventure and provides step-by-step touring plans that will eliminate an average of three hours of waiting in line on a busy day. If you plan to visit during periods of moderate to high attendance, you'll find the guide indispensable.

Knott's Berry Farm

APPEAL BY AGE	PRESCHOOL ★★★★	GRADE SCHOOL ★★★★½	TEENS ★★★★½
YOUNG ADULTS ★★★★		OVER 30 ★★★	SENIORS ★★★

8039 Beach Boulevard, Buena Park; ☎ 714-220-5200; www.knotts.com

Hours *October–May:* Monday–Friday, 10 a.m.–6 p.m.; Saturday, 10 a.m.–10 p.m; Sunday, 10 a.m.–7 p.m.; *summer:* Sunday–Friday, 10 a.m.–10 p.m.; Saturday, 10 a.m.–11 p.m. **Admission** $52 adults, $23 children ages 3–11; parking $10, RVs $15, handicapped $6. **Touring time** Average 8 hours; minimum 4 hours. **Rainy-day touring** Limited. **Restaurants** Yes. **Alcoholic beverages** Yes. **Disabled access** Yes. **Wheelchair rental** Yes; call ahead for electric. **Baby-stroller rental** Yes. **Lockers** Yes. **Pet kennels** No. **Rain check** No. **Private tours** Yes.

DESCRIPTION AND COMMENTS   This really was a berry farm once upon a time, and today it takes pride in its claim to be the country's first theme park. The theme gets a little confused from time to time, but in general the rides, shows, and amusements relate to early California and the Wild West.

Unlike Disneyland, Knott's can be great fun and not overwhelming for the 3- to 7-year-old-set, thanks to Camp Snoopy. Thoughtfully located close to the park's entrance, Camp Snoopy is a self-contained minipark with rides scaled to little kids; when our youngest was 5, she was terrified of thrill rides, but she wanted to do this just-thrilling-enough little roller coaster over and over. She also loved the Charlie Brown speedway, Red Baron ride, and Snoopy bounce. You can easily visit Camp Snoopy and then leave without dragging a cranky preschooler through other distractions.

If you have older kids, you'll want to explore the park's other areas, each of which has its own intense thrill rides. In Mexican-themed Fiesta Village, for instance, preteens and teens line up for Jaguar, a high-speed, 2,700-foot-long roller coaster; equally popular is Montezooma's Revenge, an intense, high-speed loop-the-loop, and the new Pony Express, where riders sit on a

unofficial **TIP**
One caveat: though it's not as nationally famous as Disneyland, Knott's can also attract fearsome crowds.

carousel-style pony—but instead of going round and round, these ponies go from 0 to 38 mph in a few seconds, causing tweens to scream like crazy. If you don't want to get wet, stay off the Bigfoot Rapids. If you have teens, they'll probably want to hang around the Boardwalk area, near some of the most intense thrill rides and full of midway games (which are too difficult, not to mention expensive, for younger kids).

What we most like about Knott's are the serendipitous items tucked around the park. Near Camp Snoopy, for instance, there's a trash can in the shape of a bear; when you walk by, it asks for trash, and when you put trash in its mouth, it thanks you. Our kids loved this bear so much that they went scavenging for trash. Elsewhere around the grounds you'll find a life-size replica of a great white shark; a ranger station (near Bigfoot

unofficial **TIP**
Camp Snoopy is labor-intensive, requiring you to help toddlers up and down steps, and it loses much of its appeal to 4-year-olds who spend all their time waiting in line. You'll have a much better visit with young children if you visit on a weekday, first thing in the morning.

Rapids) in which kids can hold insects and spiders; a one-room schoolhouse; informal bluegrass performances in the Old West Ghost Town; Native American artisans who will show kids how they make flutes, canoes, and jewelry; and a collection of Native American tepees and tents in which kids can play. And hokey though it is, they all love panning for gold, even jaded 15-year-olds. One daughter spent an hour watching in fascination as other visitors cracked open geodes with a hammer before she finally decided on which rock to select for herself to see what crystals lurked inside.

This is also a very good park for teens, with music, dancing, and special shows and holiday events (sometimes requiring separate nighttime admission). You really can drop 'em off and pick 'em up later.

Knott's Soak City

APPEAL BY AGE	PRESCHOOL ★★	GRADE SCHOOL ★★★★	TEENS ★★★★
YOUNG ADULTS ★★★★		OVER 30 ★★★★	SENIORS ★★

8039 Beach Boulevard, Buena Park; ☎ 714-220-5200; www.knotts.com/soakcity

Hours Open Memorial Day weekend–September; hours vary considerably, so check first. **Admission** $30 adults, $20 children ages 3–11 and seniors age 62 and older; after 3 p.m., $20 adults and children ages 3–11; $10 parking. **Touring time** Average 4–6 hours; minimum 1 hour. **Rainy-day touring** Limited. **Restaurants** Snack bars. **Alcoholic beverages** No. **Disabled access** Yes. **Wheelchair rental** Yes. **Baby-stroller rental** No. **Lockers** Yes. **Pet kennels** No. **Rain check** No. **Private tours** No.

DESCRIPTION AND COMMENTS   Built on the site of Knott's Berry Farm's former parking lot, this 13-acre water park is themed to the 1950s and 1960s—the golden days of California beach and surf culture. Ten ride areas contain various slides (including Banzai Falls, which has six high-speed slides, and the four-person Pacific Spin raft ride), a third-of-a-mile-long "lazy river" for folks who like to float, and a three-story fun house. There's a 750,000-gallon wave pool and a play area with nozzles, faucets, secret rooms, and surprise showers. Toddlers get a quiet lagoon with a submarine and an inactive octopus.

FAMILY-FRIENDLY RESTAURANTS

Goofy's Kitchen
Disneyland Hotel, 1150 Magic Way, Anaheim; ☎ 714-956-6755; disneyland.disney.go.com

Meals served Breakfast, lunch, and dinner. **Cuisine** American. **Entree range** Breakfast and lunch, $37.16 adults, $19.82 children ages 3–12; dinner, $44.60 adults, $19.82 children ages 3–12, free for children age 2 and under; prices include tax and tip. **Reservations** Recommended. **Payment** All major credit cards.

IF YOUR 2- TO 10-YEAR-OLD isn't terrified of oversize, mute Mickeys and Goofys, bring her or him here for an all-you-can-eat meal, and it will be one of the highlights of your trip to Disneyland. Perfectly tolerable food is served buffet-style, which the kids adore because they can have exactly what they want. Plan on a leisurely meal so your kids will have time to hug, follow around, and get autographs from Goofy and other wandering characters.

Inka Anaheim

400 South Euclid Street, Anaheim; ☎ 714-772-2263; www.inkaanaheim.com

Meals served Lunch and dinner. **Cuisine** Peruvian. **Entree range** $10–$21. **Kids' menu** Yes. **Reservations** Accepted only Friday–Saturday. **Payment** All major credit cards.

IF THE BLANDNESS AND STERILITY of the chain restaurants that clog Anaheim depress you, take the family on an adventure to this swell little joint, just a notch above a fast-food restaurant—it's home to superb roast chicken and interesting dishes involving French fries and other forms of potato (Peru is, after all, the birthplace of the potato). While a bit exotic, the food is simple enough for kids to enjoy, and the prices are hard to beat.

Medieval Times

7662 Beach Boulevard, Buena Park; ☎ 888-935-6878 or 714-521-4740; www.medievaltimes.com

Meals served Daily, dinner. **Cuisine** American. **Entree range** Set price of $52. **Kids' menu** Set price of $35. **Reservations** Strongly advised the day before. **Payment** All major credit cards.

IF YOU BLOW INTO TOWN in the late afternoon or evening and are looking for something to do in the way of entertainment, you could do worse than joining the bus tour groups and birthday parties at Medieval Times. You'll eat ribs and chicken legs while watching knights joust and fair maidens faint; the crowd gets into the action with lots of whoops and hollers. The littlest ones might get scared by the jousting and shouting, but all in all, if your kids are ages 5 to 15, you'll have a fine time. The performers are Hollywood hopefuls and, as such, sometimes genuinely quite talented.

Mrs. Knott's Chicken Dinner Restaurant

8039 Beach Boulevard, Buena Park; ☎ 714-220-5080; www.knotts.com/camplace

Meals served Breakfast, lunch, and dinner. **Cuisine** American. **Entree range** Breakfast, $6–$10; lunch, $6–$9; dinner, $15. **Kids' menu** Yes. **Reservations** Taken on a limited basis for parties of 12 or more. **Payment** All major credit cards.

EVERY EVENING, the front door to this legendary place is blocked by a line that stretches around the building, and that line helps further the restaurant's reputation. In truth, however, the family-style fried-chicken dinner is not worth an hour's wait. If you time it right (early or late) and can get in quickly, your kids will enjoy the Jell-O, biscuits, chicken, corn, and ice cream, and you'll enjoy the low prices, but don't let the crowds get your hopes up for a memorable meal. However, the take-out window just down the way from the restaurant entrance is a great option for folks staying nearby. The food's hot, hearty, and ready to go immediately, and you don't have to drive around looking for another stop to make.

Napa Rose
Disney's Grand Californian Hotel, Disneyland Resort; 1600 South Disneyland Drive, Anaheim; ☎ 714-300-7170; disneyland.disney.go.com

Meals served Dinner and Sunday brunch. **Cuisine** Modern American/Californian. **Entree range** $32–$42. **Kids' menu** Yes. **Reservations** Strongly advised. **Payment** All major credit cards.

IF YOUR KIDS ARE the sort who can appreciate a special-occasion meal in an elegant restaurant—or if you're leaving them in the nearby Pinocchio's Workshop evening child-care center—live it up with dinner at this surprisingly good and amazingly handsome place. Disney lured Andrew Sutton, one of California's most talented chefs, to head Napa Rose, which celebrates the wine country and California cuisine. The warm, glowing Arts and Crafts–style dining room has soaring windows and beautiful vineyard murals. The wine list is rich in California notables, the cooking is excellent, and the kids' menu is the most appealing we've ever seen.

PART THREE

LOS ANGELES AND VICINITY:
South Bay, Pasadena, Mountain Towns, Deserts, and Catalina Island

DESPITE ITS FABLED SUNSHINE and its laid-back attitude, **Los Angeles** has not traditionally been an easy city to visit. But continuing improvements and additions to the transit system make it easier to get around without a car, and an improving pool of hotels has made it possible to stay and play in some good, family-friendly "home base" areas such as **Santa Monica, Universal City,** and **Long Beach.** Because there is no compact city center, distances between destinations are sometimes considerable, so parents should select their home base carefully.

LA's attractions are many and diverse. You can sled in the local mountains and boogie-board at the beach in the same weekend. You can go from a Mexican street fair to an African-American art show to a Korean barbecue restaurant in the same day. You can take in the illusions of **Hollywood** at **Universal Studios,** then decompress in a Japanese garden at Pasadena's **Huntington Gardens.** You can join the crowds exploring Santa Monica's **Third Street Promenade,** or ride a ferry to sleepy, sun-washed **Catalina Island.**

If you decide to stay in **Redondo Beach,** which is south of Los Angeles International Airport and a 30- to 60-minute drive from downtown LA, accept that you may not be able to do **Universal Studios, Magic Mountain,** and Hollywood in the same weekend. Conversely, if Universal Studios and Hollywood are tops on your family's list, maybe you should save the beach for next time and stay in Universal City or Hollywood.

This chapter breaks the vast LA area into several geographical units, in the following order: the South Bay, composed of the beach towns of **Long Beach, Redondo Beach,** and **Manhattan Beach;** Catalina Island, a two-hour ferry ride from **San Pedro;** LA's Westside, including **Santa Monica, Marina del Rey,** and **West LA;** Central LA, ranging

unofficial **TIP**
The secret to a successful visit to LA is twofold: careful planning and judicious editing. Make a list of everything you want to do, find a place you'd like to stay, review your wish list with a map in hand, and start cutting your list down.

los angeles and vicinity

● **BEACHES AND PARKS**
1. El Dorado East Regional Park
2. Griffith Park
3. Indian Canyons
4. Joshua Tree National Park
5. Lacy Park
6. Leo Carrillo State Beach
7. Malibu Creek State Park
8. Malibu Lagoon (Surfrider)
   State Beach
9. Manhattan Beach
10. Paradise Cove
11. Redondo Beach
12. Solstice Canyon
13. Venice Beach
14. William S. Hart County Park
15. Will Rogers State Historic Park
16. Zuma Beach

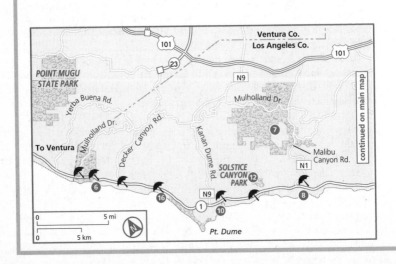

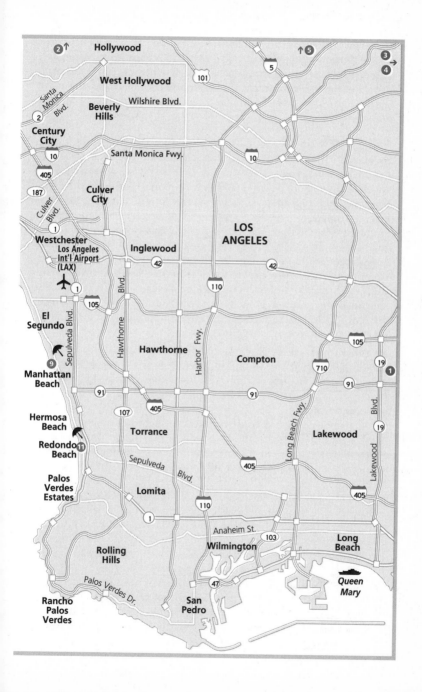

from **Beverly Hills** to downtown and encompassing the majority of the attractions, from the **California Science Center** south of downtown to **Universal CityWalk** in the Hollywood hills; side trips to the suburbs of **San Dimas** (**Raging Waters**) and Valencia (**Six Flags Magic Mountain**); **Pasadena,** the city just northeast of downtown that is home to **Old Pasadena,** the **Huntington Gardens,** and **Kidspace;** the **Mountains,** including **Big Bear** and **Lake Arrowhead;** and the deserts, including **Palm Springs** and **Joshua Tree.**

GETTING THERE

BY PLANE   Almost all major airlines serve the region's main airport, **Los Angeles International** (LAX; ☎ 310-646-5252; **www.lawa.org**), which is only about 15 minutes south of Santa Monica via the **405 freeway (Interstate 405)**—if there's no traffic, which is rare. If you're staying somewhere on the Eastside—in downtown, Studio City, or Pasadena—you'll be better off flying via **Bob Hope Airport** (BUR; 2627 North Hollywood Way, Burbank; ☎ 818-840-8840; **www.bob hopeairport.com**), a pleasantly small-scale operation used heavily by commuter flights. Also easy to manage is **Long Beach Airport,** (LGB; 4100 East Donald Douglas Drive, Long Beach; 562-570-2619; **www .longbeach.gov/airport**) home of the excellent airline JetBlue. Shuttle services, taxis, buses, and private car services link the airports to many locations across the region.

BY TRAIN   **Amtrak** delivers visitors from Northern California, the Pacific Northwest, the South, and the Midwest to **Union Station,** a gorgeous mission-style building in downtown that is every child's notion of what a train station should be. Call ☎ 800-USA-RAIL; **www.amtrak.com.**

After many years of construction, LA's light-rail system is often a practical, affordable, and even enjoyable way to get around town. From downtown's lovely Union Station (worth seeing on its own), you can take the **Red Line** to Hollywood (including the Hollywood & Highland Center) and Universal City. The Red Line also connects to the **Blue Line,** which heads south to Long Beach, where you'll find fun beaches, lively Belmont Shore, the Aquarium of the Pacific, and the *Queen Mary.* The **Gold Line** connects Union Station with Chinatown, Highland Park, South Pasadena, and Pasadena, including Old Pasadena. Part of the system now is the well-run **FlyAway** express bus (☎ 866-435-9529; **www.lawa.org/flyaway**) that runs from Union Station to LAX. Getting information is a little confusing, because the light-rail system is under the purview of the bus-based Metropolitan Transit Authority instead of the Metrolink system, which shares Amtrak's rails. For fare and route information, your best bet is to call ☎ 800-COMMUTE or visit **www.metro.net.**

BY CAR   The freeway rules in LA, so there are major highways leading to the urban area from every which way. Visitors from the north and south arrive via **Interstate 5,** the artery connecting the Mexican and Canadian borders; the coastal route from the north into LA is the **101 Freeway (US 101),** which travels via Santa Barbara. Travelers entering from almost anywhere east, from Palm Springs to Chicago, will arrive via **Interstate 10.** Once you get into the city area, the freeway numbers explode: There's the 210 (Interstate 210), and the 91 (CA 91), and the 110 (Interstate and CA 110), and the 22 (CA 22), and the 60 (CA 60), and the 134 (CA 134)—so do not arrive without a good map. (The Thomas Bros. map book is the bible, but a basic folding map will suffice for freeway navigation.)

HOW TO GET INFORMATION BEFORE YOU GO

- **Beverly Hills Conference & Visitors Bureau**
  239 South Beverly Drive, Beverly Hills 90212; ☎ 800-345-2210; **www.beverlyhillsbehere.com**
- **Catalina Island Visitors Bureau**   1 Green Pier, Avalon;
  ☎ 310-510-1520; **www.visitcatalina.org**
- **Long Beach Area Convention and Visitors Bureau**   1 World Trade Center, Suite 300, Long Beach 90831; ☎ 800-452-7829 or 562-436-3645; **www.visitlongbeach.com**
- **Los Angeles Convention and Visitors Bureau**   333 South Hope Street, 18th Floor, Los Angeles 90071; ☎ 213-624-7300; **www.lacvb.com**
- **Palm Springs Desert Resorts Convention and Visitors Authority**
  70–100 Highway 111, Rancho Mirage 92270; ☎ 800-967-3767 or 760-770-9000; **www.palmspringsusa.com**
- **Pasadena Convention and Visitors Bureau**   171 South Los Robles Avenue, Pasadena 91101; ☎ 800-307-7977 or 626-795-9311; **www.pasadenacal.com**
- **Santa Monica Convention and Visitors Bureau**   1920 Main Street, Suite B, Santa Monica 90405; ☎ 800-544-5319 or 310-319-6263; **www.santamonica.com**

CHILD CARE AND BABYSITTING

WE SIT BETTER   A licensed, bonded agency providing babysitters throughout LA; ☎ 818-997-1421.

BABYSITTERS GUILD   L.A.'s oldest babysitting agency has a staff of 50 sitters of all ages, and each is carefully screened and has CPR training and child-care experience; ☎ 310-837-1800.

A **CALENDAR** of **FESTIVALS** and **EVENTS**

January

TOURNAMENT OF ROSES PARADE   *Colorado Boulevard in Pasadena.* January 1. Every year, untold millions watch this parade on TV, and lots of them decide right then to move to LA. If you've never been, get tickets—kids adore it; ☎ 626-449-ROSE; **www.tournamentofroses.com.**

February

CHINESE NEW YEAR'S PARADE   *Chinatown*. Huge dragons snake through Chinatown's streets, and the costumes are great; note that Chinese New Year sometimes falls in January, so dates can vary; ☎ 213-617-0396; **www.lagoldendragonparade.com.**

March

LOS ANGELES MARATHON   *Throughout LA*. The city becomes gripped with marathon fever, and everyone tries to find a spot to watch the runners, walkers, skaters, wheelchair riders, and cyclists (including lots of middle- and high-school kids) go; ☎ 310-444-5544; **www.lamarathon.com.**

April

BLESSING OF THE ANIMALS   *Olvera Street, downtown*. Saturday before Easter. Hundreds of people bring their pets—from dogs to hamsters—to be blessed in this festive procession; ☎ 213-680-2525; **www.olvera-street.com.**

FIESTA BROADWAY   *Downtown*. The last weekend in April kicks off Cinco de Mayo season when 36 downtown blocks are shut to traffic and thousands of revelers enjoy performances on several stages, with Latin pop stars headlining; ☎ 310-914-0015; **www.fiestabroadway.la.**

LOS ANGELES TIMES FESTIVAL OF BOOKS   *Dickson Plaza, UCLA*. Includes a large children's area and lots of good storytelling events; ☎ 800-LA-TIMES, ext. 7BOOK; **www.latimes.com.**

BASEBALL OPENING DAY   *Dodger Stadium*.   A festive family outing; ☎ 323-224-1500; **www.dodgers.com.**

May

CHILDREN'S DAY   *Little Tokyo (downtown LA)*. A traditional Japanese celebration of the child, featuring footraces, games, arts and crafts; ☎ 213-628-2725; **www.jacdc.org.**

VALLEY GREEK FESTIVAL   *Northridge*. Memorial Day party with music, food, more; ☎ 818-886-4040; **www.valleygreekfestival.com.**

June

LONG BEACH BAYOU FESTIVAL   *Rainbow Lagoon, Long Beach*. Rollicking music, dance lessons, Cajun food, and children's amusements; ☎ 562-427-3713; **www.longbeachfestival.com.**

July

FOURTH OF JULY CELEBRATION   Queen Mary, *Long Beach*. One of the best fireworks shows in LA County; ☎ 562-435-3511 or **www .queenmary.com.**

AMERICAFEST *Rose Bowl, Pasadena.* A rousing event with live music and a boffo fireworks show; ☎ 626-577-3101; **www.rosebowl stadium.com.**

LOTUS FESTIVAL *Echo Park.* In the park surrounding pretty little Echo Park Lake, home to a large lotus bed, is a celebration of Asian food and arts, with dragon-boat races, kiddie rides, and pedal boat rides on the lake; ☎ 213-485-1310; **www.laparks.org/grifmet/lotus.htm.**

August

AFRICAN MARKETPLACE AND CULTURAL FAIRE *Location varies, LA.* Hundreds of booths, a Youth Village, and live entertainment celebrating African cultures; ☎ 323-293-1612; **www.africanmarketplace.org.**

September

LA COUNTY FAIR *County Fairplex Fairgrounds, Pomona.* An 18-day extravaganza of carnival rides, pie-eating contests, deep-fried Snickers, livestock shows, and live entertainment; ☎ 909-623-3111; **www .fairplex.com.**

October

CALABASAS PUMPKIN FESTIVAL Juan *Bautista de Anza Park, Calabasas.* A street fair lines Lost Hills Road, and in the park is a lively festival with pumpkin sales, haunted houses, country music, mummy wrapping, and pumpkin seed spit-offs; ☎ 818-222-5680; **www.calabasas pumpkinfestival.com.**

November

DIA DE LOS MUERTOS *Olvera Street, downtown.* November 1 or 2. A lively, colorful celebration of the Day of the Dead, including a candlelit procession; ☎ 213-485-9769; **www.olvera-street.com.**

DOO DAH PARADE *Old Pasadena.* Sunday after Thanksgiving, but date can vary. A goofy, eccentric spoof of the Rose Parade; ☎ 626-205-4029; **www.pasadenadoodahparade.info.**

ROSEBUD PARADE *Lake Avenue, Pasadena.* Sponsored by Kidspace Museum, this miniature version of the Rose Parade is a wonderful family event. Children parade in or on self-decorated wagons, bikes, trikes, and skateboards, and those who sign up in advance can take a float-making class at Kidspace; ☎ 626-449-9144; **www.kidspace museum.org.**

December

CHRISTMAS BOAT PARADE *Burton Chace Park, Marina del Rey.* Come after dark to watch the decorated, colorfully lit boats parade by; ☎ 310-670-7130; **www.mdrboatparade.org.**

HOLIDAY CONCERT SEASON *Walt Disney Concert Hall, downtown LA.* Several of these holiday-themed concerts held in spectacular Disney Hall are great for families; ☎ 323-850-2000; **wdch.laphil.com.**

The BEST BEACHES and PARKS

EL DORADO EAST REGIONAL PARK Your kids will have to try hard to be bored in this huge inland park in Long Beach. The 450 acres include four fishing lakes (stocked with trout, catfish, and bass), pedal boats, playgrounds, miles of level biking trails, an archery range used in the 1984 Olympics, and a fun, one-mile steam train ride (closed Monday in summer and Monday and Tuesday off-season). The biggest attraction here is the **El Dorado Nature Center,** which takes up 100 acres of the park. Its museum has cool stuff kids can touch and explore, such as skulls and antlers, as well as insect and reptile houses, animal displays, and summer-camp programs. Outside are stroller-accommodating trails and a pond that's home to turtles and ducks. Call the Nature Center to reserve a spot in one of the guided family night walks or campfires. 7550 East Spring Street, Long Beach; ☎ 562-570-1745 (Nature Center) or 562-570-1771 (park); **ci.long-beach.ca.us/park.** Open daily, 7 a.m. to dusk; closed Christmas. Parking $4 weekdays, $7 weekends, $8 holidays.

 GRIFFITH PARK One of the country's great urban parks (it is, in fact, the nation's largest city park), Griffith Park is a world unto itself, home to many excellent amusements for children and worth a full day trip, if not two. On the park's eastern edge are the **Los Angeles Zoo** and the **Museum of the American West** (see respective attraction profiles, both on page 164). A little west of there you'll find the pony rides (☎ 323-664-3266) and kiddie train ride (☎ 323-664-6788) loved by generations of LA children. On the north (Burbank) side is **Travel Town** (☎ 323-662-5874; **www.traveltown.org**), a marvelous collection of old trains that kids can climb into and explore; a small-scale train ride circles the area. Children also love the old carousel (although the deafening music terrified our 3-year-old), which is surrounded by playground areas and rolling lawns that are perfect for picnics. Extras include two golf courses, tennis courts, equestrian trails, a fern preserve, soccer fields, and woodlands. There are many entrances: zoo and Museum of the American West from Zoo Drive off I-5; pony and train rides and carousel from Griffith Park Boulevard north of Los Feliz Boulevard; Travel Town from Victory Boulevard on Burbank side; observatory, golf course, Greek Theatre, picnic areas, and trailheads from Vermont Avenue north of Los Feliz Boulevard; ☎ 323-913-4688; **www.laparks.org/dos/parks/griffithpk.** Open daily, 6 a.m. to 10 p.m.

INDIAN CANYONS Some come for the tchotchke-filled gift shop, but we come for the hiking and the almost miraculously lush beauty of this desert oasis, a stream-fed, palm-rich hideaway in the mountain rocks. There's easy hiking near the base of the trails. If your kids are old enough to ride horses, a great way to see the canyons is on horseback; contact **Smoke Tree Stables** (☎ 760-327-1372; **www.smoketreestable.com**). The

Canyons are the property of the local Cahuilla Tribe, which maintains the land and charges admission for entrance. 38500 South Palm Canyon Drive, Palm Springs; ☎ 760-323-6018; **www.indian-canyons.com.** Open daily, 8 a.m. to 5 p.m. (Friday, Saturday, and Sunday only from July through September); admission $8 adults, $6 for seniors, students, and military, $4 ages 6 to 12; equestrians $10, free for children under age 6; guided hikes, $2 to $3.

JOSHUA TREE NATIONAL PARK   A desert unlike any other, Joshua Tree borders on the mystical. Gigantic boulders are strewn everywhere, like God's rough-hewn marbles; they're so awesome they almost seem alive. Add mysteriously soft and white sand and the armies of prickly Joshua trees reaching their arms heavenward, and you have a place of great beauty, beloved by rock climbers, naturalists, hikers,

unofficial **TIP**
Consider taking a family rock-climbing lesson in Joshua Tree, and prepare to be amazed at how quickly your children might take to such a challenging and intense sport.

and stargazers. Allow time to stop at the **Oasis Visitor Center** to get oriented and take the short nature walk to an oasis; ask for a map so you can find the fun one-mile trail in Hidden Valley and the cool Jumbo Rocks area. For kids, the best bet is a private family lesson from **Joshua Tree Rock Climbing School** (☎ 800-890-4745; **www.joshua treerockclimbing.com**) or **Vertical Adventures** (☎ 800-514-8785; **www .vertical-adventures.com**). There are several campgrounds; one of the best is White Tank, where the boulders are grand and the sand is soft. Visit in spring and fall only, and bring lots and lots of water—the entire park has none. If that makes camping sound too intense, the **Twentynine Palms Motel** will make a fine base. 74485 National Park Drive (off I-10), Twentynine Palms; ☎ 760-367-5525; **www.nps.gov/ jotr**. Free admission but $15 per vehicle for parking.

LACY PARK   One of the prettiest urban parks anywhere, Lacy is carefully hidden in the wealthy enclave of San Marino, near Pasadena. So skillful is its design that it seems to go on for miles, with the trees blocking any hint of residential development. It has an excellent, large playground, vast lawns, softball fields, a bike and skate path ringing the park, and complete picnic and restroom facilities. A popular day camp is held here in summer, and the Fourth of July festivities are legendary. This is a good play stop if you're staying either downtown or in the Pasadena area. 1485 Virginia Road (north of Monterey), San Marino; ☎ 626-300-0790; **ci.san-marino.ca.us/ lacy.htm.** There is a $4 fee for nonresidents on weekends.

LEO CARRILLO STATE BEACH   Many a Southern California school goes field tripping to this Malibu beach, and for very good reason. Kids (and parents) adore it here, especially in the quieter fringe seasons, such as May and October. The tide pooling is the best in the LA area; everything is protected, so kids aren't allowed to take even a shell from the tide pool preserve. There are sea caves to

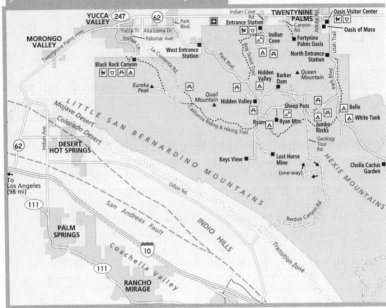

joshua tree national park

explore, rocks to climb, a sandy beach, good ocean swimming, a playground, nature trails, and a good campground with 300 sites for tents (no hookups for RVs). Lifeguards are on duty in summer. It can get pretty chilly, so bring jackets for your whole crew. 35000 West Pacific Coast Highway, between Point Mugu and Point Dume, Malibu; ☎ 818-880-0350; **parks.ca.gov.** Parking $6; campsites $25; for campsite reservations, call Reserve America, ☎ 800-444-7275; **www .reserveamerica.com.**

MALIBU CREEK STATE PARK   One of the many wonders of the Santa Monica Mountains, this park has lots to offer. You can ride mountain bikes, hike the **Malibu Creek Trail** (a beautiful hike, and not too challenging for school-age kids), fish for bass and bluegill in **Century Lake,** picnic, and swim in the rock pool near the visitors center. Parents take note that three miles in on the Malibu Creek Trail is the former set of the TV show *M*A*S*H.* Don't miss the visitors center, which has maps, children's information, and a little museum. There's also a nice campground. 1925 Las Virgenes Road, Calabasas; ☎ 818-880-0367; **parks.ca.gov.** Parking $5 per vehicle per day.

MALIBU LAGOON (SURFRIDER) STATE BEACH   If you have a surfer in the family, or someone who thinks surfers are cool, head for these adjacent beaches on the north side of the Malibu Pier. The

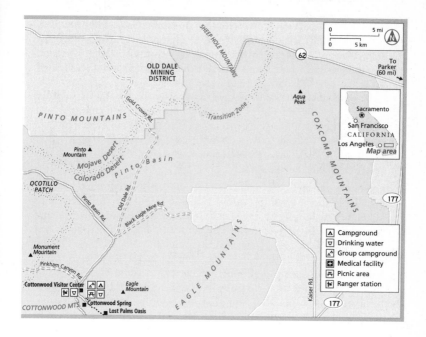

longboarding capital of LA, Surfrider was one of the birthplaces of the California surfing scene in the 1940s and 1950s, thanks to its consistent (but rarely huge) cruiser waves. The **Malibu Surfing Association Classic** contest is held here each September. The pier is a good fishing spot, and the state beach just north of Surfrider is home to a natural lagoon with great bird-watching, tide pools, a nature center, and easy little trails. Guided tours are offered; call ☎ 310-456-8432 for details. 23000 block of Pacific Coast Highway (0.5 miles south of Cross Creek Road), Malibu; ☎ 310-880-0350; **parks.ca.gov.** Parking $3 to $8, depending on season; limited parking available along PCH.

MANHATTAN BEACH   Broad and long, this is a classic Southern California beach, with a pier, bike path, volleyball courts, snack bars, summertime lifeguards, great people-watching, and lots of sunshine. The generally good waves for bodysurfing, bodyboarding, and board surfing make this a better beach for solid swimmers, usually kids older than age 8; our favorite spot is on the north side of the pier. If you have time to hit only one good all-around beach on an LA trip, this is the one to hit. The downside is the lack of parking—come early to find a metered spot. 1200 The Strand, Manhattan Beach; ☎ 310-545-5621; **beaches.co.la.ca.us.**

PARADISE COVE If you loathe giant, crowded beaches and want a nice family place—and if outrageous parking fees don't bother you—head west from Santa Monica via Pacific Coast Highway (CA 1) to this lovely private beach fronting what must surely be the most attractive, upscale trailer-park community in the country. The sand is soft, the cove and small pier are picturesque, and the shallow shoreline lets kids have lots of wave fun without getting pounded. Extras include showers, restrooms, a basketball court, and a summer lifeguard, but no snack bar; you can avoid the parking charge if you eat in the beachfront restaurant, a decent seafood cafe owned by Bob Morris of Gladstone's fame. 28128 Pacific Coast Highway, Malibu; ☎ 310-457-2503; **www.paradisecovemalibu.com.** Parking $25 if you aren't eating at the restaurant.

REDONDO BEACH A large, sweeping sand beach complete with a pier, Redondo is popular with groups of teens and young families alike. The fishing from the pier is surprisingly good; down on the sand, there are waves, volleyball courts, a bike path, concession stands, lifeguards, and good restroom and shower facilities. On the King Harbor end of the beach, you can sign up for a whale-watching trip in winter–spring or a sportfishing trip in summer. In July and August, the pier is often home to free concerts and festivals. Consider bringing your bikes and riding to neighboring Manhattan Beach. 1101 Esplanade, Redondo Beach; ☎ 310-372-2166; **beaches.co.la .ca.us**. Parking ranges from free to $8.

SOLSTICE CANYON A hike that's so easy you can do a major part of it with a stroller is the big draw here. A shaded, paved former ranch road leads through the canyon, often next to the babbling, rock-strewn creek, to an 18th-century adobe and several fine picnic areas and on to the ruins of a house that was built almost into a rock grotto and falls. This is a perfect turnaround point, about an hour each way, although real hikers can continue. Make sure to allow time for playing in the grotto and in the creek along the way. We like to pick up gourmet picnic supplies in Malibu, take a hike here, then spend some time on the beach. Water, restrooms, dogs allowed on leash. Off Corral Canyon Road, Malibu; ☎ 805-370-2301; **www.nps.gov/ samo.** Admission free.

VENICE BEACH When Angelenos host out-of-town visitors, they almost always bring them to Venice, but not to swim or sunbathe. The scene is the draw here, and what a scene it is: the boardwalk teems with merchants (T-shirts, jewelry, tie-dyes, junk of every description), tattooed acrobatic skaters, snake handlers, cycling musicians, chain-saw jugglers, street rappers, bodybuilders, and all manner of folk your Aunt Martha will never see in Topeka. Of the various food vendors, **Jody Maroni**'s sausage stand is the hands-down winner. You might see some awesome basketball action (along with intense, often-foul street language) at the public courts, and the famed **Muscle Beach** is still going strong. It's at 2300 Ocean Front Walk, between Marina del Rey Channel and the Santa Monica city line, Venice; ☎ 310-577-5700; **www.laparks.org/venice.** Parking in the county lot is $3 on weekdays and $8 on weekends.

WILLIAM S. HART COUNTY PARK Buffalo graze behind fences, you can often spot deer, and kids can feed the barnyard animals—sheep, horses, burros, ducks, chickens. When you're ready to move, you can hike any of the 265 acres. The tour of the former home of Western-movie star William Hart can be frustrating for some kids because they can't touch, but others like seeing some of the Western gear, especially the bearskin rug and old guns. Also on site is a sweet little train-station museum (open weekend afternoons only) with a steam locomotive out front and a nifty model train inside. 24151 North San Fernando Road, Newhall, Santa Clarita Valley; ☎ 661-259-0855; **www.hartmuseum .org.** Admission and parking are free.

WILL ROGERS STATE HISTORIC PARK The great storyteller's former house, still furnished as if he lived there, won't interest your kids in the slightest ("Will *who*?"), but they'll probably get a kick out of the visitors center video showing Will doing his rope tricks. After the video, head out for the one-mile (each way) hike to **Inspiration Point,** where the Pacific view is glorious, then return to the polo fields for a picnic or barbecue. Other trails link to Topanga State Park. 1501 Will Rogers State Park Road (off Sunset Boulevard), Pacific Palisades; ☎ 310-454-8212; **parks.ca.gov.** Parking is $7.

ZUMA BEACH LA's coolest teens hang out at this northern Malibu beach near the Ventura County line. Keep young children and inexperienced swimmers out of the water—strong riptides prevail—but enjoy the playgrounds, sandy beach, volleyball, and people-watching, especially if you have teens. Lifeguards, concession stands, restrooms. 30050 Pacific Coast Highway, between Trancas Canyon Boulevard and Westward Beach Road; ☎ 310-457-2525; **beaches.co.la.ca.us.** Parking $8; limited free parking along PCH.

FAMILY OUTDOOR ADVENTURES

BICYCLING–IN-LINE SKATING Cycling in this car-obsessed city isn't for the timid, but at the beach, the cyclist (and skater) is king. A smooth, paved bike path wends along the sand from the north end of **Santa Monica Beach** (in the Pacific Palisades neighborhood) for more than 20 level miles, all the way south to **Redondo**

unofficial **TIP**
Our kids' favorite is to ride bikes from Manhattan Beach south to Redondo Pier for lunch and/or ice cream, then ride back and swim at Manhattan Beach Pier.

Beach. The path gets pretty congested on warm-weather weekends, so consider a week-day outing. Bike- and skate-rental shops are plentiful near the path in Santa Monica, in Venice, and down in the South Bay. Mountain-bike trails also abound in the Santa Monica and San Gabriel Mountains; for more information on how to find them, pick up *Mountain Bike! Los Angeles County* (Menasha Ridge Press), or call the Santa Monica Mountains National Recreation Area; ☎ 818-597-9192; **www.nps.gov/samo.**

BOATING   See the "Catalina Island" section later in this chapter.

FISHING   Surprisingly good fishing is found off the Redondo Beach and Malibu piers; both have tackle shops. If you're ready for a sea-fishing trip, try **Redondo Sport Fishing Company** (233 North Harbor Drive, Redondo Beach; ☎ 310-372-2111; **www.redondosportfishing. com**) or go with **L.A. Harbor Sportfishing** (Berth 79, San Pedro Harbor; ☎ 310-547-9916; **www.laharborsportfishing.com**). Both offer half-day charters that are good for school-age children.

HIKING   Entire books have been published on the hiking opportunities in the LA area, so rich are the choices. With young children, we particularly like **Solstice Canyon** (see "The Best Beaches and Parks," page 126) and the easy trails at **Eaton Canyon** (1750 North Altadena Drive, Pasadena; ☎ 626-398-5420; **www.ecnca.org**), which offers wonderful family nature walks every Saturday morning. **Big Bear** and **Lake Arrowhead** also offer lots of great family hiking; see the "Mountains" section later in this chapter. You'll also find good trails in some of the other parks in "The Best Beaches and Parks," especially **Will Rogers, Leo Carrillo,** and **Griffith parks.**

HORSEBACK RIDING   One of our favorite outings in Los Angeles is the Friday-night sunset horseback ride through Griffith Park offered by **Sunset Ranch** (3400 North Beachwood Drive, Hollywood; ☎ 323-469-5450; **www.sunsetranchhollywood.com**)—it's a wonderful evening to spend with teenagers. A guide takes you over the mountain and down into Burbank at sunset, with dusk settling on the wild scrub and scurrying jackrabbits; you tie up at a (pretty bad) Mexican restaurant in Burbank and ride back over after dinner, guided by a bright moon if you're lucky. Children as young as age 5 are welcome on daytime rides; the stable is home to some very gentle horses. Another place to find high-quality horses and access to many park trails is the **Los Angeles Equestrian Center** (480 West Riverside Drive, Burbank; ☎ 818-840-8401; **www .la-equestriancenter.com;** horse rentals $25 per hour, cash only). See also Indian Canyons in "The Best Beaches and Parks."

SURFING–OCEAN SPORTS   You're in the land of the Beach Boys, and you (or your kids) won't have experienced it fully if you don't get some wave action. Our favorite place to learn is the **Surf Academy** in Santa Monica and Manhattan Beach (☎ 310-372-2790; **www.surfacademy.com**), created by a former surf champ who's also a mother of five. It offers both private lessons and terrific weeklong summer surfing day camps, along with great classes for moms and families, too. Another good choice is **Malibu Ocean Sports** (south side of Malibu Pier; ☎ 310-456-6302; **www.malibumikes.com**). A one-hour private lesson, including board and wet suit, is $100; lessons are usually held at famed Surfrider beach. The same company also has windsurfing lessons for the same fee. To try your hand at the easier sport of kayaking, head to **Action Watersports** in Marina del Rey (4144 Lincoln Boulevard; ☎ 310-827-2233).

> *unofficial* **TIP**
> Know your swimming strength and ability—if lifeguards have posted riptide or high-surf warnings, respect the power of the ocean and stay out.

If you just want to get into the surf without the cost and trouble of surfing lessons, rent a bodyboard at any of dozens of concessions in Malibu, Santa Monica, Redondo Beach, or any other beach town, and ride the waves on your own.

TIDE POOLING   The best tide pooling in town is at **Leo Carrillo State Beach** (see "The Best Beaches and Parks"). The snorkeling there is superb as well, but you'll need to bring your own gear, as there's no equipment rental on site.

 WHALE WATCHING   We've enjoyed the morning whale-watching expeditions by **Redondo Sportfishing Company** (233 North Harbor Drive, in Redondo Beach; ☎ 310-372-2111; **www.redondo sportfishing.com**), some of which have a docent from the Cabrillo Marine Aquarium on board to answer questions. On our last trip, we saw at least a half-dozen gray whales, along with dolphins and sea lions. On your way in or out of the Redondo harbor area, make sure to stop for a look at the gigantic Wyland whale- and sea-life mural on the side of the PG&E building. Another good whale-watching outfit is **L.A. Harbor Sportfishing** (Berth 79, San Pedro Harbor; ☎ 310-547-9916; **www.laharborsportfishing.com**).

KID CULTURE:
Theater, Literature, and the Arts

FORGET THE TALK-SHOW JOKES about bubble-headed LA—contrary to popular opinion, Angelenos and their children are voracious readers and patrons of the arts. Here are our favorite kid-oriented cultural centers, for a civilized break from the theme-park sights.

BOB BAKER MARIONETTE THEATER   Skillful puppeteers ply their craft, making their creations sing, dance, and interact with each other and the audience. An LA kid favorite since 1963. 1345 West First Street, downtown LA; ☎ 213-250-9995; **www.bobbaker marionettes.com;** tickets $10.

CHILDREN'S BOOK WORLD   If you're staying on the Westside, head over here on Saturday morning for a generally captivating (and free) story time. Author signings are also sometimes offered. Call for schedules. 10580 West Pico Boulevard, West LA; ☎ 310-559-2665; **www.childrensbookworld.com;** admission free.

FAMILY THEATRE MUSICALS, SANTA MONICA PLAYHOUSE   Every Saturday and Sunday, once or twice in the afternoon, professional actors stage high-quality children's musical theater—typically variations on popular fairy tales—in a 92-seat playhouse. Day-camp theater programs for kids are offered in summer. 1211 Fourth Street, Santa Monica; ☎ 310-394-9779; **www.santamonicaplayhouse.com;** admission $10 to $15 per person.

GETTY CENTER   Events and activities that engage kids are plentiful at the Getty, from folk-music concerts and storytelling to the half-hour Family Art Stop, which helps kids get up close and personal with a single work of art. 1200 Getty Center Drive, West LA; ☎ 310-440-7300; **www.getty.edu;** admission free, parking $8.

YOUTH EDUCATION/ENTERTAINMENT SERIES, MORGAN-WIXSON THEATRE   Accomplished performances of children's theater are held on Saturdays and Sundays. 2627 Pico Boulevard, Santa Monica; ☎ 310-828-7519; **www.morgan-wixson.org;** admission $7 adults, $5 children and seniors. Los Angeles Philharmonic Symphonies for Youth To introduce 6- to 12-year-olds to symphonic music, reserve early for one of the Philharmonic's Symphonies for Youth, typically held seven times a year. The daytime weekend concerts start with hands-on preconcert activities such as art projects and instrument demonstrations; the concert features music that appeals to children. Preschool children get their own performances at the Open House Series. Walt Disney Concert Hall, Music Center, 111 South Grand Avenue, downtown LA, ☎ 323-850-2000; **www.laphil.org;** admission $20.

STORYBOOK THEATRE   *Theatre West*   Saturdays at 1 p.m., this theater near Universal Studios puts on a lively, interactive musical play aimed at children ages 3 to 8. 3333 Cahuenga Boulevard West, Universal City; ☎ 818-761-2203; **www.theatrewest.org;** admission varies.

STORYOPOLIS   We know childless adults who hang out at this newly relocated children's art gallery and bookstore—that's how wonderful it is. You'll find original works and limited-edition prints from the finest artists in children's literature, as well as high-quality books; on Saturdays, children gather for craft workshops, story hours, and author signings. 14945 Ventura Boulevard, Sherman Oaks; ☎ 818-509-5600; **www.storyopolis.com;** admission $6 for Saturday events, otherwise free.

SUMMERSOUNDS AT THE HOLLYWOOD BOWL   A superb summer program that combines hands-on activities (puppet making, folk-dancing lessons) with performances, aimed at children ages 3 to 10. After a jazz concert, for instance, children will make their own instruments. Performances are Monday through Friday, 10 a.m. and 11:15 a.m., early July to mid-August; prices by event. Top of Highland Avenue, Hollywood; ☎ 323-850-2000; **www.hollywoodbowl.org.**

WILL GEER THEATRICUM BOTANICUM   Theater settings don't get much better than this—a natural amphitheater space set in the oaks and eucalyptus of Topanga Canyon. This is a serious theater company with first-rate actors, but many of its productions are family-friendly, particularly the Shakespeare comedies, which have captivated our kids; look for the special productions that include a preshow discussion, which really helps everyone understand what's going on. The classes and summer camps for young people are renowned. 1419 North Topanga Canyon Boulevard, Topanga; ☎ 310-455-2322; **www.theatricum.com.**

THE SOUTH BAY:
Manhattan Beach to Long Beach

SOUTH OF LOS ANGELES INTERNATIONAL AIRPORT is a string of beach communities linked by the 405 freeway: **Manhattan Beach, Hermosa Beach, Redondo Beach, Torrance, San Pedro,** and **Long Beach.** They're better known for their suburbia than their tourist appeal, but if you're seeking a fun beach day, some of these towns make for fine day trips (see "The Best Beaches and Parks"). We especially like Redondo, which has a lively pier popular with fishermen, a broad beach, and a harbor out of which run whale-watching trips. Manhattan is ideal for sun, surf, sand play, and cycling. Although San Pedro is a fairly gritty port town, full of smokestacks and cargo containers, it has real visitor value as the departing point for the Catalina ferries (see Catalina Island section) and home of the hokey but amusing **Ports o' Call Village** (a shopping and seafood area on the waterfront) and the **Cabrillo Marine Aquarium.**

> *unofficial* **TIP**
> On the bay shore in Belmont Shore is a protected sand beach that's well used by young families, thanks to its shallow, warm, wave-free water.

The largest city in this region, Long Beach, is aiming to be a world-class family destination with the **Aquarium of the Pacific.** (The *Queen Mary* has been here for years, but our kids find it a snooze.) Long Beach is also home to a miles-long beach popular with kite fliers, and the charming villages of **Belmont Shore** and **Naples**—good walking neighborhoods with canals, boutiques, restaurants, and lots of summer street life. Second Street is lots of fun for teens to stroll, shop, and people-watch.

FAMILY LODGING

Crowne Plaza Redondo Beach and Marina
300 North Harbor Drive, Redondo Beach; ☎ 800-368-9760 or 310-318-8888; www.crowneplaza.com; $216 and up; children under age 18 stay free; parking, $16 daily

THE MASSIVE SALTWATER AQUARIUM in the lobby is a kid magnet, as is Redondo's saltwater lagoon just across the street. (There's also a huge pool,

the south bay: manhattan beach to long beach

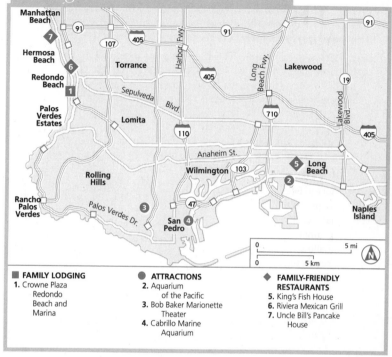

■ **FAMILY LODGING**
1. Crowne Plaza Redondo Beach and Marina

● **ATTRACTIONS**
2. Aquarium of the Pacific
3. Bob Baker Marionette Theater
4. Cabrillo Marine Aquarium

◆ **FAMILY-FRIENDLY RESTAURANTS**
5. King's Fish House
6. Riviera Mexican Grill
7. Uncle Bill's Pancake House

but it's kind of barren and not nearly as much fun as the lagoon.) Overlooking Kings Harbor, this upscale (if generic) hotel is well located for families interested in whale watching, sportfishing, biking the beach path, or enjoying summer days on Redondo Beach. Children younger than age 12 eat free in the restaurant when accompanied by a paying parent, and room service offers a kids' menu. The 339 well-maintained rooms are done in a subtle tropical style. Extras include a tennis court, bike rentals, and SeaLab, a touch-tank program for families run by the LA Conservation Corps.

ATTRACTIONS

 ## Aquarium of the Pacific

APPEAL BY AGE	PRESCHOOL ★★★	GRADE SCHOOL ★★★★	TEENS ★★★★
YOUNG ADULTS ★★★		OVER 30 ★★★★	SENIORS ★★★★

100 Aquarium Way (off Shoreline Drive), Long Beach; ☎ 562-590-3100; www.aquariumofpacific.org

Hours Daily, 9 a.m.–6 p.m.; closed Christmas Day. **Admission** $21 adults, $12 children ages 3–11, children under age 3 free, $18 seniors age 60 and over; parking $7. **Touring time** Average 3–4 hours; minimum 1½ hours. **Rainy-day touring** Yes. **Restaurants** Yes. **Alcoholic beverages** No. **Disabled access** Yes. **Wheelchair rental** Yes. **Baby-stroller rental** Yes. **Lockers** No. **Pet kennels** No. **Rain check** No. **Private tours** Yes.

DESCRIPTION AND COMMENTS   This huge, impressive aquarium, part of the Rainbow Harbor area of Long Beach, lies across the channel from the *Queen Mary* (the two are linked by a water taxi) and down the waterfront promenade from Shoreline Village, a charming collection of shops and restaurants. For visitors staying at any of the major Long Beach hotels, it's all part of a convenient waterfront entertainment area.

Inside the dramatic aquarium building (its roof is designed to look like waves), more than 12,500 ocean animals are on display. In the huge entry hall is a 142,000-gallon predator tank filled with leopard sharks and giant sea bass. Passageways lead to three major underwater worlds, each focusing on a different Pacific Rim marine habitat. The Southern California and Baja world is where you'll find Kid's Cove, with a touch tank and an outdoor area devoted to up-close viewing of seals and sea lions. The Northern Pacific section features exhibits of animals native to cold-water areas of Canada, Alaska, Russia, and Japan, including puffins, sea otters, and a giant octopus. The Tropical Pacific gallery has above- and below-water viewing, a tube walkway that takes visitors right through the middle of an enormous aquarium, and spectacular, colorful fish and coral. Ours kids' favorites are the Shark Lagoon and the audio-video whale exhibit that puts you in the middle of whale conversations.

Family-friendly extras include a kids-only register in the educational-goodies-packed store; such special events as Grandparents' Morning and kayak expeditions; the 3-D film *Monsters of the Abyss*; and a changing roster of interactive, staff-supervised activities throughout the facility.

Cabrillo Marine Aquarium

APPEAL BY AGE	PRESCHOOL ★★★	GRADE SCHOOL ★★★★	TEENS ★★★
YOUNG ADULTS ★★★	OVER 30 ★★★		SENIORS ★★★

3720 Stephen White Drive (off Pacific Avenue and 36th Street), San Pedro; ☎ 310-548-7562; www.cabrilloaq.org

Hours Tuesday–Friday, noon–5 p.m.; Saturday and Sunday, 10 a.m.–5 p.m. **Admission** Free; suggested donation, $5 adults, $1 children and seniors; parking, $7 per car. **Touring time** Average 1½ hours; minimum 45 minutes. **Rainy-day touring** Yes. **Restaurants** No. **Alcoholic beverages** No. **Disabled access** Yes. **Wheelchair rental** Yes; call ahead for beach wheelchairs. **Baby-stroller rental** No. **Lockers** No. **Pet kennels** No. **Rain check** No. **Private tours** No.

DESCRIPTION AND COMMENTS   More modest than the grandiose Aquarium of the Pacific in nearby Long Beach, this collection of sea life is also much less crowded, which counts for a lot. To do this place right, bring a picnic lunch and plan on spending much of the day here. First, spend a couple of hours playing, exploring, and swimming at adjacent Cabrillo Beach. Then, after lunch head into the aquarium to delve deeper into local sea life. They'll see all the critters that share the Pacific with us, from corbina fish to moray eels to leopard sharks; they'll touch sea stars and anemones at the touch tank; they'll feel whale bones and shark skin; and they can marvel up close at the life-size models of a killer whale and dolphin. Ask about the seasonal grunion runs and the guided tours of the nearby marine refuge during very low tides.

FAMILY-FRIENDLY RESTAURANTS

King's Fish House
100 West Broadway, Long Beach; ☎ 562-432-7463; www.kingsfishhouse.com

Meals served Lunch and dinner. **Cuisine** American, seafood. **Entree range** Lunch, $10–$20; dinner, $14–$45. **Kids' menu** Yes. **Reservations** Recommended. **Payment** All major credit cards.

IN THE HEART OF "OLD" DOWNTOWN Long Beach, close to the Aquarium of the Pacific, King's is the best seafood restaurant in these parts, offering everything from clam chowder and tuna sandwiches to Ecuadorean mahimahi and live Maine lobster—or, for the less adventurous, burgers and chicken parmigiana. Good kids' menu, handsome setting, professional service, and some tables out on the sidewalk.

Riviera Mexican Grill
1615 South Pacific Coast Highway, Redondo Beach; ☎ 310-540-2501

Meals served Lunch and dinner. **Cuisine** Mexican. **Entree range** Lunch, $6–$10; dinner, $8–$20. **Kids' menu** Yes. **Reservations** Recommended on weekends. **Payment** All major credit cards.

FRESH, TASTY, MODERN, surfer-style Mexican food—shrimp tacos, creative quesadillas—is the order of the day in this lively grill a block from Redondo Beach. It's filled with surf photos and memorabilia, which charms kids, and the patio is perfect for summer evenings.

Uncle Bill's Pancake House
1305 Highland Avenue, Manhattan Beach; ☎ 310-545-5177

Meals served Breakfast and lunch. **Cuisine** American. **Entree range** $6–$11. **Kids' menu** Yes. **Reservations** Not accepted. **Payment** All major credit cards.

OCEAN VIEWS, LOW PRICES, great waffles and pancakes—it's no wonder there's always a wait at Uncle Bill's, a funky old coffee shop that's legendary in these parts. Try to visit during the week when the wait isn't as bad.

CATALINA ISLAND

BOTH A ROMANTIC'S RETREAT and a hugely popular summertime family destination, this island is a great escape for two or three days. Centered on the dinky town of **Avalon,** life here is outdoors and active: swimming at the small beaches, snorkeling and diving in the crystal-clear waters, boating, fishing, cycling, and hiking or horseback riding into the rugged backcountry. You can wear shorts just about anywhere, and the kids never seem to get all the sand out of their hair. Beyond the one square mile of Avalon, there's nothing but wilderness, except for the tiny village of **Two Harbors,** a popular campsite and boat harbor.

The fastest seagoing way to reach Catalina is on the high-speed ferries (75 to 90 minutes) run by **Catalina Express** (☎ 800-481-3470 or 310-519-1212; **www.catalinaexpress.com**), out of San Pedro or Long Beach, or the Catalina Flyer (☎ 800-830-7744; or 949-673-5245 **www.catalinainfo.com**) out of Newport Beach. For general Catalina information, links to **Discovery Tours,** and other Catalina Island Company offerings, go to **www.scico.com.**

OUTDOOR ACTION

BOATING/WATERCRAFT You can rent every watercraft imaginable: kayak, Jet Ski, pedal boat, raft, even paddleboard; our kids have had lots of fun kayaking around the harbor. **Joe's Rent-a-Boat** on the pier (☎ 310-510-0455; **www.catalina.com/rent-a-boat.html**) is a good vendor.

CRUISES Several one-hour cruises are good for families, including a cruise to **Seal Rock** ($12 to $16) and a night cruise to see flying fish ($15 to $20). Tickets available at mainland boat terminals and at the pier, boat landing, and **Discovery Tours Center** on the island (☎ 310-510-TOUR; **www.scico.com/avalon/Tours.php**).

CYCLING Bikes are rented at concessions for riding around town. There's great mountain biking inland, but you have to spend $90 for an annual family permit from the **Catalina Island Conservancy** (125 Claressa Avenue; ☎ 310-510-2595, ext. 100; **www.catalinaconservancy.org**).

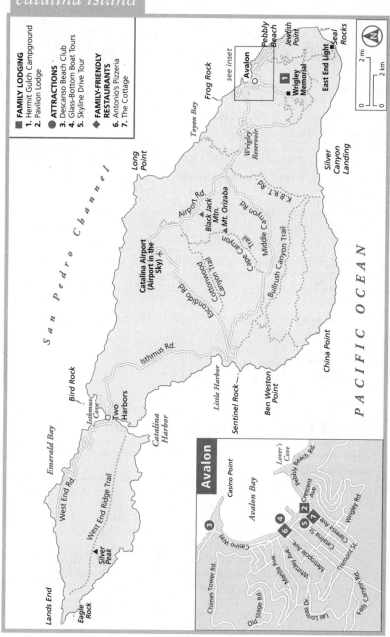

catalina island

FAMILY LODGING
1. Hermit Gulch Campground
2. Pavilion Lodge

ATTRACTIONS
3. Descanso Beach Club
4. Glass-Bottom Boat Tours
5. Skyline Drive Tour

FAMILY-FRIENDLY RESTAURANTS
6. Antonio's Pizzeria
7. The Cottage

San Pedro Channel

Long Point

Toyon Bay

Frog Rock

see inset

Avalon

Pebbly Beach

Jewfish Point

Seal Rocks

Wrigley Memorial

East End Light

2 mi

2 km

Wrigley Reservoir

Silver Canyon Landing

Airport Rd.

Black Jack Mtn.

Mt. Orizaba

K.B.R.T. Rd.

Middle Canyon Rd.

Catalina Airport (Airport in the Sky)

Cottonwood Canyon Trail

Cape Canyon Trail

Bullrush Canyon Trail

Escondido Rd.

PACIFIC OCEAN

China Point

Isthmus Rd.

Bird Rock

Isthmus Cove

Two Harbors

Catalina Harbor

Little Harbor

Sentinel Rock

Ben Weston Point

Emerald Bay

West End Rd.

West End Ridge Trail

Silver Peak

Lands End

Eagle Rock

Avalon

Casino Point

Lover's Cove

Avalon Bay

Pebbly Beach Rd.

Crescent Ave.

Wrigley Rd.

Catalina St.

Claressa Ave.

Casino Way

Chimes Tower Rd.

Old Stage Rd.

Maiille Ave.

Whittley Ave.

Metropole Ave.

Tremont St.

Las Lomas Dr.

Falls Canyon Rd.

FISHING   Kids ages 10 and up won't soon forget the thrill of reeling in a 25-pound white sea bass or bluefin tuna. Of the many fishing charters in Avalon, we like **Afishinado Charters** (☎ 323-447-4669; **www.afishinados.com**).

GOLF CARTING   Families with toddlers might enjoy a one-hour golf-cart ride around Avalon, although there isn't a lot of territory to cover. You must be 25 or older to rent. Go to **Cartopia Golf Cart Rental** (☎ 310-510-2493).

HIKING   The trails can be pretty intense here, so keep walks with young children confined to the Avalon area. But if you have sturdy walkers older than age 8 or so, pick up a map and free permit from the **Catalina Island Conservancy** (125 Claressa Avenue; ☎ 310-510-2595, ext. 100; **www.catalinaconservancy.org**). When you get into the interior, you may see lots of wildlife, including bald eagles and wild boar.

HORSEBACK RIDING   Families with horse-knowledgeable children older than age 8 can join guided rides into the mountains above Avalon. Call **Catalina Stables** (☎ 310-510-0478).

SNORKELING AND DIVING   Catalina Divers Supply on the pier (☎ 310-510-0330; **www.catalinadiverssupply.com**) can outfit you with gear to snorkel at Lover's Cove, found on the other side of the boat landing area. The snorkeling here is superb, and the gentle water is accommodating to very young children. Teens and parents can consider a scuba-diving lesson.

FAMILY LODGING

 ## Hermit Gulch Campground

A half mile from Avalon, at the top of Avalon Canyon (transportation by shuttle bus, by taxi, or on foot); ☎ 310-510-TENT; www.scico.com/ avalon/camp_hermitGulch.php; $6 per night for children, $12 for adults; reservations required

THIS PRIVATELY OWNED CAMPGROUND is one of many fine family camping sites on Catalina; its selling point is its proximity to the town of Avalon, a half mile away. (So what it loses in isolation, it makes up for in convenience.) It's a pleasant, surprisingly quiet location in the hills overlooking the ocean; if you don't have your own tent, you can stay in a cabin or tepee. Town is a pretty easy walk, but there's a shuttle bus, too. Barbecue pits, fire rings, picnic tables, hot showers, flush toilets, hiking trails.

Pavilion Lodge
513 Crescent Avenue, Avalon; ☎ 800-851-0217 or 310-510-1788; www.pavilionlodge.com; $258–$309; children age 11 and under stay free in parents' room

WHEN THE WEATHER'S FINE, families pack into this renovated 73-room motel a few feet from the beach. There are no suites, but rooms are large enough for a small family, and some rooms connect. Room rates include beach towels, Continental breakfast, HBO and Disney Channel on the TV, Internet access, and mini-refrigerators. Restaurants, shops, and the beach are a stone's throw away.

ATTRACTIONS

Descanso Beach Club

APPEAL BY AGE	PRESCHOOL ★★★★	GRADE SCHOOL ★★★★	TEENS ★★★★
YOUNG ADULTS ★★★		OVER 30 ★★★	SENIORS ★★★

1 Descanso Way (just past casino building), Avalon; ☎ 310-510-7410

Hours Daily, 11 a.m.–6 p.m.; Friday and Saturday BYOB barbecue Memorial Day–October, 6–9 p.m.; closed mid-October–mid-April. **Admission** $2 for beach; everything else free. **Touring time** Average 3–4 hours; minimum 1 hour. **Rainy-day touring** No, closed for rain. **Restaurants** Yes. **Alcoholic beverages** Yes. **Disabled access** Yes. **Wheelchair rental** Patio and grass area only. **Baby-stroller rental** No, chairs only. **Lockers** Yes. **Pet kennels** No. **Rain check** No. **Private tours** No.

DESCRIPTION AND COMMENTS   If main Crescent Beach gets too crowded, consider a beach day at this private club on the other side of the casino; you can become a "member" for just $2 a day. You can rent everything from beach chairs to rafts to kayaks to snorkeling gear. The beach is large and pretty, with tiny waves, lawns and rough sand, and clear, clear water. Showers, changing rooms, lifeguards, and full food and bar service.

Glass-Bottom Boat Tours

APPEAL BY AGE	PRESCHOOL ★★★	GRADE SCHOOL ★★★★	TEENS ★★★
YOUNG ADULTS ★★★		OVER 30 ★★★	SENIORS ★★★

Discovery Tours, Green Pleasure Pier, Avalon; ☎ 800-851-0217

Hours Daily, 10 a.m.–5 p.m.; conditional on weather and visibility. **Admission** $16 adults, $12 age 11 and under. **Touring time** Average 40–45 minutes. **Rainy-day touring** Yes. **Restaurants** No. **Alcoholic beverages** No. **Disabled access** Yes. **Wheelchair rental** No. **Baby-stroller rental** No. **Lockers** No. **Pet kennels** No. **Rain check** No. **Private tours** No.

DESCRIPTION AND COMMENTS   To get a glimpse of why Catalina is a diver's paradise, take this 45-minute boat tour to meet the local sea life. The water is amazingly clear, and when you get over to the kelp beds, you'll see vivid orange garibaldi, yellow giant kelpfish, bat rays, bass, maybe even a sea lion or some dolphins. The night cruise is cool, offering a look at nocturnal fish. The same company runs semisubmersible boat tours, but they aren't worth the substantial extra bucks.

Skyline Drive Tour

APPEAL BY AGE	PRESCHOOL ★★★	GRADE SCHOOL ★★★★	TEENS ★★★
YOUNG ADULTS ★★★		OVER 30 ★★★	SENIORS ★★★

Leaves from Island Plaza, Avalon; ☎ 800-851-0217

Hours *Summer:* tours 11 a.m., 1 p.m., and 3 p.m.; fewer off-season. **Admission** $34 adults, $30.50 seniors age 55 and over, $25.50 children ages 2–11; tickets available from kiosks around the island and at the mainland terminal. **Touring time** Average 3 hours; minimum 1 hour. **Rainy-day touring** Yes. **Restaurants** No. **Alcoholic beverages** No. **Disabled access** No. **Wheelchair rental** Yes. **Baby-stroller rental** No. **Lockers** No. **Pet kennels** No. **Rain check** No. **Private tours** No.

DESCRIPTION AND COMMENTS   First-timers to Catalina should take the two-hour narrated tour. It introduces you to the natural environment, animal life, and geography of the island. Kids love taking the ride and looking for wild boar and buffalo, and you'll love the views. Midway, everyone gets out for a leg stretch, so kids can blow off steam and see the nature center at the Island Conservancy. Reservations are essential in the busy season.

FAMILY-FRIENDLY RESTAURANTS

Antonio's Pizzeria
230 Crescent Avenue, Avalon; ☎ 310-510-0008;
www.catalinahotspots.com

Meals served Breakfast, lunch, and dinner; call ahead because hours vary. **Cuisine** Italian. **Entree range** Lunch and dinner, $9–$25. **Kids' menu** No. **Reservations** Accepted for large parties. **Payment** AE, MC, V.

THE FOOD'S A BIT ON THE HEAVY SIDE—pizzas, spaghetti with meat sauce, meatball sandwiches—but the setting is kid-friendly, with peanut shells on the floor and country music on the stereo.

The Cottage
118 Catalina Avenue, Avalon; ☎ 310-510-0726;
www.menu4u.com/thecottage

Meals served Breakfast, lunch, and dinner; closed December–January. **Cuisine** American. **Entree range** Breakfast, $7–$10; lunch, $10–$19; dinner $10–$21. **Kids' menu** Yes. **Reservations** Not accepted. **Payment** Personal checks and cash only.

YOU NAME IT, they'll make it: omelets and pancakes of any description, waffles, Mexican dishes, sandwiches—the menu is vast, and most of the food is just fine. The fresh-fruit pancakes are particularly good. Breakfast is served all day.

LOS ANGELES:
Westside

IT HAS CONSIDERABLY FEWER ATTRACTIONS and museums than central LA, but the Westside is our favorite family-vacation base nonetheless. Development in recent years has favored the pedestrian, so you can now stroll from your Ocean Avenue hotel to the **Santa Monica Pier** and its amusement park, to the beach, to the walking path along **Palisades Park,** the bluff overlooking the beach, and to a wealth of restaurants, shops, movie theaters, and small amusements, many of which are found on the car-free Third Street Promenade and the indoor mall across the street. The **Tide Shuttle** minibus (50¢) operates every 15 minutes among downtown Santa Monica, the beach, and the promenade. Active families can hop on bikes and ride the bike path down to **Venice Beach** and even on to the **South Bay.**

unofficial **TIP**
In the car-crazed LA area, we recommend choosing a hotel in **Santa Monica,** where you can actually stay quite happily without a car.

From the Santa Monica area, downtown LA is 30 minutes by freeway, Disneyland is about an hour, and Hollywood and Universal Studios are 30 to 40 minutes away. That's assuming that the freeways aren't congested, which seems increasingly rare, so factor in more time if you're traveling even remotely near rush hours. For a prettier drive, head north on the Pacific Coast Highway toward Malibu to explore some of the beaches and parks (see "The Best Beaches and Parks").

FAMILY LODGING

Best Western Jamaica Bay Inn
4175 Admiralty Way, Marina del Rey; ☎ 888-823-5333 or 310-823-5333; www.bestwestern-jamaicabay.com; $179–$279

YOUNG FAMILIES GET AN EXCELLENT location-to-price ratio here: this upscale motel is right on Marina del Rey's Mother's Beach. Many of the 42 rooms in the low-slung two-story building have patios or balconies overlooking the marina, and the rooms with two queen beds are large enough to handle a family (some have microwaves and refrigerators). Outside are

los angeles: westside

N1

2

13

27

TOPANGA STATE PARK

405

West-wood

Brentwood

8

Sunset Blvd.

SOLSTICE CANYON PARK

v1

PACIFIC PALISADES

Pacific Coast Hwy.

To
← 6

1

19 22

West Los Angeles

0   3 mi
0   3 km

Santa Monica Bay

MALIBU

Santa Monica

Lincoln Blvd.

Ocean Park

Venice

see inset at left

To 18→

San Vicente Blvd.

Pacific Coast Hwy

Lincoln Blvd.

4th St.

Montana Ave.

26th St.

16

Santa Monica

Wilshire Blvd.

21

18 12

20

Santa Monica Blvd.

2

9

Colorado Ave.

17

Olympic Blvd.

10

11

14

1

Pico Blvd.

10 →

Santa Monica Pier

3

5

Ocean Park Blvd.

4

1

Main St.

Rose Ave.

23

Abbot Kinney Blvd.

Lincoln Blvd.

Walgrove Ave.

Pacific Ave.

Venice Blvd.

187

Venice

7

Washington Blvd.

Venice Pier

1

1

Admiralty Way

15

Marina del Rey

Marina del Rey

0   1 mi
0   1 km

■ FAMILY LODGING

1. Best Western Jamaica Bay Inn
2. Circle X Ranch Campground
3. Loews Santa Monica Beach Hotel
4. Sea Shore Motel
5. Shutters on the Beach
6. Sycamore Canyon Campground

● ATTRACTIONS

7. The Cove Skatepark
8. The Getty Center
9. Magicopolis
10. Museum of Tolerance
11. Pacific Park
12. Santa Monica Playhouse
13. Will Geer Theatricum Botanicum
14. Santa Monica Pier Aquarium

◆ FAMILY-FRIENDLY RESTAURANTS

15. Aunt Kizzy's Back Porch
16. Back on the Beach
17. Broadway Deli
18. California Pizza Kitchen (2 locations)
19. Duke's Malibu
20. El Cholo
21. Johnnie's New York Pizza
22. Malibu Seafood
23. Typhoon

a playground, a small pool, a spa, a lawn, a coffee shop, bike rental, and an excellent beach for young children.

Circle X Ranch Campground

12898 Yerba Buena Road, Malibu; reservations ☎ 805-370-2300, ext. 1702; www.nps.gov/samo; $2 per person per night

A HIDEAWAY IN THE SANTA MONICA MOUNTAINS, this national-park group campground is more ranchlike than beachy, but it's popular with surfers because the beach is a short drive away. Amenities include a swimming pool, basketball courts, drinking water, toilets, barbecues (charcoal only; no wood), and miles of hiking trails to wonderful locations, including grottoes, subterranean caverns, and a waterfall; there's plenty of easy hiking for little ones.

Loews Santa Monica Beach Hotel

1700 Ocean Avenue, Santa Monica; ☎ 800-23-LOEWS or 310-458-6700; www.loewshotels.com; $350–$600, suites $850–950

FAMILIES ARE ACTIVELY COURTED at this 342-room, atrium-style beachfront resort. The pool is huge and kid-friendly, the concierge will provide babysitters, kids can borrow games and DVDs from the lending library, the Santa Monica Pier is a short walk down the beach, and a concession rents kid-size bikes (the great Santa Monica bike path is right out front). You'll also find a beach playground and children's menus for both the restaurant and room service. Rooms are modern, comfortable, and well equipped.

Sea Shore Motel

2637 Main Street, Santa Monica; ☎ 310-392-2787; www.seashoremotel.com; $105–$275

YOU CAN'T BEAT THE LOCATION and family-friendliness for the money at this fairly basic motel. It's on the north end of Main Street, the shopping-dining-browsing street that's great fun for teens to explore, and Ocean Park beach is a two-block walk. (It's also close to the Sunday-morning Farmers' Market, a particularly kid-friendly market with face painting, kiddie rides, and live music.) The best deals are the one-bedroom apartments with full kitchens (including dishwashers) and comfortable living rooms with balconies. Extras include free parking (a big asset around here), free Wi-Fi, a laundromat next door, and a location on the route of the Tide Shuttle—a zippy 50¢ bus that will take you to the Third Street Promenade and Venice Beach.

Shutters on the Beach

1 Pico Boulevard, Santa Monica; ☎ 800-334-9000 or 310-458-0030; www.shuttersonthebeach.com; $520–$825

THE ONLY LA-AREA HOTEL that sits right on the sand, Shutters is a luxury lodging, its gray shingles and white trim and shutters evoking a grand Cape Cod beach house. It has ceded the kid's-club market to neighboring competitor Loews, but many families still choose this place, willing to give up family amenities for Shutters' architecture, service, art collection, and location. There's a lovely ocean-view pool with poolside service, and a concession that rents adult- and kid-size bikes. The concierge can supply sand toys and babysitters, and the restaurant's children's menu is available for room service as well. Rooms are beautiful, done in pale ocean colors, with sliding shutters opening to small balconies.

 ## Sycamore Canyon Campground

Point Mugu State Park (off Pacific Coast Highway north of Deer Creek Road), Malibu; ☎ 818-880-0350; parks.ca.gov; reservations: Reserve America, ☎ 800-444-7275; www.reserveamerica.com; campsites $25

A CLEAN, SAFE, BEAUTIFUL family beach retreat in the LA area, near multimillion-dollar movie-star houses—for $20 a night? Yes, that's the happy truth about this campground in north Malibu. This former Chumash Native American settlement sits at the mouth of a canyon, a site that keeps visitors warm in winter and cool in summer. It's a short walk to a gorgeous white-sand beach, known for frequent visits from dolphins; in the canyon itself, you'll find sycamores, wild roses, monarch butterflies, a stream, and poison oak, so watch out on hikes. If you don't feel like cooking, drive a couple of miles south to Neptune's Net, a good ocean-side seafood shanty. Because of all this, the campground is extremely popular, so reserve very early. Best times are in spring wildflower season and in late summer after the June gloom burns off.

 # ATTRACTIONS

 ## The Cove Skatepark

APPEAL BY AGE	PRESCHOOL –	GRADE SCHOOL ★★★★	TEENS ★★★★½
YOUNG ADULTS ★★★		OVER 30 ★★	SENIORS ½

Memorial Park, 1401 Olympic Boulevard, Santa Monica; ☎ 310-458-8228; www.smgov.net/comm_progs/skatepark

Hours *Summer:* Daily, 11 a.m.–10 p.m.; *winter:* hours vary, so call first; park subject to closure for rain. **Admission** Adult nonresidents $5.50, adult residents $5, children ages 6–17 $3; quarterly and annual passes available. **Touring time** Average 2 hours; minimum 1 hour. **Rainy-day touring** No. **Restaurants** No. **Alcoholic beverages** No. **Disabled access** Yes. **Wheelchair rental** No. **Baby-stroller rental** No. **Lockers** No. **Pet kennels** No. **Rain check** No. **Private tours** No.

DESCRIPTION AND COMMENTS   With 20,000 square feet of concrete bowls, stairs and rails, this is a first-rate public skate park and a must-visit for families with skaters. Kids have to be at least age 6 to skate or bike here, parents must first sign a liability release, and helmets and protective gear are required (but not supplied, so bring your own). The day is broken into three sessions; the early one is for smaller kids, the afternoon one is for midlevel skaters, and evenings are usually filled with more aggressive, older skaters.

 The Getty Center

APPEAL BY AGE	PRESCHOOL ★★★	GRADE SCHOOL ★★★★½	TEENS ★★★★
YOUNG ADULTS ★★★★½		OVER 30 ★★★★½	SENIORS ★★★★½

1200 Getty Center Drive, off the 405 freeway; ☎ 310-440-7300; www.getty.edu

Hours Sunday, Tuesday–Thursday, 10 a.m.–6 p.m.; Friday and Saturday, 10 a.m.–9 p.m. **Admission** Free, but parking is $8 (cash only). **Touring time** Average 3–4 hours; minimum 1 hour. **Rainy-day touring** Yes. **Restaurants** Yes. **Alcoholic beverages** Yes. **Disabled access** Yes. **Wheelchair rental** Yes, free. **Baby-stroller rental** Yes, free. **Lockers** No. **Pet kennels** No. **Rain check** No. **Private tours** No; museum tours daily.

DESCRIPTION AND COMMENTS   Perched like a Pacific Rim Parthenon on a ridge above the San Diego Freeway, the Getty Center commands a view of the ocean on one side and miles of metropolitan Los Angeles on the other. Its Richard Meier–designed buildings, too, signal that this is a Grand and Important Place. Because the plazas and balconies are filled with visitors from all over the world, speaking different languages, it really does feel like the center of something.

If the Getty Center offered just grandeur, we wouldn't recommend it for children (what's impressive to an adult can be merely big to a 5-year-old), but the Getty is a kid-friendly place from the start. Upon arrival, patrons are whisked up the hill on a monorail, which, of course, delights children. As they disembark and enter the main plaza, kids are drawn to the outsides of the buildings, which are sheathed in sand-colored Italian travertine and embedded with fossil prints (we've spotted shells, leaves, and fish). Sometimes we rent an audio guide, which we tune to the special family track that offers stories, fun facts, and sound effects related to the artworks (as opposed to the scholarly discourse on the main track). Sometimes, we head straight for the Family Room to check out "Perplexing Paintings" or the "Getty Art Detective" game box, so that moving through the museum becomes a treasure hunt. Before or after our tour, we snap photos of the kids posed in costumes and backdrops that re-create famous paintings.

With older kids, we stop in the Art Information rooms of galleries that intrigue them and spend time doing projects or playing with interactive exhibits. Weekend workshops that combine gallery visits with art projects are offered for children ages 5 to 13 accompanied by a parent (sign up at the information desk in the entrance hall).

Magicopolis

APPEAL BY AGE	PRESCHOOL ★	GRADE SCHOOL ★★★★	TEENS ★★★★
YOUNG ADULTS ★★★★		OVER 30 ★★★★	SENIORS ★★★★

**1418 Fourth Street, Santa Monica; ☎ 310-451-2241;
www.magicopolis.com**

Hours Showtimes vary but are generally Tuesday–Sunday evenings with matinees on weekends. **Admission** Ticket prices range from $22 to $27 depending on the show. **Touring time** Average 2 hours; minimum 1 hour. **Rainy-day touring** Yes. **Restaurants** Snack bar. **Alcoholic beverages** No. **Disabled access** Yes. **Wheelchair rental** No. **Baby-stroller rental** No. **Lockers** No. **Pet kennels** No. **Rain check** No. **Private tours** Birthday parties.

DESCRIPTION AND COMMENTS   This theater has been welcomed heartily by young magic-lovers in LA, because the two other showcases for the region's great pool of magic talent are nightclubs. And because a little magic appeals to everyone, Magicopolis is a good idea for any family looking for special-occasion live entertainment in a family atmosphere. Choose a show in either the 150-seat theater or the 50-seat close-up theater. Some famous and soon-to-be famous performers can be seen here, and performances range from the traditional to the more modern and innovative.

 Museum of Tolerance

APPEAL BY AGE	PRESCHOOL ★	GRADE SCHOOL ★★★	TEENS ★★★★½
YOUNG ADULTS ★★★★½		OVER 30 ★★★★½	SENIORS ★★★★½

**9786 West Pico Boulevard, Century City; ☎ 310-553-8403;
www.museumoftolerance.com**

Hours Monday–Friday, 10 a.m.–5 p.m.; Sunday, 11 a.m.–5:00 p.m.; closed Saturday. **Admission** $13 adults, $11 seniors, $10 students and children. **Touring time** Average 2 hours; minimum 1 hour. **Rainy-day touring** Yes. **Restaurants** Cafeteria. **Alcoholic beverages** No. **Disabled access** Yes. **Wheelchair rental** Yes, free. **Baby-stroller rental** No. **Lockers** No. **Pet kennels** No. **Rain check** No. **Private tours** Yes.

DESCRIPTION AND COMMENTS   Far too intense for young children, the Museum of Tolerance can be life-changing for middle and high schoolers. It's devoted to increasing humankind's tolerance of differences by both exploring intolerance and celebrating diversity. This is achieved through several state-of-the-art exhibits, most famously the one on the Holocaust, which left our 13-year-old both stunned and motivated to make a difference. (This exhibit is not recommended for children younger than age 12.) Other worthwhile displays include the Point of View Diner, a 1950s diner counter that "serves" high-tech, interactive displays on topics related to personal responsibility, from drunk driving to hate speech; a video wall that explores America's struggle for civil rights; and the Millennium Machine, which both illustrates the human-rights abuses going on around the world and helps visitors look for solutions. Your teens would rather be at Universal Studios, but they'll never forget a visit here.

Pacific Park

APPEAL BY AGE	PRESCHOOL ★★★★	GRADE SCHOOL ★★★★	TEENS ★★★
YOUNG ADULTS ★★		OVER 30 ★★	SENIORS ★★

380 Santa Monica Pier, Santa Monica; ☎ 310-260-8744;
www.pacpark.com

Hours *Summer:* Sunday–Thursday, 11 a.m.–11 p.m.; Friday and Saturday, 11 a.m.–12:30 a.m.; times vary after Labor Day; call for more information. **Admission** Rides $3–$5; parking $7 on weekends, less on weekdays; unlimited ride wristbands, under 42" tall, $10–$11; over 42" tall, $20–$22; discount for online ticket purchases. **Touring time** Average 2 hours; minimum 1 hour. **Rainy-day touring** No. **Restaurants** Snack bar. **Alcoholic beverages** No. **Disabled access** Yes. **Wheelchair rental** No. **Baby-stroller rental** No. **Lockers** No. **Pet kennels** No. **Rain check** No. **Private tours** No.

DESCRIPTION AND COMMENTS   A new but old-fashioned amusement park on the planks of the Santa Monica Pier, Pacific Park is a fun beach excursion, if only for the coastline view from the Ferris wheel. If your children are younger than 10, come as close as possible to opening time, when the crowds are minimal and the clientele is other young families; late afternoon and evening draw swarms of teens and young adults on dates. Its small size makes it not too overwhelming for little ones, who get their own area on the shore side of the pier: bumper cars, mini–Ferris wheel, imitation Dumbo ride, and such. Older kids get a short but fast roller coaster, a couple of other modest thrills, and video-arcade games; steer them away from the outrageously expensive "skill" games. Don't miss the wonderful old indoor carousel on the other end of the parking lot, and allow extra time for running around the vast sandy expanse of Santa Monica Beach.

Santa Monica Pier Aquarium

APPEAL BY AGE	PRESCHOOL ★★★	GRADE SCHOOL ★★★★	TEENS ★★★
YOUNG ADULTS ★★★		OVER 30 ★★★	SENIORS ★★★

Under the pier, 1600 Ocean Front Walk, Santa Monica;
☎ 310-393-6149; www.healthebay.org/smpa

Hours Tuesday–Friday, 2–6 p.m.; Saturday and Sunday, 12:30–6 p.m. **Admission** $5 suggested for adults and children over 12; free for children 12 and under with adult. **Touring time** Average 1 hour; minimum ½ hour. **Rainy-day touring** Yes. **Restaurants** No. **Alcoholic Beverages** No. **Disabled access** Yes. **Wheelchair rental** No. **Baby-stroller rental** No. **Lockers** No. **Pet kennels** No. **Rain check** No. **Private tours** No.

DESCRIPTION AND COMMENTS   This small and very friendly under-the-pier aquarium is run by Heal the Bay, the homegrown nonprofit that has had a huge impact in reducing pollution along Southern California beaches. It has excellent touch tanks, a good octopus aquarium and a big tank that shows what the sea life looks like right under the pier. Weekday mornings are devoted to school field trips, and weekend mornings are hugely popular with local families for birthday parties.

FAMILY-FRIENDLY RESTAURANTS

Aunt Kizzy's Back Porch
Villa Marina, 523 Washington Boulevard, Marina del Rey;
☎ **310-578-1005; www.auntkizzys.com**

Meals served Lunch, dinner, and Sunday brunch. **Cuisine** Southern American. **Entree range** Lunch, $9–$17; dinner, $10–$19; all-you-can-eat brunch, $17. **Kids' menu** Yes. **Reservations** Not accepted. **Payment** All major credit cards.

BURSTING WITH LIVELINESS and conviviality, Aunt Kizzy's is a great place for a casual, hearty family meal: meat loaf, fried chicken, peach cobbler, and lemonade. The children's menu lets kids have the same good food the adults are having, only in smaller portions. Expect a wait on weekends.

Back on the Beach
445 Pacific Coast Highway, Santa Monica; ☎ **310-393-8282;**
www.backonthebeach.com

Meals served Breakfast, lunch, and dinner. **Cuisine** American. **Entree range** Breakfast and lunch, $6–$13; dinner, $6–$18. **Kids' menu** Lunch and dinner menu only. **Reservations** For 6 or more, inside only. **Payment** AE, MC, V.

THE FOOD IS BASIC, but stick to eggs-and-pancakes fare, which is what most kids want anyway, and you'll get a good, inexpensive breakfast right on the sand, with a swing set structure nearby to boot. We know families who start their weekends with breakfast here, then take advantage of the parking and restroom and spend the whole day on the beach. Sometime in 2009, Back on the Beach will become part of the new Annenberg Community Beach Club at the site of the old Marion Davies estate next door, but it will still be the same unfussy place.

Broadway Deli
1457 Third Street Promenade, Santa Monica; ☎ **310-451-0616;**
www.broadwaydeli.com

Meals served Breakfast, lunch, and dinner. **Cuisine** American/Californian. **Entree range** Breakfast, $8–$18; lunch and dinner, $8–$25. **Kids' menu** Yes. **Reservations** Not accepted. **Payment** All major credit cards.

MORE A YUPPIE DINER than a deli, this teeming place on the edge of the Promenade packs 'em in for everything from omelets and coffee to frou-frou California pizzas and Bordeaux wines. The huge booths can handle big families, the noise level is forgiving, and the children's menu offers all the standards and then some.

California Pizza Kitchen

11677 San Vicente Boulevard, Brentwood; ☎ 310-826-3573
210 Wilshire Boulevard, Santa Monica; ☎ 310-393-9335; www.cpk.com

Meals served Lunch and dinner. **Cuisine** Californian. **Entree range** $10–$20. **Kids' menu** Yes. **Reservations** Accepted for large parties. **Payment** All major credit cards.

THERE'S SOMETHING FOR EVERYONE at this slick chain. We like the shrimp-scampi pizza, field-green salads, wine by the glass, and the modest prices. Our kids like the mini-pizzas, the coloring menus, the booths, and the kid's drinks in take-home cups, complete with lids and bendy straws.

Duke's Malibu

21150 Pacific Coast Highway, Malibu; ☎ 310-317-0777;
www.dukesmalibu.com

Meals served Lunch, dinner, and Sunday brunch. **Cuisine** American, seafood. **Entree range** Lunch, $9–$14; dinner, $18–$35; Sunday buffet brunch, $24. **Kids' menu** Yes. **Reservations** Recommended. **Payment** All major credit cards.

DUKE'S MALIBU IS DEVOTED to the father of surfing, Duke Kahanamoku. Beautifully located right on top of the Malibu ocean, Duke's is a casual, lively place decorated with old surfboards and surf photos, offering modern surf 'n' turf fare: a mighty fine Caesar salad and straight-forward grilled Hawaiian fish, with burgers and the like for kids. If you're headed south, check out the Duke's in Huntington Beach, also right on the beach.

unofficial **TIP**
If your kids are enamored of surf culture, bring them to Duke's, a swell Malibu branch of the popular Waikiki original.

El Cholo

1025 Wilshire Boulevard, Santa Monica;
☎ 310-899-1106; www.elcholo.com

Meals served Lunch and dinner. **Cuisine** Mexican. **Entree range** $7–$16. **Kids' menu** Yes. **Reservations** Necessary. **Payment** All major credit cards.

THE ORIGINAL EL CHOLO, in the heart of central LA, is loved by several generations of Angelenos for its tasty Cal-Mex food and margaritas; this sprawling branch in Santa Monica continues the tradition honorably. Tile work, fountains, plants, and painted walls are the set, costumed waitresses are the performers, and families crowd in for the chips 'n' guac, saucy cheese enchiladas, fajitas, soft tacos, and other nonauthentic but nonetheless-delicious classics.

Johnnie's New York Pizza

1444 Third Street Promenade, Santa Monica; ☎ 310-395-9062
22333 Pacific Coast Highway, Malibu; ☎ 310-456-1717;
www.johnniesnypizza.com

Meals served Lunch and dinner. **Cuisine** Italian, pizza. **Entree range** $7–$19. **Kids' menu** No. **Reservations** Not accepted. **Payment** AE, MC, V.

JOHNNIE'S MAKES ONE of the best pizzas in LA. It's a traditional New York pizza—thin-crusted, herby, and cheesy—and it's really terrific. Both branches are noisy, casual, and New Yorkish, even if they are packed with tanned Angelenos.

Malibu Seafood
25653 Pacific Coast Highway, Malibu; ☎ 310-456-3430; www.malibuseafood.com

Meals served Lunch and dinner. **Cuisine** Seafood. **Entree range** Lunch, $3.75-$15.50; dinner $5.45-$15.50. **Reservations** No. **Payment** MC, V.

A FISH MARKET JUST ACROSS PCH from a small beach in south Malibu, Malibu Seafood is the best place on the coast for inexpensive, paper-plate fresh-seafood meals, which you take outside to a picnic table on the three-level outdoor patio blessed with amazing ocean views (it can get chilly, so bring sweatshirts). Kids will love the fish-and-chips or clam chowder in a sourdough bowl; parents often go for the ahi burger or broiled snapper; locals in the know get the crab-and-shrimp Louie, which is not on the menu but is made to order.

Typhoon
Santa Monica Airport, 3221 Donald Douglas Loop South, Santa Monica; ☎ 310-390-6565; www.typhoon.biz

Meals served Lunch and dinner; closed Saturday lunch; Sunday brunch. **Cuisine** Pacific Rim. **Entree range** Lunch, $15–$20; dinner, $15–$20. **Kids' menu** No. **Reservations** Recommended. **Payment** All major credit cards.

AT FIRST GLIMPSE, this might not seem like a great family restaurant, what with the serious bar (featuring the sorts of Technicolor drinks that have the word "killer" in their names) and preponderance of beautiful people. But take a second look, and you and your kids will love it. Request a table by the windows or on the balcony overlooking the runway of Santa Monica Airport, which still looks as if it could be the set for the airport in *Casablanca;* the kids will love watching the small planes take off, and if you time it right, you might get a great sunset to boot. The menu wanders the Asian continent, offering everything from Thai *satay* to Filipino chicken *adobo* to Korean barbecue, and it's all terrific; for kids who find such exotica yucky, there are simple noodles and delicious egg rolls. Yuckiest of all are the insect dishes—really!—which will surely fascinate your kids. Just knowing this place serves Manchurian ants and Thai-style crispy sea worms is cool, even if you don't try them.

CENTRAL LOS ANGELES

"CENTRAL" LOS ANGELES as we're describing it here is not a neighborhood in any way—in fact, we'll be touching on sights and attractions in **Hollywood, West Hollywood, Wilshire Center,** downtown, **Exposition Park, Griffith Park,** and **Universal City.** But all of these communities are geographically contiguous in a mostly flatland area best defined by freeway boundaries: the Santa Monica Freeway is to the south, the Ventura Freeway to the north, the Hollywood Freeway to the east, and the San Diego Freeway to the west. It's home to many of LA's major museums and cultural centers as well as a multicultural triangle of eating/shopping districts: **Chinatown, Little Tokyo,** and **Olvera Street.** Finally, it contains one of California's premier theme parks, the movie lovers' **Universal Studios,** which is a better Hollywood destination than the actual Hollywood itself.

unofficial **TIP**
Now that the Hollywood Roosevelt Hotel has gone hipster, we don't even recommend staying in Hollywood. Universal City, downtown, or the area just east of Beverly Hills makes a better home base for families.

FAMILY LODGING

 Four Seasons Hotel Los Angeles at Beverly Hills

300 South Doheny Drive, LA; ☎ 800-819-5053 or 310-273-2222; www.fourseasons.com; $405–$555; suites $625–$5,500

THE FOUR SEASONS PEOPLE know how to cater to kids, and this elegant hotel succeeds in making both children and movie stars happy. The location, on the eastern border of Beverly Hills, is terrific, and the 284 rooms and 42 suites are appointed with every convenience and luxury. The pool area is one of the most glamorous in LA, with a view over palm-tree tops across the city. In spite of being a major power hangout, it's a great place for families ready to do the upscale thing. Gift bags are given to children upon check-in, and milk and cookies are served to them that night. A babysitter service is available, and tasty kids' menus are offered through room service, at the elegant restaurant, and at the acclaimed Sunday brunch.

downtown los angeles

■ **FAMILY LODGING**
1. Millennium Biltmore
      Hotel Los Angeles

● **ATTRACTIONS**
2. California Science Center
3. Dodger Stadium Tour
4. Los Angeles Central Library
5. Olvera Street
6. Walt Disney Concert Hall
7. The Watts Tower of Simon
      Rodia State Historic Park

◆ **FAMILY-FRIENDLY RESTAURANT**
8. Empress Pavilion

Information ⓘ
Parking 🅿

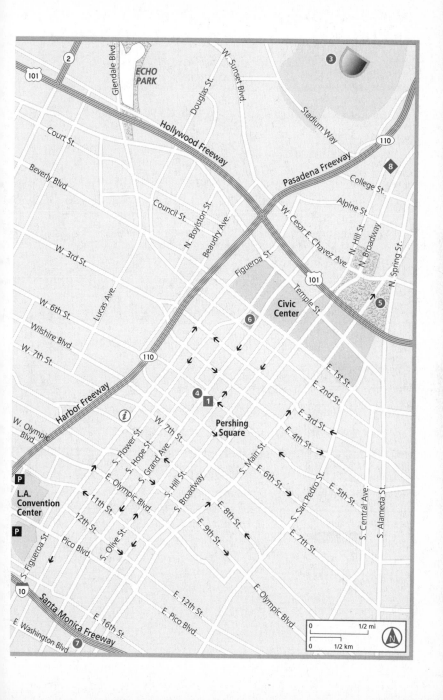

ECHO
PARK

101
2

Glendale Blvd.

Douglas St.

W. Sunset Blvd.

Stadium Way

3

110

8

Court St.

Hollywood Freeway

Pasadena Freeway

College St.

Beverly Blvd.

Alpine St.

Council St.

N. Boylston St.

Beaudry Ave.

W. Cesar E. Chavez Ave.

N. Hill St.

N. Broadway

N. Spring St.

W. 3rd St.

Figueroa St.

101

Lucas Ave.

Temple St.

Civic
Center

5

W. 6th St.

6

Wilshire Blvd.

W. 7th St.

110

E. 1st St.

Harbor Freeway

E. 2nd St.

4   1

E. 3rd St.

W. Olympic
Blvd.

i

W. 7th St.

Pershing
Square

E. 4th St.

S. Flower St.

S. Hope St.

S. Grand Ave.

S. Hill St.

S. Main St.

E. 5th St.

E. Olympic Blvd.

S. Broadway

E. 6th St.

San Pedro St.

E. 5th St.

S. Central Ave.

S. Alameda St.

P

L.A.
Convention
Center

11th St.

12th St.

S. Olive St.

E. 8th St.

E. 9th St.

E. 7th St.

P

S. Figueroa St.

Pico Blvd.

10

Santa Monica Freeway

E. 16th St.

E. 12th St.

E. Pico Blvd.

E. Olympic Blvd.

E. Washington Blvd.

7

| 0 | | 1/2 mi |
| 0 | | 1/2 km |

N

hollywood

FAMILY LODGING

1. Four Seasons Hotel
   Los Angeles at
   Beverly Hills
2. The Orlando

ATTRACTIONS

3. ArcLight Cinemas
4. Children's Book World
5. Hollywood & Highland
6. Hollywood Walk
   of Fame
7. La Brea Tar Pits and
   Page Museum

8. Los Angeles County
   Museum of Art
9. Los Angeles Zoo
10. Museum of the
    American West
11. The Paley Center
    for Media
12. Petersen Automotive
    Museum
13. Sony Pictures
    Entertainment
    Studio Tour
14. SummerSounds

15. Travel Town Transportation
    Museum

**FAMILY-FRIENDLY
RESTAURANTS**

16. El Cholo
17. Fabiolus Cafe
18. Farmers Market
19. House of Blues
20. Johnny Rockets
21. Pink's

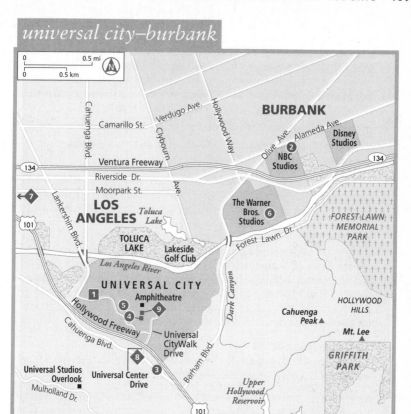

universal city–burbank

FAMILY LODGING
1. Sheraton Universal

ATTRACTIONS
2. NBC Studio Tour
3. Storybook Theatre

4. Universal CityWalk
5. Universal Studios
   Hollywood
6. Warner Brothers
   Studios VIP Tour

FAMILY-FRIENDLY
RESTAURANTS
7. Caioti Pizza Cafe
8. Poquito Más
9. Wolfgang Puck
   Cafe

Millennium Biltmore Hotel Los Angeles
**506 South Grand Avenue, downtown LA; ☎ 800-245-8673 or
213-624-1011; www.millenniumhotels.com; $225–$279; higher for suites**

THIS STATELY, WELL-MAINTAINED DOWAGER is a good choice if you're
bringing kids on a downtown business/pleasure trip or if you want to focus
on such cultural activities as theater at the Music Center and story time
at the Central Library. It sits in the heart of downtown, about 30 minutes
east of Santa Monica beach and 20 minutes southeast of Universal Studios.
We've found that kids actually enjoy the grand landmark hotels—the many

differently decorated areas, the ornateness, and the various nooks and crannies seem to appeal to them. It's fun to dress up and take tea in the historic lobby-lounge, with its hand-painted beams overhead; this has been a location in countless movies and TV shows. Less formal settings are also around, including a cafe and an indoor pool. You can catch a DASH bus to all sorts of downtown destinations, from Chinatown to Staples Center sports arena; the wonderful Los Angeles Central Library is an easy walk.

The Orlando
8384 West Third Street, LA; ☎ 800-62-HOTEL or 323-658-6600; www.theorlando.com; $209–$349

FORMERLY THE BEVERLY PLAZA, this smallish (98 rooms) hotel was totally overhauled a few years back and is now a pretty swank spot, but the price is reasonable given the location (a block and a half east of the Beverly Center shopping mall) and amenities. It's not quite in Beverly Hills, but it's close enough for your luxury-loving shoppers, and yet near enough to the major streets that will carry you to other parts of town. The nearest attractions are the Petersen Automotive Museum, La Brea Tar Pits, Farmers Market and its adjacent shopping center–cineplex, the Grove, and Hollywood, and there's plenty of walking and dining nearby. There's a wonderful saltwater swimming pool, a fitness center, wireless Internet, and a very good, high-end Italian restaurant; the front desk rents iPods and DVD players.

Sheraton Universal
333 Universal Hollywood Drive, Universal City; ☎ 888-625-5144 or 818-980-1212; www.sheraton.com; $209 and up

A WELL-RUN LINK IN THE SHERATON CHAIN, this 442-room, 23-suite modern high-rise hotel is a good bet for families planning a Universal City visit because its packages with the park offer savings and convenience. One recent package, for instance, combined a room and two adult tickets to Universal Studios for $245, and discounted children's tickets can be bought in the hotel gift shop. Universal City and CityWalk are a free tram ride or a five-minute walk away. Game room, large heated pool, children's menus, and good-sized, comfortable rooms, some with killer views of the Valley.

ATTRACTIONS

California Science Center

APPEAL BY AGE	PRESCHOOL ★★	GRADE SCHOOL ★★★★½	TEENS ★★★★
YOUNG ADULTS ★★★★		OVER 30 ★★★★	SENIORS ★★★

700 State Drive, Exposition Park; ☎ 323-724-3623; www.casciencectr.org

Hours Daily, 10 a.m.–5 p.m.; closed Thanksgiving, Christmas, and New Year's Day.
Admission Free with $6 parking; IMAX admission $8 adults, $6 seniors age 60 and

older, students, and ages 12–17, $5 children ages 3–11. **Touring time** Average 3 hours; minimum 1½ hours. **Rainy-day touring** No. **Restaurants** Yes. **Alcoholic beverages** No. **Disabled access** Yes. **Wheelchair rental** Yes, free. **Baby-stroller rental** No. **Lockers** Yes. **Pet kennels** No. **Rain check** No. **Private tours** No.

DESCRIPTION AND COMMENTS   Los Angeles parents, teachers, and kids love this ambitious museum, which has revitalized the Exposition Park complex south of downtown. When our daughter first visited on a school field trip, crowds prevented her and her classmates from even getting near Tess, the 50-foot model woman with the see-through body that lets you see how the body's systems work. (What they missed was a 15-minute animatronic demonstration of a virtual soccer game that Tess plays; lights, sounds, and visual tricks help explain what's happening in her body while she runs and kicks.) But on a later visit, when the crowds had abated, our group did get a chance to operate the high-wire bicycle and experience a simulated earthquake. The kids also enjoyed pulling, maneuvering, and playing with lots of hands-on science experiments and displays. And, of course, they love the IMAX movies. The secret to visiting this place in relative peace is to come on a school day between 1 and 3 p.m. The field-trip kids will have left, and the after-school crowd hasn't hit yet. The exhibits are so dynamic, fun, and educational that they're worth missing a day of school.

Dodger Stadium Tour

APPEAL BY AGE	PRESCHOOL ★	GRADE SCHOOL ★★★	TEENS ★★★
YOUNG ADULTS ★★		OVER 30 ★★★	SENIORS ★★★

Stadium, 1000 Elysian Park Avenue; ☎ 866-DODGERS; www.dodgers.com

Hours Tours April–September, 10 and 11:30 a.m. on days without a day game; reservations required, call ☎ 323-227-1507. **Admission** $15 adults, $10 children 14 and under. **Touring time** Average 1–1½ hours; minimum 1 hour. **Rainy-day touring** No. **Restaurants** No, snack bars closed on nongame days. **Alcoholic beverages** No. **Disabled access** Yes. **Wheelchair rental** No. **Baby-stroller rental** No. **Lockers** No. **Pet kennels** No. **Rain check** No. **Private tours** Yes.

DESCRIPTION AND COMMENTS   If you have a baseball nut in your family, this behind-the-scenes tour offers the kind of up-close experience so hard to come by in our electronic age. A guide takes you into the press box, clubhouse area, bullpen, and dugout and onto the field. Reservations required.

Hollywood & Highland Center

APPEAL BY AGE	PRESCHOOL ★	GRADE SCHOOL ★★★	TEENS ★★★★½
YOUNG ADULTS ★★★★		OVER 30 ★★	SENIORS ★★

Hollywood Boulevard at Highland Avenue, LA; ☎ 323-817-0220; www.hollywoodandhighland.com

Hours Monday–Saturday, 10 a.m.–10 p.m.; Sunday, 10 a.m.–7 p.m.; theaters, clubs, and some restaurants have extended hours. **Admission** Free to shopping center; various admissions for theaters. **Touring time** 2 hours. **Rainy-day touring** Yes for theaters; mall is outdoors. **Restaurants** Yes. **Alcoholic beverages** Yes. **Disabled access** Yes. **Wheelchair rental** No. **Baby-stroller rental** No. **Lockers** No. **Pet kennels** No. **Rain check** No. **Private tours** No.

DESCRIPTION AND COMMENTS   Hollywood has tried to gussy itself up for many years to little avail, but the tide has finally turned with this ambitious development built around the famed Grauman's Chinese Theatre. At its core, it's really just another glorified mall, home to—you'll be amazed to discover!—a Gap, Victoria's Secret, and M.A.C. Scattered around the shopping venues are the Kodak Theatre, home of the Academy Awards and the site of some worthwhile concerts; a cineplex; the famed Chinese Theatre; a bunch of hip restaurants; the chic Lucky Strike Lanes bowling alley, which is kid-friendly most of the time but gets nightclubby later at night; The Road to Hollywood, an intriguing on-the-ground art piece that serves as a tribute to the Hollywood of fantasy and reality; a couple of courtyards and outdoor performing spaces; and an adjacent upscale hotel.

 ## La Brea Tar Pits and Page Museum

APPEAL BY AGE	PRESCHOOL ★★★★	GRADE SCHOOL ★★★½	TEENS ★★★★
YOUNG ADULTS ★★★★		OVER 30 ★★★★½	SENIORS ★★★★½

5801 Wilshire Boulevard, Hancock Park, LA; ☎ 323-934-PAGE (7243); www.tarpits.org

Hours Monday–Friday, 9:30 a.m.–5 p.m.; Saturday, Sunday, and holidays, 10 a.m.– 5 p.m. **Admission** $7 adults, $4.50 seniors and students, $4.50 ages 13–17, $2 children ages 5–12, free for age 4 and under; free first Tuesday of every month. Parking $6–$8. **Touring time** Average 1½ hours; minimum 30 minutes. **Rainy-day touring** Yes. **Restaurants** No. **Alcoholic beverages** No. **Disabled access** Yes. **Wheelchair rental** Yes, free. **Baby-stroller rental** No. **Lockers** No. **Pet kennels** No. **Rain check** No. **Private tours** Yes.

DESCRIPTION AND COMMENTS   Every young Angeleno comes here at one time or another and pulls up on the poles suspended in tar-pit goo to get a feel for what it must have been like to be a prehistoric animal stuck in the bubbling ooze. This museum is architecturally interesting and pleasantly compact, with an inventive range of varied exhibits, from a film and holograms to models and a window through which visitors can watch paleontologists cleaning and studying bones. The exhibits are tightly focused—all pertain to fossils found on this very site.

 ## Los Angeles Central Library

APPEAL BY AGE	PRESCHOOL ★★★	GRADE SCHOOL ★★★	TEENS ★★★
YOUNG ADULTS ★★★		OVER 30 ★★★★	SENIORS ★★★★

630 West Fifth Street, Downtown LA; ☎ 213-228-7000; www.lapl.org

Hours Monday–Thursday, 10 a.m.–8 p.m.; Friday and Saturday, 10 a.m.–6 p.m.; Sunday, 1–5 p.m.; closed major holidays. **Admission** Free; parking in selected lots $2 with library card. **Touring time** Average 2 hours; minimum 1 hour. **Rainy-day touring** Excellent. **Restaurants** Yes. **Alcoholic beverages** No. **Disabled access** Yes. **Baby-stroller rental** No. **Lockers** Yes. **Pet kennels** No. **Rain check** No. **Private tours** Docent tours.

DESCRIPTION AND COMMENTS The hordes of office workers leave downtown LA on weekends, so parking is easier and cheaper than during the week, and that's when the historic and gorgeous Central Library is a real treat. Children's programs (theater, puppets, or video) on Saturday and Sunday give a shape and purpose to the outing, but it's great fun to simply browse the beautiful, 1930s-era, restored children's room, play on the computers in the room adjacent, ride the escalators through the glass-walled, four-story atrium with its cartoonlike giant chandeliers, and get lunch at the Chinese buffet restaurant with terrace seating.

Los Angeles County Museum of Art

APPEAL BY AGE	PRESCHOOL ★★	GRADE SCHOOL ★★★	TEENS ★★★★
YOUNG ADULTS ★★★★½	OVER 30 ★★★★½		SENIORS ★★★★½

5905 Wilshire Boulevard, Miracle Mile, LA; ☎ 323-857-6000 or 323-857-6010 (tickets); www.lacma.org

Hours Monday, Tuesday, Thursday, noon–8 p.m.; Friday, noon–9 p.m.; Saturday and Sunday, 11 a.m.–8 p.m.; closed Wednesdays, Thanksgiving, and Christmas. **Admission** $12 adults, $8 seniors and students age 18 and over with valid ID, free for children age 17 and under; some special-fee shows; free second Tuesday of every month after 5 p.m.; parking $7–8. **Touring time** Average a half day; minimum 2 hours. **Rainy-day touring** Good. **Restaurants** Yes. **Alcoholic beverages** Yes. **Disabled access** Yes. **Wheelchair rental** Yes, free. **Baby-stroller rental** No. **Lockers** No. **Pet kennels** No. **Rain check** No. **Private tours** No.

DESCRIPTION AND COMMENTS This big-city art museum is a complex of buildings on the same parklike block as the La Brea Tar Pits and Page Museum. Don't try to see everything in a single visit—just pick a single period, floor, or section, enjoy it, and be done. Some strong holdings that might appeal to certain kids are the costume and fashion collection (try it on middle schoolers), the photo collection (good for teens, too disturbing for little ones), the modern-art wing (whose huge paintings and bright colors appeal to elementary-age kids), and the sacred art of India—stone sculptures are impressive at any age. A separate but related facility is the Japanese Pavilion, with a specialized collection not likely to be appreciated by many children. The best bets for families are the special events, especially the occasional family music concerts and the Family Sundays (every Sunday at 12:30 p.m.), which typically offer hands-on art-making projects and storytelling. Note that kids age 17 and under get in free.

Los Angeles Zoo

APPEAL BY AGE	PRESCHOOL ★★★★	GRADE SCHOOL ★★★★	TEENS ★★★
YOUNG ADULTS ★★★		OVER 30 ★★★	SENIORS ★★★

5333 Zoo Drive, off I-5 freeway, Griffith Park, LA; ☎ 323-644-4200; www.lazoo.org

Hours Daily 10 a.m.–5 p.m.; closed Christmas. **Admission** $12 adults (age 13 and older), $9 seniors age 62 and older, $7 children ages 2–12, free for children under age 2; free parking. **Touring time** Average 3 hours; minimum 1 hour. **Rainy-day touring** Limited. **Restaurants** Yes. **Alcoholic beverages** Yes. **Disabled access** Yes. **Wheelchair rental** Yes. **Baby-stroller rental** Yes. **Lockers** No. **Pet kennels** Yes. **Rain check** No. **Private tours** Yes.

DESCRIPTION AND COMMENTS   A zoo membership is a must for many LA families—special events abound at this large, inviting attraction, and many are for kids. For visitors, this means you'll find plenty of entertainment in addition to animals to look at. There are excellent demonstrations and shows (schedules available at gate), as well as fun educational installations at various points (such as "What Does a Bear Smell?"). There's a children's zoo and baby-animal nursery. Overnight camps and family camping nights are occasionally offered in the summer.

Museum of the American West

APPEAL BY AGE	PRESCHOOL ★★	GRADE SCHOOL ★★★★	TEENS ★★★
YOUNG ADULTS ★★★		OVER 30 ★★★	SENIORS ★★★★½

4700 Western Heritage Way, Griffith Park, LA; ☎ 323-667-2000; www.autry-museum.org

Hours Tuesday–Sunday, 10 a.m.–5 p.m.; Thursday, 10 a.m.–8 p.m. **Admission** $9 adults, $5 seniors age 60 and over, $5 students ages 13–18, $3 children ages 2–12, free for children under age 2. **Touring time** Average 2½ hours; minimum 1 hour. **Rainy-day touring** Yes. **Restaurants** Cafeteria-style cafe. **Alcoholic beverages** No. **Disabled access** Yes. **Wheelchair rental** Yes, free. **Baby-stroller rental** Yes, free. **Lockers** No. **Pet kennels** No. **Rain check** No. **Private tours** Yes.

DESCRIPTION AND COMMENTS   This is a perfect outing for grandparents and their grandchildren, or older parents and their kids. If you're over 60, chances are good that you idolized such stars as Gene Autry and Tom Mix—and along with often-worthy exhibitions of paintings, sculpture, and other works from Western and Native American artists, you'll find great collections of Hollywood cowboy memorabilia, from costumes to posters. Our kids love the full-size jail cell, the dioramas reenacting the shootout at the OK Corral, the collections of sheriff's badges and pistols, and especially the hands-on Children's Discovery Gallery, where kids get to experience the life of Chinese immigrants to America in the 1800s—there's even a Chinese restaurant in which they can pretend to cook, serve, and eat. Elsewhere in the museum is a "movie studio" in which kids are inserted digitally into an old Western chase scene. The gift shop is a major kid pleaser, with lots of fun Native American and cowboy stuff. Weekends often bring free performances of cowboy music and children's art classes.

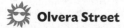

Olvera Street

APPEAL BY AGE	PRESCHOOL ★★	GRADE SCHOOL ★★★★	TEENS ★★★★
YOUNG ADULTS ★★★★		OVER 30 ★★★★	SENIORS ★★★★

845 North Alameda Street, Downtown; ☎ 213-628-1274; www.olvera-street.com

Hours Daily, 10 a.m.–7 p.m.; *summer:* daily, 10 a.m.–10 p.m. **Admission** Free. **Touring time** Average 2½ hours, with meal; minimum 1 hour. **Rainy-day touring** Limited. **Restaurants** Yes. **Alcoholic beverages** Yes. **Disabled access** Limited. **Baby-stroller rental** No. **Lockers** No. **Pet kennels** No. **Rain check** No. **Private tours** No.

DESCRIPTION AND COMMENTS   When we first came to LA, we thought Olvera Street was corny, but when we worked downtown, we started to hang out here, and we came to appreciate its sidewalk cafes and strolling mariachis; its varied shops with colorful, often-seasonal goods; and its lively street scene. Our daughter was enthusiastic after a school field trip that included a tour of the historic adobe and the vintage fire station. And everybody loves the shopping, which is every bit as good as on the main tourist strip in Ensenada, Mexico. We've been happy with purchases of blankets, purses, silver jewelry, piñatas, paper flowers, and jumping beans. As for food, eat at the tiny hole-in-the-wall called Juanita's, and save the fancier joints for margaritas (virgin or regular) and mariachis. This historic little street is part of the larger El Pueblo de Los Angeles, the birthplace of the city, which includes a lovely restored plaza and several historic buildings. Union Station is across the street, so Olvera Street is easily reached from the Gold Line, Purple Line, or Red Line trains.

Petersen Automotive Museum

APPEAL BY AGE	PRESCHOOL ★★★	GRADE SCHOOL ★★★★	TEENS ★★★★½
YOUNG ADULTS ★★★★		OVER 30 ★★★★	SENIORS ★★★★

6060 Wilshire Boulevard, Miracle Mile, LA; ☎ 323-930-2277; www.petersen.org

Hours Tuesday–Sunday, 10 a.m.–6 p.m.; Discovery Center: Tuesday–Friday, 10 a.m.–4 p.m.; Saturday and Sunday, 10 a.m.–5 p.m. **Admission** $10 adults, $5 seniors age 62 and older and students with valid ID, $3 children ages 5–12, free for children age 4 and under; parking, $8. **Touring time** Average 2½ hours; minimum 1 hour. **Rainy-day touring** Limited. **Restaurants** Mini-mart. **Alcoholic beverages** No. Disabled access. Yes **Baby-stroller rental** No. **Lockers** No. **Pet kennels** No. **Rain check** No. **Private tours** No.

DESCRIPTION AND COMMENTS   California's car culture is honored and explored in this unusual museum. More than 150 classic cars, hot rods, Indy cars, trucks, motorcycles, and custom vehicles are displayed in settings that bring the period or use of the car to life. It won't feel like a museum as you and the kids walk through settings from the horse-and-buggy era to the space-age future, each with motor vehicles of the period. Some visitors will like the vintage signage and other historically accurate parts of the environments (complete in some cases with sounds) as much as the gleaming motor vehicles. The second-floor exhibits are more traditional but include some favorites such as hot rods and celebrity cars. The Family Discovery Center brings welcome interactivity to the museum.

Travel Town Transportation Museum

APPEAL BY AGE	PRESCHOOL ★★★	GRADE SCHOOL ★★★	TEENS ★★
YOUNG ADULTS ★★		OVER 30 ★★	SENIORS ★★

5200 West Zoo Drive, Griffith Park, LA; ☎ 323-662-5874; www.traveltown.org

Hours Monday–Friday, 10 a.m.–4 p.m.; Saturday and Sunday, holidays, 10 a.m.–5 p.m.; closed Christmas. **Admission** Free. **Touring time** Average 1 hour; minimum 8 minutes for the ride only. **Rainy-day touring** No. **Restaurants** No. **Alcoholic beverages** No. **Disabled access** Yes. **Wheelchair rental** No. **Baby-stroller rental** No. **Lockers** No. **Pet kennels** No. **Rain check** No. **Private tours** Yes.

DESCRIPTION AND COMMENTS   A fond memory from our own childhoods, Travel Town is now enchanting a new generation of young train lovers who can climb into old engines, scramble through cabooses, and ride a miniature train around the park. Our Thomas-obsessed nephew wants to come here every weekend. It's basically just a bunch of old train cars and engines, but that's enough for fun.

Universal CityWalk

APPEAL BY AGE	PRESCHOOL ★★	GRADE SCHOOL ★★★★	TEENS ★★★★½
YOUNG ADULTS ★★★★		OVER 30 ★★★	SENIORS ★★★

100 Universal City Plaza, Universal City; ☎ 818-622-4455; www.citywalkhollywood.com

Hours Sunday–Thursday, 11 a.m.–11 p.m.; Friday and Saturday, 11 a.m.–midnight. **Admission** Free; self-parking, $10-$12; valet parking with validated ticket from any CityWalk vendor, $3–$12. **Touring time** Average 2 hours; minimum 1 hour. **Rainy-day touring** So-so; mall area is outdoors. **Restaurants** Yes. **Alcoholic beverages** Yes. **Disabled access** Yes. **Wheelchair rental** Yes. **Baby-stroller rental** No. **Lockers** No. **Pet kennels** No. **Rain check** No. **Private tours** No.

DESCRIPTION AND COMMENTS   Universal CityWalk aggressively courts the family (and date-night) market, and judging by the size of the crowds, it is succeeding beautifully. In addition to the movie theaters, nightclubs, restaurants, and shops, there's an IMAX theater, an indoor-skydiving adventure, a rock 'n' roll bowling alley, a bunch more restaurants, and even more of the CityWalk shops that sell such quintessential inessentials as windup toys, nostalgic clothing, science fiction memorabilia, magic tricks, and hair-braiding accessories. The entire place is as phony as a three-dollar bill (there's no actual city here), and it's shamelessly shallow, materialistic, and deafeningly loud, but there's no denying that it's fun. You'll have to pry teenagers out of here with a crowbar.

Universal Studios Hollywood

| APPEAL BY AGE | PRESCHOOL ★ | GRADE SCHOOL ★★★★ | TEENS ★★★★½ |
| YOUNG   ADULTS   ★★★★ | | OVER   30   ★★★★ | SENIORS   ★★★★ |

(See map on following pages.)

100 Universal City Plaza, Universal City; ☎ 800-UNIVERSAL**;
www.universalstudioshollywood.com**

Hours *Mid-April–September:* 9 a.m.–9 p.m. Monday–Thursday, 9 a.m.–8 p.m. Friday–Sunday (box office: 8:30 a.m.–4 p.m.); *October–March:* 10 a.m.–6 p.m. **Admission** $64 adults, $54 children under 48" tall, children under 3 free; parking $12 general, $20 preferred. **Touring time** Average 8 hours; minimum 4 hours. **Rainy-day touring** Not great, but the rain thins crowds. **Restaurants** Yes. **Alcoholic beverages** Yes. **Disabled access** Yes. **Wheelchair rental** Yes. **Baby-stroller rental** Yes. **Lockers** Yes. **Pet kennels** Yes. **Rain check** Yes. **Private tours** Yes.

DESCRIPTION AND COMMENTS   If your children are younger than age 8, you might want to postpone a trip here—it costs a fortune to get in, and the money is mostly wasted on the very young, for whom most of the special-effects rides are too scary. Although attractions for younger kids have been added, little kids are too young to be impressed by the behind-the-scenes moviemaking aspect of the park, the main point of the place.

That said, a trip to Universal Studios can be a tremendously enjoyable day for the right group, especially older elementary-school kids, teenagers, and adults who haven't experienced it before. Although sometimes hokey, the one-hour, often-updated tram ride is essential for first-timers, both for its back-lot peek at sets from many popular movies and TV shows and for its thrills—the parting of the Red Sea isn't as cool as it used to be, but the simulated earthquake is impressively realistic (and scary for Angelenos!), and the *War of the Worlds* set is astonishing. As for the rides, most of their thrills come from special effects, not roller-coaster speed—although the Revenge of the Mummy indoor roller coaster is both fast and scary—and those thrills are remarkable. *Jurassic Park:* The Ride and the new Simpsons Ride are amazing feats of movie-ride technology, not to mention big fun. *Backdraft*—not a ride, really, but a close-up view of special effects used in that firefighting movie—is also breathtaking, but if you take a fearful kid on this one, you'll be sorry. Instead, head for *Universal's Animal Actors* or the Curious George interactive playground.

When we brought a pack of elementary-school boys here, what they really remembered wasn't the rides but the spectacular *Waterworld* show. What flopped on the screen is great fun on an outdoor stage—stuntmen and stuntwomen in fabulous rags fighting on personal watercraft and diving from towers. In fact, any show is worth a look,

universal studios hollywood

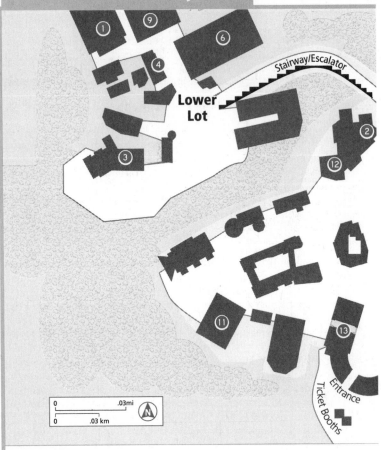

1. *Backdraft*
2. *Fear Factor Live*
3. *Jurassic Park:* The Ride
4. *Lucy—A Tribute*
5. Nickelodeon Blast Zone
6. Revenge of the Mummy
7. *Shrek 4-D*

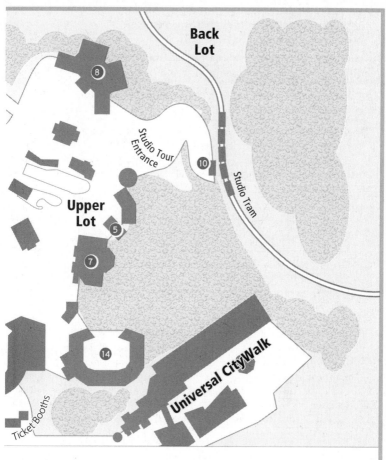

8. The Simpsons Ride
9. Special Effects Stages
10. Studio Tour

11. *Terminator 2: 3-D*
12. *Universal's Animal Actors*
13. Universal's House of Horrors
14. *Waterworld*

because the studio connection attracts talented producers and performers. Also, the *Shrek 4-D* film is a gas.

The Watts Towers of Simon Rodia State Historic Park

| APPEAL BY AGE | PRESCHOOL ★ | GRADE SCHOOL ★★★★ | TEENS ★★★★ |
| YOUNG ADULTS ★★★★ | | OVER 30 ★★★★ | SENIORS ★★★★ |

1765 East 107th Street, LA; ☎ 213-847-4646, (Arts Center); www.wattstowers.us

Hours Guided tours every half hour Tuesday–Saturday, 10 a.m.–4 p.m. **Admission** $2 adults, free for children with paying adult. **Touring time** Average 1 hour. **Rainy-day touring** None. **Restaurants** No. **Alcoholic beverages** No. **Disabled access** Yes. **Wheelchair rental** No. **Baby-stroller rental** No. **Lockers** No. **Pet kennels** No. **Rain check** No. **Private tours** No.

DESCRIPTION AND COMMENTS   After years of being closed for repairing and reinforcing after the 1994 Northridge earthquake, and then for a late-2008 renovation, the Watts Towers are reopened, and we have been reminded of what a treasure they are. In the early 1920s, an illiterate Italian tile-factory worker named Simon Rodia bought an odd-shaped lot in Watts, south of downtown Los Angeles, and spent every free moment of the next 33 years creating his own fantasyland of folk art. This is art that speaks to children—so much so that we'd advise not bringing toddlers and preschoolers, because they'll want to touch it all, and in the interest of preservation, touching is not allowed. Embedded in the concrete towers, walls, benches, fountains, and floor is a colorful, fanciful panoply of objects Rodia found at the factory and the nearby train tracks: broken tile, glass, bottles, teapots, ceramic animals, and such. The towers can be seen up close only with a guided tour, but be glad for that, because the guide's stories add much to the experience, especially for kids. After your visit, your kids will be sure to want to create some towers or folk art of their own.

FAMILY-FRIENDLY RESTAURANTS

Caioti Pizza Café
4346 Tujunga Avenue, Studio City; 818-761-3588; www.caiotipizzacafe.com

Meals served Lunch, dinner, and weekend brunch. **Cuisine** Italian/Californian. **Entree range** Lunch and dinner, $9–$16. **Kids menu** No. **Reservations** Not accepted. **Payment** MC, V.

CONTRARY TO POPULAR OPINION, the California pizza was invented by neither Wolfgang Puck nor California Pizza Kitchen. It was the brainchild of a chef named Ed LaDou, who consulted for Puck. LaDou passed away a couple of years ago, but he left behind this lively, friendly cafe, where fantastic individual pizzas come out of a wood-burning oven all day and night. Good salads and grilled entrees, too, but pizza's the thing to get. It's a five-minute drive from Universal Studios and the Sheraton Universal; consider eating here instead of at CityWalk.

El Cholo

1121 South Western Avenue, Mid-Wilshire, LA; ☎ 323-734-2773; www.elcholo.com

Meals served Lunch and dinner. **Cuisine** Mexican. **Entree range** $7–$16. **Kids' menu** Yes. **Reservations** Recommended. **Payment** All major credit cards.

SINCE 1921, El Cholo has been home to the city's best margaritas and green-corn tamales—and the enchiladas, chiles rellenos, taco tray, carnitas, and guacamole are pretty swell, too. A multiethnic cross-section of LA folk fills the maze of painted, tiled, adobe-style dining rooms, served by waitresses in flouncy costumes. The children's menu has a burger, but they're better off with the junior quesadilla or enchilada. The location is midway between downtown and the La Brea Tar Pits.

Empress Pavilion

988 North Hill Street, Chinatown; ☎ 213-617-9898; www.empresspavilion.com

Meals served Breakfast (dim sum), lunch, and dinner. **Cuisine** Chinese. **Entree range** Dim sum plates, $5–$10; dinner, $7–$26. **Kids' menu** No. **Reservations** Accepted for dinner only. **Payment** DC, MC, V.

THE PROBLEM WITH VISITING THE BEST dim sum restaurant in Chinatown is that everyone in LA knows it's the best dim sum restaurant, so the wait is an hour long by noon on weekends, and the good stuff is gone by 12:30 p.m. So arrive at this Chinatown minimall by 10:30 a.m. on weekends to share with your kids the spectacle of a vast, teeming dining room being serviced by surly women pushing metal steam carts of superb dumplings and buns of every possible description (ask for *bao* buns, pot stickers, and *sui mai*, which are the most agreeable to children). Come nighttime, the dim sum vanishes and some very good Cantonese cooking takes over, from excellent seafood to Peking duck.

Fabiolus Cafe

6270 Sunset Boulevard, Hollywood; ☎ 323-467-2882; www.fabiolus.org

Meals served Lunch and dinner. **Cuisine** Italian. **Entree range** $10–$22. **Kids' menu** No. **Reservations** Not necessary. **Payment** All major credit cards.

IF YOU'RE DOING THE TINSELTOWN tourist thing and don't want to eat at the Hollywood & Highland mall, head over to this friendly, inexpensive trattoria, a few doors east of the ArcLight and Cinerama Dome and walking distance to the Pantages, where *Wicked* has set up shop seemingly forever.

The pastas and salads are delicious, the setting is casual, and though there's no children's menu, the kitchen is happy to make a plain pasta or pizza.

 Farmers Market

6333 West Third Street, LA; ☎ 866-993-9211 or 323-933-9211; www.farmersmarketla.com

Meals served Breakfast, lunch, and early dinner. **Cuisine** Variety. **Entree range** $8–$18. **Kids' menu** Yes, at some stands. **Reservations** Not accepted. **Payment** Varies by stand.

ONE OF THE CITY'S GREAT MEETING SPOTS and melting pots, Farmers Market is beloved of senior citizens and children alike. Area retirees meet to chat, nosh, play cards, and shop for high-quality produce, meat, seafood, and specialty foods; children love to cruise the open-air merchants, looking for candy vendors and seeking kid paradise: Bob's, home of the best doughnuts in town. Come early to snag a good table strategically located between the most interesting food vendors, so everyone can get what he or she wants—a slice of pizza for one, a corned-beef sandwich for another, a bowl of gumbo for another. Next door to Farmers Market is the Grove, a luxe shopping center with serene restaurants and a trolley that kids adore.

House of Blues
8430 Sunset Boulevard, West Hollywood; ☎ 323-848-5136; www.hob.com

Meals served Dinner, Sunday brunch. **Cuisine** American, Southern. **Entree range** Brunch $40.50 for adults (senior discount), $19 for children ages 5–12, free for children age 4 and under. **Reservations** Essential. **Payment** All major credit cards.

NOT TOO MANY FAMILIES come to this music club for dinner, though if you're bringing teens to a concert, it can be fun. But the whole family will love the Sunday Gospel Brunch—and, in fact, you'll see tables filled with families, from great-grandmas down to preschoolers. The Southern cooking—fruit salads, homemade waffles, biscuits and gravy, Cheddar cheese grits, fried chicken, peach cobbler—is served as an all-you-can-eat buffet, and the gospel acts are foot-stompin', spirit-liftin', world-class performers. Dress nicely—it's Sunday, after all—and be prepared for a Sunday brunch you'll never forget.

Johnny Rockets
7507 Melrose Avenue, LA; ☎ 323-651-3361; www.johnnyrockets.com

Meals served Lunch and dinner (open late). **Cuisine** American. **Entree range** $7–$10. **Kids' menu** $5–$7. **Reservations** Not accepted. **Payment** All major credit cards.

MELROSE ISN'T QUITE AS HIP as it once was, but teens will still find it worth a gander, and this slick, rather overpriced chain is well located in the heart of the action. Basic burgers, fries, and shakes are served in a blindingly lit, red-and-white diner to a sound track of rock oldies. There are several other local branches, including on Santa Monica's Third Street Promenade and in Old Pasadena.

Pink's
709 North La Brea Avenue, LA; ☎ 323-931-4223; www.pinkshollywood.com

---

Meals served Lunch and dinner. **Cuisine** Hot dogs, turkey dogs, turkey burgers. **Entree range** $3–$7. **Kids' menu** No. **Reservations** Not accepted. **Payment** No credit cards.

A HOLLYWOOD LANDMARK, this roadside stand is known partly for its chili dog but more for its scene than anything else—the ever-present line is one of LA's more entertaining sidewalk social gatherings. Kids can get plain dogs, of course, and sloppy burgers as well. Be warned that the chili is likely to wreak havoc on your stomach, though you'll be loving it while it's going down.

Poquito Más
3701 Cahuenga Boulevard West, Studio City; ☎ 818-760-8226; www.poquitomas.com

---

Meals served Lunch and dinner. **Cuisine** Mexican. **Entree range** $3–$9. **Kids' menu** Yes. **Reservations** Not accepted. **Payment** AE, D, V.

FOR A TASTE OF WHAT ANGELENOS really eat, skip the tourist traps in Universal City and travel a mile or so to this strip-mall joint. You order at the counter and sit on plastic tables in the parking lot, and you're as likely to see a star here as in the studio. The carnitas (juicy pork) are among the best in town, the fish tacos are delicious, and the burritos are generous.

Wolfgang Puck Cafe
Universal CityWalk, 100 Universal City Plaza, Universal City; ☎ 818-985-9653; www.wolfgangpuck.com

---

Meals served Lunch and dinner. **Cuisine** Californian. **Entree range** $12–$25. **Kids' menu** Yes. **Reservations** Not accepted. **Payment** All major credit cards.

YOU HAVE TO RESERVE THREE MONTHS ahead and spend a car payment to have dinner at Wolfgang Puck's flagship Spago in Beverly Hills, but at this colorful, loud cafe, you can put your name in, browse CityWalk for a while, then enjoy affordable modern American boomer food: BBQ chicken pizzas, baby-green salads, homey desserts. Kids get a fine coloring menu of their own.

WHERE *to* FIND *the*
REAL HOLLYWOOD

THE GLAMOUR IS COMING BACK to landmarks of the movie business, as studios and vintage movie theaters in Los Angeles are restored and renovated and proud owners show them off to the public. Just remember that visiting Hollywood means not simply exploring the not-very-interesting neighborhood of that name, but rather wandering through working studios (there are now four different tours), TV-show tapings, museums, and restored movie palaces throughout the city. Most tours and tapings have age restrictions, but the younger kids won't appreciate those experiences anyway. Even if they're not movie-mad, however, most junior-high kids and older kids have seen and heard enough about show business to enjoy a look behind the scenes. And don't forget, Universal Studios is a real studio as well as a theme park, and its back-lot tram tour often features a glimpse of moviemaking in progress.

Please note that security measures have tightened at the studios. Video cameras, large bags, and weapons of any type (such as pocket knives) are not allowed. Be prepared to be checked by a metal detector and have your belongings inspected.

ARCLIGHT CINEMAS   6360 West Sunset Boulevard, Hollywood; ☎ 323-464-1478; **www.arclightcinemas.com.** Including and encompassing the historic Cinerama Dome theater, the ArcLight is LA's premier movie-watching venue and is a great place to take older kids. You pay more for the tickets, but you get reserved seats, real ushers, no commercials, an audience that doesn't talk, a chic cafe and bar, and state-of-the-art theaters. The gift shop will enthrall hip teens. Note that this is also a great spot for spotting stars—but do what the locals do and let them watch their movie in peace. The massive used-and-new-record store across the street, **Amoeba,** is teen heaven.

AUDIENCES UNLIMITED   For free tickets to tapings, call ☎ 818-753-3470, ext. 321, or go to **www.tvtickets.com** for show schedules, maps and directions, minimum age requirements, and other information. Peak taping season is August through March. Tickets are available for shows taped in Hollywood, Burbank, Culver City, and Universal City–North Hollywood.

> *unofficial* **TIP**
> Studio representatives often pass out free tickets to TV-show tapings at Grauman's Chinese Theatre, so you might keep your itinerary flexible in case something appeals to your group.

HOLLYWOOD BOULEVARD MOVIE PALACES: EGYPTIAN THEATRE, GRAUMAN'S CHINESE THEATRE, EL CAPITAN THEATRE   Three restored movie-palace jewels adorn the crown of Hollywood Boulevard (a fourth is the legit house, the **Pantages Theater**) and allow visitors to really understand what the hoopla was all about in the 1930s and 1940s, when these theaters were the scenes of grand premieres. Begin at the **Egyptian Theatre** (6712 Hollywood Boulevard, Hollywood; ☎ 323-466-FILM; **www.egyptiantheatre .com**), which offers several daily screenings of a one-hour film ($5 to $7). A compilation of golden-age documentaries, classic movie clips, and interviews with current Hollywood celebrities, this movie is the perfect way to give your kids some background before they look at the footprints in the court of **Grauman's Chinese Theater** (6925 Hollywood Boulevard, Hollywood; ☎ 323-464-8111; **www.manntheatres .com/chinese**). Most of the stars who've left their marks here will otherwise be unfamiliar to your kids. Surrounding the Chinese is the new **Hollywood & Highland Center,** which includes the **Kodak Theatre,** home of the Academy Awards. If you have younger kids, their Hollywood highlight will be the **El Capitan Theatre** (6838 Hollywood Boulevard, Hollywood; ☎ 323-467-7674; **www.elcapitantickets.com**), gloriously renovated in a joint venture with Disney, and the location of premiere showings of the latest Disney releases, complete with glittering curtains and spotlights, special stage shows, and sometimes souvenirs, interactive exhibits, and other extras.

HOLLYWOOD WALK OF FAME On Hollywood Boulevard between Gower Street and La Brea Avenue and on Vine from Yucca Street to Sunset Boulevard; ☎ 323-469-8311; **www.hollywoodchamber.net** (Hollywood Chamber of Commerce). Just ignore the **Hollywood Wax Museum** (unless you're way into kitsch) and **Ripley's Believe It or Not!** as you walk along, reading the names on the stars embedded in the sidewalk.

THE PALEY CENTER FOR MEDIA 465 North Beverly Drive, Beverly Hills; ☎ 310-786-1025; **www.paleycenter.org;** Wednesday through Sunday, noon to 5 p.m.; free admission with suggested donation; $10 adults, $8 students and seniors, $5 children age 13 and under. Another good pre–Chinese Theater stop is this museum, where you can view a tape of the classic *I Love Lucy* episode in which Lucille Ball visits the Chinese Theater and gets her foot stuck in a bucket of wet (quick-drying) cement. This small, ultramodern facility is heavily supported by the industry because it's really an archive that collects and preserves tapes of radio and TV shows, many of which had been previously preserved only by individuals. Your visit can include an hour in the screening room to see a scheduled show of select TV clips, 20 minutes in the living room–like "radio listening room" with headsets and access to a vintage radio show, and a visit to the TV library. In the library, visitors select footage choices from the museum's computer database, then move to private consoles to view their choices of vintage or historic TV clips (ranging from episodes of *Welcome Back, Kotter* to moon-walk footage).

NBC STUDIO TOUR 3000 West Alameda Avenue, Burbank; ☎ 818-840-3537; tours leave weekdays 9 a.m. to 3 p.m.; $18.50 adults, $15.50 seniors age 60 and older, $15.50 children ages 6 to 12, free for children age 5 and younger. This isn't a big movie studio with entire streets built as sets, but rather an indoor TV taping facility with several separate stages, including the one where *The Tonight Show* has been filmed for decades. It isn't glitzy, but the tour is geared for kids, and the studio's real—we walked past "hot" prop tables, coiled cables, and "live" sets. The 70-minute walking tour includes a video, an NBC sports presentation, and a look at wardrobe, makeup, and set construction.

SONY PICTURES ENTERTAINMENT STUDIO TOUR   10202 West Washington Boulevard, Culver City; ☎ 323-520-TOUR; **www.sonypicturesstudiotours .com;** $28 per person; several departures a day, weekdays only; no children younger than age 12 permitted. The former MGM Studios was once the most glamorous of all the movie lots, and Sony has worked hard to restore the Art Deco and age-old buildings (there are some 1920s-era window-walled buildings that are among the earliest movie industry buildings anywhere). The two-hour walking tour weaves in and out of soundstages and onto some working sets as the workers go about their jobs. Highlights include a stroll through wardrobe and a peek at artists at work in a backdrop studio with a seven-story-high canvas in front of them. The tour begins with a video and ends on a street of picturesque facades where participants can get an ice-cream cone and shop in the studio store. Call **Audiences Unlimited** (☎ 818-753-3470; **www.audiences unlimited.com**) to attend a taping at Sony or nearby Culver Studios to coincide with your tour day.

☼ **WARNER BROS. STUDIOS VIP TOUR**   3400 Riverside Drive (park at Gate 6), Burbank; ☎ 818-846-1403; **wbsf.warnerbros.com;** $45 per person, children younger than age 8 not permitted). Group tours of this famous lot are held Monday through Friday, 8:20 a.m. to 4 p.m., with extended hours in the summer and fall; reservations are required. It's not cheap, but you will get an insider's look at a working studio— and unlike at Sony, kids ages 8 to 12 are welcome. No more than 12 people spend two and a half hours wandering through soundstages, past historic dressing rooms and offices, onto the set of a current TV show, and through working studio areas. Part of the trip will be via golf cart and part on foot. Time your visit so you can have lunch before or after at the Studio Plaza cafe, where many Warner employees eat.

SIDE TRIPS

Raging Waters

APPEAL BY AGE	PRESCHOOL ★★	GRADE SCHOOL ★★★★	TEENS ★★★★½
YOUNG ADULTS ★★★		OVER 30 ★★	SENIORS ½

111 Raging Waters Drive (off the 210 freeway), San Dimas;
☎ **909-802-2200; www.ragingwaters.com**

Hours *Late April–May:* Saturday and Sunday, 10 a.m.–6 p.m.; *June and September:* Monday–Friday, 10 a.m.–6 p.m.; Saturday and Sunday, 10 a.m.–7 p.m.; *July:* Monday–Thursday, 10 a.m.–7 p.m.; Friday–Sunday, 10 a.m.–8 p.m.; *August:* Monday–Thursday, 10 a.m.–7 p.m.; Friday–Sunday, 10 a.m.–8 p.m.; hours vary daily, so call first; park closes at end of September. **Admission** By height: 48" or taller $35; shorter than 48" $20; under age 2 free. **Touring time** Average 6 hours; minimum 2 hours. **Rainy-day touring** No. **Restaurants** Yes. **Alcoholic beverages** No. **Disabled access** Yes. **Wheelchair rental** No. **Baby-stroller rental** No. **Lockers** Yes. **Pet kennels** No. **Rain check** Half-price coupon for another visit. **Private tours** No.

DESCRIPTION AND COMMENTS   Raging Waters is worth a side trip to hot-and-smoggy San Dimas if you have preteens and teens and the weather's hot. (It's a solid 45-minute drive from the Westside and 20 minutes from Pasadena.) Plan on an all-day excursion, and be prepared for crowds. If your kids are younger, there's plenty for them to enjoy, but the real target audience is anyone crazy enough to slide down steep, slick waterslides. Tickets are sold in advance, so call ahead to make sure the park hasn't been bought out before you arrive.

Six Flags Hurricane Harbor Water Park

APPEAL BY AGE PRESCHOOL ★★★★½ GRADE SCHOOL ★★★★½ TEENS ★★★★
YOUNG ADULTS ★★★★   OVER 30 ★★   SENIORS ★★

26101 Magic Mountain Parkway (off I-5), Valencia; ☎ 661-255-4527; www.sixflags.com

Hours Weekdays, 10 a.m.–6 p.m.; weekends, 10 a.m.–8 p.m.; hours vary tremendously by season, so call or visit Web site first. **Admission** Adults $30; children less than 48" tall $21; children age 2 and under free; online discount offered; combo tickets, $70 for both Hurricane Harbor and Magic Mountain; parking $15. **Touring time** Average 4–6 hours; minimum 2 hours. **Rainy-day touring** Not good. **Restaurants** Yes. **Alcoholic beverages** No. **Disabled access** Yes, but no assisted slides. **Wheelchair rental** Yes. **Baby-stroller rental** Yes. **Lockers** Yes. **Pet kennels** Yes. **Rain check** No. **Private tours** No.

DESCRIPTION AND COMMENTS   This water park is so much fun in the summer that we recommend it over Magic Mountain (next door and more expensive), unless you have roller-coaster–loving teens. And even then, why not let the older kids do Magic Mountain by themselves while you relax on a chaise longue and the younger kids play at Castaway Cove, a toddler wading area; ride tubes around an island; roll with the waves in a giant concrete sea; or hit the waterslides? Older kids and teens love Lizard Lagoon, where they can play water basketball and volleyball, and the thrill slides, such as the 75-foot-high Tornado. It's not as crowded as Magic Mountain, either, and the tropical jungle theme is played out in nice landscaping. Valencia is north of LA, about a half-hour drive from downtown or 45 minutes from Santa Monica (much longer at rush hour).

Six Flags Magic Mountain

APPEAL BY AGE PRESCHOOL ★★ GRADE SCHOOL ★★★★ TEENS ★★★★½
YOUNG ADULTS ★★★★   OVER 30 ★★★   SENIORS ½

26101 Magic Mountain Parkway (off I-5), Valencia; ☎ 661-255-4100; www.sixflags.com

Hours *Mid-spring–late fall:* daily, open 10 a.m.; closing times vary with season and weather; rest of year, open 11 a.m. **Admission** Adults $60; children less than 48" tall $30; children age 2 and under free; significant online discount; combo tickets, $70 for both Hurricane Harbor and Magic Mountain; parking $15. **Touring time** Average 5 hours; minimum 3 hours. **Rainy-day touring** No. **Restaurants** Yes. **Alcoholic beverages** No. **Disabled access** Yes. **Wheelchair rental** Yes. **Baby-stroller rental** Yes. **Lockers** Yes. **Pet kennels** Yes. **Rain check** In some instances. **Private tours** No.

DESCRIPTION AND COMMENTS   This cornucopia of hyperintense roller coasters (it seems as if a new one opens every year) is heaven for teens and thrill-mad preteens, but it could be hell for younger ones. They do, however, get their own smaller-thrill area, with such Looney Tunes–inspired kiddie rides as Elmer's Weather Balloons and Foghorn Leghorn's Railway. But the real reason to come here is for the white-knuckle, stomach-flipping thrill rides, our 14-year-old's reason for living. From Superman The Escape (which accelerates to 100 mph in seven seconds) to the wonderful Colossus (the tallest, fastest wooden roller coaster in the West), these rides are designed to make you scream. Valencia is north of LA, about a half-hour drive from downtown, or 45 minutes from Santa Monica (much longer at evening rush hour).

PASADENA

THE LITTLE OLD LADY FROM PASADENA isn't much in evidence anymore—these days, Pasadena is packed with families, both ones who live on its stately old tree-lined streets and ones who are visiting this LA satellite city, just ten minutes north of downtown. Over the last 15 years, formerly seedy **Old Pasadena** has become one of the hottest outdoor mall–restaurant-nightlife areas in Southern California, beloved by SUV-driving moms and tattooed teens alike—and now you can take the MTA's Gold Line from downtown LA to Old Pasadena.

unofficial **TIP**
With its family-friendly destinations and proximity to downtown LA and Universal City, Pasadena is a fine vacation base, particularly in the winter, when being by the beach isn't so appealing.

On weekends, street musicians, balloon-animal makers, and magicians amuse passersby; in summer, don't miss the nightly free concerts at **Levitt Pavilion** in Memorial Park on the edge of Old Town (☎ 626-683-3230; **www.levittpavilion pasadena.org**); Wednesday nights are aimed at children, but all concerts are family-friendly. Also in summer are Friday- and Saturday-night free outdoor movie screenings or concerts in the **One Colorado** courtyard (☎ 626-564-1066; **www.onecolorado .net**); all are fun for families. Elsewhere in Old Town are a movie-theater complex, teen-haven stores, candy and frozen-yogurt shops, a **Barnes & Noble** with a children's area, excellent restaurants, and a plaza with climb-on-me sculptures. About a mile east on Colorado Boulevard is a stylish outdoor mall, **Paseo Colorado,** with the requisite multiplex and hip chain restaurants; it's where Pasadena's middle-school set hangs out. If we have a spare weekend hour, we take our children to **Vroman's Bookstore** (695 East Colorado Boulevard; ☎ 626-449-5320; **www .vromansbookstore.com**), one of the great independent booksellers, with a wonderful kids' section and first-rate storytelling programs.

Elsewhere in town are a bounty of museums and parks, the most family-friendly of which are listed below; see also **Lacy Park** under "The Best Beaches and Parks" and **Eaton Canyon** under "Hiking" in "Outdoor Family Adventures." And see the Calendar of Events to learn about the town's famous parades: the **Rose Parade,** the **Rosebud Parade,** and the **Doo Dah Parade.**

pasadena

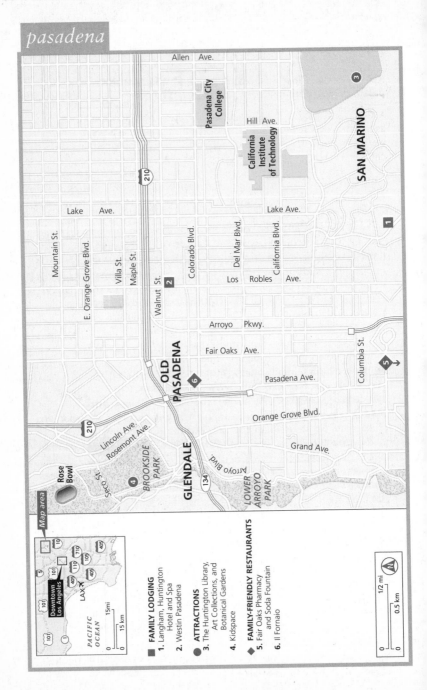

FAMILY LODGING
1. Langham, Huntington Hotel and Spa
2. Westin Pasadena

ATTRACTIONS
3. The Huntington Library, Art Collections, and Botanical Gardens
4. Kidspace

FAMILY-FRIENDLY RESTAURANTS
5. Fair Oaks Pharmacy and Soda Fountain
6. Il Fornaio

FAMILY LODGING

Langham, Huntington Hotel & Spa

1401 South Oak Knoll Avenue, Pasadena; ☎ 626-568-3900;
pasadena.langhamhotels.com; $299–$399 and up

A GRAND, GORGEOUS, AND HISTORIC hotel from Pasadena's early days
as a posh winter resort, the Huntington is a pretty formal place, but it's still
welcoming to children. The pool is beautiful, the poolside restaurant has a
children's menu, and the pastry chef offers baking classes for kids. As with
all Pasadena hotels, it books up months before for the Rose Parade.

Westin Pasadena

191 North Los Robles Avenue, Pasadena; ☎ 888-625-5144 or
626-792-2727; www.starwoodhotels.com; $239–$425

THIS PLEASANT, MODERN HOTEL is well located for visitors, near Paseo
Colorado (shops, theaters, restaurants), the Pasadena Playhouse, and
Vroman's Bookstore; Old Town and its Gold Line subway station are just
a few blocks away. There's no kids' program, but there's a rooftop pool,
a children's menu in the restaurant, a California Pizza Kitchen next door,
ticket packages for Universal Studios, and a wonderful plaza outside full of
waterways and little fountains that kids love to explore.

ATTRACTIONS

The Huntington Library, Art Collections, and Botanical Gardens

APPEAL BY AGE	PRESCHOOL ★★★	GRADE SCHOOL ★★★	TEENS ★★★
YOUNG ADULTS ★★★★	OVER 30 ★★★★½		SENIORS ★★★★½

1151 Oxford Road, San Marino; ☎ 626-405-2100; www.huntington.org

Hours *September–May:* Monday and Wednesday–Friday, noon–4:30 p.m.;
Saturday and Sunday, 10:30 a.m.–4:30 p.m.; *June–August:* Wednesday–Monday,
10:30 a.m.–4:30 p.m.; closed major holidays. **Admission** $15 adults on
weekdays, $20 weekends, $12 seniors on weekdays, $15 weekends, $10 students
ages 12–18 (with full-time student ID), $6 children ages 5–11, free for children
age 5 and under; groups of 15 or more $11 each; free (with advance tickets)
first Thursday of month; no picnics allowed. **Touring time** Average 2 hours;
minimum 1 hour. **Rainy-day touring** Yes, but you'll get wet. **Restaurants** Cafe,
tearoom. **Alcoholic beverages** No. **Disabled access** Yes. **Wheelchair rental**
Free, reserve. **Baby-stroller rental** No. **Lockers** Yes. **Pet kennels** No. **Rain
check** No. **Private tours** Arranged for mornings.

DESCRIPTION AND COMMENTS An internationally famous treasure found in
sleepy San Marino, a wealthy suburb just south of Pasadena, this cultural

center has appeal to both preschoolers and teenagers. The little ones love to run through the extraordinary gardens: world-class roses, a desert garden, a new Chinese garden, a Zen garden, a jungle garden, and, most of all, the extraordinary Children's Garden, an interactive experience designed for children ages 2 to 7. They can walk under a rainbow, disappear into a sea of fog, make music with pebbles, and more. The Conservatory for Botanical Science has hands-on exhibits that appeal to all ages, including the Carnivorous Plant Bog (cool!) and the Field Lab. Older children, especially bookworms, will be wowed by some of the venerable books in the library, including a Gutenberg Bible and first editions of Shakespeare. In-between kids will have fun searching for Gainsborough's *Blue Boy* in the art gallery. The beautiful Rose Garden Tea Room is a wonderful place to celebrate a birthday or occasion; the Café is more informal and inexpensive.

 ## Kidspace

APPEAL BY AGE	PRESCHOOL ★★★★½	GRADE SCHOOL ★★★★½	TEENS ★★
YOUNG ADULTS ★★	OVER 30 ★★★		SENIORS ★★★

**480 North Arroyo Boulevard; ☎ 626-449-9144;
www.kidspacemuseum.org**

Hours Daily, 9:30 a.m.–5 p.m.; closed major holidays. **Admission** $8; free for age 1 and under. **Touring time** Average 3 hours; minimum 1 hour. **Rainy-day touring** Yes, for the indoor activities. **Restaurants** Yes. **Alcoholic beverages** Yes. **Disabled access** Yes. **Wheelchair rental** No. **Baby-stroller rental** No, strollers not allowed. **Lockers** No. **Pet kennels** No. **Rain check** No. **Private tours** No.

DESCRIPTION AND COMMENTS   Once a modest play place in a borrowed space, Kidspace is now one of the finest interactive children's museums in the West, and it's worth a detour. In Brookside Park near the Rose Bowl, it pays tribute to the site's original tenant, the Fannie Morrison Horticultural Center, by making the outdoors as much a part of the experience as the indoors. Shows and story times take place in the outdoor amphitheater, and gardens include the Bumpy Fuzzy Garden, Interpretive Arroyo (a scaled-down version of the Arroyo Seco, in which Kidspace sits), the Spider Web Climber, tricycle tracks, and much more. Indoors are a wonderful digging exhibit for budding paleontologists, an earthquake zone, the Bug Inn, climbing towers, and more.

FAMILY-FRIENDLY RESTAURANTS

Fair Oaks Pharmacy and Soda Fountain
**1526 Mission Street, South Pasadena; ☎ 626-799-1414;
www.fairoakspharmacy.net**

Meals served Lunch daily. **Cuisine** American. **Entree range** $4–$9. **Kids' menu** No. **Reservations** Not accepted. **Payment** AE, MC, V.

A PROPER SMALL-TOWN PHARMACY in the historic small town of South Pasadena, this place has a vintage 19th-century soda fountain complete with marble counter. You can get a simple, kid-pleasing lunch (hot dogs, grilled cheese) every day; and ice-cream concoctions in the afternoon. Fun gifts, too.

Il Fornaio
24 West Union Street, Pasadena; ☎ 626-683-9797; www.ilfornaio.com

---

Meals served Lunch, dinner and Sunday brunch. **Cuisine** Italian. **Entree range** Lunch $11–$23, dinner $12–$30 **Kids' menu** Yes. **Reservations** Recommended. **Payment** All major credit cards.

IDEALLY LOCATED IN THE HEART of Old Pasadena, Il Fornaio is on the upscale side, but it's welcoming to families, with an excellent children's menu, high chairs, and an outdoor terrace overlooking the One Colorado courtyard, home to summertime movie screenings and concerts. While the kids have Italian-style mac and cheese, you can enjoy a delicious seafood tagliolini or grilled salmon. If they get bored waiting for you to finish your glass of Barbera, they can go outside to play on the *Working Man* sculpture.

THE MOUNTAINS:
Big Bear, Lake Arrowhead, and Idyllwild

LOCAL SKIING IS ONE OF THE GREAT LUXURIES of Southern California life. It means that residents can be enjoying a sunny day in their hometown, drive two hours "up the hill," and get in an afternoon of skiing. And the nearby ski resorts are especially nice for introducing kids to the sport. But these charming mountain retreats are equally appealing in the summer.

A popular weekend getaway for LA residents, **Big Bear** is less pretentious and easier for the casual visitor to negotiate than Lake Arrowhead, because the entire north shore of the lake is public land (so there are boat launches, bike trails, and picnic areas), and a combination of private and city concessions offers lake access on the southern side of the lake through a public swim beach, boat docks, and fishing sites. There are many modest vintage motels and cottages in Big Bear, as well as two conference resort hotels and some bed-and-breakfasts. It's also a ski center, five minutes from Southern California's largest ski mountain, **Snow Summit.**

Lakefront property in nearby **Lake Arrowhead,** on the other hand, is almost entirely in private hands, and unless you rent a house on the shoreline (not a bad option for a family), your only access to the lake is by staying at the **Lake Arrowhead Resort** or in the shopping area known as the **Village.** Meanwhile, **Idyllwild** is in another mountain range, about two hours from LA near **Palm Springs,** and it offers a much-less-trafficked locale for mountain hiking in the summer or snow play in the winter, weather permitting.

FAMILY LODGING

Grey Squirrel Resort
39372 Big Bear Boulevard, Big Bear Lake; ☎ 800-381-5569 or 909-866-4335; www.greysquirrel.com; $94 and up

BELOVED OF MANY LA FAMILIES for weekend retreats, this cabin compound in the woods along Big Bear Lake's main drag is an excellent value. Our favorite is the Raccoon Cabin, a 75-year-old, two-bedroom house with a stone fireplace. The 16 cottages and 3 small motel units share outdoor

the mountains: big bear, lake arrowhead, and idyllwild

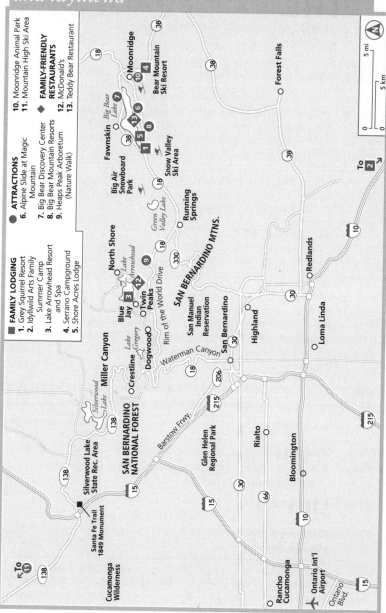

■ FAMILY LODGING
1. Grey Squirrel Resort
2. Idyllwild Arts Family Summer Camp
3. Lake Arrowhead Resort and Spa
4. Serrano Campground
5. Shore Acres Lodge

● ATTRACTIONS
6. Alpine Slide at Magic Mountain
7. Big Bear Discovery Center
8. Big Bear Mountain Resorts
9. Heaps Peak Arboretum (Nature Walk)
10. Moonridge Animal Park
11. Mountain High Ski Area

◆ FAMILY-FRIENDLY RESTAURANTS
12. McDonald's
13. Teddy Bear Restaurant

barbecue facilities, a laundry area, and a heated pool. Even the family dog is welcome. This friendly, well-maintained place is a great base for hiking, sledding, and fishing down at the lake, a short walk away.

 Idyllwild Arts Family Summer Camp

52500 Temecula Road (off CA 243), Idyllwild; ☎ 951-659-2171, ext. 365; www.idyllwildarts.org; 1-bedroom unit with 2–4 people: $1,850–$3,050 per week (includes all classes, activities, and meals)

WHEN SCHOOL IS OUT at the Idyllwild Arts School in the cool, sleepy San Jacinto Mountains above Palm Springs, families move into the dorms for weeklong arts-oriented camp fun. While young children enjoy playtime and day care and older children take part in supervised swimming, crafts, theater games, art projects, and sports, parents divide their time among their choice of arts classes—everything from ceramics and dance to writing and acting—and such outdoor pursuits as hiking and mountain biking. Everyone sleeps in modern, new Pearson Hall, with private bathrooms and daily maid service, and all meals are included.

Lake Arrowhead Resort and Spa
27984 Highway 189 (CA 189), at entrance to Lake Arrowhead Village; ☎ 909-336-1511 or 800-800-6792; www.laresort.com; $200–$800

PERFECTLY SITED if you're not a very outdoorsy family but want to spend some time in the mountains, the 177-room Lake Arrowhead Resort is part of lakefront Arrowhead Village, a collection of shops and restaurants. The views are spectacular in the summer and Christmas card–like in the winter. The resort has its own beach for swimming in the (cold) lake, as well as a (heated) pool. The adjacent marina offers watercraft rentals.

Serrano Campground
Off CA 38, Big Bear Lake; ☎ 909-866-8021; reservations ☎ 877-444-6777; www.reserveamerica.com; campsites $26–$54

A PLEASANT CAMPGROUND in the pines, close to Big Bear Lake and the town conveniences, this national forest campground allows some of its sites to be reserved, which is always a good bet when camping with kids. Shower, flush toilets, fire rings, firewood, and ranger interpretive programs, as well as lake access for boating and fishing.

Shore Acres Lodge
40090 Lakeview Drive, Big Bear Lake; ☎ 800-524-6600 or 909-866-8200; www.shoreacreslodge.com; $165 and up (based on triple occupancy)

NOT QUITE A MOTEL, more a collection of housekeeping cabins, this lodge is well located on a quiet stretch of Big Bear Lake, and it offers good value without the hassle of working through a private-home rental agency. The choices include 12 cabins with kitchens, ranging from studio-size to a cabin that sleeps 12. All are near the shore, and some are directly on the lake. In the summer, the office also offers additional rental units in private homes. The lodge area has a playground, pool, hot tub, and boat dock.

ATTRACTIONS

Alpine Slide at Magic Mountain

APPEAL BY AGE	PRESCHOOL ★★	GRADE SCHOOL ★★★	TEENS ★★★
YOUNG ADULTS ★★		OVER 30 ★★	SENIORS ½

800 Wildrose Lane, Big Bear Lake; ☎ 909-866-4626; www.alpineslidebigbear.com

Hours *Alpine Slide:* summer, Sunday–Thursday, 10 a.m.–6 p.m.; Friday and Saturday, 10 a.m.–9 p.m.; fall: Saturday and Sunday, 10 a.m.–6 p.m.; Monday, 11 a.m.–4 p.m.; winter: Saturday and Sunday, 10 a.m.–dusk; Monday–Friday, 11 a.m.–4 p.m.; spring: Saturday and Sunday, 10 a.m.–5 p.m. *Waterslide:* mid-June–mid-September, daily, 10 a.m.–6 p.m. *Snow Play:* November–Easter: daily, 10 a.m.–4 p.m. **Admission** Single ride on Alpine Slide, $4; $12 Waterslide unlimited day pass, $22 Snow Play unlimited day pass; children age 6 and under ride free with adult; various ride packages available. **Touring time** Average 1 hour; minimum 20 minutes. **Rainy-day touring** No. **Restaurants** Snack bar. **Alcoholic beverages** No. **Disabled access** Yes. **Wheelchair rental** No. **Baby-stroller rental** No. **Lockers** No. **Pet kennels** No. **Rain check** No. **Private tours** No.

DESCRIPTION AND COMMENTS   This modest family attraction has been the highlight of a couple of winter-spring weekends in Big Bear. There was enough snow left to slide ourselves into exhaustion on the inner tube slide, climbing up the small hill with giant inner tubes and flying right back down again (big kids can grab a rope tow, but not the under-8 set, so we hoofed it). Then, since there wasn't too much snow, we had a ride on the curving, lugelike concrete slide, a little kid on our lap and the bigger kids steering their own, which was quite a thrill. Also open at various times are a go-cart track and waterslide. Go-cart rentals are $4 single, $6 double. Not for the very young.

Big Bear Discovery Center

APPEAL BY AGE	PRESCHOOL ★★	GRADE SCHOOL ★★★	TEENS ★★★
YOUNG ADULTS ★★★		OVER 30 ★★★	SENIORS ★★★

40971 North Shore Drive (north shore of Big Bear Lake on CA 38 between Fawnskin and Stanfield Cutoff; ☎ 909-866-3437; www.bigbeardiscoverycenter.com

Hours Daily, 8:30 a.m.–4 p.m. (summer); closed Christmas and New Year's Day. **Admission** Free; some activities have fees or require a Park Service Adventure Pass. **Touring time** Average 1–4 hours; minimum 15 minutes. **Rainy-day touring** Yes. **Restaurants** No. **Alcoholic beverages** No. **Disabled access** Yes, into center; varies with different programs. **Wheelchair rental** No. **Baby-stroller rental** No. **Lockers** No. **Pet kennels** No. **Rain check** No. **Private tours** Yes.

DESCRIPTION AND COMMENTS   Big Bear Discovery Center is a wonderful environmental-education facility resulting from a partnership between the federal San Bernardino National Forest and the San Bernardino National Forest Association, a private, nonprofit organization. Because budget cuts decreased the number of forest rangers available to educate, guide, or entertain the public, the Discovery Center was created to take up the slack. More than 100 volunteers (among whom are two former Big Bear Lake mayors and two former college presidents) staff the center's exhibits and displays seven days a week, and also develop and participate in programs such as campfire talks, interpretive hikes, and history tours. The Adventure Outpost store offers educational and nature-related merchandise.

After looking over the center's exhibits about local flora and fauna, families can sign up for such activities as guided hikes, campfire programs with music and storytelling (fees vary, reservations required), or, in the winter, the center's Eagle Tours, which take participants by vans into bald eagle habitat areas closed to the general public.

 ## Big Bear Mountain Resorts

APPEAL BY AGE	PRESCHOOL ★★★	GRADE SCHOOL ★★★★	TEENS ★★★★
YOUNG ADULTS ★★★		OVER 30 ★★★	SENIORS ★★

880 Summit Boulevard (just south of Big Bear Village), Big Bear Lake; ☎ 909-866-5766; www.snowsummit.com

Hours Weekdays, 8 a.m.–4:30 p.m.; weekends, 9 a.m.–4 p.m.; ski season is mid-November–mid-April; mountain biking and hiking available in off-season. **Admission** Lift tickets: adults, $51–$64; kids ages 7–12, $20–$27; ages 13–21, $41–$55; free for age 6 and under. **Touring time** Average 1 day; minimum a half day. **Rainy-day touring** Depending on conditions; resort may close. **Restaurants** Yes. **Alcoholic beverages** Yes. **Disabled access** Yes. **Wheelchair rental** No. **Baby-stroller rental** No. **Lockers** Yes. **Pet kennels** No. **Rain check** Vouchers under certain conditions. **Private tours** Private lessons.

DESCRIPTION AND COMMENTS   Two mountains, Snow Summit and Bear Mountain, are now under the same ownership, so one lift ticket will work at either mountain. If you have skilled snowboarding teenagers, they'll want to go to Bear Mountain, which is full of rails, jumps, pipes, and other extreme action. Families with younger kids or beginning skiers or snowboarders will be more comfortable at Snow Summit, which has a fun, professionally staffed children's center and a good ski and snowboard school. If your 5-year-old gets wet and miserable and doesn't want to ski anymore, he can come inside, have some juice, and play with the toys. Both mountains have only a fraction of the runs that the major Sierra resorts have, and the snow is often man-made, but there's plenty to keep a skiing family happy for a two- to three-day trip. In summer, some of Snow Summit's runs become the turf of mountain bikers, often the same teens who were snowboarding here just a few months earlier.

Heaps Peak Arboretum (Nature Walk)

| APPEAL BY AGE | PRESCHOOL ★★ | GRADE SCHOOL ★★★ | TEENS ★★ |
| YOUNG ADULTS ★★ | | OVER 30 ★★★ | SENIORS ★★★ |

CA 18 (2 miles from Lake Arrowhead turnoff); Ranger Station,
☎ **909-337-2444; www.heapspeakarboretum.com**

Hours Daily, dawn–dusk. **Admission** Free, but Adventure Pass is necessary to park ($5 for day or $30 for year); purchase from Arrowhead Ranger Station off CA 18 or vendors around Lake Arrowhead. **Touring time** Average 1½ hours; minimum 20 minutes to stretch. **Rainy-day touring** No. **Restaurants** No. **Alcoholic beverages** No. **Disabled access** Some trails limited. **Wheelchair rental** No. **Baby-stroller rental** No. **Lockers** No. **Pet kennels** No; pets not allowed on trail. **Rain check** No. **Private tours** Yes; call Ranger Station.

DESCRIPTION AND COMMENTS Located in an Arrowhead-adjacent site that makes a good first stop on reaching the top of the mountain, this nature trail is a great place to walk after being in the car for a little too long. Your kids can stretch their legs and get acquainted with the forest on an easy one-mile loop that meanders through dogwood groves (blooming in May) and wildflower meadows, across a stream or two, and through pines and chaparral. The brochure that identifies various points to stop and learn a thing or two is geared beautifully to kids.

Moonridge Animal Park

| APPEAL BY AGE | PRESCHOOL ★★★ | GRADE SCHOOL ★★★ | TEENS ★★ |
| YOUNG ADULTS ★★★ | | OVER 30 ★★★ | SENIORS ★★★ |

43285 Goldmine Drive, Big Bear Lake, near Big Bear Mountain
Ski Resort, Moonridge Road to Club View Drive to Goldmine Drive;
☎ **909-878-4200 or 909-584-1171; www.moonridgezoo.org**

Hours *June–August:* daily, 10 a.m.–5 p.m.; *September–April:* Monday–Friday, 10 a.m.–4 p.m.; Saturday and Sunday, 10 a.m.–5 p.m. (weather permitting). **Admission** $11 adults, $6 seniors and children ages 3–10, age 3 and under free. **Touring time** Average 1–2 hours; minimum 1 hour. **Rainy-day touring** Open during light rain, but closes during snowstorms. **Restaurants** No. **Alcoholic beverages** No. **Disabled access** Yes. **Wheelchair rental** No. **Baby-stroller rental** No. **Lockers** Yes. **Pet kennels** No. **Rain check** No. **Private tours** No.

DESCRIPTION AND COMMENTS As we gazed at the fierce, dignified bald eagle here, our daughter spotted a fallen feather. The docent gently took it from her, explaining to the kids that any feathers shed by the eagles are given to Native American groups for sacred use. Founded in 1959, the animal park shelters orphaned and injured animals native to the San Bernardino Mountains, releasing the recovered ones into the wild. It's also open to visitors, who can see coyotes, bears, wolves, cougars, raccoons, foxes, and birds of prey. There's a gift shop and a few educational exhibits. But check the Web site or call before visiting— Moonridge is in the middle of a capital campaign and plans to become the Living Forest Wildlife Center, with better exhibits and enclosures and a more peaceful setting.

Mountain High Resort

APPEAL BY AGE	PRESCHOOL ★★	GRADE SCHOOL ★★★	TEENS ★★★
YOUNG ADULTS ★★★		OVER 30 ★★	SENIORS ½

24510 Highway 2 (CA 2), Wrightwood; ☎ 760-249-5808 or 888-754-7878; www.mthigh.com

Hours *Mid-November–mid-April:* Monday–Friday, 8:30 a.m.–10 p.m.; Saturday and Sunday, 8 a.m.–10 p.m. **Admission** *Lift tickets:* $46, 4 hours; $51, 8 hours; children ages 7–12, $20; free for children under age 6 with paying adult and seniors age 70 and older; *night skiing:* $30 adults, $20 children ages 7–12; 5–10 p.m. **Touring time** Average 8 hours; minimum 6 hours. **Rainy-day touring** No. **Restaurants** Yes. **Alcoholic beverages** Yes. **Disabled access** Yes. **Wheelchair rental** No. **Baby-stroller rental** No. **Lockers** Yes. **Pet kennels** No. **Rain check** Vouchers under certain conditions. **Private tours** Yes, classes.

DESCRIPTION AND COMMENTS   Tucked into a sparsely populated community in the mountains north of LA, an easy 90-minute drive from downtown, this working-class ski mountain is typically filled with local teens snowboarding, skiing, and hanging out on the big wooden deck of the lodge, checking each other out. Reasonably priced lessons are available for younger children, but the facilities are minimal, with a little too much uphill walking for the littlest ones. The snow can get pretty wet at the bottom, not to mention thick with out-of-control beginning snowboarders, but if you stay on the lifts to the top of the mountain, you might be surprised at the quality of the snow, much of which is

ON THE LAKES

You don't have to own or even rent a ski or fishing boat to spend some time on the water. For one thing, if you take an afternoon tour of Big Bear Lake, your fretful preschooler may nap the time away (as ours did) in the fresh mountain air, with the hum of the boat's engine to lull him or her. For another, the view from the lake is unique, and whether you're interested in gazing at celebrity vacation homes, geological formations, or the spectacular granite slopes of San Gorgonio Mountain against a bright blue sky, you'll see it from the boat. Big Bear's scenic boat tour leaves from Pine Knot Landing at the foot of Pine Knot Avenue in Big Bear Lake for an 80-minute narrated excursion, April through November, departing every two hours 10 a.m. to 6 p.m.; fare is $13.50 adults, $11 ages 52 and older, $7 children ages 2 to 10; call ☎ 909-866-2628; **www .pineknotlanding.com.** The *Arrowhead Queen* can be boarded at Arrowhead Village for a 45-minute tour, year-round; boats leave at regular intervals daily, 11 a.m. to 5 p.m.; fare is $15, $10 children ages 3 to 12; they're sold at LeRoy's Sports; ☎ 909-336-6992.

man-made. Not for anyone who get easily spooked by raging teen snowboarders—but if you have teen snowboarders in the family, they'll want to come here.

FAMILY-FRIENDLY RESTAURANTS

McDonald's
28200 Highway 189 (CA 189), Building G, Lake Arrowhead (Lake Arrowhead Village, lower level); ☎ 909-337-0558

Meals served Breakfast, lunch, and dinner. **Cuisine** American fast food. **Entree range** $2–$7. **Kids' menu** Yes. **Reservations** Not accepted. **Payment** AE, MC, V.

THIS MAY BE THE McDONALD'S with the best view in all of California. It is indeed lakefront dining, and you won't see a bluer sky or more-sparkling water from any of the terraces at the pricier restaurants down the way. So go ahead, let the kids get their favorites—just insist on getting a terrace table and put on plenty of sunscreen.

Teddy Bear Restaurant
583 Pine Knot Avenue, Big Bear Lake; ☎ 909-866-5415

Meals served Breakfast, lunch, and dinner. **Cuisine** American. **Entree range** Breakfast and lunch, $7–$10; dinner, $8–$15. **Kids' menu** Yes. **Reservations** Not accepted. **Payment** AE, MC, V.

ONE OF OUR FAVORITE PLACES to eat in a town with pretty undistinguished dining, this coffee shop does a fine BLT, some great pancakes, and such local mountain specialties as warm hot chocolate on a chilly fall morning.

PALM SPRINGS

THE DESERT COMMUNITIES ARE LOVED BY RETIREES, of course, and driving through superquiet **Palm Springs** and its neighboring towns, **Palm Desert** and **Rancho Mirage,** on a hot day, with the empty streets (everyone's indoors) punctuated by golf courses, can make parents panic—what will we do with the kids? But real kids live here, and there are a growing number of activities for young people. Resorts include kids in the mix, especially as parents are tending to bring kids along for a weekend added to a meeting or conference. Palm Springs is beloved as a weekend getaway in winter for sun lovers (it's a two-hour drive east of downtown LA). If you're going midweek or weekends, plan to include a Thursday night in your stay. The lively street fair and market (6 to 10 p.m. in the winter, 7 to 10 p.m. in the summer) offers fun food, booths (selling everything from vintage celebrity photos to a one-minute massage), and entertainment.

unofficial **TIP**
Palm Springs can turn hellish in July and August, when temperatures sometimes hit 115°F—but those months bring incredible deals at the resorts.

FAMILY LODGING

Desert Springs, A JW Marriott Resort and Spa
74855 Country Club Drive, Palm Desert; ☎ 800-228-9290 or 760-341-2211; www.desertspringsresort.com; $119–$510; substantial discounts in summer

THIS GIGANTIC (more than 900 rooms and suites) resort hotel is loads of fun because it offers entertainment and luxury without formality. There are, for example, little motorboats to take you to the restaurants. The hundreds of people lounging poolside are serenaded by a reggae surf band playing Jimmy Buffett tunes, and the isolation of the place is not an issue because it's got everything from a cappuccino bar to a hot dog stand. We took our kids to the golf course coffee shop for breakfast, sat in the hot tub and watched colorful hot air balloons glide overhead, then spent some time playing badminton near the tennis courts. The year-round Kid's Club

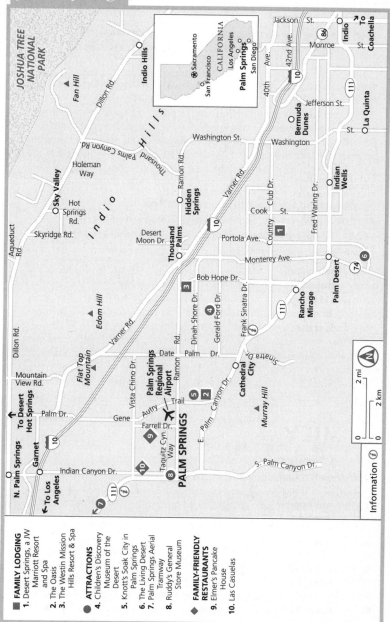

palm springs

JOSHUA TREE NATIONAL PARK

CALIFORNIA

Sacramento
San Francisco
Los Angeles
San Diego
Palm Springs

Jackson St.
Monroe
Indio
To Coachella
86
42nd Ave.
111
40th Ave.
Jefferson St.
La Quinta
Bermuda Dunes
Washington St.
Washington St.
Indian Wells
Cook Club Dr.
Fred Waring Dr.
Cook St.
1
Portola Ave.
Monterey Ave.
Palm Desert
74
6
Country Club Dr.
Bob Hope Dr.
3
Dinah Shore Dr.
Gerald Ford Dr.
4
Frank Sinatra Dr.
Rancho Mirage
111
Indio Hills
Fan Hill
Dillon Rd.
Indio Hills
Palms Canyon Rd.
Thousand
Ramon Rd.
Holeman Way
Sky Valley
Hot Springs Rd.
Skyridge Rd.
Desert Moon Dr.
Thousand Palms
Hidden Springs
Varner Rd.
10
Aqueduct Rd.
Edom Hill
Varner Rd.
Flat Top Mountain
Mountain View Rd.
Dillon Rd.
To Desert Hot Springs
Palm Dr.
Garnet
10
N. Palm Springs
To Los Angeles
Indian Canyon Dr.
111
7
Gene Autry Trail
Vista Chino Dr.
Palm Springs Regional Airport
Date
Palm Dr.
Ramon Rd.
Farrell Dr.
9
Taquitz Cyn. Way
10
8
PALM SPRINGS
S. Palm Canyon Dr.
E. Palm Canyon Dr.
Cathedral City
Murray Hill
Sinatra Dr.
5
2

Information (i)

2 mi
2 km

FAMILY LODGING
1. Desert Springs, a JW Marriott Resort and Spa
2. The Oasis
3. The Westin Mission Hills Resort & Spa

ATTRACTIONS
4. Children's Discovery Museum of the Desert
5. Knott's Soak City in Palm Springs
6. The Living Desert
7. Palm Springs Aerial Tramway
8. Ruddy's General Store Museum

FAMILY-FRIENDLY RESTAURANTS
9. Elmer's Pancake House
10. Las Casuelas

($75 per day), features organized lawn games, rock-wall climbing, arts and crafts, pizza parties, swimming parties, cartoons, and movies.

The Oasis
4190 East Palm Canyon Drive, Palm Springs; ☎ 800-444-6633 or 760-324-3422; www.vacationinternationale.com; $245–$365 for 2-bedroom condo (sleeps 6)

THIS IS A GOOD CHOICE for families from March through October, when the nearby Soak City water park is open. (Packages are often offered that include park admission.) But this isn't a hotel, really; it's the overnight rental arm of a time-share condo complex. Two- and three-bedroom condos are available, and the eight pools of the complex are open to overnight guests. The air-conditioned, fully furnished units are luxurious for the price, and although there is neither restaurant nor room service, we were happy to order pizza and relax.

The Westin Mission Hills Resort & Spa
7133 Dinah Shore Drive, Rancho Mirage; ☎ 800-WESTIN-1 or 760-328-5955; www.starwoodhotels.com; $299 and up in summer, $279 and up in late fall and winter

IT WAS HARD TO BE COMFORTABLE with a family of four in one of the small rooms at this 552-room resort, but the kids were happy in the daytime with the pool area, which includes misters at the bar and a wonderful 60-foot waterslide into the pool. Because of the many conference attendees, the Kids Club Discovery Room is pretty active for kids ages 4 to 12 (though kids older than age 8 might find it a little silly), offering a year-round program with daily morning or afternoon sessions or both ($25 to $75 each) featuring nature walks, swimming, arts and crafts, and movies. Family movies and games are available in the rooms. In the summer, two kids dine for free when accompanied by a parent. Tennis-playing families should take part in the excellent Reed Anderson Tennis Camp, held in the cooler months.

⁞ ATTRACTIONS

Children's Discovery Museum of the Desert

APPEAL BY AGE	PRESCHOOL ★★★★	GRADE SCHOOL ★★★★	TEENS –
YOUNG ADULTS –	OVER 30 ★		SENIORS ½

71–701 Gerald Ford Drive, Rancho Mirage; ☎ 760-321-0602; www.cdmod.org

Hours Tuesday–Sunday, 10 a.m.–5 p.m.; closed Monday. **Admission** $8 per person age 2 and up; all children must be accompanied by an adult. **Touring time** Average 2 hours; minimum 1 hour. **Rainy-day touring** Yes. **Restaurants** No. **Alcoholic beverages** No. **Disabled access** Yes. **Wheelchair rental** No. **Baby-stroller rental** No. **Lockers** No. **Pet kennels** No. **Rain check** No. **Private tours** For groups, special events.

DESCRIPTION AND COMMENTS A hands-on activity center where kids can paint a car, play in a grocery store, and rummage in an "attic." Special craft programs might include arts and crafts from clay to Native American gourd art. A highlight is an archaeological dig, which simulates a dig for Cahuilla Native American artifacts. Picnic area and museum store.

Knott's Soak City in Palm Springs

APPEAL BY AGE	PRESCHOOL ★★★	GRADE SCHOOL ★★★★	TEENS ★★★★
YOUNG ADULTS ★★★		OVER 30 ★★	SENIORS ★★

1500 Gene Autry Trail, Palm Springs; ☎ 760-327-0499; www.soakcityusa.com

Hours *Mid-March–Labor Day:* daily, 11 a.m.–5 p.m.; *Labor Day–October:* Saturday and Sunday, 11 a.m.–6 p.m. (on average—hours vary daily, so check Web site); closed November–mid-March. **Admission** $30 adults, $20 children ages 3–11, free for children under age 3. After 3 p.m., $20 for children and adults; parking $8. **Touring time** Average 3–4 hours; there may be lines for some of the 13 slides. **Rainy-day touring** No. **Restaurants** Snack bars. **Alcoholic beverages** No. **Disabled access** Yes. **Wheelchair rental** Yes. **Baby-stroller rental** No. **Lockers** Yes. **Pet kennels** No. **Rain check** No. **Private tours** No.

DESCRIPTION AND COMMENTS This is one of the smallest of the water parks we mention in this book, but you can believe that in the more-than-100°F temperatures of the desert, it's among the most loved. It has most of what a water park needs: a wave pool, slides, a tube river; the six-story Pacific Spin is a big hit with older kids. This place is short on shade—please take our advice and pay for a "cabana," which is actually a tent with chairs, tables, and indoor–outdoor carpeting. Otherwise, you'll fry every time you leave the water, and your kids'll get sun-addled brains.

The Living Desert

APPEAL BY AGE	PRESCHOOL ★★★	GRADE SCHOOL ★★★★	TEENS ★★★★
YOUNG ADULTS ★★★★		OVER 30 ★★★★	SENIORS ★★★★

47–900 Portola Avenue, Palm Desert; ☎ 760-346-5694; www.livingdesert.org

Hours *September 1–June 15:* daily, 9 a.m.–5 p.m.; last admission at 4 p.m. *June 16–August 31:* 8 a.m.–1:30 p.m., last admission at 1 p.m. Closed Christmas. **Admission** *September 1–June 15:* $11.95, age 13 and up, $10.50, seniors and military, $7.50, children ages 3–12, free for children age 2 and under; *June 16–August 31:* $8.75 age 13 and up, $4.75 children ages 3–12, free for children age 2 and under. **Touring time** Average 3 hours; minimum 50 minutes, for tram ride only. **Rainy-day touring** No. **Restaurants** Yes. **Alcoholic beverages** No. **Disabled access** Yes. **Wheelchair rental** Yes, free. **Baby-stroller rental** Yes, free. **Lockers** No. **Pet kennels** No. **Rain check** No. **Private tours** Yes.

DESCRIPTION AND COMMENTS To dispel any myths about deserts being barren wastelands, bring the family to this wonderful 1,200-acre preserve.

The elusive bighorn sheep clamber on hillsides as you wander through the pathways, along with the even rarer oryx, which the park is helping to save from extinction. The kids will meet coyotes, great horned owls, tortoises, mountain lions, and golden eagles of incredible grandeur. Inside is the Discovery Room, where kids can touch and feel. The desert botanical gardens will bore the kids, but sneak a peek if you can. If the day's too hot for walking, consider taking the 50-minute guided tram tour; in general, arrive right at opening time to beat the heat, unless you're visiting in winter.

Palm Springs Aerial Tramway

APPEAL BY AGE	PRESCHOOL ★	GRADE SCHOOL ★★★★	TEENS ★★★
YOUNG ADULTS ★★★		OVER 30 ★★★	SENIORS ★★★

1 Tramway Road at CA 111, Palm Springs; ☎ 888-515-TRAM or 760-325-1391; www.pstramway.com

Hours Weekdays, 10 a.m.–8 p.m.; weekends, 8 a.m.–8 p.m. **Admission** $22.25 adults, $20.25 for seniors age 60 and older, $15.25 children ages 3–12; children under age 3 ride free. **Touring time** Average 4 hours; minimum 2 hours. **Rainy-day touring** No. **Restaurants** Yes. **Alcoholic beverages** Yes. **Disabled access** Yes. **Wheelchair rental** No. **Baby-stroller rental** No. **Lockers** Yes. **Pet kennels** No. **Rain check** No. **Private tours** Yes.

DESCRIPTION AND COMMENTS   Gondola cars that rotate 360 degrees give you dizzying views as they whisk you off the desert floor and swoop you up the side of Mount San Jacinto, delivering you to a cool (sometimes even snow-filled) mountain park at 8,500 feet, with pines, trails, and picnic areas. The ride is a very big thrill for kids age 10 or younger (maybe a little too much for squeamish ones), and when the heat is wilting, it's a lovely escape. Just remember to bring a sweatshirt, because temperatures often drop 40°F or more. There's a restaurant up top, but we much prefer to bring a picnic.

Ruddy's General Store Museum

APPEAL BY AGE	PRESCHOOL ★	GRADE SCHOOL ★★	TEENS ★★★
YOUNG ADULTS ★★★		OVER 30 ★★★	SENIORS ★★★★

Village Green, 221 South Palm Canyon Drive, Palm Springs; ☎ 760-327-2156; www.palmsprings.com/points/heritage/ruddy.html

Hours *October–June:* Thursday–Sunday, 10 a.m.–4 p.m.; *July–September:* weekends, 10 a.m.–4 p.m. **Admission** 95¢ per person, children age 12 and under free. **Touring time** Average a half hour; minimum 15 minutes. **Rainy-day touring** Yes. **Restaurants** No. **Alcoholic beverages** No. **Disabled access** Yes. **Wheelchair rental** No. **Baby-stroller rental** No. **Lockers** Yes. **Pet kennels** No. **Rain check** No. **Private tours** No.

DESCRIPTION AND COMMENTS   Of the three small museums that make up Village Green in downtown Palm Springs, this one-room general store is the only one that will appeal to kids—and it's a fun and unique way to introduce them to everyday life of yesteryear. It's a facsimile of a general store circa 1930, and it's crammed with vintage packages of every imaginable product, all part of an extensive private collection. More than 6,000 unused items—from shirt collars to cigars, from soda-pop bottles to straw boater hats, from kites to toy trains—line the shelves and display cases.

FAMILY-FRIENDLY RESTAURANTS

Elmer's Pancake House

1030 East Palm Canyon Drive, Palm Springs; ☎ 760-327-8419; www.elmers-restaurants.com

---

Meals served Breakfast, lunch, and dinner. **Cuisine** American. **Entree range** $6–$12. **Kids' menu** Yes. **Reservations** Not accepted. **Payment** All major credit cards.

POPULAR WITH SENIORS and young families alike, this long-standing coffee shop does a booming breakfast business. Booths are roomy, service is friendly, and the pancakes are really good.

Las Casuelas

368 North Palm Canyon, Palm Springs; ☎ 760-325-3213

Meals served Breakfast, lunch, and dinner. **Cuisine** Mexican. **Entree range** Breakfast, $8–$15; lunch and dinner, $7–$22. **Kids' menu** Limited choice of hamburger, taco, or eggs. **Reservations** Recommended. **Payment** All major credit cards.

"LAS CAS" (as the locals call it) has been serving nachos, enchiladas, and tostadas in the desert for a couple of generations. This is the slightly more downscale original, which we like for its coziness and feel of local authenticity. A block away is the larger, fancier Las Casuelas Terraza, with a pretty sidewalk terrace and good margaritas (beer and wine only at the original location). The food at both is solid, tasty, and comforting; try the *mojo de ajos* (garlic shrimp).

PART FOUR

The
CENTRAL COAST

BEST KNOWN AS THE HOME OF THE MOST CELEBRATED stretch of California Highway 1, the Central Coast region of California has come into its own in recent years. The southern part of the Central Coast, from **Ventura** to **San Simeon,** is within easy reach of the Los Angeles metropolitan area, and the northern part, from **Big Sur** through the **Monterey Peninsula,** is weekend-getaway distance from San Francisco. Both sections of the Central Coast share a characteristic lack of urban sprawl: These are distinct and very different communities, with boundaries defined by agricultural or forest landscapes. And the pace of life is calmer here than in the urban areas.

A visit to the **Santa Barbara Zoo** or an afternoon on the **Santa Cruz Boardwalk** is no small-town experience, but each has an intimacy and ease that would be unthinkable in California's more heavily populated areas. (An exception to this rule is the internationally popular and crowded **Monterey Bay Aquarium.**) And the national restaurant or fast-food chain is not king here—many cafes are locally owned, use local produce, and create regional specialties for their menus.

We have explored this region with our children in a number of ways: by renting a beach house, by staying for the weekend during a soccer tournament, by adding time to an overnight business trip, by visiting friends and relatives. Highlights for our kids have included the unique and impressive Monterey Aquarium; Santa Barbara's charming little zoo; camping at **El Capitán State Beach,** playing in the clear, cold creek at Big Sur; apple-touring in the **Santa Ynez Valley;** getting wax impressions of their hands on the Santa Cruz Boardwalk; and, amazingly, enjoying classical music at the **Ojai Music Festival.**

To give this region its due, a week's visit is only fair. If you have only two or three days, focus on one end or the other. On the Southern California end, you can spend a few days based in Santa Barbara, exploring the beaches, the zoo, **Cachuma Lake, Solvang,** the playgrounds, and the parks. Or set up camp in **San Luis Obispo,** from which you can venture to

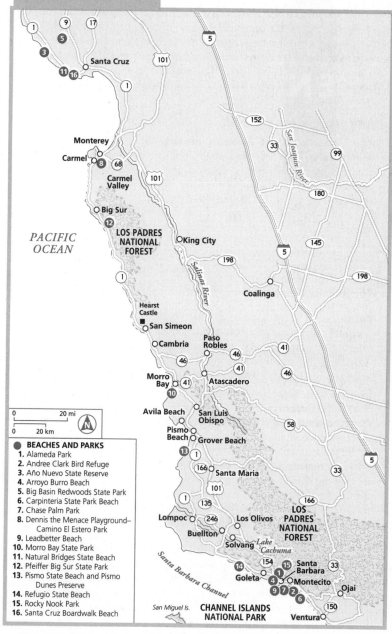

the central coast

PACIFIC
OCEAN

Santa Cruz

Monterey
Carmel
Carmel
Valley

Big Sur

LOS PADRES
NATIONAL
FOREST

King City

Hearst
Castle
San Simeon

Cambria

Paso
Robles

Morro
Bay
Atascadero

Avila Beach
San Luis
Obispo
Pismo
Beach
Grover Beach

Santa Maria

Lompoc
Los Olivos
Buellton
Solvang
Lake
Cachuma

Coalinga

LOS
PADRES
NATIONAL
FOREST

Goleta
Santa
Barbara
Montecito
Ojai

San Miguel Is.
CHANNEL ISLANDS
NATIONAL PARK
Ventura

San Joaquin River
Salinas River
Santa Barbara Channel

0   20 mi
0   20 km

● **BEACHES AND PARKS**
1. Alameda Park
2. Andree Clark Bird Refuge
3. Año Nuevo State Reserve
4. Arroyo Burro Beach
5. Big Basin Redwoods State Park
6. Carpinteria State Park Beach
7. Chase Palm Park
8. Dennis the Menace Playground–
   Camino El Estero Park
9. Leadbetter Beach
10. Morro Bay State Park
11. Natural Bridges State Beach
12. Pfeiffer Big Sur State Park
13. Pismo State Beach and Pismo
    Dunes Preserve
14. Refugio State Beach
15. Rocky Nook Park
16. Santa Cruz Boardwalk Beach

Morro Bay, Pismo Beach, and even **Hearst Castle.** If you're coming from the northern end, you can easily devote three days to **Monterey,** with its aquarium and other attractions, or spend a day in Big Sur and a couple of days in Monterey. In summertime, Santa Cruz also makes a fine base, with lots of beach-oriented activities and a great boardwalk. You won't get a whit of the region's cherished intimacy and relaxed charm if you zoom through it all, so pick a couple of spots and focus, allowing time to wander through a farmers' market or picnic by a waterfall. The rest will wait for another trip.

GETTING THERE

BY PLANE   **Monterey Peninsula Airport** (MRY; ☎ 831-648-7000; www.montereyairport.com) is serviced by four airlines: American Eagle, Allegiant Air, United Express, and US Airways. Flights are to and from San Francisco, Phoenix, Denver, Las Vegas, and LA, with connections beyond. The busiest terminal on the Central Coast, however, is **Santa Barbara Airport** (SBA; ☎ 805-967-7111; www.flysba .com), which is served by eight airlines that fly nonstop to such destinations as Denver, Portland, Las Vegas, San Diego and San Francisco. Four airlines fly in and out of San Luis Obispo County Regional Airport (SBP; ☎ 805-781-5205; www.sloairport.com).

BY TRAIN   Amtrak's *Coast Starlight* from LA to Seattle stops in Santa Barbara and San Luis Obispo. Otherwise, there are commuter trains several times daily from LA to Santa Barbara, and the Pacific Surfliner, which mostly connects L.A. to Orange County and San Diego, also runs a few trains to Santa Barbara and San Luis Obispo most days. Trains from the north to the Santa Cruz or Monterey areas originate in Oakland. ☎ 800-USA-RAIL; www.amtrak.com.

BY CAR   The Central Coast area as we're defining it stretches from Ventura to Santa Cruz; it is best accessed from the north by CA 1 and from the south by US 101. Tour this region by enjoying some part of its famous coast drive.

We recommend driving US 101 from LA to Santa Barbara (about a two-hour drive) and from Santa Barbara to San Luis Obispo (another two hours). From SLO to San Simeon, take CA 1, allowing about an hour with no stops. You'll continue on the same road for about the same amount of time to drive from San Simeon to Big Sur. Allow at least 3½ hours total from San Luis Obispo to Monterey.

Heading south from San Francisco, take CA 1 through Half Moon Bay to Santa Cruz (about an hour and a half). Monterey is an hour's drive in light traffic from Santa Cruz on CA 1.

Between Monterey and San Luis Obispo, US 101 runs roughly parallel to CA 1, but inland through the Salinas Valley. Between San Luis Obispo and Santa Barbara, CA 1 is not exactly on the coast (Vandenberg Air Force Base controls that land) but is west of US 101 and goes through the little towns of Lompoc and Guadeloupe.

HOW TO GET INFORMATION BEFORE YOU GO

- **California State Parks** P.O. Box 942896, Sacramento 94296; ☎ 800-777-0369 or 916-653-6995; **parks.ca.gov**
- **Monterey Convention and Visitors Bureau** 150 Olivier Street, Monterey 93942; ☎ 888-221-1010; **www.montereyinfo.org**
- **Morro Bay Chamber of Commerce** 845 Embarcadero Road, Suite D, Morro Bay 93442; ☎ 800-231-0592 or 805-772-4467; **www.morrobay.org**
- **Ojai Valley Chamber of Commerce and Visitors Bureau** 201 South Signal Street, Ojai 93023; P.O. Box 1134, Ojai 93024; ☎ 805-646-8126; **www.ojaichamber.org**
- **Pismo Beach Visitors Information Center** 581 Dolliver Street, Pismo Beach 93449; ☎ 800-443-7778 or 805-773-4382; **www.classiccalifornia.com**
- **San Luis Obispo County Visitors and Conference Bureau** 811 El Capitan Way, ☎200, San Luis Obispo 93401; ☎ 800-634-1414 or 805-541-8000; **www.sanluisobispocounty.com**
- **San Simeon Chamber of Commerce** 250 San Simeon Drive, Suite 3A, San Simeon 93452; ☎ 800-342-5613 or 805-927-3500; **www.sansimeonchamber.org**
- **Santa Barbara Conference and Visitors Bureau** 1601 Anacapa Street, Santa Barbara 93101; ☎ 800-549-5133 or 805-966-9222; **www.santabarbaraca.com**
- **Santa Cruz County Conference and Visitors Council** 1211 Ocean Street, Santa Cruz 95060; ☎ 800-833-3494 or 831-425-1234; **www.santacruzca.org**
- **Solvang Conference and Visitors Bureau** P.O. Box 70, Solvang 93464; ☎ 800-468-6765 or 805-688-6144; **www.solvangusa.com**
- **Ventura Visitors and Convention Bureau** 101 South California Street, Ventura 93001; ☎ 800-333-2989 or 805-648-2075; **www.ventura-usa.com**

The BEST BEACHES and PARKS

ALAMEDA PARK Santa Barbara's kids designed the Kids' World playground in this lovely midcity park. The result is a playground worth a detour, with such creations as an eel-shaped slide, a giant shark, and a really cool, tree house–style climbing structure. 1400 Santa Barbara Street, Santa Barbara; ☎ 805-564-5418; **www.sbparks andrecreation.com.**

ANDREE CLARK BIRD REFUGE An easy bike or surrey ride along Santa Barbara's oceanfront path from Stearns Wharf, this lagoon is just past the zoo. Bring some bread crumbs for the kids to toss to the birds. 1400 East Cabrillo Boulevard, Santa Barbara; ☎ 805-564-5418; **www .sbparksandrecreation.com.**

AÑO NUEVO STATE RESERVE   This one-of-a-kind animal refuge is on the coast north of Santa Cruz. In the winter, by reservation, rangers bring visitors along a roped path right into the breeding rookery of the remarkable elephant seals. These enormous sea mammals (bulls can get up to 20 feet long, and some weigh four tons) can be seen up close, lying in the sand with their pups or bellowing at each other. (A summer highlight is the molting of the seals, when they "haul out" to shore and shed their skin.) In some frightening cases, visitors witness the bulls attacking each other in the waves. Sea otters are also within camera range. Visitors must be able to walk for two and a half hours on a three-mile round-trip trail that is sandy and uneven (or call for access information). CA 1–New Year's Creek Road, Pescadero; reservations: ☎ 800-444-4445; equal-access program: ☎ 650-879-2033; general information: ☎ 650-879-0227; **parks.ca.gov.** Wildlife viewing offered December 15 through March 31. Advance reservations highly recommended. Individual exploration allowed during other parts of the year, but sensitive areas are controlled by rangers or well-trained volunteer "Roving Naturalists," who are happy to answer any questions. Open 8 a.m. to sunset.

ARROYO BURRO BEACH   Santa Barbara locals with kids skip city-center Cabrillo Beach and head to this fine beach park, where whales and sea lions are sometimes spotted. The surf is usually calm enough for younger kids, and creature comforts—restrooms, showers, snack bar, lifeguard—are good, too. 2981 Cliff Drive, Santa Barbara; ☎ 805-687-3714. Open 8 a.m. to sunset.

BIG BASIN REDWOODS STATE PARK   More than 100 miles of trails lead visitors on explorations of the cool groves of towering, 2,000-year-old redwoods in this acclaimed coastal park north of Santa Cruz. The short Redwood Nature Trail takes you into a grove of ancient trees, including the Mother of the Forest, a 330-foot monster. If your kids are more than 8 years old, you should hike the Sequoia Trail, which leads past lush ferns and azaleas to Sempervirens Falls. There are several wonderful campgrounds, including a cluster of tent cabins for those who want to rough it only to a point. 21600 Big Basin Way, Boulder Creek (CA 1 north of Santa Cruz to CA 9 to CA 236); ☎ 831-338-8860; **www.mountainparks .org.** Open 6 a.m. to 10 p.m.; $6 day-use parking fee.

*un*official **TIP**
Carpinteria has been called the world's safest beach. Its natural breakwater makes the surf peaceful and allows for a mile of great swimming with lots of shallow water and no riptides.

CARPINTERIA STATE PARK BEACH   This beach was named by the Spanish for the Chumash canoe-building carpentry shop once located here. There's lots of calm, shallow water plus a lagoon and tide pools. An area of the beach not protected by the offshore shelf offers surfing. There are 260 developed campsites, 111 with RV hookups; camping fees are approximately $25 per night but vary with dates; day-use fee is $8. Ranger walks include topics from tide pool life to maritime history, and campfire programs include Chumash Native American lore. Restaurant, groceries, restrooms, showers. At the bottom of Linden Avenue, Carpinteria (via CA 224 off US 101), 12 miles south of Santa Barbara; ☎ 805-684-2811. To make reservations, call ☎ 800-444-7275 or visit **www.reserveamerica.com.**

CHASE PALM PARK Santa Barbara's newest city park is a Pacific Coast jewel. Across the street from the ocean, this meticulously crafted and landscaped public space is composed of grassy knolls, ponds, a skate park, a lavish fountain, perfectly situated benches, a vintage carousel, murals painted by local artists, an unobtrusive snack bar, clean restrooms, picnic tables, and a superb playground that reflects the style and history of the region. Climb-on-me whales, half submerged in the sand, spout mist throughout the day. A mock mission is great for pretend play, as are ship-themed climbing structures. We took a gang of 10-year-olds who couldn't get enough of the stand-up slide. Bring a picnic lunch and hang out for a while. East Cabrillo Boulevard at Santa Barbara Street, Santa Barbara; ☎ 805-564-5418; **www.sbparksandrecreation.com.**

DENNIS THE MENACE PLAYGROUND–EL ESTERO PARK We have vivid childhood memories of playing on the locomotive here, so on a recent visit to Monterey, we took the kids on a pilgrimage. Time hadn't faded the park's charm for toddlers and preschoolers in particular, although it seemed modest to the over-four-footers. Designed by cartoonist Hank Ketcham, it does indeed still have the train engine, as well as slides, a bridge, and a maze. In the park at Camino El Estero, Monterey; ☎ 831-646-3866; **www.monterey.org/rec/locations.html.** Open 10 a.m. to dusk, daily (closed Tuesdays, September through May); admission free. A little lake in the same park offers pedal boats for $15 a half hour, $20 an hour; call ☎ 831-375-1484 for hours.

LEADBETTER BEACH An unforeseen side effect of construction created this excellent sand beach—when the city built Santa Barbara Harbor, the flow of sand and water altered, and this harbor-adjacent spot at the foot of Santa Barbara City College filled with sand. This may have angered some down-coast towns, which sued the city for their loss of sand, but Santa Barbara's residents no doubt benefited from the situation. Today, Leadbetter is a well-populated family beach known for its easygoing but consistent surf. This is where local kids learn to boogie-board and board-surf. The beach adjoins Shoreline Park, with its grassy areas, picnic areas, outdoor showers, and restrooms, and the cherished Shoreline Beach Café. Shoreline Drive west of the harbor; limited free street parking and more plentiful paid lot parking; ☎ 805-564-5418; **www.sbparksandrecreation.com.**

MORRO BAY STATE PARK This is one of the most varied-use state parks around, with a golf course (featuring a tree planted in the 1930s by the Civilian Conservation Corps), a museum (see the Museum of Natural History profile on page 239), a boat harbor with launch and rental facilities, a bayside restaurant, a bird sanctuary that protects peregrine falcon nesting sites, and campgrounds. You can rent a boat or kayak, fish in the surf or from a boat, go clamming, picnic, and hike. State Park Road, one mile south of Morro Bay, ☎ 805-772-7434; **parks.ca.gov;** reservations: ReserveAmerica, ☎ 800-444-7275; **www .reserveamerica.com.** Open daily; free day use. Campsites with electricity and water are $29 to $34, and sites for a tent or self-contained vehicle are $15 to $18.

NATURAL BRIDGES STATE BEACH Named for a natural stone bridge that heads out into the ocean, this gorgeous Santa Cruz beach is home to some 100,000 monarch butterflies each winter, when they come to roost and feed. Year-round it's also a great spot for tide pooling, watching for otters, seals and whales, and general beach play. The docent tours during butterfly season (October through February) are highly recommended. West Cliff Drive, just west of Santa Cruz; ☎ 831-423-4609. Open 8 a.m. to sunset daily; Monarch-butterfly tours offered weekends from mid-October through February. Day-use fee $8 per car.

PFEIFFER BIG SUR STATE PARK Every campsite in this park is taken during the summer and over holiday weekends, when Californians bring their kids here to relive their own childhood memories of making dams in the cool, clear creeks under the canopy of redwoods, sycamores, and willows. Adults will remember the spectacular drive to and from the park on the often-photographed stretch of CA 1 that winds on cliffs above the rugged shoreline. But kids will remember the canyon, stopping for a picnic (at least), an overnight in the park's motel-like lodge, or several quiet days of riverside camping. Junior Ranger programs, guided walks, and ranger programs. Off CA 1, Big Sur; ☎ 831-667-2315; **parks.ca.gov;** reservations: ReserveAmerica, ☎ 800-444-7275; **www.reserveamerica.com.** Day-use fee $10; campsites $25 to $35.

PISMO STATE BEACH AND PISMO DUNES PRESERVE This huge (eight-mile) beach runs through the towns of Oceano, Grover City, and Pismo Beach. At the turn of the 19th century, Pismo Beach was a tourist mecca, with visitors coming to dig clams and play in the sand. Today, the monarch butterflies are the greater wildlife attraction—one of the largest colonies to winter in the United States is found in and around a grove of pine and eucalyptus south of North Beach campground from November to March. Ironically, the sand dunes of this beach are known on the one hand for dune buggies and other off-road riding (see "Family Outdoor Adventures," right), and on the other hand for the Pismo Dunes Preserve, a protected area with unique and rare vegetation as well as archaeological sites. You'll find the Dunes Preserve via Oso Flaco Lake Road, at the end of which is a parking lot that is open from 8 a.m. to 6 p.m.; the dunes may be reached after a ten-minute walk. Passenger vehicles may drive along the beach from Grand Avenue in Grover City and Pier Avenue in Oceano. The state park has two campgrounds, food service, a visitors center, exhibits, and programs. Pismo State Beach information is ☎ 805-489-1869; **parks.ca.gov.** Campground reservations through ReserveAmerica, ☎ 800-444-7275; **www.reserveamerica .com.** Campsites $25 to $34 per day.

 REFUGIO STATE BEACH   About 20 minutes west of Santa Barbara lies this lovely, palm-rimmed cove nestled below US 101 and the train tracks. Campsites are tough to come by; if you can't score one, visit for the afternoon. The sand is soft, the swimming and bodyboarding are great, and the tide pools on the north end are stunning. Bring bikes to ride the 2.5-mile path to neighboring El Capitán State Beach; our kids also loved riding bikes in Refugio's paved areas. Lawns, barbecue facilities, showers, restrooms, summer lifeguard. US 101 at Refugio Road, Goleta, ☎ 805-968-1033; **parks.ca.gov.** Campground reservations via ReserveAmerica, ☎ 800-444-7275; **www .reserveamerica.com.** Campsites $25 per day. Day-use fee $8.

ROCKY NOOK PARK   With 19 acres in the heart of Santa Barbara near the mission and the Museum of Natural History, this park is great for a picnic with need-to-run kids after too much touring. No grassy lawns, but big boulders for climbing along Mission Creek, as well as picnic and barbecue areas and playground equipment. 610 Mission Canyon Road, Santa Barbara; ☎ 805-568-2461; **www.sbparks.org.**

SANTA CRUZ BOARDWALK BEACH   Why not spread your towel on the sand, with the sparkling Pacific before you and the colorful roller coasters and sky buckets of the boardwalk as a backdrop? There's a lot of sense in breaking up the hours spent on rides with a dip in the sea and a nap in the sun. ☎ 831-426-7433 or 831-423-5590; **www.beachboardwalk.com.**

FAMILY OUTDOOR ADVENTURES

ATV DRIVING ON THE SAND DUNES   All-terrain vehicles are welcome at **Oceano Dunes State Vehicular Recreation Area.** All off-road vehicles must be transported by street-legal vehicles to the off-road area, from which they may explore almost 2,000 acres of sand. Drivers younger than age 18 may operate ATVs on public land only if they have an ATV Safety Certificate of Completion. All riders are advised to wear helmets and protective clothing; vehicles must have an adequate roll bar and other safety features. For information call Oceano Dunes at ☎ 805-473-7220; **ohv.parks.ca.gov.** There are ATV-rental companies in Grover Beach and Oceano, including **BJ's ATV Rentals,** 197 Grand Avenue, Grover Beach; ☎ 805-481-5411; **www.bjsatvrentals.com.**

EAGLE CRUISE AT CACHUMA LAKE   The personable and regionally famous ranger Liz Mason was our guide the last time we took the 75-minute boat tour of Cachuma Lake, a man-made reservoir with camping areas about 18 miles northeast of Santa Barbara. She enthralled grandmother and 7-year-old alike as she pointed out and identified birds for us, then pulled up to the shoreline and clipped a piece of "miner's lettuce" for us to see, and held open the palm of her hand to show us how a particular seed "walked." In winter months, visitors cruise to see eagle-nesting areas as well as migratory birds such as Canada geese. Summer cruisers see other birds (more than 275 species, both year-round residents and migrants), including great blue herons, ospreys, hawks, and woodpeckers. There's a small natural history museum on shore that complements the experience.

Amenities for campers at Cachuma include yurts (tentlike cabins sleeping six) to rent, 500 campsites, a general store, laundry facilities, showers, a snack bar, a marina, a bait-and-tackle shop, picnic tables, barbecues, corrals for campers on horseback, fireside theater programs, summer movies, and weekend nature walks. Access available for travelers with disabilities. Cachuma Lake Recreation Area, Santa Barbara County Park Department, CA 154. Boat-tour reservations: ☎ 805-686-5050 weekdays, ☎ 805-686-5055 weekends; $15 adults, $7.50 children under age 12. Camping and yurt reservations: ☎ 805-686-5050, ☎ 805-686-5055 weekends; **www.sbparks.org.**

☀ **HIKING**   If you never do any other outdoor activities in California, we urge you to get out of your car and take a few hikes or nature walks while in Central California. There are several good trails for children in this area.

To reach **Cold Springs Canyon** in Santa Barbara (for older kids), off US 101 south of the San Ysidro Road exit, take San Ysidro east to Mountain Drive, turn left and continue 1.25 miles to the trailhead, where a creek crosses the road. Walk on the trail for a quarter-mile, then head right at the main (east) fork, which leads to lovely pools in the creek.

To reach **Rattlesnake Canyon Trail** in Santa Barbara, take the Mission Street exit north from US 101 and continue past Mission to Foothill Road. Turn right on Foothill, left on Mission Canyon, and right on Las Canoas Road; the trailhead is about a mile from the turn at a stone bridge in Skofield Park–Rattlesnake Canyon Wilderness Area. The trail leads to pools and a small waterfall.

Aliso Canyon Nature Trail is three miles from the Santa Barbara District Rangers Office at Sage Hill Campground. Call ☎ 805-967-3481 for directions.

Nojoquoi Falls County Park Trail is seven miles southwest of Solvang on Alisal Road. This easy trail travels alongside a creek under the California coastal oaks and comes to the 164-foot falls. The park is open 8 a.m. to dusk; admission is free.

Big Basin Redwoods State Park in Santa Cruz offers the four-mile Sequoia Trail through the big trees, which culminates at a waterfall; see more details in "The Best Beaches and Parks." Call ☎ 831-338-8860;

Even the little ones can handle **Pfeiffer Falls Trail,** a less-than-half-mile loop up to see the waterfall. In Pfeiffer Big Sur State Park; ☎ 831-667-2315; **parks.ca.gov.**

KAYAKING OR CRUISING Before or after learning about the special marine ecology of the huge and magnificent Monterey Bay (with Santa Cruz on the north end and Monterey on the south), school-age and older kids can sign up for an outing in the **Monterey Bay National Marine Sanctuary** (☎ 831-647-4201; **montereybay.noaa .gov;** interpretive center at Santa Cruz Harbor), which is a stellar ocean-kayaking site thanks to its sheltered waters and remarkable wildlife (otters, sea lions, gray whales). **Adventure Sports Unlimited** (303 Potrero Street, Suite 15, the Old Sash Mill, Santa Cruz; ☎ 831-458-3648 or 888-839-4286; **www.asudoit.com**) offers an intensive but not-too-long combination that includes training in sit-on-top kayaks and an excursion to the sanctuary. You begin in the evening with classroom and heated-pool instruction, then, the next day, enjoy an outing to the sanctuary, complete with a "cooperative" brunch and an end-of-the-day hot-tub soak. **Kayak Connections** sets off from two locations in the Monterey Bay Sanctuary, at Santa Cruz Harbor (413 Lake Avenue, Santa Cruz; ☎ 831-479-1121;) and in Moss Landing, 20 miles south of Santa Cruz, at Elkhorn Yacht Club (2370 Highway 1, Moss Landing; ☎ 831-724-5692). Rentals, guided tours, and instruction. The Monterey Bay Sanctuary tour is Sundays at 8:30 a.m., and private tours are held by request.

Nonpaddlers can take a two-hour guided natural-history tour on an easy-riding, 27-foot pontoon boat. The **Elkhorn Slough Safari** takes you ten miles into the coastal wetlands of the Monterey Bay National Marine Sanctuary. Fares, which include guide, refreshments, and use of binoculars, are $32 adults, $30 seniors, and $24 children ages 3 to 12 (no one younger than age 3 permitted); tours depart from Moss Landing. Guided nature walks. Day-use fee $5. Call ☎ 831-633-5555, or go to **www.elkhornslough.com.**

SURF SPORTS Certain beaches of the Central Coast are prime areas for surf sports, from boogie boarding to bodysurfing to surfing.

In Santa Barbara, **Greg Lewis's Santa Barbara Surf School** offers day camps, private lessons, and even surf-yoga classes; ☎ 805-745-8877; **www.santabarbarasurfschool.com.** If you want to try it yourself, you can rent a soft longboard at **Rincon Designs Surfboards,** ☎ 805-684-2413; at the East Beach Cabrillo Pavilion, on Cabrillo Boulevard in Santa Barbara. The **Cabrillo Bathhouse** at 1118 East Cabrillo Boulevard also rents and sells equipment and sundries; call ☎ 805-564-5418.

In Santa Cruz, the place to learn to surf is **Club Ed Surf Schools and Camps,** established by "the Professor of Surfing" at the University of California Santa Cruz, Ed Guzman, a third-generation Santa Cruz surfer (his grandmother learned to surf in 1915!). The school offers lessons, rentals, excursions, and camps; it's on Cowell's Beach in front of the Santa Cruz Dream Inn in Santa Cruz, ☎ 800-287-SURF or 831-464-0177; **www.club-ed.com.** Private lessons are $110 an hour; two-hour group lessons are $85 for the first lesson, with two-hour group follow-ups at $65, including equipment. A solid alternative surf academy is **Richard Schmidt Surf School,** 849 Almar Avenue, Santa Cruz; ☎ 831-423-0928; **www.richardschmidt.com.**

NOSHING *through* *the* CENTRAL COAST

AGRICULTURE IS AS IMPORTANT AS SURFING (maybe even more so!) in the Central Coast, so the food is often wonderful. Here are the edible souvenirs to look for:

TUB OF BUTTER COOKIES FROM SOLVANG (year-round). Available from several bakeries, but we like the quality of the cookies and other goods at the **Solvang Bakery** (☎ 805-688-4939; **www.solvangbakery .com**), near the big visitors' parking lot on the mission side of town. Layers of different kinds of butter cookies (marble, cherry-in-center, chocolate crescents) are packed between sheets of baker's paper in a plastic tub with a handle. We always think it'll take a week to empty, but it's never made it past two days.

BAG OF APPLES BOUGHT FROM STREET-SIDE APPLE STAND IN SANTA YNEZ VALLEY (September and October). Farmers in the area grow several varieties, and fresh-picked ones are available from card tables in driveways and other roadside stands. We usually stop by Mr. Dittmar's stand at **Greenhaven Orchard** (2275 Alamo Pintado Road; ☎ 805-686-5858) near the little town of Ballard, just down the way from the miniature-horse farm. The startling superiority of fresh Fujis and Granny Smiths makes it easy for kids to enjoy a healthy snack from a bag carried along on your travels.

 STRAWBERRIES AND CORN FROM ROADSIDE STANDS IN OXNARD AND VENTURA (May and June). The corn is usable only if you have a kitchen, but a basket of strawberries is a wonderful addition to a picnic or tailgate lunch. Stand locations vary, but they can often be found alongside US 101 after descending the big grade heading north. Check by the Las Posas exit or in Ventura at the end of Telephone Road at Olivos Park.

CENTRAL COAST TRI-TIP SANDWICH FROM AN OUTDOOR BARBE-CUE STAND AT THE THURSDAY NIGHT FARMERS' MARKET IN SAN LUIS OBISPO (year-round; ☎ 805-541-0286; **www.downtownslo.com**). The essence of Central Coast cowboy culture (formerly 19th-century rancho culture) is carried in the aroma of grilling beef that emanates from competing barbecues set up during this weekly farmers' market and street fair. Tri-tip is the locally favored cut of beef (the top portion of choice sirloin), and it makes for a tasty sandwich. For the ultimate picnic, stop by **El Rancho Market** near Solvang (2886 Old Mission Drive; ☎ 805-688-4300; **www.elranchomarket.com**), where, on the weekends, a barbecue wagon is set up outside the market and whole tri-tips, chicken, sausage, ribs, and turkey breast are grilled over oak and sold by the pound.

PISMO BEACH CLAM CHOWDER In the late 19th century, Pismo Beach visitors would come for the sweet, succulent shellfish, so numerous then that it's said they could be dug with the toes (the earliest limits were 200 a day per person). Today, visitors with a fishing license and a clamming fork can try to bag the current limit of ten clams per person a day, but they're not as easily found. If you're not the hunter-gatherer type, order some chowder at one of the beach-shanty cafes in town.

PICK-YOUR-OWN OLALLIEBERRIES AT AVILA VALLEY BARN (late May or early June); call ☎ 805-595-2810; **www.avilavalleybarn.com;** 560 Avila Beach Drive, a half mile west of US 101 near San Luis Obispo. If you're too late for berry season, you can pick peaches, apples, or pumpkins. There's also a bakery and gift shop, and a place to picnic. The overall season is approximately Memorial Day through Thanksgiving.

FRESH STEAMED ARTICHOKES The eastern Monterey Peninsula borders on the rich agricultural lands of the Salinas Valley. Wineries abound, as do a variety of farms, but the area is most famous for its artichokes. Locals will be bagging produce here, but you can stop and eat fresh steamed artichokes at the **Pezzini Farms** stand off CA 1 three miles from Castroville, north of Monterey. Open year-round at Nashua Road and CA 1; ☎ 800-347-6118 or 831-757-7434; **www.pezzinifarms.com.**

APPLE JUICE Young apple-juice guzzlers will delight not only in drinking the fresh-pressed apple juice from Gizdich Ranch in Watsonville near Santa Cruz (see profile, page 257), but also in watching it made.

A **CALENDAR** of **FESTIVALS** and **EVENTS**

February

JOHN STEINBECK BIRTHDAY PARTY *Cannery Row, Monterey.* Tours, entertainment, refreshments; ☎ 831-392-0120; **www.canneryrow.org.**

MIGRATION FESTIVAL *Natural Bridges State Beach, Santa Cruz.* Exhibits, slide programs, music, and crafts in celebration of "the fantastic journeys of migrating animals"; ☎ 831-423-4609; **parks.ca.gov.**

March

SOLVANG CENTURY BIKE RIDE *Solvang.* A huge event open to participants age 10 and up, who take part in a 100-mile ride; ☎ 562-690-9693; **www.bikescor.com/solvang.**

April

SANTA MARIA STRAWBERRY FESTIVAL *County Fairgrounds, Santa Maria.* Locals celebrate the kickoff of the typically bounteous strawberry season with a lively carnival and festival that's great for kids; ☎ 805-925-8824; **www.santamariafairpark.com.**

May

CALIFORNIA STRAWBERRY FESTIVAL *Oxnard.* This multievent celebration includes soccer tournaments, arts and crafts, entertainment, and special events; ☎ 888-288-9242 or 805-385-4739; **www.strawberry-fest.org.**

CHILDREN'S FESTIVAL *Alameda Park, Santa Barbara.* ☎ 805-965-1001; **www.fsacares.**

GREAT MONTEREY SQUID FESTIVAL *Monterey Fairgrounds.* There are cooking demonstrations, exhibits on the commercial fishing industry, touch tanks, entertainment, arts, and crafts; ☎ 831-649-6544.

I MADONNARI ITALIAN STREET PAINTING FESTIVAL *Mission Santa Barbara.* Over Memorial Day weekend, artists (including plenty of kids) turn the steps of the old mission into a tapestry of artworks; live music, Italian food, free evening concerts; ☎ 805-964-4710, ext. 4411; **www.imadonnarifestival.com.**

SANTA CRUZ LONGBOARD CLUB INVITATIONAL *Santa Cruz.* Western surf clubs compete in this amateur competition; ☎ 831-017-4371; **www.santa-cruz-longboard-union.com.**

June

LIVE OAK MUSIC FESTIVAL *San Luis Obispo.* A three-day, family-style festival of music including traditional, blues, Cajun, and classical. Concerts, barn dance, food, crafts, camping; ☎ 805-781-3020; **www.liveoakfest.org.**

LOMPOC VALLEY FLOWER FESTIVAL *Lompoc.* Kids will go for the floral floats, marching bands, and carnival; gardening parents will love the tours of the region's great flower fields; ☎ 805-735-8511; **www .springartsfestival.org.**

SUMMER SOLSTICE CELEBRATION *Central Santa Barbara, with music festival in Alameda Park.* The antidote to overblown theme parks. No motorized floats, no amplified music, just one of the most joyous, freewheeling parades you'll ever see; ☎ 805-965-3396; **www .solsticeparade.com.**

July

FOURTH OF JULY CELEBRATION *Monterey.* Music, parade, and fireworks; ☎ 831-646-3427; **www.monterey.org/four.**

PACIFIC GROVE FEAST OF LANTERNS *Pacific Grove.* For more than 90 years, this small community next to Monterey has celebrated with a week of activities. The event concludes with a pageant, barbecue, boat parade, and fireworks on the city beach; ☎ 831-373-8295; **www .feast-of-lanterns.org.**

SANTA BARBARA COUNTY FAIR *County Fairgrounds, Santa Maria.* An A-list county fair with everything from pie-eating contests to concerts by some of the country's best musicians; ☎ 805-925-8824; **www .santamariafairpark.com.**

SHAKESPEARE SANTA CRUZ *Santa Cruz.* Outdoor and indoor theater festival that runs from mid-July through August at UC Santa Cruz; ☎ 831-459-2121; **www.shakespearesantacruz.org**.

Late July–early August

MID-STATE FAIR *Paso Robles.* ☎ 800-909-FAIR or 805-239-0665; **www.midstatefair.com.**

August

OLD SPANISH DAYS FIESTA *Held at sites throughout Santa Barbara.* The many activities include a children's parade and Tardes de Ronda, a children's variety show; ☎ 805-962-8101; **www.oldspanish days-fiesta.org.**

September

CAPITOLA BEGONIA FESTIVAL *Capitola.* An unusual flower-boat parade—floats are constructed of flowers wired onto pontoons and sailed down Soquel Creek and under Stockton Bridge while onlookers gaze from the banks. Also a sand-castle contest, a children's art event, and much else; ☎ 831-476-3566; **www.begoniafestival.com.**

CARMEL MISSION FIESTA *Carmel.* At the lovely site of the mission, a farmers' market, art fair, children's games, and entertainment; ☎ 831-624-8322.

DANISH DAYS   *Solvang.* Parade, special events to celebrate the town's Danish heritage. Third weekend in September; ☎ 800-468-6765; www.solvangusa.com.

SANTA ROSALIA FESTIVAL   *Monterey.* Outdoor Mass, parade, blessing of the fleet, entertainment, arts and crafts, food; ☎ 831-238-6740; www.festaitaliamonterey.com.

October

HERITAGE HARVEST FESTIVAL   *Wilder Ranch State Park, Santa Cruz.* Showcases antique tractors, draft horses, historic farming techniques; celebrates local produce harvest. Food, games, children's activities; ☎ 831-426-0505; parks.ca.gov.

MORRO BAY HARBOR FESTIVAL   *Morro Bay.* Various events and locations, including entertainment, boat rides, and seafood fair; ☎ 800-366-6043; www.mbhf.com.

PISMO BEACH CLAM FESTIVAL   *Downtown pier parking lot and other locations, Pismo Beach.* Third weekend in October. Clam digging for prizes, clam chowder cook-off, fishing derby. Parade featuring Pam and Sam Clam walking along and greeting kids. Admission free; ☎ 805-773-4382; www.classiccalifornia.com.

WELCOME BACK MONARCHS DAY   *Natural Bridges State Beach, Santa Cruz.* The butterflies return to Santa Cruz. Music, food, games; ☎ 831-423-4609; parks.ca.gov.

December

CAROLING UNDER THE STARS   *Santa Cruz.* Rain or shine, families gather on successive weekends to carol at Lighthouse Point and Municipal Wharf; ☎ 831-420-5273.

DOWNTOWN HOLIDAY PARADE   *State Street, Santa Barbara.* A fun small-town children's event with Santa, school marching bands, karate kids, junior dancers and gymnasts; ☎ 805-962-2098; www.santabarbaradowntown.com.

VENTURA

IF YOU'RE TAKING A COAST VACATION in short stages, Ventura offers a nice enough balance of beach, marina areas, agricultural landscapes, and suburban shopping to keep a family busy for a day or two, and it's a dandy half-day stop as well. As you approach from the south, the first thing you may notice is an expansive farming setting: on roads just off the freeways, you'll see orange groves as full of fruit and blossoms as on any picture postcard. The old downtown area east of the freeway has a fun midcentury main street with vintage storefronts in various stages of renovation and reuse. On the other side of the freeway (but accessible by foot) is a wide, sandy beach, with a pedestrian and bike path on a rise above the beach. It's great for walking, people-watching, and admiring vendors' wares when mini–arts fairs are set up. A few miles south, the **Ventura Harbor** area has shops, restaurants, boat slips, a merry-go-round, and the Channel Islands visitors center (see profile, page 215).

FAMILY LODGING

Crowne Plaza Ventura Beach Hotel

450 East Harbor Boulevard (off California and Harbor Boulevard), Ventura; ☎ 800-842-0800 or 805-648-2100; www.cpventura.com; $119 and up, winter; $150 and up, summer

THE PEOPLE'S BEACH RESORT, this high-rise hotel has a terrific location and affordable rooms. That means it is very popular, and although there are 260 rooms and 16 suites, it's often sold out in summer. There's a pedestrian walkway to a plaza with shops and cafes adjacent; the pool overlooks the public beach promenade and sands. You just walk across the sidewalk to reach the beach. There are no kids' programs or children's menus, but there is a game room.

Embassy Suites Mandalay Beach—Hotel & Resort

2101 Mandalay Beach Road, Oxnard; ☎ 800-EMBASSY or 805-984-2500; www.embassysuites.com; weekends $200–$400; weekdays $175 and up

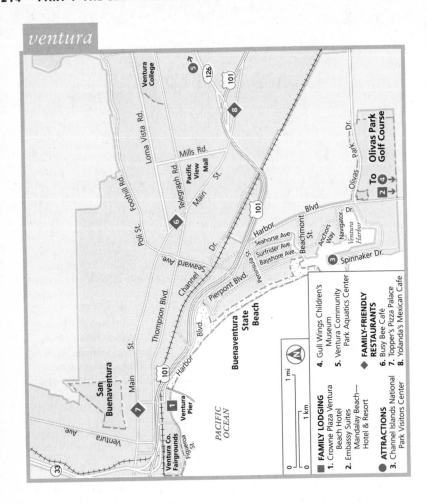

ventura

FAMILY LODGING
1. Crowne Plaza Ventura
   Beach Hotel
2. Embassy Suites
   Mandalay Beach—
   Hotel & Resort

ATTRACTIONS
3. Channel Islands National
   Park Visitors Center
4. Gull Wings Children's
   Museum
5. Ventura Community
   Park Aquatics Center

FAMILY-FRIENDLY RESTAURANTS
6. Busy Bee Café
7. Topper's Pizza Palace
8. Yolanda's Mexican Cafe

A RESORT THAT'S BEEN run by one chain after another, this little-known, all-suite (two-bedroom, two-bath) hotel has a choice on-the-beach location—but beware: it often doesn't get sunny in this region until July. The 248 suites are roomy and comfortable, and the oceanfront ones could make a family happy for several days. Other rooms overlook a landscaped courtyard. Extras include a pool, tennis court, fitness room, paddle tennis, pool table, children's activities, and children's menus; a full breakfast is included in the rates.

ATTRACTIONS

☀ Channel Islands National Park

APPEAL BY AGE	PRESCHOOL ★★	GRADE SCHOOL ★★★★½	TEENS ★★★★½
YOUNG ADULTS ★★★★½	OVER 30 ★★★★½		SENIORS ★★★

1901 Spinnaker Drive, Ventura Harbor; ☎ 805-658-5730; www.nps.gov/chis

Hours *Visitors center:* Daily year-round, 8:30 a.m.–5 p.m.; closed Thanksgiving, Christmas. **Admission** Free; all-day boat excursion and guided hike to Anacapa Island: $45 adults, $41 seniors, $28 children; contact Island Packers, ☎ 805-642-1393; **www.islandpackers.com. Touring time** All-day trip to Anacapa is 7–8 hours; half-day trip to Anacapa is 3–4 hours; minimum touring time 30 minutes to walk through visitors center only and see nature exhibits. **Rainy-day touring** Yes, to visitors center; boat excursions occur weather permitting. **Restaurants** No. **Alcoholic beverages** No. **Disabled access** Yes, to visitors center. **Wheelchair rental** No. **Baby-stroller rental** No. **Lockers** No. **Pet kennels** No. **Rain check** No. **Private tours** No.

DESCRIPTION AND COMMENTS Ever wanted to visit the Galápagos Islands? A visit to Channel Islands National Park is easier and way cheaper, and it offers similarly amazing wildlife experiences. The park includes five islands and their surrounding one nautical mile of ocean with kelp forests. The ocean for six miles around each island is designated as a National Marine Sanctuary, and the isolation of the islands has

unofficial **TIP**
California's famous "June gloom" means Ventura is often overcast in May and June; if you want a sunny beach vacation, August and September are your best bets.

preserved many unique plant and animal species. The park is home to more species of seals and sea lions (pinnipeds) than anywhere else in the world; between 180,000 and 200,000 individuals live on and around the islands. Pelicans, seagulls, and other sea birds nest here, and the ocean around the islands often teems with dolphins. For families, the day trips to Anacapa Island are wondrous. Sometimes, seagulls are nesting along the one-mile path the ranger leads you on, or schools of dolphins surround your boat, or whales are spotted along the way. You have to be able to climb a ladder (or be carried in a backpack) and a few flights of stairs; otherwise, the 1.5-mile island is easily accessible. Land-lubbers can stop by the visitors center, on the mainland in a waterfront complex of shops and cafes, and combine a look at the island exhibits and indoor tide pool with a ride on the carousel and stop for lunch. In the center store, you can pick up a copy of *Island of the Blue Dolphins*, required reading in many fifth-grade classrooms and based on a true story of the Channel Islands.

Gull Wings Children's Museum

APPEAL BY AGE	PRESCHOOL ★★★★½	GRADE SCHOOL ★★★	TEENS ½
YOUNG ADULTS ★		OVER 30 ★	SENIORS ½

418 West Fourth Street, Oxnard; ☎ 805-483-3005; www.gullwings.org

Hours Tuesday–Saturday, 10 a.m.–5 p.m.; closed Sunday–Monday. **Admission** $4 adults, free for children under age 2. **Touring time** Average 3 hours; minimum 2 hours (no point in rushing the little ones). **Rainy-day touring** Excellent. **Restaurants** No. **Alcoholic beverages** No. **Disabled access** Yes. **Wheelchair rental** No. **Baby-stroller rental** No. **Lockers** No. **Pet kennels** No. **Rain check** No. **Private tours** No.

DESCRIPTION AND COMMENTS   An excellent, homegrown, low-tech children's museum, best for kids younger than age 9. Our little ones spent happy hours with the bubble exhibit, puppet theater, pretend campground with tent, pretend farmers' market, and touchable fossils. Not glitzy like the big-city children's museums, but not overwhelming for the little ones in any way, so for some families it will be actually more fun and hands-on.

Ventura Community Park Aquatics Center

APPEAL BY AGE	PRESCHOOL ★★★★	GRADE SCHOOL ★★★★	TEENS ★★★
YOUNG ADULTS ★		OVER 30 ★	SENIORS ½

901 South Kimball Road, Ventura; ☎ 805-654-7511; www.cityofventura.net/aquatics

Hours Monday–Friday, 1–4 p.m. (Monday and Wednesday, night sessions 7–8:30 p.m.), Saturday–Sunday noon–4:30 p.m. **Admission** $5 adults, $3 children 3–9 and seniors, free for children age 2 and under. **Touring time** Average 3 hours; minimum 1 hour. **Rainy-day touring** Yes, but closed if risk of lightning. **Restaurants** No. **Alcoholic beverages** No. **Disabled access** Yes. **Wheelchair rental** No. **Baby-stroller rental** No. **Lockers** Yes (you provide lock). **Pet kennels** No. **Rain check** No. **Private tours** No.

DESCRIPTION AND COMMENTS   Ventura has grand plans for this 100-acre park, which it's developing in stages. Fortunately for locals and visitors, the first stage, now completed, is the most fun: an aquatics center with a competition pool, a recreation pool, two 25-foot water slides, a colorful children's water playground, picnic areas, and a locker and shower center. Savvy locals line up a half-hour before opening time because the park caps the number of visitors at 400—which makes for an easygoing experience. Once in, you can get your hand stamped to come and go. A relaxed, cooling, and affordable afternoon's outing on a hot summer day. Check the Web site or call first, because hours can vary.

FAMILY-FRIENDLY RESTAURANTS

Busy Bee Cafe
478 East Main Street, Ventura; ☎ 805-643-4864; www.busybeecafe.biz

Meals served Breakfast, lunch, and dinner. **Cuisine** American. **Entree range** Breakfast, lunch, and dinner, $4–$11.50. **Kids' menu** Yes. **Reservations** Not accepted. **Payment** All major credit cards.

SOME RETRO-AMERICAN DINERS pretend to have history, but the Busy Bee really does date to the *Leave It to Beaver* era, having been founded by the Warren family in 1963. This red-and-white diner has all the soda-shop standards—pancakes, eggs, burgers, sandwiches, shakes, ice-cream sundaes—plus such modern additions as Caesar salads and "Chablis."

Topper's Pizza Place
3940 East Main Street, Ventura; ☎ 805-385-4444

Meals served Lunch and dinner. **Cuisine** American. **Entree range** Lunch, $4.50–$6; dinner, $7–$18. **Kids' menu** No. **Reservations** Not necessary. **Payment** MC, V.

THIS SMALL LOCAL CHAIN (seven restaurants in Ventura County) is a good, reliable eat-in, take-out, or deliver-to-your-hotel-room restaurant. The pizzas are fine, and the six-inch sandwiches are fresh and tasty. If you eat in, there's a salad bar, games, and a big-screen TV.

Yolanda's Mexican Cafe
2753 East Main Street, Ventura; ☎ 805-643-2700; www.yolandasmexicancafe.com

Meals served Lunch, dinner, and Sunday brunch. **Cuisine** Mexican. **Entree range** Lunch, $9–$11; dinner, $11–$18. **Kids' menu** Yes. **Reservations** Recommended. **Payment** All major credit cards.

ONE OF THE BEST CAL-MEXICAN restaurants in Southern California, this large, cheerful place is nevertheless completely kid-friendly. You'll find terrific homemade food here, made from the freshest ingredients, some obtained from local farms. Try the veggie combo plate, the enchiladas rancheras, and the flautas. It's a local chain, and there's another beach-town location down the coast in Oxnard.

SANTA BARBARA

SANTA BARBARA IS CONSIDERED BY ITS RESIDENTS to be an unparalleled paradise of perfect weather, fine restaurants, and beautifully maintained residential neighborhoods. Strict zoning laws have kept the city's famous red-tile-roof building style so predominant that even major shopping malls are discreetly tucked into the traditional Mediterranean silhouette (and in some cases into the historic buildings themselves).

unofficial **TIP**
The trick is to focus on the area's unbeatable outdoor attractions: glorious beaches, lovely hiking trails to rock-strewn waterfalls, pastoral agricultural areas of horse ranches, and apple orchards.

For some families, the lack of theme parks and glitzy attractions will make Santa Barbara look like a sleepy, ho-hum sort of place, but we think that whether you're making a day trip up from LA, stopping for a couple of nights en route north or south, or making a week-long vacation of it, Santa Barbara is a great place for a family trip making the most of the area's terrific outdoor resources. Making these outdoor pleasures family-friendly is easy to do—rent a bike, sign up for boogie-board lessons, hang out at the kiddie wading pool on a sunny afternoon, or pack a picnic and look for the trailhead. Overnight options range from retro-appealing postwar motels with kitchenettes near the main city beaches to full-service, five-star resorts to a vintage ranch resort.

FAMILY LODGING

Casa del Mar
18 Bath Street, Santa Barbara; ☎ 800-433-3097 or 805-963-4418; www.casadelmar.com; $179–$289

BUILT AS A COURTYARD APARTMENT complex, this 1930s Spanish charmer offers a lot of comfort and location for the price (which includes breakfast). The downside for kids is the lack of a pool, but the large hot tub is lovely. Cabrillo Beach is just around the corner, and the 20 apartment-style accommodations are ideal for a family, offering kitchens, fireplaces, and plenty of room for everyone.

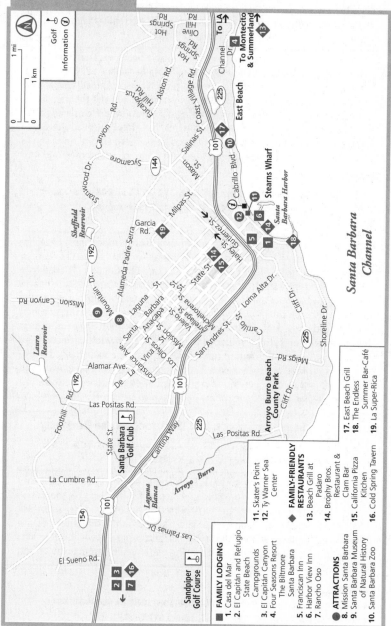

santa barbara

N

Golf
Information ⓘ

1 mi
1 km
0
0

Hot Springs Rd.
Olive Hill Rd.
Hot Springs Rd.
Channel Dr.
To LA
4
13
To Montecito & Summerland
East Beach
225

Eucalyptus Hill Rd.
Alston Rd.
Salinas St.
Coast Village Rd.
Mason St.
101
17
10
Cabrillo Blvd.

Canyon Rd.
Stanwood Dr.
Sycamore Canyon Dr.
144
Stearns Wharf
11
ⓘ
12
6
14
Santa Barbara Harbor

Sheffield Reservoir
Garcia Rd.
19
Milpas St.
Gutierrez St.
5
1
18
192

Alameda Padre Serra
Haley St.
14
15
State St.

Mission Canyon Rd.
Mountain Dr.
9
8
Laguna St.
Santa Barbara St.
Anacapa St.
Santa Barbara Channel

Lauro Reservoir
Santa Barbara St.
Valerio St.
Mission St.
Los Olivos St.
Vina Viña
De La Vina
Loma Alta Dr.
Cliff Dr.
Shoreline Dr.
Carrillo St.

Alamar Ave.
Constance Ave.
101
San Andres St.
Meigs Rd.
Cliff Dr.
225

192
Las Positas Rd.

Foothill Rd.
State St.
Santa Barbara Golf Club
Cantina Way
Las Positas Rd.
225
Arroyo Burro Beach County Park

La Cumbre Rd.
Arroyo Burro
Laguna Blanca

154
101
Las Palmas Dr.

El Sueno Rd.
2 3 16
7
↓
Sandpiper Golf Course

FAMILY LODGING
1. Casa del Mar
2. El Capitán and Refugio State Beach Campgrounds
3. El Capitán Canyon
4. Four Seasons Resort The Biltmore Santa Barbara
5. Franciscan Inn
6. Harbor View Inn
7. Rancho Oso

11. Skater's Point
12. Ty Warner Sea Center

FAMILY-FRIENDLY RESTAURANTS
13. Beach Grill at Padaro
14. Brophy Bros. Restaurant & Clam Bar
15. California Pizza Kitchen
16. Cold Spring Tavern

ATTRACTIONS
8. Mission Santa Barbara
9. Santa Barbara Museum of Natural History
10. Santa Barbara Zoo

17. East Beach Grill
18. The Endless Summer Bar-Café
19. La Super-Rica

El Capitán and Refugio State Beach Campgrounds

**US 101 between Santa Barbara and Gaviota; ☎ 805-968-1033;
parks.ca.gov; reservations: ReserveAmerica, ☎ 800-444-7275;
www.reserveamerica.com; campsites $25–$34**

VERY POPULAR WITH LOCALS seeking a simple beach vacation, El Capitán
and Refugio are about 20 minutes west of Santa Barbara. At El Capitán, you
camp in a grassy, oak-shaded area on a bluff overlooking the sea, with a good
beach below; request a campsite as far away from US 101 and the train tracks
as possible, or you'll be up all night. Refugio's campsites are closer together
and therefore less private than El Capitán's, but there's a beautiful beach
right in front, and the train noise isn't a problem. There are fire rings, showers, flush toilets, picnic tables, and a lifeguard on beach in summer.

El Capitán Canyon

**11560 Calle Real, Santa Barbara; ☎ 866-352-2729 or 805-685-3887;
www.elcapitancanyon.com; $145–$350 (April–November),
$125–$310 (December–March)**

IF YOU'D LIKE TO EXPERIENCE some of the rustic outdoorsiness of camping but can't travel with all the camping gear—or don't actually want to
sleep on the ground—bring the kids to El Capitán Canyon. Tucked in a
sycamore-and-oak–shaded canyon just inland from El Capitán State Beach,
it's a rustic-chic resort with "safari tents" (think *Out of Africa* goes to the
beach) and cedar cabins with willow furniture, comfy beds, front porches,
fire pits, and barbecues. The tin-roofed market has a good deli counter that
offers kits with everything you need to make dinner on your barbecue. It's a
kid paradise here, with room to run, a creek to play in, a solar-heated swimming pool, guided naturalist hikes, El Capitán beach a short walk away, and
Saturday-night campfire concerts in summer. The safari tents are too small
for a family, but many of the cabins sleep four to six comfortably.

 ## Four Seasons Resort The Biltmore Santa Barbara

**1260 Channel Drive, Montecito; ☎ 800-332-3442 or 805-969-2261;
www.fourseasons.com/santa barbara; $550 and up**

TO FIND THE CALIFORNIA DREAM, look no further than this famed luxury
hotel facing the Pacific. From the spectacular flower beds to the envel-
oping king-size beds, every detail is perfect. The arches, tiles, and thick
stucco walls evoke the romance of old California, but the amenities are
thoroughly modern—such as the free children's program, which keeps kids
happily swimming, exploring, and making crafts while parents play tennis,
get massages, or nap on the beach. e.

Franciscan Inn

**109 Bath Street, Santa Barbara, ☎ 800-663-5288 or 805-963-8845;
www.franciscaninn.com; $99–$185, suites $125–$295**

IF YOU WANT TO STAY CLOSE to the waterfront without breaking the bank, consider this 1920s Spanish-style lodge about a block and a half from the harbor. A good family choice is the standard suite, which has a queen bedroom, a living room with a queen sleeper, and a kitchenette. It has the all-important pool, plus Wi-Fi, free Continental breakfast, and laundry facilities.

Harbor View Inn

28 West Cabrillo Boulevard; ☎ 800-755-0222 or 805-963-0780; www.harborviewinnsb.com; $325 and up; no charge for kids under age 16

THIS HANDSOME, RED-TILE-ROOFED Spanish motel has a large pool, a wading pool, and a whirlpool, as well as the breadth of Cabrillo Beach right across the street, with Stearns Wharf a three-minute walk. The newest of the cool, well-appointed rooms (coffeemakers, fridges, movies) are relatively large, so you may fit comfortably in one room without having to spring for one of the suites. The rates include a tasty Continental breakfast and afternoon refreshments.

Rancho Oso

3750 Paradise Road (off CA 154), Santa Barbara; ☎ 805-683-5686; www.rancho-oso.com; wagons $59–$69, cabins $89–$99

JUST UP THE SAN MARCOS PASS from downtown Santa Barbara lies a rustic family retreat that offers a lot of fun for not much money. Originally a riding stable, Rancho Oso has evolved into a small guest ranch, with five simple cabins (each sleeps four) and the kids' favorite, ten covered wagons, which are fitted with army cots to sleep four. Luxuries are few—restrooms are outside—but the fun quotient is high. Kids age 8 and up (and their parents) can head out on the several daily horseback rides; littler ones enjoy escorted pony rides. When you're not riding, you can swim in the two pools, soak in the spa, play in the playground, fish in the creek, or head out for nature hikes. A chuck wagon feeds guests hearty cowboy fare.

❚ ATTRACTIONS

Mission Santa Barbara

APPEAL BY AGE	PRESCHOOL ★	GRADE SCHOOL ★★	TEENS ★★
YOUNG ADULTS ★★★	OVER 30 ★★★★	SENIORS ★★★★	

East Los Olivos and Laguna streets, Santa Barbara; ☎ 805-682-4149; www.sbmission.org

Hours Daily, 9 a.m.–5 p.m.; closed Easter, Thanksgiving, and Christmas. **Admission** $4 adults, free for children age 12 and under. **Touring time** Average 2 hours; minimum 1 hour. **Rainy-day touring** Not recommended. **Restaurants** No. **Alcoholic beverages** No. **Disabled access** Limited; some steps. **Wheelchair rental** No. **Baby-stroller rental** No. **Lockers** No. **Pet kennels** No. **Rain check** No. **Private tours** No.

DESCRIPTION AND COMMENTS   We don't list all the California missions in this book because we think they're pretty confusing for the youngest kids and more interesting to adults than to even many school-age kids. But Santa Barbara's mission is well preserved, well restored, and quite kid-friendly in the exhibits. Completed in 1820, this mission now features a self-guided tour with stops including a padre's bedroom, a Chumash Native American room, and the chapel and cemetery.

Santa Barbara Museum of Natural History

APPEAL BY AGE	PRESCHOOL ★★★	GRADE SCHOOL ★★★	TEENS ★★
YOUNG ADULTS ★★		OVER 30 ★★★	SENIORS ★★★

**2559 Puesta del Sol Road (behind the mission), Santa Barbara;
☎ 805-682-4711; www.sbnature.org**

Hours Daily, 10 a.m.–5 p.m.; closed Thanksgiving, Christmas, and New Year's Day, and at 3 p.m. Christmas Eve. **Admission** $10 adults, $7 seniors age 65 and over and teens ages 13–17, $6 children ages 3–12; children under age 3 free. The third Sunday of every month except September is free admission. **Touring time** Average 1½ hours; minimum 45 minutes. **Rainy-day touring** Yes. **Restaurants** No. **Alcoholic beverages** No. **Disabled access** Yes. **Wheelchair rental** Yes, free. **Baby-stroller rental** No. **Lockers** No. **Pet kennels** No. **Rain check** No. **Private tours** No.

DESCRIPTION AND COMMENTS   A graceful, elegant complex of red-tile-roofed buildings, this museum prides itself on programming that focuses on the local environment, so it makes for an enlightening stop for visitors unfamiliar with California's ecology. Native animal and bird species are shown (stuffed) in dioramas and through models, such as the full-size (33-foot) giant squid. Other highlights are the Chumash Indian Hall, a planetarium, and an observatory. The museum also runs the Ty Warner Sea Center on Stearns Wharf; see profile, page 224.

Santa Barbara Zoo

APPEAL BY AGE	PRESCHOOL ★★★★½	GRADE SCHOOL ★★★★	TEENS ★★
YOUNG ADULTS ★★		OVER 30 ★★★	SENIORS ★★★

**500 Niños Drive (off Cabrillo Boulevard), Santa Barbara;
☎ 805-962-6310 or 805-962-5339, ext. 54; www.santabarbarazoo.org**

Hours Daily, 10 a.m.–5 p.m.; closed Thanksgiving and Christmas. **Admission** $11 adults, $8 seniors age 60 and older, $8 children ages 2–12, children under age 2 free; parking $4. **Touring time** Average 3–4 hours; minimum 2 hours. **Rainy-day touring** Yes, but you'll get wet. **Restaurants** Yes. **Alcoholic beverages** No. **Disabled access** Yes. **Wheelchair rental** Yes, $5. **Baby-stroller rental** Yes, $5 single, $8 double. **Lockers** No. **Pet kennels** No. **Rain check** No. **Private tours** No.

DESCRIPTION AND COMMENTS   Neatly hidden on the east end of town, between Cabrillo Beach and the bird refuge, this gem of a zoo fits a lot into a compact space. The skillful wending of paths and exhibits through the former private estate makes this a wonderful place for even the littlest kids, who might get overwhelmed at huge, crowded animal parks and theme parks.

SANTA BARBARA FINDS

Lil' Toot   Santa Barbara's water-taxi fleet consists of one boat, an adorable yellow tugboat named Lil' Toot. It runs on biodiesel, it connects the harbor and Stearns Wharf, and it's every young kid's notion of what a tugboat should be. Kids can even come up to the pilothouse and help Captain Fred steer the boat. A one-way ride is $4 for adults and $1 for kids 12 and under. Ticket stations at Stearns Wharf and Santa Barbara Harbor; ☎ 805-896-6900; **www.sbwatertaxi.com.**

One Thousand Steps Beach   An unbelievably long staircase to the beach from the Mesa neighborhood on Santa Cruz Boulevard below Shoreline Drive. There's a landing midway, so you can stop to enjoy the view and catch your breath.

Santa Barbara Arts and Crafts Show   Held Sundays and holidays, 10 a.m. to dusk year-round, at Chase Palm Park between Cabrillo Boulevard and the ocean, this permanent arts show attracts vendors of all kinds and is patronized by locals for gift shopping. The sales are direct and the prices often very reasonable; ☎ 805-897-1982; **www.sbaacs.com.**

Santa Barbara Trolley Tour   Every half hour from 10 a.m. to 4 p.m., the Santa Barbara Trolley leaves from Stearns Wharf on its way to the Santa Barbara Courthouse. The 60-minute tour ($19 adults, free children 12 and under; online discounts available) gives a pleasant overview of the town, pointing out landmarks such as the bird refuge, zoo, Moreton Bay Fig Tree, mission, and so forth. Your ticket is good for boarding all day. Call ☎ 805-965-0353; **www.sbtrolley.com.**

UC Santa Barbara Family Vacation Center   Families return year after year to this summertime program on the University of California, Santa Barbara campus. It's an all-inclusive week of camp, including room and board (nothing fancy, but family-suite campus housing that is just fine), kids' programs, and all the activities you and your kids could want: tennis, swimming, basketball, hiking, board games, campfires, talent shows, a family carnival, soccer, and more; for an extra fee you can golf, kayak, get a massage or go wine tasting. UCSB students run the terrific kids' camps, for ages 1 month to 18 years (some families come with teens as part of a college tour). Rates are $859 per person for a week, with discounts for kids and UCSB alums. For information, call ☎ 805-893-3123 or visit **www.familyvacationcenter.com.**

The elephants, giraffes, and lions are a big hit, as is the reptile house. Our preschool nephew insisted on three rides on the miniature train; other extras include a playground, an excellent gift shop, and a lovely picnic area. A unique gorilla-viewing area is a replica of Dian Fossey's African field station and allows kids to walk into a room with desk, hammock, and everyday objects left as if the famous scientist were just outside.

Skater's Point

APPEAL BY AGE	PRESCHOOL ★★	GRADE SCHOOL ★★★★	TEENS ★★★★
YOUNG ADULTS ★★		OVER 30 ★★	SENIORS ½

Chase Palm Park, East Cabrillo Boulevard at Garden Street, Santa Barbara; ☎ 805-564-5418; www.santabarbaraca.gov/parks

Hours Daily, 8 a.m.–half hour after sunset. **Admission** Free. **Touring time** Average 1 hour; minimum 30 minutes. **Rainy-day touring** Yes, but it'll be slippery. **Restaurants** Nearby. **Alcoholic beverages** No. **Disabled access** No. **Wheelchair rental** No. **Baby-stroller rental** No. **Lockers** No. **Pet kennels** No. **Rain check** No. **Private tours** No.

DESCRIPTION AND COMMENTS   The latest addition to the beachfront Chase Palm Park has been a huge hit with Santa Barbara's kids. This 14,600-square-foot, ocean-view skate park is chock-full of rails, ramps, hips, ledges, a half pipe, and a six-foot-deep bowl. Some skate parks can be intimidating for all but the best skaters, but this one is as likely to have a 5-year-old girl in a pink helmet going down a ramp as it is a shaggy-haired 16-year-old skate dude. (A rule of thumb is to bring younger kids before noon—the older ones run the show in the afternoons.) Helmets and pads required.

Ty Warner Sea Center

APPEAL BY AGE	PRESCHOOL ★★★★	GRADE SCHOOL ★★★★	TEENS ★★★
YOUNG ADULTS ★★★		OVER 30 ★★★	SENIORS ★★★

Stearns Wharf, State Street at Cabrillo Boulevard, Santa Barbara;
☎ **805-962-2526; www.sbnature.org/seacenter**

Hours Daily, 10 a.m.–5 p.m.; closed Thanksgiving, Christmas, New Year's Day, and 3 p.m. Christmas Eve. **Admission** $8 adults, $7 teens ages 13–17, $5 children ages 2–12, $7 students and seniors; children under 2, free. **Touring time** Average 1 hour; minimum 30 minutes. **Rainy-day touring** Yes. **Restaurants** Nearby. **Alcoholic beverages** No. **Disabled access** Yes. **Wheelchair rental** No. **Baby-stroller rental** No. **Lockers** No. **Pet kennels** No. **Rain check** No. **Private tours** No.

DESCRIPTION AND COMMENTS   Run by the Museum of Natural History, this small, easy-to-digest marine-education center is right on picturesque Stearns Wharf. After a morning of beach fun, bring the kids here to learn about the critters they were just swimming with. Kids get to help with the scientific research that goes on here by testing water samples, examining miniature sea life under microscopes, and observing tide pool life. They can also crawl through a tunnel inside a 1,500-gallon surge tank and then wonder at the exhibit of tiny local sharks (sharks aren't all great whites!). Check the Web site for the fun events.

FAMILY-FRIENDLY RESTAURANTS

 Beach Grill at Padaro

3765 Santa Claus Lane, Carpinteria; ☎ **805-566-3900;**
www.beachgrillpadaro.com

Meals served Breakfast, lunch, and dinner. **Cuisine** American. **Entree range**

Lunch and dinner, $10–$20. **Kids' menu** Yes. **Reservations** Not accepted. **Payment** All major credit cards.

WHEN THE WEATHER IS FINE, there is no better family restaurant in the Santa Barbara area. Order at the counter inside the restaurant, then take your food (good salads, fresh fish sandwiches, burgers, pizzas) to one of the picnic tables on the huge, grassy lawn just across the train tracks from the ocean. After the kids wolf down their food, they can run and play (there's even a giant sandbox) while parents have a few moments of ocean-air peace, perhaps accompanied by a glass of wine. Even the family dog is welcome. Beach Grill at Padaro is in the little beach town of Carpinteria, a few miles east of Santa Barbara.

Brophy Bros. Restaurant & Clam Bar

119 Harbor Way, Santa Barbara; ☎ 805-966-4418; www.brophybros.com

Meals served Lunch and dinner. **Cuisine** American, seafood. **Entree range** Lunch, $6–$13; dinner, $17–$22. **Kids' menu** Yes. **Reservations** No. **Payment** AE, MC, V.

FOR THE BEST WATERFRONT SEAFOOD in town, head to this informal, family-friendly, harbor-front restaurant, where the locals flock to get the tastiest clam chowder, calamari, cioppino, and oyster shooters this side of Monterey. Kids love the views of the seagulls and boats as much as parents do. Plenty of kid-pleasing choices. Come early to avoid a long wait.

California Pizza Kitchen

719 Paseo Nuevo, State Street, Santa Barbara; ☎ 805-962-4648; www.cpk.com

Meals served Lunch and dinner. **Cuisine** Californian. **Entree range** $10–$18. **Kids' menu** Yes. **Reservations** Not accepted. **Payment** All major credit cards.

A CHAIN, YES, BUT A GREAT ONE for families, well located in downtown's Paseo Nuevo shopping center. The vegetarian soups, field-green and Caesar salads, designer pizzas, and California wines keep parents happy, and the simpler pizzas and pastas are perfect for younger kids.

Cold Spring Tavern

5995 Stagecoach Road, Santa Barbara; ☎ 805-967-0066; www.coldspringtavern.com

Meals served Lunch and dinner; breakfast Saturday and Sunday only. **Cuisine** American. **Entree range** Lunch, $8–$13; dinner, $18–$29. **Kids' menu** Yes. **Reservations** Yes. **Payment** AE, MC, V.

WELL WORTH THE 20-MINUTE DRIVE up CA 154 to the San Marcos Pass in the hills above Santa Barbara, this place has so much atmosphere, you can practically cut it with a knife. A century-old stagecoach stop set in an oak grove, it looks like a restaurant Tom Sawyer would love, with stone fireplaces, hidden nooks and crannies, and battered wooden walls hung with such things as barbed-wire displays and hunting trophies. Outside, a cook mans a huge, oak-burning barbecue, grilling marinated tri-tips, while over in front of the separate bar (a Harley riders' hangout), musicians play Grateful Dead and Crosby, Stills & Nash songs for tips. Add a creek with a small waterfall and a kids' menu offering ribs, pasta, and giant hot dogs, and you've got a very fun family outing, especially at lunchtime, when the kids can scamper around outside and the (harmless) bikers aren't yet drinking seriously.

East Beach Grill
1118 East Cabrillo Boulevard, Santa Barbara; ☎ 805-965-8805

Meals served Breakfast and lunch. **Cuisine** American. **Entree range** $4-$9. **Kids' menu** No. **Reservations** Not accepted. **Payment** MC, V.

YOU CAN'T BEAT THE SETTING: plastic outdoor tables and chairs sit right on the edge of the beach bike path at the Cabrillo Bathhouse on East Beach in the heart of Santa Barbara. Order at the counter, don't expect more than good beach basics (omelets, burgers, quesadillas, ice cream), and snag a beachfront table to watch the passing parade. Restless kids can head for the adjacent swing set and play area.

The Endless Summer Bar-Café
113 Harbor Way, Santa Barbara; ☎ 805-564-4666;
www.endlesssummerbarcafe.net

Meals served Lunch and dinner. **Cuisine** American, seafood. **Entree range** $7–$15. **Kids' menu** Yes. **Reservations** Accepted. **Payment** All major credit cards.

UPSTAIRS FROM THE FANCIER WATERFRONT GRILL, on the north end of the harbor with a fabulous view of the boats, the coastline, and the city, this place is a find for families who want a good meal in a great setting—a great setting, that is, with a tolerance for 4-year-olds who jump on the banquettes. Kids are welcomed with a smile, crayons, and a kids' menu, and parents are rewarded with delicious clam chowder, seafood salads, simple grilled fish, and other chic, beachy fare. Before and after your meal, the kids can run around the harbor paths, looking at the boats and chasing seagulls.

La Super-Rica
622 North Milpas Street, Santa Barbara; ☎ 805-963-4940

Meals served Lunch and dinner. **Cuisine** Mexican. **Entree range** $3–$7. **Kids' menu** No. **Reservations** Not accepted. **Payment** No credit cards.

THIS ORDER-AT-THE-COUNTER ROADSIDE JOINT draws people from 100 miles away. This is great Mexican soul food: beans, *queso fundido,* posole, homemade tortillas, tamales, and cold sodas and Coronas. You eat in a tarp-covered patio on rickety plastic furniture, and you'll probably have to wait in a long line, but it's still an absolute must-visit. Plenty of plain options (cheese quesadillas, steak tacos) for picky eaters.

SIDE TRIP: *Ojai*

A HAVEN FOR PAINTERS, WRITERS, and the sorts of crafty folks who make jewelry, Ojai is also a fine family getaway for a day or two. We passed a near-perfect weekend here, staying at the serene Ojai Valley Inn and riding the inn's bikes into the dinky town for ice cream, a browse at open-air Bart's Books, a romp at Libbey Park, and a fun shopping trip at the Sunday farmers' market. The town trolley is also a hoot for kids. Try to get in a short hike in the local hills to get a view over this gorgeous valley, once a Chumash paradise and later the set for the movie *Lost Horizon*. A trail map is available at the Ojai Chamber; ☎ 805-646-8126; **www.ojaichamber.org.**

FAMILY LODGING

Ojai Valley Inn and Spa
905 Country Club Road, Ojai; ☎ 888-697-8780 or 805-646-1111; www.ojairesort.com; $330–$450, more for suites

THIS RESORT SITS IN THE MIDDLE of a lovely golf course at the base of the Topa Topa Mountains, with access to hiking and equestrian trails; tennis courts, a full-service spa, two beautiful swimming pools, and a lap pool are also on site. For kids ages 5 to 12, Camp Ojai is one of the better hotel children's programs we've experienced (it's pricey—$60 half day, $100 full day, though on some holidays, the evening program is offered for $50 per child). Our kids fished, played Ping-Pong, had their faces painted, decorated hats, played in the Chumash hut, and rode bikes. At press time the resort was just completing a new family pool and children's area, which will have a snack bar and Camp Ojai activity areas. We love the beamed, tiled rooms in the old adobe wing, but the modern, upscale-motel rooms are a good value. The restaurant has a large and lovely terrace and one of the best children's menus around.

ATTRACTION

Fillmore & Western Railway Company

APPEAL BY AGE	PRESCHOOL ★		GRADE SCHOOL ★★★	TEENS ★★
YOUNG ADULTS ★★★★		OVER 30 ★★★		SENIORS ★★★★

Boarding at railway depot, 250 Central Avenue, Fillmore; ☎ 805-524-2546; reservations: ☎ 800-773-8724; www.fwry.com

Hours Trains depart at various times; call or check Web site for more information. There are seasonal special trains, such as the Pumpkin Liners in October and Christmas Tree trains (cut your own tree and bring it back on the train) in December. There are also special dinner trains, including Murder Mystery with special whodunit-type fun. **Admission** Tickets $22 adults, $20 seniors age 60 and over, $12 children ages 4–12, $6 kids ages 2–3, free kids under 2; for special trains, prices are subject to change; 48-hour cancellation notice for refunds. **Touring time** Excursions average 2½ hours round-trip; dinner trains 3½–4 hours. **Rainy-day touring** Yes. **Restaurants** Dinner trains. **Alcoholic beverages** Yes. **Disabled access** Some. **Wheelchair rental** No. **Baby-stroller rental** No. **Lockers** No. **Pet kennels** No. **Rain check** No. **Private tours** No.

DESCRIPTION AND COMMENTS   Southeast of Ojai is this little vintage-train line that travels through a beautiful stretch of California nostalgia. Fillmore, where the rides begin and end, is one of the last pretty little rural towns in California; the various excursions take you through orange groves and agricultural lands. You ride in restored vintage cars, and, depending on the time, you might enjoy a murder mystery, musical entertainment, or such activities as pumpkin picking and Christmas-tree cutting. Meals range from celebrity-chef demonstrations and wine-tasting rides to family-friendly "Shake, Rattle & Rail" 1950s and '60s music trips. Weekend day excursions have lunch service (extra charge).

FAMILY-FRIENDLY RESTAURANT

 Boccali's
3277 Ojai-Santa Paula Road, Ojai; ☎ 805-646-6116; www.boccalis.com

Meals served Lunch and dinner; closed Monday and Tuesday lunch. **Cuisine** Italian-American. **Entree range** $9–$18. **Kids' menu** No. **Reservations** Not accepted. **Payment** Cash only.

WHAT LOOKS LIKE AN ORDINARY ROADSIDE DINER, with picnic tables and a generic PIZZA & PASTA sign, turns out to be a fantastic place that grows its own produce in an adjacent garden, makes its own wine, turns out delicious pizzas and garlic bread, has superb fresh-tomato salads in season and is justly famed for its strawberry shortcake, made from local strawberries in summer. It's the kind of place where local neighbors run into each other and visitors can't believe their luck. In fall there's a pumpkin patch with hayrides.

SOLVANG

SOLVANG IS THE TOWN THAT TOURISM MADE. Its perfect placement as a stopping point on the long trip between LA and San Francisco—combined with the bright idea some decades ago for local businesses to emphasize the region's Danish heritage—turned it into a popular disembarking point for massive tour buses, but it's also a stop for Southern California families looking for a Sunday-drive destination.

Although Solvang is kitschy, it is visitor-friendly, and we recommend it as an overnight base if you plan on exploring the area's authentic attractions such as the Cachuma Lake nature cruise (see "Family Outdoor Adventures").

It's especially nice for those families with several age groups. One parent can stay with little kids at the pool and not really miss anything (it's hot, hot, hot here from late spring through fall), while older kids are let out on their own to wander the village and another parent goes to the art-gallery town of Los Olivos or, with grandmother, heads for the flower fields of Lompoc.

BALLARD SCHOOL

It's fun to drive or bike past this little red 1883 schoolhouse and tell your kids that it's still in use. It's at Cottonwood and School streets in the village of Ballard, a few miles north of Solvang; ☎ 805-688-4812; **www.ballardschool.org.**

FAMILY LODGING

Alisal Guest Ranch & Resort

1054 Alisal Road, Solvang; ☎ 800-4-ALISAL or 805-688-6411; www.alisal.com; $475–$610 double occupancy, including breakfast and dinner; extra charge of $85 per child ages 6–12 and $55 per child ages 3–5; children age 2 and under free

ALISAL, AN OLD-MONEY, intentionally low-key family resort, is the kind of place where even though the setting is outdoorsy, active, and rustic (with horseback riding, fishing, and canoeing), people are expected to

solvang

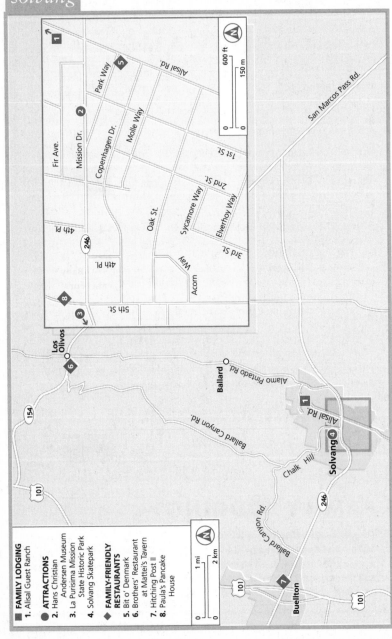

FAMILY LODGING
1. Alisal Guest Ranch

ATTRACTIONS
2. Hans Christian Andersen Museum
3. La Purísima Mission State Historic Park
4. Solvang Skatepark

FAMILY-FRIENDLY RESTAURANTS
5. Bit o' Denmark
6. Brothers' Restaurant at Mattei's Tavern
7. Hitching Post II
8. Paula's Pancake House

dress for dinner and children to be on their best behavior. Golf is the central focus, but there are tennis courts, a swimming pool, and a private lake. There are neither phones nor TVs in the 73 rooms and cottages. Kids ages 6 to 12 are invited to join free activities, such as a pool bash, nature hikes, reptile nights, and a mini-rodeo; occasional teen nights are also offered. The whole family joins together for barbecues and bingo night. Although it is just outside Solvang, about a half hour from Santa Barbara, guests rarely leave the property.

ATTRACTIONS

Hans Christian Andersen Museum

APPEAL BY AGE	PRESCHOOL ★★	GRADE SCHOOL ★★	TEENS ★★
YOUNG ADULTS ★★		OVER 30 ★★	SENIORS ★★

1680 Mission Drive, Solvang; ☎ 805-688-2052;
www.solvangca.com/museum/h1.htm

Hours Daily, 10 a.m.–5 p.m. **Admission** Free. **Touring time** Average 30 minutes; minimum 15 minutes. **Rainy-day touring** Yes. **Restaurants** No. **Alcoholic beverages** No. **Disabled access** No. **Wheelchair rental** No. **Baby-stroller rental** No. **Lockers** No. **Pet kennels** No. **Rain check** No. **Private tours** No.

DESCRIPTION AND COMMENTS   A small gallery, this is actually the upstairs part of a building shared with a bookstore and feels like an exhibition space at a library. Fans of "The Princess and the Pea," "The Little Mermaid," and "The Ugly Duckling" will like the little models of scenes from Andersen's life and stories, original letters by and photographs of the writer, whimsical artwork he created, and hundreds of first and early editions, as well as specially illustrated volumes of his works.

La Purisima Mission State Historic Park

APPEAL BY AGE	PRESCHOOL ★★	GRADE SCHOOL ★★★★	TEENS ★★★
YOUNG ADULTS ★★★		OVER 30 ★★★★	SENIORS ★★★★

2295 Purisima Road (off CA 246), Lompoc; ☎ 805-733-3713;
www.lapurisimamission.org

Hours Daily, 9 a.m.–5 p.m.; closed Thanksgiving, Christmas, and New Year's Day. **Admission** $4 per vehicle, $10 for large passenger commercial vans; call for rates for buses. **Touring time** Average 2 hours; minimum 1 hour, 3 hours with living-history program. **Rainy-day touring** OK. **Restaurants** No. **Alcoholic beverages** No. **Disabled access** Yes. **Wheelchair rental** No. **Baby-stroller rental** No. **Lockers** No. **Pet kennels** No; pets allowed on leash, even in buildings. **Rain check** No. **Private tours** Yes.

DESCRIPTION AND COMMENTS   This tiny and beautiful mission is marvelous to visit when the monthly living-history program is going on, so check ahead and see if your trip will coincide. Always on a Saturday from 11 a.m. to 2 p.m., it features costumed docents going about their mission-era business, with visitors eavesdropping on them and observing as they do their tasks with period tools and techniques.

Solvang Skatepark

APPEAL BY AGE	PRESCHOOL ★	GRADE SCHOOL ★★★★	TEENS ★★★★
YOUNG ADULTS ★★		OVER 30 ★	SENIORS ½

Hans Christian Andersen Park, Atterdag Road, Solvang; ☎ 805-688-7529; www.cityofsolvang.com/skatepark.html

Hours Daily, 10 a.m.–a half hour before sunset. **Admission** Free. **Touring time** Average 2 hours; minimum 1 hour. **Rainy-day touring** No. **Restaurants** No. **Alcoholic beverages** No. **Disabled access** Yes. **Wheelchair rental** No. **Baby-stroller rental** No. **Lockers** No. **Pet kennels** No. **Rain check** No. **Private tours** No.

IF YOUR 12-YEAR-OLD SON is not terribly interested in seeing the Lompoc flowers or tasting Solvang's *abelskiver* pastries, consider sending him here while you do the tourist stuff. It's a very good park, well respected by serious local skaters, and it's free. You don't need to sign a liability waiver for your kids to skate here, but the helmet laws are enforced—we know a kid who got a $395 ticket for not wearing protective gear.

FAMILY-FRIENDLY RESTAURANTS

Bit o' Denmark
473 Alisal Road, Solvang; ☎ 805-688-5426

Meals served Breakfast, lunch, and dinner. **Cuisine** American, Danish. **Entree range** Breakfast, $9–$10; lunch, $10–$16; dinner, $17–$27. **Kids' menu** $9–$11. **Reservations** Accepted. **Payment** All major credit cards.

MANY VISITORS FEEL OBLIGED to try smorgasbord while in Solvang, and this pleasant restaurant offers a nice sampling of salads, smoked fish, and other Danish dishes, as well as American entrees. In spring and fall, the patio is a nice place to be, and there's a full bar.

☀ Brothers' Restaurant at Mattei's Tavern
2350 Railway Avenue off CA 154, Los Olivos; ☎ 805-688-4820; www.matteistavern.com

Meals served Dinner, nightly. **Cuisine** American. **Entree range** Dinner, $16–$44. **Kids' menu** Yes. **Reservations** Recommended. **Payment** MC, V.

RUN BY BROTHERS AND CHEFS Matt and Jeff Nichols, this 1886-built stagecoach stop turned restaurant is a beloved Santa Barbara wine country way station. With its massive stone fireplace, garden grounds, and upscale menu (tuna tartare, prime rib, rack of lamb), this is a special-occasion restaurant, but one that welcomes families and offers a children's menu.

Hitching Post II
406 East CA 246 (1 mile from US 101), Buellton; ☎ 805-688-0676; www.hitchingpostwines.com

---

Meals served Dinner. **Cuisine** American steak house. **Entree range** $21–$49. **Kids' menu** Yes. **Reservations** Recommended. **Payment** AE, MC, V.

MADE FAMOUS BY THE MOVIE *Sideways,* this steak and barbecue restaurant is particularly nice in the early part of the evening while seniors are enjoying the early-bird specials and the kids are ravenous. The steaks and game are cooked over an open oak fire, the French fries are highly recommended, and for the over-21 members of your family, the wine list is great.

Paula's Pancake House
1531 Mission Drive, Solvang; ☎ 805-688-2867

Meals served Breakfast and lunch. **Cuisine** American-Danish. **Entree range** $8–$11. **Kids' menu** No, but small and split portions available. **Reservations** Not accepted. **Payment** All major credit cards.

IF THE LOCAL PASTRY SHOPS aren't enough fortification, head for this cheerful breakfast haven for buttermilk or thin Danish pancakes, sausages, omelets, and waffles.

SAN LUIS OBISPO

THIS SMALL CITY IS A MODEL OF WORKABILITY. Its renovated downtown is lively with students from the nearby university as well as families and businesspeople. The mission plaza, also restored, features a running creek that's the centerpiece of the park. Although the suburbs hint at the growth that's come to the area, the city center itself is as tree-lined and friendly as ever.

There's a visitors center at 1039 Chorro Street and a free trolley that runs along a downtown corridor of several blocks, but this is not a tourist-attraction town. It's a good base for visits to Hearst Castle to the north and nearby beach towns: Pismo Beach, Morro Bay, and the closest, Avila Beach, just four miles from town. Take a stroll on Avila's pier, below which sea lions await scraps thrown over by fishermen, and allow time to pick seasonal fruit at the Avila Valley Barn (560 Avila Beach Drive; ☎ 805-595-2810; **www.avilavalleybarn.com**). In the fall, the Barn is duded up with pumpkins, and a tractor-pulled hayride and a hay maze are provided.

MISSION PLAZA

Between Broad and Chorro streets in downtown San Luis Obispo, this former eyesore was redesigned and transformed in the 1960s into a city-center gathering place where workers eat their brown-bag lunches, children wade in the creek, and tourists head for the mission or the historic adobe.

FAMILY LODGING

Embassy Suites Hotel
333 Madonna Road, San Luis Obispo; ☎ 800-EMBASSY or 805-549-0800; www.embassysuites.com; $159 and up in winter; $179 and up in summer

THIS BRANCH OF THE NATIONAL CHAIN has 196 suites and is connected to the Central Coast Mall, so teens can roam and younger kids can enjoy the swimming pools, but downtown is too far to walk. Breakfast included, kids' menu in restaurant and room service, video-game systems in rooms.

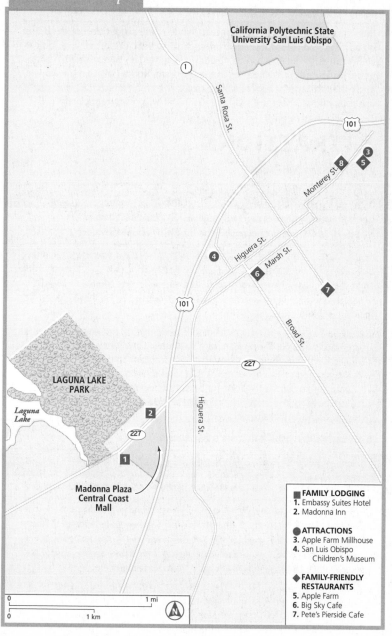

san luis obispo

California Polytechnic State
University San Luis Obispo

■ **FAMILY LODGING**
1. Embassy Suites Hotel
2. Madonna Inn

● **ATTRACTIONS**
3. Apple Farm Millhouse
4. San Luis Obispo
    Children's Museum

◆ **FAMILY-FRIENDLY**
    RESTAURANTS
5. Apple Farm
6. Big Sky Cafe
7. Pete's Pierside Cafe

Madonna Inn
100 Madonna Road, San Luis Obispo; ☎ 800-543-9666 or 805-543-3000; www.madonnainn.com; $179–$449; children under age 12 stay free

MOST PEOPLE JUST STOP HERE to have a bite to eat and peek at the elaborately overdecorated restrooms, and to visit the office and look at the pictures of the 109 rooms, including 5 suites (no two are alike), outrageously themed along the lines of the Caveman Room (with a rock shower) and other fantasies. If you're willing to pay for a high-kitsch joke, you might like a stay here. There are kids' menus in the two restaurants.

ATTRACTIONS

Apple Farm Millhouse

APPEAL BY AGE	PRESCHOOL ★★★	GRADE SCHOOL ★★★	TEENS ★★
YOUNG ADULTS ★★		OVER 30 ★★★	SENIORS ★★★

2015 Monterey Street, San Luis Obispo; ☎ 800-255-2040 or 805-544-2040 (ask for restaurant or inn); www.applefarm.com

Hours Daily, 9 a.m.–6 p.m. **Admission** Free. **Touring time** Average 30 minutes; minimum 30 minutes. **Rainy-day touring** Better on a nice day; interior quite small. **Restaurants** Next door. **Alcoholic beverages** Yes. **Disabled access** Yes. **Wheelchair rental** No. **Baby-stroller rental** No. **Lockers** No. **Pet kennels** No. **Rain check** No. **Private tours** No.

DESCRIPTION AND COMMENTS   Within the buildings of the Apple Farm Inn, behind the Apple Farm restaurant, is a replica of a 19th-century mill. It's a working mill, constructed with such attention to period detail (using salvaged parts from other mills) that local schoolchildren come here for field trips to see the 14-foot-high waterwheel move the gears that turn the stones to grind the wheat or press the apples. Products made here are sold in the gift shop and restaurant.

San Luis Obispo Children's Museum

APPEAL BY AGE	PRESCHOOL ★★★★	GRADE SCHOOL ★★★★	TEENS ½
YOUNG ADULTS ★		OVER 30 ★	SENIORS ½

1010 Nipomo Street, San Luis Obispo; ☎ 805-545-5874; www.slocm.org

Hours Tuesday–Saturday, 9:30 a.m.–5 p.m., Sunday, 10:30 a.m.–5 p.m. **Admission** $8; children age 2 and under free. **Touring time** Average 2 hours; minimum 1 hour. **Rainy-day touring** Yes. **Restaurants** No. **Alcoholic beverages** No. **Disabled access** Yes. **Wheelchair rental** No. **Baby-stroller rental** No. **Lockers** No. **Pet kennels** No. **Rain check** No. **Private tours** No.

DESCRIPTION AND COMMENTS   After years of a from-the-ground-up reconstruction, this wonderful children's museum is back in action. The focal point is the second-floor, kid-size "town" of San Luis Obispo, with a fire station, diner, 16-foot-tall climbable clock tower, and more, and the top

Held on Higuera Street on Thursdays (year-round, 6 to 9 p.m.), this is a lively and fun street fair and market that our kids loved. In addition to the usual farmers' market offerings of produce, flowers, and herbs, this festive gathering includes food booths of many kinds (don't miss the famous SLO tri-tip) and such street entertainment as puppet shows, musicians, and jugglers.

floor pays homage to SLO's railroad heritage with a train-themed play area for preschoolers. Opening in 2009 is a "scientific research station" where kids can explore the mock volcano that starts in underground "caverns" and climbs up through the building's three floors.

FAMILY-FRIENDLY RESTAURANTS

Apple Farm

2015 Monterey Street, San Luis Obispo; ☎ 805-544-6100; www.applefarm.com

Meals served Daily, breakfast, lunch, and dinner. **Cuisine** American. **Entree range** Breakfast, $7–$15; lunch, $10–$15; dinner, $10–$25. **Kids' menu** Yes. **Reservations** Recommended. **Payment** All major credit cards.

WHAT WAS ONCE A CUTE, grandma-ish roadside cafe has become a phony theme restaurant, but the pancakes and cinnamon-roll French toast are still terrific, and kids are well catered to.

Big Sky Cafe

1121 Broad Street, downtown San Luis Obispo; ☎ 805-545-5401; www.bigskycafe.com

Meals served Breakfast, lunch, and dinner. **Cuisine** Californian. **Entree range** Breakfast, $5–$10; lunch, $7–$14; dinner, $9–$19. **Kids' menu** Yes. **Reservations** Not accepted. **Payment** AE, MC, V.

A FUNKY-CHIC CAFE that's noisy, lively, colorful, and earnestly Californian, featuring local organic products and local wines. The kitchen turns out great sandwiches, salads, Latin dishes, and homey desserts.

Pete's Pierside Cafe

Harford Pier, Avila Beach Drive, Avila Beach; ☎ 805-595-7627

Meals served Lunch and dinner. **Cuisine** Californian. **Entree range** $5–$12. **Kids' menu** No. **Reservations** Not accepted. **Payment** All major credit cards.

DELICIOUS, CHEAP WATERFRONT CHOW—shrimp tacos, clam chowder, sandwiches, calamari—is served out on a real working fishermen's pier without the usual tourist shops but with frequent visits from sea lions and seabirds. Some of the fresh-fish dishes will have been caught just the night before.

Splash Café
1491 Monterey Street, San Luis Obispo; ☎ 805-544-7567; www.splashbakery.com

---

Meals served Breakfast, lunch, and dinner. **Cuisine** Seafood, American. **Entree range** Lunch and dinner, $3.95–$9.95. **Kids' menu** No. **Reservations** Not accepted. **Payment** MC, V.

THE FAMOUS CLAM-CHOWDER DIVE from Pismo Beach has come to SLO, only here the cafe is a little nicer, and it has the added bonus of a wonderful chocolate shop, selling confections made upstairs from organic Fair Trade ingredients. Everyone gets the clam chowder in a sourdough bowl, and you should, too. There's also an on-site bakery that sells good breads.

SIDE TRIP: *Morro Bay*

unofficial **TIP**
One of the best family adventures we've ever had was renting kayaks and paddling past otters to Montaña de Oro State Park, where we ran down soft sand dunes.

NO ONE WHO DRIVES THIS STRETCH OF COAST will forget the sight of Morro Rock looming 578 feet tall in this city's harbor, even if the sight lines are obstructed at some vantage points by the equally looming power plant next to the rock. The pleasures here include a bustling harbor, a tranquil bird sanctuary, and hotels and cafes that bring you close to the shore and its wildlife. You could also stay here and combine a visit to Hearst Castle with nature-loving time.

FAMILY LODGING

Gray's Inn
561 Embarcadero, Morro Bay; ☎ 805-772-3911; www.graysinnandgallery.com; $110–$159, winter; $154–$181, spring and fall; $176–$187, summer

---

THIS TINY INN IS RIGHT ON THE WATERFRONT in a building that also houses an art gallery. It has only three rooms, but each has a living room and kitchen, so this is a good value for small families who like a lively setting. No restaurant.

The Inn at Morro Bay
60 State Park Road, Morro Bay State Park; ☎ 800-321-9566 or 805-772-5651; www.innatmorrobay.com; $169–$449

SITUATED IN MORRO BAY STATE PARK in a spot that's notable for birds, the inn has rooms with fireplaces and French-country design touches;

THE EMBARCADERO

This waterfront area has restaurants, fish markets, art galleries, and such, and its small-craft harbor is the embarkation point for boat cruises and fishing charters. A giant chessboard in a park along the way has hand-carved two- and three-foot-tall game pieces. The aquarium and commercial fishing docks are here, too.

two-thirds of them have ocean views, and most have mini–hot tubs on their balconies. Sea otters live in the waters in front. It's a peaceful, quiet spot away from the town center, with very good views. There are five family-size rooms, children's menus, a heated pool, and free bikes, and kayak rentals are available nearby.

ATTRACTIONS

Morro Bay Aquarium

APPEAL BY AGE	PRESCHOOL ★★★	GRADE SCHOOL ★★	TEENS ★★
YOUNG ADULTS ★★		OVER 30 ★★	SENIORS ★★

595 Embarcadero (on the waterfront), Morro Bay; ☎ 805-772-7647; www.morrobay.com/morrobayaquarium

Hours Daily, 9:30 a.m.–5:30 p.m. (may be open as late as 6 p.m.). **Admission** $2, $1 children ages 5–11, free for children age 4 and under. **Touring time** Average 30 minutes; minimum 10 minutes to see the seals. **Rainy-day touring** Bring umbrellas for outside sites. **Restaurants** No. **Alcoholic beverages** No. **Disabled access** Yes. **Wheelchair rental** No. **Baby-stroller rental** No. **Lockers** No. **Pet kennels** No. **Rain check** No. **Private tours** No.

DESCRIPTION AND COMMENTS   Although this small facility doesn't hold a candle to the high-tech, superdesigned glamour of the big-time aquariums, it's not crowded, either, and small children won't be overwhelmed by mobs and noise. Kids can feed seals and sea lions and check on marine mammals being cared for in a rescue center, as well as look at eels, small sharks, and the like in 14 small tanks.

Morro Bay State Park Museum of Natural History

APPEAL BY AGE	PRESCHOOL ★★	GRADE SCHOOL ★★★	TEENS ★★★
YOUNG ADULTS ★★★		OVER 30 ★★★	SENIORS ★★★

Morro Bay State Park Road, Morro Bay State Park; ☎ 805-772-2694; www.morrobaymuseum.org

Hours Daily, 10 a.m.–5 p.m.; closed Thanksgiving, Christmas, and New Year's Day. **Admission** $2 adult, free for children age 16 and under. **Touring time** Average 1 hour; minimum 30 minutes. **Rainy-day touring** No problem. **Restaurants** No. **Alcoholic beverages** No. **Disabled access** Yes. **Wheelchair rental** No. **Baby-stroller rental** No. **Lockers** No. **Pet kennels** No. **Rain check** No. **Private tours** No.

DESCRIPTION AND COMMENTS   Overlooking the bay from a high, rocky bluff, the revamped museum also overlooks a large heron rookery and has several trailheads to viewing areas. Worthwhile exhibits and dioramas focus on the flora and fauna (including marine life) of the area, as well as on geology and Native American history.

FAMILY-FRIENDLY RESTAURANTS

 Bayside Cafe
10 State Park Road, Morro Bay State Park; ☎ 805-772-1465

Meals served Lunch daily, dinner Thursday–Sunday. Cuisine Cal-Mexican and seafood. Entree range Lunch, $6–$15; dinner, $6–$25. Kids' menu Yes. Reservations Not accepted. Payment No credit cards.

IN THE STATE PARK'S MARINA AREA, this terrific find looks out over the waters of the back bay. It's less expensive than the waterfront restaurants, but the clam chowder and other seafood dishes are just as fresh, and the generous lunches satisfy hearty appetites.

Dorn's Original Breakers Cafe
801 Market Street, Morro Bay; ☎ 805-772-4415; www.dornscafe.com

Meals served Breakfast, lunch, and dinner. Cuisine American. Entree range $11–$23. Kids' menu Yes. Reservations Recommended. Payment All major credit cards.

THIS IS A GREAT PLACE FOR BREAKFAST, with a view of Morro Rock and such specialties as seafood omelets and blueberry pancakes. Lunch and dinner dishes include seafood and meats. Located in the same white-clapboard, Cape Cod–style building since 1942, Dorn's is in great shape, with a new deck and a well-maintained decor. Parents of hungry kids, take note: Dorn's begins serving dinner at 4 p.m.

Margie's Diner
1698 Main Street, Morro Bay; ☎ 805-772-2510; www.margiesdiner.com

Meals served Breakfast, lunch, and dinner. Cuisine American. Entree range Breakfast and lunch, $7–$12; dinner, $16–$20. Kids' menu Yes. Reservations Not accepted. Payment No credit cards, but personal checks okay.

A PROPER DINER, not a trendy imitation, serving chicken-fried steak, big omelets, hamburgers, shakes, and homemade pie. There is a kids' menu; regular adult portions are large, but they'll split plates at no extra charge.

Taco Temple
2680 Main Street, Morro Bay; ☎ 805-772-4965

Meals served Lunch and dinner; closed Tuesday. Cuisine Mexican-Californian. Entree range Lunch and dinner, $5-$12. Kids' menu Yes. Reservations Not accepted. Payment Cash only.

CALLING ITSELF A "FUSION" TAQUERIA, Taco Temple showcases fresh, local, often organic produce—quite unusual at an order-at-the-counter taco joint. Excellent garlic-calamari, crab-cake, or Baja shrimp tacos.

SIDE TRIP: *Pismo Beach*

THIS BEACH TOWN PRIDES ITSELF on being in a bit of a time warp, with shell shops like Grandma used to shop in, and lots of chowder shacks and postwar beach-town motels.

FAMILY LODGING

Sandcastle Inn
100 Stimson Avenue, Pismo Beach; ☎ 800-822-6606 or 805-773-2422; www.sandcastleinn.com; $139–$439

BOASTING AN ENVIABLE BEACHFRONT location, this place offers fine ocean views and a beachfront hot tub. Among the 60 rooms in three stories are several family-size junior suites, one with a kitchenette.

FAMILY-FRIENDLY RESTAURANT

Giuseppe's
891 Price Street, Pismo Beach; ☎ 805-773-2870; www.giuseppesrestaurant.com

Meals served Lunch and dinner. **Cuisine** Italian. **Entree range** $13–$26. **Kids' menu** No. **Reservations** Not accepted. **Payment** All major credit cards.

SURELY THE BEST PLACE IN TOWN, with or without kids, this homey, noisy, informal Italian eatery is a terrific family restaurant.

SIDE TRIP: *San Simeon and Cambria*

THE FIRST FEW TIMES we came to San Simeon, we didn't even know Cambria had a name. It seemed to be simply an area of motels and coffee shops near Hearst Castle. And that's what it is. But it is a convenient place to stay, and our kids had a great time splashing with other traveling families in a sheltered pool after a long drive.

Meanwhile, Cambria is just too cute for most active families—a veritable capital of bed-and-breakfasts, Cambria is on the curve as the highway heads to the sea, between San Luis Obispo and San Simeon.

unofficial **TIP**
Your best bet is to arrive in the late afternoon the day before your early morning Hearst Castle tour. Swim, eat, sleep, and hit the castle the next day.

FAMILY LODGING

Best Western Cavalier Oceanfront Resort
9415 Hearst Drive, San Simeon; ☎ 800-826-8168 or 805-927-4688; www.cavalierresort.com; $109–$319

A UTILITARIAN MOTEL with 90 large rooms, many of which have stunning views of the ocean from the bluff above. Some rooms have terraces, some have fireplaces, and all have DVD players. Extras include two pools, a day spa, a gym, kids' menus for the restaurant and room service, and binoculars for whale watching.

Bluebird Inn
1880 Main Street, Cambria; ☎ 800-552-5434 or 805-927-4634; www.bluebirdmotel.com; $50–$220

STARTING AT JUST $50 IN WINTER, rooms are a great value at this modest but friendly and tidy motel. Amenities are few, and there's no pool, but Santa Rosa Creek runs through the pretty rear gardens, and the Main Street location puts restaurants and shops a short walk away.

Cambria Pines Lodge
2905 Burton Drive, Cambria; ☎ 800-445-6868 or 805-927-4200; www.cambriapineslodge.com; $69–$299

A SMALL-SCALE RESORT with something for everyone, Cambria Pines is set in 25 wooded acres, so there's room for kids to explore. Housing ranges from studios to family suites to cabins; extras include an indoor pool, a day spa, gorgeous gardens and lawns, and a very short trail that leads to town. Some of the suites can comfortably sleep six. There's a good restaurant that uses organic produce grown on-site, and such extras as wireless Internet access and evening room service.

ATTRACTION

 Hearst Castle–Hearst San Simeon State Historical Monument

APPEAL BY AGE	PRESCHOOL ★	GRADE SCHOOL ★	TEENS ★★
YOUNG ADULTS ★★	OVER 30 ★★★★		SENIORS ★★★★

Off CA 1, San Simeon; ☎ 805-927-2020; ☎ 800-444-4445 (reservations); www.hearst-castle.org

Hours *March–September:* daily, 8 a.m.–6 p.m.; *October–February:* Monday–Friday, 9 a.m.–5 p.m.; Saturday and Sunday, 9 a.m.–3 p.m. Closed Thanksgiving, Christmas, and New Year's Day. **Admission** $24 adults, $12 children ages 6–17, free for children age 5 and under. **Touring time** Average 1 hour 45 minutes. **Rainy-day touring** Yes. **Restaurants** Concession stand. **Alcoholic beverages** No. **Disabled access** Yes. **Wheelchair rental** Free; call for special tours. **Lockers** Yes. **Pet kennels** No. **Baby-stroller rental** No; strollers not allowed on tour. **Rain check** No. **Private tours** Call ☎ 805-927-2070.

DESCRIPTION AND COMMENTS   Face it: this isn't a great stop for young children. They just don't get it. And why should they? It's hard enough for adults to grasp the beautiful weirdness of a place that is largely made up of pieces and parts of European churches and palaces that are older than the state they are visiting (having been disassembled, shipped across the seas, and reassembled here as dining room walls and corridor embellishments). Even official brochures warn that "young children may find the stairs, museum restrictions, and group format challenging." But school-age kids and teens will make it through one of the shorter tours, all of which include the cool swimming pools. The latest add-on is a 40-minute *National Geographic* movie, which is shown as part of the shortest tours. Make sure to book your tour in advance—this place draws the crowds!

SIDE TRIP: *Big Sur*

GETTING THERE, ESPECIALLY FROM THE SOUTH, can be hell with a car-sickness-prone kid, but if you have to keep pulling over, at least you'll have the awesome view as a reward. Once you get to Big Sur, you'll find a town in which the clocks seem to have stopped back in 1971—the hippie lives here, and lives well. Oh, sure, things have gotten fancy with the big-bucks Post Ranch Inn, but you'll still see rusted-out VW vans and tie-dyes. The only thing for families to do in Big Sur is soak in the natural beauty, preferably among the redwoods in **Pfeiffer Big Sur State Park,** where you can pass happy days camping or staying in the lodge. A horseback ride on the beach is lots of fun; we also love hiking the gorgeous trails and playing on the beaches. We're happy to report that after the fire of 2008, the town is back in full swing.

FAMILY LODGING

Deetjen's Big Sur Inn

CA 1 at south end of town, Big Sur; ☎ 831-667-2377; www.deetjens.com; $80–$200

RICH WITH FUNKY, EX-HIPPIE Big Sur charm, Deetjen's is a ragtag collection of cottages tucked among the redwoods in a setting of great beauty. Walls may be thin, beds a little creaky, and housekeeping on the simple side, but you won't find a motel more atmospheric than this one. The restaurant serves a killer breakfast (get the pancakes), but you'll need reservations.

Pfeiffer Big Sur State Park Campground and Big Sur Lodge

Off CA 1, Big Sur; ☎ 831-667-2315; parks.ca.gov; reservations: ReserveAmerica, ☎ 800-444-7275; www.reserveamerica.com; campsites $25–$35

A BELOVED FAMILY CAMPGROUND, this park has 218 campsites nestled among the redwoods just inland from the breathtaking Big Sur coast. Each site has tables, stoves, and food lockers; some are next to Big Sur River, and some are in the redwoods, while others rest in oak groves or meadows.

There are no hookups, but there are showers, laundry facilities, a store, and a cafe. A more luxurious choice (in relative terms) is the park's Big Sur Lodge, where you can rent a simple, motel-style cottage in the redwoods, perhaps even with a fireplace, for $189 to $359 (for reservations, call ☎ 800-424-4787 or 831-667-3100, or visit **www.bigsurlodge.com**—well in advance). See also the park description in "The Best Beaches and Parks."

 Treebones Resort

71895 CA 1, Big Sur, ☎ 877-424-4787; www.treebonesresort.com; $155–$280

THANKS TO THESE SNUG AND COMFORTABLE YURTS, you can have a Big Sur resort experience with jaw-dropping views without paying Post Ranch Inn prices. Treebones is a wonderful, family-friendly (for kids 6 and older only) hideaway on a hilltop with stunning, 360-degree views of the Big Sur coast. Rates include a waffle breakfast and accommodations in a tentlike yurt with good bedding, electricity, sinks, and creature comforts; bathrooms are a short walk away. There's a beautiful heated pool, a clubhouse, a good restaurant, and nice people who can set you up with a guided hike or kayak adventure.

FAMILY-FRIENDLY RESTAURANTS

 ## Big Sur Bakery and Restaurant

**CA 1 (middle of town), Big Sur; ☎ 831-667-0520;
www.bigsurbakery.com**

Meals served Breakfast, lunch, and dinner. **Cuisine** American and Mediterranean. **Entree range** Breakfast and lunch, $12–$18; dinner, $27–$36. **Kids' menu** No. **Reservations** Recommended. **Payment** MC, V.

A SERIOUS RESTAURANT disguised as a casual-funky, indoor-outdoor bakery, this place has fantastic food. The couple who do the cooking—she is the baker, and he is the chef—produce a hearty cuisine that's appealing to everyone. Carnivores adore the grilled prime rib and roasted Niman Ranch pork loin, and vegetarians have tons to choose from, too. The wood-fired pizzas are outstanding; our kids pronounce the cheeses-and-tomato-sauce pizza to be the best one they've ever had. Save room for one of the amazing desserts.

Nepenthe and Cafe Kevah
CA 1 (south end of town), Big Sur; ☎ 831-667-2345

Meals served Breakfast, lunch, and dinner. **Cuisine** American. **Entree range** Lunch, $13–$16; dinner, $13–$37. **Kids' menu** No. **Reservations** Not necessary. **Payment** AE, MC, V.

SURELY THE BEST-VIEW RESTAURANT on the California coast, Nepenthe and its outdoor-cafe sibling, Cafe Kevah, can be forgiven if the food isn't memorable. We've had a decent burger and some mighty good fries, however, which tasted even better on the terrace, with the famed Big Sur coastline tumbling down below. Teenagers will like the downstairs gift shop, featuring local crafts. A fine refueling stop after the long drive from the south.

MONTEREY

MONTEREY IS A BEAUTIFUL CITY, and since its remarkable aquarium has become a top tourist attraction, it's on most must-see lists for travelers to California. And how wonderful that is, because Monterey is as much a part of how Californians feel about themselves, thanks to the novels of John Steinbeck and the recordings of the Monterey Jazz Festival, as the waterfalls of Yosemite or the star-studded sidewalks of Hollywood.

California's regions can each be symbolized by a tree that dominates the landscape. In the south, it's the palm tree; in the north, the redwood; and in the north-central coast, here on the Monterey Peninsula, it's the cypress tree. The Monterey cypress survives only on Point Lobos, where the dramatic trees, twisted into starkly artistic shapes by the wind, are preserved in a state reserve. But other varieties of cypresses are planted throughout the city, giving it a special, dark-green canopy. Another striking characteristic of Monterey is its preserved, 19th-century historic district, a rarity in California, but not an attraction we recommend spending a lot of time in with young children. Instead, look to the gem in the crown of the revitalized waterfront: the Monterey Bay Aquarium, one of the largest in the country.

EASY MONTEREY OUTINGS

CANNERY ROW Several self-contained mini-malls now reside in the former sardine canneries made famous by novelist John Steinbeck; most are just tourist shops, which will interest a 13-year-old but not a 6-year-old. But kids of all ages like the Oceans 18 indoor miniature golf course in the American Tin Cannery (125 Ocean Boulevard; ☎ 831-643-9215; **www.oceans18minigolf.com/rates.htm**). And for a souvenir with soul, go to Friends of the Sea Otter, also inside the American Tin Cannery (☎ 831-642-9037; **www.seaotters.org**), which sells books, gifts, and educational materials; all proceeds benefit the otters. For a Cannery Row Resource Guide, call ☎ 831-649-6690 or go to **www.canneryrow.com**.

FISHERMAN'S WHARF Even kids who think seafood is yucky (seafood restaurants being the main attraction at Fisherman's Wharf) will get a kick out of the sea lions who frequent the pier area. Charter fishing boats and sightseeing boats tie up here.

☀ **MONTEREY PENINSULA RECREATION TRAIL**   This 18-mile trail connects parks and paths between Asilomar State Beach in Pacific Grove and the city of Castroville. It is a multiuse trail for walkers, bikers, and surrey pedalers and goes along the shore past Point Pinos Lighthouse, the Monterey Bay Aquarium, Cannery Row, the Custom House Plaza, and De Monte Beach. The trail is equipped with drinking fountains, bike racks, and benches at various points.

OLD MONTEREY MARKETPLACE   Tuesday afternoons year-round, this farmers' market is a great way for families to enjoy Old Monterey (as opposed to, say, a docent walking tour of the historic buildings). There are produce stalls, flowers, and arts and crafts, as well as food and entertainment; ☎ 831-655-8070; **www.oldmonterey.org.**

FAMILY LODGING

Casa Munras
700 Munras Avenue, Monterey; ☎ 800-222-2446 or 831-375-2411; www.hotelcasamunras.com; $199–$249 summer, $179–$219 winter

A NICE CHANGE FROM COOKIE-CUTTER MOTELS, this hotel near Fisherman's Wharf fills an 1824 building on acres of landscaped grounds. The 171 rooms are decorated in soft earth tones and have good beds and DVD players; some have fireplaces. Outside is a heated pool with a large shallow end for kids; other amenities include a new fitness center, a business center, homemade cookies at check-in and fresh fruit on hand for hungry kids.

Hyatt Regency Monterey Resort & Spa
1 Old Golf Course Road, Monterey; ☎ 800-633-7313 or 831-372-1234; www.hyatt.com; $179–$369

THE FREE CAMP HYATT PROGRAM attracts 3- to 15-year-olds with garden-variety activities. Around the 575-room property, you'll find two pools, spas, a game room, a volleyball court, tennis, a golf course, a sports bar, and a bike-rental concession. Children's menus are offered.

Lighthouse Lodge & Suites
1150 and 1249 Lighthouse Avenue, Pacific Grove; ☎ 800-858-1249 or 831-655-2111; www.lhls.com; $89–$204

CLEVER NEW OWNERS took two motel properties and jazzed them up with families in mind. On one side of the street is a former Best Western, comfortably furnished with a few upscale touches, including 32-inch TVs and robes; the rooms (including double-doubles that are popular with families) surround a pool, at which a free barbecue (hamburgers and hot dogs) is held every evening. On the other side of the street is a smaller building with 31 suites, some of which are ideal for families. Room rates

monterey

■ **FAMILY LODGING**
1. Casa Munras
2. Hyatt Regency Monterey
   Resort & Spa
3. Lighthouse Lodge & Suites
4. Manresa State
   Beach Campground
5. Quality Inn Monterey

● **ATTRACTIONS**
6. Monterey Bay Aquarium
7. M. Y. Museum
8. Peter Hay Golf Course
9. Point Pinos Lighthouse

◆ **FAMILY-FRIENDLY
   RESTAURANTS**
10. Abalonetti Seafood
    Trattoria
11. John Pisto's Whaling
    Station
12. Jose's
13. Old Monterey Cafe

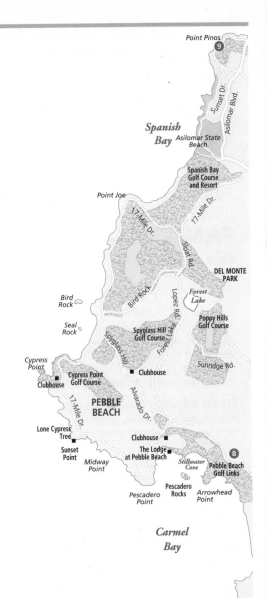

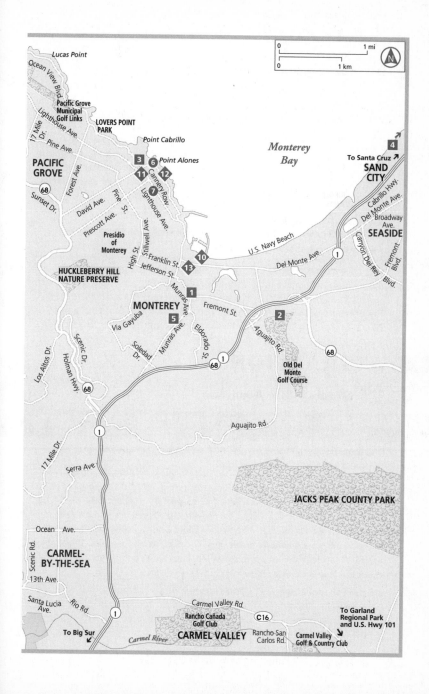

include a full breakfast and the aforementioned barbecue; typically on offer are good package deals that include admission to the aquarium or whale-watching trips.

 ## Manresa State Beach Campground

205 Manresa Beach Road (off San Andreas Road), La Selva Beach;
☎ **831-761-1795; parks.ca.gov; reservations: ReserveAmerica,**
☎ **800-444-7275; www.reserveamerica.com; campsites $25**

BEACH CAMPGROUNDS don't get any more peaceful and lovely than this small tent-camping retreat, which forbids RVs. The location is gorgeous, on a bluff overlooking Monterey Bay, shaded by Monterey pines and eucalyptus; a trail leads down to the long sand beach. Fire rings, picnic tables, showers, flush toilets.

Quality Inn Monterey

1058 Munras Avenue, Monterey; ☎ 800-361-3835 or 831-372-3381;
www.qualityinnmonterey.com; $80-$249

THIS IS A COMFORTABLE, GOOD-VALUE family hotel with an indoor pool and hot tub, which are nice when it's cold and foggy in Monterey—which it often is. Rates include an exceptionally generous Continental breakfast. Some rooms even have fireplaces. The TVs have HBO, but no games or DVD players—however, you don't come to Monterey to play Guitar Hero.

 # ATTRACTIONS

 ## Monterey Bay Aquarium

APPEAL BY AGE	PRESCHOOL ★★★★	GRADE SCHOOL ★★★★½	TEENS ★★★★½
YOUNG ADULTS ★★★★½	OVER 30 ★★★★½	SENIORS ★★★★½	

886 Cannery Row, Monterey; ☎ 831-648-4800; advance tickets:
☎ **800-756-3737; www.mbayaq.org**

Hours *June–August:* daily, 9:30 a.m.–6 p.m.; *rest of year:* 10 a.m.–6 p.m.; closed Christmas. **Admission** $24.95 adults; $22.95 seniors, students ages 13–17, and college students with ID; $15.95 for guests with disabilities and children ages 3–12. **Touring time** Average 4 hours; minimum 2 hours. **Rainy-day touring** Yes. **Restaurants** Yes. **Alcoholic beverages** Yes. **Disabled access** Yes. **Wheelchair rental** Yes, free. **Baby-stroller rental** No. **Lockers** Yes. **Pet kennels** No. **Rain check** No. **Private tours** Yes, $75 and up.

DESCRIPTION AND COMMENTS Don't despair. If you forget to call way, way ahead for advance tickets to the aquarium for the day of your visit, you can avoid waiting in line for too long. Ask at your hotel—many sell tickets good for the next day or two.

Is it really that crowded? Yes. Is it really worth it? Yes. You haven't seen an aquarium until you've seen the Outer Bay exhibit, a million-gallon

tank filled with sharks, sea turtles, barracuda, and tuna, and the spectacular, three-story Kelp Forest tank, which holds hundreds of species.
Because the tanks tower from floor to ceiling, you have the sensation of
actually being on the ocean floor looking up.

But to really enjoy the aquarium, you should consider a few things.
The youngest children won't find cartoon-cute animals that jump and
play with balls as at SeaWorld, and you may discover that the beautiful,
impressive tanks of jellyfish and other animals don't hold preschoolers'
attention for long (although some will put nose to the glass and not
move for hours). Let the little ones hang out and watch the antics of
the sea otters, those charismatic mammals that swim on their backs and
seem to grin at spectators. Then take them to the Splash Zone, an expe-
riential, interactive museum-within-a-museum designed for children
from toddlers to about age 9. Young ones can climb and crawl through
shore habitats, sit in a giant clam chair, feel sea critters in a touch pool,
and go "inside" a penguin community. While 3- to 9-year-olds stage
underwater plays in the costume and puppet area, babies and toddlers
can play in Coral Babies, a place just for tiny ones.

School-age kids will want to spend a lot of time at the bat-ray pool,
another pet-the-fish area. The 100 or so exhibits include an aviary and
a video feed from underwater in Monterey Bay. And don't forget to
check for the feeding times, which are posted—they make for a good
show. There's a restaurant and several gift shop–bookstores.

M. Y. Museum

APPEAL BY AGE	PRESCHOOL ★★★★		GRADE SCHOOL ★★★★	TEENS ½
YOUNG ADULTS ★		OVER 30 ★		SENIORS ½

**425 Washington Street, Monterey; ☎ 831-649-6444;
www.mymuseum.org**

Hours Monday–Saturday, 10 a.m.–5 p.m.; Sunday, noon–5 p.m.; closed
Wednesday, Easter, Thanksgiving, Christmas, and New Year's Day. **Admission**
$5.50, free for children under age 2. **Hours** and prices subject to change. **Touring
time** Average 2 hours; minimum 1 hour. **Rainy-day touring** Yes. **Restaurants**
No. **Alcoholic beverages** No. **Disabled access** Yes. **Wheelchair rental** Yes.
Baby-stroller rental Yes. **Lockers** Yes. **Pet kennels** No. **Rain check** No. **Private
tours** Photo Caravan, age 8 and older, $65–$89.

DESCRIPTION AND COMMENTS M. Y. stands for "Monterey Youth" at this
interactive children's museum, relocated just as we went to press in a
prime spot near Dennis the Menace Park and the Wharf. The new space
is more than triple the size of the old, and the number of hands-on,
action-oriented activities—including life-size environments that let very
young kids fish from a boat, "buy" food and supplies, be a cook or a
customer in a restaurant, and make a puppet show—has grown from 25
to 80. At the old museum, our kids' favorite exhibits were the Magnetic
Center, where they make structures out of magnetic pieces, and Build-
a-House, where they don hard hats and build brick walls, fix plumbing,

and hang wallpaper. The new one promises many more intelligent, engaging offerings like these.

Peter Hay Golf Course

APPEAL BY AGE	PRESCHOOL ★	GRADE SCHOOL ★★★	TEENS ★★★
YOUNG ADULTS ★★★		OVER 30 ★★	SENIORS ★★★

17 Mile Drive, Pebble Beach; ☎ 831-622-8723; www.pebblebeach.com

Hours Daily, 6:30 a.m.–dark; call to make sure there are no golf clinics. **Admission** $25 for as many rounds as you like. **Touring time** Average 1 hour; minimum 45 minutes. **Rainy-day touring** No. **Restaurants** Yes. **Alcoholic beverages** Yes. **Disabled access** Yes. **Wheelchair rental** No. **Baby-stroller rental** No. **Lockers** No, storage available. **Pet kennels** No. **Rain check** No. **Private tours** Lessons.

DESCRIPTION AND COMMENTS   For the budding Tiger Woodses in your family, stop at the Peter Hay par three public golf course in Pebble Beach. It's a pitch-and-putt that's part of the complex of famous courses that includes the Pebble Beach Golf Links and the Links at Spanish Bay. No reservations needed for tee times, but call ahead in case a golf clinic is scheduled.

Point Pinos Lighthouse

APPEAL BY AGE	PRESCHOOL ★	GRADE SCHOOL ★★★	TEENS ★★★
YOUNG ADULTS ★★★		OVER 30 ★★★	SENIORS ★★★

Asilomar Avenue at Lighthouse Avenue; ☎ 831-648-5716; www.ci.pg.ca.us/lighthouse

Hours Thursday–Sunday, 1–4 p.m. . **Admission** Free; requested donation $2 for adults, $1 for kids. **Touring time** Average 45 minutes; minimum 20 minutes. **Rainy-day touring** Not pleasant. **Restaurants** No. **Alcoholic beverages** No. **Disabled access** No. **Wheelchair rental** No. **Baby-stroller rental** No. **Lockers** No. **Pet kennels** No. **Rain check** No. **Private tours** No.

DESCRIPTION AND COMMENTS   The oldest lighthouse still in operation on the West Coast, Point Pinos dates from 1855. This is a quick stop—the kids can run up the stairs to the top of the lighthouse, and there's a little museum room downstairs.

FAMILY-FRIENDLY RESTAURANTS

Abalonetti Seafood Trattoria
57 Fisherman's Wharf, Monterey; ☎ 831-373-1851; www.abalonettimonterey.com

Meals served Lunch and dinner. **Cuisine** American/seafood. **Entree range** Lunch, $9–$17; dinner, $15–$25. **Kids' menu** Yes. **Reservations** Recommended. **Payment** All major credit cards.

IT MAY LOOK LIKE A TOURIST TRAP, but this wharf restaurant turned out to be one trap we were glad to get caught in. Famed for its calamari (squid), prepared every way imaginable, it's also a good, straightforward Italian trattoria with wood-fired pizzas and decent pastas. Kids get choices that include pizza, pasta, or fish-and-chips, or they can get half portions from the regular menu. We passed a happy early evening here, eating irresistible fried calamari and sipping Chianti (and sodas) while we watched the sea lions put on a show right outside the window.

John Pisto's Whaling Station
763 Wave Street, Monterey; ☎ 831-373-3778; www.whalingstationmonterey.com

Meals served Dinner. **Cuisine** American, seafood. **Entree range** $23–$53. **Kids' menu** Yes. **Reservations** Recommended. **Payment** All major credit cards.

JUST ABOVE CANNERY ROW, this old warhorse has been lightened and brightened for a new era, but it's still known for the prime rib and prime steaks. Yet although this is an elegant place, the Whaling Station is exceptionally welcoming to children. When you see the soft lighting, huge French posters, and crisp white linens, you'll be tempted to flee and take your 5-year-old to McDonald's—but before you know it, your child will be warmly greeted and presented with a children's menu; very little ones are given Goldfish crackers to keep hunger at bay. The mesquite-grilled prime steaks, chops, and fresh fish are excellent, as is the famed chilled Castroville artichoke appetizer.

Jose's
638 Wave Street, Monterey; ☎ 831-655-4419

Meals served Lunch and dinner. **Cuisine** Mexican. **Entree range** $7–$10. **Kids' menu** Yes. **Reservations** Not accepted. **Payment** All major credit cards.

THIS GOOD TAQUERIA is ideally located two blocks from the aquarium. Order your quesadillas, soft tacos, burritos, and chips at the counter, then snag a table outside when the weather's good.

Old Monterey Cafe
489 Alvarado Street, Monterey; ☎ 831-646-1021; www.cafemonterey.com

Meals served Breakfast and lunch. **Cuisine** American. **Entree range** $5–$12. **Kids' menu** Yes, and will serve a half portion. **Reservations** Not accepted. **Payment** D, MC, V.

A GOOD DOWNTOWN CHOICE, near Dennis the Menace Park, this popular cafe is known for its cappuccino, hefty four-egg omelets, homemade muffins, and from-scratch hash browns; breakfast is served through the lunch hour as well, but not to the exclusion of traditional lunch dishes, which include homemade soups and half-pound burgers. Children are welcomed and much in evidence.

SANTA CRUZ

THIS BEAUTIFULLY SITUATED TOWN is known for the university on a hill in the redwoods, as well as (nowadays) for its many recently arrived, well-heeled residents who supported the downtown businesses that were rebuilt after earthquake damage—so now the little town center is more picturesque (and pricey) than ever before.

unofficial TIP
In winter, when the seaside attractions are shuttered or open only on weekends, the area assumes an off-season charm. Bargains abound in lodgings, and the beaches are good for soulful walks, if not sunbathing. And the redwoods know no seasons.

Vacationing families will gravitate toward neither of these, however, but instead will make for the waterfront, where the pier, boardwalk, beach, and train station come together to form a bright, cheerful summertime-amusement area. Lots of motels and cafes compete for the visitor's attention, but the area is still low-key. It's a beach town, true, but not everyone who's strolling in the sun looks rich or beautiful, and fancy cars don't block the narrow streets. Rather, working-class families from inland (Salinas and east) come to the shore for much-deserved recreation to join traveling families of all income levels. We also like the tiny beach town of **Aptos** a few miles east of Santa Cruz, which has modest but good family resorts, along with the glorious **Seacliff State Beach.**

FAMILY LODGING

Best Western Seacliff Inn
7500 Old Dominion Court, Aptos; ☎ 800-367-2003 or 831-688-7300; www.seacliffinn.com; $160–$200

IDEALLY LOCATED A TWO-BLOCK walk from spectacular Seacliff State Beach, this handsomely landscaped motel has a large pool in a protected area. Because you can walk to the beach, you don't have to pay the vehicle entrance fee at Seacliff. In-room movies and games, a fitness center, a laundry, a restaurant, and a free Continental breakfast round out the amenities.

santa cruz

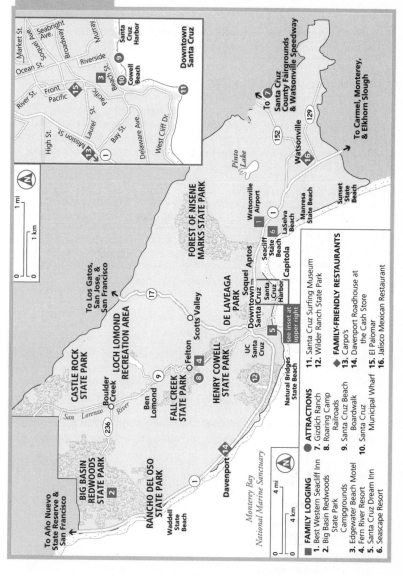

Market St.
Seabright Ave.
Soquel Ave.
Broadway
Murray
Santa Cruz Harbor
Ocean St.
Riverside
Beach St.
9
10
Cowell Beach
Downtown Santa Cruz
11
River St.
Front
15
Pacific
3
High St.
Laurel St.
Pacific
Bay St.
Delaware Ave.
West Cliff Dr.
Mission St.
13
1

7
To
Santa Cruz County Fairgrounds & Watsonville Speedway
129
152
Watsonville
16
To Carmel, Monterey, & Elkhorn Slough

Pinto Lake

Watsonville Airport

FOREST OF NISENE MARKS STATE PARK

To Los Gatos, San Jose, & San Francisco

17

LOCH LOMOND RECREATION AREA

Scotts Valley

DE LAVEAGA PARK

Soquel
Aptos
1
Seacliff State Beach
6
LaSelva Beach
Manresa State Beach
Sunset State Beach
Capitola

CASTLE ROCK STATE PARK

Boulder Creek

9

Ben Lomond

Felton
4
8
FALL CREEK STATE PARK

HENRY COWELL STATE PARK

UC Santa Cruz
12

Downtown Santa Cruz
5
see inset at upper right
Santa Cruz Harbor

San Lorenzo River

236

BIG BASIN REDWOODS STATE PARK

RANCHO DEL OSO STATE PARK

Davenport
14
1

Natural Bridges State Beach

Waddell State Beach

To Año Nuevo State Reserve & San Francisco

Monterey Bay National Marine Sanctuary

0   1 mi
0   1 km

0   4 mi
0   4 km

■ **FAMILY LODGING**
1. Best Western Seacliff Inn
2. Big Basin Redwoods State Park Campgrounds
3. Edgewater Beach Motel
4. Fern River Resort
5. Santa Cruz Dream Inn
6. Seascape Resort

● **ATTRACTIONS**
7. Gizdich Ranch
8. Roaring Camp Railroads
9. Santa Cruz Beach Boardwalk
10. Santa Cruz Municipal Wharf
11. Santa Cruz Surfing Museum
12. Wilder Ranch State Park

◆ **FAMILY-FRIENDLY RESTAURANTS**
13. Carpo's
14. Davenport Roadhouse at the Cash Store
15. El Palomar
16. Jalisco Mexican Restaurant

Big Basin Redwoods State Park Campgrounds

21600 Big Basin Way (off CA 1 north of Santa Cruz); ☎ 831-338-8860;
parks.ca.gov; reservations: ReserveAmerica, ☎ 800-444-7275;
www.reserveamerica.com; campsites $25, tent cabins $65

ONE OF THE MOST BEAUTIFUL state parks in California, Big Basin is home
to some seriously big redwoods and some seriously fine campgrounds. If
sleeping on the ground makes you grumpy, reserve one of the 35 sweet
little cabins in Huckleberry Camp, each equipped with two double beds
and a woodstove (bring your own sleeping bags, pillows, and wood). Huckleberry also has tent sites a short walk from the parking area, and the RV
campsites at Blooms and Sempervirens are among the loveliest we've seen.
Lots of good hiking. Picnic tables, fireplaces, showers, flush toilets.

Edgewater Beach Motel

525 Second Street, Santa Cruz; ☎ 888-809-6767 or 831-423-0440;
www.edgewaterbeachmotel.com; $249–$379 summer; $219–$329 winter

THIS PLEASANT MOTEL is near the beach and boardwalk, and it has a
garden setting to enjoy in the summer as well as fireplaces to warm that
year-round chill. There are 17 rooms, including 10 suites with kitchenettes.
We liked the barbecue and picnic area and the heated pool.

Fern River Resort

5250 CA 9, Felton; ☎ 831-335-4412; www.fernriver.com;
$69–$151 low season; $99–$218 high season

THIS VINTAGE RESORT brings you into the mountains near the redwood
parks and Roaring Camp, where the popular train ride originates. The
inexpensive accommodations include 13 cabins, most with fireplaces and
kitchenettes; two of them sleep up to six people. Youngsters enjoy exploring the private beach on the San Lorenzo River (the river is just wading
depth); playing volleyball, tetherball, horseshoes, and indoor games; and
feeding the ducks. The basic rooms are equipped with Sony PlayStations
and Nickelodeon.

Santa Cruz Dream Inn

175 West Cliff Drive, Santa Cruz; ☎ 866-774-7735 or 831-426-4330;
www.dreaminnsantacruz.com; $279–$419 summer; $219–$299 winter

TOTALLY RENOVATED AND RENAMED to honor its heritage (most recently
called the Coast Santa Cruz Hotel, it was originally the Dream Inn), this
1970s-modern hotel next to the boardwalk and wharf represents the high
end in these parts. It's right on the sand, and all 155 rooms and 10 suites
face the ocean. In addition to having direct beach access, guests enjoy an
outdoor pool with kids' and adult hot tubs, a restaurant (with kids' menu),
room service (also with kids' menu), and such touches as in-room iPod
docking stations and media hubs for game consoles.

Seascape Resort
1 Seascape Resort Drive, Aptos; ☎ 800-929-7727;
www.seascaperesort.com; $320-$652

ON CLIFFS ABOVE THE APTOS BEACHES just east of Santa Cruz is this high-end condo resort with a golf course, tennis courts, a fitness center, spa services, basketball and sand volleyball courts, lap and children's pools, paddle tennis, and much more—it's an athletic family's heaven, and it books up far in advance for summer. There's a path to the beach (or they'll give you a ride on a golf cart), and you can walk for miles and miles at low tide. Summertime brings a kids' camp that includes such things as tennis, hikes, and bonfires. Seascape is great for family reunions and multifamily groups, but it works well for a small family, too.

ATTRACTIONS

Gizdich Ranch

APPEAL BY AGE	PRESCHOOL ★★★	GRADE SCHOOL ★★★★	TEENS ★★
YOUNG ADULTS ★★★	OVER 30 ★★★		SENIORS ★★★

55 Peckham Road, Watsonville; ☎ 831-722-1056;
www.gizdich-ranch.com

Hours *January–March:* weekends, 9 a.m.–5 p.m.; *April (apple-blossom time):* daily, 9 a.m.–5 p.m.; *May 1–July 31 (berry season):* daily, 8 a.m.–5 p.m.; *August–December 31 (apple season):* daily, 9 a.m.–5 p.m. **Admission** Free. **Touring time** Average 2 hours with picking; minimum 1 hour. **Rainy-day touring** Not recommended. **Restaurants** Yes. **Alcoholic beverages** No. **Disabled access** Shops. **Wheelchair rental** No. **Baby-stroller rental** No. **Lockers** No. **Pet kennels** No. **Rain check** No. **Private tours** For groups.

DESCRIPTION AND COMMENTS If your visit to the Santa Cruz area coincides with berry season, your kids will enjoy picking their own strawberries, boysenberries, and raspberries—and apples are on the trees for pickin' in the fall. There's a bake shop where you can watch bakers prepare pies (available for sale). You can also see apple juice pressed. Boxes of apples can be shipped.

Roaring Camp Railroads

APPEAL BY AGE	PRESCHOOL ★★★★	GRADE SCHOOL ★★★★	TEENS ★★★
YOUNG ADULTS ★★★	OVER 30 ★★		SENIORS ★★★

Graham Hill Road, Felton (6 miles north of Santa Cruz); ☎ 831-335-4484;
www.roaringcamp.com

Hours Vary per trip and season. **Admission** Redwood forest trip: $19.50 adults, $13.50 children ages 3–12, free for children under age 3 with an adult; beach trip: $21.50 adults, $16.50 children ages 3–12, free for children under age 3 with an adult. **Touring time** Average 3 hours to beach; 75 minutes to redwoods; minimum 75 minutes. **Rainy-day touring** Not recommended. **Restaurants** Picnicking. **Alcoholic beverages** No. **Disabled access** Yes; no motorized wheelchairs. **Wheelchair rental** No. **Baby-stroller rental** No. **Lockers** No. **Pet kennels** No, but pets allowed. **Rain check** Yes. **Private tours** No.

DESCRIPTION AND COMMENTS   Roaring Camp Railroads operates two trains, including America's last steam-powered passenger railroad with year-round passenger service, in excursions from a colorful "camp" that has a general store and outdoor barbecue. The attraction re-creates a logging camp of 100 years ago, when trains hauled timber out of the mountain areas. This is one of those great tourist activities that is extremely well run. There are two separate railroads: Santa Cruz, Big Trees & Pacific Railway Company diesel trains take you through beautiful forest land southbound to the beach. Roaring Camp & Big Trees Narrow Gauge Railroad steam trains head north to the redwoods. On each round-trip ride, passengers may disembark at midpoint (to hike or picnic in the redwoods or stroll along the beach and boardwalk in downtown Santa Cruz) and take a later train back (space permitting, so be careful during crowded months).

Santa Cruz Beach Boardwalk

APPEAL BY AGE	PRESCHOOL ★★★★	GRADE SCHOOL ★★★★½	TEENS ★★★★
YOUNG ADULTS ★★★		OVER 30 ★★★	SENIORS ★★

400 Beach Street, Santa Cruz; ☎ 831-423-5590; www.beachboardwalk.com

Hours *Memorial Day–Labor Day:* daily, 11 a.m.–8 p.m.; *spring and fall:* Saturdays and Sundays, 11 a.m.–7 p.m. **Admission** Free to boardwalk, but rides cost $2–$4; full-day passes for unlimited rides $30; 60 tickets for $40 (good if you have more than 1 child); parking, $10. **Touring time** Average 3–4 hours; minimum 2 hours. **Rainy-day touring** Not good. **Restaurants** Yes. **Alcoholic beverages** Yes. **Disabled access** Yes. **Wheelchair rental** Free. **Baby-stroller rental** Yes. **Lockers** Yes. **Pet kennels** No. **Rain check** No. **Private tours** No.

DESCRIPTION AND COMMENTS   There's nothing quite like the screams of roller coaster riders mingling with the smell of hot dogs and salt air. Adults will be content just to stroll along the sunny beachfront boardwalk, on one hand admiring the ocean view and on the other enjoying the colorful amusement-park atmosphere. The famous Giant Dipper Roller Coaster dates from 1924 and the carousel from 1911, but there are also up-to-date amusements such as laser tag and virtual reality. There's a special little-kid area with gentle rides as well as fun booths of games, wax hand-dipping, and ice-cream vendors.

Santa Cruz Municipal Wharf

APPEAL BY AGE	PRESCHOOL ★★★★	GRADE SCHOOL ★★★★	TEENS ★★★★
YOUNG ADULTS ★★★★		OVER 30 ★★★★	SENIORS ★★★★

Beach Street, Santa Cruz; ☎ 831-420-6025;
www.ci.santa-cruz.ca.us/pr/wharf

Hours Daily, 5 a.m.–2 a.m. **Admission** Free; parking $2 per hour. **Touring time** Average 1 hour; minimum half-hour stroll. **Rainy-day touring** Not recommended. **Restaurants** Yes, many. **Alcoholic beverages** In some restaurants. **Disabled access** Yes. **Wheelchair rental** No. **Baby-stroller rental** No. **Lockers** No. **Pet kennels** No. **Rain check** No. **Private tours** No.

DESCRIPTION AND COMMENTS   This is among the best spots in the Monterey Bay Sanctuary to give the kids a glimpse of the appealing sea lions native to these waters. Just walk out on the wharf and look over the railings. There, beneath the surface, you'll see the lithe, balletic bodies of the sea lions as they swim. The bait shops on the wharf sell bags of fish to toss down to the mammals. Eight gift shops, restaurants, charter boats.

Santa Cruz Surfing Museum

APPEAL BY AGE	PRESCHOOL ★★	GRADE SCHOOL ★★★	TEENS ★★★
YOUNG ADULTS ★★★		OVER 30 ★★★	SENIORS ★★★

Mark Abbott Memorial Lighthouse, 701 West Cliff Drive, Santa Cruz;
☎ 831-420-6289; www.santacruzsurfingmuseum.org

Hours *Summer:* Wednesday–Monday, 10 a.m.–5 p.m.; *winter:* Thursday–Monday, noon–4 p.m. **Admission** Free; donation requested. **Touring time** Average 1 hour; minimum 30 minutes. **Rainy-day touring** Yes. **Restaurants** No. **Alcoholic beverages** No. **Disabled access** Yes. **Wheelchair rental** No. **Baby-stroller rental** No. **Lockers** No. **Pet kennels** No, but pets allowed. **Rain check** No. **Private tours** No.

DESCRIPTION AND COMMENTS   This museum actually holds some interest for nonsurfers, thanks to its atmospheric location in the Mark Abbott Memorial Lighthouse on a pretty coastal stretch. Surf-history fans can check out the small but appealing collection of old photos, vintage boards, and local surf history, while others watch the sea-lion colony and the surfers outside.

Wilder Ranch State Park

APPEAL BY AGE	PRESCHOOL ★★★	GRADE SCHOOL ★★★★	TEENS ★★★
YOUNG ADULTS ★★★		OVER 30 ★★★	SENIORS ★★★

1401 Coast Road, Santa Cruz; ☎ 831-426-0505

Hours *Historic complex:* Thursday–Sunday, 10 a.m.–4 p.m.; ranch activities on weekends; park open daily, sunrise–sunset. **Admission** Free, but $6 for a day pass to park. **Touring time** Average 3 hours with hike; minimum 1 hour. **Rainy-day touring** Yes, but wet. **Restaurants** No. **Alcoholic beverages** No. **Disabled access** Yes. **Wheelchair rental** No. **Baby-stroller rental** No. **Lockers** No. **Pet kennels** No. **Rain check** No. **Private tours** No.

DESCRIPTION AND COMMENTS   At this park just west of Santa Cruz, you can see what ranch life was like 100 years ago. There's a great old farmhouse, chicken coops, a working blacksmith, and a storybook barn, as well as trails and such natural wonders as a beachside fern grotto. Call to ask about the schedule of living-history weekends, when docents dress in costume and go about daily ranch life circa 1890. The horse-drawn wagon tour of the ranch is a big hit with younger kids.

FAMILY-FRIENDLY RESTAURANTS

Carpo's
2018 Mission Street, Santa Cruz; ☎ 831-427-1800; www.carposrestaurant.com

Meals served Lunch, dinner. **Cuisine** American. **Entree range** Lunch and dinner, $3.75–$15.95. **Kids' menu** No. **Reservations** Not accepted. **Payment** All major credit cards.

WELL LOCATED OFF US 101, Carpo's is where soccer and Little League teams come to celebrate and kids have birthday parties. Low prices; great fish-and-chips, burgers, and fresh peach or olallieberry pies.

Davenport Roadhouse at the Cash Store
1 Davenport Avenue (9 miles northwest of Santa Cruz on CA 1); ☎ 831-426-8801; www.davenportinn.com

Meals served Breakfast, lunch, and dinner. **Cuisine** Californian. **Entree range** Breakfast, $9–$15; lunch, $9–$20; dinner, $9–$28. **Kids' menu** Yes. **Reservations** Not accepted. **Payment** All major credit cards.

PERFECTLY SITED FOR TRAVELERS who decide to head north to San Francisco without having a big lunch in Santa Cruz, this is a very popular stop. Sometimes there's a long wait, but the cinnamon French toast is worth it. We enjoyed the woodsy, airy room and the beautifully prepared pastas, salads, and wood-fired pizzas. Vegetarian dishes are a specialty.

El Palomar
1336 Pacific Avenue, Santa Cruz; ☎ 831-425-7575; www.elpalomarcilantros.com

Meals served Lunch, dinner, and Sunday brunch. **Cuisine** Mexican. **Entree range** Lunch and dinner, $10–$25. **Kids' menu** Yes. **Reservations** Yes. **Payment** All major credit cards.

THIS NOISY, LIVELY RESTAURANT and bar has several high-ceilinged, beamed dining rooms and some striking murals, thanks to its location in a historic landmark hotel. It's everybody's favorite restaurant, busy even on weeknights, so it's overwhelming for the youngest ones but fun for older kids. You'll enjoy excellent Mexican regional dishes such as mole, fabulous fish tacos, and specialties such as funnel-shaped tacos—a cut above your average Cal-Mex establishment, but still casual and reasonably priced.

Jalisco Mexican Restaurant
618 Main Street, Watsonville; ☎ 831-728-9080;
www.jaliscorestaurant.com

Meals served Lunch, dinner, and weekend breakfast. **Cuisine** Mexican. **Entree range** $13–$17; combination dinners $13–$16. **Kids' menu** No. **Reservations** Necessary on Friday night. **Payment** All major credit cards.

LOCALS COME HERE ON FRIDAY NIGHTS to hear the real mariachis perform, and their music typically captivates kids. The food is straightforward, authentic Mexican, everything from the kid-quesadilla basics to saucy entrees.

PART FIVE

The
SIERRA NEVADA

LITERARY GIANTS AND LEGENDARY EXPLORERS have put their pens to use in describing the sights found in the regions in and around the **Sierra Nevada** mountain range of eastern California. From **Lake Tahoe**'s blue, blue water to **Half Dome**'s moonlit granite curve to the awe-inspiring sequoias, the wonders contained in these landscapes are so extraordinary that Americans have enshrined all or parts of them as national parks, forests, and preserves. From south to north, we will consider the following destinations in this Sierra Nevada chapter: **Death Valley, Sequoia–Kings Canyon, Mammoth Lakes** (with side trips to **Bodie** and **Mono Lake**), **Yosemite,** and Lake Tahoe (the California section of **South Lake Tahoe** as well as **North Lake Tahoe**). The areas we'll discuss in this chapter are for the most part mountainous (except for Death Valley, which is the lowest point on the continent), and they stretch in length along more than half the state.

unofficial **TIP**
Don't be too ambitious in planning visits to the Sierra's remarkable landscapes. Do as Californians do, and concentrate on one or two activities at a time.

Though our enthusiasm for California's national parks is unbounded, our children have had occasion to groan about driving another four hours "to see some more big rocks." Unless you are literally going to be traveling for several weeks, don't try to see all the parks or destinations mentioned in this chapter. Make plans to stay in the park you select or its vicinity and consider a few activities or excursions to bring variety to your days: a guided tour, a horseback ride, a rope-climbing session, a river swim, or even an outlet-shopping day.

Let the season be your first guide in planning your visit to this region. Death Valley is most pleasant and popular from October through April, with high season being in March (although European visitors often prefer the extreme heat of summer, we don't advise it with kids—they'll be most uncomfortable). **Mammoth Mountain** and

the sierra nevada

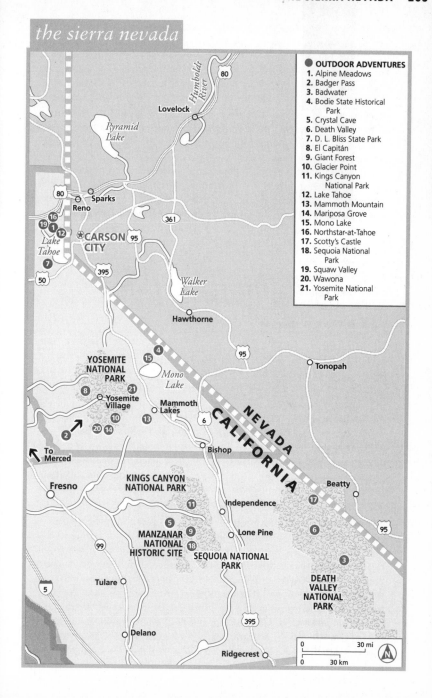

● OUTDOOR ADVENTURES
1. Alpine Meadows
2. Badger Pass
3. Badwater
4. Bodie State Historical Park
5. Crystal Cave
6. Death Valley
7. D. L. Bliss State Park
8. El Capitán
9. Giant Forest
10. Glacier Point
11. Kings Canyon National Park
12. Lake Tahoe
13. Mammoth Mountain
14. Mariposa Grove
15. Mono Lake
16. Northstar-at-Tahoe
17. Scotty's Castle
18. Sequoia National Park
19. Squaw Valley
20. Wawona
21. Yosemite National Park

the town of Mammoth Lakes have two peak seasons—winter for skiing and other snow sports and summer for hiking, fishing, and mountain biking. Sequoia–Kings Canyon has traditionally been a spring-summer-fall destination, but family snow play is burgeoning there, and rangers now lead snowshoe walks and other activities in the winter months. Yosemite is popular all year round—its beauty chronicled by photographers and writers in every season—although summer is its busiest. And Tahoe has distinctly different pleasures in summer (boating, swimming, waterskiing, and hiking) and winter (skiing, snowboarding, and snow play).

You don't have to be a camper to enjoy these national parks and big wonders, but camping is a wonderful option at all of these sites. It is necessary to plan ahead and make reservations whenever possible. There are also lodges and motels in every area, but a limited number of rooms, so advance planning (several months before summer) is necessary to secure the most desirable accommodations. Camping reservations may (and should) typically be made three months in advance. Mammoth and Lake Tahoe have full-fledged towns, with shopping and movie theaters (and, in the case of the Nevada side of South Lake Tahoe, casinos) in addition to lodging and restaurants.

FOR SKIERS ONLY

WE COULDN'T POSSIBLY DO JUSTICE to the many, many ski mountains in the Sierra. Instead, we'll give you the short list of our five favorite Sierra family ski resorts. For more-comprehensive information on skiing, see *The Unofficial Guide to Skiing & Snowboarding in the West*.

ALPINE MEADOWS   This large North Tahoe mountain has excellent snow; less of a scene than glitzier Squaw; and what may be the best children's ski school, staffed by first-rate instructors, in the state. There are more snowboarders than there used to be, which may please your 12-year-old (if not you), but skiers have hardly been forced out. 2600 Alpine Meadows Road, Tahoe City; ☎ 800-949-3296 or 530-583-4232; **www.skialpine.com.**

BADGER PASS   The conditions aren't always ideal, and the quality of skiing is on the lower end, but that didn't stop us from falling in love with this place. It's the ski mountain that time forgot, with a small, beamed lodge, the cheapest ski-mountain cafeteria in the West, friendly people, good Nordic trails, and a very good learn-to-ski program for children and adults. The beginner-to-intermediate runs are great for learning and cruising, and the lift tickets and packages are the least expensive we've seen. Good skiers and cool teens, however, might get bored. The mountain is easily reached from accommodations on the valley floor. Yosemite National Park; ☎ 209-372-8430; **www.yosemite park.com.**

MAMMOTH MOUNTAIN   We learned to ski at Mammoth as teenagers, and it remains a teen haven to this day—in fact, it's a haven for every sort of skier, because its vastness can accommodate everyone, and the quality and diversity of its runs are among North America's best. It'd take you a week to ski every run. Good children's programs and lessons are run out of both the main lodge and Canyon Lodge, and nearby condos are plentiful. The downside is the crowding during holidays, but the addition of more high-speed lifts has dramatically improved the situation. For details, see the Mammoth Mountain attraction profile in the Mammoth Lakes section.

NORTHSTAR-AT-TAHOE   This is a large, upscale snow resort with well-designed and well-maintained areas for downhill skiers, snowboarders, and Nordic skiers. The children's programs and ski schools are impressive. For details, see the Northstar attraction profile in the Lake Tahoe section.

SQUAW VALLEY   Like Mammoth, this mountainous resort is so huge that skiing it all takes days. Unlike the ones at Mammoth, Squaw Valley's lift lines are short, if they exist at all. Lots of beginner runs, lots of expert runs, even more groomed intermediate runs, and a separate children's ski area. For details, see the Squaw Valley attraction profile in the Lake Tahoe section.

A **CALENDAR** of **FESTIVALS** and **EVENTS**

February

NORTH LAKE TAHOE SNOWFEST   *Lake Tahoe.* Tahoe's ten-day Snowfest celebration includes more than 100 events, ranging from parades and a snow-sculpture contest to a polar swim and costume parties; ☎ 530-583-7167; **www.tahoesnowfestival.com.**

March

SOUTH LAKE TAHOE ANNUAL WINTER CELEBRATION   *Lake Tahoe.* Includes ski and snowboard races, concerts, and an ice-sculpting contest; ☎ 530-544-5050.

April

EASTER EGG HUNT AND PLAYDAY   *Mammoth Lakes.* ☎ 760-934-8989; **www.visitmammoth.com.**

CONVICT LAKE SPRING TROUT DERBY   *Convict Lake Resort, Mammoth Lakes.* Lots of kids join their parents in trying to catch the biggest fish at this Eastern Sierra lake; ☎ 800-992-2260 or 760-934-3800; **www.convictlakeresort.com.**

May

BISHOP MULE DAYS   *Bishop.* A rootin'-tootin' rodeo and fair, with coon jumping, mule dressage, barrel racing, country-western concerts, barbecue dinners, and a parade; ☎ 760-872-4263; **www.muledays.org.**

June

AMERICA'S MOST BEAUTIFUL BIKE RIDE   *Lake Tahoe.* Hundreds of cyclists ride the 72-mile shoreline road around the lake; ☎ 800-565-2704; **www.bikethewest.com.**

MOVIES UNDER THE STARS   *The Village, Mammoth Lakes.* Family-friendly movies are shown outdoors at the Village from mid-June to early September. The films are free, and proceeds from snack sales go to local youth programs; ☎760-935-4356; **www.villageatmammoth.com.**

July

CHILDREN'S FISHING FESTIVAL   *Mammoth Lakes, Snowcreek Ponds.* For age 12 and younger. Kids learn to fish, with free tackle provided; ☎ 760-934-2712; **www.visitmammoth.com.**

FOURTH OF JULY CELEBRATION   *Lake Tahoe.* Includes fireworks at the beach in Tahoe City, and a parade and party in Truckee; ☎ 530-587-2757; **www.truckee.com.**

FOURTH OF JULY CELEBRATION   *Mammoth Lakes.* Includes Lions Club pancake breakfast, a very popular parade, Fire Department open house, U.S. Forest Service Fire Department open house, and fireworks at Crowley Lake; ☎ 888-466-2666, 760-934-6717, 760-934-2712; **www.visitmammoth.com.**

LAKE TAHOE MUSIC FESTIVAL   *Lake Tahoe.* Extends for several weeks at various locations around the lake; ☎ 530-583-3101; **www.tahoe music.org.**

MAMMOTH LAKES JAZZ JUBILEE   *Mammoth Lakes.* Lots of mostly traditional jazz (Dixieland, swing, and big-band), dancing, food, and more; ☎ 877-686-5299 or 760-934-2478; **www.mammothjazz.org.**

August

LAKE TAHOE CONCOURS D'ELEGANCE   *Lake Tahoe.* Show of antique and vintage wooden boats and other maritime events; ☎ 530-581-4700; **www.laketahoeconcours.com.**

September

LABOR DAY ARTS AND CRAFTS FESTIVAL   *Mammoth Lakes.* A village arts celebration of the end of summer; ☎ 760-873-7242; **www.mono arts.org.**

MILLPOND MUSIC FESTIVAL   *Bishop.* A sweet, family-friendly outdoor music festival, emphasizing folk and world music. Bring a picnic and a guitar; ☎ 760-873-8014; **www.inyo.org/millpond.**

October

KOKANEE SALMON FESTIVAL   *Taylor Creek Visitors Center.* Two-day festival celebrating the spawning of local salmon, with family activities such as art displays, nature walks, and interpretive talks at the fish windows of the Forest Service's Taylor Creek Visitors Center; ☎ 530-543-2674; **www.fs.fed.us/r5/ltbmu/recreation/visitor-center.**

December

MAMMOTH LAKES TOWN CHRISTMAS TREE LIGHTING CEREMONY *Mammoth Lakes.* ☎ 760-934-8989; **www.visitmammoth.com.**

BREAKFAST WITH SANTA   *Mammoth Lakes.* ☎ 760-924-5500.

GETTING THERE

BECAUSE THE TERRITORY COVERED IS SO HUGE, we will devote a section of each destination's coverage to getting there.

HOW TO GET INFORMATION BEFORE YOU GO

- **Caltrans Highway Conditions**   (For winter driving in mountains); ☎ 800-427-7623; **dot.ca.gov**
- **Death Valley National Park**   Death Valley 92328; ☎ 760-786-2331; **www.nps.gov/deva**
- **Lake Tahoe Visitor Information**   North Shore: ☎ 888-434-1262; **www.gotahoenorth.com;** South Shore: ☎ 800-AT-TAHOE; **www.bluelaketahoe.com**
- **Mammoth Lakes Visitors Bureau**   P.O. Box 48, Mammoth Lakes 93546; ☎ 888-466-2666; **www.visitmammoth.com**
- **Mammoth Visitor Center and Ranger Station**   Has up-to-date information on opening dates of campgrounds (700 sites at elevations above 7,500 feet) in Inyo National Forest; ☎ 760-924-5500; **www.fs.fed.us/r5/inyo**
- **National Parks Camping Reservations**   ☎ 877-444-6777; international callers, ☎ 518-885-3639; **www.recreation.gov**
- **Sequoia and Kings Canyon national parks**   ☎ 559-565-3134; **www.nps.gov/seki;** Guest Services (authorized concessionaire handling lodging except for camping and other services in the two parks): 47050 Generals Highway, Three Rivers 93271; ☎ 559-565-3341

The BEST PARKS

THIS ENTIRE CHAPTER IS NOTHING BUT THE BEST PARKS, so they're not listed under this heading—they're described in detail throughout the chapter, as "town" descriptions and sometimes under "Attractions." Look for specifics under the particular area that interests you.

FAMILY OUTDOOR ADVENTURES

AGAIN, THIS CHAPTER IS NOTHING BUT. They're not listed separately here because they're plentiful at every spot in these wilderness areas. Check for details in individual geographic areas.

LITTLE MOMENTS IN BIG PLACES

SOMETIMES THE VASTNESS of these remarkable Western landscapes—big skies, big mountains, big lakes—is just too much for kids to absorb, and they respond with indifference or ennui. We always look for ways to bring the wonders of the region down to their scale. Here are some activities and strategies that have worked for us.

1. While a sports-loving middle schooler and Mom went for a challenging hike in Yosemite (up many, many steps to **Vernal Falls**), Dad and a younger sister rented bikes and took a leisurely ride along the flat, paved bike path of **Yosemite Valley** that winds through meadows and campgrounds. Deer, squirrels, and other kids were out in view, and those easy two hours live on the younger sister's memory.

2. After panning for gold in **Gold Country,** we began our time in Yosemite by stopping for a picnic at a spot where the **Yosemite River** makes a sweeping curve and **Half Dome** can be seen rising majestically above the treetops. The kids didn't even look up at the mighty landmark, though, because while wading in the icy stream, they realized that the water was flecked with gold. Instead, they began to gather and scrutinize every pebble just in case one was a real nugget.

3. At **Montecito Summer Family Camp,** the youngest children are taken on a "fishing trip," in which they lie facedown on a dock over the little lake and reach down with nets to try to scoop up the tadpoles and guppies they can see below. Our daughter now indignantly says the nets had holes big enough to allow every fish to swim through, but at the time (at age 4), she was an enthralled sportswoman.

4. Because of the uniquely sudden coolness of the desert night, the **Furnace Creek Inn** in Death Valley has a huge fireplace in the pool area. Our daughter floated in the 85°F pool water (heated by natural hot springs), gazing at the early-rising "children's moon" as the sky started to glow pink with a dramatic desert sunset. After getting out, she wrapped herself in a big towel and warmed herself happily by the fireplace. The juxtaposition charmed her.

5. On an inspired moment while enjoying a condo vacation in **Mammoth,** we agreed to stop (after hiking and before hitting the pool) at a bead shop and let the kids each browse among the bins with a muffin tin. They picked out a variety of beads and something to string them on, and left with little bags and triumphant airs. That night, the usual plea for a movie on DVD was replaced by the quiet sounds of kids creating.

6. At **Mono Lake,** the adults read interpretive plaques and shook their heads over water-use controversies, but the kids didn't come alive until we joined a ranger walk at lake's edge and the story of those teeny-tiny brine shrimp (specimens scrutinized) and the funny little fly larvae was revealed.

BIG ADVENTURES FOR BIGGER KIDS

WHILE LOOKING FOR SMALL FOCAL POINTS is the right thing to do with younger children, older kids and teenagers are mature enough to grasp the grandeur of the Sierra—and they're often ready to be physically challenged, too. Here are some of our favorite mountain-country adventures, ranging from an hour to a week.

Gondola mountain biking. In the summertime, Mammoth Mountain's gondola delivers bike riders and their mounts halfway up the mountain, or all the way to the 11,063-foot peak. How hard could it be to ride downhill? Answer: terrifyingly hard. Some of the trails are steep, narrow, rocky and unstable—and lots of teenagers find it absolutely thrilling. See page 285 for details

Rock climbing in Yosemite. Older kids (and their parents) are typically dazzled by the world-class climbers inching up Half Dome. To get a taste for just how insanely difficult that is, have the whole family take a rock-climbing lesson (best for ages 10 and up). See page 296 for information.

Guided High Sierra Camp Hikes. Taking one of these five- to seven-day guided backcountry trips is a rite of passage for many California families. A National Park Service ranger leads a small group to several High Sierra tent camps. You carry your personal supplies, but the food, water and camp gear is provided. The camps are six to ten miles apart, making this a manageable and incredibly memorable adventure for teenagers; outdoorsy and fit 9-and-ups can handle it, too. These trips are in high demand, with spaces for summer outings being booked by lottery during the previous September, October, and November, so plan early; ☎ 801-559-4909; **www.yosemitepark.com.**

Conquering Mt. Whitney. This is a very serious adventure, and you need to be in shape for it, but making it to the top of the largest peak in the lower 48 is entirely within the reach of reasonably fit teenagers and their active middle-aged parents. But forget what your friends said about climbing it in one day—it's technically possible, but you'll all be likely to lose your lunch by the side of the trail, and your kids will hate you forever. Instead, give yourself a few days for the adventure, and consider doing it with a reputable guide service, such as **Sierra Mountain Center** (☎ 760-873-8526; **www.sierramountaincenter.com**). Trips typically depart out of Lone Pine in the Eastern Sierra.

DEATH VALLEY

OFTEN, CITY OR SUBURB DWELLERS discover that gazing on open vistas refreshes the mind and broadens mental horizons. In contrast to the close-up visual density of our daily lives (from nearby computer screen to a horizon cluttered with buildings), there are places where emptiness is neither a sign of failure nor simply an affront to commercial enterprise. This vast area is one such place.

In Death Valley, we found the spaces to be affirmingly expansive and the views cleansing—barren mountains, untrafficked roads stretching empty for miles in both directions, sky as a presence. The children felt it, too, though they didn't articulate the sensation. Still, they fell silent and gazed about when we stopped for cold drinks and directions.

As we explored the area, its vastness was broken up into little sections—each with a history, a personality, and a name. Such places as **Scotty's Castle** and **Badwater** became real to us. Where there seemed to have been a great nothingness, we found a little bit of everything.

GETTING THERE

BY CAR Death Valley is about 300 miles northeast of LA and 525 miles southeast of San Francisco. It's a long drive no matter which way you come, and you can't cross those mountains just anywhere. From LA, take **CA 14** north to **US 395** north to a fork in the road called **Olancha,** where you pick up **CA 190** (scenic route) east to Death Valley. From San Francisco, your best bet is to pick one or two other parks to include in your trip and to access Death Valley after visiting Yosemite or Sequoia, both directly between San Francisco and your goal.

FAMILY LODGING

Furnace Creek Campground
CA 190, Death Valley; ☎ 877-444-6777; www.recreation.gov; park information, ☎ 760-786-3200; www.nps.gov/deva; $18

PART OF DEATH VALLEY NATIONAL PARK, this campground is a good bet for families. There are 20 tent spaces and 180 tent or RV spaces with fireplaces, tables, water, and flush toilets. Not all campsites have shade.

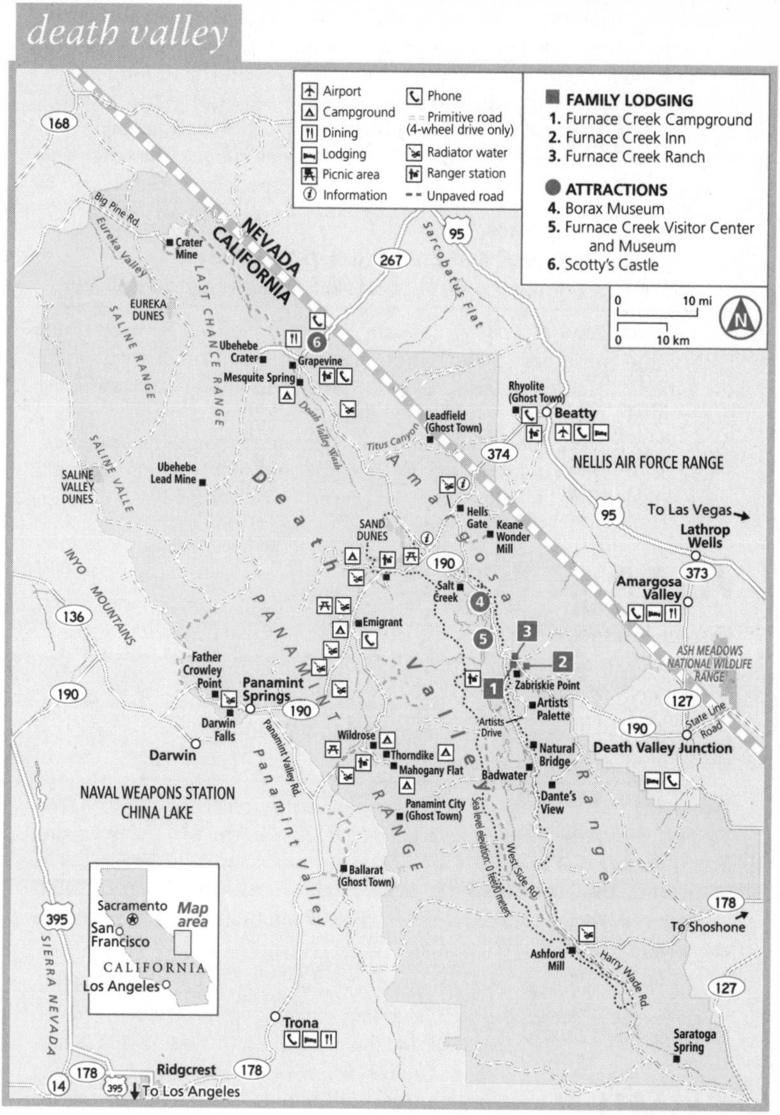
death valley
Airport
Campground
Dining
Lodging
Picnic area
Information
Phone
Primitive road (4-wheel drive only)
Radiator water
Ranger station
Unpaved road
FAMILY LODGING
1. Furnace Creek Campground
2. Furnace Creek Inn
3. Furnace Creek Ranch
ATTRACTIONS
4. Borax Museum
5. Furnace Creek Visitor Center and Museum
6. Scotty's Castle
0 10 mi
0 10 km
N
NEVADA
CALIFORNIA
Big Pine Rd.
Eureka Valley
Crater Mine
LAST CHANCE RANGE
EUREKA DUNES
SALINE RANGE
Ubehebe Crater
Grapevine
Mesquite Spring
Death Valley Wash
Sarcobatus Flat
Rhyolite (Ghost Town)
Beatty
Leadfield (Ghost Town)
Titus Canyon
NELLIS AIR FORCE RANGE
SALINE VALLEY DUNES
SALINE VALLEY
Ubehebe Lead Mine
Death Valley
Amargosa Range
Hells Gate
Keane Wonder Mill
SAND DUNES
To Las Vegas
Lathrop Wells
Amargosa Valley
INYO MOUNTAINS
Salt Creek
Emigrant
ASH MEADOWS NATIONAL WILDLIFE RANGE
Father Crowley Point
Panamint Springs
PANAMINT RANGE
Zabriskie Point
Artists Palette
Artists Drive
Darwin Falls
Darwin
Panamint Valley Rd.
Wildrose
Thorndike
Mahogany Flat
Natural Bridge
Badwater
State Line Road
Death Valley Junction
NAVAL WEAPONS STATION CHINA LAKE
Panamint City (Ghost Town)
Dante's View
Sea level elevation: 0 feet/0 meters
West Side Rd.
Panamint Valley
Ballarat (Ghost Town)
Sacramento
Map area
San Francisco
CALIFORNIA
Los Angeles
To Shoshone
Ashford Mill
Harry Wade Rd.
SIERRA NEVADA
Trona
Saratoga Spring
Ridgecrest
To Los Angeles
168
95
267
374
190
373
136
127
178
395
14

Furnace Creek Inn

CA 190, Death Valley; ☎ 800-236-7916 or 760-786-2345; www.furnacecreekresort.com; $305–$400

DESIGNED BY NOTED EARLY-20TH-CENTURY ARCHITECT Albert C. Martin, this 66-room luxury hotel is truly something special, offering real comfort in an incredibly isolated location. You might be hot and dusty from a hike, but after a shower, a swim in the warm, spring-fed pool, and a cool drink on your room's balcony, you'll feel lucky indeed. The rooms, remodeled in the late 1990s, are true to their 1920s roots in a decor that fits nicely with the desert setting. The dining room was too formal for us to enjoy with the kids except at breakfast (although there is a kids' menu). The hotel is on a hill above the valley, so views are spectacular—especially at sunrise.

Furnace Creek Ranch
CA 190, Death Valley; ☎ 800-236-7916 or 760-786-2345;
www.furnacecreekresort.com; $124–$192; kids under age 18 stay free

AT THE BOTTOM OF THE HILL is the other part of the Furnace Creek Resort, the more boisterous motel- and camping-focused area, where restaurants, laundry services, tennis courts, and spring-fed swimming pools serve visitors in a grassy, shady oasis. The 224 units range in quality from okay to very good, depending on whether they've been upgraded. There are three restaurants on the grounds, and plenty of kids running around playing basketball, tennis, and (desert) sand volleyball.

ATTRACTIONS

Borax Museum

APPEAL BY AGE	PRESCHOOL ★★	GRADE SCHOOL ★★	TEENS ★★
YOUNG ADULTS ★★★	OVER 30 ★★★		SENIORS ★★★

Furnace Creek Ranch, Death Valley; ☎ 760-786-2345;
www.furnacecreekresort.com

Hours Daily, 8:30 a.m.–4 p.m.; closed noon–1 p.m. for lunch. **Admission** Free. **Touring time** Average 40 minutes; minimum 20 minutes. **Rainy-day touring** Yes (it doesn't rain anyway). **Restaurants** At resort. **Alcoholic beverages** At restaurants. **Disabled access** Yes. **Wheelchair rental** At registration. **Baby-stroller rental** No. **Lockers** No. **Pet kennels** No. **Rain check** No. **Private tours** No.

DESCRIPTION AND COMMENTS   Whether or not you stay at Furnace Creek Inn or Furnace Creek Ranch, you'll end up spending some time at the ranch because of the amenities, including horseback riding. You can while away some time by strolling through the old mining-equipment graveyard behind this museum or, if the hour is right, through the museum itself. The brand name "20 Mule Team Borax" doesn't mean much to those too young to have seen the Ronald Reagan commercials in the early 1960s, but if you think about it and talk about it a bit, the idea of actually handling a team of 20 mules will begin to sink in.

unofficial **TIP**
Don't bother with the Borax horseback trail ride—it's a dull walk.

Furnace Creek Visitor Center and Museum

APPEAL BY AGE	PRESCHOOL ★★	GRADE SCHOOL ★★	TEENS ★★
YOUNG ADULTS ★★		OVER 30 ★★★	SENIORS ★★

Death Valley National Park, Death Valley; ☎ 760-786-3200; www.nps.gov/deva

Hours Daily, 9 a.m.–5 p.m. **Admission** $10. **Touring time** Average 1 hour for exhibits, slide show, and questions; minimum 30 minutes. **Rainy-day touring** Yes. **Restaurants** At ranch. **Alcoholic beverages** At restaurants. **Disabled access** Yes. **Wheelchair rental** No. **Baby-stroller rental** No. **Lockers** No. **Pet kennels** No. **Rain check** No. **Private tours** No.

DESCRIPTION AND COMMENTS   The central source for visitor information while in Death Valley, the center has an hourly slide-show orientation, a small museum, and schedules of programs offered at campsites around the valley. The bookstore operated by Death Valley History Association has a number of children's publications.

 Scotty's Castle

APPEAL BY AGE	PRESCHOOL ★★	GRADE SCHOOL ★★★★	TEENS ★★★★½
YOUNG ADULTS ★★★★½		OVER 30 ★★★★½	SENIORS ★★★★½

Death Valley Ranch, Death Valley National Park, Death Valley; ☎ 760-786-2392 or 760-786-2331; www.nps.gov/deva

Hours Tours daily, winter 9 a.m.–5 p.m., summer 9:30 a.m.–4 p.m. **Admission** $11 adults, $6 disabled adults, $9 seniors, $6 children ages 6–15, free for children age 5 and under. **Touring time** Average 50 minutes; minimum 50 minutes. **Rainy-day touring** Yes, for inside. **Restaurants** Snack bar. **Alcoholic beverages** No. **Disabled access** Yes. **Wheelchair rental** Yes, free. **Baby-stroller rental** No. **Lockers** No. **Pet kennels** No. **Rain check** No. **Private tours** No.

DESCRIPTION AND COMMENTS   Together with Hearst Castle and the Will Rogers House, Scotty's Castle forms a picture of a grand period in California in the late 1920s and early 1930s, when personalities and the houses they occupied were larger than life. This remarkable mansion museum is shown today by docents who offer living-history tours, pretending that you are arriving guests of the owner, Chicago millionaire Albert Johnson, while showing you around. In its own way, Scotty's Castle rivals the stately homes and castles of Europe, with its carpets from Majorca, ceramics from Italy, custom wrought-iron fixtures in fantasy shapes, and huge redwood beams. The kids listened intently to the story of the trickster caretaker Scotty, who persuaded many that this was his house. At the end, it was extraordinary in a goofy way to stand in the resonating vibration of the player organ as it boomed "Pomp and Circumstance" and we wended our way down the circular steps of a turret.

SEQUOIA *and* KINGS CANYON NATIONAL PARKS

THESE TWIN PARKS ARE ADMINISTERED JOINTLY but were established separately, Sequoia in 1890 and Kings Canyon in 1940. Today's visitors might not know, as they drive from place to place in the pine forests, whether they are entering Kings Canyon or leaving Sequoia. Overall, most of the park acreage is given over to wilderness areas, but 90 miles of paved roads allow for access to the groves of sequoias and some other natural wonders. A special experience is a stay at **Montecito Summer Family Camp,** (see listing under "Family Lodging," page 276). Sequoia is home to the world's largest tree, the **General Sherman,** found in the **Giant Forest.**

GETTING THERE

BY CAR **CA 198** leads into Sequoia National Park from the southwest; **CA 180** provides access to the parks from the Fresno area. The **Generals Highway** connects Highways 198 and 180 and also connects Sequoia and Kings Canyon parks. The **Foothill Visitors Center** (☎ 559-565-3135; **www.nps.gov/seki**) is located at the entrance to the park. It's the park headquarters, and rangers here will collect an entrance fee.

FAMILY LODGING

Buckeye Tree Lodge
46000 Sierra Drive, Three Rivers; ☎ 559-561-5900;
www.buckeyetree.com; $79–$153

THERE ARE SEVERAL MOTELS in Three Rivers, which is a short distance from the entrance to Sequoia National Park, and this is one of the more comfortable. It has 12 rooms, and it's in a woodsy setting next to a river; some rooms have balconies overlooking the river. One room has a kitchenette; our favorite is the two-bedroom cottage with a fireplace and a kitchen. Pool and a playground, refrigerators in the rooms, and a restaurant nearby.

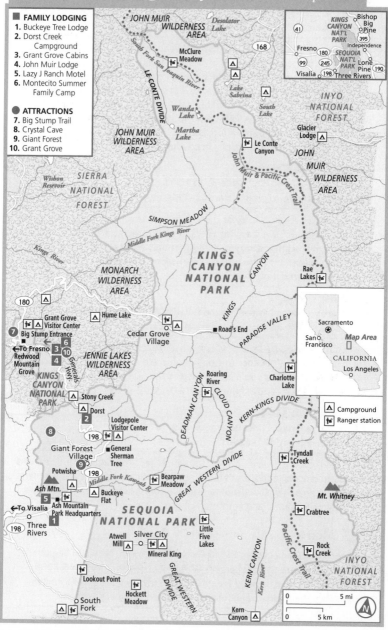

sequoia and kings canyon national parks

FAMILY LODGING
1. Buckeye Tree Lodge
2. Dorst Creek Campground
3. Grant Grove Cabins
4. John Muir Lodge
5. Lazy J Ranch Motel
6. Montecito Summer Family Camp

ATTRACTIONS
7. Big Stump Trail
8. Crystal Cave
9. Giant Forest
10. Grant Grove

JOHN MUIR WILDERNESS AREA
Desolator Lake
McClure Meadow
South Fork San Joaquin River
LE CONTE DIVIDE
Wanda Lake
Martha Lake
JOHN MUIR WILDERNESS AREA
Lake Sabrina
South Lake
Le Conte Canyon
John Muir & Pacific Crest Trail
Glacier Lodge
JOHN MUIR WILDERNESS AREA

KINGS CANYON NAT'L PARK
41
Bishop
Big Pine
395
Independence
Fresno
180
SEQUOIA NAT'L PARK
Lone Pine
190
99
245
Visalia
198
Three Rivers

INYO NATIONAL FOREST

Wishon Resevoir
SIERRA NATIONAL FOREST
JOHN MUIR WILDERNESS AREA
SIMPSON MEADOW
Middle Fork King River
Kings River
MONARCH WILDERNESS AREA
KINGS CANYON NATIONAL PARK
KINGS CANYON
Rae Lakes

180
Grant Grove Visitor Center
Big Stump Entrance
←To Fresno
Redwood Mountain Grove
Hume Lake
Cedar Grove Village
Road's End
PARADISE VALLEY
Sacramento
San Francisco
Map Area
CALIFORNIA
Los Angeles

JENNIE LAKES WILDERNESS AREA
Generals Hwy.
KINGS CANYON NATIONAL PARK
Stony Creek
Dorst
Lodgepole Visitor Center
198
Giant Forest Village
General Sherman Tree
Potwisha
198
Middle Fork Kaweah R.
Bearpaw Meadow
Ash Mtn.
Buckeye Flat
←To Visalia
Ash Mountain Park Headquarters
Three Rivers
198
SEQUOIA NATIONAL PARK
Atwell Mill
Silver City
Mineral King
Little Five Lakes
Lookout Point
Hockett Meadow
South Fork

Roaring River
DEADMAN CANYON
CLOUD CANYON
Charlotte Lake
KERN-KINGS DIVIDE
GREAT WESTERN DIVIDE
Tyndall Creek
Mt. Whitney
Crabtree
Rock Creek
KERN CANYON
GREAT WESTERN DIVIDE
Pacific Crest Trail
Kern River
Kern Canyon
INYO NATIONAL FOREST

△ Campground
🚹 Ranger station

0   5 mi
0   5 km

N

Dorst Creek Campground
Off Generals Highway, a few miles north of the Lodgepole Visitors Center; ☎ 559-565-3341; www.nps.gov/seki; reservations, ☎ 877-444-6777; www.recreation.gov; campsites $18

THE BEST FAMILY CAMPGROUND in Sequoia–Kings Canyon is Dorst, which also happens to be one of the many national-park campgrounds that accept reservations—so make them very, very early. Kids run wild here, making friends at other tent sites, jumping in gentle Dorst Creek, and romping in the meadowy areas. This is a great base for exploring the redwood forests and hiking to little peaks and creeks. Hume Lake, an excellent swimming and fishing destination, is close by, and you can pick up supplies easily at Lodgepole. Flush toilets, fireplaces, picnic tables, food lockers.

Grant Grove Cabins
Grant Grove, ☎ 866-522-6966 or 559-335-5500; www.rescentre.com/grant.htm; $62–$140

THE 56 SMALL CABINS look far more picturesque on the outside than they feel on the inside—we'd advise taking a picture here rather than staying. But if you must camp here, you'll find that only nine cabins have electricity and indoor plumbing. The others have kerosene lanterns, outdoor woodstoves, and shared bathhouses.

John Muir Lodge
Grant Grove, Kings Canyon National Park; ☎ 866-522-6966 or 559-335-5500; www.sequoia-kingscanyon.com; $79–$180

THE LODGE IS WOODSY on the outside and basic-motel on the inside, but the beds are comfortable, the bathrooms are new, and the location is great. No kitchens, so you'll have to eat in the cafe or pack picnics, and no TV, which is a very good thing in such a beautiful place.

Lazy J Ranch Motel
39625 Sierra Drive, Three Rivers; ☎ 559-561-4449; www.bvilazyj.com; $75–$250

AN 18-ROOM MOTEL with a real ranch feel—cottages are scattered around meadows, and there's a path that leads down to the river. Several units have one or two bedrooms, and five cottages have kitchens. There's a pool, a playground, and laundry facilities.

Montecito Summer Family Camp
Montecito Sequoia Lodge, 63410 Generals Highway, between Sequoia and Kings Canyon national parks; ☎ 800-227-9900 or 559-565-3388; www.mslodge.com; weekly 7-day, 6-night stay in cabin, $1,495 and up, depending on number of people; all meals and activities included

WHEN WE STAYED HERE it was like a California version of Lake Wobegon: all the men were good-looking, and all the women were above average.

Something about the mountain-air atmosphere and the choice to be with your kids at summer camp made for a lot of conviviality among the adults. Parents never had to cook a meal, but plenty gathered at the camp "bar" for a glass of wine in the early evening hours or gathered early in the morning at the daily songfest before activities.

Kids are divided into age groups with counselors, and they can spend specified hours in the counselors' care while you pursue your own camp activities (archery, anyone?) or leave the premises to hike or sightsee. Meals are taken together, and evening activities such as games and costume parties are designed for the whole family. This is truly the best of both worlds for those who'd rather join their kids at camp than send them (especially the too-young ones). This former girls' camp is on Sequoia National Forest land between the national parks, within easy distance of Crystal Cave and some of the most famous big trees. Open all year, it offers cross-country skiing and ice skating on the lake in the winter, and waterskiing, horseback riding, pool swimming, and many other activities in the summer. There are 29 rustic, motel-type rooms with private baths, and 13 family camping cabins (with beds, but bring your own linens; they have electricity and wood-burning stoves, but no running water—bathhouses are nearby).

ATTRACTIONS

Big Stump Trail

APPEAL BY AGE	PRESCHOOL ★★	GRADE SCHOOL ★★★	TEENS ★★
YOUNG ADULTS ★★★	OVER 30 ★★★		SENIORS ★★★

Near the entrance to Sequoia National Park; ☎ 559-335-2856; www.nps.gov/seki

Hours Daily, 24 hours, weather permitting. **Admission** Free. **Touring time** Average 3 hours; minimum 30 minutes. **Rainy-day touring** No, and hard to tour in snow. **Restaurants** In Grant Grove. **Alcoholic beverages** Yes. **Disabled access** No. **Wheelchair rental** No. **Baby-stroller rental** No. **Lockers** No. **Pet kennels** No. **Rain check** No. **Private tours** No.

DESCRIPTION AND COMMENTS   This one-and-a-half-mile nature loop has a wonderful disaster theme that appeals to school-age kids. It shows, in its short distance, all sorts of natural and human-caused damage that the sequoias have endured. There's one tree that was hit by lightning, another that was shattered by loggers, and a huge stump that was created when one of the largest sequoias was felled for display in New York.

Crystal Cave

APPEAL BY AGE	PRESCHOOL ★★★	GRADE SCHOOL ★★★★	TEENS ★★★
YOUNG ADULTS ★★★	OVER 30 ★★★		SENIORS ★★

9 miles from Lodgepole Visitor Center, Sequoia National Park; ☎ 559-565-3341; www.sequoiahistory.org

Hours *Mid-May–October:* daily 1-hour tours, usually starting at 10:30 or 11 a.m.; last tour as early as 2 p.m. or as late as 5 p.m.; call for schedule. **Admission** $11 adults, $10 seniors, $6 children ages 6–12, free for children age 5 and under (tickets at Lodgepole or Foothill visitors centers only). **Touring time** Average 2 hours; minimum 1-hour tour plus time to hike steep ½-mile trail from parking area to cave entrance. **Rainy-day touring** Okay. **Restaurants** No. **Alcoholic beverages** No. **Disabled access** No. **Wheelchair rental** No. **Baby-stroller rental** No. **Lockers** No. **Pet kennels** No. **Rain check** No. **Private tours** No, group tours only.

DESCRIPTION AND COMMENTS   Not far from the Giant Forest (see profile below) is the Crystal Cave. We like cave tours when there are plenty of people and the caves aren't too dark and spooky but, rather, full of stalactites and stalagmites. So we like the one-hour tour of Crystal Cave with the Organ Room and the Marble Room. And it's nice in the summer to spend some time in the cool underground. Note that this tour is neither stroller- nor wheelchair-accessible, and backpacks are not allowed. Also, the 2008 touring season ended early due to forest fires in the area, so check the Web site or call for any updates in the 2009 schedule.

Giant Forest

APPEAL BY AGE	PRESCHOOL ★★★★	GRADE SCHOOL ★★★★	TEENS ★★★★
YOUNG ADULTS ★★★★		OVER 30 ★★★★	SENIORS ★★★★

Generals Highway, Sequoia National Forest; ☎ 559-565-3782; www.nps.gov/seki/lpvc.htm

Hours Vary by season and conditions; call before you go. **Admission** Free (park has $20 vehicle-entrance fee). **Touring time** Average 2–3 hours; minimum 30 minutes without the walk. **Rainy-day touring** Come prepared and you won't be miserable. **Restaurants** Yes. **Alcoholic beverages** No. **Disabled access** Limited. **Wheelchair rental** No. **Baby-stroller rental** No. **Lockers** No. **Pet kennels** No. **Rain check** No. **Private tours** No.

DESCRIPTION AND COMMENTS   In the Giant Forest, you'll find the General Sherman Tree and the Congress Trail. The 2,500-year-old tree is one of those superlatives every visitor to the region must pay homage to. It's the biggest measured tree in the world, as tall as a 27-story building. Near this giant specimen in Sequoia National Park is the Congress Trail, a two-mile, self-guided loop that makes a nice outing for walking families because it winds through several magnificent groves of sequoias. Stop at Lodgepole Visitor Center for trail and other information.

Grant Grove

APPEAL BY AGE	PRESCHOOL ★★★★	GRADE SCHOOL ★★★★	TEENS ★★★★
YOUNG ADULTS ★★★★		OVER 30 ★★★★	SENIORS ★★★★

Kings Canyon National Park; ☎ 559-335-2856; www.nps.gov/seki/ggvc.htm

Hours Daily, 8 a.m.–5 p.m. **Admission** Free (park has $20 vehicle-entrance fee). **Touring time** Average 2 hours with visitors center, refreshments, and self-guided nature walk; minimum 1 hour. **Rainy-day touring** No; plus, it's hard to tour in the snows. **Restaurants** Yes. **Alcoholic beverages** Yes. **Disabled access** Yes. **Wheelchair rental** No. **Baby-stroller rental** No. **Lockers** No. **Pet kennels** No. **Rain check** No. **Private tours** No, interpretive hikes available.

DESCRIPTION AND COMMENTS   This mountain village is a kind of headquarters for Kings Canyon. It's a few miles from the park entrance and adjacent to the General Grant Grove stand of giant sequoias. In the village are a couple of lodges, a little market, and a visitors center. The grove itself is an impressive stand of sequoias that was not too much for us to enjoy in an hour's part-drive–part-stroll from tree to tree. There's a twin-sisters tree, with two trees growing from a single trunk; a fallen, 21-foot-diameter tree with a tunnel cut into it; and the General Grant, the third-largest known tree in the world, at 267 feet high, with a circumference of almost 108 feet.

MAMMOTH LAKES

THIS IS THE EASIEST MOUNTAIN RESORT in California to recommend to visitors, because you don't have to be a certain kind of traveler to enjoy it. It has such a wide range of options that two very different families could spend time here and never cross paths. Some visit only during ski season, but we had one of the most fun summer family vacations ever by staying a week in a condominium, which is the housing of choice for most visitors. Family-friendly and plentiful, Mammoth's condos range from the swank and expensive to the dated and cheap; now that developer Starwood is pumping zillions into this once-funky resort town, prices are climbing. Summer or winter, **Mammoth Mountain** is the scene of many sports competitions, from mountain biking to snowboarding (a number of Olympic snowboarders hail from Mammoth), and there are marathons weekly throughout the nonsnow season. If you happen upon one of these events, let the kids hang out for a while and watch—they may see a young sports hero followed around by a TV crew.

GETTING THERE

BY PLANE Horizon Air has begun twice-daily service from Los Angeles International Airport to little **Mammoth Yosemite Airport** (MMH) during the winter ski season.

BY CAR This is one of the easiest mountain communities in the world to take kids to—the approaches via **US 395** from Bishop in the south and Yosemite out of Lee Vining in the northeast are on a mostly multilane modern highway whose broad pavement curves slowly and gradually up into the higher elevations. There's none of the hours of switchbacks that so often unnerve (and make ill) the little ones. From LA, plan on a five-hour drive; it's about 100 miles from Yosemite Valley, but you can't take the direct route in winter, when snow closes the roads.

mammoth lakes

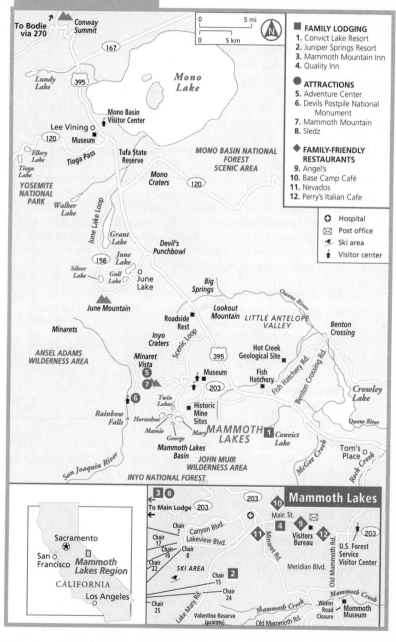

FAMILY LODGING
1. Convict Lake Resort
2. Juniper Springs Resort
3. Mammoth Mountain Inn
4. Quality Inn

ATTRACTIONS
5. Adventure Center
6. Devils Postpile National Monument
7. Mammoth Mountain
8. Sledz

FAMILY-FRIENDLY RESTAURANTS
9. Angel's
10. Base Camp Café
11. Nevados
12. Perry's Italian Cafe

- Hospital
- Post office
- Ski area
- Visitor center

FAMILY LODGING

CONDO RENTALS

MOST MAMMOTH VISITORS rent a condominium for a few nights or a week, and there are hundreds of choices. Unfortunately, there's no one central reservations service, so you'll have to surf some Web sites or call around to find a place right for you. The ones close to Canyon or Little Eagle (aka Juniper Springs) lodges are best suited to skiers and those who want mountain and lift access. Main Lodge is the hub of summer activity, from the climbing wall to the mountain-bike lift rides. Snow Creek is great for golfers, tennis players, and hikers. The developments near town are best for those who want to eat, shop, and be central to everything. Three of our favorite developments and/or rental agencies are **Mammoth Mountain Reservations,** representing two developments near Canyon Lodge (☎ 888-204-4692; **www.mammothres.com**); **Mammoth Properties,** which represents many different developments all over the area (☎ 888-MAMMOTH; **www.mammoth-lodging.com**); and **Mammoth Estates,** which is a good value near the Village development and not far from Canyon Lodge (☎ 800-228-2884; **www.mammothestates.com**).

 Convict Lake Resort

2000 Convict Lake Road (off US 395), just southeast of Mammoth Lakes;
☎ **800-992-2260 or 760-934-3800; www.convictlake.com; $139–$1099**

FAMILIES RETURN TO THIS FRIENDLY COMMUNITY of cabins summer after summer, often for generations. About ten minutes southeast of the town of Mammoth Lakes and two miles off the highway, it's as peaceful and quiet as you can get. A five-minute walk takes you to Convict Lake, bordered on three sides by majestic Sierras peaks. The fishing, swimming, and boating is lots of fun here, and you can also ride horseback, bike, or hike around the lake. Kids also love fooling around at Convict Creek. The kitchen-equipped cabins range from the tiny and quite rustic to the large and homelike; you can also camp at the Forest Service campground (no reservations accepted) alongside the creek. The general store is stocked with everything you might need, and the surprisingly upscale restaurant is famous for what might be the best cooking in the Eastern Sierra.

Juniper Springs Resort
4000 Meridian Boulevard, Mammoth Lakes; ☎ 800-626-6684 or
760-924-1102; www.mammothmountain.com; $169–$349 summer,
$379–$549 winter, $449–$795 holidays for studio to 3-bedroom condos

THIS WOODSY LODGE-CONDO was built as phase one of the ambitious plan to turn Mammoth into a ski resort with the swank of, say, Whistler. Located at the base of the Eagle Express six-person chairlift, Juniper Springs combines the services of a hotel—daily maid service, bell service, coffee shop, concierge, ski check—with the convenience of condo living.

Each of the 174 units, even the studios, has a full kitchen. It's more expensive than renting a condo in one of the many nearby complexes, but because of the ski-in–ski-out location (on an easy run that beginners can handle) and the full-service aspect, many families consider it money well spent. Extras include a pool, hot tubs, and laundry room. Be forewarned that in spring the snow melts first on this side of the mountain, so you may have to take a shuttle or drive over to Canyon Lodge or Main Lodge.

Mammoth Mountain Inn

CA 203 next to ski area, Mammoth Lakes; ☎ or 800-626-6684 or 760-934-2581; www.mammothmountain.com; $239–$825

THIS UPGRADED LODGE IS TERRIBLY CONVENIENT, right in front of the Main Lodge, gondola, summer activities, and children's ski school (though it's several miles from town). Many families are pleasantly surprised to find that they can afford one of the 213 rooms, 43 two-bedroom units, or 14 three-bedroom units, and since skiing families tend to arrive with an SUV stuffed with gear and tired children, they practically weep with joy to discover that there's bell service and a free ski check right by the door. There's also a child-care center (sometimes with storytellers and magicians), a game room, and kids' menus. In summer, the mountain-bike park, climbing wall, and Devil's Postpile shuttle are just outside the door. All the rooms have been refurbished within the last few years, but some are larger than others; ask for a roomy one.

Quality Inn

3537 Main Street, Mammoth Lakes; ☎ 877-424-6423 or 760-934-5114; $99–$220; kids under age 12 stay free.

THE SECOND-FLOOR LOUNGE of this well-run motel makes for a less claustrophobic feel for guests in the winter. There are 61 rooms (with coffeemakers, microwaves, refrigerators, and free movies), an indoor hot tub, and the best free Continental breakfast in town.

▌ ATTRACTIONS

Adventure Center

APPEAL BY AGE	PRESCHOOL ★	GRADE SCHOOL ★★★★	TEENS ★★★★
YOUNG ADULTS ★★★★½		OVER 30 ★★★★	SENIORS ★★

1 Minaret Road, Mammoth Mountain Ski Area; ☎ 760-934-2571; www.mammothmountain.com

Hours *Late June–late September:* daily, 8:30 a.m.–6 p.m. **Admission** *Zip line:* single zip, $10; 2 zips, $15; *climbing wall:* $10 single climb, $25 1 hour. **Touring time** Average 1 hour; minimum 30 minutes. **Rainy-day touring** No. **Restaurants** Cafe. **Alcoholic beverages** Yes. **Disabled access** Limited, but programs available. **Wheelchair rental** No. **Baby-stroller rental** No. **Lockers** No. **Pet kennels** No, pets may be tied up. **Rain check** Yes. **Private tours** Yes, and classes.

DESCRIPTION AND COMMENTS   Unfortunately, the wonderful ropes course is no longer offered, but the multisided climbing towers outside Main Lodge are a big hit, offering everyone from beginners (4-year-olds to grandmas) to experienced climbers a challenge and a chance to succeed. Don't waste your money on a $10 single climb, which could be completed in minutes—instead, spend the $20 for an hour of climbing and try various routes. A friendly staff helps kids and parents into harnesses and provides tips and support. There's nothing like watching a scared 8-year-old make it to the top of a climbing wall and beam with joy and a sense of achievement.

Devils Postpile National Monument

APPEAL BY AGE	PRESCHOOL ★★★★	GRADE SCHOOL ★★★★½	TEENS ★★★★½
YOUNG ADULTS ★★★★½		OVER 30 ★★★★½	SENIORS ★★★★½

Mammoth Visitor Center and Ranger Station; board shuttle in front of Mammoth Mountain Inn at the ski area; ☎ 760-934-2289; www.nps.gov/depo

Hours Last bus leaves Mammoth Mountain at 7 p.m. and Red's Meadow at 7:45 p.m. **Admission** Shuttle $7 adults, $4 children. **Touring time** Average half to full day; minimum 2 hours. **Rainy-day touring** Not recommended. **Restaurants** Cafe at Red's Meadow. **Alcoholic beverages** At cafe and resort store. **Disabled access** No, private cars admitted. **Wheelchair rental** No. **Baby-stroller rental** No. **Lockers** No. **Pet kennels** No. **Rain check** No. **Private tours** No.

DESCRIPTION AND COMMENTS   Don't miss the Devils Postpile National Monument. We set aside about two-thirds of a day and boarded the shuttle (the only way to enter the park), getting off at the Devils Postpile trailhead. Before we'd walked five minutes, we found a lovely picnic spot next to a roaring river. We continued to the Postpile (an easy half-mile walk from the bus stop) and then on to Rainbow Falls, where scores of people either looked at the 100-foot falls from a viewpoint or continued down stairs and a steep path to the bottom of the falls to fully enjoy the thundering waters of the San Joaquin River. Rainbow Falls is a one-and-a-half-mile walk from the bus stop through mostly dusty flatland. Other shuttle bus stops include lakes, falls, and Red's Meadow Resort—a pack station for trail rides with a cafe and a store for campers.

unofficial **TIP**
We prefer the beautiful, easy hike from the Devils Postpile to Minaret Falls, a wonderful place for children to play in splashing, cascading water.

Mammoth Mountain

APPEAL BY AGE	PRESCHOOL ★★	GRADE SCHOOL ★★★★½	TEENS ★★★★½
YOUNG ADULTS ★★★★½		OVER 30 ★★★★½	SENIORS ★★★★½

Mammoth Lakes: ☎ 800-MAMMOTH; bike park: ☎ 760-934-2571, ext. 3671; www.mammothmountain.com

Hours Vary by activity. **Admission** Varies by activity. **Touring time** Average depends on your sign-up choices; minimum at least 1 hour to get the lay of the land. **Rainy-day touring** Sometimes. **Restaurants** Yes, several. **Alcoholic beverages** Yes. **Disabled access** Limited. **Wheelchair rental** No. **Baby-stroller rental** No. **Lockers** Yes. **Pet kennels** No. **Rain check** No. **Private tours** Ski, snowboard, and mountain bike.

DESCRIPTION AND COMMENTS   The official ski area and the condos and restaurants adjacent to it are known as Mammoth Mountain. To visitors,
it simply feels like a few little complexes at several bases around the
mountain above the town of Mammoth Lakes.

In winter, this is one of the best ski mountains in the West, serviced
by seemingly endless high-speed lifts; in summer, the gondola continues
to run as a scenic ride and mountain-bike hauler to the top of the mountain. Winter skiing and snowboarding options for families include group
and individual lessons, a good half-day and all-day ski and snowboard
school for children (all-day includes lunch and supervision), and a three-
day snowboard camp for groups of five or more compatible kids.

In the summer, a mountain-bike trail area, the Mammoth Mountain
Bike Park, is created in the trails accessed via the Main Lodge, and it
includes a "little riders fun zone" for kids age 4 and up who are just
learning to ride. Some lifts carry bikes and riders up the mountain, but
you should start on the most modest hills—it can be scarier than you
might think to point a bike down these steep trails; try the Little Eagle
chair over by Juniper Springs for easier runs (mountain bikes are rented
here). Main Lodge is also home to a zip line for kids age 12 and under
and a big climbing wall for all ages, so everyone can try rock climbing,
complete with ropes and harnesses. Main Lodge is also the place to
catch the shuttle to the Devils Postpile (see previous profile) and many
great backcountry lakes and hikes. In the summer, an outdoor barbecue
cafe is set up in the middle of the whole scene.

Sledz

APPEAL BY AGE	PRESCHOOL ★★★★	GRADE SCHOOL ★★★★	TEENS ★★★★
YOUNG ADULTS ★★★★		OVER 30 ★★★★	SENIORS ★★★

CA 203, between town and Main Lodge; ☎ 760-934-7533

Hours Winter: daily, 10 a.m.–4 p.m.; spring: daily, 4:30–7:30 p.m.; weather and
snow permitting. **Admission** $10 per person (any age) for an hour of sledding.
Touring time 1 hour. **Rainy-day touring** Closes in rain; good if it's snowing.
Restaurants No. **Alcoholic beverages** No. **Disabled access** No. **Wheelchair
rental** No. **Baby-stroller rental** No. **Lockers** No. **Pet kennels** No. **Rain check**
No. **Private tours** No.

DESCRIPTION AND COMMENTS   If you haven't had a good, whooping laugh
with your kids in a while, come here and take a ride (or ten) on an inner
tube down a wide, luge-style snow chute. Ten bucks gets you an hour
of sledding, which is plenty. An iron rope tow takes you up to the top

of the 500-foot run, and then you come bouncing and barreling down, which generally involves a lot of screaming and hooting. It's safe enough for preschoolers, and many inner tubes are big enough for a parent and child to ride together.

FAMILY-FRIENDLY RESTAURANTS

 Angel's

3516 Main Street, Mammoth Lakes; ☎ 760-934-7427

Meals served Lunch and dinner. **Cuisine** American-Mediterranean. **Entree range** Lunch, $7–$10; dinner, $10–$30. **Kids' menu** Yes. **Reservations** Not accepted. **Payment** All major credit cards.

THIS MAMMOTH LAKES INSTITUTION is often jam-packed at peak times, and it doesn't take reservations, so try to come on the early or late side. We love the hearty lunch-or-dinner sandwiches (triple-stacked grilled club, Ortega-chile melt, tuna-avocado melt, chicken Caesar wrap), the acclaimed ribs, the homemade soups, and the hickory-roasted barbecued chicken.

Base Camp Café

3325 Main Street, Mammoth Lakes; ☎ 760-934-3900; www.basecampcafe.com

Meals served Breakfast, lunch, and dinner. **Cuisine** American. **Entree range** $5–$19. **Kids' menu** Yes. **Reservations** Not accepted. **Payment** All major credit cards.

THIS LOCALS' HANGOUT is the best place in town for a bargain meal, whether it's a hearty breakfast, take-out sandwiches for a hikers' picnic, or a dinner of soup, chili, pasta, or steak. Good kids' menu, nice people.

Nevados

Main Street and Minaret Road, Mammoth Lakes; ☎ 760-934-4466

Meals served Dinner. **Cuisine** American/Californian. **Entree range** $16–$30. **Kids' menu** Yes. **Reservations** Recommended. **Payment** All major credit cards.

THE FOOD AT THIS STYLISH, upscale restaurant could pretty much hold its own in LA, which is not true of most Mammoth restaurants. And despite the niceness of the place, children are welcome, with a fixed-price $10 menu (steak, pasta, or shrimp, including salad and dessert). We particularly liked the creative pasta dishes, and there's a pretty good wine list.

Perry's Italian Cafe

3399 Main Street, Mammoth Lakes; ☎ 760-934-6521

Meals served Breakfast, lunch, and dinner. **Cuisine** Italian. **Entree range** Lunch,

HAPPY TRAILS

For a memorable way to take your children into the Sierras, head out on horse-back. Several outfitters offer everything from half-hour hand-led rides for 6-year-olds and younger to weeklong pack trips into the John Muir Wilderness. Here are three favorite outfitters:

Convict Lake Resort ☎ 800-992-2260 or 760-934-3800; **www.convict lake.com.** The 75-minute horseback ride around this beautiful lake is easy and ideal for kids (age 7 and up), who do not need to be accompanied by parents. Littler ones can be guided by their parents on a 30-minute walk.

McGee Creek Pack Station ☎ 800-854-7407; **www.mcgeecreekpack station.com.** The possibilities are vast here, from a one-hour ride along McGee Creek to a day trip into historic McGee Canyon to weeklong riding or pack-mule trips into the John Muir Wilderness. A popular family option is a ride-in camping trip to McGee's wilderness base camp; the horses return home, leaving you to hike, fish, and sing around the campfire until they return to collect you a few days later.

Red's Meadow Pack Station ☎ 800-292-7758 or 760-934-2345; **www .redsmeadow.com.** Near Devils Postpile and Rainbow Falls, this is a tidy mountain resort complete with cabins, a general store, and a cafe. The Tanner family leads all sorts of outings, from two-hour rides to a five-day parent-child summertime pack trip up into either the Ansel Adams or John Muir Wilderness area, in which families with children as young as age 5 sleep at two well-equipped base camps.

$7–$9; dinner, $8–$25. **Kids' menu** Yes. **Reservations** Not accepted. **Payment** All major credit cards.

A FRIENDLY, FAMILY-ORIENTED PLACE, Perry's is popular, bright, and lively—perhaps a little too lively during peak seasons, when the wait can top an hour. The food is simple and satisfying fare: a good salad bar, pizzas, burgers, and pastas. Our kids love the "old-fashioned" video games (Pac-Man!), and the TV in the bar is always tuned to a game.

SIDE TRIPS

 Bodie State Historic Park

APPEAL BY AGE	PRESCHOOL ★	GRADE SCHOOL ★★★★	TEENS ★★★★
YOUNG ADULTS ★★★★		OVER 30 ★★★★	SENIORS ★★★★

20 miles east of Bridgeport via US 395 and CA 270; ☎ **760-647-6445; parks.ca.gov**

Hours *Memorial Day–Labor Day:* daily, 8 a.m.–7 p.m.; *rest of year:* daily, 9 a.m.–4 p.m. *Note:* The park is often closed because of inaccessible roads in winter, so call ahead. **Admission** $3 per adult, $1 per child. **Touring time** Average 2–3 hours; minimum 1 hour (not counting drive time). **Rainy-day touring** Not recommended. **Restaurants** No. **Alcoholic beverages** No. **Disabled access** No. **Wheelchair rental** No. **Baby-stroller rental** No. **Lockers** No. **Pet kennels** No, pets must be leashed, $1 fee. **Rain check** No. **Private tours** No.

DESCRIPTION AND COMMENTS　This remarkable ghost town is all alone in its remote valley, so it's the fullest experience of the real Old West available today. It's north of the turnout to Yosemite from US 395; from the highway, you take CA 270 east for 13 miles—the last three miles of which are hard-packed, unpaved dirt, which is unplowed in winter and accessible then only by cross-country skis or snowmobile. (The park is actually open and staffed by rangers, but no one visits.) The only services in Bodie are restrooms near the parking lot and a small museum and bookstore that is sometimes staffed by volunteers. There's no snack bar, so bring water and a picnic lunch.

The ghost town is preserved by the park service in a state of "arrested decay," which means the rangers and volunteers keep the buildings from falling down (by strengthening foundations, replacing broken glass, and such) while allowing them to look as if they might actually fall down at any moment. Bodie had 10,000 residents in its lawless, 19th-century heyday (it was a gold-mining town with dozens of saloons, no churches, and lots of gunfights); a much smaller number of people lived here until 1932, when a fire devastated the town. Artifacts inside and outside the buildings—furniture, wagons, trucks, mining equipment, beauty-shop fixtures, curtains—are left from all periods of the town's occupation. Visitors walk around the dirt streets on a self-guided tour, peeking into houses and churches, the schoolhouse (with a map showing the world as it was just before World War I), the big old mine, and the mortuary. A detailed brochure tells about the inhabitants of each address and what is known of their fates, and a very good film about life in Bodie's very wild Wild West days shows in an old barn.

unofficial **TIP**
School-age kids love the ghostly exploration of Bodie's Wild West past, but little ones don't really get it.

We took a group of young teens who were enthralled by the voyeuristic thrill of looking into the windows and doors. Even though this is the coldest spot in the lower 48, the summer sun can be strong, so wear hats and stay hydrated.

Mono Lake

APPEAL BY AGE	PRESCHOOL ★	GRADE SCHOOL ★★	TEENS ★★
YOUNG ADULTS ★★		OVER 30 ★★★	SENIORS ★★★

(Add ★★ to each rating if ranger walk included.)

US 395 near Lee Vining; ☎ 760-647-6595; www.monolake.org

Hours *Summer:* daily, 9 a.m.–4:30 p.m.; limited hours in winter. **Admission** $3 in visitors center. **Touring time** Average 1 hour for visitors center and nature walk, 1½ hours for ranger walk; minimum 30 minutes for visitors center and lake-viewing area. **Rainy-day touring** Not recommended. **Restaurants** In Lee Vining. **Alcoholic beverages** In Lee Vining. **Disabled access** Visitors center, viewing veranda. **Wheelchair rental** No. **Baby-stroller rental** No. **Lockers** No. **Pet kennels** No. **Rain check** No. **Private tours** No.

DESCRIPTION AND COMMENTS   Families spending time in the Mammoth Lakes area should consider an excursion to Mono Lake to experience a strange and beautiful landscape: a large, flat lake in a desertlike setting with shoreline formations of tufa-rock columns rising like stalagmites above the surface of the water. We had stopped at the Mono Basin Scenic Area Visitors Center to enjoy the view and walk the nature trail when we learned that a ranger walk was scheduled soon, so we joined it and had a wonderful experience. The walk included touching, tasting, smelling, and looking through binoculars and magnifying glasses, and was conducted right along the lake's shore. The center also offers a stargazing and storytelling program, a "sounds of the creek" walk, and additional hikes and talks at campgrounds and other sites around the Inyo National Forest. The early-morning guided canoe and kayak tours can be extraordinarily beautiful.

FAMILY-FRIENDLY RESTAURANT

 Whoa Nellie Deli

Tioga Gas Mart, CA 120 at US 395, Lee Vining; ☎ 760-647-1088; www.thesierraweb.com/tiogagasmart

Meals served Breakfast, lunch, and dinner, April–October only. **Cuisine** American. **Entree range** $7–$19. **Kids' menu** Yes. **Reservations** Not accepted. **Payment** All major credit cards.

THIS AIN'T YOUR TYPICAL MOBIL MART—the setting overlooks Mono Lake, the shop stocks REI-quality gear, and the deli counter goes way beyond the gas-station orange-cheese-nachos standards. Chef Matt Toomey runs an amazing kitchen here, serving everything from grilled-salmon salads to lobster taquitos—but your kids can get chicken fingers, too. The pizzas are superb, as is the barbecue potato salad. Call ahead, and they'll pack picnic boxes for a Mono Lake outing or Sierra hike. An absolute must-stop between Mammoth and Yosemite in summertime.

YOSEMITE

SO MANY GIFTED WRITERS AND PHOTOGRAPHERS have turned their talents to portraying Yosemite that we can't possibly do it justice. Suffice it to say that this national park is one of the world's natural treasures, a place of great beauty, grandeur, and even mysticism. And while the awesomeness of **Yosemite Valley** may not leave your children as speechless as you, it will provide plenty of opportunities to imprint itself on their memories. Whether they're climbing up **Vernal Falls,** riding a bike under **Half Dome,** or searching the **Merced River** for frogs, your kids will find their own reasons to love Yosemite.

Yosemite is also, of course, a place with roads, visitors centers, and campgrounds, because this is a national park. This infrastructure was greatly damaged in a 1997 flood; restoration work has been going on for years and is almost complete. After the flood, the park service put into immediate effect a long-term plan designed to update, upgrade, and improve Yosemite's infrastructure and make visitor facilities more environmentally friendly: not all structures were rebuilt; there are fewer campsites in the valley itself and more in the surrounding areas (which are well worth exploring); public transportation has improved and cars greatly discouraged; and overall, the park service says summer crowds aren't as overwhelming as they once were, although you might not agree if you visit in August. Critics complain that the number of affordable motel-style lodgings have decreased in favor of higher-end accommodations, but there is no doubting the benefit of fewer cars in the valley.

Campsite reservations may be made beginning at the 15th of each month up to five months in advance by calling ☎ 877-444-6777 or going to **www.recreation.gov.** Reservations for hotels, motels, and tent cabins within Yosemite may be made up to a year in advance; call ☎ 801-559-5000 or 801-559-4884, or go to **www .yosemitepark.com.**

*un*official **TIP**
Yosemite's popularity demands that visitors make reservations as early as possible.

The camp entrance fee is $20 per car (an annual Yosemite pass is $40, and an annual National Park Service pass is $50). Once you've arrived and settled into your camp or cabin,

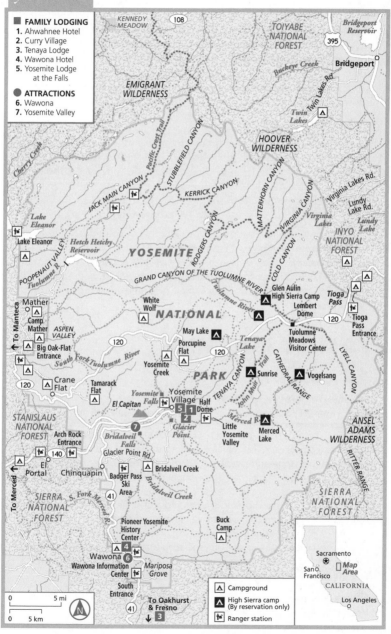

yosemite

■ **FAMILY LODGING**
1. Ahwahnee Hotel
2. Curry Village
3. Tenaya Lodge
4. Wawona Hotel
5. Yosemite Lodge
   at the Falls

● **ATTRACTIONS**
6. Wawona
7. Yosemite Valley

please try to use your car as little as possible and take the park's convenient free shuttle service to get to trailheads and other areas.

There are several Yosemite Web pages to explore. The National Park Service site is at **www.nps.gov/yose** and has park information and "Yosemite Notebooks" with visuals. The Yosemite Association's site, **www.yosemite.org,** has visitor information, a bookstore, class listings, and a live camera view of **Glacier Point.** The Yosemite Concessions Services page at **www.yosemitepark.com** has lodging and park activity information, links to other Yosemite sites, and an online gift shop.

GETTING THERE

BY CAR The most common approach to the park is from the west via the town of **Merced,** which is reached by taking **Interstate 5** south from San Francisco or north from LA and then transitioning to **CA 140** east. Visitors who are also seeing Mammoth Lakes, Death Valley, or Lake Tahoe might approach from the east, via the town of Lee Vining, by taking **US 395** north or south, then **CA 120** west into the park.

BY BUS Be respectful and leave your smelly car behind, traveling via the **Yosemite Area Regional Transportation System,** ☎ 877-989-2787; **www.yarts.com.** There's service along CA 140 between Merced and various park locations several times a day year-round, and on CA 120 and US 395 to Lee Vining, June Lake Loop, and Mammoth Lakes in the summer.

FAMILY LODGING

 Ahwahnee Hotel

Yosemite National Park; ☎ **801-559-5000;**
www.yosemitepark.com/accommodations.aspx; $439 and up

THIS NATIONAL HISTORIC LANDMARK HOTEL is a favorite for outdoors people and city-slicker visitors alike, and it's often sold out. Its soaring Arts and Crafts–era stone-and-wood architecture fits the majestic setting, and its Native American artifacts and decor are authentic and museum quality. In addition to 99 lodge rooms, there are 24 cottages, which are a good choice for families. It's not the most kid-friendly lodging in the park—lots of wealthy retirees visit here, and they like to sit quietly in the awesome public areas, reading or doing elaborate jigsaw puzzles; when we visited, we felt that we had to constantly hush our children and keep them away from those puzzles. On the other hand, Ahwanee does have a pool and a children's play area, and the restaurant is polite to kids and has a menu for them.

Curry Village
Yosemite National Park; ☎ **801-559-5000;**
www.yosemitepark.com; $97–$163

COMPOSED OF SOME 600 PACKED-TOGETHER rustic wooden cabins (with or without private baths) and tiny tent cabins (the least expensive lodging in the park), Curry Village is crowded and low on comfort. But the location is fun for kids because of the bustling village atmosphere, complete with a pool, cafeteria, snack bar, minimarket, and lots of other kids to make friends with. It's also a center for activities and services, including tour departures, raft rentals, cross-country ski rentals, and bike rentals. From mid-November to March there's an outdoor ice rink (rare in California!). Overall, Curry Village is lively and active; don't expect any quiet, secluded moments.

Tenaya Lodge
1122 Highway 41 (CA 41), Fish Camp; ☎ 888-514-2167 or 559-683-6555; www.tenayalodge.com; $200 and up; children free in parents' room

TWO MILES FROM YOSEMITE'S SOUTH ENTRANCE in the town of Fish Camp, this newer full-service resort makes a fine vacation base, even if it does imprint a sense of chain-corporate America on a previously funky little mountain village. Spread among the trees are 244 rooms, two restaurants, a playground, an open-air ice-skating rink, an arcade, and two pools, one indoors and one out. The best room for families is the double deluxe: a larger room with a sitting area, a sofa bed, and a balcony with a forest view. At the activities desk, you can sign up for a flashlight hike for the kids, a narrated bus tour of the valley, and a guided ten-mile hike to a 30-foot waterfall; other fun stuff to do includes mountain-bike rentals, horseback riding, volleyball, and fishing at nearby Bass Lake. Adventure Club, the program for children ages 5 to 12, is offered on weekday mornings year-round (if at least four kids sign up) and includes lunch as well as such amusements as hikes, climbing on the rock wall, and watching movies.

Wawona Hotel
CA 41, Wawona, 27 miles south of Yosemite Valley, Yosemite National Park; ☎ 801-559-5000; www.yosemitepark.com; $119–$183

LOCATED IN THE MARIPOSA GROVE AREA, nearly 30 miles from the valley, the Wawona (like the Ahwahnee) is a National Historic Landmark. There's an almost secluded feeling to the hotel, a favorite with Yosemite lovers who want to avoid the hustle and bustle of the valley. Come here in the off-season and you're likely to see deer, coyotes, and foxes right in front of the hotel. The homey, rustic rooms are spread among whitewashed turn-of-the-19th-century buildings with great front porches; ask for spacious or connecting rooms as there are a variety of options among the 105 rooms (50 with private baths). There's a big lawn with a pool, tennis courts, and a nine-hole golf course, plus an on-site restaurant and a store nearby.

Yosemite Lodge at the Falls
Yosemite National Park; ☎ 801-559-5000; www.yosemitepark.com; $98–$170

CONVENIENTLY LOCATED AND NEITHER as grand as the Ahwahnee nor as funky as Curry Village, Yosemite Lodge provides the middle-ground noncamping accommodations in the park. Activities right around the lodge are plentiful. The short walk to Yosemite Falls begins just across the street; the lodge has a bike-rental shop, many paved trails adjacent, and a terrific pool. There are three restaurants, one with a children's menu. Learn-to-ski packages for Badger Pass are offered midweek in the winter.

ATTRACTIONS

Wawona

APPEAL BY AGE	PRESCHOOL ★★★	GRADE SCHOOL ★★★★	TEENS ★★★★½
YOUNG ADULTS ★★★★½		OVER 30 ★★★★½	SENIORS ★★★★½

CA 41 south of Yosemite Valley; ☎ 209-375-9501; off-season: ☎ 209-372-0200; www.yosemite.org

Hours *Spring and summer:* Wawona Information Station open daily, 9 a.m.– 5 p.m.; off-season hours limited. **Admission** $20 per vehicle at park entrance. **Touring time** Average several days; minimum 1 day and 1 night. **Rainy-day touring** Possible. **Restaurants** Yes. **Alcoholic beverages** Yes. **Disabled access** Some. **Wheelchair rental** No. **Baby-stroller rental** No. **Lockers** No. **Pet kennels** No. **Rain check** No. **Private tours** No.

DESCRIPTION AND COMMENTS This south-entrance area of Yosemite is loved by some visitors as a base because of its relative peace and quiet. There's never a lack of things to do since this is where the Mariposa Grove and the Pioneer Yosemite History Center are found. You can stay in the charming, rustic (and inexpensive), white-sided Wawona Hotel (see listing in "Family Lodging," page 292).

The Wawona Information Station, at the park's south entrance, has maps, wilderness permits, trail guides, and books. A free shuttle bus from the information station takes visitors to the Mariposa Grove of giant sequoias; it operates daily in the summer from mid-May, 9 a.m. to 6 p.m.

Yosemite Valley

APPEAL BY AGE	PRESCHOOL ★★★	GRADE SCHOOL ★★★★½	TEENS ★★★★½
YOUNG ADULTS ★★★★½		OVER 30 ★★★★½	SENIORS ★★★★½

Yosemite Village west of the main post office; ☎ 209-372-0200; www.yosemite.org

Hours Visitors center open daily, 8 a.m.–5 p.m. **Admission** $20 per vehicle at park entrance. **Touring time** Average several days; minimum a half day. **Rainy-day touring** Possible, can be pretty and quiet. **Restaurants** Yes. **Alcoholic beverages** Yes. **Disabled access** Yes, ask at visitors center. **Wheelchair rental**

No. **Baby-stroller rental** No. **Lockers** Food lockers vs. bears. **Pet kennels** No. **Rain check** No. **Private tours** No.

DESCRIPTION AND COMMENTS   Much is written in travel literature about Yosemite being more than the Yosemite Valley itself, and it's true—the famous park has miles of wilderness for hiking and camping, and plenty of room in which to spread out if you get off the beaten path. We know many Californians who return (often with kids in tow) year after year to the valley to settle in for a week of hiking, biking, and campfire-going. These re-peaters tell us that Yosemite is a large park with a varied topography and that they do go on excur-sions, such as taking the easy walk to Mirror Lake or one of a zillion incredible hiking trails. But they still love the valley.

unofficial TIP
Visitors don't need to apologize for actually liking the valley, with its ranger talks, world-famous waterfalls, much-photographed views, abundant wildlife, and scenic bike rides.

Along with the Yosemite Valley Visitors Center, in Yosemite Village west of the main post office, you'll find a museum, a gallery, a wilderness supply shop, and trailheads to two nature trails.

YOSEMITE'S LITTLE JOYS

BIKE RIDING   Bikes can be rented at Yosemite Lodge or Curry Village, and there are level trails crisscrossing the entire valley floor. This is lots of fun for school-age kids.

EARLY-MORNING PHOTOGRAPHY WALKS   These leave around 8:30 a.m. and last for one hour from either the Ahwahnee or Yosemite Lodge.

EL CAPITÁN   Take some moments while you're in Yosemite to look at this granite wall at different times of the day. There are often climbers working their way up the face, and if you go to the meadow across from it with binoculars, you can watch their progress. At night, you can see the climbers' lights, or on a full-moon night, simply admire the dazzling rock itself. See "Rock-climbing Classes" (next page) for your own adventurous climbing kids.

FAMILY WALKS   These begin at the Valley Visitors Center, and they're led by a ranger-naturalist.

GLACIER POINT   Most families stop here for just a half hour on their way into or out of the valley, but don't neglect to make the stop. It's the picture-postcard view of your dreams, and even the kids will be awestruck. The scenic overlook is 30 miles (one hour) from the valley, and the road is open from late spring through early fall. A snack stand is open 9 a.m. to sundown.

HORSEBACK RIDING   Weather permitting, two-hour and half-day rides depart spring through fall from stables in the valley and at Wawona. Call ☎ 209-372-8348 for more information.

LE CONTE MEMORIAL LODGE CHILDREN'S CENTER   In the summer months, there are programs for kids ages 5 to 10. ☎ 209-372-4542.

MARIPOSA GROVE   The largest of three sequoia groves in Yosemite has been a magnet for visitors since the mid–19th century. The grove's Grizzly Giant Tree, 2,700 years old, is believed to be the oldest living sequoia. There's a small log cabin museum at the grove (open May 22 through fall, 10 a.m. to 5 p.m.). To reach the grove, take the free shuttle bus from Wawona, then follow the interpretive trail signs for a self-guided walking tour. Weather permitting in the summer, a guided tram tour ($25.50 adults, $18 for kids ages 5 to 12, children under age 4 free) leaves every 20 minutes for a one-hour tour through the upper and lower groves. For reservations, call ☎ 209-375-1621.

PIONEER YOSEMITE HISTORY CENTER   This cluster of historic buildings at Wawona is the center of living-history programs and other activities for children. A jailhouse, miner's cabin, and covered bridge can be explored in a 30-minute self-guided tour; there's a stagecoach ride, and, depending on the season, there are sometimes demonstrations and crafts, such as soap making, yarn spinning, and Christmas crafts. The bookstore is open 9 a.m. to 5 p.m. in the summer.

ROCK-CLIMBING CLASSES   Yosemite Mountaineering School and Guide Service (☎ 209-372-8344; **www.yosemitepark.com**). Rock climbing is hugely popular here, and it can be a wonderful adventure for older kids. Beginning rock-climbing classes are offered from Easter through mid-October; kids must be at least 10 years old. Mike Corbett's one-hour talk and walk about the history of climbing in Yosemite leaves from either the Ahwahnee or the Yosemite Lodge twice a week at 8:30 a.m.

TOURS OF THE VALLEY   Two-hour, half-day, and all-day summer tours of the major landmarks of Yosemite Valley are given daily, in part to reduce the flow of auto traffic on the few roads on the valley floor. The summer tour vehicle is completely open-air and allows riders to see in all directions; winter tours are in heated buses. There's also a two-hour moonlight tour in the summer. We thought the tour was an easy, helpful way to get the lay of the land, and we found the guide's comments on wildlife particularly interesting. Call Yosemite Lodge at ☎ 209-372-1240 (**www.yosemitepark.com/accommodations .aspx**) for fees and times.

WATERFALLS   Waterfalls from below and waterfalls from above are one of the main attractions at Yosemite, but depending on the time of year and the amount of snowmelt the area is receiving, some of the falls may or may not be filled with water. One of the most popular hikes in Yosemite is up to the top of Vernal Falls, and for purists it's probably a discouraging experience—literally hundreds of people at a time are working their way up and down the waterside trail that goes from the base of the falls to a pool (where people swim) at the top (from which some hikers continue on up to other pools). But families with active preteens and teens may find this a great way to participate in the democratic appreciation of a great national park. The other hikers are from all over the country and the world, and it makes for a fine outdoor social occasion, if not a wilderness experience. Lower Yosemite Falls and Bridalveil Falls can be enjoyed with just short, easy walks from shuttle stops. Yosemite Falls, with its 2,425-foot drop, can be seen from Glacier Point.

WILDLIFE   Please, please review safety information about sharing the park with bears and mountain lions, and watch your children closely at all times. You will also see deer, coyotes, squirrels, and other smaller animals. Do not feed or disturb wildlife—doing so is not only dangerous but a violation subject to fine.

LAKE TAHOE

THIS IS A BIG LAKE, TO BE SURE—it's 22 miles long and 12 miles wide, with 72 miles of shoreline—but the special characteristic remembered by most visitors here is not the size but the beautiful deep, dark blue of the water. Surrounded by pine forests and visible from above on some scenic roads and hikes, Lake Tahoe makes an indelible impression. That inky blue water will turn swimmers blue, too—it seldom gets warmer than 60°F, even in the middle of summer. We love it for instantly soothing aching muscles or swelling feet after a hike in the hot sun, but parents of little ones will want to pull them out of the water for a towel rubdown every now and then.

Two-thirds of the lake is in California and one-third in Nevada. The several communities on the lake's shore are quite different and are concentrated either north or south. The North Shore California towns of **Tahoe City** and **Tahoe Vista** are summer sports centers, where the best personal-watercraft rentals are located and where water-skiers rule. The South Shore includes some Nevada territory, so there are casinos, but the town of **South Lake Tahoe** also offers family-friendly swim beaches, hikes, and sightseeing excursions. There is skiing on both sides of the lake. The west side of the lake offers access to the hiking trails of the **Desolation Wilderness** and **El Dorado Village;** the east side offers highway junctions to Nevada's gambling centers and historic silver-mining towns.

GETTING THERE

BY PLANE   Among the airlines serving **Reno-Tahoe International Airport** (RNO; 60 miles east of the lake area; ☎ 775-328-6400; **www.reno airport.com**) are Alaska Airlines, Allegiant, American, Continental, Delta, ExpressJet, Horizon, US Airways, Southwest, and United.

BY CAR   Lake Tahoe is most easily reached by car from San Francisco; it's 200 miles northeast of the Bay Area. Your route will depend on whether you're headed for the North or South Shore. For North Shore, take **Interstate 80** east to Truckee; for South Lake Tahoe, take **US 50** east.

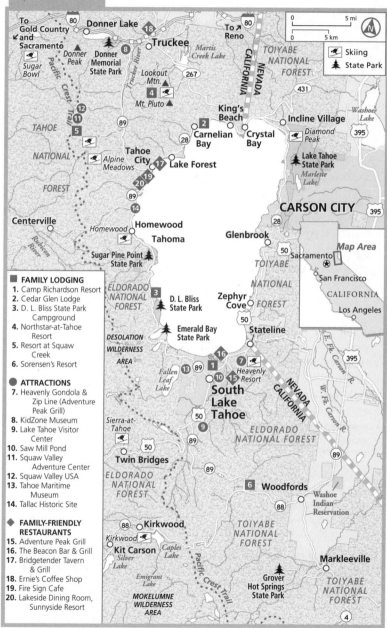

lake tahoe

FAMILY LODGING
1. Camp Richardson Resort
2. Cedar Glen Lodge
3. D. L. Bliss State Park Campground
4. Northstar-at-Tahoe Resort
5. Resort at Squaw Creek
6. Sorensen's Resort

ATTRACTIONS
7. Heavenly Gondola & Zip Line (Adventure Peak Grill)
8. KidZone Museum
9. Lake Tahoe Visitor Center
10. Saw Mill Pond
11. Squaw Valley Adventure Center
12. Squaw Valley USA
13. Tahoe Maritime Museum
14. Tallac Historic Site

FAMILY-FRIENDLY RESTAURANTS
15. Adventure Peak Grill
16. The Beacon Bar & Grill
17. Bridgetender Tavern & Grill
18. Ernie's Coffee Shop
19. Fire Sign Cafe
20. Lakeside Dining Room, Sunnyside Resort

Skiing
State Park

To Gold Country and Sacramento
Donner Lake
Truckee
To Reno
Sugar Bowl
Donner Peak
Donner Memorial State Park
Lookout Mtn.
Mt. Pluto
Martis Creek Lake
TOIYABE NATIONAL FOREST
King's Beach
Incline Village
Washoe Lake
Carnelian Bay
Crystal Bay
Diamond Peak
TAHOE
Tahoe City
Lake Forest
Alpine Meadows
Lake Tahoe State Park
Marlette Lake
NATIONAL
FOREST
CARSON CITY
Centerville
Homewood
Homewood
Tahoma
Glenbrook
Map Area
Sugar Pine Point State Park
Sacramento
San Francisco
TOIYABE
ELDORADO NATIONAL FOREST
D. L. Bliss State Park
Zephyr Cove
NATIONAL
FOREST
CALIFORNIA
Los Angeles
Emerald Bay State Park
Stateline
DESOLATION WILDERNESS AREA
Fallen Leaf Lake
Heavenly Resort
South Lake Tahoe
NEVADA
CALIFORNIA
Sierra-at-Tahoe
E. Fk. Carson R.
W. Fk. Carson R.
ELDORADO NATIONAL FOREST
Twin Bridges
ELDORADO NATIONAL FOREST
Woodfords
Washoe Indian Reservation
Kirkwood
Kit Carson
Kirkwood
Silver Lake
Caples Lake
TOIYABE NATIONAL FOREST
Markleeville
Emigrant Lake
MOKELUMNE WILDERNESS AREA
Grover Hot Springs State Park
TOIYABE NATIONAL FOREST
Pacific Crest Trail
Rubicon River
Truckee River

FAMILY LODGING

 Camp Richardson Resort

1900 Jameson Beach Road, South Lake Tahoe; ☎ 800-544-1801
or 530-541-1801; www.camprich.com; $105–$325 summer,
$95–$250 winter

THIS UNIQUELY RUSTIC RESORT has been home to vacationing families
for more than 70 years—it's no grand ski complex, but rather a jumble of
lodges, cabins, and campsites (for both tents and RVs) in a pine woods at
the shore of the lake. The lodge has a pleasant public space with a big stone
fireplace and the wonderful Beacon restaurant. The beach is the big draw
for many; it's one of the best for swimming, and the full-service marina is
a bustling center of water sports, kayak rentals, windsurfing gear, and
more. The 36 lodge rooms and 39 cottages vary in decor and layout; some
have terraces, fireplaces, and kitchens, but the cabins don't have TVs or
phones. Also on premises are an ice-cream shop and cafe-bakery, children's playground, bike-rental shop, and stable.

Cedar Glen Lodge

6589 North Lake Boulevard, Tahoe Vista; ☎ 800-500-TAHOE or
530-546-4281; www.cedarglenlodge.com; $79–$139

A VERY GOOD VALUE FOR FAMILIES, this small, recently spruced-up cabin
motel is across the highway from a nice beach in Tahoe Vista on the North
Shore. It's tucked into the pine woods, with a playground, pool, hot tub,
and barbecues. Two two-bedroom units with kitchens are among the
rooms and cabins. There's no restaurant, but most rooms have refrigerators and many have kitchens.

D. L. Bliss State Park Campground

CA 89, Tahoma; ☎ 530-525-7277; parks.ca.gov; reservations:
ReserveAmerica, ☎ 800-444-7275; www.reserveamerica.com;
campsites $20 plus $5 entrance fee; beach sites $35

IT'S BLISSFUL HERE ALL RIGHT, especially for children, who never tire of
scrambling over the boulders, playing hide-and-seek behind the pines, and
exploring the gorgeous white-sand Lester Beach or close-by Emerald Bay.
Bliss has three clumps of campsites; if you want to be closest to Lester
Beach, reserve a site between 141 and 168. Hot showers, flush toilets,
picnic tables, fire pits, wood for sale.

Northstar-at-Tahoe Resort

CA 267 north of Lake Tahoe, 6 miles south of Truckee; ☎ 530-562-1010
or 800-466-6784; www.skinorthstar.com; $139–$1379

THIS SQUAW VALLEY RIVAL RESORT has everything an active family could
dream of spread over its 600 acres. You and your kids can mountain bike,
ride a pony, join guided hikes, ski, tackle a climbing wall, learn orienteering,

take a ropes course, swim in heated pools, play tennis—it's exhausting just to consider the options. The Minors' Camp program handles kids ages 2 to 12, with skiing lessons and snow play in winter and all sorts of amusements year-round. The accommodations range from upscale motel rooms to suites to fully equipped condos, found one mile from the main complex. There are seven restaurants, many of which have kids' menus.

unofficial **TIP**
Northstar is one of the most popular learn-to-ski family resorts in North America, known for its ego-enhancing runs and friendly ski school.

Resort at Squaw Creek

400 Squaw Creek Road, Olympic Valley; ☎ 800-327-3353 or 530-583-6300; www.squawcreek.com; $229–$729

MODERN MOUNTAIN ARCHITECTURE makes this a distinctly Tahoe resort, with contemporary buildings at the center of 632 acres designed so every room has a view of the Sierra. The resort is a little town, actually, and in the winter especially, families can find all they need for a vacation right within the complex: shopping, skiing (direct access to Squaw Creek mountain lifts), world-class golf, junior tennis programs, a posh new full-service spa, and even lawn games. In the summer, the Activity Center has a ropes course, climbing walls, and bungee jump, and the wonderful, landscaped pool complex boasts a waterslide; in the winter there's an ice rink. Of the 403 renovated and upscale rooms and suites, the best bet for families is a suite; some have fireplaces. The Mountain Buddies Club offers half- and full-day programs (swimming, hiking, crafts, and games) for kids ages 4 to 12, as well as separate teen programs. One drawback: the lodging is not connected to the lobby area except by outdoor walkways, so in the winter, guests must go outside to get to restaurants.

☀ Sorensen's Resort

14255 Highway 88, Hope Valley; ☎ 800-423-9949 or 530-694-2203; www.sorensensresort.com; $115–$275

HOPE VALLEY IS JUST 20 MINUTES SOUTH OF, a thousand feet higher than, and a world away from the hubbub of South Lake Tahoe. Most of the valley is pristine and undeveloped, thanks to forward-thinking preservationists who helped protect the area in perpetuity via land trusts. Sorensen's is a collection of cottages, cabins, and homes just a mile east of the CA 89–CA 88 intersection. Lodging options vary from basic one-room quarters to full-on homes with all the amenities. Nearly all of the cabins have kitchens and fireplaces or wood-burning stoves, but none have TVs or phones. If you don't feel like cooking, just head down to the Country Café for breakfast, lunch, or dinner (kids and grown-ups alike chow down on the locally famous beef stew). The main draw here, though, is the unbelievably gorgeous setting. Parents can swing in hammocks under the aspens while the kids catch and release trout in the resort's stocked pond or romp in the meadows across the way. There are loads of fun activities for kids of all ages. In winter there's cross-country skiing and sledding in Hope Valley and alpine skiing and snowboarding at Kirkwood, a 15-minute drive up the road. The West Fork of the Carson River cascades through the valley, providing fantastic opportunities for summertime trout fishing and rafting. Sorensen's has kids programs in the summer months and can set you up on llama tours with picnics, trail rides on horseback, and other excursions with local outfitters. Teens especially love heading down the road to Grover Hot Springs State Park, where they can float around a large pool heated by natural hot springs. After the Donner Party tragedy, the main emigrant route to California went through Hope Valley over Carson Pass; hence, the entire region is filled with hands-on history lessons. When they're tracing the steps of the Pony Express, kids have no idea they're in "school."

For a more rustic experience, stay at Sorensen's nearby sister property, **Hope Valley Resort and Campground** (☎ 800-423-9949; **www .hopevalleyresort.com**), which has RV and tent campsites, a trailer, and a three-bedroom vacation home along the river.

TAHOE TREASURES

D. L. BLISS STATE PARK   This park contains some great camping (168 sites; see "Family Lodging"), terrific beach and boating areas, and several wonderful trails for day hikers, including the dreamy, 4.5-mile **Rubicon Trail,** which snakes along the shore through the woods to the beach, where you can swim and picnic. Another hike, less than a mile long, takes you to an old lighthouse, and another, just one mile round-trip, takes you to the remarkable **Balancing Rock.** Nine miles north of South Lake Tahoe on CA 89; ☎ 530-525-7277 or 530-525-7982; **parks.ca.gov.**

TRUCKEE HISTORIC TOWN CENTER   Almost 100 19th-century buildings remain in this town, and visitors can get an Old West feel on **Commercial Row,** where wooden sidewalks remain. The historic area is largely cafes and shops, as well as the **Southern Pacific Railroad Depot Gallery;** the **Bar of America,** with its photos of famous outlaws; and the old **Truckee Jailhouse Museum** (10142 Jibboom Street, behind Commercial Row; ☎ 530-582-0893; **www.truckeehistory.org/jail museum.htm;** free admission, open summer weekends), which features real cells, historic photos, and Chinese American historical items. Truckee is on I-80, 20 minutes north of Lake Tahoe.

ATTRACTIONS

 Heavenly Gondola & Zip Line (Adventure Peak Grill)

APPEAL BY AGE	PRESCHOOL ★	GRADE SCHOOL ★★★★	TEENS ★★★★½
YOUNG ADULTS ★★★★½		OVER 30 ★★★★½	SENIORS ★★★★

Heavenly Mountain Resort, Wildwood Avenue and Saddle Road, South Lake Tahoe; ☎ 775-586-7000; www.skiheavenly.com

Hours *Summer:* daily, 10 a.m.–5 p.m.; *winter:* Monday–Friday, 9 a.m.–4 p.m.; Saturday, Sunday, holidays, 8:30 a.m.–4 p.m. **Admission** *Tram:* $30 adults, $26 teens ages 13–18, $20 children ages 5–12, children under age 5 free; *winter ski-lift ticket:* $20–$57. **Touring time** Average 2 hours; minimum 15 minutes. **Rainy-day touring** Not good for hiking. **Restaurants** Yes. **Alcoholic beverages** Yes. **Disabled access** Tram only. **Wheelchair rental** No. **Baby-stroller rental** No. **Lockers** In winter. **Pet kennels** No. **Rain check** No. **Private tours** No.

DESCRIPTION AND COMMENTS   Theme parks sometimes try to duplicate the thrill of a ski gondola or tram ride, but there's nothing like the real thing. The ride itself is a spectacular, mile-long ascent to a point 2,000 feet above Lake Tahoe. In summer, a chairlift will take you another 525 feet up to the top of the longest zip line in the continental United States. At $20 to $30 per ride, it's an investment, but it's not one you (or your kids) will regret. Kids must be at least 75 pounds and 52 inches tall to ride the zip.

KidZone Museum

APPEAL BY AGE	PRESCHOOL ★★★★	GRADE SCHOOL ★★★★	TEENS ★★
YOUNG ADULTS ★		OVER 30 ★	SENIORS ½

11711 Donner Pass Road, Truckee; ☎ 530-587-5437; www.kidzonemuseum.org

Hours *April–Columbus Day:* Tuesday–Sunday, 9 a.m.–1 p.m.; *Columbus Day–April:* Tuesday–Saturday, 10 a.m.–5 p.m., Sunday 10 a.m.–3 p.m. **Admission** $7, free for children under age 2. **Touring time** Average 2 hours; minimum 1 hour. **Rainy-day touring** Yes. **Restaurants** Nearby. **Alcoholic beverages** Nearby. **Disabled access** Yes. **Wheelchair rental** No. **Baby-stroller rental** No. **Lockers** Cubbyholes. **Pet kennels** No. **Rain check** No. **Private tours** No.

DESCRIPTION AND COMMENTS   This modest but growing children's museum, strongly supported by the local community, provides a welcome respite from the macho world of skiing or waterskiing for young children. A variety of educational hands-on exhibits aimed primarily at the under-7 set are here, as well as some imaginative temporary special exhibits and arts and crafts projects.

Lake Tahoe Visitor Center

APPEAL BY AGE	PRESCHOOL ★★★	GRADE SCHOOL ★★★	TEENS ★★★
YOUNG ADULTS ★★★		OVER 30 ★★★	SENIORS ★★★

CA 89, 3 miles north of South Lake Tahoe, off of Highway 89; ☎ 530-543-2674; www.fs.fed.us/r5/ltbmu/recreation/visitor-center

Hours *Mid-June–September:* daily, 8 a.m.–5 p.m.; *early June and October:* 8 a.m.–4 p.m.; closed in winter. **Admission** Free. **Touring time** Average, depends on trail chosen; minimum 30 minutes. **Rainy-day touring** Okay on paved path. **Restaurants** Nearby. **Alcoholic beverages** Yes. **Disabled access** Yes. **Wheelchair rental** Yes, free. **Baby-stroller rental** No. **Lockers** No. **Pet kennels** No, but leashed pets allowed. **Rain check** No. **Private tours** No.

DESCRIPTION AND COMMENTS   While one parent peruses the maps and brochures, another can take the kids along one of the five self-guided nature trails at this center, run by the U.S. Forest Service. Among the trail attractions is an underground fish-viewing chamber that provides a window on Taylor Creek's aquatic life. Interpretive programs (night walks, astronomy adventures, and living-history performances) are offered on site from June through Labor Day.

Saw Mill Pond

APPEAL BY AGE	PRESCHOOL ★★★★	GRADE SCHOOL ★★★★	TEENS ★★★
YOUNG ADULTS ★		OVER 30 ★	SENIORS ½

Past the Y at Lake Tahoe Boulevard and Saw Mill Road, Lake Tahoe Basin Management, 870 Emerald Bay Road, South Lake Tahoe; ☎ 530-543-2600

Hours Daily, 24 hours, year-round. **Admission** Free. **Touring time** Average 2 hours; minimum 1 hour. **Rainy-day touring** Yes, but you'll get wet. **Restaurants** 2 miles from civilization. **Alcoholic beverages** Yes. **Disabled access** No, but in the works. **Wheelchair rental** No. **Baby-stroller rental** No. **Lockers** No. **Pet kennels** No, but leashed pets allowed. **Rain check** No. **Private tours** No.

DESCRIPTION AND COMMENTS   Serious fishing families will scoff, but for non-fishing adults, this is a fine fishing hole for introducing your kids to the activity. Kids age 14 and under fish free in this pretty little pond stocked with trout by the California Department of Fish and Game, but you must supply your own bait and equipment. Visitors age 15 or over can tag along but can't fish, so parents can teach but not cast a line. The pond is popular for ice-skating and hockey in winter.

Squaw Valley Adventure Center

APPEAL BY AGE	PRESCHOOL ★	GRADE SCHOOL ★★★★	TEENS ★★★★½
YOUNG ADULTS ★★★★½		OVER 30 ★★★★	SENIORS ★★

1960 Squaw Valley Road, Squaw Valley; ☎ 800-403-0206 or 530-583-7673; www.squawadventure.com

Hours Open summers; hours vary by activity. **Admission** Varies by activity. **Touring time** Average 1 day; minimum 1 hour. **Rainy-day touring** Indoor climbing wall only. **Restaurants** Nearby. **Alcoholic beverages** In some restaurants. **Disabled access** Yes. **Wheelchair rental** No. **Baby-stroller rental** No. **Lockers** No. **Pet kennels** No, but leashed pets allowed in summer. **Rain check** No. **Private tours** Yes.

DESCRIPTION AND COMMENTS   This "center" is actually spread over three activities in three areas, all within the Squaw Valley resort. Near the Olympic Village Inn is an excellent ropes course, open for individual and family use in July and August (other months are available for groups only). It's an intense and amazing experience to walk across a swaying rope bridge 25 feet above ground while your family cheers you on. We highly recommend this adventure for teenagers, brave preteens, and parents, but it's too scary for younger ones. Even toddlers, however, will have a blast on the Skyjump, a combination trampoline and bungee jump that's safe and thrilling ($10 for a five-minute jump session). Finally, there's the Headwall Climbing Wall, which is actually two walls: a 30-foot indoor climbing structure and a summertime 40-foot outdoor wall. A day pass is a reasonable $14, plus $4 to rent climbing shoes.

Squaw Valley USA

APPEAL BY AGE	PRESCHOOL ★ ★ ★	GRADE SCHOOL ★ ★ ★ ★	TEENS ★ ★ ★ ★ ½
YOUNG ADULTS ★ ★ ★ ★ ½		OVER 30 ★ ★ ★ ★	SENIORS ★ ★ ★

1960 Squaw Valley Road, Olympic Valley; ☎ 800-403-0206 or 530-583-6985; www.squaw.com

Hours Open year-round; hours vary by activity. **Admission** Varies by activity. **Touring time** Average 1 day; minimum 2 hours. **Rainy-day touring** Not great. **Restaurants** Yes. **Alcoholic beverages** In some restaurants. **Disabled access** Yes. **Wheelchair rental** Yes. **Baby-stroller rental** No. **Lockers** Yes. **Pet kennels** No; leashed pets allowed in summer. **Rain check** No. **Private tours** No.

DESCRIPTION AND COMMENTS   There's little to remind visitors of the 1960 Winter Olympics that were held here, but there's plenty to do year-round. Summer activities include an aerial tram ride to the High Camp Bath and Tennis Club, where you can swim, mountain-bike, play tennis, and bungee-jump—all at an altitude of 8,200 feet. In winter, don't miss the chance to ice-skate in the beautiful outdoor Olympic Ice Pavilion (it's even open for roller skating in summer); in the summer, head for the Adventure Center (see previous profile). And, of course, there's the skiing: some of the best in the West, with spectacular views of the lake. Kids get their own ski area, Children's World, with a playground, ski school, day-care center, and complete facilities.

Tahoe Maritime Museum

APPEAL BY AGE	PRESCHOOL ★	GRADE SCHOOL ★ ★ ★ ★	TEENS ★ ★ ★ ★ ½
YOUNG ADULTS ★ ★ ★ ★ ½		OVER 30 ★ ★ ★ ★ ½	SENIORS ★ ★ ★ ★

5205 West Lake Boulevard, Homewood; ☎ 530-525-9253; www.tahoemaritimemuseum.org

Hours *Summer:* Thursday–Tuesday, 10 a.m.–5 p.m., closed Wednesday; *winter:* Friday–Sunday, 10 a.m.–5 p.m., closed Monday–Thursday. **Admission** Suggested donation, adults $5, children under age 12, free. **Touring time** Average 2 hours; minimum 30 minutes. **Rainy-day touring** Yes. **Restaurants** No. **Alcoholic beverages** No. **Disabled access** Yes. **Wheelchair rental** No. **Baby-stroller rental** No. **Lockers** No. **Pet kennels** No. **Rain check** No. **Private tours** Yes.

DESCRIPTION AND COMMENTS   This new 5,800-square-foot museum on the West Shore is devoted to Lake Tahoe's fascinating maritime history. View boats from many eras, from wooden fishing boats and opulent steamers to racing boats. Aquaplanes and water skis (did you know that early ones were made from barn doors and rope?) are also on exhibit, along with a huge collection of outboard motors. Younger kids will enjoy the fun, hands-on, lake-related activities in the children's area.

Tallac Historic Site

APPEAL BY AGE	PRESCHOOL ★★	GRADE SCHOOL ★★★	TEENS ★★★
YOUNG ADULTS ★★★		OVER 30 ★★★	SENIORS ★★★

CA 89, 2.5 miles north of South Lake Tahoe, next to Historic Camp Richardson Resort; ☎ 530-541-5227; www.fs.fed.us/r5/ltbmu/recreation/tallac

Hours *Mid-June–mid-September:* daily, 10 a.m.–5 p.m.; *mid–late September:* 11 a.m.–4 p.m. **Admission** Free. **Touring time** Average 2 hours; minimum 45 minutes. **Rainy-day touring** Yes, places to escape from rain. **Restaurants** Adjacent. **Alcoholic beverages** At restaurant. **Disabled access** About half of buildings. **Wheelchair rental** No. **Baby-stroller rental** No. **Lockers** No. **Pet kennels** No, but leashed pets allowed. **Rain check** No. **Private tours** Yes.

DESCRIPTION AND COMMENTS   There are several mansion museums in the Tahoe area, but the most interesting for children is a three-building complex in South Lake Tahoe called Tallac Historic Site. It's accessible by paved bike paths from the town and is adjacent to white-sand beaches and a couple of easy hiking trails, so it makes for a nice destination for a bike ride or combination sightseeing-swimming-hiking afternoon. The buildings consist of a 1921 "log cabin" estate that is now a museum, with exhibits on Washoe Native Americans and the history of the estate owners; an 1894 mansion retreat that's home to an interpretive center and summertime living-history programs; and a 1923 estate used for music and arts events, where you'll find several cabins turned over to crafts and arts exhibits and workshops for children.

FAMILY-FRIENDLY RESTAURANTS

Adventure Peak Grill
Heavenly Mountain Resort, Wildwood Avenue and Saddle Road, South Lake Tahoe; ☎ 530-544-6263

Meals served Lunch. **Cuisine** Californian/American. **Entree range** $9–$14. **Kids' menu** Yes. **Reservations** Not accepted. **Payment** All major credit cards.

ALTHOUGH THE FUN is in the getting here on the aerial tram, it's not a bad restaurant considering how far the staff has to come to cook. The fare is simple—salads, burgers, sandwiches—kid-pleasing, and not terribly overpriced, given the setting. And you can't beat the view.

The Beacon Bar & Grill
**Historic Camp Richardson Resort, 1900 Jameson Beach Road,
South Lake Tahoe; ☎ 530-541-0630; www.camprich.com**

Meals served Lunch, dinner, and weekend brunch. **Cuisine** American. **Entree range** Lunch and dinner, $10–$34. **Kids' menu** Yes. **Reservations** Recommended. **Payment** D, MC, V.

SITTING ON THE DECK HERE, eye level with that blue, blue lake, watching kids in their bathing suits pad barefoot and dripping up to the take-out window for a snow cone—it all made us want to be kids again. Then, seeing the gang of 20-somethings laughing over margaritas made us want to be footloose and single again. But then, looking around our own table at the contented smiles as we scarfed down our just-fine summer-vacation food in a carefree boat-and-beachy setting made us, of course, feel happy to be who we are and where we were.

Bridgetender Tavern & Grill
65 West Lake Boulevard, Tahoe City; ☎ 530-583-3342

Meals served Lunch and dinner. **Cuisine** American. **Entree range** $8–$12. **Kids' menu** No. **Reservations** Not accepted. **Payment** D, MC, V.

A NOISY, CASUAL LOCALS' HANGOUT in the heart of Tahoe City, the Bridgetender is known for its delicious, messy burgers, its ribs, its onion rings, its mountain-folk bar scene, and its location right next to Fanny Bridge—so named for the dozens of backsides sticking up in the air on summer days as people lean over the bridge to see (and feed) the huge, spawning trout. Older kids will like the food and scene at this place, and little ones will love tossing bread crumbs down to the fish.

Ernie's Coffee Shop
1146 Emerald Bay Road, South Lake Tahoe; ☎ 530-541-2161

Meals served Breakfast and lunch. **Cuisine** American/coffee shop. **Entree range** $6–$12. **Kids' menu** Yes. **Reservations** Not necessary. **Payment** No credit cards.

A PLACE WHERE NEIGHBORS GATHER to drink coffee and chew the fat before the day gets too far along. Families will be comfortable here.

Fire Sign Cafe
1785 West Lake Boulevard, Tahoe City; ☎ 530-583-0871

Meals served Breakfast and lunch. **Cuisine** American. **Entree range** $6–$10. **Kids' menu** Yes. **Reservations** Not accepted. **Payment** MC, V.

A GOOD STOP BETWEEN HIKES, this modern coffee shop has a nice, woodsy atmosphere and an outside deck for summertime. Choices include teriyaki steak, a turkey club sandwich, veggie baked potatoes, and awesome breakfasts, especially the buckwheat pancakes and lattes. The staff brings out a basket of toys and crayons for kids. Expect a wait on Sunday mornings.

Lakeside Dining Room, Sunnyside Resort
1850 West Lake Boulevard, Tahoe City ☎ **530-583-7200;**
www.sunnysideresort.com

Meals served Lunch and dinner. **Cuisine** American/steak house. **Entree range**
Lunch $11–$20; dinner, $14–$35. **Kids' menu** Yes, $7. **Reservations** Yes.
Payment All major credit cards.

SITTING ON THE DECK on a summer's day is indeed a sunnyside experience. Request a table on the deck's railing, and you'll be able to let the kids
go down and play on the beach (with its excellent rock-skipping opportunities) while you keep an eye on them and enjoy your Sauvignon Blanc. This is
a "nice" restaurant, with upscale seafood and steak house fare, but there's a
good kids' menu and a relaxed family atmosphere on the deck; the bar is
more of a grown-ups' scene. Make sure to order the famous crispy zucchini
sticks, which will convince even the pickiest eater to like vegetables.

PART SIX

SAN FRANCISCO BAY AREA

SIMPLY PUT, WE CAN'T GET ENOUGH OF THE BAY AREA. We've both visited it with our kids many times and still feel there's more to explore, as well as many favorites to revisit. The city of **San Francisco** appeals to every age group, though it's easiest with the 5-and-up set, who are old enough to walk the steep streets and jump on cable cars. It has something for every kid: great parks, museums (of science, art, even a prison), fun ferries, buses, subways, cable cars, cool shops, street music, and so much more. Theme-park junkies can venture out to **Vallejo** to **Six Flags Discovery Kingdom,** or south to **California's Great America** in **Santa Clara.** East in **Berkeley** are the **University of California** and the wonderful **Charles Lee Tilden Regional Park;** north in **Marin County** are redwoods, beaches, and charming small towns. Everywhere there is great food—many of the country's best restaurants are in the Bay Area, and some are even welcoming to children.

If you have only two or three days and your kids haven't experienced San Francisco, stick to the city and you won't be sorry. The city center is compact and easy to negotiate, so in just a few days you can easily hit the hot spots, from cable car and ferry rides to the **Exploratorium, Zeum,** and **Golden Gate Park.** If you have more time, you'll be able to add some wonderful adventures to the itinerary: kayaking **Tomales Bay** in Marin County, for instance, or BARTing over to Berkeley, or even tackling one of the suburban theme parks.

If you're combining a Monterey–Santa Cruz visit (see Part Four, The Central Coast) with some time in San Francisco, you may want to make **San Jose,** capital of the Silicon Valley, your gateway city, as it's midway between the two points. And San Jose's extraordinary **Tech Museum** is well worth a visit all by itself.

san francisco bay area

0 ___ 5 mi
0 ___ 5 km

Sonoma

Napa 29

121

221

12

121

12

121

29

12

Napa County Airport

29

Petaluma

116

116

101

12

Arnold Dr.

121

Infineon Raceway

Sears Point

Marin County Airport

Novato

37

Marinwood

101

Marine World Pkwy.

37

Vallejo

San Pablo Bay

Pinole

Martinez

780

4

Fairfax

San Anselmo

San Rafael

80

San Rafael–Richmond Bridge

San Pablo

Richmond

El Cerrito

See Berkeley map (page 342) for details.

Corte Madera

Larkspur

580

MT. TAMALPAIS STATE PARK Mill Valley

San Quentin

Albany

3

Berkeley

80

580

Stinson Beach

6

7

8

1

5

1

101

131

Tiburon

Marin City

Sausalito

2 *Angel Island*

Muir Beach

Rodeo Beach

Point Bonita

Golden Gate Bridge

San Francisco–Oakland Bay Bridge

Piedmont

80

PACIFIC OCEAN

GOLDEN GATE NATIONAL RECREATION AREA

101

OAKLAND

580

13

4

9

Pacific Bell Park

Alameda

61

880

580

SF Bay Area

Sacramento

SAN FRANCISCO

1

280

Oakland International Airport

61

San Leandro

San Francisco

CALIFORNIA

280

■ **3Com Park**

San Lorenzo

Los Angeles

35

Daly City

101

San Francisco Bay

South San Francisco

1

35

380

San Francisco International Airport

To Half Moon Bay ↓ Pacifica

● **BEACHES AND PARKS**
1. Agate Beach
2. Angel Island State Park
3. Charles Lee Tilden Regional Park
4. Golden Gate Park
5. Muir Woods National Monument
6. Point Reyes National Seashore
7. Stinson Beach
8. Tomales Bay State Park
9. Yerba Buena Gardens

GETTING THERE

BY PLANE   Most major airlines serve one or all three of the region's airports: **San Francisco International Airport** (☎ 650-821-8211; **www.flysfo.com**) is a 30-minute drive south of downtown; **Oakland International Airport** (☎ 510-563-3300; **www.oaklandairport.com**) is more convenient for the East Bay. **BART (Bay Area Rapid Transit)** connects Oakland Airport to downtown San Francisco. **San Jose International Airport** (☎ 408-501-7600; **www.sjc.org**) is just three miles from downtown San Jose; this airport connects with downtown San Jose via free "airport flyer" shuttle and light rail, and with San Francisco via free shuttle to Santa Clara's **Caltrain** station and then by train.

BY TRAIN   **Amtrak** delivers visitors from Southern California, the Pacific Northwest, and Midwest (☎ 800-USA-RAIL; **www.amtrak .com; www.amtrakcalifornia.com**). There is also train service via BART (☎ 415-498-2278; **www.bart.gov**) and Caltrain (☎ 800-660-4287; **www .caltrain.com**) among various Bay Area and Peninsula cities, including San Francisco, the East Bay communities, and San Jose.

BY CAR   The major highways heading into San Francisco are **US 101,** which heads south to LA and north to the Oregon border, and **Interstate 80,** which leads to Oakland, Sacramento, Lake Tahoe, and Nevada. Parking is a challenge—expect to pay dearly for hotel parking.

San Jose is reached by any of the Bay Area's main freeways: **Interstates 280, 680,** and **880,** and **CA 101.**

A **CALENDAR** of **FESTIVALS** and **EVENTS**

January

SEA-LION ARRIVAL   *Pier 39, San Francisco.* A celebration of the annual return of the sea lions to the bay from breeding; ☎ 415-705-5436; **www.pier39.com.**

February

CALIFORNIA INTERNATIONAL ANTIQUARIAN BOOK FAIR   *Concourse Exhibition Center, San Francisco.* World's largest rare-book fair, held in San Francisco in odd-numbered years, in Los Angeles in even numbered years; ☎ 415-551-5190; **www.sfbookfair.com.**

CHINESE NEW YEAR CELEBRATION   *San Francisco.* A lavish parade from Market and Second streets to Columbus Avenue, plus a festival and street fair in Chinatown; ☎ 415-986-1370; **www.chineseparade.com.**

March

ST. PATRICK'S DAY PARADE   *San Francisco.*   ☎ 415-395-8417; **www.sfstpatricksdayparade.com.**

April

CHERRY BLOSSOM FESTIVAL   *Japantown and Japan Center, San Francisco.* Japanese food, music, *taiko* drumming, martial arts, and more; ☎ 415-563-2313; **www.nccbf.org.**

SAN FRANCISCO INTERNATIONAL FILM FESTIVAL   *San Francisco.* Worthwhile for teens; more than 100 films and videos from around the world; ☎ 415-561-5000; **www.sffs.org.**

May

BAY TO BREAKERS FOOTRACE   *San Francisco.* One of the world's largest footraces is also the most colorful—most of the 65,000-plus participants don costumes; ☎ 415-359-2800; **www.baytobreakers.com.**

CINCO DE MAYO FESTIVAL   *Mission District, San Francisco.* Arts, crafts, food, music, and a parade in the city's vibrant Latino community; ☎ 415-647-1533; **www.sfcincodemayo.com.**

YOUNG AT ART   *Golden Gate Park, San Francisco.* ☎ 415-695-2441; **www.youngatartsf.com.**

June

NORTH BEACH FESTIVAL   *Grant Avenue and Green Street, San Francisco.* The city's oldest street fair is refreshingly low-key and funky, with great food, live music, and good crafts; ☎ 415-989-2220; **www .sfnorthbeach.org/NBFestival.**

ZOOFEST FOR KIDS   *San Francisco Zoo.* Festival, live entertainment, up-close encounters with animals; ☎ 415-753-7080; **www.sfzoo.org.**

July

SAN FRANCISCO CABLE CAR BELL-RINGING COMPETITION   *Union Square, San Francisco.* The much-esteemed cable car conductors put on a show; ☎ 415-474-1887; **www.cablecarmuseum.org.**

SAN FRANCISCO FOURTH OF JULY WATERFRONT FESTIVAL   *Fisherman's Wharf, San Francisco.* Food, amusements, arts, and a fabulous fireworks show; ☎ 415-392-4520.

September

SAN FRANCISCO SHAKESPEARE FESTIVAL   *San Francisco.* Free plays in the Presidio; the festival also runs earlier in the summer in Cupertino, Pleasanton, and San Mateo; ☎ 415-558-0888; **www.sfshakes.org.**

October

THE CANNERY'S HALLOWEEN FESTIVAL   *San Francisco.* For more than 20 years, kids have come to the Cannery for a costume contest, games, cookie decorating, and trick-or-treating in the shops; ☎ 415-771-3112; **www.delmontesquare.com.**

HARDLY STRICTLY BLUEGRASS   *Golden Gate Park, San Francisco.* A remarkable and free weekend music festival that includes some of the finest folk, bluegrass, and alternative-country musicians in the United States; **www.hardlystrictlybluegrass.com.**

INDIGENOUS PEOPLE'S DAY   *Berkeley.* Held the Saturday closest to October 12. Berkeley's answer to the traditional Columbus Day parade, featuring a powwow and Indian market; ☎ 510-595-5520; **www.red-coral.net/Pow.html.**

ITALIAN HERITAGE DAY CELEBRATION   *North Beach and Fisherman's Wharf, San Francisco.* Parade, Queen Isabella coronation, and celebration of Italian culture and Columbus's discovery; **www .sfcolumbusday.org.**

November

TREE-LIGHTING CEREMONY   *Ghirardelli Square, San Francisco.* Musical theatre, puppets shows, visits with Santa and a 50-foot tree decorated with giant chocolate bars; ☎ 415-775-5500.

December

CHRISTMAS AT SEA   *Hyde Street Pier, Fisherman's Wharf, San Francisco.* Santa, caroling, stories, cookies, and more on the historic ferryboat *Eureka;* ☎ 415-929-0202; **www.maritime.org.**

TELEGRAPH AVENUE HOLIDAY STREET FAIR   *Berkeley.* A vibrant street market and festival held the two weekends and the two days before Christmas; ☎ 510-234-1013; **www.telegraphfair.com.**

HOW TO GET INFORMATION BEFORE YOU GO

- **Berkeley Convention and Visitors Bureau**   2015 Center Street, Berkeley 94704; ☎ 510-549-7040 or 800-847-4823; **www.visitberkeley.com**
- **Marin County Visitors Bureau**   1 Mitchel Boulevard, San Rafael 94903; ☎ 415-925-2060 or 866-925-2060; **www.visitmarin.org**
- **San Francisco Convention and Visitors Bureau**   Visitor Information Center, Lower Level, Hallidie Plaza, 900 Market Street, San Francisco 94102-2804; ☎ 415-391-2000; **www.sfvisitor.org**
- **San Jose Convention and Visitors Bureau**   408 Almaden Boulevard, San Jose 95110; ☎ 408-295-9600 or 800-SAN-JOSE; **www.sanjose.org**
- **Sausalito Chamber of Commerce**   10 Liberty Ship Way, Bay 2, Suite 250, Sausalito 94965; ☎ 415-331-7262; **www.sausalito.org**

CHILD CARE AND BABYSITTING

AMERICAN CHILDCARE SERVICES   580 California Street, Suite 1600, San Francisco; ☎ 415-285-2300; **www.americanchildcare.com.** Activity programs and in-room care; credit cards accepted.

The BEST BEACHES and PARKS

AGATE BEACH   It's a bit of a challenge to reach this 6.6-acre beach park at the end of a 300-yard, sometimes-steep gravel path that is neither stroller- nor wheelchair-friendly. The reward, however, is considerable: an excellent tide-pooling beach teeming with sea life. (Remember, no collecting allowed.) Ranger tours are limited but possible; call the County of Marin Parks Service to arrange one; ☎ 415-499-6405. CA 1 to Elm Road, Bolinas; ☎ 415-507-2816; **co.marin.ca.us.**

ANGEL ISLAND STATE PARK   Between the congested urbanity of San Francisco and the pampered suburbanity of Tiburon lies this wonderfully unspoiled island, a terrific day or half-day trip for families. Once a Civil War garrison, then an immigration center ("Ellis Island of the West"), Angel Island is now devoted to hiking, mountain biking, kayaking, and beach fun. Ferries from San Francisco and Tiburon pull into **Ayala Cove,** where you can rent bikes or kayaks, take a tram tour, or pick up a hiking map. The paved, five-mile **Perimeter Road** is the favorite hiking and biking destination, thanks to its incredible bay and city views; some of the unpaved hiking trails may be too challenging for little kids. See also "Kayaking" under "Family Outdoor Adventures" (page 318); ☎ 415-435-1915; **www.angelisland.org.**

CHARLES LEE TILDEN REGIONAL PARK   If you visit the Berkeley area by car (BART won't get you this far), set aside a few hours to explore this storybook-perfect park in the hills. Within more than 2,000 acres are amusements for all ages, from the pony rides and petting farm to the beach at **Lake Anza** and the many hiking trails. You'll also find an old, hand-carved merry-go-round (open weekends; ☎ 510-524-6773), a miniature steam train (open weekends; ☎ 510-548-6100), playgrounds, and naturalist programs. Off Grizzly Peak Boulevard, Berkeley; ☎ 510-843-2137; **www.ebparks.org/parks/tilden.**

GOLDEN GATE PARK   One of the country's great urban parks, Golden Gate is 1,017 acres of family fun, worthy of a full day or more. Its various activities are sometimes driving-distance apart, separated by rolling acres of parkland. In "Attractions," you'll find descriptions of its museums (the **California Academy of Sciences** and the **de Young**); in "Family Outdoor Adventures," you'll find advice on biking and skating the park. But that's just the beginning. Very young children will spend several happy hours at **Stow Lake** (☎ 415-752-0347), for example. There's also a children's playground with great slides and equipment accessible to those with disabilities; a 1912 carousel ($1.50 adults, 50¢ children ages 6 to 12, free for younger kids with a paying adult) with a veritable Noah's ark of animals to ride (including frogs, cats, and zebras!); and fields and facilities for playing soccer, tennis, baseball, golf, or croquet. The **Japanese Tea Garden** is

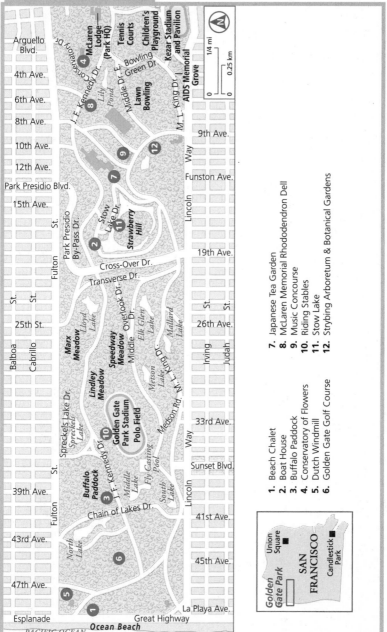

golden gate park

Arguello Blvd.

4th Ave.

6th Ave.

8th Ave.

10th Ave.

12th Ave.

Park Presidio Blvd.

15th Ave.

McLaren Lodge (Park HQ)

Tennis Courts

Children's Playground

Kezar Stadium and Pavilion

Bowling Green Dr.

Lily Pond

Lawn Bowling

AIDS Memorial Grove

9th Ave.

Way

Funston Ave.

Lincoln

19th Ave.

Stow Lake Dr.

Strawberry Hill

Park Presidio By-Pass Dr.

Cross-Over Dr.

Transverse Dr.

St.

St.

25th St.

Balboa

Cabrillo

Marx Meadow

Lloyd Lake

Speedway Meadow

Overlook Dr.

Middle Dr.

Elk Glen

Mallard Lake

St.

St.

26th Ave.

Irving

Judah

Lindley Meadow

Metson Lake

M. L. King Dr.

33rd Ave.

Speckels Lake Dr.

Golden Gate Park Stadium Polo Field

Spreckels Lake

Medson Rd.

Way

Sunset Blvd.

Lincoln

Fulton

St.

Buffalo Paddock

J.F. Kennedy Dr.

Middle Lake

Fly Casting Pool

South Lake

Chain of Lakes Dr.

39th Ave.

41st Ave.

43rd Ave.

North Lake

45th Ave.

47th Ave.

Esplanade

PACIFIC OCEAN

Great Highway

La Playa Ave.

Ocean Beach

1/4 mi

0.25 km

0

0

1. Beach Chalet
2. Boat House
3. Buffalo Paddock
4. Conservatory of Flowers
5. Dutch Windmill
6. Golden Gate Golf Course
7. Japanese Tea Garden
8. McLaren Memorial Rhododendron Dell
9. Music Concourse
10. Riding Stables
11. Stow Lake
12. Strybing Arboretum & Botanical Gardens

Golden Gate Park

Union Square

SAN FRANCISCO

Candlestick Park

unofficial **TIP**
We've circumnavigated the island of Golden Gate Park's tiny lake with a succession of 3-year-olds in pedal boats who, at rental time's end, hop onto the shore, beg us to buy popcorn, and feed the ducks for another hour.

a lovely interlude for grandparents and grandchildren. It's open daily, 9 a.m. to 6 p.m. (until 5 p.m. in winter); tea and cookies are served in the teahouse ($2 adults, $1 seniors and children; ☎ 415-752-1171). Of course, families can also picnic in the many meadows. There's a buffalo paddock, an arboretum, a Victorian greenhouse, a windmill, and access to the beach. Pick up a map to the park at McLaren Lodge (Stanyan and Fell streets) and consider taking the free guided walking tour conducted by park docents; ☎ 415-263-0991; **www.sfpt.org/default.aspx?tabid=87.** Bordered by Fulton and Stanyan streets, Lincoln Way, and Great Highway; ☎ 415-831-2700; **parks.sfgov.org.**

MUIR WOODS NATIONAL MONUMENT One of the Bay Area's last uncut stands of old-growth redwoods lives in this small national forest. The largest trees—250 tall, 14 feet across, and 1,000 years old—are found in **Bohemian Grove** and **Cathedral Grove,** both of which are accessed via stroller-friendly, less-than-a-mile trails that head out from the main parking lot. In the spring, kids can try to spot baby salmon in **Redwood Creek.** Come early to avoid the afternoon crowds, and stop at the visitors center to pick up the free, very cool Junior Ranger pack, complete with bug box and activity guide. This is a forest of awe, mystery, and beauty, appreciated by everyone from toddlers to teens. Open daily; admission $5 for adults age 16 and older, free for children age 15 and under. On CA 1 near Mill Valley, 12 miles north of the Golden Gate Bridge; ☎ 415-388-2595; **www.nps.gov/muwo.**

POINT REYES NATIONAL SEASHORE Remote and gloriously wild, this national park preserves 65,000 acres of coastal property on the north end of Marin County. It is a paradise for bird-watchers—more than 45 percent of the bird species in North America have been sighted here—for hikers, and for lovers of romantically windswept, rocky, foggy beaches. The beach hikes are fairly challenging, but for families with younger kids, there are several easy walks that begin at the **Bear Valley Visitors Center** (Bear Valley Road off CA 1 near Olema; ☎ 415-464-5100). Walk the quarter-mile trail to **Kule Loklo,** a replica of a Coast Miwok Native American village. Another short walk takes you across fern-filled gullies and scrambling over fallen logs to **Morgan Horse Ranch,** where you can watch cowboys train horses for the park rangers to use, and walk through historic stables. School-age kids like the half-mile **Earthquake Trail,** which follows a fracture zone of the famed San Andreas Fault; an exhibit displays a seismograph and photos of the 1906 quake in San Francisco. For a longer but still easy hike, take the three-mile **Bear Valley Trail.** Point Reyes Station; ☎ 415-464-5100; **www.nps.gov/pore.**

Farther afield are more treasures, most notably **Point Reyes Lighthouse,** built in 1870 and found at the bottom of a 300-step walkway (warning for parents of whiny preschoolers) on Point Reyes Headlands (Sir Francis Drake Boulevard; ☎ 415-669-1534; **www .ptreyeslight.com/lthouse.html**). The visitors center has exhibits on whales and lighthouses, and from January to April the lighthouse is a superb place to look for migrating gray whales. Elsewhere you'll find great beaches to comb (**Drakes** is a good one), but the water's too cold and rough for swimming.

STINSON BEACH   A grand, sweeping beach some three and a half miles long, Stinson is ideal for a family beach day in July and August, though the water is frosty by Southern California standards. The little town of Stinson Beach, which has a couple of restaurants and shops, is just a half block away. Picnic area, restrooms, snack bar, outdoor (cold) showers, lifeguards (in summer). CA 1 at Panoramic Highway, north of San Francisco; ☎ 415-868-1922; **www.nps.gov/goga/stbe.htm.**

unofficial **TIP**
Stinson changes from a cold, rough, riptide-laden place in the winter and spring to a peaceful, delightful, small-surf beach in the summer.

TOMALES BAY STATE PARK   A former home of the Miwok Native Americans, this is a beautiful retreat with lots of activities for families. Its several beaches include Heart's Desire, a sheltered cove with a wading lagoon, picnicking, and easy hiking trails through groves of pines. Kayaking is also popular here; see "Kayaking" in "Family Outdoor Adventures" (next page). Pierce Point Road, near Inverness; ☎ 415-669-1140; **parks.ca.gov.**

YERBA BUENA GARDENS   Atop the roof of Moscone Center, near the Museum of Modern Art, public Yerba Buena Gardens (see map on next page) has something for every kid. There's a state-of-the-art ice-skating rink, a cheerful bowling alley, a hand-carved 1906 carousel, a fabulous hands-on, high-tech arts museum (**Zeum**), a hip urban playground bordered by a child-sized botanical maze . . . and a Starbucks for Frappuccino-swilling 12-year-olds. For free fun, bring a picnic lunch to the open, grassy knolls in the center of the gardens, where kids can run behind the huge waterfall-fountain, then head over to the pit-style playground. Kids slide down giant tubes, bounce giant balls on the springy, recycled-sneaker playground surface, and lose themselves in sand-and-water play. To learn more about Zeum, see its attraction profile (page 336); for details on the other admission-charging venues, see the Yerba Buena Gardens attraction profile (page 335); **www.yerbabuenagardens.com.**

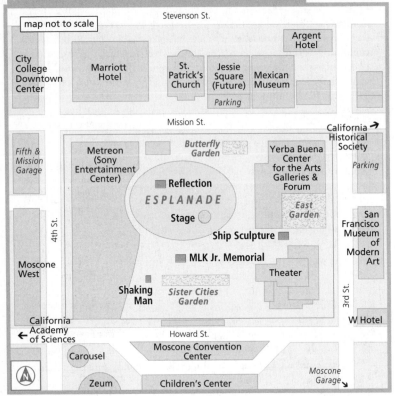

yerba buena gardens and environs

map not to scale

Stevenson St.

Argent Hotel

City College Downtown Center

Marriott Hotel

St. Patrick's Church

Jessie Square (Future)
Parking

Mexican Museum

Mission St.

Fifth & Mission Garage

Metreon (Sony Entertainment Center)

Butterfly Garden

California Historical Society

Parking →

Yerba Buena Center for the Arts Galleries & Forum

Reflection

ESPLANADE

East Garden

Stage

4th St.

Ship Sculpture

San Francisco Museum of Modern Art

Moscone West

MLK Jr. Memorial

Theater

3rd St.

Shaking Man

Sister Cities Garden

W Hotel

California Academy of Sciences ←

Howard St.

Moscone Convention Center

Carousel

Zeum

Children's Center

Moscone Garage ↘

FAMILY OUTDOOR ADVENTURES

BICYCLING At the north end of Golden Gate Park, you can rent bikes at **Golden Gate Park Bike & Skate** (3038 Fulton Street at Sixth Avenue; ☎ 415-668-1117; **www.goldengateparkbikeandskate.com**), then set off and explore the park's 1,017 acres, which are crisscrossed with paths; if you follow Kennedy Drive west, you'll hit the oceanfront bike path at Ocean Beach, which goes for three level miles. Stash a picnic in a backpack, and you've got a great family day. (Note that Kennedy is a functioning street, but it's closed to cars on Sundays.)

Also within the city limits is the starting point for a wonderful adventure: riding across the **Golden Gate Bridge.** Pick up rental bikes and a route map at **Blazing Saddles Bike Rentals** (1095 Columbus Avenue and four Fisherman's Wharf locations: 2715 Hyde Street, 465 Jefferson Street, Pier 41, and Pier 43 ½; ☎ 415-202-8888; **www.blazing saddles.com**), ride across the bridge, refuel with lunch in Sausalito, then catch the ferry back—there's a bike-return spot at the ferry terminal.

If you have older children who are avid mountain bikers, you'll want to go to **Mount Tamalpais State Park** (Panoramic Highway off CA 1, Marin County; ☎ 415-388-2070; **parks.ca.gov**), where the mountain bike was invented in 1974 by a few broke gearheads. The trails, views, and thrills are first rate. You can rent gear on the way there at **Mike's Bikes** (1 Gate 6 Road, Sausalito; ☎ 415-332-3200; **www.mikesbikes.com**).

FISHING Fishing can be a great family bonding activity, and the deep-sea fishing is good in the bay—even better when the boats venture through the Golden Gate into the Pacific in search of striped bass, salmon, and giant sturgeon. It's not cheap, though—a full day costs about $95, with kids charged roughly half price. A number of companies run boats out of the Fisherman's Wharf area. For salmon fishing, reserve a trip on the *Wacky Jacky* (473 Bella Vista Way, San Francisco; ☎ 415-586-9800; **www.wackyjackysportfishing.com**), a boat that's fast and cool.

HILL WALKING Looking for an outdoor family challenge that offers exercise, adventure, and great views? Try stair-climbing. Our favorite places to do so are the stairs up to **Coit Tower** on the edge of North Beach, off Greenwich Street, which pays off in an extraordinary view and a look at the evocative WPA murals inside the tower; the stairs up Vallejo Street in Russian Hill to **Ina Coolbrith Park,** a terraced city park with incredible views and great hide-and-seek possibilities; and, of course, a climb up **Lombard Street,** the famous winding road.

unofficial **TIP**
Try climbing San Francisco's urban mountains—in other words, stair climbing. What can be so tedious in a gym is a joy in this city, and kids feel a tremendous sense of accomplishment at cresting one of the famed peaks.

HORSEBACK RIDING To ride in the redwoods, head up to **Willow Tree Stables** in the Marin County town of Novato (3777 Vineyard Road; ☎ 415-897-8212; **www.willowtreestables.com**). This high-quality stable leads several rides daily into the oak- and redwood-covered Novato hills, following the ancient trails of the Miwok Native Americans. Children older than age 6 are welcome.

KAYAKING The hot outdoor activity of the moment is kayaking in Marin County's **Tomales Bay,** a spectacular coastal wilderness refuge. A full-service kayak company, **Blue Waters Kayaking** in Inverness (☎ 415-669-2600; **www.bwkayak.com**), can teach your family how to kayak, rent you the boats, or take you on a naturalist-led tour of the coves and sea life in the bay. The best bet for families (with kids age 8 and up) is the guided, three-hour morning paddle on weekends ($68 per person), which pairs one adult with one child in each kayak; you'll paddle to hidden beaches and look for seals, bat rays, and birds. In Sausalito, **Sea Trek** (Schoonmaker Point Marina; ☎ 415-488-1000; **www.seatrekkayak.com**) will take you paddling to see a bird refuge, sea lions, and Angel Island; it also has a three-hour guided, kid-oriented paddling adventure ($75 adults, $45 children).

SKATING   Two spots are perfect for family skating: **Marina Green,** the easy, 1.5-mile waterfront park with great bay views, and **Golden Gate Park,** especially on Sundays, when the main street is closed (rent skates at **Golden Gate Park Bike & Skate,** 3038 Fulton Street at Sixth Avenue; ☎ 415-668-1117; **www.goldengateparkbikeandskate.com**).

WHALE WATCHING   **Oceanic Society Expeditions** heads out in search of gray and humpback whales from Fort Mason Center in the Marina District, (Quarters 35 N; ☎ 415-474-3385; **www.oceanic-society.org;** reservations required several weeks in advance). The all-day outings are held Saturday and Sunday; the cost is $85 to $90. After the gray-whale season, the tours become nature cruises to the Farallon Islands in pursuit of humpback and blue whales and other marine life. These are rustic, nature-focused trips, and you'll need to bring your own food and drink. No access for persons with disabilities.

SAN FRANCISCO

EVEN THOUGH THIS POLISHED, chic waterfront city was home of the original yuppie, it's still a wonderful place to visit with children, especially school-age kids, who can appreciate the big-city energy, not to mention hop on cable cars and safely hold on all by themselves. San Francisco doesn't have theme parks, but who needs 'em when the city itself is one big theme park? Rounding a corner on a cable car, driving down **Lombard Street,** cutting through the fog on a ferry boat, paddling a kayak around **Angel Island,** cycling over the **Golden Gate Bridge**—these are thrills that a kid remembers.

Colleen took each of her daughters on a special one-on-one trip to San Francisco when they turned 7. On both trips they did the hokey tourist stuff that she'd usually avoid, and they had a ball. Here are the highlights, and any child under the age of 10 would adore the same things:

- An afternoon at the **Exploratorium,** the hands-down highlight of the trip and a winner for any child, teenager, or adult.
- Riding up and down **Nob Hill** on a cable car, hanging off the side.
- Strolling past the sidewalk vendors at **Fisherman's Wharf** and splurging on the child's most cherished memento, a $1.50 caricature of herself.
- Picking out a chocolate bar at **Ghirardelli Square.**
- Riding the **ferry to Tiburon**, then spending an hour climbing the shore rocks.
- Studying with amazement the 1906 postfire photos of the city at the **Cable Car Museum.**

Older kids and teens might find Fisherman's Wharf and Ghirardelli a bit predictable, but they'll love the video arcade at **Pier 39,** the spiffy shops of **Union Street,** the Claymation studio at **Zeum,** the now-upscale tie-dyed wares of **Haight-Ashbury,** and an inline-skating session along **Marina Green.** And since San Francisco has become a sort of sophisticated Disneyland for grown-ups, parents enjoy a family trip there as much as the kids. For starters, they're going to eat way, way better than in Anaheim.

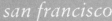

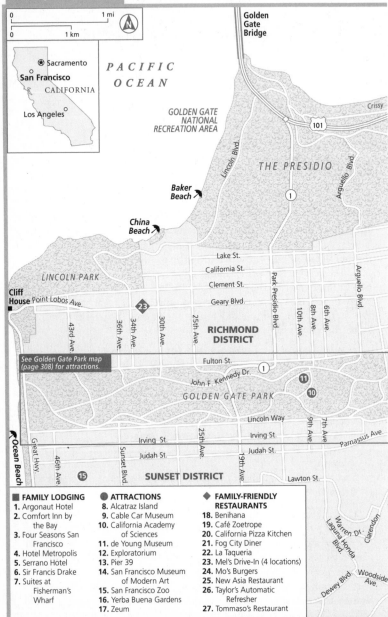

san francisco

PACIFIC OCEAN

Golden Gate Bridge

Sacramento
San Francisco
CALIFORNIA
Los Angeles

GOLDEN GATE NATIONAL RECREATION AREA

THE PRESIDIO

Baker Beach

China Beach

Lake St.
California St.
Clement St.
Geary Blvd.

LINCOLN PARK

Cliff House Point Lobos Ave.

RICHMOND DISTRICT

Lincoln Blvd.
Arguello Blvd.
Park Presidio Blvd.
10th Ave.
8th Ave.
6th Ave.
Arguello Blvd.
43rd Ave.
36th Ave.
34th Ave.
30th Ave.
25th Ave.

Fulton St.

See Golden Gate Park map (page 308) for attractions.

John F. Kennedy Dr.

GOLDEN GATE PARK

Lincoln Way
Irving St.   Irving St.
Judah St.   Judah St.
Lawton St.

Ocean Beach
Great Hwy.
46th Ave.
Sunset Blvd.
25th Ave.
19th Ave.
9th Ave.
7th Ave.
Parnassus Ave.

SUNSET DISTRICT

Crissy
101

Warren Dr.
Laguna Honda Blvd.
Clarendon
Dewey Blvd.
Woodside Ave.

■ FAMILY LODGING
1. Argonaut Hotel
2. Comfort Inn by the Bay
3. Four Seasons San Francisco
4. Hotel Metropolis
5. Serrano Hotel
6. Sir Francis Drake
7. Suites at Fisherman's Wharf

● ATTRACTIONS
8. Alcatraz Island
9. Cable Car Museum
10. California Academy of Sciences
11. de Young Museum
12. Exploratorium
13. Pier 39
14. San Francisco Museum of Modern Art
15. San Francisco Zoo
16. Yerba Buena Gardens
17. Zeum

◆ FAMILY-FRIENDLY RESTAURANTS
18. Benihana
19. Café Zoetrope
20. California Pizza Kitchen
21. Fog City Diner
22. La Taqueria
23. Mel's Drive-In (4 locations)
24. Mo's Burgers
25. New Asia Restaurant
26. Taylor's Automatic Refresher
27. Tommaso's Restaurant

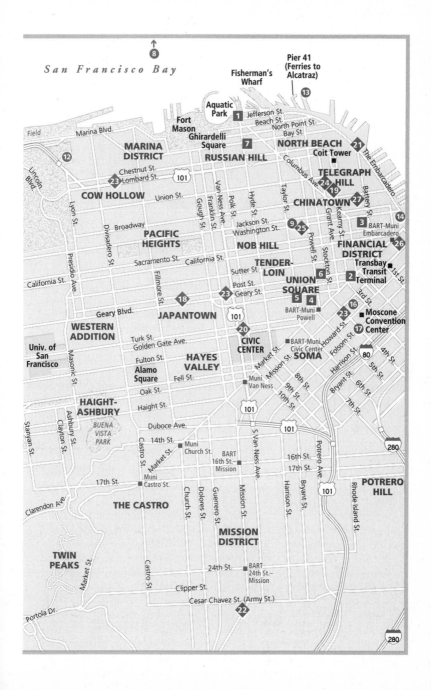

San Francisco Bay

Field

Marina Blvd.

Lincoln Blvd

Presidio Ave.

Lyon St.

Divisadero St.

Fillmore St.

California St.

Masonic St.

Ashbury St.

Clayton St.

Stanyan St.

Clarendon Ave.

Portola Dr.

Market St.

Pier 41
(Ferries to
Alcatraz)

Fisherman's
Wharf

Aquatic
Park

Fort
Mason

Ghirardelli
Square

Jefferson St.
Beach St.
North Point St.
Bay St.

MARINA
DISTRICT

RUSSIAN HILL

NORTH BEACH
Coit Tower

TELEGRAPH
HILL

Chestnut St.
Lombard St.

COW HOLLOW

Union St.

CHINATOWN

Columbus Ave.

The Embarcadero

Battery St.

Broadway

PACIFIC
HEIGHTS

NOB HILL

Van Ness Ave.
Franklin St.
Gough St.
Polk St.
Hyde St.
Taylor St.
Powell St.
Grant Ave.
Kearny St.
Stockton St.

Jackson St.
Washington St.

Sacramento St.

California St.

FINANCIAL
DISTRICT

BART-Muni
Embarcadero

TENDER-
LOIN

Sutter St.

Post St.
Geary St.

UNION
SQUARE

Transbay
Transit
Terminal

1st St.

JAPANTOWN

Geary Blvd.

WESTERN
ADDITION

Univ. of
San
Francisco

Turk St.
Golden Gate Ave.

CIVIC
CENTER

BART-Muni
Powell

Moscone
Convention
Center

3rd St.

2nd St.

Howard St.

Folsom St.

Harrison St.

Bryant St.

4th St.

5th St.

6th St.

7th St.

Fulton St.

Alamo
Square

HAYES
VALLEY

Fell St.

BART-Muni
Civic Center

SOMA

Market St.

Mission St.

8th St.

9th St.

10th St.

Muni
Van Ness

Oak St.

HAIGHT-
ASHBURY

Haight St.

Duboce Ave.

BUENA
VISTA
PARK

14th St.

Castro St.

Church St.

Muni
Church St.

BART
16th St.–
Mission

16th St.

17th St.

S Van Ness Ave.

Guerrero St.

Dolores St.

Mission St.

Harrison St.

Bryant St.

Potrero Ave.

Rhode Island St.

POTRERO
HILL

17th St.

Muni
Castro St.

THE CASTRO

MISSION
DISTRICT

TWIN
PEAKS

24th St.

BART
24th St.–
Mission

Clipper St.

Cesar Chavez St. (Army St.)

WORDS OF WISDOM

MARK TWAIN QUIPPED, "The coldest winter I ever spent was a summer in San Francisco." This may be the most overquoted line in guidebook history, but it's for a very good reason: When a fog bank moves in, you'll be chilled to the bone, even if it's July. Be prepared with warm clothing.

If you're bringing a car into the city, be aware that parking is costly and that street spots are as rare as sunny days in June. If you do find a spot, and it's on a hill, make sure to curb the wheels, or you'll face a nasty ticket (and risk a smashed car).

GETTING THERE IS ALL THE FUN

NOT ONLY IS SAN FRANCISCO HAPPILY NAVIGABLE without a car, but its various forms of public transportation—cable car, trolley, subway, ferry, taxi—are also as much fun for kids as the city's best amusements. Here are the basics on each:

CABLE CARS   Part of the city's vast **Muni** (San Francisco Municipal Railway) service, the cable cars are the city's pied pipers, an irresistible lure to children. They run on three routes in the heart of the city, connecting **Market Street–Union Square** to **Fisherman's Wharf** and Union Square to **Ghirardelli Square,** and running from the **downtown financial district** near the Ferry Building over Nob Hill to **Van Ness.** In peak tourist times (which, thanks to conventions, is almost always), expect long lines at the end stations near Union Square and the wharf; we've had better luck catching a ride several blocks up the hill from either of these stops (the cars sometimes depart not fully loaded to allow for passengers to get on at later stops). If the city is really crowded, avoid the Powell lines completely and climb up Nob Hill to catch the California Line, which is typically half empty.

The best way to enjoy cable cars the old-fashioned way (as actual transportation) is to designate one day as cable-car day. Leave your hotel very early in the morning before breakfast the way we did for one mother–daughter excursion. The cars start running at 6:30 a.m., so there we were, virtually alone, stepping onto the Powell-Mason Line car, buying an all-day pass from the conductor, transferring at the top of the hill, then riding along with the office workers down the steep and dramatic California Line to the end. We hopped off, enjoyed breakfast, and then hopped on again and headed for Chinatown. We reboarded later in Chinatown and continued to our next stop. That evening after dinner, we used our passes to board a once-again nearly vacant cable car back to our hotel. At the end of the day we'd had a half-dozen cable-car rides, hadn't waited in line for any of them, and had gotten where we were going, too. The fare is $5 (kids under age 5 ride free) for a one-way ride; Muni Passports (available throughout town) allow unlimited rides on the cable cars, trolleys, light-rail cars, and buses for $11 a day, $18 for three days, or $24 for seven days. For more information, call ☎ 311 or 415-701-2311; **www.sfmta.com.**

FERRIES The view of San Francisco from the water is one of the most memorable sights in the world, and you can thrill to it (without having your kids even realize you're spending time looking at scenery) by hopping onto one of the commuter ferries used to bring office workers from the suburbs into downtown's financial district. The fun for the kids, of course (and for adults, too), is in the boat ride, and nobody in your family will argue against a ferry to wherever and back—an hour on the bay, standing at the rail with the gulls sporting behind you and the wind in your face, will knock the airplane and hotel-room blahs right out of everyone's system.

Pier 39, within easy distance of a number of tourist attractions, is the disembarkation point for the **Blue and Gold Fleet** (☎ 415-705-5555; **www.blueandgoldfleet.com**), which will take you (famously) not only to **Sausalito** but also to **Tiburon, Muir Woods** (via a connecting shuttle bus, Memorial Day weekend through Labor Day weekend only), **Angel Island,** and Oakland's **Jack London Square** waterfront. But we've also had a great trip on a high-speed commuter ferry, buying sodas at the snack bar and then heading out to the benches on deck to shiver while passing under the majestic **Bay Bridge** on the way to **Alameda,** where the ferry docks at a decidedly less picturesque point (an abandoned military base) than in Sausalito. We found ourselves near the end of Market Street when we spied the Ferry Building, so we simply asked about the next ferry and got on for a round-trip. We might just as easily have gone to Sausalito, where you can while away a few hours in shops and cafes, or to Larkspur (**Golden Gate Ferries;** ☎ 415-455-2000; **www.goldengate.org**). Be sure to ask your hotel concierge to call for updated departure times to give yourselves an idea of the schedule (in general, the commuter ferries run for a few hours in the morning and afternoon-evening, but not at midday), then be ready to take a ride.

TROLLEYS The newest additions to San Francisco's already-great public-transportation system combine retro charm for parents with novelty for kids. Running along the refurbished **Embarcadero,** ending at Fisherman's Wharf, the **F Line** is made up of brightly colored trolleys salvaged from several American cities. Regular Muni rates apply.

SUBWAY The **BART** system carries riders under the bay from downtown San Francisco to Berkeley and Oakland. The trains are clean, quiet, and modern, and kids love the ride—not to mention the cool automated ticket dispensers and sucker-uppers at the high-tech stations. Fares are modest; children under age 4 ride free, and those ages 5 to 12 can get a huge discount from outside vendors, which are listed in brochures at every BART station. You can even board at one of the Market Street stops and go just one or two stops in either direction—it's more fun to ride an escalator underground and board a train than it is to drag a dead-tired toddler along the sidewalks of those long city blocks. For information on stations and maps, call ☎ 510-464-6000; **www.bart.gov.**

TAXIS To children who live in the suburbs, nothing is more cosmopolitan than hopping in a cab and being whisked off someplace. Our 7-year-old's first ride in a taxi was as thrilling as her first ride on Dumbo at Disneyland at age 4. Stay away from the unlicensed gypsy cabs (generally black sedans), but feel safe in any of the city's licensed cabs. The short distances within San Francisco mean that taxi rides are a real bargain, especially with three or four people; fares are typically in the $5 to $8 range. Cabs are easy to find at hotels and on downtown streets; otherwise, call or ask your restaurant host to order one. Our favorite companies are **Luxor** (☎ 415-282-4141) and **Veteran's** (☎ 415-552-1300).

SPENDING IT

COMPACT, STYLISH, AND RELENTLESSLY PROSPEROUS, San Francisco draws shoppers from all over the West, including children. Here are our kids' favorite San Francisco shops.

GHIRARDELLI CHOCOLATE MANUFACTORY   Ghirardelli Square, Northpoint and Larkin streets; ☎ 415-775-5500; **www.ghirardelli.com.** Chocolate bars, chocolate cable cars, chocolate coins—you get the picture. In the rear is a Willy Wonka fantasy: a picture window overlooking a giant vat of chocolate being stirred by mechanical paddles. Next door is an ice-cream parlor that serves great hot-fudge sundaes. Irresistible.

JEFFREY'S TOYS   685 Market Street, Union Square; ☎ 415-546-6551. Perhaps the best toy selection in town is packed into this fine indie store. Whether your kids are into board games, electronic games, comic books, crafts, collectibles, robots, Dungeons and Dragons, or dolls, they'll be enthralled here.

PUPPETS ON THE PIER   Pier 39, Fisherman's Wharf; ☎ 415-781-4435; **www.pier39.com.** From finger puppets to marionettes, they're all here, often in performance in front of the shop.

SANRIO   865 Market Street, Union Square; ☎ 415-495-3056. Hello Kitty heaven or hell, depending on where you stand on the issue.

HAIGHT STREET VINTAGE-CLOTHING SHOPS   The great **Amoeba Music** (1855 Haight Street; ☎ 415-831-1200; **www.amoeba.com**) is the hot destination in this still-hip neighborhood, made famous in the 1960s. If you have teens, you must let them wander the Haight and explore Amoeba and the many shops selling vintage and funky-new clothes, jewelry, and accessories; they'll likely encounter retro-hippies, too. **Telegraph Avenue** in Berkeley is also great for the same thing, including good street vendors on the weekends.

TWO SPECIAL FOUNTAINS

TWO FOUNTAINS IN TWO WELL-TRAVELED PARTS of the city—Ghirardelli Square and Union Square—were gifts to children from Ruth Asawa, a San Francisco–based sculptor. One, at the **Grand Hyatt** at Union Square (345 Stockton Street), is drum-shaped, straddles some steps, and can be viewed from below (as you climb the steps), from the sides, and from above. You can touch it and get as close as you want, because the drum is covered with bronze relief panels cast from sculpted figures, as well as landscape features that were fashioned by Asawa and scores of kid and adult helpers out of a dough mixture called "baker's clay." (Asawa, a mother of six, first used the medium to keep small hands busy, then came to use it in her work.) The panoramic scenes are of San Francisco itself, with some fantasy folks (like Raggedy Ann and Superman) thrown in. One could easily pass it by, but if you take a moment with kids after a day or two in the city, they'll see all the places they've visited, represented in whimsical, whirling relief: Golden Gate Bridge, Lombard Street, the Ferry Building, the parks, some schools and neighborhoods. Chinatown has a dragon, plus kite fliers, clowns, City Hall, trains, and taxis.

Over at Ghirardelli Square, toddlers and their parents spend happy times dipping fingers and toes into *Andrea,* aka the **Mermaid Fountain,** a more traditional shape with a pool and some central figures—but especially fun for kids because some of the sculpted features, such as frogs, extend out to the sides, where visitors sit and splash.

FAMILY LODGING

 Argonaut Hotel

495 Jefferson Street; ☎ 800-790-1415 or 415-563-0800; www.argonautehotel.com; $260 and up

PART OF THE SPIFFY KIMPTON HOTEL GROUP, this boutique hotel is part of the Maritime National Historic Park at Fisherman's Wharf. The location is terrific—the Cannery is on one side of the hotel, the cable-car turnaround is on the other side, and the park and bay are right out front. Many rooms have views of Alcatraz, the Golden Gate Bridge, or both, and all are done in a cheerful navy-and-yellow nautical style, with white-washed furniture and captain's chairs. Check out the Neptune's Adventure package, which includes a two-queen-bedded room for a family of four, a full breakfast, cable-car passes, Hyde Street Pier passes, and a gift for the kids. This is also one of the rare upscale city hotels that welcomes pets.

Comfort Inn by the Bay

2775 Van Ness Avenue, near Fisherman's Wharf; ☎ 877-424-6423 or 415-928-5000; www.comfortinn.com; $129 and up; children under age 19 free in parents' room; special discounts sometimes offered

THE VALUE IS GOOD AT THIS 11-STORY, 138-room motel six blocks from Ghirardelli Square on busy Van Ness Avenue. Some rooms have bay views, a generous Continental breakfast is free, and seasonal specials can bring the room rates below $100. Expect a clean, no-frills motel, and you won't be disappointed.

Four Seasons San Francisco
757 Market Street, Union Square; ☎ 800-819-5053 or 415-633-3000; www.fourseasons.com; $395–$800; children under age 18 stay free in parents' room

THIS SLICK FOUR SEASONS PROVIDES the pampering and child friendliness that are trademarks of the chain. It's next to Yerba Buena Gardens, just south of Market, making it ideal for families heading to Zeum and the Museum of Modern Art. The gleaming, 40-story tower also houses luxury condos and the 100,000-square-foot Sports Club/LA, which is free to guests 16 and older. Kids get welcome gifts, child-size robes, kids' menus, and PlayStation; parents get dazzling city views, a warmly modern decor featuring the work of local artists, and every creature comfort.

Hotel Metropolis
25 Mason Street; ☎ 800-553-1900 or 415-775-4600; www.hotelmetropolis.com; $99–$199; family suite $269

THE NICEST OF SEVERAL SAN FRANCISCO PROPERTIES in the Personality Hotels group, the ten-story, 105-room Metropolis has a three-room family suite that includes a parents' room; a bunk room complete with toys and an eMac computer; and a living room with a wet bar, fridge, and pullout sofa. It's on the edge of the Tenderloin at Mason and Third streets, a block from the Powell cable-car station and an easy walk to Yerba Buena Gardens, and it has a colorful, kid-appealing decor as well as a terrific Southern restaurant, Farmer Brown (great mac and cheese). All rooms have refrigerators, free Internet access, and Nintendo; on site are a fitness center and library. Ask about family packages here as well as at the Personality group's several other small hotels in the neighborhood.

Serrano Hotel
405 Taylor Street, Union Square; ☎ 866-289-6561 or 415-885-2500; www.serranohotel.com; $229–$399, suites $299 and up

A MEMBER OF THE STYLISH KIMPTON HOTEL FAMILY, this carefully renovated, Spanish Revival charmer boasts games as its theme, so our kids love it. The lobby has several seating areas built around chess, checkers, backgammon, and tic-tac-toe tables; rooms are equipped with playing cards, puzzles, and Nintendo; and a call to the front desk will have your room supplied with any of dozens of board games, from Twister to Trivial Pursuit. The rooms are lovely but small, so families might need a suite or adjoining rooms. The Serrano is in the theater district, three blocks west of Union Square, and has all the upscale modern essentials: fitness room, in-room high-speed Internet access, free newspapers, morning coffee, evening wine tastings, and good soundproofing.

Sir Francis Drake

450 Powell Street, Union Square; ☎ 800-795-7129 or 415-392-7755; www.sirfrancisdrake.com; $219 and up; packages and free upgrades often available

COLLEEN HAS A SENTIMENTAL ATTACHMENT to this Union Square hotel—her family stayed here on her first trip to San Francisco when she was 10 years old, and she and her sister were enthralled with the doormen in Beefeater costumes, not to mention the cable cars right out front. The Beefeaters and cable cars are still captivating children, only now the hotel is owned by the Kimpton group, and the rooms have been tastefully modernized with rustic furniture and floral fabrics; the studio-style executive rooms have sleeper sofas and are a good family choice. Some rooms have refrigerators, and the touristy but perfectly fine Cal-Italian restaurant has a kids' menu. Let the concierge book a babysitter for you, and head upstairs for a memorable grown-up night at Harry Denton's Starlight Room on the roof, a Sinatraesque 1950s throwback that's one of the city's most happening nightclubs.

Suites at Fisherman's Wharf

2655 Hyde Street, Fisherman's Wharf; ☎ 866-729-7182 or 415-771-0200; www.thesuitesatfishermanswharf.com; $179–$289; children under age 12 stay free

A GOOD BASE FOR FAMILIES who want to be near the wharf, this 24-unit, all-suites hotel is also a time-share property. Each unit is about 550 square feet, containing a bedroom with queen bed, a living room with queen sleeper sofa, and a full compact kitchen complete with dishwasher and cookware. It's two blocks up from the wharf, right on the cable car line, which means the front-facing view rooms can get noisy; if you want quiet, pick a viewless room in back. Rates include an adequate Continental breakfast and wine, tea, and cookies in the afternoon.

▮ ATTRACTIONS

 ## Alcatraz Island (via Hornblower Cruises)

APPEAL BY AGE	PRESCHOOL ★	GRADE SCHOOL ★★★	TEENS ★★★★½
YOUNG ADULTS ★★★★½	OVER 30 ★★★★		SENIORS ★★★★

Pier 33; ☎ 415-981-7625; www.alcatrazcruises.com

Hours Tours leave daily at approximately 30-minute intervals, 9 a.m.–3:55 p.m.; Night Tours leave 6:10 p.m. and 6:50 p.m. **Admission** $26 adults, $24.50 seniors 62 or older, $16 children ages 5–11, free for age 4 and under; Night Tours, $33 adults, $30.50 seniors, $32 children ages 12–17, $19.50 children ages 5–11, free for age 4 and under. **Touring time** Average 3 hours; minimum 2 hours. **Rainy-day touring** Tours run unless the captain feels it's dangerous. **Restaurants** Snack bars on boats. **Alcoholic beverages** No. **Disabled access** Yes. **Wheelchair rental** No, but ask about SEAT. **Baby-stroller rental** No. **Lockers** No. **Pet kennels** No. **Rain check** Yes. **Private tours** No.

DESCRIPTION AND COMMENTS   This fabled maximum-security prison, isolated as it is on an island with the city so tantalizingly visible, is both a powerful reality and a striking metaphor. Its thoughtful adaptation as an "attraction" has made it an important historic site. The bleak corridors, now thronged with tourists, are nevertheless strangely quiet as visitors, each with his or her audio tour set, listen to the tales of individual prisoners trying to escape, hear the sounds of the occupied prison re-created, and stand before the unimaginably small and dark isolation cells. Don't go without the audio tour—the dimension of sound is what brings the ghosts back to these sad halls.

unofficial **TIP**
Definitely too eerie for preschoolers, Alcatraz is significant and memorable for older kids and teenagers.

Cable Car Museum

APPEAL BY AGE	PRESCHOOL ★★★	GRADE SCHOOL ★★★★	TEENS ★★★
YOUNG ADULTS ★★		OVER 30 ★★★	SENIORS ★★★

1201 Mason Street, Nob Hill; ☎ 415-474-1887; www.cablecarmuseum.com

Hours *October–March:* daily, 10 a.m.–5 p.m.; *April–September:* daily, 10 a.m.–6 p.m. **Admission** Free, but donations welcome. **Touring time** Average 1 hour; minimum 30 minutes. **Rainy-day touring** Yes. **Restaurants** No. **Alcoholic beverages** No. **Disabled access** Limited. **Wheelchair rental** No. **Baby-stroller rental** No. **Lockers** No. **Pet kennels** No. **Rain check** No. **Private tours** No.

DESCRIPTION AND COMMENTS   School-age kids are fascinated by the cable car, not just because it is open-air but because it is propelled by some mysterious force that requires a strong man to yank on big metal handles. A fairly brief visit to this extremely noisy museum will dispel the mystery in a most enjoyable way. The functioning hub of the cable-car system, this 1907 redbrick building sits atop the vast pulley-and-cable network that hauls the cars up Nob Hill, and enough of that network is visible to make it understandable to kids. What our daughter found even more fascinating than the cables and the prototype cars, however, were the ancient 25-cent photo viewfinders that show before-and-after pictures from the great 1906 quake and fire—she was astounded by the devastation and amazed at how the city rebuilt itself.

California Academy of Sciences

APPEAL BY AGE	PRESCHOOL ★★★	GRADE SCHOOL ★★★★½	TEENS ★★★★½
YOUNG ADULTS ★★★★½		OVER 30 ★★★★½	SENIORS ★★★★½

55 Music Concourse Drive, Golden Gate Park, San Francisco; ☎ 415-379-8000; www.calacademy.org

Hours Daily, 9:30 a.m.–5 p.m. **Admission** $24.95 adults; $19.95 seniors, students, and youths ages 12–17; $14.95 children ages 7–11; free for children age 6 and under; free for all ages the third Wednesday of each month. **Touring time** Average 2–3 hours; minimun 1½ hours. **Rainy-day touring** Yes. **Restaurants** Yes. **Alcoholic beverages** Yes. **Disabled access** Yes. **Wheelchair rental** Yes. **Baby-stroller rental** No. **Lockers** No. **Pet kennels** No. **Rain check** No. **Private tours** Yes.

DESCRIPTION AND COMMENTS   The academy's permanent home in Golden Gate Park reopened recently after a massive ten-year renovation, and you won't want to miss a chance to experience it. The new facility is, appropriately, as green as can be, starting with its 197,000-square-foot "living roof," lushly landscaped with 1.7 million native plants and grasses. (An observation tower affords good views of this remarkable urban garden.) This place is huge, so you might want to focus on just one or two areas, coming back for another visit later if you have time. Start on the lower level, which will take you from the reaches of the universe to the depths of the ocean, via the state-of-the-art Planetarium, which gets real-time feeds from NASA missions, and the Aquarium, which includes a gorgeous deep-water Philippine-style reef, a look under California's waters, and a dazzling exhibit showing the underwater life on the floor of the Amazon rain forest in rainy season. (This exhibit continues up all three floors, so you can climb up from the bottom to the top of a rain forest.) On the main floor you'll find a fun preschooler play area, a cafe, a fun shop, and several exhibits, ranging from the traditional dioramas in the Tusher African Center to a re-created swamp stocked with real live alligators. On the top floor are the upper reaches of the simulated Amazon forest and a naturalist center where kids can help with research and examine cool things from the natural world up close. Even the Web site has a lot to explore, from penguin cams to explanations of the world's ecosystems. The admission is steep, but it includes the excellent Planetarium show.

de Young Museum

APPEAL BY AGE	PRESCHOOL ★★	GRADE SCHOOL ★★★	TEENS ★★★
YOUNG ADULTS ★★★★	OVER 30 ★★★★		SENIORS ★★★★

50 Hagiwara Tea Garden Drive, Golden Gate Park; ☎ 415-750-3600; www.famsf.org/deyoung

Hours Tuesday–Sunday, 9:30 a.m.–5:15 p.m.; open Friday until 8:45 p.m.; closed New Year's Day, Thanksgiving, and Christmas. **Admission** $10 adults, $7 youths 13–17 and college students, $7 seniors, free for children age 12 and under. **Touring time** Average 3 hours; minimum 1 hour. **Rainy-day touring** Yes. **Restaurants** Yes. **Alcoholic beverages** Yes. **Disabled access** Yes. **Wheelchair rental** Yes, free loaners. **Baby-stroller rental** No. **Lockers** Bag check. **Pet kennels** No. **Rain check** No. **Private tours** Yes.

DESCRIPTION AND COMMENTS   The beloved de Young Museum may go back to 1895, but today's version is a sleek, modern facility that offers twice the museum space of the original on a much smaller footprint. And the same beautiful Golden Gate Park surrounds it. This is a very fine fine-art museum with one of the best collections of American paintings in the nation, along with American sculpture, decorative art, and exciting collections from sub-Saharan Africa, New Guinea, the Americas, and Oceania. These latter collections are typically the most engaging for kids: the masks, totem poles, figures, charms, and weapons holders are totally cool. Try to visit on Saturday mornings, when the museum offers free drop-in art classes for kids ages 3½ to 12; Friday nights from April through November are also devoted to family activities. If you have a budding artist, stop by the Kimball Education Gallery on Wednesday through Sunday afternoons, when you can see the visiting artist of the month at work; he or she will be happy to chat with young-sters. The changing exhibitions typically feature modern American art and are often appealing to teenagers.

 ## Exploratorium

APPEAL BY AGE	PRESCHOOL ★★★★	GRADE SCHOOL ★★★★½	TEENS ★★★★½
YOUNG ADULTS ★★★★½		OVER 30 ★★★★½	SENIORS ★★★★½

Palace of Fine Arts, 3601 Lyon Street; ☎ 415-563-7337; www.exploratorium.com

Hours Tuesday–Sunday, 10 a.m.–5 p.m.; closed Mondays, Thanksgiving, Christmas Eve, and Christmas Day. **Admission** $14 adults ages 18–64, $11 seniors age 65 and older and students over age 18 with ID, $11 people with disabilities and children ages 13–17, $9 children ages 4–12, free for children age 3 and under. Free admission on the first Wednesday of each month, but groups of 10 or more must make reservations. **Touring time** Average 4 hours; minimum 2 hours. **Rainy-day touring** Yes. **Restaurants** Yes. **Alcoholic beverages** No. **Disabled access** Yes. **Wheelchair rental** Yes, free. **Baby-stroller rental** No. **Lockers** Yes. **Pet kennels** No. **Rain check** No. **Private tours** No.

DESCRIPTION AND COMMENTS   Even childless adults find themselves drawn back to the Exploratorium, so seductive are its science-geek charms. More than 650 hands-on exhibits fill a sprawling, warehouse-style space within the grand Palace of Fine Arts on the west end of the Marina District; there's so much to experience that you may want to visit twice to do the place justice. Kids and grown-ups get to feel, touch, see, and wonder at the particle accelerator, the Shadow Box, the two-way mirrors, the interactive video disks, the computer finger painting, the optical illusions—the list goes on and on. Kids older than age 7 (and their parents) who aren't claustrophobic or skittish can brave the Tac-tile Dome, where you squeeze through in total darkness, experiencing only touch sensations. Each "exhibit" is really an activity: a machine, a device, or a Rube Goldberg concoction designed to illustrate a scientific principle. These principles range from the swimming habits of fish to optical illusions to the physics of tornadoes.

On our first visit, the first floor alone (which begins with biology-related exhibits) exhausted us, so we had to return to discover the ultracool area upstairs, with its sight- and sound-perception exhibits. From this mezzanine area, we looked down on the work area where the exhibits are created and were amused and entertained to watch graduate-student types hard at work on these most appreciated of science projects.

unofficial **TIP**
The Exploratorium's grounds alone—rolling lawns, meandering pond, ducks, gorgeous trees— are worth a visit, so pack a picnic lunch to enjoy before or after your exploration.

Scattered throughout the vast space are guides (mostly college students) who love to explain the gizmos to the kids, so don't be shy about flagging them down. And before or after your visit, point your kids to the amazing Web site, where they can learn how to make a mummy, build a spectroscope, or take on any of dozens of other cool projects.

Pier 39

| APPEAL BY AGE | PRESCHOOL ★★ | GRADE SCHOOL ★★★ | TEENS ★★★★ |
| YOUNG ADULTS ★★ | | OVER 30 ★★ | SENIORS ★★ |

Beach Street and the Embarcadero; ☎ 415-981-PIER; www.pier39.com

Hours Daily; hours vary by activity, shop, or restaurant. **Admission** Free overall, but rides charge fees. **Touring time** Average 3 hours; minimum 1 hour. **Rainy-day touring** Yes, for inside activities. **Restaurants** Yes. **Alcoholic beverages** In restaurants. **Disabled access** Yes. **Wheelchair rental** No. **Baby-stroller rental** No. **Lockers** No. **Pet kennels** No, but leashed pets allowed on pier. **Rain check** No. **Private tours** No.

DESCRIPTION AND COMMENTS   This is really a kitschy, crowded mall, not an attraction, but it's a mighty seductive place for kids, and it borders on being a theme park. It can be expensive if you fall prey to the rides and shops, but one of its greatest charms is free: the thriving sea-lion community at the end of the 1,000-foot-long K pier, which fascinates toddlers and teens alike. On weekends, docents offer free programs about the sea lion; call ☎ 415-289-SEAL for details. The view is also free, and it's a doozy, taking in everything from Coit Tower to the Golden Gate Bridge.

After you've enjoyed the simple pleasures, the kids will be on you to start shopping. We'll leave that up to you.

Next, head for **Aquarium of the Bay** (☎ 888-SEA-DIVE or 415-623-5300; **www.aquariumofthebay.com;** admission $14.95 adults, $8 children ages 3 to 11, $8 seniors, family rate $37.95 for two adults and two children), where you walk through 300 feet of acrylic tunnels through a huge aquarium, surrounded by thousands of Bay Area fish. The Blue and Gold Fleet also runs its bay tours from Pier 39 (see "Ferries" under "Getting There Is All the Fun," page 324).

Older kids will want a turn on **Turbo Ride** (☎ 415-392-8872; admission $12.95 adults, $9.95 seniors and children), a simulated roller coaster with high-tech special effects that gives a pretty impressive thrill but is too scary for many young children. While the big kids are on Turbo Ride, you can take younger ones to the low-key double-decker carousel.

Other kid fun includes the 10,000-square-foot video arcade called **Riptide,** cookie vendors, and lots of shops (the **Marine Mammal Center Store,** the **National Park Store, Houdini's Magic Shop,** and **Fairyland** are big hits). If you have teens who need time away from parents, Pier 39 is a good, self-contained place to drop them off for a few hours.

San Francisco Museum of Modern Art

APPEAL BY AGE	PRESCHOOL ★★	GRADE SCHOOL ★★★	TEENS ★★★
YOUNG ADULTS ★★★★		OVER 30 ★★★★	SENIORS ★★★★

151 Third Street at Mission; ☎ 415-357-4000; www.sfmoma.com

Hours Friday–Tuesday, 11 a.m.–5:45 p.m.; Thursday, 11 a.m.–8:45 p.m.; closed major holidays and Wednesdays. **Admission** $12.50 adults, $8 seniors age 62 and older, $7 students with current ID, free for children age 12 and under; first Tuesday of each month free; Thursday 6–8:45 p.m. is half price. **Touring time** Average 3 hours; minimum 1 hour. **Rainy-day touring** Yes. **Restaurants** Yes. **Alcoholic beverages** Yes. **Disabled access** Yes. **Wheelchair rental** Yes, free. **Baby-stroller rental** No. **Lockers** No. **Pet kennels** No. **Rain check** No. **Private tours** Yes.

DESCRIPTION AND COMMENTS   This heavily patronized museum is nice and compact, so museum fatigue never gets a chance to set in. Our 11-year-old daughter had learned about Frida Kahlo and Jackson Pollock in school and was pleased to find their works represented here. The small permanent collection of 20th-century masters is a minitour of modern art, and the changing exhibits often include photography, which can be highly accessible to kids in a museum setting. A very low-key interactive area of four computers with headsets attached allowed us to click on a painting we'd seen to learn more—and the five-minute "Making Sense of Modern Art" presentation explained what parents couldn't in an hour.

San Francisco Zoo

APPEAL BY AGE	PRESCHOOL ★★★★½	GRADE SCHOOL ★★★★	TEENS ★★★
YOUNG ADULTS ★★★		OVER 30 ★★★	SENIORS ★★★

1 Zoo Road, 45th Avenue at Sloat Boulevard, Golden Gate Park;
☎ 415-753-7080; www.sfzoo.org

Hours Daily, 10 a.m.–5 p.m. **Admission** Non–San Francisco residents: $15 adults, $12 seniors age 65 and older, $9 children ages 4–14, free for children age 3 and under; discount for San Francisco residents; first Wednesday of each month free for San Francisco residents. **Touring time** Average 3 hours; minimum 1 hour. **Rainy-day touring** Limited. **Restaurants** Yes. **Alcoholic beverages** Yes. **Disabled access** Limited. **Wheelchair rental** Yes, $10. **Baby-stroller rental** Yes, single $6 and double $9. **Lockers** No. **Pet kennels** Yes. **Rain check** No. **Private tours** No.

DESCRIPTION AND COMMENTS   After years of gradual improvements, this old zoo has become a pretty wonderful place to spend an afternoon, and it's a must-visit for families with children younger than 7 or so, thanks to the exceptional Children's Zoo. Located right near the entrance, it goes far beyond the typical mangy petting area. There's the Family Farm, with plenty of animals to pet, but also a chick hatchery, a nature trail, families of mice, and an enthralling indoor Insect Zoo. Just outside its entrance is a good playground and carousel ($2 a ride). Young kids could spend an hour or two here and happily skip the larger zoo. But that's not to say it deserves skipping—there's plenty to see, in improved, more naturalistic settings. Our two favorites are the huge Jones Family Gorilla Preserve and the Primate Discovery Center, home to many species of rare and endangered monkeys, but that's just the beginning; make sure you don't miss Grizzly Gulch, a one-acre naturalistic habitat for sister grizzly bears Kachina and Kiona, whom the zoo saved from being euthanized in Montana. Our kids also loved seeing the penguins get their dinner, at 2:30 p.m. every day.

Yerba Buena Gardens

APPEAL BY AGE	PRESCHOOL ★★★★	GRADE SCHOOL ★★★★	TEENS ★★★★
YOUNG ADULTS ★★★		OVER 30 ★★★	SENIORS ★★★

(See map on page 318.)

Rooftop of Moscone Center, bordered by Mission, Third, Folsom, and Fourth streets; ☎ 415-978-2787; www.yerbabuenagardens.com; skating or bowling: ☎ 415-820-3532; www.skatebowl.com

Hours Gardens open 6 a.m.–10 p.m. daily; hours vary for attractions. **Admission** Free to gardens and playground; carousel ride $4; skating center $8 adults, $5.50 seniors age 55 and older, $6.25 children; bowling fees vary; $3 skate rental. **Touring time** Average 1 hour; minimum 30 minutes. **Rainy-day touring** Yes for indoor attractions, no for gardens. **Restaurants** Yes. **Alcoholic beverages** No. **Disabled access** Yes. **Wheelchair rental** No. **Baby-stroller rental** No. **Lockers** No. **Pet kennels** No. **Rain check** No. **Private tours** No.

DESCRIPTION AND COMMENTS   Spread over the vast squatness of the Moscone Center, this rooftop children's center has something for every kid, from sand play for toddlers to the ultracool Zeum for tech-crazy teens. For a description of the park, see "The Best Beaches and Parks" at the beginning of this chapter; for details on Zeum, see its attraction profile on the next page.

Aside from the park space and Zeum, Yerba Buena Gardens has several kid-pleasing opportunities. First is the ornate, hand-carved 1906 carousel, which is unfortunately housed in a glass structure. It's unaesthetic, but it was deemed necessary to protect the carousel from the elements and give it more operating days. Inside or out, the attraction is well worth a ride; next to it is a food cart serving hot dogs and snacks.

Past Zeum, near the playground, are the two other indoor amusements: the Ice Skating Center and the Bowling Center. Both are state of the art; the huge window in the skating rink offers a great view of downtown San Francisco, so you almost feel as if you're skating outside, and the bowling alley is spotless and cheerful, unlike most urban bowling alleys, which tend toward the grim.

An entire day could easily be passed here. Gather for a picnic in the park, then send older kids into Zeum to make a video or work on an art project while you sip a latte (yes, there's a Starbucks) and watch the little ones ride the carousel and play in the playground, then treat the whole gang to a session of skating or bowling. You could end the day by walking to the mall next door to catch a movie.

 ## Zeum

| APPEAL BY AGE | PRESCHOOL ★ | GRADE SCHOOL ★★★★½ | TEENS ★★★★½ |
| YOUNG ADULTS ★★★★ | | OVER 30 ★★★ | SENIORS ★★★ |

Yerba Buena Gardens, 221 Fourth Street, South of Market;
☎ **415-820-3320; www.zeum.org**

Hours During school year, Wednesday–Sunday, 11 a.m.–5 p.m., and specified weekday afternoons for special workshops; summer: Tuesday–Sunday, 11 a.m.– 5 p.m. **Admission** $10 adults, $8 students and seniors, $8 kids ages 3–18; free for members. **Touring time** Average 3 hours; minimum 2 hours. **Rainy-day touring** Yes. **Restaurants** No. **Alcoholic beverages** No. **Disabled access** No. **Wheelchair rental** No. **Baby-stroller rental** No. **Lockers** No. **Pet kennels** No. **Rain check** No. **Private tours** No.

DESCRIPTION AND COMMENTS   If there was ever a place that will make you wish to be 12 years old again, Zeum is it. A nonprofit, wildly creative, hands-on art and technology center, this is more a big-kid arts play place than a museum. In the Animators Studio, kids sketch characters of their own making, storyboard a story, then bring it to life in a Claymation film. They get to do every step of the process (with help from plenty of staff members if needed). It was a dream come true for our 10-year-old, who could have spent days here. In the Learning Lab, kids try digital photography and digital animation, and if that's not fun enough, they can design their own Web pages. In the Production Lab, kids work together (bring friends!) to make a multimedia video—they're the actors, directors, special-effects technicians, sound-effects technicians, and camera operators. In the Main Gallery, the artists-in-residence help kids do everything from build architectural models to publish their own books.

Zeum is heaven for kids from about the second or third grade through high school, but it's boring for younger ones, who won't have the patience or the physical skills necessary to tackle these projects. And be forewarned that this is not a quick-drop-in place—come prepared to spend the afternoon so that your children have time to become fully absorbed. The last time we were here, the city was mobbed, but Zeum was half empty, with plenty of staff members and easy access to the labs and studios.

FAMILY-FRIENDLY RESTAURANTS

Benihana
1737 Post Street, Union Square; ☎ 415-563-4844; www.benihana.com

Meals served Lunch and dinner. **Cuisine** Japanese. **Entree range** $17–$45. **Kids' menu** $8–$10. **Reservations** Recommended. **Payment** All major credit cards.

SURE, IT'S TOURISTY AND GIMMICKY, but it's great fun for kids, and the mainstream Japanese food is fine and not threatening to picky eaters. You sit around a grill as a showman chef cooks your mea while tossing knives, cutting food in midair, flipping shrimp, and making jokes. It's so entertaining that they're more likely to try some new, scary food.

Café Zoetrope
916 Kearny Street, North Beach; ☎ 415-291-1700; www.cafecoppola.com

Meals served Lunch and dinner (closed Monday). **Cuisine** Italian. **Entree range** Lunch and dinner, $11–$18. **Reservations** Recommended. **Payment** All major credit cards.

A HIT WITH TEENS, this cool North Beach trattoria is owned by filmmaker Francis Ford Coppola (whom they may know as Sofia Coppola's dad). It's full of movie mementos and North Beach personality, and the reasonably priced salads (get the Caesar), pastas, and pizzas are excellent. Parents will appreciate the good wine list, including, of course, Coppola's own vintages.

California Pizza Kitchen
524 Van Ness Avenue; ☎ 415-436-9380; www.cpk.com

Meals served Lunch and dinner. **Cuisine** Californian. **Entree range** Lunch and dinner, $7–$15. **Kids' menu** $5. **Reservations** Not accepted. **Payment** All major credit cards.

DESPITE SAN FRANCISCO'S POPULARITY as a family vacation spot, it's not always easy to find a good parent-child restaurant, especially in the Civic Center area. This import from LA is your best bet, and it's sure to make you all happy. Kids get a coloring menu, crayons, cups with lids, and tasty little pizzas and pastas; parents get chic designer pizzas and pastas, fresh salads, and wine by the glass.

Fog City Diner
1300 Battery Street, Financial District; ☎ 415-982-2000; www.fogcitydiner.com

Meals served Lunch and dinner. **Cuisine** Modern American. **Entree range** Lunch, $10–$20; dinner, $15–$25. **Kids' menu** No. **Reservations** Recommended. **Payment** All major credit cards.

A GREAT PLACE FOR PARENTS to get a taste of modern American cooking, San Francisco–style, in a lively setting. On the North Beach–Battery waterfront (but lacking a view), Fog City is a cross between a train-car diner and an old San Francisco bar and grill, with roomy booths, an open kitchen, and lots of hustle and bustle. Prices are fair, given the hipness of the place; the food is delicious; and even though there's no kids' menu per se, children are sure to find something they like—the oft-changing menu runs to such things as crab cakes, Cobb salad sandwiches, buffalo burgers, macaroni and gouda cheese with Black Forest ham and sweet peas, and homey desserts. We go in the 3-to-5-p.m. range to avoid the constant crowds.

La Taqueria
2889 Mission Street, Mission District; ☎ 415-285-7117

Meals served Lunch and dinner. **Cuisine** Mexican. **Entree range** $5–$10. **Kids' menu** No. **Reservations** Not accepted. **Payment** No credit cards.

THE LARGELY LATINO MISSION DISTRICT, south of downtown's Market Street, is blessed with many fine taco joints, and this is one of the finest. Timid eaters will be pleased with a cheese quesadilla and a fresh strawberry *licuado* (shake); braver kids will adore the huge burritos and savory soft tacos filled with *pollo* (chicken), *carnitas* (pork), or *carne asada* (grilled beef).

Mel's Drive-In
3355 Geary Boulevard, near Golden Gate Park; ☎ 415-387-2255
2165 Lombard Street, Marina; ☎ 415-921-2867
801 Mission Street; ☎ 415-227-0793
1050 Van Ness Avenue; ☎ 415-292-6358; www.melsdrive-in.com

Meals served Breakfast, lunch, and dinner. **Cuisine** American. **Entree range** Breakfast, $3–$11; lunch, $6–$7; dinner, $7–$14. **Kids' menu** Yes. **Reservations** Not accepted. **Payment** No credit cards.

THE GEARY LOCATION is on the site of an original Mel's, lionized in *American Graffiti* and beloved by many a San Francisco kid. Oldies blare, waitresses talk smart, and milk shakes are thick and good. Our kids adore the kids' menu, the crayons, the music, the floats, and the grilled-cheese sandwiches served in a toy Corvette. The Lombard Street Mel's is well located for a lively diner meal after a visit to the Exploratorium or a skate along the Marina Green.

Mo's Burgers
1322 Grant Avenue, North Beach; ☎ 415-788-3779; www.mosgrill.com

Meals served Breakfast, lunch, and dinner. **Cuisine** American. **Entree range** Breakfast, $6–$15; lunch and dinner, $6–$18. **Kids' menu** Yes. **Reservations** Not accepted. **Payment** MC, V.

THIS IS LIKELY THE BEST BURGER in San Francisco, a town that takes the burger pretty seriously. A simple, friendly spot not far from the Wharf, serving fresh, perfectly cooked burgers.

New Asia Restaurant

772 Pacific Avenue, Chinatown; ☎ 415-391-6666

Meals served Breakfast, lunch, and dinner. **Cuisine** Chinese. **Entree range** $4–$7 (per dim sum order). **Kids' menu** No. **Reservations** Not accepted. **Payment** AE, MC, V.

THE BEST FAMILY-ORIENTED RESTAURANT IN CHINATOWN, New Asia makes a mean dumpling for breakfast or lunch and fine Chinese seafood dishes for dinner. If your kids have never experienced dim sum, with waitresses wheeling around carts laden with dumplings, noodles, meats, and strange sweets, bring them here. They'll recoil in horror at the chicken feet, but they'll love the fluffy white *bao* buns stuffed with pork and the savory little *sui mai*. At dinnertime, kids are always happy with a big plate of Chinese noodles or fried rice. Come early to beat the lunchtime line.

 Taylor's Automatic Refresher

1 Ferry Building, the Embarcadero at Market Street; ☎ 866-328-3663; www.taylorsrefresher.com

Meals served Lunch and dinner. **Cuisine** American. **Entree range** $8–$15. **Kids' menu** No. **Reservations** Not accepted. **Payment** All major credit cards.

THIS SLEEK, MODERN DINER is part of the newly restored Ferry Building, a sort of food lover's mall and the site of a terrific farmers' market on Tuesdays, Thursdays, Saturdays, and Sundays. The diner aesthetic is honored with great burgers, fries, and hand-scooped shakes. But there's more than just diner fare: The ahi burger (cooked rare) is fabulous, the fish tacos are as good as any in Mexico, and the salads are made with fresh farmers' market produce. Be prepared for a long line at rush hours. Try to snag a table outside, where the people-watching is great and the kids can run.

Tommaso's Restaurant

1042 Kearny Street, North Beach; ☎ 415-398-9696; www.tommasosnorthbeach.com

Meals served Dinner. **Cuisine** Italian. **Entree range** $14–$25. **Kids' menu** No. **Reservations** Not accepted. **Payment** All major credit cards.

ALMOST A CLICHÉ of what an old North Beach pizza joint should look like, Tommaso's is the real thing, from its rickety white wooden table nooks to its old brick pizza oven and chipped walls hung with photos of the restaurant's patron saint, Francis Ford Coppola. On the way here, you may have to distract the kids' attention from the nearby triple-X theater, but once inside you'll be rewarded with superb, inexpensive food that's a far cry from Domino's. Calzones are hearty and cheesy, thin-crust pizzas are saucy and delicious, and vegetables hail from local organic farms (if you see the fresh-tomato, mozzarella, and basil salad on special, get it).

SIDE TRIP

Six Flags Discovery Kingdom

APPEAL BY AGE	PRESCHOOL ★★★★	GRADE SCHOOL ★★★★	TEENS ★★★★
YOUNG ADULTS ★★★★		OVER 30 ★★★★	SENIORS ★★★★

1001 Fairgrounds Drive (off I-80), Vallejo; ☎ 707-643-6722; www.sixflags.com

Hours *Spring and fall:* daily, 10 a.m.–8 p.m.; *summer:* daily, 10 a.m.–10 p.m.; closed November–late March. **Admission** $40 adults ($30 online), $30 children less than 48" tall, free for children age 2 and under. **Touring time** Average 6 hours; minimum 3–4 hours. **Rainy-day touring** Yes, but you will get wet. **Restaurants** Yes. **Alcoholic beverages** Yes. **Disabled access** Yes. **Wheelchair rental** Yes. **Baby-stroller rental** Yes. **Lockers** Yes. **Pet kennels** No. **Rain check** No. **Private tours** No."

DESCRIPTION AND COMMENTS   Formerly known as Marine World Africa USA, this animal-oriented theme park is now more thrill oriented (since Six Flags is the operator), but it also emphasizes the marine-life side of the park. Animal shows are the strong suit, each running 20 minutes or so, and many get quite crowded. As at SeaWorld, the killer-whale and dolphin shows are lots of fun (and wet—if you sit in front, you'll get splashed). Traveling on the moving ramp through the Shark Experience, where sharks swim around you on three sides, is a very cool experience; the sea-lion show is charming; the animal-vs.-people Olympics is a hoot; and the Dolphin Discovery, where you can touch, train, and feed bottlenose dolphins, is a hit with kids. If you get lucky, there may be a baby animal or two to see at the Veterinary Clinic's Nursery.

Out of water, you'll find lots of animals from around the world in different park zones, from camels to cougars, and the experiences are interactive whenever possible, whether it's petting an elephant or feeding a giraffe. (The Butterfly Exhibit is particularly enchanting for young ones.) In the process, kids learn quite a bit about animals, their habitats, their diets, and their fragility in a people-dominated world.

When your 6-year-old has had enough of sitting through shows and needs to blow off steam, he'll have fun trying the modest rides in Thomas Town, named for a certain train engine, or playing in the Looney Tunes play area, which also has some young-kid-friendly rides, including a carousel and a mini-coaster. Meanwhile, big kids can head for the intense thrill rides, such as Medusa, the tallest, fastest, and longest roller coaster in Northern California.

Note that families staying in San Francisco can reach Marine World via the Blue and Gold Fleet, with a combination ticket that includes both the scenic one-hour ferry ride and park admission.

BERKELEY

NATIONALLY KNOWN AS THE HOME of the **University of California, Berkeley,** and one of the birthplaces of the hippie movement, Berkeley is a dynamic little city that is particularly wonderful for teenagers. The campus is inspirational to wander, and the still-funky downtown is colorful and great fun to shop, thick with coffeehouses, bookstores, theaters, handmade jewelry, and street musicians. Kids of all ages will like the cool, hands-on **Lawrence Hall of Science** on campus, as well as the sprawling Charles Lee Tilden Park on the outskirts of town (see "The Best Beaches and Parks," page 314). East of San Francisco across the bay, this college town can be easily reached on a BART subway or by car across the Bay Bridge; taxi rides are costly.

unofficial **TIP**
Most 16-year-olds could spend a week in Berkeley and not be bored.

FAMILY LODGING

Claremont Resort and Spa
41 Tunnel Road, Berkeley; ☎ 877-551-7266 or 510-843-3000; www.claremontresort.com; $329 and up

THIS GRAND WHITE VICTORIAN RAMBLER in the Berkeley hills (on the Oakland border) is the place for society locals to have weddings and parties, and now that the former stuffiness has relaxed enough to inspire the creation of a kids' program, it's a terrific family retreat as well. Hotel guests can take advantage of The Club at the Claremont, a sort of country club within a resort; it includes two beautiful pools, ten tennis courts, a fitness center, a spa, and a comprehensive children's program including kids' tennis and yoga and a Friday-night movie.

Rose Garden Inn
2740 Telegraph Avenue, Berkeley; ☎ 800-992-9005 or 510-549-2145; www.rosegardeninn.com; $99–$245

AS SWEET A PLACE AS ITS NAME SUGGESTS, this longtime favorite of visiting professors occupies two old mansions and three other buildings in the middle of the good shopping and walking area near the UC Berkeley campus.

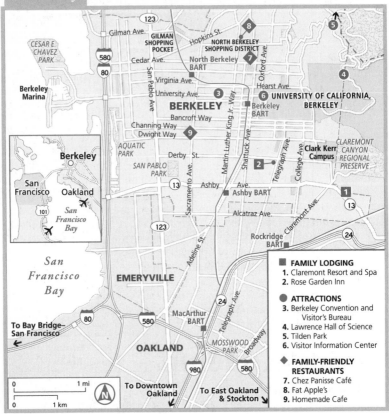

berkeley

FAMILY LODGING
1. Claremont Resort and Spa
2. Rose Garden Inn

ATTRACTIONS
3. Berkeley Convention and Visitor's Bureau
4. Lawrence Hall of Science
5. Tilden Park
6. Visitor Information Center

FAMILY-FRIENDLY RESTAURANTS
7. Chez Panisse Café
8. Fat Apple's
9. Homemade Cafe

It has all the charm of a bed-and-breakfast (fireplaces, quirky rooms, evening wine and cheese), but unlike most, it welcomes families—some rooms are big enough for several, and they'll bring in a futon for $10 more. There's a lawn to play on outside, and kids love the afternoon cookies and milk.

ATTRACTION

Lawrence Hall of Science

APPEAL BY AGE	PRESCHOOL ★★★	GRADE SCHOOL ★★★★	TEENS ★★★★
YOUNG ADULTS ★★★		OVER 30 ★★★	SENIORS ★★★

Centennial Drive below Grizzly Peak Boulevard, UC Berkeley;
☎ **510-642-5132; www.lawrencehallofscience.org**

Hours Daily, 10 a.m.–5 p.m. **Admission** $11 adults ages 19–61; $9 students ages 7–18, disabled guests, and seniors age 62 and older; $6 children ages 3–6; free for children age 2 and under. **Touring time** Average 3 hours; minimum 2 hours. **Rainy-day touring** Yes. **Restaurants** Yes. **Alcoholic beverages** No. **Disabled access** Yes. **Wheelchair rental** No. **Baby-stroller rental** No. **Lockers** No. **Pet kennels** No. **Rain check** No. **Private tours** No.

DESCRIPTION AND COMMENTS   A smaller version of San Francisco's Exploratorium, this university science museum encourages kids to touch and experience, starting with the 60-foot-long DNA model outside, which doubles as a climbing structure. A particular favorite of our kids is the Biology Discovery Lab, which on weekends and summer days allows them to examine frogs, pet snakes, and hold a tarantula. Elsewhere they can play math puzzle games, try to get magnets through a maze, look through telescopes, create their own laser-light show, and get inside the human brain. Prepare for some serious begging for a souvenir from the exceptional gift shop, stocked with gee-whiz toys, science experiments, puzzles, books, and all sorts of fun and educational kid stuff.

FAMILY-FRIENDLY RESTAURANTS

 Chez Panisse Café

1517 Shattuck Avenue, Berkeley; ☎ 510-548-5049; www.chezpanisse.com

Meals served Lunch and dinner. **Cuisine** Modern American. **Entree range** Lunch, $12–$18; dinner, $14–$34. **Kids' menu** Weekdays only. **Reservations** Not accepted. **Payment** All major credit cards.

IF YOUR KIDS ARE THE LEAST BIT INTERESTED in food—or if you are—bring them to the casual cafe above chef Alice Waters's more serious restaurant, the birthplace of California cuisine. It's lively, friendly to kids (they even get crayons), and moderately priced, considering the restaurant's international fame and the exceptional quality of the food. Thanks to Waters's slavish devotion to farm-fresh produce (most grown just for this restaurant), even the simplest cheese pizza sings with flavor. Choose from great salads, sophisticated pizzas, grilled fish, and homey desserts. To beat the crowds, we like to come for a very early lunch.

Fat Apple's
1346 Martin Luther King Jr. Way, Berkeley; ☎ 510-526-2260

Meals served Breakfast, lunch, and.dinner. **Cuisine** American. **Entree range** Lunch, $7–$10; dinner, $10–$15. **Kids' menu** No. **Reservations** Not accepted. **Payment** MC, V.

FANS DRIVE ACROSS THE BAY BRIDGE to sit in this plain coffee shop and eat some terrific diner cooking: oatmeal-apple pancakes, homemade soups, dreamy cheese puffs, perfect burgers, and fresh-berry pies. There's no need to have a kids' menu when you have a grown-up menu that speaks so profoundly to kids.

Homemade Cafe
2454 Sacramento Street, Berkeley; ☎ 510-845-1940

Meals served Breakfast (available all day) and lunch. **Cuisine** American. **Entree range** $7–$11. **Kids' menu** No. **Reservations** Not accepted. **Payment** No credit cards.

BREAKFAST NIRVANA, known for its pancakes, French toast, and egg scrambles. As is usually the case at great breakfast cafes, however, there's always a crowd, so be prepared to wait. Lunch runs to clever, tasty sandwiches.

MARIN COUNTY

WITH ITS REDWOOD FORESTS, CREEKS, ROLLING HILLS, and proximity to San Francisco just across the Golden Gate Bridge, it's no surprise that Marin County is home to some of the priciest real estate in the nation. Fortunately, you don't have to take on a million-dollar mortgage to enjoy its spectacular parks, beaches, and atmospheric small towns. Under "The Best Beaches and Parks" and "Family Outdoor Adventures," you'll find details on Marin's great outdoors, from **Muir Woods** walks to **Tomales Bay** kayaking to **Mount Tamalpais** mountain biking. En route to these adventures, you'll find spiffy towns worth a stop, stroll, and nosh, especially **Mill Valley, Larkspur, Olema,** and **San Rafael.** From San Francisco, you can reach two of the county's most popular and charming towns, **Sausalito** and **Tiburon,** by ferry; both are fun to explore.

FAMILY LODGING

Point Reyes Seashore Lodge
10021 Coastal Highway 1 (CA 1), Olema; ☎ 800-404-5634 or 415-663-9000; www.pointreyesseashore.com; $135–$295

IDEALLY LOCATED ALONGSIDE OLEMA CREEK at the edge of Point Reyes National Seashore, this country inn is more family-friendly than many places in these parts. Done in a modern Victorian style, it has 23 rooms and two cottages, and several of the accommodations can handle a family (the private Creekside Cottage, with kitchen and hot tub, is our favorite). The grounds encompass lawns, woods, walkways, Adirondack chairs for quiet reading, and a trail to the national seashore headquarters; inside is a game room and library. The neighboring restaurant, the Farm House (see profile on page 348), is a welcoming, casual place with a take-out deli attached.

marin county

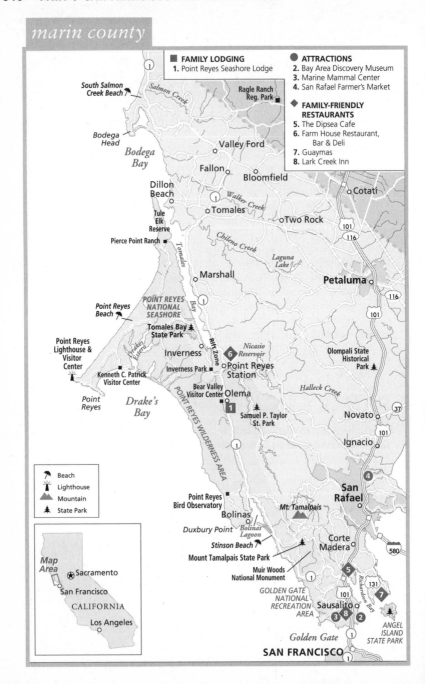

■ **FAMILY LODGING**
1. Point Reyes Seashore Lodge

● **ATTRACTIONS**
2. Bay Area Discovery Museum
3. Marine Mammal Center
4. San Rafael Farmer's Market

◆ **FAMILY-FRIENDLY RESTAURANTS**
5. The Dipsea Cafe
6. Farm House Restaurant, Bar & Deli
7. Guaymas
8. Lark Creek Inn

South Salmon Creek Beach

Salmon Creek

Ragle Ranch Reg. Park

Bodega Head

Bodega Bay

Valley Ford

Fallon

Dillon Beach

Bloomfield

Cotati

Walker Creek

Tule Elk Reserve

Tomales

Two Rock

101

116

Pierce Point Ranch

Chileno Creek

Laguna Lake

Petaluma

Marshall

116

POINT REYES NATIONAL SEASHORE

101

Point Reyes Beach

Tomales Bay State Park

Nicasio Reservoir

Point Reyes Lighthouse & Visitor Center

Inverness

Olompali State Historical Park

Inverness Park

Point Reyes Station

Kenneth C. Patrick Visitor Center

Bear Valley Visitor Center

Olema

Halleck Creek

Point Reyes

Drake's Bay

Samuel P. Taylor St. Park

Novato

37

Ignacio

101

1

🏖 Beach

🗼 Lighthouse

🔺 Mountain

🌲 State Park

Point Reyes Bird Observatory

Mt. Tamalpais

San Rafael

Bolinas

Duxbury Point

Bolinas Lagoon

Corte Madera

Stinson Beach

Mount Tamalpais State Park

580

Muir Woods National Monument

Map Area

Sacramento

San Francisco

CALIFORNIA

Los Angeles

GOLDEN GATE NATIONAL RECREATION AREA

Richardson Bay

131

Sausalito

ANGEL ISLAND STATE PARK

Golden Gate

SAN FRANCISCO

101

ATTRACTIONS

☀ Bay Area Discovery Museum

APPEAL BY AGE	PRESCHOOL ★★★★	GRADE SCHOOL ★★★★	TEENS ★★★
YOUNG ADULTS ★★		OVER 30 ★★	SENIORS ★★

Fort Baker, 557 McReynolds Road, Sausalito; ☎ 415-339-3900; www. badm.org

Hours Tuesday–Friday, 9 a.m.–4 p.m.; Saturday and Sunday, 10 a.m.–5 p.m. **Admission** $10 for adults, $8 for children. **Touring time** Average 2 hours; minimum 1 hour. **Rainy-day touring** Yes. **Restaurants** Lunch cafe. **Alcoholic beverages** No. **Disabled access** Yes. **Wheelchair rental** No. **Baby-stroller rental** No. **Lockers** No. **Pet kennels** No. **Rain check** No. **Private tours** No.

DESCRIPTION AND COMMENTS   Tucked under the Marin side of the Golden Gate Bridge, this is one of the better children's museums in California, especially for kids younger than 11. It's hands-on, interactive, and fun, emphasizing the bay-side location instead of generic kid stuff. Kids love the Underwater Sea Tunnel, which lets them crawl "under" the bay, and the full-size Fishing Boat. Other cool exhibits include Everybody Builds, where kids get to both create and climb about giant nests and webs, and the construction site for a scaled-down Golden Gate Bridge, which kids get to help build.. There's a separate, equally fun play area for toddlers, a decent cafe, and a cool gift shop. There's even a carousel for kids who insist on a theme-park ride.

Marine Mammal Center

APPEAL BY AGE	PRESCHOOL ★★	GRADE SCHOOL ★★★	TEENS ★★★
YOUNG ADULTS ★★★		OVER 30 ★★★	SENIORS ★★★

Marin Headlands, near Sausalito; ☎ 415-289-7325; www.tmmc.org

Hours Daily, 10 a.m.–4 p.m.; closed Thanksgiving, Christmas, and New Year's Day. **Admission** Free. **Touring time** Average 1½ hours; minimum 45 minutes. **Rainy-day touring** Yes. **Restaurants** No. **Alcoholic beverages** No. **Disabled access** Yes. **Wheelchair rental** No. **Baby-stroller rental** No. **Lockers** No. **Pet kennels** No. **Rain check** No. **Private tours** No, but docents available on weekends.

DESCRIPTION AND COMMENTS   Part of the Golden Gate National Recreation Area, this nonprofit organization rescues, rehabilitates, and releases ocean mammals that have been injured or orphaned or that become ill. It's one of the largest wild-animal hospitals in the world, and although it was closed for renovation at press time, by mid-2009 it will return to welcoming animal-loving children, who can observe the volunteers and vets tending to the sea lions, dolphins, seals, and otters. Exhibits teach kids about the mammals and about marine ecology and conservation.

San Rafael Farmers' Market

APPEAL BY AGE	PRESCHOOL ★★★★	GRADE SCHOOL ★★★★	TEENS ★★★★
YOUNG ADULTS ★★★★		OVER 30 . ★★★★	SENIORS ★★★★

Fourth Street, San Rafael; ☎ 415-492-8007; www.sanrafaelmarket.org

Hours April–September: Thursday, 5–8 p.m. **Admission** Free. **Touring time** Average 1 hour; minimum 30 minutes. **Rainy-day touring** Yes, but you'll get wet. **Restaurants** In town. **Alcoholic beverages** In town. **Disabled access** Yes. **Wheelchair rental** No. **Baby-stroller rental** No. **Lockers** No. **Pet kennels** No. **Rain check** No. **Private tours** No.

DESCRIPTION AND COMMENTS   One of the nation's best farmers' markets is held every Thursday evening from April through September in downtown San Rafael on Fourth Street, and it's worth a detour. The center alone is worth a look as one of the last and most significant of Frank Lloyd Wright's buildings. And the market is as much fun for kids as for food-loving baby boomers. There's usually a balloon artist and storyteller, a man on roller skates selling eggs, street musicians, and a small-town party atmosphere. Along with superb organic produce, you can buy boutique cheeses, condiments, oils, and fresh breads, and graze on tamales, pancakes, and sausage sandwiches.

FAMILY-FRIENDLY RESTAURANTS

The Dipsea Cafe
200 Shoreline Highway, Mill Valley; ☎ 415-381-0298; www.dipseacafe.com

Meals served Breakfast and lunch. **Cuisine** American. **Entree range** $8–$15. **Kids' menu** $5–$7. **Reservations** Not accepted. **Payment** All major credit cards.

A FANTASY FAMILY RESTAURANT done up like a 19th-century farmhouse, Dipsea is idyllically located creek-side, and picture windows bring in views of the footbridge and ducks outside. This is a fine spot to fuel up for a hike along one of the terrific, not-too-challenging local trails. Although the cooking can suffer from a slapdash approach, it's generally quite satisfying: pancakes, eggs, biscuits, and smoothies for breakfast, and burgers, Caesar salad, and grilled-ahi salads for lunch.

Farm House Restaurant, Bar & Deli
10005 Highway 1 (CA 1), Olema; ☎ 415-663-1264; www.olemafarmhouse.com

Meals served Lunch and dinner; breakfast on weekends only. **Cuisine** American. **Entree range** Lunch, $9–$20; dinner, $10–$25; breakfast, $5–$12. **Kids' menu** No. **Reservations** Recommended. **Payment** All major credit cards.

BOTH CONVENIENT AND CHARMING, this is a good place to eat before or after a day at Point Reyes, thanks to its location near the lighthouse, beaches, and visitors center. On your way into the 1856 farmhouse building, take a peek at the cowhide-upholstered saloon—it will wow any cowboy-loving kid. In the boarding-house-style dining room, people put away large portions of clam chowder, oyster stew, barbecued oysters, ribs, burgers, and cioppino, as well as hearty, good-quality breakfasts. There's no children's menu, but kids will have no trouble finding something good (without slimy oysters) to eat. The adjacent deli can supply you for a Point Reyes picnic.

Guaymas
5 Main Street, Tiburon; ☎ 415-435-6300; www.guaymasrestaurant.com

Meals served Lunch and dinner. **Cuisine** Mexican. **Entree range** $14–$25. **Kids' menu** No. **Reservations** Accepted. **Payment** All major credit cards.

IF THE SUN IS SHINING, take advantage of it and treat the kids to a 30-minute ferry ride to the impossibly bucolic town of Tiburon (the ferry passes right by Alcatraz, which is a thrill). This slick waterfront restaurant, just a few steps from the ferry landing, is most notable for its huge patio with a fabulous view of the bay and San Francisco. The yuppified Mexican food is perfectly fine, especially when accompanied by a margarita and the dreamy view. There's no kids' menu, but the kitchen is happy to make plain quesadillas. If you score the right patio table, you can let the kids scramble over adjacent waterfront rocks while you linger awhile and watch them from your seat.

Lark Creek Inn
234 Magnolia Avenue, Larkspur; ☎ 415-924-7766; www.larkcreek.com

Meals served Dinner, Sunday brunch. **Cuisine** Modern American. **Entree range** Brunch, $11–$17; dinner, $22–$36. **Kids' menu** Yes. **Reservations** Essential. **Payment** All major credit cards.

A VERY SPECIAL SPECIAL-OCCASION RESTAURANT, Lark Creek is a wonderful place to experience California cuisine. Located in a turn-of-the-19th-century mansion at the edge of a redwood canyon a short drive north of the Golden Gate Bridge, this is one of the best restaurants in the Bay Area, with or without kids. Unlike at the region's other top restaurants, however, children are warmly welcomed and catered to with their own menu (field-green salads, great chicken fingers, pasta). The kitchen takes American classics—crab Cobb salad, grilled quail salad, oak-roasted chicken—to lofty levels, and the desserts alone (butterscotch pudding, devil's food cake with espresso ice cream) are worth the trip. In summer, request a garden table outside.

SAN JOSE

WITH A POPULATION OF MORE THAN 900,000, San Jose may be bigger than San Francisco, but it's nowhere near the tourist destination that the City by the Bay is—although its fame as the hub of high-tech industry has made it a major business-travel destination and the home of the wonderful **Tech Museum,** which is well worth a trip in itself. It's at the southern tip of San Francisco Bay, about an hour's drive south from downtown San Francisco and a 90-minute drive from Monterey. That can make it a good stop on a road trip, especially on weekends, when hotel rates plummet to half the cost of weeknights.

San Jose's an important city historically—it was founded in 1777 and was the state's first capital—but families with computer-savvy kids will be more interested in the city's role in the future, as symbolized by **The Tech Museum of Innovation** (see profile, page 354).

Close by San Jose are a number of attractive little towns—**Los Gatos, Saratoga, Campbell,** and **Gilroy**—that we won't discuss here, but you should know that not only are they centers of adult tourist pleasures, with wineries, historic districts, hiking, and fine restaurants, but they can also be pleasant for a lunch stop or afternoon hike or park visit with kids.

 ## FAMILY LODGING

Hotel De Anza
233 West Santa Clara Street, San Jose; ☎ 800-843-3700 or 408-286-1000; www.hoteldeanza.com; $149–$299

THERE'S NO DENYING that this is primarily a business hotel, but with its discounted weekend rates, central location, and smaller size than the big convention hotels, the historic De Anza can be a good choice for families. Our kids learned to love breakfast buffets in Europe and can indulge in them here, but even more fun for night owls is the "Raid Our Pantry" program. Your room key opens the door to a lounge where a full deli buffet is set out—sandwich fixings, cookies, fruit, and surprises—seven nights a week from 10 p.m. until 5 a.m. This is a great TV-dinner choice for teens and older kids who've stayed up late at one of the big amusement parks.

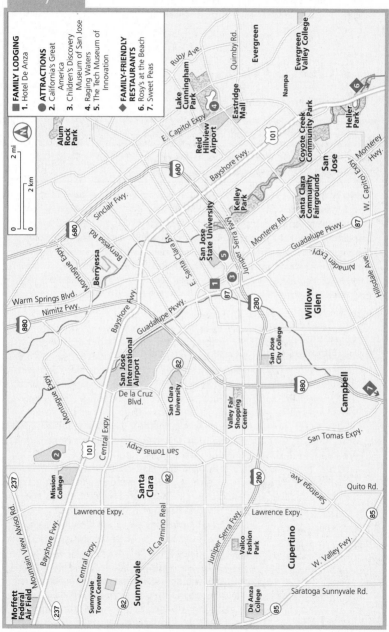

san jose

FAMILY LODGING
1. Hotel De Anza

ATTRACTIONS
2. California's Great America
3. Children's Discovery Museum of San Jose
4. Raging Waters
5. The Tech Museum of Innovation

FAMILY-FRIENDLY RESTAURANTS
6. Rosy's at the Beach
7. Sweet Peas

The hotel is just a few easily walked blocks from each of the museums listed below and is also near Guadalupe River Park, a nice city park with playground and lawns. Make sure to check out the diving lady mural at the pool.

ATTRACTIONS

 California's Great America

APPEAL BY AGE	PRESCHOOL ★★★★	GRADE SCHOOL ★★★★½	TEENS ★★★★½
YOUNG ADULTS ★★★★		OVER 30 ★★★★	SENIORS ★★

2401 Agnew Road (Great America Parkway exit off US 101), Santa Clara; ☎ 408-988-1776; www.pgathrills.com

Hours *May–end of August:* daily, 10 a.m. (closing times vary depending on month); *March–May, September, and October:* open Saturday and Sunday only; closed November–February. **Admission** $54 ages 3–61; $35 seniors age 62 and older; free for children age 2 and under. **Touring time** Average 6–8 hours; minimum 4 hours. **Rainy-day touring** Yes, rides still function and the lines are shorter. **Restaurants** Yes. **Alcoholic beverages** Yes. **Disabled access** Yes. **Wheelchair rental** Yes. **Baby-stroller rental** Yes. **Lockers** Yes. **Pet kennels** No. **Rain check** Yes. **Private tours** No.

DESCRIPTION AND COMMENTS An amusement park taken to the highest level, Great America has an American-heritage theme, with six zones devoted to different epochs in our history. But the themes are merely window dressing: this place is really about thrills. Some of its rides are so intense they leave parents a quivering mess, but 12- to 19-year-olds can't get enough of such horrors as the Drop Tower Scream Zone, the world's tallest free-fall ride, and Flight Deck, where you'll experience a zero-gravity barrel roll and 360-degree vertical loop, among other psychological and physiological challenges. Those seeking slightly less terrifying thrills have lots more to choose from, including the IMAX films (which can be too intense for little ones), a few fun water-rapids rides (expect to get wet), and the famed Grizzly, Northern California's second-largest wooden roller coaster. The newest adventure, FireFall, made us almost lose our lunch just looking at it—riders spin in 360-degree vertical arcs as they drop 60 feet through fire and water special effects.

unofficial **TIP**
Don't expect cool San Francisco weather at Great America—it's an entirely different climate, demanding plenty of sunscreen, drinking water, and hats in summertime.

Although ultimately this place is really best for children age 10 and up, younger kids are hardly neglected. They get their own area, KidZville, with small-scale rides, a cartoon carousel, a play area, and wandering Hanna-Barbera characters such as Scooby-Doo; the live music and ice shows are good for all ages as well. And our second-grader went wild for Nickelodeon Central, where she hugged SpongeBob and got slimed. In the summertime, Boomerang Bay adds a water-park element, and it has play areas for young kids, too.

If you don't want to succumb to the pricey, junky food sold in the park, pack your own lunch and enjoy it in the pleasant picnic area outside the front gates.

Children's Discovery Museum of San Jose

APPEAL BY AGE	PRESCHOOL ★★★★	GRADE SCHOOL ★★★	TEENS ½
YOUNG ADULTS ★		OVER 30 ★	SENIORS ½

180 Woz Way, San Jose; ☎ 408-298-5437; www.cdm.org

Hours Monday–Saturday, 10 a.m.–5 p.m.; Sunday, noon–5 p.m. **Admission** $8 kids and adults, $7 seniors, under age 1, free. **Touring time** 2–4 hours; minimum 1 hour. **Rainy-day touring** Yes. **Restaurants** Yes. **Alcoholic beverages** No. **Disabled access** No. **Wheelchair rental** No. **Baby-stroller rental** No. **Lockers** No. **Pet kennels** No. **Rain check** No. **Private tours** No.

DESCRIPTION AND COMMENTS   This highly regarded children's museum is adjacent to Guadalupe River Park and has a nice cafe, too, so plan at least a half-day outing and a meal indoors or out. Great for kids who are too young for the Tech Museum, it is home to a variety of semipermanent and temporary interactive, hands-on exhibitions, climbing and play areas, and such imagination-stimulating environments as a play post office and Tales from the land of Gullah.

Raging Waters

APPEAL BY AGE	PRESCHOOL ★★★★	GRADE SCHOOL ★★★★½	TEENS ★★★★½
YOUNG ADULTS ★★★★		OVER 30 ★★★★	SENIORS ★★★

2333 South White Road, San Jose; ☎ 408-238-9900; www.rwsplash.com

Hours *Mid-June–Labor Day:* weekdays, 10:30 a.m.–6 p.m.; weekends, 10:30 a.m.–7 p.m.; *May, early June, and September:* weekends only, 10 a.m.–6 p.m. **Admission** $30 over 48" tall, $22 seniors age 55 and older, $22 under 48" tall, free for children age 2 and under; after 3 p.m. $22 for all ages; parking $6; double tube rental $6, single tube rental $4, all-day locker rental $5. **Touring time** Average 6–8 hours; minimum 4 hours. **Rainy-day touring** Okay. **Restaurants** Food service. **Alcoholic beverages** No. **Disabled access** No. **Wheelchair rental** No. **Baby-stroller rental** No. **Lockers** Yes. **Pet kennels** No. **Rain check** No. **Private tours** No.

DESCRIPTION AND COMMENTS   Like its sister Raging Waters in San Dimas (see Part Three, Los Angeles and Vicinity, page 176), this huge water park with its many twisting, intense slides appeals to teens and preteens, but you'll also find some moderate slides, a few little-kids-only areas, some not-for-thrill-seekers quiet pools, and a "lazy river" for tube floating. Every vacationing kid deserves a day in a water park, and if you find yourself in the San Jose area in the peak of summer, you'll be desperate for a dunk in the wave pool, too.

The Tech Museum of Innovation

APPEAL BY AGE	PRESCHOOL ★	GRADE SCHOOL ★★★★	TEENS ★★★★½
YOUNG ADULTS ★★★★½		OVER 30 ★★★★	SENIORS ★★★★

201 South Market Street, San Jose; ☎ 408-294-8324; www.thetech.org

Hours Daily, 10 a.m.–5 p.m.; closed several days in September for annual maintenance (check ahead for dates); closed Thanksgiving and Christmas. **Admission** $8 all ages; admission includes IMAX movie. **Touring time** Average 4 hours; minimum 2 hours. **Rainy-day touring** Yes. **Restaurants** No. **Alcoholic beverages** No. **Disabled access** Yes. **Wheelchair rental** Yes. **Baby-stroller rental** No. **Lockers** No. **Pet kennels** No. **Rain check** No. **Private tours** No.

DESCRIPTION AND COMMENTS   Here in the birthplace of high tech, this wondrous warehouse of gadgets and tools takes up more than 132,000 square feet, throughout which kids and adults can try out, step into, or peer through all sorts of really cool scientific devices. More than 240 interactive displays are found in dozens of themed exhibits, many of which have changed recently as part of a large-scale updating. Our kids loved Superhero Science, a lively show and exhibit that demystifies the science behind superpowers. Another new exhibit, NetPl@net, pushes the boundaries of how people use the Internet—a kid, for instance, can arm wrestle a kid at another science museum in New York or Alaska. And still another, the Silicon Workshop, allows kids to learn about microchip programming by programming their own Mr. Potato Head. In the ocean section, you can sit in a minisubmarine, put your arm into a full-size model of a deep-sea diving suit, and manipulate its claw. Second Life aficionados will make a beeline for the Tech Virtual Test Zone, whose interactive exhibits were all created within Second Life. Elsewhere you can do everything from make a movie in a digital studio to design your own roller coaster.

unofficial **TIP**
The Tech Museum is a most worthy day-trip destination from San Francisco.

Curious adults will be as enthralled with this place as their kids, so allow plenty of time to explore and experience. The entry fee includes admission to the special IMAX Dome Theater, the first of its kind in Northern California, with an eight-story-tall domed screen and wraparound sound.

FAMILY-FRIENDLY RESTAURANTS

Rosy's at the Beach

17320 Monterey Road, Morgan Hill; ☎ 408-778-0551; www.rosysatthebeach.com

Meals served Breakfast, lunch, and dinner. **Cuisine** American. **Entree range** $8–$25. **Kids' menu** Yes. **Reservations** Recommended. **Payment** All major credit cards.

ROSY AND RICH BERGIN'S RESTAURANT isn't actually on the beach, but it is conveniently located right off the US 101 freeway in Morgan Hill, south of San Jose. It also has a swell, beachy vibe, with surfboards, beach umbrellas, tropical cocktails, and the seductive aromas of cioppino and fish-and-chips. The Bergins spent years as fish-market proprietors before becoming restaurateurs, so the quality of their grilled fresh fish, seafood chowders, and famous salmon tacos is first rate. There's a good kids' menu, and the prices are moderate.

Sweet Peas

453 North Santa Cruz Avenue, Los Gatos; ☎ 408-354-3144

Meals served Breakfast and lunch. **Cuisine** American. **Entree range** $5–$10. **Kids' menu** No. **Reservations** Not accepted. **Payment** All major credit cards.

THIS FRIENDLY, ORDER-AT-THE-COUNTER PLACE in the fetching little town of Los Gatos is one of the best cafes in the San Jose area, featuring local products and family-friendly fare: smoothies, Belgian waffles, all kinds of crepes, all sorts of sandwiches (try the chicken pesto), omelets, homemade soups, and fabulous cookies and cakes, some from old German family recipes. The only catch is the limited seating—just a couple of tables on a patio—so be prepared to wait.

PART SEVEN

GOLD COUNTRY

CALIFORNIA'S GOLD COUNTRY might sound to the uninitiated like a vaguely educational collection of musty historic sites. And indeed, parents intent on reading every paragraph of every historic marker will certainly bore their kids in this region. But the rest of us can have a grand, old-fashioned time in the villages and towns along **CA 49,** panning for gold, riding horses, exploring caves, scrambling around ruins, walking Native American trails, and even whitewater rafting.

The Gold Country consists of a string of picturesque small towns and cities strung along the grassy foothills of the **Sierra Nevada** east of **Sacramento.** It's the area called the Mother Lode by the '49ers, the thousands of gold seekers who rushed here from all over the world after John Marshall's 1848 discovery of gold at John Sutter's mill.

The area is particularly rich in Chinese American history because the Sacramento Delta was originally reclaimed by Chinese laborers, and many of these Chinese railroad workers went on to become miners. The Delta town of **Locke** was founded by Chinese immigrants, and Gold Country landmarks include 100-year-old buildings that housed stores owned by Chinese pioneers.

We'll concentrate here on the former mining boomtowns along CA 49 between **Nevada City** and **Columbia.** Sacramento is our gateway city and could be used as an airport–rental car starting point, but families might also consider touring the southern part of Gold Country before or after some time in Yosemite. (Yosemite is covered in Part Five, The Sierra Nevada.) Kids of at least elementary-school age will enjoy Gold Country the most. They should be old enough to want to pan for gold or ride a mule.

The region is anchored by six fascinating state parks, each worthy of a half-day stop. In **Grass Valley,** in the northern part of Gold Country, you'll find **Empire Mine State Historic Park,** the site of one of the oldest

unofficial **TIP**
Families should consider touring the southern part of Gold Country before or after some time in Yosemite.

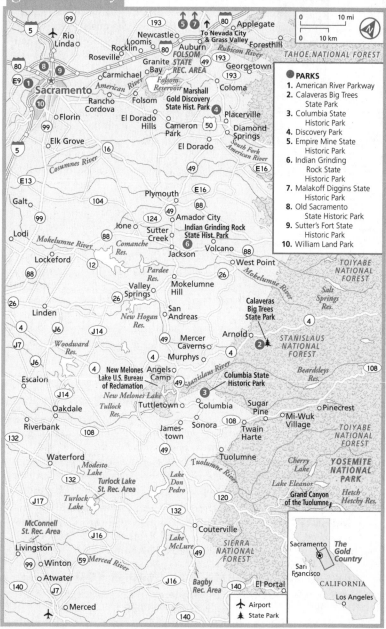

gold country

PARKS

1. American River Parkway
2. Calaveras Big Trees
   State Park
3. Columbia State
   Historic Park
4. Discovery Park
5. Empire Mine State
   Historic Park
6. Indian Grinding
   Rock State
   Historic Park
7. Malakoff Diggins State
   Historic Park
8. Old Sacramento
   State Historic Park
9. Sutter's Fort State
   Historic Park
10. William Land Park

and richest gold mines in California. In Sacramento, the riverfront **Old Sacramento State Historic Park** has 110 restored or reconstructed buildings, and **Sutter's Fort State Historic Park** has a blacksmith shop, jail, and other gold-rush-era environments. In the middle part of the region is **Indian Grinding Rock State Historic Park,** once the seasonal meeting place of the Miwok tribe and the only California state park that focuses primarily on Native American culture. A short easterly side trip from CA 49 brings you to **Calaveras Big Trees State Park,** where you will see majestic giant sequoias. In the southern section of the Mother Lode is **Columbia State Historic Park,** the most fully preserved of the gold rush towns, where old brick buildings now house museums, shops, cafes, hotels, and a theater.

Between these main attractions, various tiny gold rush towns each offer one or two interesting sites to explore, as well as such enjoyable activities as cave tours, hiking, and berry picking. The 19th-century historic districts of the towns are usually surrounded by 21st-century American commercial districts and residential areas, so travelers won't lack access to motels, minimarts, fast food, and, in some cases, fine dining.

Allow three days and two overnights in either case. For the northern part, begin with a day and a night in Sacramento, then drive on to Grass Valley and Nevada City for another day and a night. Add a day for such activities as river rafting, if you can. In the south, choose any of the gold-rush towns as a base, depending on your desired activities (historic sights, cave exploration, river rafting), for a one-day add-on (Columbia State Park only) to a Yosemite trip or a two- or three-day exploration of several different towns.

GETTING THERE

BY PLANE Sacramento International Airport (☎ 916-874-0700; **www.sacairports.org**) is 15 minutes from downtown Sacramento.

BY TRAIN Amtrak offers direct service on the *California Zephyr* east from the Bay Area and west from Chicago, and on the *Coast Starlight* south from Seattle and Portland, Oregon, and north from San Diego and Los Angeles (☎ 800-872-7245; **www.amtrak.com**). Commuter trains also run several times daily from the Bay Area and San Jose.

BY CAR From the San Francisco Bay Area, take **Interstate 80** west to **Interstate 5** north. From the LA area, take I-5 north. From Reno–North Lake Tahoe, take I-80 west; from Reno via South Lake Tahoe, take **US 50** west. From Yosemite, take **CA 99** north.

HOW TO GET INFORMATION BEFORE YOU GO

- **Amador County Chamber of Commerce**   125 Peek Street, P.O. Box 596, Jackson 95642; ☎ 209-223-0350; **www.amadorcountychamber.com**
- **Calaveras Visitors Bureau**   P.O. Box 637, Angels Camp 95222;

☎ 800-225-3764 or 209-736-0049; **www.gocalaveras.com**
- **Grass Valley and Nevada County Chamber of Commerce**
  248 Mill Street, Grass Valley 95945; ☎ 800-655-4667 or
  530-273-4667; **www.grassvalleychamber.com**
- **Nevada City Chamber of Commerce**   132 Main Street,
  Nevada City 95959; ☎ 800-655-6569 or 530-265-2692;
  www.nevadacitychamber.com
- **Old Sacramento Visitor Center**   1002 Second Street, Old
  Sacramento 95814; ☎ 916-442-7644; **www.oldsacramento.com**
- **Sacramento Convention and Visitors Bureau**   1608 I Street,
  Sacramento 95814; ☎ 800-292-2334 or 916-808-7777;
  www.discovergold.org

A **CALENDAR** *of* **FESTIVALS** *and* **EVENTS**

January

MARTIN LUTHER KING COMMUNITY CELEBRATIONS   *Sacramento*.
Parades, activities; ☎ 916-920-8655; **www.mlk365.org.**

March

MARIPOSA STORYTELLING FESTIVAL   *Mariposa*. ☎ 800-903-9936 or
209-966-3155; **www.arts-mariposa.org/storytelling.html.**

April

FESTIVAL DE LA FAMILIA   *Cal Expo, Capital City Freeway and Exposition Boulevard, Sacramento*. Held the last Sunday of each April, this
is a hugely popular festival celebrating the heritage of more than two
dozen Latin American countries. Puppet shows, games, storytelling,
music, dancing, and food; ☎ 451-6200; **www.festivaldelafamilia.com.**

OPENING DAY, SACRAMENTO RIVERCATS MINOR LEAGUE BASEBALL
Sacramento. Season goes into September at Raley Field, an old-fashioned ballpark complete with children's play area; 400 Ballpark Drive;
☎ 916-371-HITS; **www.rivercats.com.**

May

FIREMAN'S MUSTER   *Columbia*. Vintage hand-pumped fire engines, a
parade, a kids' bucket brigade, a firefighter "shootout," and more in
this weekend-long shindig; ☎ 209-532-0150; **www.columbiagazette
.com/muster.html.**

JUMPING FROG JUBILEE   *Angels Camp*. Continuing the tradition
begun by Mark Twain's story, this famed frog-jumping contest is held
the third week in May as part of the Calaveras County Fair, which
also boasts pig races, carnival rides, and a kids' play area; ☎ 209-736-
2561; **www.frogtown.org.**

PACIFIC RIM STREET FEST *Old Sacramento*. A one-day celebration of California's Asian cultures, with food, arts and crafts, and a great array of entertainment, from Polynesian dance and Thai boxing to Japanese drumming and a Chinese orchestra. ☎ 916 451-6200; **www.pacificrimstreetfest.com.**

SACRAMENTO COUNTY FAIR *Cal Expo, Capital City Freeway and Exposition Boulevard, Sacramento.* ☎ 916-263-2975; **www.sacfair.com.**

June

CRAWDAD FESTIVAL *Isleton.* ☎ 916-777-5880; **www.crawdadfestival.org.**

PLACER COUNTY FAIR *Placer County Fairgrounds, Roseville.* ☎ 916-786-2023; **www.placercountyfair.org.**

July

FOURTH OF JULY PARADE AND CELEBRATION *Mokelumne Hill.* ☎ 209-286-1401; **www.gocalaveras.com.**

SUTTER CREEK OLD FASHION FOURTH OF JULY *Minnie Provis Park, Sutter Creek.* Children's parade, games, and picnic; ☎ 209-267-1344; **www.amadorcountychamber.com.**

August

CALIFORNIA STATE FAIR *Cal Expo, Capital City Freeway and Exposition Boulevard, Sacramento.* One of the nation's largest state fairs, with rodeo riding, fireworks, and Kids Park; ☎ 916-263-3247; **www.bigfun.org.**

September

GOLD COUNTRY FAIR *Auburn.* Founded in 1889, this Placer County fair has everything from thrill rides to livestock judging and juggling performances; ☎ 530-823-4533; **www.goldcountryfair.com.**

GOLD RUSH DAYS *Old Sacramento.* Old Sacramento is closed to cars and its streets are covered with dirt during this four-day annual Labor Day event. Period-appropriate tents and booths include blacksmith's tent, jail, and apothecary; ☎ 916-808-7777; **www.discovergold.org.**

NATIVE AMERICAN FESTIVAL *Indian Grinding Rock State Park.* On the weekend following the fourth Friday in September, Native American tribes gather to celebrate their heritage with food, dances, and games; ☎ 209-296-7488; **parks.ca.gov.**

October

SPOOKOMOTIVE TRAIN RIDES *Old Sacramento.* Halloween season is celebrated with a pumpkin patch at the railroad museum and a train ride with ghouls and goblins on board; ☎ 916-445-6645; **www.californiastaterailroadmuseum.org.**

December

CORNISH CHRISTMAS STREET CELEBRATION   *Grass Valley.* Held one evening a week in December, this honors the Cornish heritage of many in this former mining center and includes performances by the Grass Valley Cornish Choir and street stalls with traditional foods and crafts; ☎ 530-272-8315; **www.ncgold.com; www.historicgrassvalley.com.**

LAMPLIGHT TOUR   *Columbia.* The town re-creates a different year in its history each December, and docents lead visitors through town by lamplight to "eavesdrop" on 19th-century goings-on; ☎ 209-532-0150; **www.columbiagazette.com/lamplight.html.**

The BEST PARKS

AMERICAN RIVER PARKWAY   This meandering park runs through Sacramento and its suburbs along the banks of the American River for 23 miles. The **Jedediah Smith Memorial Trail** winds for 32 miles from Old Sacramento to Beals Point in the town of Folsom. It's also great for jogging, horseback riding, picnics, river rafting, fishing, and birding; ☎ 916-875-6961 or 916-875-6672; **www.sacparks.net.** To rent bikes, try **River Rat Raft and Bike** (4053 Pennsylvania Avenue, Fair Oaks; ☎ 916-966-6777; **www.river-rat.com**).

DISCOVERY PARK   This Sacramento County park at the confluence of the Sacramento and American rivers is near Old Sacramento and is another starting point for bike trails. Hosts boat launching, picnic area, horseshoes, archery, restrooms, and barbecues; ☎ 916-875-6672; **www.sacparks.net.**

STATE HISTORIC PARKS   Because many state parks in Gold Country are also the region's primary historical attractions, we've placed their individual descriptions under "Attractions" in each section. We've covered **Old Sacramento State Historic Park, Sutter's Fort State Historic Park, Empire Mine State Historic Park, Indian Grinding Rock State Historic Park, Calaveras Big Trees State Park,** and **Columbia State Historic Park.** In addition, **Malakoff Diggins State Historical Park** is discussed under the listing for Chute Hill Campground in "Family Lodging" (page 373) in the Northern Gold Country section. For more information, go to **parks.ca.gov.**

WILLIAM LAND PARK   The 15-acre **Sacramento Zoo** (see attraction profile, page 370) is here, as are a public golf course, a picnic area, and an amusement area; ☎ 916-808-6060; **www.cityofsacramento.org.** For information about the terrific **Fairytale Town,** see the listing under "Attractions" (page 368) in the Sacramento section of this chapter.

unofficial **TIP**
The best thing about Land Park is Fairytale Town, a wonderful amusement park for the very young.

FAMILY OUTDOOR ADVENTURES

BICYCLING   See American River Parkway under "The Best Parks" (previous page). Also, self-guided and escorted bike tours along with equipment are available at **Bicycles Plus** next to the American River Bike Trail on Gold Lake Drive in Old Town Folsom; ☎ 916-355-8901; **www.onlinecycling.com.**

CAVING   Several cave systems first explored by miners in the 1850s are open to the public today. The world down under can be creepy or awesome, depending on your child's perspective. For an introduction to caves, check out **Mercer Caverns** near Murphys (☎ 209-728-2101; **www.mercercaverns.com**), which is open summers, Sunday through Thursday, 9 a.m. to 5 p.m.; Friday and Saturday, 9 a.m. to 6 p.m.; from October 1 to Memorial Day weekend, hours are daily, 10 a.m. to 4:30 p.m. Admission is $12 for adults and kids over age 12, and $7 for children ages 5 to 12.

An exhilarating experience for teens is to descend into **Moaning Cavern** on a 165-foot rappel (note that there are special rules for kids ages 12 to 17 that include need for parent's authorization or presence). Moaning Cavern is open year-round and offers guided, 45-minute walking tours (includes a steep spiral staircase) and a three-hour Adventure Tour (reservations required) that involves climbing and narrow passages. General admission is $14.25 adults, $7.15 children ages 6 to 12. Near Vallecito (☎ 866-762-2837 or 209-736-2708; **www.cavern tours.com**). The same company offers tours of **Black Chasm Cave** at 15701 Pioneer–Volcano Road near Volcano. The 50-minute family tour of Black Chasm costs $14.25 for adults and $7.15 for kids. There's also "gemstone mining" for the little ones at both Moaning Cavern and Black Chasm.

HOUSEBOATING   The Sacramento River Delta area offers about a thousand square miles of calm-water waterways. You can drive a houseboat more or less as you would, say, a 1958 Buick, while the kids fish, sunbathe, and watch for herons and other waterbirds. Tie up at a small-town marina on one of the many islands or to a tree stump and swim or picnic on shore.

unofficial **TIP**
Even the least water-savvy family can enjoy an afternoon on a flat-bottomed patio boat or a few lazy days on a houseboat on the Sacramento River Delta.

Houseboats are usually offered for three to seven nights and can sleep one or two families; patio or fishing boats can be rented for a day's water play. Among the houseboat companies renting in the Delta: **Forever Resorts** (☎ 800-255-5561 or 480-998-1981; **www.foreverresorts .com**) and **Seven Crown Resorts** (☎ 800-752-9669; **www.sevencrown .com**). For one-day boat rentals, contact **Paradise Point Marina** (8095

Rio Blanco Road, Stockton; ☎ 209-952-1000 or 800-752-9669; **www .sevencrown.com/lakes/california_delta**).

☀ **RIVER RAFTING** With older, water-safe kids, you can up the excitement and take a whitewater-rafting trip, ranging in thrill level from mild to wild. There are several popular rafting areas on the **American, Stanislaus,** and **Tuolumne rivers** in Gold Country, heading out of such rendezvous points as Coloma, Angels Camp, Sacramento, and Stockton. Typically ranging from two days to a week, trips are offered from April through October; the wildest rapids are in early spring, when runoff is greatest. Some outfitters offer quickie half-day rides. In many overnight trips, you camp out in style en route, with cooking and camp chores provided by staff members; at the journey's end, a van will take you back to the starting point. Some companies have overnight packages with nearby bed-and-breakfast inns or motels.

It is generally recommended that children younger than age 12 go on a raft that's steered by a guide; minimum ages vary by the excursion, with 6 being about the youngest. Fares range from $70 to $200 per person for half- or all-day excursions and include meals and transportation back to the rendezvous point.

We know several families who have had excellent whitewater adventures with an outfitter called **Whitewater Connection;** (☎ 800-336-7238 or 530-622-6446; **www.whitewaterconnection.com**). Its base is a beautiful 40-acre private campground (complete with horseshoes, fishing, and gold panning) alongside the south fork of the American River in the heart of Gold Country, next to Marshall Gold Discovery State Park. Kids older than age 6 can participate in the Class III trips, which range from a half day to two days; there's also a great, discounted two-day trip for families with little kids. Mom gets to go rafting one day and Dad the other, while the non-rafting parent plays at camp with the little ones. Some other rafting companies include **Whitewater Excitement** (☎ 800-750-2386; **www .whitewaterexcitement.com**); **All-Outdoors California Whitewater Rafting** (☎ 800-247-2387 or 925-932-8993; **www.aorafting.com**); **Arta River Trips** (☎ 209-962-7873; **www.arta.org**); and **O.A.R.S.** (☎ 800-346-6277 or 209-736-4677; **www.oars.com**).

THE SCHOOLHOUSES OF GOLD COUNTRY

NOTHING WILL BRING THE GOLD-RUSH ERA ALIVE for your kids more than the sight of the wonderful old schoolhouses of the region. Almost every historic town has one, some fully restored and open for pretending, some shuttered and awaiting renovation, and a few turned into private homes. Each is named for its town.

ALTAVILLE SCHOOL (1858) is red brick with dainty white trim; it was used until 1950 and is open to visitors.

COLOMA SCHOOL HOUSE is part of Marshall Gold Discovery State Historic Park and can be found, like other historic buildings, by referring

HATS   Bonnets for the girls can be expensive but may be cherished; miners' felt floppy hats or various historically inaccurate but fun versions of coonskin and cowboy hats are popular with boys.

MINERALS   Everywhere you look you'll find gold (and fake gold, of course). Little vials of water with microscopic gold flecks fascinate kids and are inexpensive or come from their own gold-panning efforts (for which they'll be charged a fee by a whiskered miner).

OLD BOTTLES   Gold Country is dotted with antiques shops to lure the tourist, and if parents can't resist browsing, kids might have fun picking out an old glass bottle of curious shape and color (but not of great age if you want it to be affordable).

to the guide map available at the Gold Discovery Museum; ☎ 530-622-3470; **parks.ca.gov.**

COLUMBIA SCHOOL HOUSE is at the north end of Columbia and makes for a nice walk through the residential blocks (imagine living in a state historic park) up the hill to the state's first two-story brick school building. Built in 1860, it's outfitted with the desks, inkwells, and slates that were used by 19th-century children; the old town cemetery is out back; ☎ 209-532-0150; **parks.ca.gov.**

FIDDLETOWN SCHOOLHOUSE (1862) is a beautiful shell of a building waiting to be restored. It has the classic schoolhouse shape with the little bell tower.

MURPHYS GRAMMAR SCHOOL (1860) was, until it closed in 1973, California's oldest public school. It's on a hill near the corner of Main and Jones streets and is now a church.

OLD SACRAMENTO SCHOOLHOUSE is a yellow wood-frame building, beautifully restored and dramatically situated at the waterfront with Tower Bridge rising behind it. Kids can swing in the schoolyard (note the outhouse), and the classroom's open for exploring Monday through Saturday, 10 a.m. to 4 p.m., and Sunday, noon to 4 p.m. Admission is free; ☎ 916-483-8818; **www.scoe.net/oldsacschoolhouse.**

SUTTER CREEK GRAMMAR SCHOOL (1871), an imposing two-story stone building on a hill east of the town center, is fun to drive past. It's now a community center.

VOLCANO SCHOOL has been impeccably restored and is now a private residence. Though the building is not open to the public, it does have a historical marker.

SACRAMENTO

ALTHOUGH IT SEEMS OFF THE BEATEN TRACK because of its inland location, Sacramento was once a major hub thanks to its busy riverfront (now a vital outdoor recreation area) and its position as a gateway to Gold Country, the Sierra, and the agricultural valley areas of the state. As the state capital, it's often filled with California schoolkids visiting the buildings where legislators make the laws, and its **Old Sacramento** and **Sutter's Fort state historic parks** allow kids to visit environments that bring history to life. The **DASH trolley,** linking tourist areas and hotels, is free from 11 a.m. to 3 p.m. daily; ☎ 916-321-BUSS; **www.sacrt.com.**

For vacationing families, Sacramento can be a convenient base for several days of varied activities in the region, but we don't recommend an extended stay in the city unless you're visiting friends. Accommodations, although often very competitive in price, are geared to the capital's many business visitors, and only a few hotels (see profiles following) are in family-friendly areas (most of the chains are in desolate, freeway-adjacent locations). Bed-and-breakfast inns are isolated in quiet residential areas throughout the city.

Instead, plan a convenient overnight at the beginning or end of a few days devoted to houseboating on the Delta or exploring Gold Country, especially if you're arriving in the area by plane.

▌FAMILY LODGING

Holiday Inn Capitol Plaza
300 J Street, Sacramento; ☎ 916-446-0100; www.holidayinnsacramento.com; $80–$122, suites $175–$350; children under age 18 stay free

LOCATED AT CAPITOL PLAZA, this 364-room motel is in a mixed-use area that includes an upscale shopping plaza with movie theaters, restaurants, a pedestrian walkway (under the freeway) to Old Sacramento, and pedestrian access to the city's business district. From here your teens can walk to the movies while you and the toddlers play in the pool, and then you can all stroll out to one of the lively restaurants nearby. There is a coffee shop

sacramento

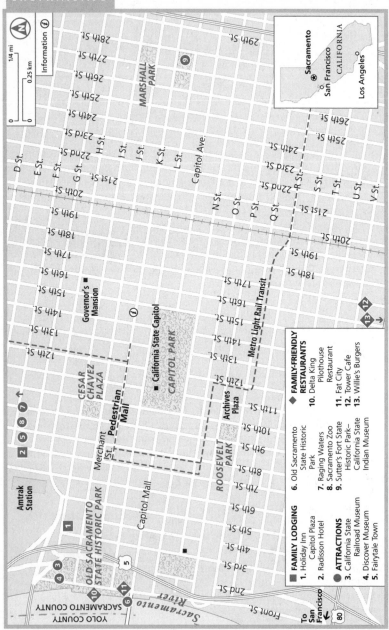

FAMILY LODGING
1. Holiday Inn Capitol Plaza
2. Radisson Hotel

ATTRACTIONS
3. California State Railroad Museum
4. Discover Museum
5. Fairytale Town
6. Old Sacramento State Historic Park
7. Raging Waters
8. Sacramento Zoo
9. Sutter's Fort State Historic Park–California State Indian Museum

FAMILY-FRIENDLY RESTAURANTS
10. Delta King Pilothouse Restaurant
11. Fat City
12. Tower Cafe
13. Willie's Burgers

with a kids' menu; room service has its own menu that includes kids' items. Five rooms are suites with refrigerators. Babysitting is available. There are no special kids' programs.

Radisson Hotel
500 Leisure Lane, Sacramento; ☎ 800-333-3333 or 916-922-2020; www.radissonsac.com; $79–$180

ONE OF THE FEW RESORTLIKE LODGINGS in the area, this 335-room motor inn is on 18 acres with a small lake; some rooms have patios or decks. Kids are welcomed, and they stay free in their parents' room, with an extra charge for roll-away beds. Includes some suites, a pool, bike rentals, and pedal boats.

■ ATTRACTIONS

 California State Railroad Museum

APPEAL BY AGE	PRESCHOOL ★★	GRADE SCHOOL ★★★	TEENS ★★
YOUNG ADULTS ★★	OVER 30 ★★★		SENIORS ★★★★

111 I Street, Old Sacramento; ☎ 916-445-6645 or 916-445-7387; www.californiastaterailroadmuseum.org

Hours Daily, 10 a.m.–5 p.m.; closed Thanksgiving, Christmas, and New Year's Day. **Admission** $8 adults, $3 children ages 6–17, free for children age 5 and under. Train ride: same prices as above, but separate admission. **Touring time** Average 3 hours; minimum 2 hours. **Rainy-day touring** Yes. **Restaurants** No. **Alcoholic beverages** No. **Disabled access** Yes. **Wheelchair rental** Yes. **Baby-stroller rental** No. **Lockers** No. **Pet kennels** No. **Rain check** No. **Private tours** No, but docents are available.

DESCRIPTION AND COMMENTS An impressive museum that grabs visitors in several ways, with movies, miniatures, and hands-on experiences. Displays include 21 restored locomotives and train cars, some of which you can walk through. Ticket allows for admission to the nearby, restored Central Pacific Passenger Station, and on weekends April through September there are hourly, six-mile-long steam train rides from the Central Pacific Freight Depot.

Discovery Museum: The Sacramento Museum of History, Science, and Space Technology

APPEAL BY AGE	PRESCHOOL ★	GRADE SCHOOL ★★★	TEENS ★★★
YOUNG ADULTS ★★★	OVER 30 ★★		SENIORS ★★

History Center: 101 I Street, Old Sacramento; ☎ 916-264-7057 Science and Space Center: 3615 Auburn Boulevard; ☎ 916-575-3941; www.thediscovery.org

Hours *History Center:* June–August, daily, 10 a.m.–5 p.m.; September–May, Tuesday–Sunday, 10 a.m.–5 p.m. *Science and Space Center:* July–August, daily,

10 a.m.–5 p.m.; September–June, Tuesday–Friday, noon–5 p.m.; closed major holidays. **Admission** $5 adults, $4 seniors age 60 and over, $4 children ages 13–17, $3 children ages 4–12, children age 3 and under free. **Touring time** Average 1–2 hours; minimum 1 hour. **Rainy-day touring** Yes. **Restaurants** No. **Alcoholic beverages** No. **Disabled access** Yes. **Wheelchair rental** No. **Baby-stroller rental** No. **Lockers** No. **Pet kennels** No. **Rain check** No. **Private tours** No, but docents are available.

DESCRIPTION AND COMMENTS   Two separate facilities—the Museum of History and the Science and Space Center—share management and a common hands-on approach. A visit to the History Center's Gold Gallery (entered through a miner's shaft) is a great way to kick off a driving tour of the Gold Country; it includes fun, hands-on exhibits that allow kids to touch real gold and see a miner's cabin. In the Science Center, you'll find a planetarium, the Challenger Learning Center, and such rotating exhibits as the Bone Zone, an exploration of the human body. The Challenger Learning Center offers simulated space missions on occasional Friday evenings, 5:45 to 8:30 p.m.; $20, $18 each for two people, $15 each for three or more people. Reservations: ☎ 916-485-8836.

Fairytale Town

APPEAL BY AGE	PRESCHOOL ★★★★½	GRADE SCHOOL ★★★	TEENS ½
YOUNG ADULTS ★	OVER 30 ★		SENIORS ½

3901 Land Park Drive, Sacramento; ☎ 916-264-5233; www.fairytaletown.org

Hours *Summer:* daily, 9 a.m.–4 p.m.; *November–February:* Thursday–Sunday, 10 a.m.–4 p.m. **Admission** $4.50 weekends and holidays, $3.75 weekdays, children age 2 and under free. **Touring time** Average 2 hours; minimum 1 hour. **Rainy-day touring** Yes, but you'll get wet. **Restaurants** No. **Alcoholic beverages** No. **Disabled access** Some. **Wheelchair rental** No. **Baby-stroller rental** No. **Lockers** No. **Pet kennels** No. **Rain check** No. **Private tours** No.

DESCRIPTION AND COMMENTS   Across the street from the Sacramento Zoo, Fairytale Town makes a wonderful stop for families with toddlers to kids about age 8. *Play* is the operative word here—the 2.5-acre non-profit park comprises some 25 play sets where kids can pretend, climb, slide, and explore. Inspired by children's literature, the fun includes the Sherwood Forest play fort, a slide down Jack's beanstalk, a race along the Crooked Mile path (actually an eighth of a mile), a slide down Alice's Rabbit Hole, and an exploration of Mr. McGregor's Garden. The petting-zoo animals include three Nigerian dwarf goats (the Three Billy Goats Gruff), Peter Rabbit and his sisters, and three Vietnamese pot-bellied pigs (the Three Little Pigs); time your visit for the afternoon if your kids want to witness feeding time.

Old Sacramento State Historic Park

APPEAL BY AGE	PRESCHOOL ★★	GRADE SCHOOL ★★★	TEENS ★★
YOUNG ADULTS ★	OVER 30 ★★		SENIORS ★★★

Old Sacramento is bounded by Capitol Mall, the I Street Bridge, Interstate 5, and the Sacramento River; ☎ 916-442-7644; www.oldsacramento.com

Hours Vary by area and attraction. **Admission** Free to area; some attractions charge. **Touring time** Average 4 hours; minimum 2 hours. **Rainy-day touring** Not great for enjoying the walk around district. **Restaurants** Yes, many. **Alcoholic beverages** In some cafes and clubs. **Disabled access** Yes. **Wheelchair rental** No. **Baby-stroller rental** No. **Lockers** No. **Pet kennels** No. **Rain check** No. **Private tours** No.

DESCRIPTION AND COMMENTS   This restored historic district has an especially attractive waterfront, where wooden walkways face the river. Here you'll find Tower Bridge, the unique *Delta King* paddlewheel boat hotel, and boat docks where visiting cruise ships and yachts tie up for an hour or a day. The area is home to several museums, including the California State Railroad Museum (see profile, page 367), the California Military Museum, and the Discovery Museum (see profile, page 367). But overall, there are more souvenir shops and cafes than historic points of interest, so the effect can sometimes be of a completely commercial, tourist-tacky area. We recommend a morning visit with a stroll around the waterfront, followed by a museum visit, lunch, and a bit of shop-crawling.

Raging Waters

APPEAL BY AGE	PRESCHOOL ★★★★½	GRADE SCHOOL ★★★★½	TEENS ★★★★½
YOUNG ADULTS ★★★★		OVER 30 ★★★	SENIORS ★★

Cal Expo, 1600 Exposition Boulevard; ☎ 916-924-3747; www.ragingwaters.com

Hours *Early May–late September:* daily, 10:30 a.m.–6 p.m.; hours and days vary at other times of the year. **Admission** $25 adults, $20 seniors, $20 for children under 48" tall, free for children age 2 and under; tubes $2; parking $7. **Touring time** Average 5 hours; minimum 3 hours. **Rainy-day touring** No. **Restaurants** Yes. **Alcoholic beverages** Yes. **Disabled access** Yes. **Wheelchair rental** No. **Baby-stroller rental** No. **Lockers** Yes, $5. **Pet kennels** No. **Rain check** Yes. **Private tours** No.

DESCRIPTION AND COMMENTS   The summer heat here is unrelieved by ocean breezes. We love water parks for a great change from sightseeing, a chance for adults to read and talk, a safe environment for kids to splash, and a cool, summery time for all. Raging Waters has all the features a family looks for in a water park: a wave pool, a wading area for toddlers, a moving-water river-tubing area, an activity lagoon, and, of course, slides ranging from the modest to the terrifying. The most popular is the Honolulu Halfpipe, a four-story "wave" slide that's a good screamer.

unofficial **TIP**
The summer heat in this part of the state can be startling, even overwhelming—which is why a water park can make a good destination.

Sacramento Zoo

APPEAL BY AGE	PRESCHOOL ★★★★	GRADE SCHOOL ★★★★	TEENS ★★
YOUNG ADULTS ★★		OVER 30 ★★	SENIORS ★★

3930 West Land Park Drive; ☎ 916-808-5885; www.saczoo.com

Hours *February–October:* daily, 9 a.m.–4 p.m.; *November–January:* daily, 10 a.m.–4 p.m.; closed Thanksgiving and Christmas. **Admission** $8.50 adults, $6 children ages 3–12, free for children age 2 and under. **Touring time** Average 3–4 hours; minimum 1 hour. **Rainy-day touring** Yes. **Restaurants** Snack bars. **Alcoholic beverages** No. **Disabled access** Yes. **Wheelchair rental** Yes, free. **Baby-stroller rental** Yes. **Lockers** No. **Pet kennels** No. **Rain check** No. **Private tours** No.

DESCRIPTION AND COMMENTS   Zoo camps and overnight safaris are among the special kids' activities at this friendly midsize (400-animal) zoo. There are weekend animal talks, and you can learn about animals the high-tech way by taking the self-guided Cell Phone Safari audio tour. If you have little ones, buy a combination ticket for the zoo and the neighboring Fairytale Town, a swell play place for the under-7 set.

Sutter's Fort State Historic Park and California State Indian Museum

APPEAL BY AGE	PRESCHOOL ★★	GRADE SCHOOL ★★★	TEENS ★★
YOUNG ADULTS ★★		OVER 30 ★★	SENIORS ★★★

Sutter's Fort: 2701 L Street at 27th; ☎ 916-445-4422
Indian Museum: 2618 K Street; ☎ 916-324-0971; general information: ☎ 916-324-0539; parks.ca.gov

Hours Daily, 10 a.m.–5 p.m.; closed holidays. **Admission** Fort and Indian Museum separate admissions: $6 adults, $4 children ages 6–12, free children age 5 and under. **Touring time** Average 2 hours each; minimum 1 hour each. **Rainy-day touring** Yes. **Restaurants** No. **Alcoholic beverages** No. **Disabled access** Limited. **Wheelchair rental** No. **Baby-stroller rental** No. **Lockers** No. **Pet kennels** No. **Rain check** Yes. **Private tours** No.

DESCRIPTION AND COMMENTS   Built by early California rancher John Sutter in 1839, this fort was abandoned after one of Sutter's employees, James Marshall, found gold at a sawmill Sutter was building; within a year, everyone was looking for gold. Costumed docents demonstrate spinning, weaving, and cooking in this reconstructed fort; the several buildings include a candle-making room, cooperage, trading post, and blacksmith shop. The audio wands for a self-guided tour are free and fun.

unofficial **TIP**
Call first to find out when this state park has living-history events scheduled—they provide kids with an engaging, three-dimensional view of the past.

The California State Indian Museum is part of the complex and has exhibits that connect well with youngsters—featuring artifacts that include games, toys, feather baskets, and jewelry. It includes some hands-on exhibits.

Sutter's Fort Trade Store sells period toys, games, and clothing.

FAMILY-FRIENDLY RESTAURANTS

Delta King Pilothouse Restaurant
1000 Front Street, Old Sacramento; ☎ 916-441-4440; www.deltaking.com

Meals served Lunch Monday–Saturday, dinner nightly, and Sunday buffet brunch. **Cuisine** American. **Entree range** Lunch, $8–$10; dinner, $17–$35; brunch, $26. **Kids' menu** Yes. **Reservations** Recommended, especially on weekends. **Payment** AE, MC, V.

WHEN YOU SEE THE HISTORIC LANDMARK paddlewheeler at the dock in Old Town, your kids will clamor to go on board, but be forewarned: this is the kind of restaurant that seniors select for a picturesque lunch or dinner, and noisy preschoolers will disrupt the atmosphere. With elementary-age or older kids, go ahead and give it a try, but know that the food doesn't live up to its slightly pretentious presentation—and besides, the views of the river can be had from the dock itself. On the other hand, it's a good bet for a one-grandparent, one-child brunch, lunch, or dinner that's to be a bit special.

 ## Fat City

1001 Front Street, Old Sacramento; ☎ 916-446-6768; www.fatsrestaurants.com

Meals served Lunch, dinner, and weekend brunch. **Cuisine** American. **Entree range** Lunch and brunch, $10–$16; dinner, $10–$25. **Kids' menu** Yes. **Reservations** Accepted for large parties only. **Payment** AE, MC, V.

RUN BY THE FAT FAMILY, descendants of Chinese-immigrant railroad workers and now the city's leading restaurateurs, Fat City is the best family-oriented restaurant in Old Town. It's a pretty place, with a fine view of the river and passing carriages. The straightforward California fare—salads, sandwiches, fresh fish, and burgers—is quite good.

 ## Tower Cafe

1518 Broadway, William Land Park; ☎ 916-441-0222; www.towercafe.com

Meals served Breakfast, lunch, and dinner. **Cuisine** Californian. **Entree range** Breakfast, $5–$12; lunch, $8–$13; dinner, $8–$18. **Kids' menu** $6. **Reservations** Not necessary. **Payment** AE, MC, V.

ONE OF THOSE FUN RESTAURANTS that are discovered by a new generation of hipsters every few years, the Tower Cafe is in a landmark building that also houses a foreign- and independent-movie theater. It serves creative, reasonably priced fusion cuisine of the Asian-burrito variety, as well as burgers, pastas, and good wine by the glass. The outdoor tables are wonderful in spring and early summer, and at Saturday and Sunday brunch there's a mean French toast. The location, at the entrance to William Land Park, is perfection.

Willie's Burgers
2415 16th Street, William Land Park; ☎ 916-444-2006; www.williesburgers.com

Meals served Lunch and dinner. **Cuisine** American. **Entree range** $2–$5. **Kids' menu** No. **Reservations** Not accepted. **Payment** Cash only.

ACROSS FROM LAND PARK, this plain but clean joint makes the best (and messiest) burger in town. The fries and shakes are also outstanding.

NORTHERN GOLD COUNTRY:
Grass Valley and Nevada City

NORTHERN GOLD COUNTRY extends into the mountains above Sacramento, but distances are greater and the driving harder between attractions, so we recommend a beginning or end at Nevada City. **Grass Valley** and **Nevada City** are small cities so close together that they alternate Fourth of July celebrations between them. Both have beautiful, hilly settings with historic town centers of 19th-century buildings given over, for the most part, to such contemporary uses as shops and galleries. Grass Valley is the busier of the two, but Nevada City is better for overnighting and is great for antiquing and strolling to admire Victorian houses. We recommend a half-day visit to **Empire Mine State Historic Park.**

FAMILY LODGING

 ### Chute Hill Campground

23579 North Bloomfield Road, Nevada City; ☎ 530-265-2740; reservations through ReserveAmerica, ☎ 800-444-7275; www.reserveamerica.com; tent sites $15, cabins $35

THE BEST FAMILY CAMPGROUND IN GOLD COUNTRY, Chute Hill is part of Malakoff Diggins State Historical Park, comprising the old mining town of North Bloomfield and the old Diggins hydraulic mining operation, which in its heyday was an environmental nightmare. Today, there are 30 excellent tent and camper sites as well as three old prospectors' cabins under huge ponderosa pines overlooking the town and Diggins. Kids will love walking to the museum town, with its general store and blacksmith; swimming in Blair Lake, which has a wooden raft in its center; and taking flashlights on a hike to Hiller Tunnel, a cool remnant from mining days. Amenities include water, flush toilets, wood for sale, picnic tables, and fire rings.

Northern Queen Inn
400 Railroad Avenue, Nevada City; ☎ 800-226-3090 or 530-265-5824; www.northernqueeninn.com; $99–$154

THIS PLEASANT FACILITY is an affordable haven. Its 86 rooms, suites, and efficiency units are adjacent to easy parking but built along a woodsy

northern gold country: grass valley and nevada city

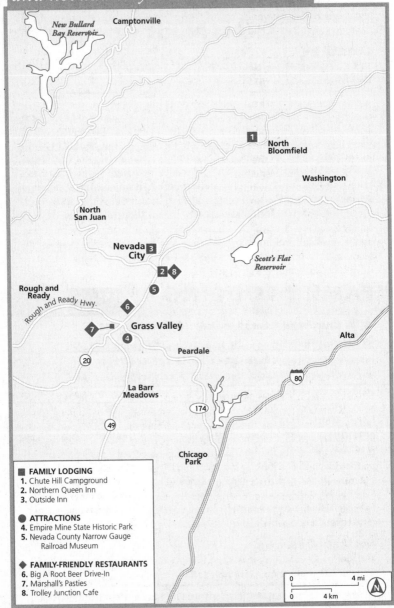

FAMILY LODGING
1. Chute Hill Campground
2. Northern Queen Inn
3. Outside Inn

ATTRACTIONS
4. Empire Mine State Historic Park
5. Nevada County Narrow Gauge Railroad Museum

FAMILY-FRIENDLY RESTAURANTS
6. Big A Root Beer Drive-In
7. Marshall's Pasties
8. Trolley Junction Cafe

creek. Some are individual cottages with lofts, decks or terraces, kitchens, and wood-burning stoves or fireplaces; even the basic rooms have little refrigerators and coffeemakers. Our kids found blackberry bushes on the hillside behind the deck. There's a picnic area, a good restaurant (see profile, page 377) that overlooks the creek's huge waterwheel, and restored train cars next door. Children younger than age 6 stay free.

Outside Inn
575 East Broad Street, Nevada City; ☎ **530-265-2233; www.outsideinn.com; $75–$180**

JUST TWO BLOCKS FROM DOWNTOWN, this quirky inn, run by active outdoor buffs, appeals to nature-loving families with a sense of humor. The complex includes 12 rooms and suites plus 3 cottages—each celebrating a particular theme. Kids into river rafting love staying in the Paddler's Suite; parents and teens like the Celestial Room, which celebrates the 1960s with glowing stars and beaded curtains. Some rooms have kitchenettes. The staff can connect you with a range of outdoor-adventure options and tell you how to find all the best river pools to soak in.

ATTRACTIONS

 Empire Mine State Historic Park

APPEAL BY AGE	PRESCHOOL ★	GRADE SCHOOL ★★★	TEENS ★★★
YOUNG ADULTS ★★★		OVER 30 ★★★★	SENIORS ★★★★

10791 East Empire Street, Grass Valley; ☎ **530-273-8522; www.empiremine.org**

Hours *May–September:* daily, 9 a.m.–6 p.m.; *September–April:* daily, 10 a.m.–5 p.m.; closed Thanksgiving, Christmas, and New Year's Day. **Admission** $3 adults, $1 children age 16 and under, free for children under age 6. **Touring time** Average 3 hours; minimum 1 hour. **Rainy-day touring** No. **Restaurants** No. **Alcoholic beverages** No. **Disabled access** Limited. **Wheelchair rental** No. **Baby-stroller rental** No. **Lockers** No. **Pet kennels** No, leashed dogs only. **Rain check** No. **Private tours** No.

DESCRIPTION AND COMMENTS This state park is quite undervisited, which is a shame. Kids who spend a few hours here will get a real sense of mining, from the individual miner's point of view (witness the Cornish dinner pails on exhibit) to an

unofficial **TIP**
If you take the time, Empire Mine takes you beyond the legends and stories.

overview of how gold is extracted from rock. The Empire Mine was one of the oldest and richest mines in California. Cornish miners dug 367 miles of tunnels here, going more than 10,000 feet deep underground.

Call ahead for tour times and bring a picnic lunch; there's no food for sale at the park, and the brisk mountain air made us ravenous in minutes. Begin in a little screening room at the visitors center with a viewing of movies with vintage footage of miners at work, and then, by all means, join a ranger walk for a guided tour of the site owner's mansion, mining offices (with period office fixtures), clubhouse, and mine-shaft entrance. Then get out your camera for a stroll around a graveyard of rusty mining equipment. If you hike, you can enjoy 12 miles of trails here, too. At the end of your visit, allow a little time to browse the gift shop. Restoration and interpretive exhibit work is ongoing, and construction has begun on the Underground Tour, an interactive tram ride into a mine shaft.

 Nevada County Narrow Gauge Railroad Museum

APPEAL BY AGE	PRESCHOOL ★	GRADE SCHOOL ★★★	TEENS ★★★
YOUNG ADULTS ★★★	OVER 30 ★★★★		SENIORS ★★★★

5 Kidder Court, Nevada City; ☎ 530-470-0902; www.ncngrrmuseum.org

Hours *May–October:* Friday–Tuesday, 10 a.m.–4 p.m., closed Wednesday and Thursday; *November–April:* open Saturday and Sunday only, 10 a.m.–4 p.m. **Admission** Free, donations appreciated. **Touring time** Average 1 hour; minimum 1 hour. **Rainy-day touring** Yes. **Restaurants** No. **Alcoholic beverages** No. **Disabled access** Limited. **Wheelchair rental** No. **Baby-stroller rental** No. **Lockers** No. **Pet kennels** No. **Rain check** No. **Private tours** No.

DESCRIPTION AND COMMENTS   Train buffs of all ages think they're in railroad heaven at this new museum, a local transportation-history showcase with all sorts of artifacts from the narrow-gauge railroad era. To get the most out of the visit, take a docent-led tour of the museum, rail yard, and restoration shop. In the main gallery, you'll see Engine 5, a sturdy 1875 Baldwin that hauled passengers, lumber, and other freight, and later in its storied life starred in movies at Universal Studios in Hollywood. There are also exhibits on electric streetcars, steam-powered cars, and the nation's first commercial airport. A collection of wooden rail cars fills the rail yard, and budding engineers can watch volunteers restore them in the adjacent shop. Load up on train-related souvenirs in the gift shop at the end of the tour.

FAMILY-FRIENDLY RESTAURANTS

 Big A Root Beer Drive-In

810 Main Street, Grass Valley; ☎ 530-273-3243

Meals served Daily, lunch and dinner. **Cuisine** American. **Entree range** $3–$10. **Kids' menu** Yes. **Reservations** None. **Payment** All major credit cards.

THIS OLD-FASHIONED DRIVE-IN with a traditional menu, updated for 21st-century palates, serves more than 20 types of burgers, numerous salads, and, of course, root beer in every way, shape, and form, including fabulous floats.

Our kids are partial to the giant Korn Dog, and health-minded parents tend to order the fresh salads such as the ahi niçoise, but everyone who comes here raves about the juicy burgers.

 ## Marshall's Pasties

203 Mill Street, Grass Valley; ☎ 530-272-2844

Meals served Daily, lunch and takeout. **Cuisine** Cornish. **Entree range** $4–$5. **Kids' menu** No. **Reservations** No. **Payment** No credit or debit cards.

THE MINERS IN THIS PART OF THE WORLD hailed from Cornwall, England, and their staple food was Cornish pasties, the specialty of Marshall's. Hand-rolled, these large pastries are stuffed with savory fillings such as sausage and broccoli and cheese. You can eat them at a little table upstairs or take them on a picnic.

 ## Trolley Junction Cafe

Northern Queen Inn, 400 Railroad Avenue, Nevada City; ☎ 530-265-5259

Meals served Daily, breakfast and lunch; Thursday–Sunday, dinner. **Cuisine** American. **Entree range** Breakfast, $5–$10; lunch, $9–$12; dinner, $9–$25. **Kids' menu** Yes. **Reservations** Recommended. **Payment** All major credit cards.

THERE'S A LOT OF CHARM AND GOOD FOOD at this fun place overlooking the woods, creek, and waterwheel, but for kids, the biggest appeal is the train ride across the parking lot. The train runs in summer (tickets are $12 for kids and $7 for adults). From the French toast to the omelets to the prime rib, the food is generous and carefully prepared, and the children's menu is extensive.

CENTRAL GOLD COUNTRY:

Jackson, Volcano, and Murphys

THIS IS THE ROAD-TRIP PART OF GOLD COUNTRY. CA 49 leaves the more developed areas along the Sacramento-to-Tahoe thoroughfare and becomes more countrified. The highway goes through the business or historic centers of some gold-rush towns; others are a few miles off the main drag. There are too many small towns, each with a historic landmark or two, to mention here; one of the most attractive is **Sutter Creek,** a Victorian/New Englandy–looking town that's home to many artisans. **Volcano,** a town that was a highlight for our kids, is listed following as an attraction. This is also the region for cave touring (see "Family Outdoor Adventures," page 362) and the site of **Indian Grinding Rock** and **Calaveras Big Trees state parks.**

FAMILY LODGING

El Campo Casa Resort Motel
12548 Kennedy Flat Road, Jackson; ☎ 209-223-0100; www.elcampocasa.com; $48–$72

AN OLDER MOTEL, not quite dating back to the gold-rush days (its restrooms have 1950s-era tile), but it has some good features for families. Its 15 rooms are comfortable if not spacious, and there's a playground, a swimming pool with an extra-shallow section, and a barbecue for guest use.

Jackson Lodge
850 North Highway 49, Jackson; ☎ 866-333-0486 or 209-223-0486; www.thejacksonlodge.com; $69–$130; children under age 16 stay free

A KITCHEN AWAY FROM HOME is sometimes a blessing, and this place (renovated in 2005) has eight duplex housekeeping cottages, some with their own patios. The pool is refreshing in the summer and heated in the winter. It's right on CA 49 but not too noisy.

Murphys Historic Hotel
457 Main Street, Murphys; ☎ 800-532-7684 or 209-728-3444; www.murphyshotel.com; $70–$155; children age 12 and under stay free

central gold country: jackson, volcano, and murphys

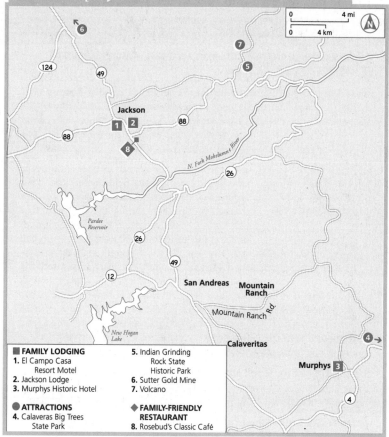

0 | 4 mi
0 | 4 km

FAMILY LODGING
1. El Campo Casa
   Resort Motel
2. Jackson Lodge
3. Murphys Historic Hotel

●**ATTRACTIONS**
4. Calaveras Big Trees
   State Park

5. Indian Grinding
   Rock State
   Historic Park
6. Sutter Gold Mine
7. Volcano

◆**FAMILY-FRIENDLY**
   RESTAURANT
8. Rosebud's Classic Café

FOR FAMILIES WHO WILL BE SPENDING TIME in the caves near Murphys, this well-maintained hostelry (part 1856 landmark, part new rooms) is quite serviceable, and the tree-shaded town center offers restaurants and shops. The restaurant and old saloon are popular stops for weary modern '49ers. If you're visiting in summer, be warned that the historic rooms are not air-conditioned; in the spirit of historic accuracy, they also don't have TVs or phones (but rooms in the newer annex do).

ATTRACTIONS

 ## Calaveras Big Trees State Park

APPEAL BY AGE	PRESCHOOL ★★★	GRADE SCHOOL ★★★★	TEENS ★★★★
YOUNG ADULTS ★★★★		OVER 30 ★★★★	SENIORS ★★★★

**4 miles northeast of Arnold, 20 miles northeast of Murphys on CA 4;
☎ 209-795-2334; parks.ca.gov**

Hours Daily, sunrise–sunset. **Admission** $6 per car, $2 per dog. **Touring time** Average 2 hours; minimum 1 hour. **Rainy-day touring** No. **Restaurants** No. **Alcoholic beverages** No. **Disabled access** Yes, except trails. **Wheelchair rental** No. **Baby-stroller rental** No. **Lockers** No. **Pet kennels** No. **Rain check** No. **Private tours** No.

unofficial **TIP**
The North Grove's self-guided 1.5-mile trail and the "Three Senses" Trails are the best for nonhiking families.

DESCRIPTION AND COMMENTS Native Americans had known about and held sacred the giant sequoias of this grove for eons when it was discovered by outsiders during the gold rush. For the next 20 years, although the big-tree groves of Yosemite and Sequoia national parks also had been found, the Calaveras site was the most visited and best known. Its tourist hotels continued as popular and stylish destinations until the turn of the 19th century. Today, the park is less well known, and its South Grove remains secluded and primeval; it is home to the park's largest tree, the Louis Agassiz, which is 250 feet tall and more than 25 feet in diameter 6 feet above the ground. Creek swimming, developed campgrounds with 129 campsites, and a rustic recreation hall make it one of the most attractive Gold Country camping areas.

Indian Grinding Rock State Historic Park

APPEAL BY AGE	PRESCHOOL ★★★	GRADE SCHOOL ★★★	TEENS ★★★
YOUNG ADULTS ★★★		OVER 30 ★★★	SENIORS ★★★

14881 Pine Grove–Volcano Road; ☎ 209-296-7488; parks.ca.gov

Hours Daily, sunrise–sunset. **Admission** $6 per private vehicle. **Touring time** Average 2 hours; minimum 1 hour. **Rainy-day touring** No. **Restaurants** No. **Alcoholic beverages** No. **Disabled access** Yes. **Wheelchair rental** No. **Baby-stroller rental** No. **Lockers** No. **Pet kennels** No. **Rain check** No. **Private tours** No.

DESCRIPTION AND COMMENTS You get the idea that there are rocks here, but few visitors are prepared for the sight of hundreds of feet of flat limestone outcropping spread out over the rolling countryside. A closer look reveals more than a thousand mortar cups (or *chaw'ses*) chiseled into the largest rock, which also displays 363 petroglyphs. The mortar cups were used for grinding acorns and seeds, staple foods in the Miwok people's diet. The Regional Indian Museum exhibits and slide show illuminate the hunting and gathering way of life of ten Sierra Nevada tribes, and a full-scale model roundhouse, bark conical dwelling, and football field provide further insight into daily Native American life more than 100 years ago. Twenty-one campsites have tables, stoves, piped water, and restrooms, but no showers.

 ## Sutter Gold Mine

APPEAL BY AGE	PRESCHOOL ★	GRADE SCHOOL ★★★★	TEENS ★★★★
YOUNG ADULTS ★★★	OVER 30 ★★★		SENIORS ★★★

13660 Highway 49 between Sutter Creek and Amador City;
☎ **888-818-7462 or 209-736-2708; www.caverntours.com**

Hours *Summer:* daily, 9 a.m.–5 p.m.; *winter:* weekdays, 10 a.m.–4 p.m.; weekends and holidays, 10 a.m.–5 p.m. **Admission** *Family tour:* $17.50 adult, $11.50 child. *Moaning Cavern rappel:* $65 per ticket, age 12 and up only; gold panning, $5. **Touring time** Average 2 hours; minimum 1 hour. **Rainy-day touring** Yes. **Restaurants** Volcano General Store. **Alcoholic beverages** Bar in town. **Disabled access** Limited. **Wheelchair rental** No. **Baby-stroller rental** No. **Lockers** No. **Pet kennels** No. **Rain check** No. **Private tours** No.

DESCRIPTION AND COMMENTS   It's one thing to pan for gold in a creek—it's another experience entirely to descend into a real underground mine shaft. You and your crew will be fitted with hard hats before descending for a one-hour tour, during which you'll see lots of mining equipment (including a huge haul truck) and learn

unofficial **TIP**
The typical 11-year-old will pronounce this underground mine-shaft adventure totally cool.

how to distinguish real gold from pyrite. Above ground, you can mine for gemstones, pan for gold, and see a film on gold mining and its history. The same outfitter operates tours into nearby Moaning Cavern, the state's largest cave chamber; the walking tour down 234 stairs is fun for the whole family, and the rappel, dropping 165 feet into the huge main chamber, is a tremendous thrill for kids 12 and up—but be advised that they'll be allowed to descend only if parents sign a waiver; if a parent isn't present, a signed and notarized waiver must accompany the child.

Volcano

APPEAL BY AGE	PRESCHOOL ★	GRADE SCHOOL ★★★	TEENS ★★★
YOUNG ADULTS ★★★	OVER 30 ★★★		SENIORS ★★★

Choose a loop trip from CA 49. We took Gopher Flat Road from Sutter Creek, which turns into Shake Ridge Road and winds 13 miles to Daffodil Hill (first planted in the 1800s and bursting with 400,000 flowers in the spring). The exciting Ram's Horn Grade was a dramatic 3-mile descent to Volcano. We took Pine Grove–Volcano Road out to Indian Grinding Rock State Historic Park.

Touring time Average 1 hour; minimum 30 minutes. **Rainy-day touring** No. **Restaurants** Volcano General Store. **Alcoholic beverages** Bar in town. **Disabled access** Limited. **Wheelchair rental** No. **Baby-stroller rental** No. **Lockers** No. **Pet kennels** No. **Rain check** No. **Private tours** No.

unofficial **TIP**
Volcano General Store has a wonderfully atmospheric old soda-shop counter that serves such kid chow as burgers and hot dogs.

DESCRIPTION AND COMMENTS Traveling south, you'll see Plymouth, Amador City, and Sutter Creek before you come to the turnoff for Volcano. Sutter Creek appeals to many adults because its historic buildings mix so pleasantly with its tasteful modern development. But we recommend a Volcano side trip combined with a visit to Indian Grinding Rock State Historic Park. There are four different scenic routes that converge in Volcano, where you'll find a park with grassy mounds and ruins, a few places to get refreshments, and some charming residential blocks. You can also check out the Black Chasm Cave's 50-minute Family Tour (a few restrictions apply regarding children and backpacks; ☎ 866-762-2837; **www .caverntours.com**). See this chapter's "Family Outdoor Adventures" section (page 362) for more info.

FAMILY-FRIENDLY RESTAURANT

Rosebud's Classic Café
26 Main Street, Jackson; ☎ 209-223-1035

Meals served Breakfast and lunch. **Cuisine** American. **Entree range** $5–$12. **Kids' menu** Yes. **Reservations** Not accepted. **Payment** MC, V.

A SWEET LITTLE CAFE WITH an Art Deco look and a wonderful children's menu offering waffles, junior cheese omelets, even a small turkey hot plate with homemade mashed potatoes. Parents can get a proper latte and a good meal, too. Breakfast is served all day.

SOUTHERN GOLD COUNTRY:
Columbia and Sonora

IF IT'S LIVING HISTORY YOU WANT, this part of the Mother Lode is the place to get it before heading on to the scenic wonders of Yosemite, or back north or south to big-city civilization. Enjoy the oak- and pine-dotted hills and the river vistas—but be prepared for hot, hot weather in the summer.

FAMILY LODGING

Best Western Sonora Oaks
19551 Hess Avenue, Sonora; ☎ 800-532-1944 or 209-533-4400; www.bestwestern.com; $122 and up

THIS 101-ROOM MOTEL.may be part of a chain, but it nevertheless has a rural feel, with an oak grove in its backyard and a pool that's a necessity in the summer. Ask for a deluxe king room, which has both a king bed and a queen sleeper sofa. There's an adjacent coffee shop with a children's menu, and children younger than age 12 stay free.

ATTRACTION

 Columbia State Historic Park

APPEAL BY AGE	PRESCHOOL ★★	GRADE SCHOOL ★★★★	TEENS ★★★★
YOUNG ADULTS ★★★		OVER 30 ★★★	SENIORS ★★★

4 miles north of Sonora on CA 49, Columbia; ☎ 209-588-9128 (visitor services), ☎ 209-532-0150 (park office), ☎ 209-532-3120 (theater info), ☎ 209-588-0808 (stagecoach and horseback riding); parks.ca.gov

Hours Daily, 10 a.m.–5 p.m. for most businesses; tours at 11 a.m. Saturday and Sunday. **Admission** Free to park, various charges at concessions. **Touring time** Average 4 hours; minimum 2 hours. **Rainy-day touring** No. **Restaurants** City Hotel; ice-cream parlor. **Alcoholic beverages** Yes. **Disabled access** No. **Wheelchair rental** No. **Baby-stroller rental** No. **Lockers** No. **Pet kennels** No, leashed dogs only. **Rain check** No. **Private tours** No.

southern gold country: columbia and sonora

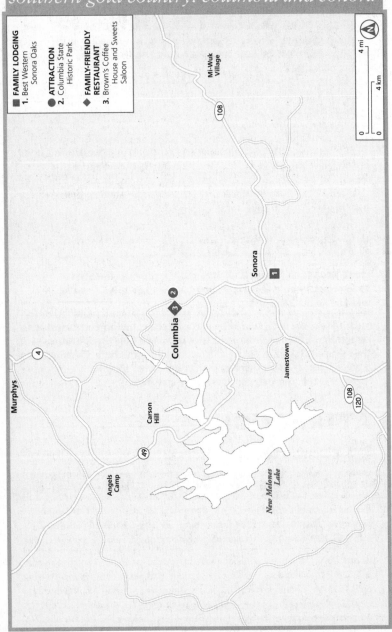

FAMILY LODGING
1. Best Western
   Sonora Oaks

ATTRACTION
2. Columbia State
   Historic Park

FAMILY-FRIENDLY RESTAURANT
3. Brown's Coffee
   House and Sweets
   Saloon

Mi-Wuk Village

108

Sonora

1

2
3

Columbia

Jamestown

108
120

Murphys

4

Carson Hill

49

Angels Camp

New Melones Lake

0   4 mi
0   4 km

DESCRIPTION AND COMMENTS   More modest than a theme park (by far), more honky-tonk than you'd expect in something called a historic park, Columbia is actually a perfect stop for school-age kids. It's a historic landmark, a four-block area of intact 1850s and 1860s buildings (which survived because the town was rebuilt almost entirely in brick after a fire), but it's also a tourist town. There are concessions operating within the park that allow you to pan for gold, go on a tour of a working mine (☎ 209-532-9693), and go on a horseback or stagecoach ride throughout the town. You can brave the ghosts and stay in a restored historic hotel right in the park (☎ 209-532-1479; operated by hotel students at a nearby community college), attend a play at the town playhouse (though it will likely be a modern show), sip a sarsaparilla and listen to bluegrass music at the saloon, watch the blacksmith work, browse for souvenirs and knickknacks, or head for the ice-cream parlor.

FAMILY-FRIENDLY RESTAURANT

Brown's Coffee House & Sweets Saloon
22760 Main Street in Columbia State Historic Park, Columbia;
☎ 209-532-1850; finendandy.biz/columbiacoffee.htm

BEFORE YOU LET YOUR KIDS PICK OUT SOME CANDIES or jumbo chocolate-chip cookies in this sweets shop in the historic saloon building, fortify yourselves with respectable sandwiches (turkey, vegetarian, PB&J) or hot dogs that you can take to one of the picnic tables outside. To drink, try a real sarsaparilla or a good espresso.

PART EIGHT

NORTHERN CALIFORNIA

SPARSELY POPULATED AND RICH IN DRAMATIC LANDSCAPES, Northern California is given over in large part to national forest land. The coastal area (roughly **Sonoma, Mendocino,** and **Humboldt counties**) begins in the south as rugged, beautiful beach country and leads to the **Redwood Coast,** home of the big trees. It's bounded on the east by the north–south chain of mountains known as the **Coast Range.** Immediately to the east of the range is a huge swath of forest. From south to north, **Mendocino National Forest** merges into **Shasta-Trinity National Forest,** which in turn merges into **Klamath National Forest.** In northern midstate is **Lake Shasta,** a man-made lake of immense proportions and a major recreation site, and **Mount Shasta.** Directly north of San Francisco is the famous wine-producing Napa Valley, not covered in any detail here as its primary pleasures are adults-only.

Many of the small towns and cities of Northern California have neighborhoods catering to tourists and travelers, but these are sometimes simply a few motels and chain restaurants near the freeways. In this region, the fact that a town has a larger population may mean that it has more industry and jobs, not more vacation options, so we've organized this chapter around counties instead of cities. We feature only selected Northern California counties with significant family-vacation options.

Along the coast, these include the counties of **Sonoma,** for its agricultural producers and historic sites; **Mendocino,** for whale watching, the **Skunk Train,** tide pools, and picturesque, shop-filled towns; and **Humboldt,** with three giant-redwood state parks and the huge, primeval oasis of **Redwood National Park.** Inland, we'll focus on **Trinity** and **Shasta counties** for the **Whiskeytown-Shasta-Trinity National Recreation Area,** with **Lake Shasta** as its centerpiece (allow a few days for houseboating or personal-watercraft riding here).

A significant number of city, state, and county parks in this region have summer swimming options, so when you load up the car in the

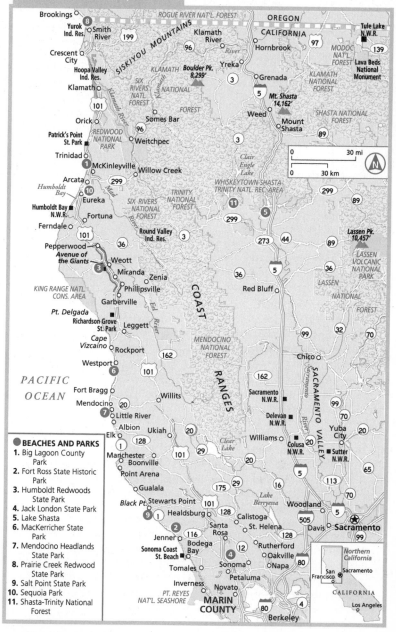

northern california

Brookings ○ ⑧
Yurok ○ Smith
Ind. Res.   River   199
ROGUE RIVER NAT'L. FOREST   OREGON
CALIFORNIA
Tule Lake
N.W.R.

Crescent ○
City
96
Klamath
River
Hornbrook
97
MODOC
NAT'L.
FOREST
139
Lava Beds
National
Monument

Hoopa Valley
Ind. Res.
SIX
KLAMATH
Yreka
5   Mt. Shasta
14,162'
KLAMATH
NATIONAL
FOREST

Klamath ○
101
RIVERS
NAT'L.
FOREST
Boulder Pk.
8,299'
3
Grenada
Weed
Mount
Shasta
SHASTA NATIONAL
FOREST

Orick ○
Somes Bar
FOREST
89

Patrick's Point
St. Park ■
Trinidad ○
REDWOOD
NATIONAL
PARK
96
Weitchpec
3
Clair
Engle
Lake
30 mi
0   30 km

McKinleyville
Willow Creek
WHISKEYTOWN-SHASTA-
TRINITY NATL. REC. AREA
299
89

Arcata ○
Humboldt
Bay
299
⑩
Eureka
TRINITY
NATIONAL
FOREST
⑪
5

Humboldt Bay ■
N.W.R.
SIX RIVERS
NATIONAL
FOREST
299
Lassen Pk.
10,457'

Fortuna ○
273   44
89

Ferndale ○
101
Round Valley
Ind. Res.
3
5
36
LASSEN
VOLCANIC
NATIONAL
PARK

Pepperwood
Avenue of
the Giants
36
③   Weott
Miranda
Zenia
36
5
LASSEN
NATIONAL

KING RANGE NATL.
CONS. AREA
Phillipsville
Red Bluff
FOREST

Garberville
COAST
99   32   70

Pt. Delgada
Richardson Grove
St. Park
Leggett
MENDOCINO
NATIONAL
FOREST
SACRAMENTO

Cape
Vizcaino ○ Rockport
162
Chico ○

Westport ○
⑥
101
RANGES
162

PACIFIC
OCEAN
Fort Bragg ○
Willits
Sacramento
N.W.R.
99
VALLEY

Mendocino ○
⑦ ○ Little River
20
Delevan
N.W.R.
70
Yuba
City

Albion ○
Ukiah
20
Williams ○
Colusa
N.W.R.
■ Sutter
N.W.R.
20

Elk ○
①
128
Clear
Lake
5
113
65

● BEACHES AND PARKS
1. Big Lagoon County
   Park
2. Fort Ross State Historic
   Park
3. Humboldt Redwoods
   State Park
4. Jack London State Park
5. Lake Shasta
6. MacKerricher State
   Park
7. Mendocino Headlands
   State Park
8. Prairie Creek Redwood
   State Park
9. Salt Point State Park
10. Sequoia Park
11. Shasta-Trinity National
    Forest

Manchester ○
○ Boonville
Point Arena ○
Gualala ○
Black Pt.
⑨ ① Stewarts Point
Jenner ○ ②
Sonoma Coast
St. Beach ■
Tomales ○
Inverness ○
PT. REYES
NAT'L. SEASHORE
101   29
29
175
16
Lake
Berryessa
Healdsburg ○
128
Calistoga ○
Santa
Rosa
St. Helena ○
116
Bodega
Bay
12
Rutherford ○
○ Oakville
Sonoma ○ ○ Napa
Petaluma ○
Novato ○
**MARIN
COUNTY**
Woodland ○
505   5
128
Davis ● **Sacramento**
99
80
Berkeley

*Northern
California*
San ⊛ Sacramento
Francisco
CALIFORNIA
Los Angeles

morning, keep bathing suits and inflatable rafts within easy reach. Your midday stop can be a festive highlight at a beautiful redwood-forest recreation area, where you can swim, play a little catch, and picnic.

Because children are famously indifferent to scenery, the spectacular but challenging winding roads of the Northern California coast should be carefully reviewed before setting out on road trips. Parents of children who get motion sickness should also plan carefully.

The same is true for inland scenic routes. Although the Shasta-Trinity National Forest is a beautiful region of pine-covered slopes and rocky chasms plunging to rivers far below, it took us much longer to cover the miles than we had anticipated. On one vacation, we had to change our itinerary midtrip (cutting down on the places we would visit) to allow enough time to actually get out into the outdoors we had spent so much time driving through.

GETTING THERE

BY PLANE   If you're flying into the western United States, you can investigate connecting regional air service into one of Northern California's small-city airports and rent a car on arrival. For example, **Horizon Air** serves Eureka/Arcata and Redding airports from Portland, Oregon; **United Express** offers service to Eureka/Arcata and Redding from San Francisco.

BY TRAIN   Amtrak's *Coast Starlight* goes from Sacramento through Chico, Redding (access to Lake Shasta), and Dunsmuir (access to Mount Shasta) before continuing on to Seattle. Call ☎ 800-USA-RAIL, or go to **www.amtrak.com.**

BY CAR   **CA 1** north of San Francisco takes you to the Mendocino coast. Continue on **US 101** from San Francisco to get to Sonoma and the Redwood Empire area. For a direct drive to the Shasta-Trinity area, take **Interstate 5** north from Sacramento.

HOW TO GET INFORMATION BEFORE YOU GO

- **California State Parks information**   P.O. Box 942896, Sacramento 94296-0001; ☎ 800-777-0369 or 916-653-6995; **parks.ca.gov**
- **Fort Bragg–Mendocino Coast Chamber of Commerce**   P.O. Box 1141, Fort Bragg 95437; ☎ 707-961-6300; **www.mendocinocoast .com;** more info at ☎ 866-GO-MENDO; **www.gomendo.com**
- **Greater Trinidad Chamber of Commerce**   P.O. Box 356, Trinidad 95570; ☎ 707-677-1610; **www.trinidadcalif.com**
- **Humboldt County Convention and Visitors Bureau**   1034 Second Street, Eureka 95501; ☎ 800-346-3482 or 707-443-5097; **www.redwoodvisitor.org**
- **Santa Rosa Convention & Visitors Bureau**   9 Fourth Street, Santa Rosa 95401; ☎ 800-404-7673 or 707-577-8674; **www.visitsantarosa.com**
- **Sonoma County Convention and Visitors Bureau**   420 Aviation

Boulevard, Suite 106, Santa Rosa 95403; ☎ 800-576-6662 or 707-522-5800; **www.sonomacounty.com**
- **Sonoma Valley Visitors Bureau**   453 First Street East, Sonoma 95476; ☎ 707-996-1090; **www.sonomavalley.com**

The BEST BEACHES and PARKS

NOTE: SWIMMING IS NOT PERMITTED at some of Northern California's rugged beaches because of dangerous water conditions. Never leave children unattended near the ocean anywhere in this region.

BIG LAGOON COUNTY PARK   Although it's a popular park, the setting here is one of splendid isolation, and although it's adjacent to the highway and thus easily accessed, the huge expanses of beach, water, and sky make it seem remote. It's a county (read: low-budget) campground, so it's more rustic than amenity-laden. The site makes a nice break between the northern redwoods and Eureka. There is a fee for day use and camping; amenities include boat launching, picnicking, camping, fishing, swimming, sanitary facilities, and cold running water. Reservations are not accepted; campsites are on a first-come, first-served basis. Seven miles north of Trinidad, exit US 101 at Big Lagoon Park Road; 707-445-7651; **co.humboldt.ca.us/portal/living/county_parks.**

> *unofficial* **TIP**
> The chance to camp in the redwoods is not to be missed.

HUMBOLDT REDWOODS STATE PARK   The most famous part of Humboldt Redwoods State Park is the dramatic **Avenue of the Giants,** a winding bypass road with turnouts and parking areas, that curves along the south fork of the Eel River through a magnificent forest of redwoods. You feel as if you're moving through a green undersea world as you drive for miles under the forest canopy, only occasionally coming into a sunny meadow. Slanting beams of sunlight impart that sense of sanctuary and awe so often remarked upon in connection with the big trees. You'll find picnicking, swimming, and other recreation along the drive, as well as towns about every six miles.

The hours spent in those awe-inspiring groves are unlike any other camping experience. See "Family Lodging" (page 408) for details. The park has remarkable scenic picnic areas, and the campgrounds are near trails in the most important redwood groves. Gentle, easy, self-guiding nature trails may be found at several locations; don't miss the half-mile **Founder's Grove Nature Loop,** which leads to the massive **Founder's Tree** and the **Dyerville Giant,** a 500-ton redwood that crashed to the ground several years ago. There are bike trails, and a park auto tour is available. Humboldt Redwoods State Park is 45 miles south of Eureka on US 101. The visitors center is next to Burlington Campground, two miles south of Weott; ☎ 707-946-2409; **www.humboldtredwoods.org.**

MACKERRICHER STATE PARK You won't find sunbathers and bikini-clad skaters on this stretch of rugged, often-foggy coastline, but rather hikers, bikers, anglers, horseback riders, and whale and seal watchers. Look for the **Seal Point Trail,** a short walk leading out to **Seal Rocks,** where you'll find loads of sunbathing seals. North of Seal Rocks is a popular spot for ocean fishing, and the whole area has great tide pooling at low tide. For a great adventure, contact **Ricochet Ridge Ranch** (☎ 888-873-5777 or 707-964-7669; **www.horse-vacation .com**) about its guided horseback rides on the beach or in the redwoods. The park has many wheelchair-accessible areas as well as superb tent and RV campsites (for reservations, call ☎ 800-444-7275 or go to **www. reserveamerica.com**). MacKerricher is three miles north of Fort Bragg on CA 1 near Cleone; ☎ 707-937-5804; **parks.ca.gov.**

SALT POINT STATE PARK A 6,000-acre park encompassing six miles of rugged coastline, Salt Point is a well-loved tide-pooling spot. There are trails for hiking and horseback riding, but it's the hidden coves, with their secret nooks and strange sandstone formations, that appeal to little ones (Tuesday through Sunday, 10 a.m. to 5 p.m.; open until 7 p.m. in summer; admission $4 adults, $3 seniors 60 or older and military personnel, $2 children ages 3 to 12, free children age 2 and younger; ☎ 707-441-4263; **www.sequoiaparkzoo.net**). Good camping, too. The park is 20 miles north of Jenner on CA 1; ☎ 707-847-3221 or 707-865-2391; **parks.ca.gov.**

SEQUOIA PARK This lovely city park in Eureka has a free zoo where you can see animals native to the area, such as bears, elk, and deer, as well as exotic species. There are also picnic areas, a playground, a duck pond, and more than 50 acres of North Coast redwoods. In the summer months, a petting zoo is open Tuesday through Sunday, 11:30 a.m. to 3:30 p.m. The zoo is closed Mondays, but the park itself is open every day. W and Glatt streets, Eureka; ☎ 707-441-4263.

FAMILY OUTDOOR ADVENTURES

 BOATING ON LAKE SHASTA One of the most memorable days of our Northern California vacation was spent on a patio boat on Lake Shasta. We donned bathing suits and sunscreen, packed rented fishing poles, packed hot dogs for barbecuing, grabbed the two-person inflatable rowboat and some rope, and headed for the rental dock. Over the next idyllic hours, we took turns driving the flat-bottomed boat over calm lake waters while marveling at how close the forested mountains looked in the clear, high-elevation air. We cooked on the grill and took turns swimming off the side or floating in the inflatable rowboat tied behind the bigger boat. We tied up on shore from time to time, fished over the side, and waved to other patio boaters as they passed. Motel reservations the night before and the night after at Bridge Bay Resort at Lake Shasta allowed us to fully enjoy the long day on the lake. Contact **Seven Crowns Resorts** (☎ 800-752-9669; **www.sevencrown.com**) or **Silverthorn Resort** (☎ 800-332-3044; **www.silverthornresort.com**) for information on lodging and renting houseboats or patio boats.

HIKING   Whether it's poking along a half-mile, stroller-friendly trail in a redwood forest or negotiating a beach trail for an entire morning, you are guaranteed to spend time hiking in Northern California. So integral is the experience that we won't even get into details here, because this chapter is loaded with descriptions of state, national, and regional parks and their trails.

HORSEBACK RIDING   Although horseback riding for casual visitors is available throughout the state, Northern California–area trail rides lead you along routes that are really the stuff of fantasy. Picture yourself cantering along the beach? The one-and-a-half-hour ride at **Ricochet Ridge Ranch** (24201 North Highway 1, Fort Bragg; ☎ 888-873-5777 or 707-964-7669; **www.horse-vacation .com;** both group and private rides are available) takes you out to MacKerricher State Park for a good portion of the saddle time, and you'll ride right along the tide line and be able to see seals on the offshore rocks—and, in season, whales.

Thinking of spending a few days or a full vacation at a family-oriented ranch resort? See the lodging listing for **Coffee Creek Ranch** (page 413). Do you have preteen and teen riders ready for the adventure of an overnight pack trip into the wilderness, or at least a daylong trip along the Klamath River? Combine a wilderness pack ride with a ranch stay, or try a "saddle and paddle" package that combines trail rides with rafting or mountain biking at **Marble Mountain Ranch** (see lodging profile, page 409).

How about a moonlight trail ride with your kids? Try the guided trail rides (children must be 8 or older) through **Sugarloaf Ridge State Park** with the **Triple Creek Horse Outfit** near Kenwood, 30 minutes north of Sonoma (☎ 707-887-8700; **www.triplecreekhorseoutfit.com**); $90 per person for a two-hour ride. Group rates available.

RIVER RAFTING   The ocean may be wilder way up north, but the rivers tend to be milder, making for excellent, not-too-scary rafting trips suitable for kids as young as age 4. One of the best rivers for families is the **Trinity,** which wanders along the Trinity Alps Wilderness. Companies to try include **Bigfoot Rafting** (Willow Creek; ☎ 530-629-2263 or 800-722-2223; **www.bigfootrafting.com**) and **Trinity River Rafting** (Big Flat; ☎ 800-307-4837 or 530-623-3033; **www .trinityriverrafting.com**), which have half- to two-day trips on Class I and II stretches for families; children 12 and older can sign up for Class III and IV adventures.

unofficial **TIP**
It's not necessary to take a boat to see whales—the high bluffs along the shoreline in the Mendocino area offer ideal viewing from land.

Over Shasta way, the Klamath River is another gentle one that can be great for family rafting; **Turtle River Rafting** (Mount Shasta; ☎ 800-726-3223 or 530-926-3223; **www.turtleriver.com**) offers trips geared to children ages 4 to 11.

WHALE WATCHING ON THE MENDOCINO COAST If you're a winter or spring visitor to Northern California, be sure to join locals for the annual whale-watching rites. Gray whales pass this coast on their way south to Baja California from December through February and on their return home to the Bering Sea from mid-March through April. There are programs and docent-led walks at MacKerricher State Park near Fort Bragg, **Mendocino Headlands State Park** in Mendocino, and **Point Cabrillo Light Station** near Mendocino; call ☎ 707-964-9112 for MacKerricher, ☎ 707-937-5804 for Mendocino Headlands, and ☎ 707-937-0816 for Point Cabrillo.

When looking from shore, it's hard to fully appreciate the size of these mammals, so many wildlife enthusiasts take a whale-watching boat trip. **Noyo Harbor** in Fort Bragg is an embarkation point for several such charters, which cost about $35 to $80 per person for a two-hour trip. For information, contact **Anchor Charters** (☎ 707-964-4550; **www.anchorcharterboats.com**); **All Aboard Adventures** (☎ 707-964-1881; **www.allaboardadventures.com**), or **Telstar Charters** (☎ 707-964-8770; **www.gooceanfishing.com**).

SONOMA COUNTY:

Sonoma, Santa Rosa, Windsor, Forestville, Guerneville, and Glen Ellen

NOW AS FAMOUS AS NAPA VALLEY for its wine, Sonoma County is actually a mixed agricultural area with a variety of outstanding products, including cheese, apples, wine, and carnivorous plants. Families traveling on US 101 will find such rest-stop recreations as skating rinks, bumper cars, and a steam railway in the city of **Santa Rosa,** which also has one of the area's airports. The historic town center of **Sonoma** is a nice lunch stop—a stroll through the fort where the **Bear Flag Revolt** took place can be combined with a meal and a look at the cheese-making process. But although some of the wineries serve juice or soda, we don't recommend tasting-room stops for families. **Guerneville,** a fetching little town on the Russian River, makes a fine family base, especially in summer, when the canoeing conditions are ideal and the riverside beach is a fun warm-afternoon destination.

Much is made of the **Jack London State Park,** but we don't think kids get it, even if they've read *White Fang* (how to explain the connection between the stories and the ruins of a dream house?); however, the outdoor activities at this park can be fun.

FAMILY LODGING

Best Western Sonoma Valley Inn
550 Second Street, West Sonoma; ☎ 800-334-5784 or 707-938-9200; www.sonomavalleyinn.com; $129–$269

A PLEASANT 80-ROOM MOTEL just a block from Sonoma Plaza, with a pool and garden setting. Courtyard rooms have private balconies and fireplaces, all rooms have coffeemakers and refrigerators, and a Continental breakfast is delivered to your room. Children younger than age 16 stay free; activity packages and babysitting are available.

Creekside Inn
16180 Neeley Road, Guerneville; ☎ 800-776-6586 or 707-869-3623; www.creeksideinn.com; cottages $130–$270

IN ADDITION TO ITS STABLE OF HOMEY, family-focused cottages in the redwoods, Creekside recently added a dozen sustainable "Nature's *sonoma county*

HENDY WOODS
STATE PARK
Ukiah

COW
MOUNTAIN
RECREATION
AREA

MENDOCINO
NATIONAL
FOREST

Indian Valley Reservoir

Russian River

29

Lakeport

Clear Lake

CLEAR LAKE
STATE PARK

175

16

MENDOCINO
COUNTY

128

ANDERSON
MARSH NATIONAL
PRESERVE

Gualala

Cloverdale

175

KRUSE
RHODODENDRON
STATE RESERVE

Lake Sonoma

101

29

Middletown

Sea
Ranch

Geyserville

SONOMA
COUNTY

ROBERT LOUIS
STEVENSON
STATE PARK

Lake Berryessa

SALT POINT
STATE PARK

Healdsburg

128

Calistoga

ARMSTRONG
REDWOODS
STATE RESERVE

Windsor

NAPA
COUNTY

Salt Point

4

FORT ROSS STATE
HISTORIC PARK

6

Jenner

2

Guerneville

Forestville

BOTHE-NAPA
STATE PARK

St. Helena

Napa R.

*PACIFIC
OCEAN*

5

116

3

7

Rutherford

Sebastopol

12

Santa
Rosa

12

Bodega Bay

10

Glen Ellen

Yountville

Bodega Head

Bodega Bay

PETALUMA
ADOBE
S.H.P.

8

9

Napa

11

Sonoma

Tomales
Point

Petaluma

116

121

TOMALES
BAY
STATE
PARK

MARIN COUNTY

37

1

*San Pablo
Bay*

PT. REYES
NATIONAL
SEASHORE

*Point
Reyes*

*Drakes
Bay*

San Rafael

80

Richmond

580

MT. TAMALPAIS
STATE PARK

GOLDEN GATE
NAT'L. REC. AREA

Sausalito

Tiburon

Farallon
Islands

San
Francisco

80

101

Oakland

■ **FAMILY LODGING**
1. Best Western
   Sonoma Valley Inn
2. Creekside Inn
3. Flamingo Conference
   Resort & Spa
4. Salt Point State Park

● **ATTRACTIONS**
5. California Carnivores
6. Fort Ross State
   Historic Park
7. Redwood Empire
   Ice Arena
8. Sonoma Plaza
9. Traintown

◆ **FAMILY-FRIENDLY
RESTAURANTS**
10. Garden Court Cafe
    and Bakery
11. Juanita Juanita
12. Omelette Express

0   16 mi

0   16 km

N

Cottages," built to exacting green standards and equipped with all the modern essentials, from Wi-Fi to flat-screen TVs. It also has a small bed-and-breakfast operation, but that's aimed more at wine-touring couples. The cottages and grounds, however, are perfect for families. On-site are a pool, a billiards table, pinball games, picnic areas, and lawns for romping. A short walk away is one of the first miniature golf courses in Northern California, as well as the town of Guerneville, which boasts shops, restaurants, an old-fashioned five-and-dime, bike- and canoe-rental outfits, and Johnson's Beach, with paddleboat rentals, a kiddie swim area, and a snack bar. A canoe trip on the river is a great family excursion. The Creekside will also point you toward local farms that welcome visitors.

Flamingo Conference Resort & Spa
2777 Fourth Street, Santa Rosa; ☎ 800-848-8300 or 707-545-8530; www.flamingoresort.com; $119–$339 May–October, less in off-season; children younger than age 12 stay free

A FAMILY-RUN RESORT with 170 rooms spread over ten acres of grounds and spa facilities, this Santa Rosa hotel boasts a playground, lawn games, a pool, a wading pool, and tennis courts. All the public areas are smoke-free. The hotel's spa (Montecito Heights; ☎ 707-526-0529) offers a daytime child-care program with games, arts, and crafts for kids from 3 months to 12 years old, for the modest fee of $6 an hour. For ages 3 months to 16 months, add $1.50 per hour; reservations are essential.

Salt Point State Park
CA 1, north of Jenner; ☎ 707-847-3221; parks.ca.gov; reservations: ReserveAmerica, ☎ 800-444-7275; www.reserveamerica.com; campsites $25 (less for walk-ins)

THIS GORGEOUS PARK on the rugged Sonoma Coast is rich with family pleasures: hiking and horseback trails, a sandy beach, a marine reserve with tide pools, and proximity to Fort Ross. Pack warm clothes, even for August, but know that warm, sunny days happen, too. Facilities include fire rings, picnic tables, water, and restrooms, but no showers.

▐ ATTRACTIONS

California Carnivores

APPEAL BY AGES	PRESCHOOL ★★★	GRADE SCHOOL ★★★	TEENS ★★
YOUNG ADULTS ★★		OVER 30 ★★	SENIORS ★★

2833 Old Gravenstein Highway South, Sebastopol; ☎ 707-824-0433; www.californiacarnivores.com

Hours Thursday–Monday, 10 a.m.–4 p.m.; closed Tuesdays, Wednesdays, Thanksgiving, Christmas Eve, Christmas, and New Year's Day. **Admission** Free. **Touring time** Average 1 hour; minimum 30 minutes. **Rainy-day touring** Yes, no problem in greenhouses. **Restaurants** No. **Alcoholic beverages** No. **Disabled**

access Yes. **Wheelchair rental** No. **Baby-stroller rental** No. **Lockers** No. **Pet kennels** No pets allowed. **Rain check** No. **Private tours** No.

DESCRIPTION AND COMMENTS   This nursery and farm specializes in insect-eating plants, a fact that makes it the coolest nursery in the world for a 10-year-old. Some 350 varieties are on display, and many are for sale. Picnic areas are available. Kids must be accompanied by adults, but there's no age limit.

 ## Fort Ross State Historic Park

APPEAL BY AGE	PRESCHOOL ★★★	GRADE SCHOOL ★★★★	TEENS ★★★★
YOUNG ADULTS ★★★★		OVER 30 ★★★★	SENIORS ★★★

19005 Coast Highway 1, Jenner; ☎ 707-847-3286; parks.ca.gov or www.fortrossstatepark.org

Hours *Park:* daily, sunrise–sunset; *fort:* daily, 10 a.m.–4:30 p.m.; closed Thanksgiving, Christmas, and New Year's Day. **Admission** $6 per private vehicle. **Touring time** Average 2 hours; minimum 1 hour. **Rainy-day touring** Not recommended. **Restaurants** Nearby. **Alcoholic beverages** No. **Disabled access** Limited. **Wheelchair rental** No. **Baby-stroller rental** No. **Lockers** No. **Pet kennels** No. **Rain check** No. **Private tours** Yes.

DESCRIPTION AND COMMENTS   Its spectacular location on a high bluff above the roiling ocean would be reason enough to stop here, but Fort Ross is also a great reconstruction of the Russian-American Company's 1812 outpost. Here's one of the few places to learn about a foreign power's one-time foothold on continental America. You'll see reconstructed 12-foot-high stockades, soldiers' barracks, and an octagonal Orthodox chapel, as well as museum displays on Native American, Russian, and Yankee culture. Russian Orthodox services are held Memorial Day and the Fourth of July. Try to allow time to explore either Sandy Beach or North Cove, both of which have terrific tide pools when the conditions are right. And if you visit in spring, you'll be present for harbor-seal pupping season; call ☎ 707-869-9177 for information.

Redwood Empire Ice Arena

APPEAL BY AGE	PRESCHOOL ★★★★	GRADE SCHOOL ★★★★	TEENS ★★★
YOUNG ADULTS ★★		OVER 30 ★★	SENIORS ★★

1667 West Steele Lane, Santa Rosa; ☎ 707-546-7147; www.snoopyshomeice.com

Hours Complicated because of many ice shows, but call for skate times; consider reserving for an ice show; some public hours daily, but hours vary. **Admission** $9 adults, $7 ages 11 and under; skate rental $3 per person. **Touring time** Average 3 hours to skate and shop; minimum 1 hour to see gallery and gift shop. **Rainy-day touring** Just dandy. **Restaurants** Yes. **Alcoholic beverages** No. **Disabled access** Yes. **Wheelchair rental** No. **Baby-stroller rental** No. **Lockers** Yes. **Pet kennels** No. **Rain check** No. **Private tours** No, but limited private rentals possible.

DESCRIPTION AND COMMENTS   Built and operated by *Peanuts* creator Charles Schulz, this rink (decorated with huge photo murals of Switzerland and life-size trees) offers rentals, public skating sessions, and ice shows. It's a great place to burn off some kid energy on rainy or cold days—or to cool off on hot days.

Sonoma Plaza

APPEAL BY AGE	PRESCHOOL ★★	GRADE SCHOOL ★★	TEENS ★★★
YOUNG ADULTS ★★★		OVER 30 ★★★★	SENIORS ★★★★

Spain and First streets, Sonoma; Sonoma Valley Visitors Center; ☎ 707-996-1090

Hours *State Historic Park:* daily, 10 a.m.–5 p.m.; closed Thanksgiving, Christmas, and New Year's Day; shops and cafe hours vary. **Admission** *Mission and Vallejo Home:* $2, kids age 17 and under free. **Touring time** Average 2 hours; minimum 1 hour. **Rainy-day touring** Not recommended. **Restaurants** Yes. **Alcoholic beverages** At some restaurants. **Disabled access** Yes. **Wheelchair rental** No. **Baby-stroller rental** No. **Lockers** No. **Pet kennels** No. **Rain check** No. **Private tours** No.

DESCRIPTION AND COMMENTS   California was proclaimed a republic when the Bear Flag was raised here in 1846; a few weeks later it became a state. The plaza itself, created in 1835, is now a National Historic Landmark. Sonoma State Historic Park is also here; it includes a hotel and barracks, a mission, and, at another location, a historic residence. The mission has exhibits of religious and ranching life, and on weekends children can help bake bread in the garden workshop area (call ☎ 707-938-1519). Historic buildings are interspersed with contemporary shops and restaurants, all surrounding a pleasant park square.

Traintown

APPEAL BY AGE	PRESCHOOL ★★★★½	GRADE SCHOOL ★★★★	TEENS ★
YOUNG ADULTS ★		OVER 30 ½	SENIORS ½

20264 Broadway, Sonoma; ☎ 707-938-3912; www.traintown.com

Hours *September–May:* Friday–Sunday, 10 a.m.–5 p.m.; *June–Labor Day:* daily, 10 a.m.–5 p.m. **Admission** Train rides, $4.25; carousel, Ferris wheel, and other carnival rides, $2.50 per ride. **Touring time** Average 1½ hours; minimum 45 minutes. **Rainy-day touring** Not recommended. **Restaurants** Snack bar. **Alcoholic beverages** No. **Disabled access** Yes. **Wheelchair rental** No. **Baby-stroller rental** No. **Lockers** No. **Pet kennels** No. **Rain check** Unused tickets can be used another time. **Private tours** No.

DESCRIPTION AND COMMENTS   Take a ride on a quarter-scale railroad that replicates a steam train of the 1890s used in the mountains. The 20-minute trip winds through ten acres of forest, past lakes, and through tunnels to a miniature town. There's also a merry-go-round and petting zoo. This is heaven for your typical 4-year-old.

FAMILY-FRIENDLY RESTAURANTS

Garden Court Cafe and Bakery
13647 Arnold Drive, Glen Ellen; ☎ 707-935-1565;
www.gardencourtcafe.com

Meals served Breakfast and lunch. **Cuisine** American. **Entree range** $6–$12 (breakfast and lunch). **Kids' menu** Yes. **Reservations** Not accepted on weekends. **Payment** MC, V.

THE BRIGHT, PEACEFUL INTERIOR of this countryish cafe is perhaps the best place to sit, because sometimes the body shop next door makes the patio a bit noisy. The children's menu is cheerful, with choices ranging from Goldilocks porridge (an oatmeal that's not too hot, not too cold, but just right) to turkey sandwiches and small salads.

Juanita Juanita

19114 Arnold Drive, Sonoma; ☎ 707-935-3981;
www.juanitajuanita.com

Meals served Lunch and dinner. **Cuisine** Mexican. **Entree range** $5–$12. **Kids' menu** No. **Reservations** Not accepted. **Payment** No credit cards.

A FRIENDLY LOCAL RESTAURANT, this place puts a healthy spin on Mexican standards. Aside from the usual tacos and burritos, you can get a veggie tamale and a grilled-mushroom quesadilla. Kids love the home-made chips; parents like sampling from the roster of beers, including some locally brewed. This is the best Mexican food for miles around.

Omelette Express
112 Fourth Street, Railroad Square, Santa Rosa; ☎ 707-525-1690;
www.omelette.com

Meals served Breakfast and lunch. **Cuisine** American. **Entree range** $6–$12. **Kids' menu** Yes. **Reservations** Not accepted. **Payment** MC, V.

THIS BRIGHT, CHEERFUL DINER is a good spot for breakfast or lunch en route north or south, serving bagels, omelets, sandwiches, burgers, and the like.

MENDOCINO COUNTY:
Mendocino, Fort Bragg, Willits, and Leggett

IT'S CONSIDERED ONE OF THE MOST BEAUTIFUL and romantic places in the world, but the **Mendocino Coast** loses some of its charm if you have a 4-year-old throwing up in the backseat. Travel time along the scenic 80-mile "Dramamine Drive" (**Coast Highway 1,** also known as CA 1) between **Bodega Bay** and **Fort Bragg** can take twice as long as you might think from looking at a mileage chart. The pace is slow due to hairpin turns—but you're grateful it's slow when you encounter the careening log trucks. It all makes for a much longer time between bathroom stops than the map might suggest.

Traveling at a leisurely pace, and with plenty of picnic supplies for tailgate lunches (and with kids capable of scrambling down a fern-covered gully for a desperation rest stop), we have had a wonderful and memorable family drive along CA 1. But if your children are younger than age 6 or prone to car sickness, or if you want to cover a lot of miles (say, to get to the redwoods near **Eureka** or the Oregon border), we suggest the drive along US 101, showcasing a rolling agricultural landscape instead of dramatic ocean cliffs. You can access the major Mendocino attractions using connecting roads from US 101.

The towns of **Mendocino** and **Fort Bragg** make the best overnight bases for families. Fort Bragg is less picturesque, but it's the best point to board the area's major family attraction, the **Skunk Train.**

FAMILY LODGING

Emandal

16500 Hearst Post Office Road, Willits; ☎ 707-459-5439; www.emandal.com; 1-week July–August family camps, $725 adults, $182–$505 kids (varies by age); shorter family camps June–September; seasonal themed weekends throughout the year

A LAID-BACK FAMILY CAMP with few structured activities, this is a working ranch and farm complete with pigs, cows, and pickle making (it's inland from Mendocino near Willits). Don't expect luxury—the charming

mendocino county

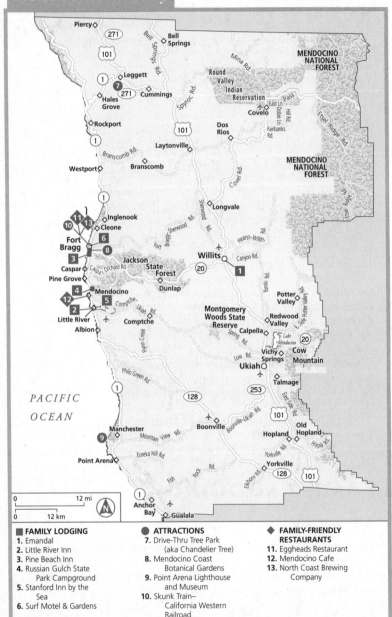

Piercy
271
101
Bell Springs Rd.
Bell Springs
MENDOCINO NATIONAL FOREST
Mina Rd.
1
Leggett
7
271
Cummings
Spyroc Rd.
Round Valley Indian Reservation
East Ln.
Dobie Ln.
Hill Rd.
Hales Grove
Covelo
Rockport
101
Dos Rios
Fairbanks Rd.
Etsel Ridge Rd.
1
Laytonville
MENDOCINO NATIONAL FOREST
Branscomb Rd.
Covel Rd.
Westport
Branscomb
Sherwood Rd.
Etsel Ridge
1
Inglenook
Cleone
10 11 13
6
Fort Bragg
8
Bragg-Sherwood Rd.
Hearst-Willits Rd.
3
Jackson State Forest
Willits
Canyon Rd.
1
Caspar
Orchard Rd.
20
Caspar
Tomki Rd.
Pine Grove
Dunlap
4
Mendocino
12
5
Compche-Ukiah Rd.
Montgomery Woods State Reserve
Potter Valley
2
Comptche
Redwood Valley
Little River
Albion
Calpella
20
Lake Mendocino
Spring Rd.
Cow Mountain
Philo Creek
Vichy Springs
Ukiah
Low Gap Rd.
PACIFIC OCEAN
Philo Green Rd.
1
128
253
Talmage
East Side Rd.
Manchester
Boonville
Mountain View Rd.
Boonville-Ukiah Rd.
Hopland
Old Hopland
101
9
Eureka Hill Rd.
Yorkville Rd.
Hopla
Point Arena
Fish Rock Rd.
Elkhorn Rd.
Yorkville
128
101
0   12 mi
0   12 km
N
1
Anchor Bay
Gualala

■ **FAMILY LODGING**
1. Emandal
2. Little River Inn
3. Pine Beach Inn
4. Russian Gulch State Park Campground
5. Stanford Inn by the Sea
6. Surf Motel & Gardens

● **ATTRACTIONS**
7. Drive-Thru Tree Park (aka Chandelier Tree)
8. Mendocino Coast Botanical Gardens
9. Point Arena Lighthouse and Museum
10. Skunk Train– California Western Railroad

◆ **FAMILY-FRIENDLY RESTAURANTS**
11. Eggheads Restaurant
12. Mendocino Cafe
13. North Coast Brewing Company

little redwood cabins lack hot water, and you'll have to walk a bit to the bathrooms and showers—but do expect reasonable comfort and lots of old-fashioned farm charms, from hearty, organic home-cooked meals to swimming holes in the Eel River, hiking trails, campfire songs, berry-picking, even helping with such farm chores as feeding the chickens.

Little River Inn
7901 North Highway 1, Little River; ☎ ☎ 888-466-5683 or 707-937-5942; www.littleriverinn.com; $130–$365

IDEALLY LOCATED ABOVE THE OCEAN and next to Van Damme State Park (which has an excellent beach and an easy trail through a pygmy forest of dwarf pines), this is a terrific small resort that's more welcoming than most here in the land of romantic bed-and-breakfasts. There's a good family suite in the main complex as well as comfortable rooms, most with superb views. Extras include a nine-hole golf course, tennis, gardens, and a highly regarded restaurant with a children's menu.

Pine Beach Inn
16801 North Highway 1, south of Fort Bragg; ☎ 888-987-8388 or 707-964-5603 ; www.pinebeachinn.com; $69 and up

THERE'S ROOM TO RUN at this moderately priced, family-friendly coastal inn four miles south of Fort Bragg. The 50 rooms (including nine two-bedroom suites, some with kitchenettes) sit on an 11-acre site that spills onto a sandy beach cove fed by a small creek. Elsewhere on the grounds are two tennis courts, lawns, and a good Thai restaurant (closed Tuesdays).

Russian Gulch State Park Campground

Off CA 1 just north of Mendocino; ☎ 707-937-5804; parks.ca.gov; reservations: ReserveAmerica, ☎ 800-444-7275; www.reserveamerica.com; campsites $25

TUCKED UNDER A PICTURESQUE BRIDGE just north of Mendocino, this is a beautiful little campground that's perfect for family tent or RV camping. There are only 30 sites, each with a picnic table and fireplace, and what it lacks in isolation it makes up in beauty and convenience. The campground itself is nestled in a little canyon; just across the stream is a white-sand beach, which is warmer and more protected than most in these parts. The town of Mendocino—with shops, food, and charm galore—is an easy hike of less than a mile. You can fish, swim, explore, and cycle, as well as rent a canoe from **Catch-a-Canoe and Bicycles, Too!** (two-person canoe, $20 per hour or $60 per day; four-person canoe, $22 per hour or $66 per day; call ahead for tide information; ☎ 707-937-0273; **www.catchacanoe.com**). You can paddle on the Big River estuary to look for seals and ospreys. Amenities include showers, flush toilets, and wood for sale.

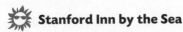 **Stanford Inn by the Sea**

44850 Comptche–Ukiah Road, Mendocino; ☎ 800-331-8884 or
707-937-5615; www.stanfordinn.com; $195–$785;
$25 children ages 3–18; $35 pet fee

THIS FOUR-DIAMOND HOTEL describes itself as a "self-sustaining eco-system." Its ten acres of landscaped grounds include a certified organic garden, nursery, and working farm, and guests can take classes in yoga—it's all so Mendocino here. You'll also enjoy the indoor swimming pool, complimentary full breakfast, video library, and mountain bikes. There are 33 wood-paneled rooms and suites, many with four-poster beds and wood-burning stoves or fireplaces. Amenities include babysitting, VCRs and DVDs, mini-refrigerators, coffeemakers, and a vegetarian restaurant (breakfast and dinner only).

Surf Motel & Gardens
1220 South Main Street, Fort Bragg; ☎ 800-339-5361 or 707-964-5361;
www.surfmotelfortbragg.com; $49 and up; $10 children over age 9;
apartment units, $100–$250

A GOOD CHOICE FOR FAMILIES ON A BUDGET, this motel is well located in Fort Bragg, not far from the Skunk Train. The two apartment units sleep up to six and are a particularly good value. Outside there's a barbecue and picnic area, landscaped grounds, and fish-cleaning facilities. Refrigerators and microwave in all rooms. There's no restaurant, but the kids will be happy to spot the McDonald's right across the street.

 # ATTRACTIONS

Drive-Thru Tree Park (aka Chandelier Tree)

APPEAL BY AGE	PRESCHOOL ★★★	GRADE SCHOOL ★★★	TEENS ★★★
YOUNG ADULTS ★★★		OVER 30 ★★	SENIORS ★★

US 101 in Legget; ☎ 707-925-6363; www.drivethrutree.com

Hours *Memorial Day–mid-October:* daily, 8:30 a.m.–8:30 p.m.; *rest of year:* daily, 9 a.m.–sunset. **Admission** $5 per vehicle. **Touring time** Average 15 minutes; minimum 5 minutes. **Rainy-day touring** Okay. **Restaurants** No. **Alcoholic beverages** No. **Disabled access** Yes. **Wheelchair rental** No. **Baby-stroller rental** No. **Lockers** No. **Pet kennels** No. **Rain check** No. **Private tours** No.

DESCRIPTION AND COMMENTS   On US 101 in Leggett, a town situated where Coast Highway (CA 1) veers in and meets US 101, you'll find the famed drive-through tree: a privately owned 315-foot-tall redwood, 21 feet in diameter, which had a car-sized tunnel carved into it in the mid-1930s. Weird but memorable. Picnic facilities are on site.

Mendocino Coast Botanical Gardens

APPEAL BY AGE	PRESCHOOL ★★	GRADE SCHOOL ★★★	TEENS ★★★
YOUNG ADULTS ★★★		OVER 30 ★★★	SENIORS ★★★★

18220 North Highway 1 (2 miles south of Fort Bragg); ☎ 707-964-4352; www.gardenbythesea.org

Hours *March–October:* daily, 9 a.m.–5 p.m.; *November–February:* daily, 9 a.m.– 4 p.m. **Admission** $10 adults, $7.50 seniors age 60 and over, $4 teens ages 13–17, $2 children ages 6–12, free for children age 5 and under. **Touring time** Average 3 hours; minimum 1 hour. **Rainy-day touring** Not recommended. **Restaurants** Yes, garden setting. **Alcoholic beverages** No. **Disabled access** About 1 mile of paved trails. **Wheelchair rental** Electric carts. **Baby-stroller rental** No. **Lockers** No. **Pet kennels** No. **Rain check** Yes. **Private tours** Yes.

DESCRIPTION AND COMMENTS Botanical gardens, with their smooth paths and landscaped environments, can make a pleasant, parklike stop for families with strollers and young children who need some safe, easy running time. This 47-acre facility is known for its rhododendrons and fuchsia gardens. Families will enjoy the easy, one-mile loop trail to the ocean and the Fern Canyon section with its six small, wooden bridges over the creek. Food, a gift shop, and a retail nursery are on-site.

 ## Point Arena Lighthouse and Museum

APPEAL BY AGE	PRESCHOOL ★★★	GRADE SCHOOL ★★★★	TEENS ★★★★
YOUNG ADULTS ★★★★		OVER 30 ★★★★	SENIORS ★★★

Off CA 1 just north of Point Arena; ☎ 877-725-4448 or 707-882-2777; www.pointarenalighthouse.com

Hours *April–September:* daily, 10 a.m.–4:30 p.m.; *October–March:* daily, 10 a.m.– 3:30 p.m. **Admission** $5 adults, $1 children under age 12. **Touring time** Average 1 hour; minimum 30 minutes. **Rainy-day touring** Yes. **Restaurants** No. **Alcoholic beverages** No. **Disabled access** No. **Wheelchair rental** No. **Baby-stroller rental** No. **Lockers** No. **Pet kennels** No. **Rain check** No. **Private tours** No.

DESCRIPTION AND COMMENTS The first lighthouse at this location was destroyed in the 1906 San Francisco earthquake; the current historic building, just reopened after yet another renovation, dates from 1908. It towers 115 feet over the ground, which makes for a swell view and a moderately challenging and fun climb to the top for all but the littlest kids; in spring, this is a great place to look for migrating whales. A small museum is in the 1896 Fog Signal Building, next to the lighthouse.

 ## Skunk Train–California Western Railroad

APPEAL BY AGE	PRESCHOOL ★★★★	GRADE SCHOOL ★★★★½	TEENS ★★★
YOUNG ADULTS ★★★★		OVER 30 ★★★★½	SENIORS ★★★★½

CA 1 and Laurel Street, Fort Bragg; ☎ 800-866-1690 or 707-964-6371; www.skunktrain.com

Hours Half-day trips from Fort Bragg available March–November and from Willits May–August plus September. **Admission** *Round-trip Fort Bragg–Northspur fares:* $47 and up for adults, $22 and up for kids ages 3–11. **Touring time** Average 4–5 hours for half-day trip, including boarding time and the like; minimum half-day ride is 3½ hours. **Rainy-day touring** Not recommended. **Restaurants** Snack bar at Northspur. **Alcoholic beverages** Yes. **Disabled access** Yes. **Wheelchair rental** No. **Baby-stroller rental** No. **Lockers** No. **Pet kennels** In the area. **Rain check** Yes. **Private tours** Yes.

DESCRIPTION AND COMMENTS   It's a family joke that Mom liked this train ride even more than the kids did, but part of the pleasure in the excursion was the happy-surprise variety. Especially pleasing was the go-the-extra-mile attitude of this recreational-railroad company.

We boarded the vintage passenger cars of the diesel train (some trains are pulled by older steam locomotives) at the Skunk Depot in Fort Bragg and settled in to enjoy the 40-mile round-trip through forest and meadowland, over bridges and trestles, through tunnels, and around curves. Mom was happy enough, and then a friendly strolling guitar player began walking through the cars, adding a festive touch with railroad-themed folk songs. At Northspur, the round-trip midpoint railroad camp, we disembarked and enjoyed a cool interlude in a shady grove where picnic tables, refreshment stands, and souvenir stands offer a country-fair feeling. The round-trip from Fort Bragg to Northspur is about three and a half hours, and reservations are advised during high season. Real buffs can inquire about riding in the cab with the engineer.

FAMILY-FRIENDLY RESTAURANTS

Eggheads Restaurant
326 North Main Street, Fort Bragg; ☎ 707-964-5005; www.eggheadsrestaurant.com

Meals served Breakfast and lunch. **Cuisine** American. **Entree range** $6–$13. **Kids' menu** No. **Reservations** Not accepted. **Payment** MC, V.

A FANCIFUL PLACE devoted to the land of Dorothy and Toto (it used to be called Egghead Omelettes of Oz), this is a great place to know about, if only for its location one block from the Skunk Train depot. Fortunately, the food is as appealing as the location: every sort of omelet imaginable, carefully prepared and happily split in two for kids, along with great pancakes and, at lunch, salads and burgers.

Mendocino Cafe

10451 Lansing Street, Mendocino; ☎ 707-937-2422

Meals served Lunch and dinner. **Cuisine** California, International. **Entree range** Lunch, $8–$16; dinner, $12–$26. **Kids' menu** Yes, $7–$8. **Reservations** Accepted. **Payment** MC, V.

TELL THE KIDS IT'S CHINESE or Mexican food, but know that you're settling in for some Pacific Rim–Latin–contemporary American cuisine, prepared with organic Mendocino flair: nachos with black beans, Vietnamese chicken salad, St. Louis–style ribs, Brazilian seafood stew, Thai *tom yum* soup, scampi. The menu is all over the map, and it's all tasty. There's a good kids' menu, too.

North Coast Brewing Company
455 North Main Street, Fort Bragg; ☎ 707-964-2739;
www.northcoastbrewing.com

Meals served Lunch and dinner. **Cuisine** American. **Entree range** $10–$32. **Kids' menu** No. **Reservations** Recommended. **Payment** All major credit cards.

OK, MAYBE A BREWPUB doesn't seem like the ideal place for kids, but this one is relaxed and family-friendly, and the food is terrific. Try the North Beach sandwich, the shrimp and chips, the huge burger, or the Carolina-style barbecued pulled pork. Enjoy excellent local wines on the outdoor patio.

HUMBOLDT *and* DEL NORTE COUNTIES:
Eureka, Redwoods, and Trinidad

THE MOST NORTHERLY COAST OF CALIFORNIA is big country—big trees, big rivers, big mountains, and big distances. There are both state and national redwood parks, quaint seaport villages, and plenty of opportunities for outdoor adventures from river rafting to rock climbing. The city of **Eureka** is the best base for exploring the area, and it's where you'll connect to the highway east to **Lake Shasta**.

Whatever you do up here, make sure to visit **Humboldt Redwoods State Park,** especially **Avenue of the Giants,** where the road winds through an astounding, primeval redwood forest (see lodging listing on the next page). If at all possible, you should camp out in the state park, one of the most beautiful family campgrounds in the country.

Eureka's renovated, Victorian-era Old Town neighborhood brings the days of the free-spending lumber barons to mind, but **Old Town Eureka** also makes for a fun afternoon of dining and shopping. We don't recommend taking the kids on the historic walking tours, but look for the local children's museum with interactive exhibits, **Discovery Museum** (see profile, page 409). Also see "The Best Beaches and Parks" for several important sites.

With a picturesque village perched on a promontory above a tiny harbor with a pier, a lighthouse (replica of the 1871 original), and a dozen pretty shops and cafes, **Trinidad** is home to some motels and bed-and-breakfasts that make for a restful overnight stay on the way to or from the redwoods. We hiked the **Trinidad Head Trail** to look down on the beach, had supper in the harbor, and had a fine time shopping in the crafts stores.

FAMILY LODGING

Bishop Pine Lodge
1481 Patrick's Point Drive, Trinidad; ☎ 707-677-3314;
www.bishoppinelodge.com; $115 for 4 people; $125 with kitchen;
$15 extra person and pet fee

A FUNKY BUT UTTERLY CHARMING little cabin resort in the pines behind the village of Trinidad. We loved the old-fashioned playground and the

humboldt and del norte counties

■ FAMILY LODGING
1. Bishop Pine Lodge
2. Humboldt Redwoods State Park Campgrounds
3. Jedediah Smith Redwood State Park Campground
4. Lost Whale Inn
5. Marble Mountain Guest Ranch

● ATTRACTIONS
6. Arcata Skate Park
7. Discovery Museum
8. Fort Humboldt State Historic Park
9. Humboldt Bay Harbor Cruise
10. Prairie Creek Redwood State Park

◆ FAMILY-FRIENDLY RESTAURANTS
11. Samoa Cookhouse
12. Seascape

PACIFIC OCEAN

DEL NORTE CO.

Smith River
Fort Dick
199
Patrick Creek
SISKIYOU CO.
Gasquet
3
Hiouchi
SMITH RIVER
SISKIYOU WILDERNESS
Crescent City
101
NATIONAL RECREATION AREA
Clear Creek (Pick-a-Wish)
96
Requa
169
Klamath
Klamath Glen
DEL NORTE CO.
HUMBOLDT CO.
10
YUROK INDIAN RES.
SIX
5
Somes Bar
101
REDWOOD
RIVERS
Orleans
Orick
169
96
NATIONAL
Weitchpec
NATIONAL
Big Lagoon Park
PARK
HOOPA VALLEY INDIAN RES.
FOREST
12
1
Hoopa
4
Trinidad
101
Crannell
Fieldbrook
McKinleyville
299
Willow Creek
Trinity Village
Blue Lake
6
Arcata
Korbel
Salyer
7
8
Manila
Bayside
Indianola
Hawkins Bar
11
Eureka
Myrtletowne
Maple Creek
Burnt Ranch
Fairhaven
9
Cutter
Freshwater
Fields Lndg.
Kneeland
SIX
211
Loleta
Fernbridge
Fortuna
RIVERS
Ferndale
Hydesville
Carlotta
Rio Dell
Alton
NATIONAL
Capetown
Bridgeville
36
Scotia
Pepperwood
FOREST
101
Shively
Holmes
Redcrest
Petrolia
HUMBOLDT REDWOODS
Weott
McCann
TRINITY CO.
STATE PARK
2
Whitlow
Blocksburg
KING RANGE
Honeydew
254
Myers Flat
Miranda
Eel Rock
Ft. Seward
NATIONAL CONSERVATION AREA
Phillipsville
Alderpoint
Zenia
Ettersburg
Kettenpom

0   20 mi
0   20 km

unofficial **TIP**
The best way to help your family absorb the majesty of the giant redwoods is to live with them for a day or two at one of the park's campgrounds.

chance to sit on the porch and look at those bright, bright stars in the rural sky. There are 12 wooden cottages and two two-bedrooms, some with kitchens and barbecues on the decks. Outside is a barbecue area.

 ## Humboldt Redwoods State Park Campgrounds

45 miles south of Eureka off US 101, Weott;
☎ **707-946-2409; www.humboldtredwoods.org; reservations: ReserveAmerica,** ☎ **800-444-7275, www.reserveamerica.com; campsites $12–$20**

TRY TO SPEND MORE TIME in this remarkable state park than just what it takes to drive through to see the incredible old-growth redwoods— although whether you camp here or not, you must take the 32-mile drive called Avenue of the Giants. The three campgrounds here are Albee; Burlington, near the park headquarters; and Hidden Springs. Each area has restrooms, hot showers, and laundry tubs, as well as evening campfire programs and interpretive programs in the summer.

Jedediah Smith Redwood State Park Campground

4241 Kings Valley Road, Crescent City; ☎ **707-458-3018; reservations: ReserveAmerica,** ☎ **800-444-7275; www.reserveamerica.com; campsites $20 and up**

THE HAPPIEST STAY of our family's see-the-redwoods trip when we were kids, Jedediah Smith continues to be a superb family campground in a setting of God-fearing beauty. The Smith River runs right through the redwood-studded campground, and kids love to splash, fish, and paddle rafts in it. This park is warmer than some of the coastal camps because it's inland enough to avoid most fog. A footbridge over the river leads to the marvelous Simpson-Reed Discovery Trail, an educational loop that's easy even for toddlers. Amenities include flush toilets, showers, picnic tables, and fireplaces.

Lost Whale Inn
3452 Patrick's Point Drive, Trinidad; ☎ **800-677-7859 or 707-677-3425; www.lostwhaleinn.com; May–October: $260–$375; November–April: $170–$230; extra adult $25, extra child $20**

USUALLY, A BED-AND-BREAKFAST on a prime piece of coastal land like this is aimed at romancing couples, and children are as welcome as earthquakes. Not so here. Some of the rooms and suites are great for families (ask for one with a sleeping loft), and while they're certainly charming, with wood floors and ocean views, they're not full of delicate antiques. The kids won't mind the lack of TV when they can pick berries, play croquet and boules, pet the two friendly dogs, explore the beach, and look for whales or sea lions. The rough beach is fun for (supervised) tide pooling, otter spotting, and rock climbing, but not swimming—but the kids can take a cold shower in the waterfall. While Dad's at the beach with the kids, Mom can get an in-room hot-stone massage.

Marble Mountain Guest Ranch

92520 Highway 96, Somes Bar; ☎ 800-552-6284 or 530-469-3322; www.marblemountainranch.com; housekeeping cabins $125 for 2 people, plus $20 per extra person (kids under age 6 stay free); deluxe cabin homes $250–$275 (kids under age 6 stay free); tent sites and RV hookups $15; all-inclusive family vacations offered; packages include accommodations, meals, and 1 activity per day

FOR THE AMBITIOUS, this guest ranch at the edge of the Marble Mountain Wilderness offers pack trips into the wild. For the rest of us, it's possible to enjoy a night or a week in the company of the ranch's 18 horses and various dogs, goats, and chickens. Self-guided activities include horseback riding and, in fall, drift-boat fishing; guided excursions include rafting, mountain biking, and horseback riding (one-hour to custom multiday adventures). The lodge serves family-style meals nightly and a weekend Western barbecue, and the deli packs lunches to take along on hikes. Accommodations vary from RV hookups and tent sites to no-frills housekeeping cabins (which sleep up to six) and fancier "deluxe cabin homes." Kids (and parents) never get bored here, thanks to the games (air hockey and Ping-Pong), zip cable, swings, swimming pool, bocce ball, petting farm, casting pond, and sparkling lake for swimming and fishing.

■ ATTRACTIONS

Arcata Skate Park

APPEAL BY AGE	PRESCHOOL ★	GRADE SCHOOL ★★★★	TEENS ★★★★
YOUNG ADULTS ★★		OVER 30 ★	SENIORS ½

900 Sunset Avenue, Arcata; ☎ 707-822-7091; www.skateboardparks.com/california/arcata

Hours Open daily in daylight hours. **Admission** Free. **Touring time** Average 2 hours; minimum 1 hour. **Rainy-day touring** No. **Restaurants** No. **Alcoholic beverages** No. **Disabled access** No. **Wheelchair rental** No. **Baby-stroller rental** No. **Lockers** No. **Pet kennels** No. **Rain check** No. **Private tours** No.

DESCRIPTION AND COMMENTS   Skateboard heaven, right off US 101, with three bowls, good rails, a fun box, and lots of vertical edges. Helmets are required.

Discovery Museum

APPEAL BY AGE	PRESCHOOL ★★★★	GRADE SCHOOL ★★★	TEENS ½
YOUNG ADULTS ★		OVER 30 ★	SENIORS ½

Third and F streets, Eureka; ☎ 707-443-9694; www.discovery-museum.org

unofficial **TIP**
The Discovery Museum is a godsend for young children on a rainy day.

Hours Tuesday–Saturday, 10 a.m.–4 p.m.; Sunday, noon–4 p.m. **Admission** $4, free for children age 2 and under. **Touring time** Average 2 hours; minimum 1 hour. **Rainy-day touring** Yes. **Restaurants** No. **Alcoholic beverages** No. **Disabled access** Some. **Wheelchair rental** No. **Baby-stroller rental** No. **Lockers** No. **Pet kennels** No. **Rain check** No. **Private tours** No.

DESCRIPTION AND COMMENTS   The sweeping vistas, big trees, and dramatic scenery of the North Coast are best suited to older kids—so we're thankful for this friendly haven for the little ones. It's a cheerful, small-town children's museum with a dozen or so interactive, play-based exhibits that are great for preschoolers and early-elementary kids. They can play in a mini–grocery store, learn about North Coast ecology, pretend to captain a ship, and do much more.

Fort Humboldt State Historic Park

APPEAL BY AGE	PRESCHOOL ★	GRADE SCHOOL ★★	TEENS ★★
YOUNG ADULTS ★★		OVER 30 ★★	SENIORS ★★

Fort Avenue off Highland Avenue, Eureka; ☎ 707-445-6567 or 707-488-2041; parks.ca.gov

Hours Daily, 8 a.m.–5 p.m. **Admission** Free. **Touring time** Average 1 hour; minimum 1 hour. **Rainy-day touring** Not great. **Restaurants** No. **Alcoholic beverages** No. **Disabled access** Yes. **Wheelchair rental** No. **Baby-stroller rental** No. **Lockers** No. **Pet kennels** No. **Rain check** No. **Private tours** No, docents available.

DESCRIPTION AND COMMENTS   This 19th-century fort has been partly reconstructed and is a testimony to some of the grim, violent history of the area. Exhibits highlight gold mining, logging, and Native American history; look for junior ranger activities in summertime.

 ## Humboldt Bay Harbor Cruise

APPEAL BY AGE	PRESCHOOL ★★★★	GRADE SCHOOL ★★★★	TEENS ★★★
YOUNG ADULTS ★★★		OVER 30 ★★★★	SENIORS ★★★★

Foot of F Street, Eureka; ☎ 707-444-9440; www.humboldtbaymaritimemuseum.com

Hours *May–October:* cruises depart Wednesday–Saturday at 1 p.m., 2:30 p.m., and 4 p.m.; Sunday–Tuesday, 1 p.m. and 2:30 p.m. **Admission** $18 adults, $16 seniors age 55 and older and children ages 13–17, $10 children ages 5–12, children 4 and under free. **Touring time** Average 3 hours; minimum 2 hours (allow for boarding and the like). **Rainy-day touring** Not recommended. **Restaurants** No. **Alcoholic beverages** Yes. **Disabled access** Yes. **Wheelchair rental** With notice. **Baby-stroller rental** No. **Lockers** No. **Pet kennels** No, but pets are allowed on cruise. **Rain check** Yes. **Private tours** No.

DESCRIPTION AND COMMENTS A tiny, storybook-like 1910 ferry (which holds just 49 people) takes visitors on a 75-minute tour of the Humboldt Bay area, past sawmills, a former Native American village, and bird habitats. The narration will bore little ones, but the stories are interesting enough to engage older children. Kids can watch for fishing boats, otters, and special birds, while Mom and Dad can belly up to the smallest licensed bar in the state.

 Prairie Creek Redwood State Park

APPEAL BY AGE	PRESCHOOL ★★★★	GRADE SCHOOL ★★★★	TEENS ★★★
YOUNG ADULTS ★★★★		OVER 30 ★★★★	SENIORS ★★★★

US 101, 6 miles north of Orick; ☎ 707-465-7347; parks.ca.gov

Hours Daily, open 24 hours. **Admission** Day-use fee $6; $2 per dog (leashed only); limited number of day-use permits issued. **Touring time** Average a half day; minimum 2 hours. **Rainy-day touring** Not great. **Restaurants** No. **Alcoholic beverages** No. **Disabled access** Some trails. **Wheelchair rental** No. **Baby-stroller rental** No. **Lockers** No. **Pet kennels** No. **Rain check** No. **Private tours** No.

DESCRIPTION AND COMMENTS This state park also happens to be a UNESCO-designated World Heritage Site , along with Del Norte Coast Redwoods State Park, Jedediah Smith Redwoods State Park, and Redwood National Park. It's particularly worth a family visit because of its daily (in summer) one-hour junior ranger programs for children ages 7 to 12. The other great reason to visit, aside from the amazing forests of redwoods, is the herd of protected, native Roosevelt elk roaming the 14,000 acres, often in the meadow near the highway. The 75 miles of trails include wheelchair-accessible routes. Interpretive exhibits on the elk and other flora and fauna of the region are offered as well. A nature walk near the visitors center takes you to Chimney Tree, where a family lived in the 1930s; little kids love the half-mile loop trail into Fern Canyon. You also might consider camping here—there are 100 family campsites, including some on the beach.

FAMILY-FRIENDLY RESTAURANTS

Samoa Cookhouse
511 Vance Avenue, Samoa; ☎ 707-442-1659;
www.samoacookhouse.net

Meals served Breakfast, lunch, and dinner. **Cuisine** Lumberjack American. **Entree range** $10–$16. **Kids' menu** $4–$7; children under age 5, free. **Reservations** Not accepted. **Payment** All major credit cards.

IF YOU HAVE AN OVEREATER in the family, don't stop here. It's an old lumber-camp cookhouse, and it serves meals as if we are all lumberjacks. Diners seat themselves at long tables, and family groups are brought platters heaped with chicken, ham, or fish (depending on what the cook's up to that night), vegetables, breads, and dessert—it's an all-you-can-eat feast. Equally hearty breakfasts and lunches are served. For anyone with the willpower to avoid a stomachache, it's a fun stop—the tables have checkered cloths, and there's a mini-museum of old-time kitchen and logging equipment.

Seascape
Trinidad Harbor at the foot of Bay Street, Trinidad; ☎ 707-677-3762

Meals served Breakfast, lunch, and dinner. **Cuisine** American. **Entree range** $8–$25. **Kids' menu** $5. **Reservations** Accepted only for 5 or more. **Payment** MC, V.

RIGHT AT THE HARBOR IN TRINIDAD, this place is notable mostly for its views of the pier, bay, and harbor seals right outside the window. The food is fine: good breakfasts (try the blackberry pancakes), basic burgers, fish-and-chips, omelets, and, at dinner, fresh seafood.

TRINITY *and* SHASTA COUNTIES

WE'RE TALKING AN AREA AS BIG AS SOME STATES when it comes to these two counties, and the landscapes they encompass are impressive Western mountain pine forests and big-deal rivers—the kind that inspire people to build dams.

The city of **Redding** is where the **Central Valley** meets the mountains, but it's no vacation mecca—that honor is reserved for the awkwardly named **Whiskeytown-Shasta-Trinity National Recreation Area.** Above it all towers **Mount Shasta,** a dormant volcano whose slopes are home to seven living glaciers. A mountain that has figured in legends and lore of several cultures, its snow-shrouded peak is often circled with mysteriously shaped clouds.

FAMILY LODGING

Bridge Bay Resort
10300 Bridge Bay Road, Shasta Lake; ☎ 800-752-9669 or 530-275-3021; www.sevencrown.com; $85–$190

A SO-SO 40-ROOM MARINA MOTEL that we nevertheless valued highly because we were just knocked out after days of fresh air and water—we simply couldn't get back into the car and cover more miles. So we extended our stay, relaxed in the air-conditioned room, and floated in the pool. You'll want to stay in this motel the night before you patio-boat or begin a houseboat vacation, or the night after you spend a day or two on the lake. A restaurant and minimart are on-site, and some larger units have kitchens.

Coffee Creek Ranch

Coffee Creek Road off CA 3, Trinity Center; ☎ 530-266-3343 or 800-624-4480; www.coffeecreekranch.com; $1,275–$1,295 per week for adults, $400–$1,195 per week for children, $1,255–$1,275 per week for teens; daily rates $195–$259; riding in summer is extra

A WELL-REGARDED FAMILY DUDE RANCH, Coffee Creek is in the Trinity Alps at 3,100 feet elevation. Guests should be inclined to spend a lot of time on horseback, as that's the main activity. Other activities include volleyball,

trinity and shasta counties

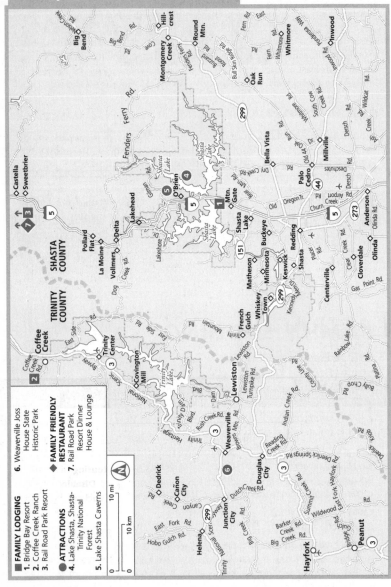

■ FAMILY LODGING
1. Bridge Bay Resort
2. Coffee Creek Ranch
3. Rail Road Park Resort

● ATTRACTIONS
4. Lake Shasta, Shasta–Trinity National Forest
5. Lake Shasta Caverns

6. Weaverville Joss House State Historic Park

◆ FAMILY FRIENDLY RESTAURANT
7. Rail Road Park Resort Dinner House & Lounge

archery, canoeing, square dancing, pedal-boating, basketball, and hayrides. The ranch also has a pool, rifle range, and trout pond. Children's programs include the Kiddie Corral, with supervised play for toddlers; games, hikes, and pony rides for 3- to 5-year-olds; and horsemanship, roping, and hiking programs for older kids. Fifty guests a week can be accommodated in the rustic, comfortable cabins, all with fireplaces or potbellied stoves. Riders must be at least 5 years old for all rides; no one under 8 years of age is permitted on all-day trips, but lessons are available for kids age 4 and up.

 ### Rail Road Park Resort

100 Railroad Park Road, Dunsmuir; ☎ 530-235-4440; www.rrpark.com; $115–$120, plus $10 for each person over 2 people; rooms sleep up to 5; $15 pet fee; camping fees $22–$30

IN THE TOWN OF DUNSMUIR, just south of Mount Shasta and near Castle Crags State Park, a collection of old freight-train cabooses are linked together to make an atmospheric family motel. The cabooses surround a pool, hot tub, and deck; inside the cabooses are motel rooms, each decorated differently. Also on the property are four cabins with kitchens, a restored water tower, a huge logging steam engine, and an RV campground with a creek, swimming hole, and convenience store. The train-car restaurant is a fun place to eat.

 # ATTRACTIONS

 ### Lake Shasta, Shasta-Trinity National Forest

APPEAL BY AGE	PRESCHOOL ★★★★	GRADE SCHOOL ★★★★	TEENS ★★★★
YOUNG ADULTS ★★★★		OVER 30 ★★★★	SENIORS ★★★★

2400 Washington Avenue, Redding; ☎ 530-275-1587; www.fs.fed.us/r5/shastatrinity

Hours Vary. **Admission** Free; fees for boat rental; camping $16–$26 per night. **Touring time** Average 1 day; minimum 4 hours. **Rainy-day touring** Not great. **Restaurants** Mostly snack bars. **Alcoholic beverages** Limited. **Disabled access** Some. **Wheelchair rental** No. **Baby-stroller rental** No. **Lockers** No. **Pet kennels** No. **Rain check** No. **Private tours** No.

DESCRIPTION AND COMMENTS This man-made lake is so large that once you chug away from the dock on your houseboat, patio boat, or water-ski boat, you'll feel as if you could get lost for days. The water is cool and exhilarating for swimming, fishermen pull up 21 varieties of fish, and the slopes surrounding the lake are covered in pine forest. See "Family Outdoor Adventures" for more on patio boating and houseboating. For camping reservations in the forest, call ☎ 800-365-CAMP.

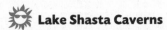 **Lake Shasta Caverns**

| APPEAL BY AGE | PRESCHOOL ★★ | GRADE SCHOOL ★★★★ | TEENS ★★★★ |
| YOUNG ADULTS ★★★ | OVER 30 ★★★ | SENIORS ★★★★ |

**20359 Shasta Caverns Road, Lakehead; ☎ 800-795-CAVE or
530-238-2341; www.lakeshastacaverns.com**

Hours *Summer:* daily, 9 a.m.–4 p.m., with tours every half hour; *April, May, and
September:* daily, 9 a.m.–3 p.m., with tours every hour; winter: tours leave at
10 a.m., noon, and 2 p.m. **Admission** $20 adults,, $12 children ages 3–15, free
for children age 3 and under. **Touring time** Average 2 hours; minimum 2 hours.
Rainy-day touring No problem. **Restaurants** Snack bar. **Alcoholic beverages**
No. **Disabled access** No. **Wheelchair rental** No. **Baby-stroller rental** No.
Lockers No. **Pet kennels** Staff will care for. **Rain check** No. **Private tours** No.

DESCRIPTION AND COMMENTS   We took a day off from the sun, sunburn, and
water sports of Lake Shasta to descend into the cool, eerie depth of
Lake Shasta Caverns. This is not an excursion for little ones or anyone
who has trouble walking—the day begins with a steep descent to a boat
that takes you across Lake Shasta to board a bus that takes you, gears
grinding, up a narrow, steep road to the top of a mountain. In the
course of visiting the cave, you'll go up or down more than 600 steps.
But for the energetic and hardy, it's a worthwhile look at those always-
amazing underground formations, culminating in a 60-foot room of
crystal-studded "draperies."

Weaverville Joss House State Historic Park

| APPEAL BY AGE | PRESCHOOL ★★ | GRADE SCHOOL ★★★★ | TEENS ★★★★ |
| YOUNG ADULTS ★★★ | OVER 30 ★★★ | SENIORS ★★★★ |

**Main Street, , near intersection of CA 299 West and CA 3, Weaverville;
☎ 530-623-5284 or 530-225-2065; parks.ca.gov**

Hours Wednesday–Sunday, 10 a.m.–5 p.m., with tours on the hour, 10 a.m.–
4 p.m. **Admission** $2 adults, free for kids under age 16. **Touring time** Average
1 hour; minimum 30-minute walk-through tour of temple. **Rainy-day touring**
Adjustments made on the tours. **Restaurants** Nearby. **Alcoholic beverages** No.
Disabled access With assistance. **Wheelchair rental** No. **Baby-stroller rental**
No. **Lockers** No. **Pet kennels** No. **Rain check** No. **Private tours** Yes.

DESCRIPTION AND COMMENTS   On the road to Shasta Lake from the North
Coast is a reminder that California's ethnic diversity is no new devel-
opment. The Weaverville Joss House is the oldest continuously used
Chinese temple in California, named by its builders "The Temple of the
Forest beneath the Clouds" (an apt description of its setting). Descen-
dants of the gold miners who built this temple still worship here in the
Taoist tradition. Art objects, mining tools, and other artifacts are on
display. The temple is open to the public only for guided tours.

FAMILY-FRIENDLY RESTAURANT

Rail Road Park Resort Dinner House & Lounge
100 Railroad Park Road, Dunsmuir; ☎ 530-235-4611; www.rrpark.com

Meals served Dinner, mid-April–mid-November, Friday and Saturday only. **Cuisine** American. **Entree range** $10–$19. **Kids' menu** Yes. **Reservations** Recommended. **Payment** All major credit cards.

A COLLECTION OF 100-YEAR-OLD TRAIN CARS makes up this charming family restaurant next to the Rail Road Park Resort motel. Kids love the setting, and they're welcomed with a children's menu. The food is straightforward, moderately upscale dinner-house American, and there's a full bar.

INDEX

Unofficial Guide Reader Survey

If you'd like to express your opinion about traveling in California with kids or this guidebook, complete the following survey and mail it to:

> *Unofficial Guide* Reader Survey
> P.O. Box 43673
> Birmingham, AL 35243

Inclusive dates of your visit:_____

Members of your party:

	Person 1	Person 2	Person 3	Person 4	Person 5
Gender:	M F	M F	M F	M F	M F
Age:					

How many times have you been to California? _____
On your most recent trip, where did you stay? _____

Concerning your accommodations, on a scale of 100 as best and 0 as worst, how would you rate:

The quality of your room? _____   The value of your room? _____
The quietness of your room? _____   Check-in/checkout efficiency? ___
Shuttle service to the airport? _____ Swimming pool facilities? _____

Did you rent a car?_____   From whom?_____

Concerning your rental car, on a scale of 100 as best and 0 as worst, how would you rate:
Pickup-processing efficiency?_____ Return processing efficiency?____
Condition of the car?____   Cleanliness of the car?____
Airport shuttle efficiency?____

Concerning your dining experiences:
Estimate your meals in restaurants per day? _____
Approximately how much did your party spend on meals per day? _____
_____

Favorite restaurants in California: _____
_____

Did you buy this guide before leaving? _____ While on your trip?_____

How did you hear about this guide? (check all that apply)

Loaned or recommended by a friend ☐   Radio or TV ☐
Newspaper or magazine ☐   Bookstore salesperson ☐
Just picked it out on my own ☐   Library ☐
Internet ☐

What other guidebooks did you use on this trip? _____

_____

_____

_____

On a scale of 100 as best and 0 as worst, how would you rate them?

_____

_____

_____

Using the same scale, how would you rate the *Unofficial Guide*(s)?

_____

Are *Unofficial Guides* readily available at bookstores in your area? _____

Have you used other *Unofficial Guides*? _____

Which one(s)? _____

_____

_____

Comments about your California trip or the *Unofficial Guide*(s):

_____

_____

_____

_____

_____

_____

_____

_____

_____

_____

_____

_____

_____

_____

_____

_____

_____